MW00527634

Black Art of Windows Game Programming

Eric R. Lyons

WAITE GROUP PRESS™
CORTE MADERA, CA

PUBLISHER Mitchell Waite
EDITOR-IN-CHIEF Charles Drucker
ACQUISITIONS EDITOR Jill Pisoni
EDITORIAL DIRECTOR John Crudo
MANAGING EDITOR Kurt Stephan
CONTENT EDITOR Heidi Brumbaugh
TECHNICAL REVIEWER Jeff Bankston
COPY EDITOR Janna Hecker Clark
PRODUCTION DIRECTOR Julianne Ososke
PRODUCTION MANAGER Cecile Kaufman
PRODUCTION TRAFFIC COORDINATOR Ingrid Owen
DESIGNERS Sestina Quarequio, Christi Fryday
PRODUCTION Christi Fryday, Tom Debolski
ILLUSTRATIONS Kristin Peterson, Tom Debolski
COVER ILLUSTRATION James Dowlen

Published by Waite Group Press™, 200 Tamal Plaza, Corte Madera, CA 94925.

Printed in the United States of America

95 96 97 • 10 9 8 7 6 5 4 3 2 1

Library of Congress Cataloging-in-Publication Data

Lyons. Eric R., 1960-
Black art of Windows game programming / Eric R. Lyons.
p. cm.
Includes index.
ISBN 1-878739-95-6 : $34.95 ($50.95 Can.)
1. Computer games--Programming. 2. C (Computer programming language). 3. Microsoft Windows (Computer file). I Title.
QA76. 76. C672L96 1995
794.8' 15265--dc20 95-18956
CIP

Dedication

This book is dedicated to Connor and Claire.

Message from the **Publisher**

Welcome to Our Nervous System

Some people say that the World Wide Web is a graphical extension of the information superhighway, just a network of humans and machines sending each other long lists of the equivalent of digital junk mail.

I think it is much more than that. To me the Web is nothing less than the nervous system of the entire planet—not just a collection of computer brains connected together, but more like a billion silicon neurons entangled and recirculating electro-chemical signals of information and data, each contributing to the birth of another CPU and another Web site.

Think of each person's hard disk connected at once to every other hard disk on earth, driven by human navigators searching like Columbus for the New World. Seen this way the Web is more of a super entity, a growing, living thing, controlled by the universal human will to expand, to be more. Yet unlike a purposeful business plan with rigid rules, the Web expands in a nonlinear, unpredictable, creative way that echoes natural evolution.

We created our Web site not just to extend the reach of our computer book products but to be part of this synaptic neural network, to experience, like a nerve in the body, the flow of ideas and then to pass those ideas up the food chain of the mind. Your mind. Even more, we wanted to pump some of our own creative juices into this rich wine of technology.

Taste our Digital Wine

And so we ask you to taste our wine by visiting the body of our business. Begin by understanding the metaphor we have created for our Web site—a universal learning center, situated in outer space in the form of a space station. A place where you can journey to study any topic from the convenience of your own screen. Right now we are focusing on computer topics, but the stars are the limit on the Web.

If you are interested in discussing this Web site, or finding out more about the Waite Group, please send me email with your comments and I will be happy to respond. Being a programmer myself, I love to talk about technology and find out what our readers are looking for.

Sincerely,

Mitchell Waite

Mitchell Waite, C.E.O. and Publisher

200 Tamal Plaza
Corte Madera CA 94925
415 924 2575
415 924 2576 fax
Internet email:
mwaite@waite.com
CompuServe email:
75146,3515
Website:
http://www.waite.com/waite

Creating the Highest Quality Computer Books in the Industry

Waite Group Press
Waite Group New Media

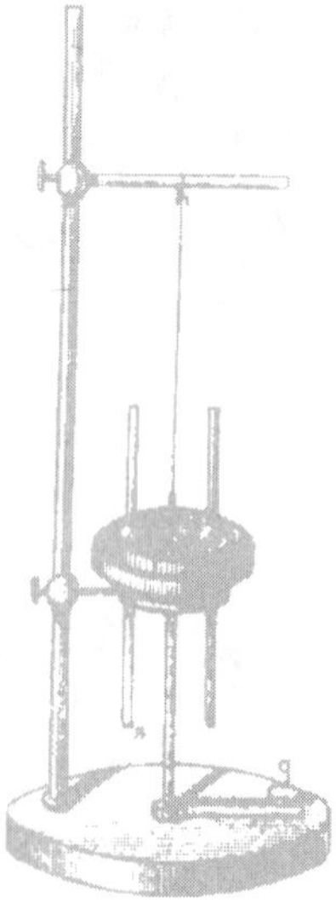

About the Author

Eric Lyons has been programming computers for 15 years, writing mostly graphics and computer-aided design software. He spent seven years at CAD market leader Autodesk, where as director of advanced technology, he headed the company's virtual reality project and later co-created its Multimedia Products Division, from which Autodesk Animator and Autodesk 3D Studio emanated. He also co-founded Altamira Software Corporation (recently acquired by Microsoft) and wrote the Windows user interface for its Altamira Composer application.

Mr. Lyons has written many articles on VR, CAD, graphics programming, entertainment software, and personal computing in general. Although much of his time in the last six years has been spent managing programmers, he is considerably happier being one instead.

Contents

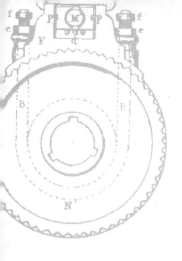

Table of Contents

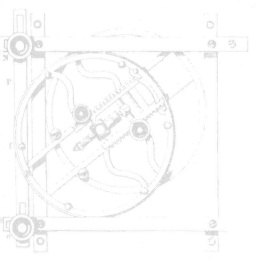

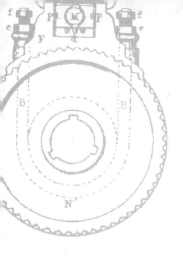

Acknowledgments

A book project like this one takes the work of many people. First and foremost, I'd like to thank the contributing authors Paul Tyma, David Black, and John Barrus for their great work in the second part of the book. A very special thanks goes to Zane Thomas, who developed the BugBots game. Next, heartfelt thanks to all the people at Waite Group Press, especially my tireless editor Kurt Stephan, and Mitchell Waite, who believed in me (and re-believed in me after every long delay). Mitchell is the best publisher in this business, and I am honored to have done this book for him.

More thanks to Heidi Brumbaugh for her insightful editing (again, I was lucky to have the best), and to my old friend Mauri Laitinen for editing and encouragement. I'd also like to thank my partner, friend, and boss at Altamira Software, Alvy Ray Smith, for encouragement, understanding, and most of all, inspiration.

Finally, thank you to my wonderful wife, Sheila, who put up with all of my various mental states throughout this project (and all my other projects, for that matter) and encouraged and supported me every day.

Introduction

Welcome to the world of game programming under Windows! Writing computer games is one of the most creatively rewarding pursuits in the computer software business. It can also be a very lucrative activity. With the PC's installed base nearing the 100 million mark, any good PC game is poised to attract a huge market—a market that is rapidly moving to Microsoft Windows, making Windows the new environment of choice for PC game programmers.

What's This Book About?

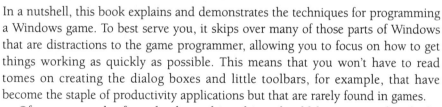

In a nutshell, this book explains and demonstrates the techniques for programming a Windows game. To best serve you, it skips over many of those parts of Windows that are distractions to the game programmer, allowing you to focus on how to get things working as quickly as possible. This means that you won't have to read tomes on creating the dialog boxes and little toolbars, for example, that have become the staple of productivity applications but that are rarely found in games.

Of course, much of any book on this subject should be concerned with the Windows programming environment in general. *Black Art of Windows Game Programming* is no exception. It's all the more important to cover these topics because Windows has traditionally been anathema to most self-respecting DOS game programmers. As a result, few game developers know much about programming under this environment. Given market forces, though, such ignorance is likely to become a serious liability in the near future.

Why Windows?

Microsoft Windows, long accepted by the business community, is finally being embraced by home users. Rarely does a newly purchased computer now go home without Windows installed on it, and the plethora of home productivity applications for Windows have finally displaced most of their DOS-based counterparts, at least on all but the oldest and slowest machines. This is a trend that game developers would be wise to note.

It's certainly true that in the world of games, DOS still rules as a host operating system. Any graphical user interface, Windows or otherwise, adds an unavoidable amount of overhead to any application running under it. Windows has earned a pretty poor reputation for graphics speed, and many game developers are loathe to give up a large measure of performance for a little convenience.

With the growing popularity of Windows, though, DOS is slowly being relegated to obsolete status. DOS may make it possible for the programmer to squeeze the absolute maximum performance out of the PC's architecture, but DOS is plagued with configuration problems, an archaic command-line interface, and the burdens of compatibility with past Intel microprocessor architectures. These faults, coupled with the extreme difficulty of running DOS-based games and Windows on the same computer and Microsoft's promise to do away with DOS completely in Windows 95, make DOS' abandonment inevitable.

Fortunately, Microsoft has recently made this bitter pill easier for game programmers to swallow. Recognizing that it needed to improve speed if it was to convince game programmers to develop games under Windows, Microsoft created WinG—a set of extensions and a programming interface that can dramatically improve the display speed of Windows applications, particularly games. The successful introduction of WinG is having a significant impact on the number of game titles being produced for Windows, encouraging more and more game programmers to consider this environment.

Who Should Read This Book?

This book is aimed at the intermediate to advanced C programmer who has some DOS game programming experience and who needs to learn Windows game programming with a minimum of fuss and pain.

If you've already built the ultimate DOS-based game and want it to run under Windows, don't worry—this is the book for you, too. It gives you all the key information you'll need to port a game from DOS to Windows, no matter how the game was originally written.

If you're new to game programming, you might want to start with a book that covers that subject specifically. There are many appropriate Waite Group Press titles. Christopher Lampton's pair, *Flights of Fantasy* and *Gardens of Imagination*, provide excellent examples of DOS-based game programming techniques.

Why C and Not C++?

All the programs and examples in this book are in the C programming language, rather than in C++. One reason for this is that C++ must often be used in conjunction with a particular development environment's class library. Windows class-library implementations vary greatly between development environments—Microsoft's MFC is quite different than Borland's OWL, for example. Understanding and using the various class libraries is a subject unto itself, putting it beyond the scope of this book.

Another reason I've used C is that most of the popular programming texts for Windows are still written for the C language. This is important because you will find a good *general* Windows programming reference to be indispensable to your efforts to develop Windows games. The Waite Group Press has several excellent offerings, such as Robert Lafore's *Windows API Bible* and *Windows Programming Made Easy.*

If you're used to writing in C++, don't be concerned. Although written in C, the code in this book draws on an object-oriented model. (After all, object-oriented programming wasn't the innovation of C++, but rather the reverse.) This means you should find that my code is at least aesthetically compatible with your mode of thinking.

Windows 95 and Win32

The code in this book and on the accompanying CD-ROM will, for the most part, compile and run under both 16-bit and 32-bit development environments. It might be obvious why I've written for a 32-bit environment: The release of Windows 95 will make a true 32-bit programming and run-time environment for the PC widely available. (If you've never programmed in a 32-bit environment, you'll learn a little about its advantages and pitfalls in Chapter 14.) However, I'm also aware that Windows 3.1 is still a very viable operating system for games, especially with the release of WinG, and that many DOS game programmers are still saddled with 16-bit development environments.

Microsoft designed WinG specifically to improve display speed under Windows 3.1, but it is also compatible with Windows 95 and Windows NT. This means that you can create a game that runs at optimum display speed under *all three* operating systems by using WinG, as either a 16-bit or a 32-bit application.

Software Requirements

To compile and run the code on the CD-ROM that comes with this book, you'll need a 16-bit or 32-bit Windows development environment. Microsoft, Borland, Symantec, and Watcom all produce suitable tools. Keep in mind that while you shouldn't need to modify the code, you might need to edit or recreate certain aspects—project or make files, for example—depending on your tool choice.

The code on the CD-ROM was compiled with Microsoft Visual C++, versions 1.5 (16-bit) and 2.0 (32-bit). The make files are therefore compatible with these two environments.

Integrated development environments (like Microsoft Visual C++) make life a lot easier. They integrate a Windows-based debugger, source-code editor, resource editor, and compiler/linker into a seamless package for producing Windows code. Microsoft, Borland, Symantec, and Watcom all provide IDEs for Windows.

All the code here will work on Windows 3.1 and Windows for Workgroups 3.11. It should also work under suitable configurations of Windows NT and Windows 95, although the latter has not been officially released as of this writing and therefore has not been tested in this context.

How This Book Is Organized

The chapters of this book are grouped into two parts. Part I, "The Essence of Windows Game Programming," contains Chapter 1 through Chapter 14. Part II, "Advanced Gaming Concepts," runs from Chapter 15 through Chapter 21, and includes Appendix A.

In Part I, you'll learn all about programming under Windows—how Windows messaging works, how to create a minimal Windows program, how to work with bitmaps and palettes under Windows, how to use sound, and so on. Chapters 1 through 9 (and the corresponding code examples on the CD-ROM) build on each other to culminate in the development of the sprite engine introduced in Chapter 10. Chapters 11 through 14 introduce other important aspects of Windows and games, like sound, file handling, optimization, and the implications of 32-bit programming.

Part II covers more advanced concepts like scoring and saving, integrating various types of complex motion, creating artwork for games, and even 3D programming. Appendix A provides an overview of BugBots, the complete game included on the CD-ROM. The game uses the sprite engine developed in Part I along with a complete BASIC-like interpreter for creating your own robots to compete with each other on a playing field.

Here's a breakdown of what's covered in each chapter:

Part I: The Essence of Windows Game Programming

Chapter 1: Windows—The User's Perspective

This chapter unveils important aspects of the *outer* workings of Windows, explaining just why users like Windows and how certain features affect games in particular. Although this chapter is mostly nontechnical, it provides you, the game programmer, with information crucial to forming a basic understanding of Windows's user interface concepts. This chapter is especially important for game programmers who have a limited familiarity with Windows.

Chapter 2: Windows—The Programmer's Perspective

This chapter looks into the real guts of Windows. It explores all the basic inner workings and covers fundamental Windows programming concepts. You'll create your first Windows program here (a version of the seminal "Hello, world" program). You'll also learn about Windows' resource files and how to conveniently store data with your program for quick and easy retrieval.

Chapter 3: Windows Memory Management

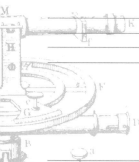

In this chapter, you'll learn about how Windows manages that ever-precious system resource: main memory. The concepts in this chapter are valid for both 16-bit and 32-bit Windows programs. I also include certain tricks and shortcuts to make memory management as painless as possible.

Chapter 4: Input Systems

This chapter is all about the various input devices (and metadevices) that Windows can handle: the mouse, the keyboard, the joystick, timers, and user interface pseudo-devices. In this chapter, I make it simpler for the DOS programmer to understand the concepts of message-driven input by comparing them to the polling-loop system typically used in DOS-based game programs.

Chapter 5: The Graphical Device Interface

This chapter discusses the Windows Graphical Device Interface, the subsystem responsible for all graphical output on a Windows device, in detail. The GDI is a complex and fickle beast; this chapter gives you the information essential for keeping the GDI happy with your program. I provide a full explanation of devices and device contexts, the WM_PAINT message, and GDI objects and their uses here.

Chapter 6: Windows Bitmaps—The Device-Dependent Bitmap

This is the first of three chapters describing the way Windows works with bitmaps. Although the device-dependent bitmap is seldom used in Windows game programming directly, an understanding of this type of bitmap is essential to comprehension of the other two bitmap types.

Chapter 7: Windows Bitmaps—The Device-Independent Bitmap

This chapter explains how to use device-independent bitmaps, or DIBs, and examines how they interact with the GDI. The DIB, which represents a general-purpose way of storing bitmap data that can then be copied to a device without regard for the physical storage format of that device, is at the heart of Windows bitmap programming.

Chapter 8: Palette Management Under Windows

Using 256-color images, the current standard, means using a palette—and using a palette under Windows is a far cry from using a palette under DOS. This chapter presents the important facts about Windows palette management and covers how to integrate palettes with the DIBs I discuss in Chapter 7. DIBs and palettes are inextricably related, and this chapter (and its accompanying code) builds on the knowledge you'll gain from Chapters 6 and 7.

Chapter 9: Fast Windows Bitmaps—The WinG Bitmap

This chapter introduces WinG, the Windows game programming development subsystem that makes DIBs run fast and that integrates them more completely with the

GDI. Here, I cover how to use the examples in the WinG SDK (included on the CD-ROM) and how to integrate WinG into your game application. Chapters 6, 7, and 8 will prepare you for understanding this topic.

Chapter 10: Bringing It All Together—Sprite Animation

This chapter brings together all the concepts introduced thus far to create a working 2D sprite engine based on WinG. I cover the code for the sprite engine in detail, and introduce subjects like transparency, z-order, dirty-rectangle updating, page flipping, and off-screen buffering.

Chapter 11: Using Sound Under Windows

In this chapter, I introduce the three kinds of sound handled under Windows: CD audio, waveform audio, and MIDI audio. This chapter also introduces the Media Control Interface, a high-level system for controlling audio and other devices under Windows. I also discuss authoring MIDI files for different classes of Windows audio devices, and the use of the Wavemix DLL, which allows multichannel waveform audio playing.

Chapter 12: Windows and Files

This short chapter gives the game programmer all the essential knowledge for using files under Windows, including initialization (.INI) files.

Chapter 13: Optimization

In this chapter, I demonstrate how you can dramatically improve the performance of the sprite engine developed in Chapter 10 through the use of assembly language functions. This chapter also addresses general game-program optimization.

Chapter 14: 32-Bit Programming

This chapter discusses how 16-bit programming and 32-bit programming under Windows differ, and explains the differences between the three primary Windows 32-bit platforms: Windows 3.1 with Win32s, Windows 95, and Windows NT. Although it isn't a full introduction of the Win32 programming environment, this chapter offers important details for game programmers in particular. This chapter also includes an explanation of various portability tricks.

Part II: Advanced Gaming Concepts

Chapter 15: Sprite Movies

This chapter builds on Chapter 10's sprite engine, enhancing it with the ability to play sprite "movies" or multiframe sprites. I explain how you can use this enhancement for everything from giving a sprite different images for different directions of travel to creating short movies of explosions or character movements.

Chapter 16: Detecting and Reacting to Collisions

This chapter also builds on the sprite engine introduced in Chapter 10, this time by adding the ability to detect sprite collisions.

Chapter 17: WinToon

This chapter describes the use of WinToon, the Windows cartoon engine developed by Microsoft and available license-free for use in games and other programs. The complete WinToon engine and sample code is included on the CD-ROM.

Chapter 18: Game Smarts (AI)

This chapter explores how to make your game intelligent—artificially intelligent, that is. Here, I introduce concepts that can help you create interesting character motion, implement evasive responses, and program simple automatons.

Chapter 19: Backgrounds and Foregrounds

This chapter discusses the technical as well as creative aspects of producing artwork for your game. I cover the use of automatic scenery generators, 3D modeling programs, and palette-processing tools.

Chapter 20: Scoring and Saving

Most computer games have winners and losers—and the score is what distinguishes between the two. This chapter introduces the basic concepts of scoring, and explains how important scoring can be to the overall "playability" of a game. It also discusses what "saving a game" can mean in different contexts.

Chapter 21: Entering the Third Dimension with OpenGL

The hottest trend in computer gaming is true 3D games. This introduction to OpenGL, a graphics library originally available only from Silicon Graphics but now available under Windows NT as well, will give you a basic understanding of 3D programming concepts and how they can be used in a game.

Appendix A: BugBots—Under the Lens

This appendix presents an overview of BugBots, the game included on the CD-ROM. BugBots is a complete game that uses a BASIC-like programming language to create animated robots that compete on a playing field. Here, you'll learn how you can program the sprites to hunt, chase, evade, and fire at each other.

The CD-ROM

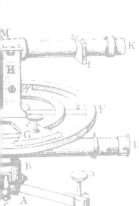

The code on the CD-ROM is organized into directories named after the chapters of this book. To install the code, you can copy the entire source directory and its subdirectories to your hard disk, or you can just copy the directories chapter by chapter to save room. (Many of the chapters in Part I build on each other, so the code you'll find in the CHAP5 directory, for example, will have all the examples created for the CHAP4 directory.) Remember that the make files included on the CD-ROM were created with Microsoft Visual C++ versions 1.5 and 2.0, so if you have a different compiler you may have to edit or create new project/make files.

The CD-ROM also contains complete installations for both WinG and the WinToon engine. To install these, change to the WINGINST or WINTINST directory and run SETUP. You can choose where to put these components on your hard disk, but you may have to edit the make files of the chapter projects to point to the right location of the libraries.

You can find the BugBots program and source code under the BUGBOTS directory.

There are also a couple of bonus directories on the CD-ROM. One (RWARE) contains a demonstration of the RenderWare 3D graphics library for Windows. This is a very capable and high-performance 3D rendering library especially well-suited to game development. In the N3D directory you'll find the shareware version of Nitemare 3D, a complete 3D maze game for Windows that uses WinG.

Look at the README.TXT file for complete information about the contents of the CD-ROM.

Part I

The Essence of Windows Game Programming

Aequinoctiums
Aequator

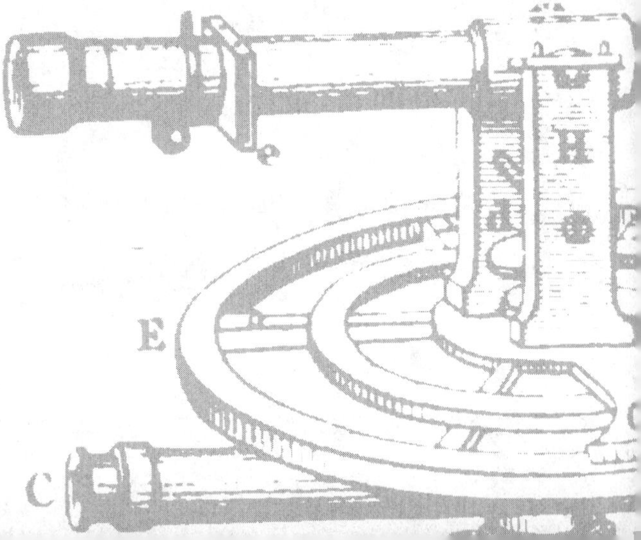
I
H
E
C

1

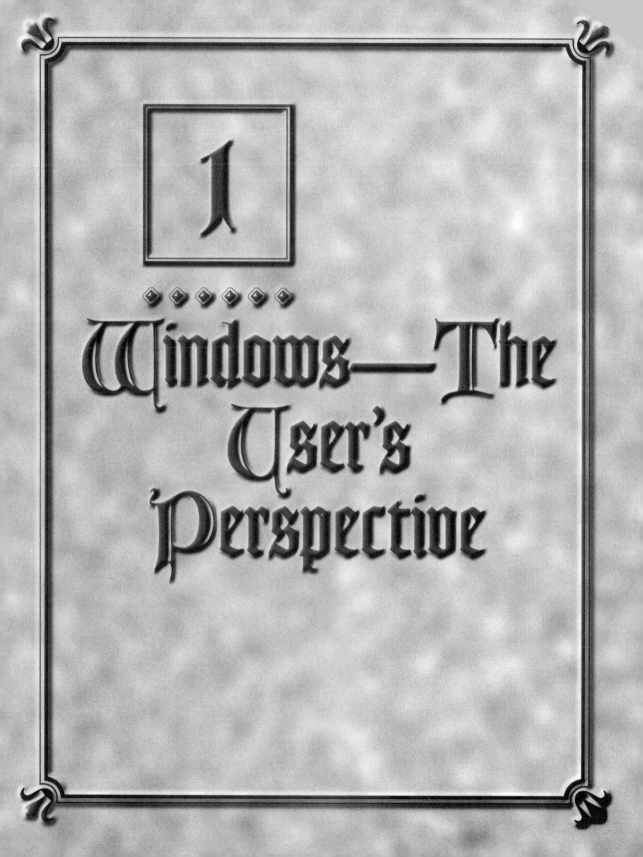

Windows—The User's Perspective

[illegible]ome debbe stare le manovelle [illegible] le quali si movano e s'alza
e i gran pesi [illegible] [illegible]
forzare nella [illegible] maggiore della manovella perchè quan[illegible]
la forza è più [illegible] più vale.

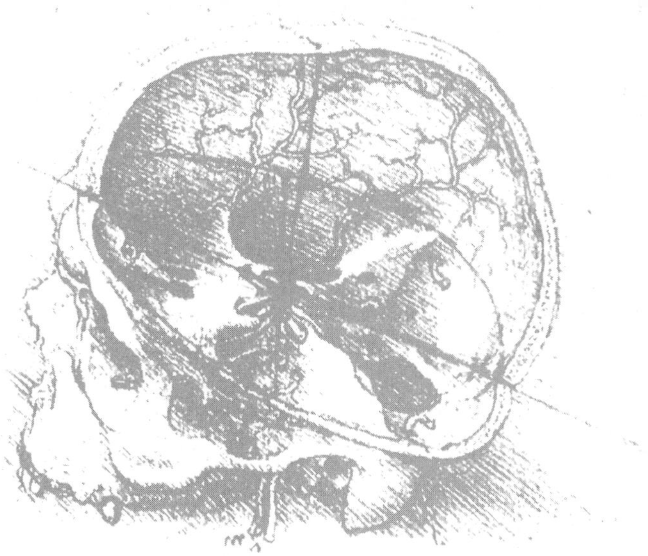

1

Windows—The User's Perspective

What is this thing called Windows, and why is it taking over the world? As a game developer, you probably consider Windows a mixed blessing, if a blessing at all. The performance penalty for graphics applications under Windows—especially games—has been hard for you to swallow. If you're coming from the DOS world, you have had the advantage of complete freedom to do just about anything with the computer you like: no multitasking to worry about, no interface "standards" to limit your creativity, and no overhead demands from another operating system layer. But it's computer *users* that benefit from all the advantages of a graphical user interface and, ultimately, they set the standard.

I'll admit to having been one of the most GUI-phobic programmers of the last decade, but I have since seen the light and embraced the Event-Driven Way. In this chapter, you'll learn a little bit about why tens of millions of others have made Microsoft Windows their GUI of choice. Of course, we'll also look at some dirty laundry, lest you imagine Windows to be the great panacea of GUIs. And I'll touch on some of the things that Microsoft is doing to make Windows even better—for users and developers alike. For example, you'll learn all about the WinG extensions that vastly improve graphics performance, finally making high-performance games practical under Windows.

First, let's take a look at some Windows games and see how they compare to DOS games.

Such a classic it's almost a cliché, Microsoft Solitaire (see Figure 1-1)—which ships with every copy of Windows—is possibly *the* most widely played Windows game. The number of Carpal Tunnel Syndrome casualties lost to Solitaire must be in the tens of thousands.

Solitaire is certainly not what you would call a complex game. Perhaps its most advanced feature is the ability it gives the user to choose from 12 patterns for the back of the cards. There's also a little bit of animation apparent when you try to make a wrong move—the cards snap back to their original positions. A zillion shareware variants of this game have popped up over the years and it remains an all-time favorite, maybe because *everyone* knows how to play Solitaire. Another reason for its popularity (besides the fact that it is one of only a couple of games that come free with Windows) is that it's a simple, unobtrusive little game. It's played within its own window and looks a lot like a regular Windows productivity application—though perhaps *anti*productivity has more to do with its appeal.

Microsoft took a similar approach when it launched its Arcade series of games. On one disk you get five classic arcade games from the 1970s and early 1980s—Asteroids, Battle Zone, Centipede, Missile Command, and Tempest—all ported to Windows (Figure 1-2 shows the Battle Zone screen after an unsuccessful run). Each of the games is exactly like its arcade predecessor—same colors, same shapes, same sound, everything. The only difference is that these games run inside a window on your screen. The performance of the Arcade series games is even the same as that of the original games—hardly a challenge, given the speed of even an 80386-based Windows machine.

The Arcade series was really a stroke of genius. After all, a goodly number of Windows users grew up pouring coins into Asteroids all afternoon long. It was a young

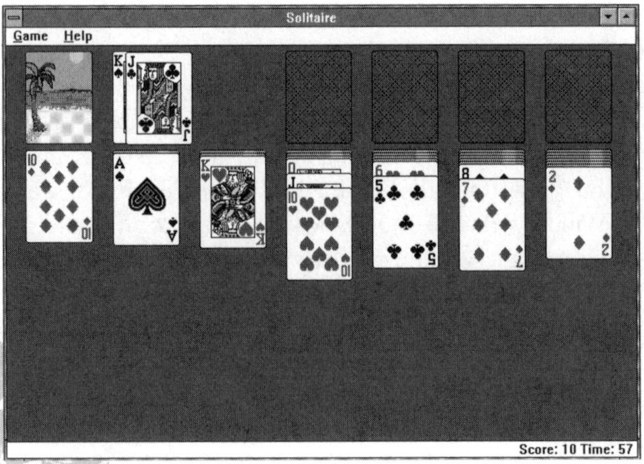

FIGURE 1-1
Microsoft's Solitaire

FIGURE 1-2

Battle Zone

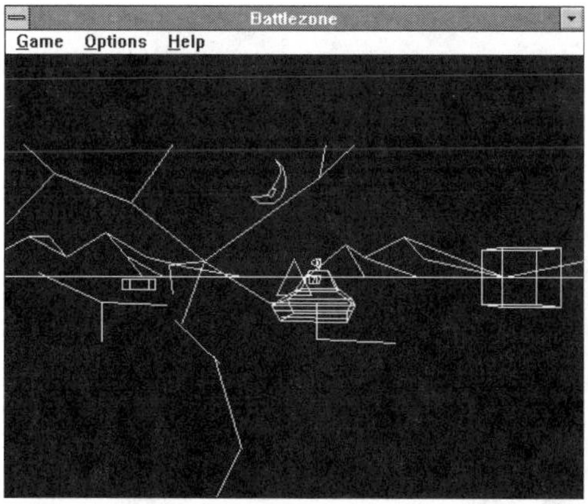

wrist-twitcher's dream to have a personal Asteroids machine at home. The amazing thing is how well these games hold up today.

Another classic ported to Windows is Chessmaster. The most current rendition is Chessmaster 3000, from Mindscape (formerly Software Toolworks). Figure 1-3 is one of several configurations that you can choose in this highly configurable chess game.

Chessmaster is a good example of a game that uses a lot of Windows user interface elements—multiple windows, buttons, and menus. These elements are more typical of board-based games than role-playing or simulation games, which should be more "immersing" experiences.

There's certainly no shortage of Windows games that take over the entire screen to provide the same level of immersion as their DOS-based counterparts. Figure 1-4 is an example of one of the highly successful series of Living Books CD-ROMs from Broderbund; this one is Ruff's Bone.

FIGURE 1-3

Chessmaster 3000

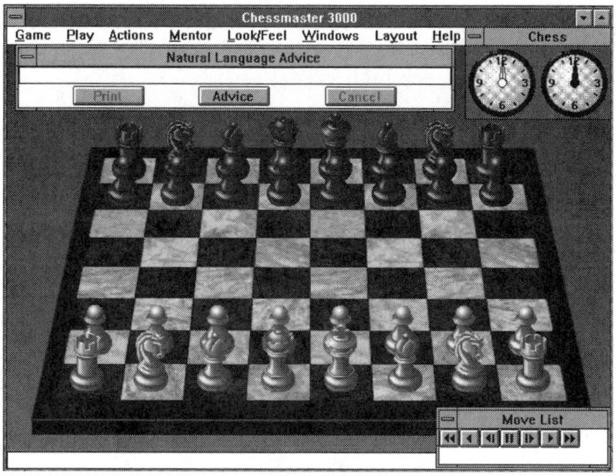

FIGURE 1-4

Ruff's Bone

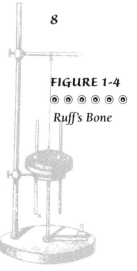

Although the Living Books games take over the screen, they are still well-behaved Windows applications. While playing, you can switch to another task by pressing ALT-TAB, just as you can with any other Windows program. You can close the game with ALT-F4, like you can in any other Windows application, as well. But while it's running, such a game is indistinguishable from its DOS counterpart because of its full-screen implementation.

Users appreciate a game like Ruff's Bone because it installs easily under Windows—click on the setup program and it's there. There's nothing to configure, no interrupts to figure out, no DOS commands to struggle over. A three-year-old could do it—in fact, three-year-olds are a big part of the target market for the Living Books series.

Plenty of shareware games are available under Windows these days. Hexagames for Windows is an example of a program with good sound, nice animation, and fancily rendered 3D objects (see Figure 1-5).

Quatra Command (Figure 1-6) is another shareware game that uses detailed graphics. It's also an excellent performer under Windows, although it was introduced prior to the WinG extensions for increased speed. You can play the game either windowed or full-screen.

Hyperoid is a turbo version of the die-hard Asteroids that comes complete with source code (as shown in Figure 1-7). It, too, can be played full-screen or windowed.

These games are all good examples of what can be done under Windows today, even without the speed benefit of the WinG extensions. All are well-behaved Windows applications—they run well with other applications and use certain standard keystrokes and graphical elements for common Windows functions, like closing the

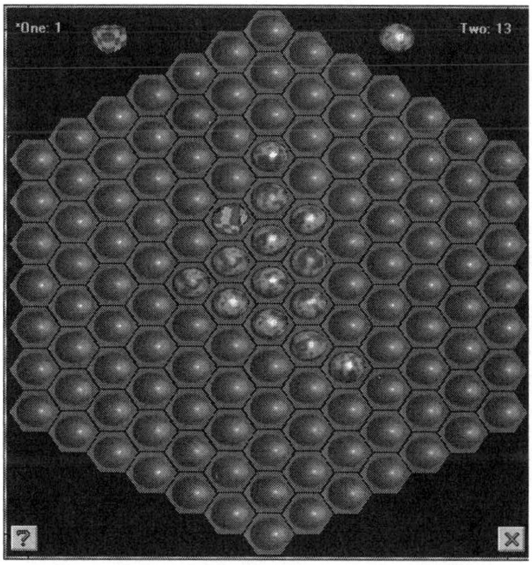

FIGURE 1-5

Hexagames

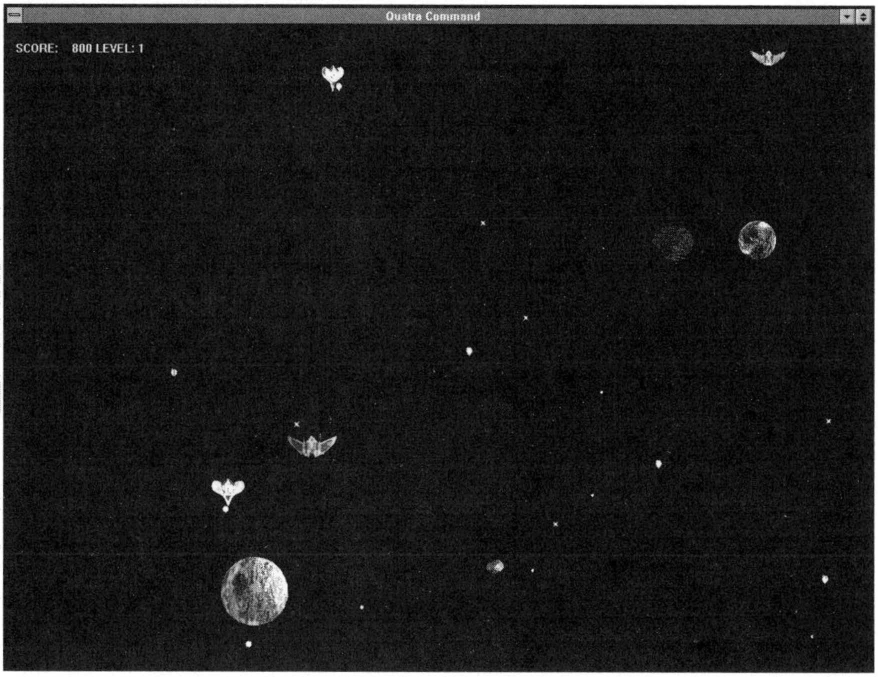

FIGURE 1-6

Quatra Command

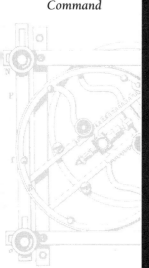

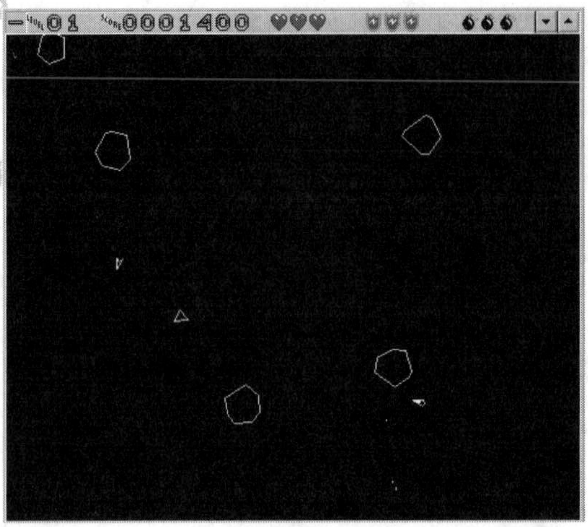

FIGURE 1-7

Hyperoid

program and resizing its windows. Understanding these Windows standards is important to producing a popular Windows game, because users have come to expect a certain amount of standards compliance from the programs they buy—even games. In this chapter, you'll learn a little about what those standards are and how they apply—and sometimes *don't* apply—to Windows games.

First, to understand what the GUI craze is all about, we need some history.

A Little GUI History

Back during the First Age of Enlightenment of computer interfaces (after the Dark Ages of the card deck, but before the personal computer), the command line ruled. The interactive terminal gave computer operators the unbelievable power to do computing *interactively,* rather than as a batch process. Still, the interactivity left a lot to be desired: Typing commands and trying to scan the scrolling results were hardly processes anyone would call "user friendly."

Thence came the Menu, and it was good. At least the Menu gave us something that truly *felt* interactive, even if the response time wasn't exactly instantaneous. Menus begat more menus, and soon there was no space on the screen for the sheep to roam.

Enter Doug Engelbart

In 1968, at the ARPA-funded Stanford Research Institute laboratory known as the Augmentation Research Center, a talented computer programmer named Doug Engelbart came up with the idea of slicing the screen into overlapping stacks of information, much in the same way that our limited desk space has overlapping pieces of paper on it. The overlapping panes of (at the time, textual) information were called *windows,* and whenever you wanted to get at one that was underneath another, you would just pop it to the top. This made things visible while at the same time saving screen space.

How to select the desired window was another dilemma. Doug needed some form of pointing device that he could use to quickly select a window and pop it to the top. The only pointing device around at the time was the light pen, a device whose flaws were serious obstacles to extended use. So Doug, having invented windows, sat down and invented that icon of graphical computing—the mouse. His original mouse differed only cosmetically from what has now become the ubiquitous computer pointing device.

Xerox PARC: 1970

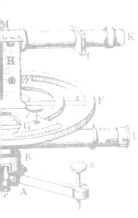

Doug's influence was evident in what was to become the center of the graphical computing universe: Xerox's Palo Alto Research Center. At PARC, folks were working on the genesis of the first personal computer. The very notion of dedicating a *whole computer* to a *single user* was heresy to most of computerdom in those days. Besides, the majority thought, such a computer would be either a toy lacking significant processing power, or a waste of processing power on a single person. PARC's notion, though, was to use processing power for innovations that would have the greatest social effect: any innovations that made computers *easier to use.* So the PARC researchers set about creating the first *graphical* user interface.

The Alto computer was the culmination of their efforts. The Alto was unlike any other computer of its time: The display had a small, pointed cursor that tracked (well, mostly tracked) the position of the attached mouse. It could display text with unprecedented precision, prompting the researchers to coin the term *What You See Is What You Get* (yes, WYSIWYG was a PARC invention, too) to describe it. Like Doug Engelbart's windows, the Alto, too, had windows, but they could display much more than just text. The first interactive computer paint program was designed and implemented on the Alto.

The Alto also gave us the so-called *desktop metaphor:* the notion that the computer screen was a sort of simulacrum of the overlapping pieces of paper and information sitting on an ordinary desktop. (In retrospect, I think that the desktop metaphor was poorly named—who's desk has menus, buttons, cursors, and other such stuff that jumps out at you when you poke it with a stick?) In any case, the desktop metaphor—combined with the personal computer—would forever change our perception of computing.

But enough history already. What is it that the GUI actually *does* for computer users?

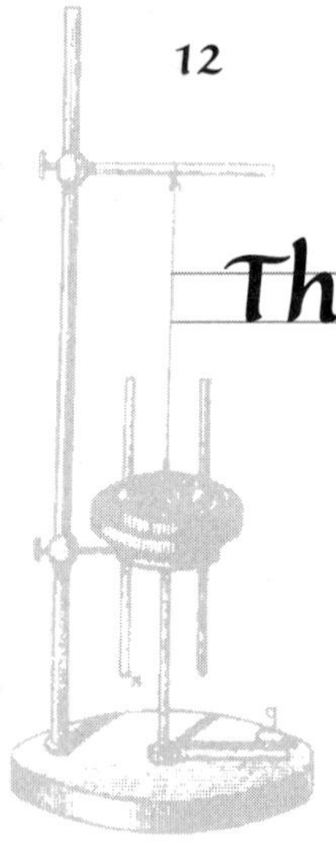

The Benefits of GUIs

One of the main benefits that graphical user interfaces like Windows bring to users is that of commonality among applications. A GUI standardizes (or at least attempts to standardize) certain functions that virtually all applications have in common. For example, consider the functions of opening and closing files, adjusting windows, entering text and numbers, scrolling data, and selecting objects. Many applications share these functions, and it's only logical that programs should perform them in essentially the same way. This not only makes it easier for a user to move from one application to another, but it also rationalizes buying more software, since the overhead of learning a new package is reduced. Good for users, good for software developers.

In my early, cynical, years of intense GUI-phobia, I was quick to accept the argument of many of my colleagues against the GUI germ. "GUIs stifle innovation and creativity," we'd all moan, "because they standardize stuff that could be improved on or even ultimately eliminated."

I'd listen to the Mac aficionados with their favorite torment: "I like the Mac because once I've learned one application, I know 90 percent of what I need for the next one."

"If that's so," I'd say, "then there must be only a 10 percent difference in what the applications actually *do.*"

So I've been there. But after using a GUI every single day for the last five years, I can honestly say that I appreciate it *much* more than "having a different user interface for every application I use." I can think of one possible exception: games. As you'll learn later in this chapter, I believe that the "user interface" is a concept that cannot necessarily be separated from the immersing nature of a good computer game. Fortunately, Microsoft Windows and its users are particularly flexible in this regard.

Let's move on to the common components that make up a GUI, and then Windows in particular.

Common GUI Elements

What most people think of when asked about the term *user interface* (or what they think of first, anyway) is the graphical *look* of the program on the screen. And a good portion of that look *is* controlled by the GUI. Let's explore the list of elements that make up the most common GUIs, and then see how Windows differentiates itself.

Windows

Ever since Doug Engelbart put overlapping text windows on the screen, they've been part and parcel of virtually every modern GUI. The Mac, Microsoft Windows, X Windows, Open Look, OS/2, and most everything else use them as the basic element for encapsulating the data of an application.

On the simplest level, a window is just a rectangle onto which the program draws text and graphics. Windows are so basic to the GUI that most of them have very similar characteristics: a title bar, a border, and some buttons for opening and closing the window. The title bar is almost always at the top, and you can usually grab it with the mouse to drag the window around on the screen. You can often use the mouse to select the borders, as well, allowing you to resize the window. It's this *resizable* aspect of windows that most distinguishes a GUI from an old-style full-screen application, by putting the allocation of screen real estate directly into the hands of the user.

Another common GUI element, the *desktop,* is really a byproduct of having windows. There has to be a background for those windows, after all.

Input Devices

A GUI isn't complete without some kind of pointing device. Doug Engelbart's ubiquitous mouse is the obvious winner in this category. But however ideal a mouse is for specifying general locations on the two-dimensional screen, it is not necessarily a great device for other kinds of input. Joysticks, for example, are vastly more popular for certain game programs, where the motions of the joystick map more closely to, say, those of a real jet fighter's joystick. Most GUIs don't support a joystick as the cursor-control device (Windows is no exception), and so the task of providing joystick support is usually left to the developer who needs it. In Chapter 4, we'll learn about Windows joystick support and how you can access it without having to write your own driver.

Menus

Menus are so common, even in non-GUI programs, that there's not much I can say here that will add to your knowledge of them. Figure 1-8 shows three common menu types.

There are at least a couple of ways to select an item from a menu. The Macintosh's operating system, for example, uses the click-and-drag method—the user holds down the mouse button while dragging over the selections and releases the button when the cursor is over the desired item. Other systems use the click-move-click technique, in which the user clicks once to open the menu, moves the cursor until it is over the desired item, and then clicks the mouse button again. As we'll see, Windows integrates these two methods so that you can select items in either way.

You open most menus by clicking on a visible menu item, but there are a few menu systems out there that you open simply by moving the mouse over the menu area. They are in the tiny minority.

FIGURE 1-8

Menu types

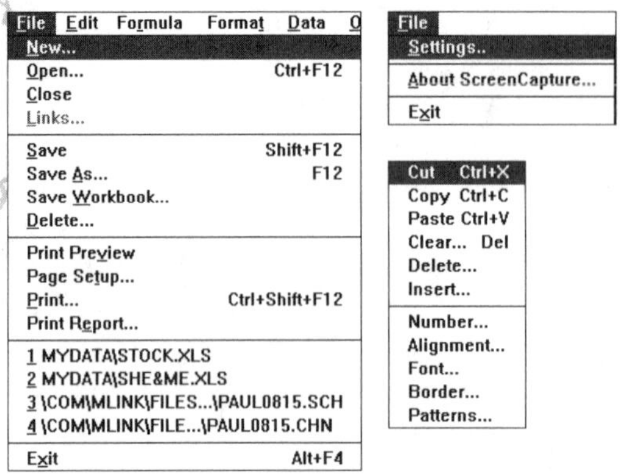

In addition, menus that you pop up at the cursor position by pressing the right mouse button are becoming more popular.

Controls

Controls are the little tidbits that are the most visibly distinguishing characteristic of a GUI. Various buttons, list boxes, scrollbars, text and number fields, and so on all fall into this category. There has been a consistent trend toward fancier and fancier controls—partly because they *are* the most visible and distinguishing part of the GUI and partly because innovative controls can actually make a program easier to learn and use. The move toward "3D-looking" buttons and other controls is probably the most noticeable trend in recent years. It's not certain that an OK button that appears to stick out a little from the dialog box is actually better than a flat rectangle that says "OK," but it sure *looks* better.

Dialog Boxes

Dialog boxes were designed to be screen real-estate savers. Each consists of a window with a bunch of controls on it—buttons, list boxes, and so on. Dialog boxes usually come up when you select a menu item. They let you set some values by tweaking the controls and then go away when you click on the appropriately labeled button (which, if you're lucky, always has the same label). These are called *modal* dialog boxes, because once they come up, the program won't allow you to do anything else until you put them away. There are also *nonmodal* dialog boxes that stay up while you go on to do other things (a text-search dialog box is the most common example). Figure 1-9 shows a typical Windows dialog box.

Programs usually employ dialog boxes to get the user to set certain global or modal parameters, like text font and height in a word processing package, for example. In general, it's bad design to have a dialog box come up as part of an interactive function; dialog boxes should appear always as the result of a user-initiated function.

Games rarely use dialog boxes, and almost never as part of the game play. Occasionally, a game will use a dialog box for entering setup or configuration information, or perhaps to specify a file name.

The Desktop and File System

Certain GUIs extend their relationship with the computer to include the whole concept of the file system. The Macintosh is the preeminent example: What the user thinks of as a filing system is neatly integrated into the way the whole desktop works. Obviously, there are considerable ease-of-use benefits to an integrated file system and desktop.

Contrast this with Windows, whose DOS heritage shows in the form of a separate application—File Manager—that single-handedly performs all file-management functions. Fortunately, Microsoft has fixed some of these shortcomings in Windows 95. (By the way, some of the UNIX-based GUIs don't address the file system at all. They rely on the user's command-line prowess to display, move, delete, rename, and back up files.)

Multitasking

Though not technically part of the GUI itself, the multitasking aspect of a system allows a single user to run more than one application at once. For this to work, the GUI must present a consistent multitasking model and method for switching between applications.

The two most popular multitasking GUI systems are the Macintosh and Windows. Both are so-called *cooperative multitasking systems*. Under a cooperative multitasking system, each application must be coded in such a way as to allow other applications

FIGURE 1-9

A dialog box

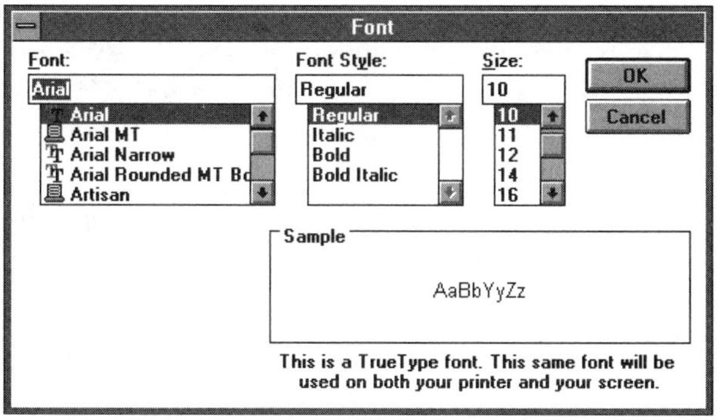

a slice of processor time. In other words, a given program must yield control back to the operating system at various times so that other programs can run.

It might at first seem difficult to design a program in such a way that it willingly gives up control every once in a while, and it might seem especially difficult to do so for game programs that have, essentially, no idle time. As it turns out, the event-driven architecture of the GUI makes this less of a problem than you might think. We'll explore the event-driven architecture of Windows in Chapter 2.

The alternative to cooperative multitasking is *preemptive multitasking,* where the operating system itself doles out time to the running applications, interrupting them without so much as asking. There are certain efficiencies that you can gain through preemptive multitasking, and it's generally—though not always—friendlier to the user. Windows 95 allows preemptive multitasking among 32-bit applications, but limits all the 16-bit programs to cooperative multitasking.

The Microsoft Windows Environment

Now that we know about the general features of a GUI, let's see how Windows compares. I'll examine Windows from the point of view of a "GUIologist"—pointing out its outstanding features along with a few of its holes.

Windows as Operating System

The first thing that a GUIologist might observe about Windows is that it's considerably more than just a graphical user interface—it's really more like an entire operating system unto itself. Windows has a say in just about everything that's important to a programmer: memory usage, display and other device access, printing, networking, and even file operations, to some extent. The fact that DOS exists "underneath" it (in the case of Windows 3.1, anyway) could almost be imperceptible to the user, were it not for things like configuration and the plethora of DOS-only programs (games, in particular) that people still run. Indeed, it's the DOS/Windows nightmare that Microsoft would like to replace with both Windows 95 and the WinG extensions for Windows games. Windows 95 doesn't require DOS at all, though it offers DOS emulation in a manner similar to Windows 3.1.

Not that long ago, many game publishers targeted platforms that were simply too underpowered to run Windows effectively, like 80286-based computers. Today, it's rare to see a game program that doesn't demand at least an 80386-based PC, often coupled with other requirements like a joystick and sound card. Many of these same PCs are running Windows. In fact, the majority of new computers sold today are sold with Windows *preinstalled,* so that the user doesn't have to figure out how to configure the machine to run it.

The problem comes when the poor user tries to install his or her first DOS-based game on their shiny new Windows-based machine. Understanding how to edit the AUTOEXEC.BAT and CONFIG.SYS files (among others) so that a DOS game and Windows can coexist is well beyond the capabilities of most home computer users. Consequently, these users frequently end up on the phone to the product support department of the DOS game's publisher, which more often than not explains to them how to make a boot disk so that they can run the game in a "clean" configuration. Between the support hassles and the general inconvenience of running DOS games, more and more users are turning to Windows games, even if the performance doesn't match that of their DOS counterparts.

Less Religion

To a GUIologist, the look and feel of a particular interface is only part of the story. Equally important is the largely undocumented *culture* that surrounds a given GUI; its *religion,* if you will. Every computing platform—and in particular, GUI-based ones—comes complete with its ministers, evangelists, and other zealots that preach the benefits of Conformance to the Great Way (of their GUI). Their bible is sometimes written, sometimes not. If it is, it's usually called *The XXX System Interface Guidelines,* and it spells out the commandments dutiful programmers should follow to make all applications running under the GUI similar. It warns against being seduced by Unwarranted Innovation for the sake of Distinction, and tells us horrifying tales of woe about the wayward programmers who chose to stray down the path of Unbridled Creative Interface Design, only to find themselves lost in the limbo of Consumer Rejection.

The theory behind such a GUI religion is that the consumer research and development done by its creator is best leveraged when the independent software vendor sticks to The Plan—by creating applications that closely follow the interface guidelines for their GUI. Deviations from the standard generally don't pay off, the GUI creator says, for two reasons: (a) The creator has already figured out what works and what doesn't, and (b) the GUI's entire purpose is to improve comprehensibility through familiarity of interface (meaning that deviations are antithetical). Most evangelists argue that there is still plenty of room for innovation within the guidelines, and that the guidelines attempt to enforce only a common, low-level interface look and feel.

Of course, every religion has its heretics. In the case of GUIs, sometimes the heretics innovate what becomes the next de facto standard of interface look and feel. Other times, their efforts are dubbed "quirky" and fail in the market.

In the GUI-less world of straight DOS programming, every single *program* can—and often does—have its very own interface religion. This is an important reason why the transition from DOS programming to Windows programming is so difficult for many—there's not just the steep learning curve associated with understanding Windows, but also the cultural shock brought about by having to put one's faith in someone else's user interface paradigm. A reassurance that there's plenty of room for innovation *within* the guidelines is hardly a consolation to someone who's put a great deal of time and effort into creating an entirely new (and, in their mind at least, *better*) system for doing menus, for example.

So where is Windows on the scale of religious temperance? Granted, this assessment is based on my (totally subjective) opinion only, but I believe that the Windows culture—perhaps because of its DOS heritage—is more accepting of interface innovations than are other GUI cultures. After all, a large percentage of current Windows users (though it's undoubtedly a shrinking proportion) grew up on DOS applications, with all their widely differing interfaces. Perhaps these users had a respect for innovation when it actually seemed to help make things go faster—like shortcut keys and other power-user features. Perhaps, at first, they also had a contempt for GUIs' need for constant "mousing around." These users came to Windows reluctantly, maybe even pushed there by corporate edicts rather than their own self-interest. (The conversion (brainwashing?) sometimes takes a long time—I relied on the crutch of the DOS Box regularly for the first three years I used Windows.) But once they crossed the bridge, there was no going back.

The willingness of Windows users to accept interface innovation is a good sign for applications developers, and probably an even better sign for game developers. It means that there's room to push the envelope in places that might be rejected on other GUIs.

There is, in fact, an official Interface Guideline book for Windows, but it generally can't keep up with the state of the art. In some cases, the guidelines even contradict what Microsoft does with their own applications.

Enough religion. Let's take a look at what Windows really looks like to the user, and what things the average user expects to be consistent among applications. We'll also look at various implementations of games under Windows and how they both do and don't follow the religion.

Windows

What every user sees when he or she starts an application is usually the standard application window. Figure 1-10 shows the application window for the standard Windows accessory Notepad.

Although the elements of this window should be familiar to even the most casual Windows user, I'll assume nothing here and describe each element briefly. (If you're an experienced Windows user, you might want to skip over the next few sections.)

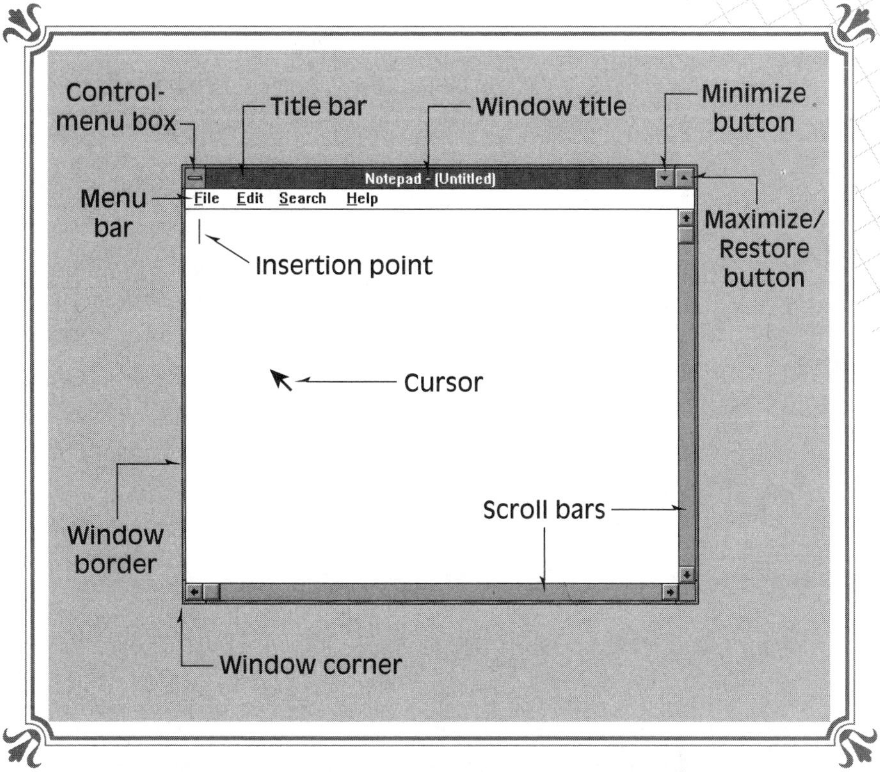

FIGURE 1-10

An application window

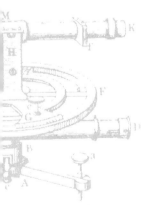

- The *Control-menu box* is in the upper left corner of the window. The Control menu is used primarily by keyboard users, although you can double-click the box itself to quickly close the window (and the application).
- The *title bar* shows the name of the application or document. If more than one window is open, the title bar for the *active* window (the one in which you are working) is a different color or intensity than other title bars. You can drag the window around the desktop by dragging the title bar.
- The *window title,* depending on the type of window in which it appears, can be the name of an application and a document, or the name of a group, directory, or file. If a document has not been saved, a placeholder such as "(Untitled)" usually appears as part of the window title.
- The *menu bar* lists the available menus. Most applications have at least a File menu, an Edit menu, and a Help menu. The underlined characters in the menu bar represent the character you type in conjunction with ALT to select that menu (more on this in a moment).

- By using *scrollbars,* you can move parts of a document into view when the entire document doesn't fit in the window. You can also use scrollbars to view unseen portions of lists and other information that cannot fit in the allotted space. Not all windows or applications require scrollbars, of course.
- Using a mouse, you can click the *Maximize button* to enlarge the active application window so that it fills the entire desktop, or you can click the *Minimize button* to reduce the window to an icon.
- After you enlarge a window, the Maximize button is replaced by the *Restore button,* which contains both an up arrow and a down arrow. You can click the Restore button to return the window to its previous size.
- The *window border* is the outside edge of a window. You can lengthen or shorten the border on each side of a window by clicking and dragging.
- You can use the *window corner* to shorten or lengthen two adjoining sides of a window border at the same time.
- The *insertion point* shows where you are in a document, and can take different forms depending on the application. The insertion point marks the place where text and graphics appear when you begin typing or drawing.
- The *mouse pointer* or *cursor* moves with the mouse.

The standard application window is but one type of window that Windows can display. The elements listed here are only *optional* parts of a standard applications window, though most applications have all of them. For example, you might find an application that has a fixed-size window, in which case there would be no Maximize button and the borders might have a slightly different look to indicate that they were not resizable.

The Mouse

Using the mouse under Windows is very similar to using a mouse with most GUIs, like the Macintosh. The main difference is that the Mac has a strictly one-button mouse, and most mice for Windows have either two or three buttons. Until Windows 95, the primary mouse button (by default, this is the left button) was the only button to which Windows proper paid attention. (You can change the primary-button setting if you prefer to designate another mouse button as the primary one.) The three primary-button operations are:

- Click and release
- Click, drag, and release
- Double-click

How these three actions are used within any given application is largely up to the application programmer; the standard varies with the type of application.

With Windows 95, use of the right (or secondary) mouse button begins to be standardized. The new standard for the right mouse button is as an object *inspector:* Right-clicking (that is, clicking with the right mouse button) on something brings up a pop-up menu of that particular object's properties.

Menus

Menus in Windows have some characteristics that are unique among GUIs. As a GUIologist, I'll have to give Microsoft credit for some real innovations here that aren't seen in other systems.

When Microsoft first introduced Windows in 1984, one of its goals was to make a GUI that was equally effective for keyboard-only users and mouse users. Most applications you'll find on Windows today (and, indeed, Windows 95 itself) require a mouse, but the ALT-character menu-selection method is still a very useful component of the Windows menu system. Every menu item has a unique underlined character in its title, and you can select that menu item by holding down ALT while pressing the underlined letter. Once you've "pulled down" a menu, you can make subsequent menu selections by just typing the underlined character of the desired menu item. This gives power users the ability to navigate menus without ever having to take their hands from the keyboard (see Figure 1-11).

FIGURE 1-11

ALT- character usage for menu selection

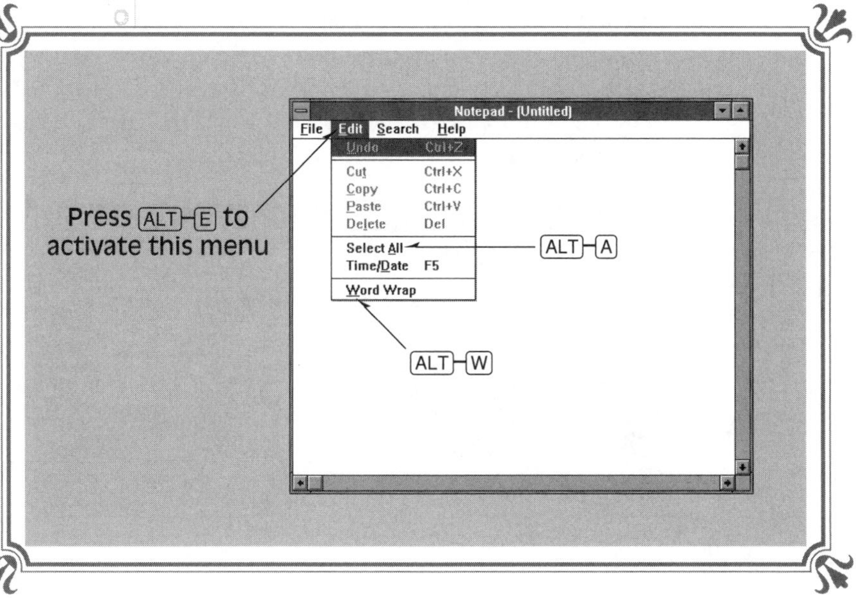

In Windows, each application window has its *own* menu. The Mac, on the other hand, has a single menu bar across the top of the screen that changes when you switch applications. The question of which method is better could be argued for days on end by zealots representing both sides. Really, the choice is an outgrowth of exactly where an application *lives* under each GUI, which is another topic of some debate.

Another difference between the Mac's and Windows' menu systems is that Windows allows you to choose a menu item with either a click-release-select operation *or* a click-drag-release operation, whereas the Mac allows only the latter.

Cascading menus (sometimes called *pull-right* menus—see Figure 1-12) are also fairly common among Windows applications. General GUI wisdom holds that the use of cascading menus should be restricted to only the more obscure functions, since such menus are substantially more difficult for the user to navigate.

Besides appearing at the top of an application window, under Windows, menus can appear at the click of the mouse. These are called *pop-up* menus. As I mentioned previously, these are becoming a more and more commonly accepted part of the Windows interface when coupled appropriately with the right mouse button.

Menu shortcut keys or *accelerators* are different from the ALT-character combinations for selecting menus. An accelerator key combination appears to the right of its equivalent menu item, and you can type it at any time to choose that function.

Windows has a few current standards for accelerator keys, along with a few evolving standards. For example, ALT-F4 is the standard accelerator key combination for closing an application and is, in fact, hard-wired into the Windows message-handling loop. If you *don't* want your application to use the ALT-F4 combination, you must include code to specifically override that accelerator (although it would be highly unwise for a programmer to make this kind of decision, given that this accelerator key combination is one of Windows' genuine standards). Likewise, F1 is the Windows standard accelerator key for Help. Typically, it opens the Windows Help system to the context-appropriate topic. Unlike ALT-F4, F1 isn't hard-wired into Windows, so each application must decode this accelerator.

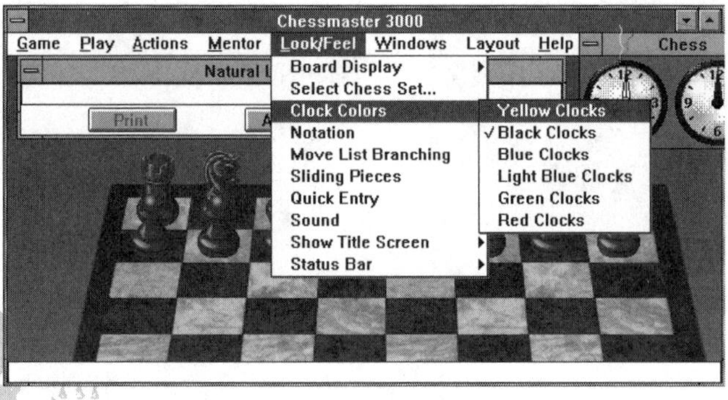

FIGURE 1-12

Cascading menus

Most Windows applications are starting to mimic the Macintosh standard for many menu operations. For example, CTRL-S is quickly becoming the universal standard key combination for saving the current file, which is considerably better than SHIFT-F12, the old Microsoft standard. You can now execute the Cut, Copy, and Paste commands by pressing CTRL-X, CTRL-C, and CTRL-V, respectively.

You can also use menu items in Windows to indicate modal settings or program states through the use of *graying, check marks,* and *bullets.* Menu items that aren't appropriate for a given selection or state of the program are grayed to prevent access. This provides an important visual clue to the user that, for example, the item can be chosen only when a selection is active. Check marks appear next to menu items to indicate that toggled (binary) options are on. Bullets distinguish mutually exclusive options. When you select one item, the bullet moves from the previously selected item to the current one.

Finally, it's standard practice to include an ellipsis (...) at the end of a menu item that calls up a dialog box, our next subject.

Dialog Boxes

As we learned before, a dialog box is a special window filled with controls that the user can tweak to set certain operating parameters. Windows has three basic kinds of dialog boxes: modal dialog boxes, nonmodal dialog boxes, and system modal dialog boxes. They differ not in how they look, but in how they act.

A modal dialog box is the type you see most often. It's called modal because once it's up, you can't do anything else in the application until you make the dialog box go away. A *message box* is probably the most commonly encountered modal dialog box. It typically contains a message and one or more command buttons offering choices like Yes or No, or Save or Cancel. The user can't go any further in the program without pushing one of the buttons, dismissing the dialog box.

A nonmodal dialog box is one that doesn't prevent the user from doing other things in the application. The most common example is probably the Find Text dialog box you can find in most text-processing applications. The user can alternate back and forth between the dialog box and the main application window (or windows) without having to put the dialog box away. Nonmodal dialog boxes are far less common than modal ones.

A system modal dialog box is one that prevents you from doing *anything at all* before you put away the dialog box. It blocks you even from selecting another application window. Programmers typically use system modal dialog boxes for times when the application is accessing a shared system resource, during time-critical operations, or for when something very bad happens and the programmer needs to keep the user from changing the state of the system.

Controls

As I mentioned earlier, controls are the various little interface objects that Windows uses to allow the user to display and select information in standard ways. There are surprisingly few standard Windows controls. Many of the controls we see in applications are custom-designed by their creators. Windows has a robust mechanism for turning a standard control into a custom control, as well as many ways for creating a custom control from scratch. Here's a list of the standard controls:

- *Command buttons* typically initiate an immediate action, like opening a new window or closing an existing one. If you push the OK button on a modal dialog box, for example, you dismiss the dialog box and keep its current settings.
- *Option buttons,* sometimes called *radio buttons,* come in groups that represent mutually exclusive settings.
- *Check boxes* allow users to select or clear an option.
- *Edit fields* let users enter alphanumeric information. An edit field can be a single line of text or multiple lines. Within an edit field, you can use standard Windows text-selection and editing keys (the arrow keys, SHIFT, and so on) to navigate and select characters.
- A *list box* is a box that contains several lines of text, allowing the user to select one (or sometimes more) lines. If there are more lines than can fit in the box, a *scrollbar* appears to allow the user to scroll the list.
- *Scrollbars* are vertical or horizontal controls that you use to scroll a window's contents.
- A *combo box* is a combination of an edit field and a list box, and allows a user to type in information as well as select it from the list. These also come in a space-saving *drop-down* variant that has a little button. You push the button to reveal the list.
- A *static* control is one that just displays uneditable text information.

As I mentioned, it's possible to customize controls to look or behave differently than the standard Windows variety. For example, you might have a list box that has pictures rather than text, or a combination of both. A standard Windows button has a textual label; you might make it a picture instead. Or you might create an entirely new control, like the status bar display found at the bottom of the main application window in many programs.

Windows also provides a set of common dialog boxes for performing certain operations that all applications typically share, like opening and saving files, selecting text fonts, and so on. These are "canned" dialog boxes that don't have to be designed separately by every application developer.

Multitasking in Windows

Earlier, we learned that Microsoft Windows is a cooperative multitasking system. This means that each application running under Windows must be written in such a way that it yields control back to Windows periodically, which in turn passes control on to the other running applications. In Chapter 2, we'll learn why this is less difficult than it may sound. But what does cooperative multitasking really mean to the Windows user?

First of all, multitasking means that the user can easily switch between running tasks. There are several ways to do this under Windows, none of which is particularly ideal. First, if the window of the task to which you want to switch is visible, you can simply click the mouse on that window and it will pop to the foreground, replacing whatever program was current. Clicking on another application's window can be difficult or impossible, however—if the current application is maximized, then no other windows are visible.

Several key combinations are dedicated to the task of switching applications, as well. For example, the ALT-TAB combination cycles through a list of the running applications as the user successively presses TAB while holding down ALT. Releasing ALT brings that program to the foreground. Pressing ALT-ESC does the same thing, but rather than cycling through a list, the system actually switches from one application to another as the user successively presses ESC while holding down ALT. Also, pressing CTRL-ESC brings up a dialog box containing a list of all the running applications; double-clicking on one of the names in the list switches you to that application.

The fact that the user can switch applications easily is important to the game programmer. You can't assume that your running game will always be the foreground application. When the user switches to another program, it shouldn't have a deleterious effect on the game. For most games, the kind thing to do is to suspend play until the game becomes the foreground application again. Some games implement a "boss" key that, when pressed, suspends the game and minimizes it, activating the last foreground application (presumably a spreadsheet or some other suitable productivity application). The Microsoft Arcade games all respond to the ESC key in this way.

Windows Sound

Back in 1990, before Windows 3.1 was introduced, Microsoft unveiled the Multimedia Extensions for Windows 3.0. The MME enabled Windows to include sound support, among other things. Before the MME, using sound hardware under Windows was completely nonstandard; every application had to write drivers for all the various sound cards on the market, and users had no uniform way to configure sound cards. The Multimedia Extensions really helped solidify the sound-card market, and were included as a standard part of Windows 3.1 when it shipped.

Thanks to the MME, a suitably equipped Windows PC can handle the following types of sound:

- Waveform (sampled) audio
- MIDI audio
- CD audio

Waveform audio is sound that has been digitized at some sampling rate and resolution. Waveform audio has the advantage of being able to represent anything, since it's a true digital recording, but it has the disadvantage of high bandwidth and disk-space requirements. For example, CD-quality stereo audio—2 channels of 16-bit samples at 44.1 kHz—requires over 10 MB of disk space per recorded minute. Many applications don't require the full fidelity of CD-quality audio, and indeed, a lot of audio hardware is incapable of fully resolving that level of quality anyway. But at least Windows is capable of supporting the complete range.

MIDI audio is musical performance data stored in the internationally standardized Musical Instrument Digital Interface format. MIDI audio doesn't represent the actual recorded waveform of the sound, but rather the *notes* as they would be played on a variety of digitally simulated musical instruments. MIDI data takes the form of a series of note-on and note-off messages that you can play on a wide variety of sound hardware. MIDI represents *instrumental music only,* and has nothing to do with recorded voice or other sounds. Because it represents only the performance data and not the actual waveform itself, MIDI data can be quite compact—you can store many hours of music in several hundred thousand bytes.

CD audio is the stuff found on the CDs you buy in record stores. This is often called Red Book audio, after the original Sony/Philips specification book for CD manufacturing. Since all CD-ROM drives are also capable of playing Red Book audio if so commanded, Windows provides access to the drives in a way similar to that used by a regular home CD player. It's even possible to mix Red Book audio and CD-ROM data on the same disk, although handling access to the various parts in a seamless way is no small programming challenge.

Installation and Setup

Once upon a time, the installation process was an afterthought, exempt from all the ease-of-use mandates that governed the actual application program. It wasn't unusual for a user to have to install a Windows program by running a batch file from DOS—before running Windows itself!

Today, users expect nothing less than a professional, Windows-based installation program that guides them through all aspects of the installation process. Besides allowing the user to determine into which directory the program will be loaded, most installation programs also check for free disk space and allow the customization of certain options to save space when it's appropriate.

The majority of Windows programs use the standard Microsoft installation program—Setup. The Setup Toolkit (available from Microsoft, and often included in some of their SDKs) provides a complete set of tools for creating your own setup program. There's a floppy-disk layout tool that compresses all the source files and packs them optimally onto the minimum number of floppy disks for you. Setup can handle updates as well as new installations, and you can even program it to read standard version numbers that are buried inside Windows program modules.

There are other installation products available on the market for building installation programs. The key point here is that whether or not you use the Microsoft Setup Toolkit to create an installation program, user expectations are such that whatever you do must be Windows-based.

There's a topic related to installation that's been getting more and more attention lately, and that's *de*installation. As often as not, an installed Windows program doesn't just deposit a few files into one directory and leave the rest of your system untouched. There are usually DLLs, .INI files, and perhaps even drivers and font files strewn about on your hard disk, not to mention the program groups created in File Manager. The poor user who wants to remove a program from his or her system for whatever reason has at best an arduous task ahead of him or her, and at worst an impossible one. There's no standard for defining what files belong to a given application, and indeed, applications sometimes share resources like DLLs to such an extent that their removal would unintentionally cripple remaining applications. A growing trend seems to be to include the *removal* of the program as an option in the setup or installation program, especially for programs that scatter their guts across the user's hard disk.

The Nasty Bits

Notwithstanding its remarkable market acceptance, it would be hard to call Windows the perfect GUI, even if such a thing existed (which, of course, it doesn't). From the user's perspective, there are decidedly unremarkable aspects of Windows. Complaints about some of these tend to be voiced frequently and contribute to Windows' sometimes tarnished image.

Before beating up on Windows too much, I should mention a few important facts. First, a lot of what's bad about Windows is really attributable to DOS. Half the battle of getting Windows configured properly on a given PC is getting *DOS* configured properly. Second, Windows was designed to move users from a GUI-less world to a GUI-full one that offered *both* compatibility and ease of use—two goals that are, often as not, mutually incompatible. In this regard, Windows is quite an accomplishment. Lastly, most or all of the following list of "idiosyncrasies" are fixed in Windows 95.

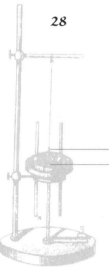

But inasmuch as these little deficiencies account for the vast majority of problems that users—and hence, the product support staffs of software companies—encounter, it seems only fair to dig into them here.

Different Strokes

Although Windows was designed to be both a mouse-based *and* keyboard-based GUI, some of the choices Microsoft made about what keystrokes to use for certain functions were, perhaps, a little obscure. For example, there are probably millions of Windows users that have never learned that ALT-TAB switches between running applications. Then again, it *is* explained on page 56 of the Windows 3.1 User's Guide, along with another (equally obscure) method for switching—double-clicking on the desktop to bring up a list. The latter is, of course, impossible to do if the current application covers the whole desktop, as is commonly the case in Windows games. For such contingencies, you're undoubtedly familiar with the completely obvious CTRL-ESC combination, no?

Another favorite key combination I mentioned earlier is ALT-F4, which closes the current application. This, too, is explained in the User's Guide (page 63), but a large portion of Windows users miss this reference. It's especially significant for Windows games, because they often don't have a visible File menu from which the user can choose Exit, the other method mentioned on page 63. Of course, it isn't Windows' fault if a program doesn't make it clear how to quit, but you'd think Microsoft could have used *something* a little more intuitive than ALT-F4. Some of the philosophy of keystroke usage in Windows appears to have come from the idea that the application should be allowed to use as many easily accessible keystrokes as possible for its own purposes. So instead of CTRL-Q for Quit, we end up with ALT-F4, in case some application wants to use CTRL-Q for Query or something.

Windows has a whole host of standard key combinations that are shortcuts for mouse operations; users never learn most of them. One of my favorites is CTRL-/, the key combination you can use to select all items in any standard Windows list box. Try doing *that* one in front of a new (or even veteran) Windows user—you'll be anointed Guru in an instant. The many common Windows shortcut keys are listed in the User's Guide, starting on page 583.

While some might consider the sheer quantity of key combinations a detractor from ease of use, the shortcut keys are just that—*shortcuts*. All the operations they perform you can do with the mouse, usually more intuitively. The shortcut keys really are convenient for power users only.

Driver Mania

Windows is a very unique GUI because of its model of device independence. While most GUIs claim to be device-independent at their core, the fact is that Windows has the burden of supporting a vastly wider range of hardware than any other GUI. Most popular GUIs are captive to the hardware on which they run, and are developed by the same company that manufactures that hardware: The Macintosh is an obvious example. But Microsoft had to create a GUI that was as open to add-on hardware as the PC architecture itself is. This, of course, allows competition in the market and, hence, prompts prices to drop steadily and performance to improve. All this open architecture comes at a price, though; namely, configuration of the system through the use of device drivers.

As you probably know, a *device driver* is a code module that is loaded at run time and that interfaces between a system or application and some kind of physical hardware. In Windows, there are several kinds of device drivers (or just drivers, for short). There are display drivers, printer drivers, sound-card drivers, MCI drivers, mouse drivers, network card drivers, and even some special low-level drivers for disk drives and other basic components.

The process of installing some hardware and configuring it through its driver varies, depending on the type of device. For example, display, mouse, and keyboard drivers are configured with the Windows Setup program, whereas sound-card and other drivers are configured from the Control Panel program under the Drivers icon, just to make things confusing. The drivers themselves have varying degrees of dissimilarity problems and generate other ease-of-use concerns. Some have slick Windows installation programs that guide you through each step; others require a considerable degree of knowledge from the user about things like IRQ settings and I/O addresses.

Worse yet, you can't alway configure Windows for certain types of hardware solely within Windows itself. Some drivers require changes to CONFIG.SYS and AUTOEXEC.BAT files, which in turn bring on new configuration problems. Complicating matters further are hardware conflicts that usually can't be resolved except by moving physical jumpers on the cards themselves, if then.

Admittedly, not all these problems are strictly Windows' fault. The hardware architecture of the PC makes it difficult to resolve all of them completely. The plug-and-play standard introduced by Microsoft in Windows 95 promises to make a significant dent in this problem. Over time, all hardware manufacturers will begin to use the features of this specification, if for no other reason than the support-cost savings.

System Resources

Here's a real nasty one. It comes from Windows' tradition of running on machines with relatively scant memory and is, unfortunately, buried rather deep in Windows 3.1's core.

The problem has to do with how Windows handles memory for certain system resources that are shared among all running applications. Sadly, the memory for these resources come from fixed-size pools—small pools (64k), at that. Because of this fact, running multiple applications under Windows is an activity often limited not by the total amount of available application memory, but by the availability of memory in the system resource pools (or *heaps*, as they're called). There are four such heaps that constitute the system resources:

- The GDI heap
- The user heap
- The menu heap
- The string heap

Each of these heaps is 64k in size and is shared among all running applications. Users typically have no idea what these heaps are used for, and more importantly, shouldn't have to think about them at all. (A user usually learns about heaps shortly after he or she has opened one too many applications and their system starts to slowly fall apart, even if the amount of available memory seems like it should be adequate.)

System-resource handling was improved slightly in Windows 3.1, and is radically improved again (but not made perfect) under Windows 95.

Enhanced Mode vs. Standard Mode

Windows 3.0 and later were designed to run on Intel 80286 and better microprocessors. It doesn't take a computer scientist to understand that there is a world of difference between the Intel 80286 and the 80386. The 386 has 32-bit processing power, contains a built-in memory-management unit, supports external caching, and offers a host of other improvements over the older 286 design. Unfortunately, the installed base of 286 machines was, at least at one time, considerable enough to make Microsoft take them into account in the design and enhancement of Windows. This has probably been one of the greatest limitations on Windows' design. With Windows 95, which runs only on 386 and higher microprocessors, Microsoft has finally abandoned the 286.

Depending on which microprocessor it detects, Windows 3.1 runs in either Standard mode (286) or Enhanced mode (386 and above). Enhanced mode provides several additional features:

- Multiple DOS sessions
- Windowed DOS sessions
- More addressable memory
- Virtual memory

Of these, virtual memory is certainly of the greatest overall benefit to the user. Virtual memory uses hard-disk space to make the system appear to have more memory than it has physical RAM. Whenever the system needs more memory than it can make room for in RAM (a so-called overcommitted memory condition), it *swaps* or *pages* the least-recently used segments of RAM out to disk to free up RAM memory. Whenever a program tries to access a memory address that isn't physically available, the CPU generates a *page fault* and the memory-management unit tells the operating system that it should load the requested page or pages of information from disk.

Virtual memory is a godsend for most applications, because it can both allow larger programs to run and, in a multitasking system like Windows, allow *more* programs to run. The performance hit you take when paging is felt only when swapping to a different application, so long as there's enough physical memory for the largest application.

The problem arises when there *isn't* enough memory for the current application, in which case the virtual memory system *thrashes*—constantly pages sections of the program and its data to and from a disk. Unfortunately, it is difficult to tell if your system is thrashing. If it seems like it's running slowly and the hard-disk light is blinking all the time, then your system probably *is* thrashing and you should install more RAM. It's likely there are many Windows users who could greatly increase the performance of their machines with a few hundred dollars' worth of RAM, if they could only identify the problem.

DOS and Windows: An Unhappy Marriage

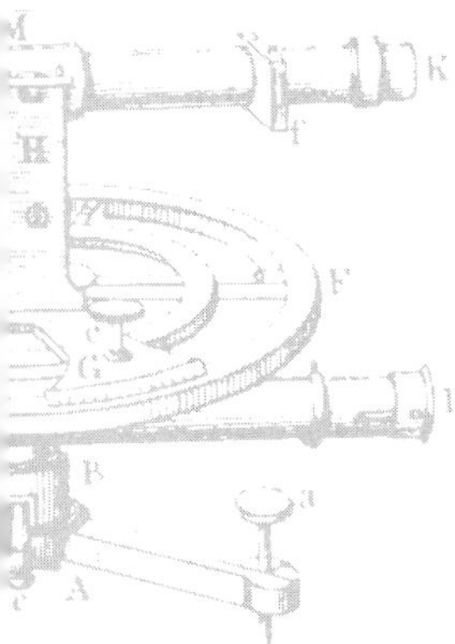

By far the worst problems with Windows aren't with Windows at all, but with its relationship to DOS. All the various drivers that must be loaded via CONFIG.SYS and AUTOEXEC.BAT files are a starting point for the difficulties the average user must contend with to get a system up and running. In the early days of DOS, when 640k was more than enough memory to run virtually all popular applications (does anybody remember that far back?), an average CONFIG.SYS and AUTOEXEC.BAT file had maybe five simple statements. Today, the conflagration of memory managers, disk caches, device drivers, and other programs has made configuration almost unmanageable for the average user. Understanding EMS, XMS, LIM, DPMI, MSCDEX, and how the various settings of STACKS and BUFFERS affect performance can be a career in itself.

This becomes a particularly difficult dilemma for the Windows user who needs to run DOS-based games, of course. The nature of most games requires that the whole system be tuned to their benefit—and Windows has the same requirement. A junior genius might be lucky enough to come up with a set of configuration options that allows DOS games to run so long as Windows *isn't* running—but it takes a master guru (and a miracle) to find the configuration that allows even a few DOS games to run in a DOS box *under* Windows. The situation becomes worse with each piece of hardware that's added to the system. Windows drivers trying to access sound-card hardware, for example, can conflict with DOS-based programs and vice versa. It's easy to see why one environment under which all applications run is the only reasonable solution.

Games and Windows

Although DOS-based games are still in the vast majority, more and more game and education titles appear for Windows every day, even without the performance enhancements provided by WinG. What are the common characteristics of these games and the user expectations of them?

The User Interface Is the Game

I think it's safe to say that for most game developers, the story or idea behind a game and its user interface are inseparable concepts. Game developers try to present a compelling, immersing, and entertaining experience by using whatever means necessary. Many of the concepts behind a GUI, however, are antithetical to games—GUIs were designed to provide a consistent metaphor for working with different applications, making it possible for a user to move from application to application with the least amount of effort. For some games, *challenging* the user may be the whole point! Breaking the rules is what most game developers consider to be their job, and frequently the most popular games are ones that toss aside conventional assumptions about interactivity and invent a whole new way of doing things.

Given all this, how do Windows games get around Windows' inherent desire to control consistency?

To Make It Full-Screen or Not to Make It Full-Screen

Windows games fall largely into two classes, depending on how they use screen real estate: There are *full-screen* games, and there are *windowed* games. Occasionally, there are games that belong to both classes.

A full-screen game is, obviously, one that takes over the entire Windows screen when it runs. There are no standard Windows elements visible to the user: no title bar, menu bar, borders, Minimize or Maximize button, nothing. The game is responsible for every aspect of the interaction between the computer and the user. Obviously, this is the class of games that are most like today's DOS-based games.

There are many Windows games that operate in this way, and they have been well-accepted by the market. Many game developers consider the standard Windows elements to be a distraction from the immersing nature of certain types of games. Having a menu bar staring at you from the top of the screen sort of destroys the illusion that you are, say, flying a WWII fighter plane over enemy territory. Windows users may prefer a standard user interface for productivity applications like spreadsheets and word processors, but they are happy to abandon the usual screen elements for the sake of a more immersing game.

The other variant of Windows games works within a window, similar to most productivity applications (see Figure 1-13). Simple examples include the games that come free with Windows, like Minesweeper. The windows these games run in look very much like any standard application window, with a title bar, menu bar, system menu button, and often Minimize and Maximize buttons and resizable borders.

A windowed game gives the user a few advantages, like the ability to easily switch between the game and other applications, at the cost of being less immersing than a full-screen game.

In a windowed game that has a Maximize button, the user can choose to display the game "full-screen," albeit while retaining the title bar and menu bar. It's conceivable that you could program a windowed game to eliminate the title bar and menu bar from the display when maximized, but I'm not certain what game would benefit from such a shift in perspective.

Important Factors for Windowed Games

The question of which method is *best* is, of course, a matter of design choice. But there are a few important technical issues that profoundly affect the choice, primarily having to do with a game's *scalability*.

A window that has resizable borders creates certain assumptions in a user's mind. He or she assumes that when the window is resized, its contents will somehow change to suit the new size. This typically means one of two things: Either the contents will

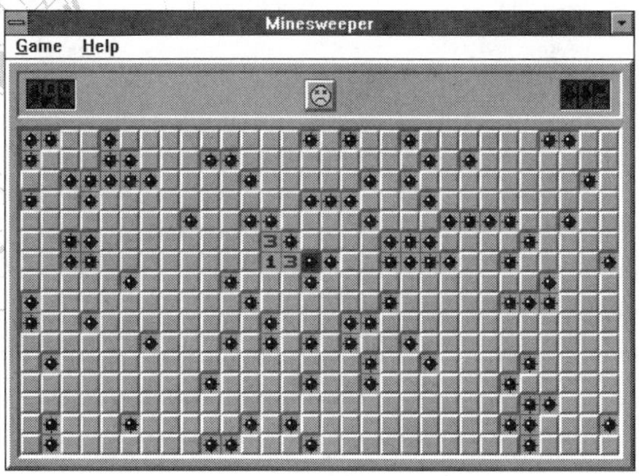

FIGURE 1-13

A windowed game: Minesweeper

FIGURE 1-14

Scaling vs. scrolling

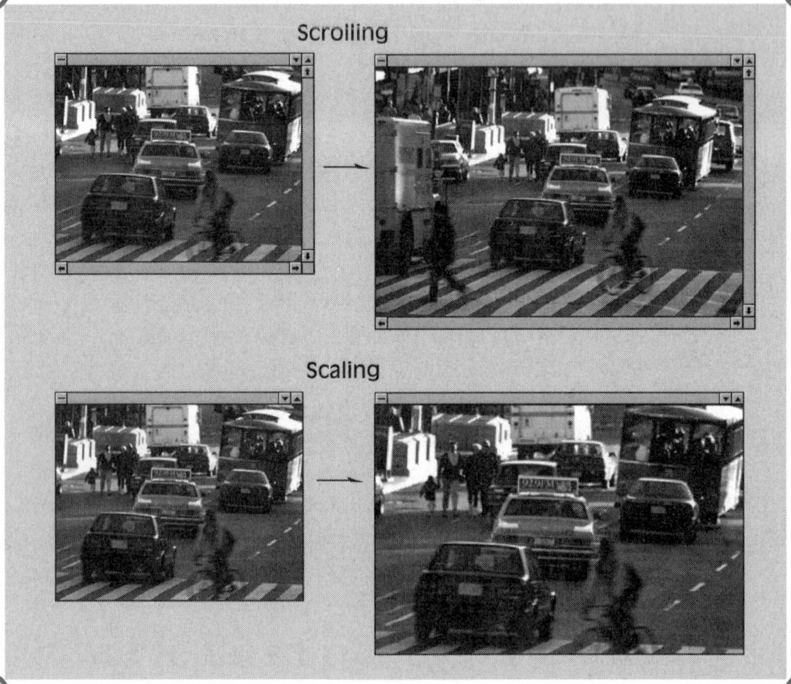

stretch or shrink to fit (the process is called *scaling*), or the program will show more or less of the contents (in which case, the user will need to scroll). The latter is vastly more common—take text-processing applications, for example. When you resize a word processor's window, it reveals more or less of the displayed document. Scrollbars appear along one or two sides of the window to allow the user to "pan" the view of the document.

Scrolling is not only more common, but usually considerably easier for a programmer to accommodate. Only applications that use a lot of geometry-based objects can effectively scale their window contents. Even then, it doesn't always makes sense for a program to do so. Even most drawing programs, which are fundamentally geometry-based, assume that contents will be scrolled rather than scaled when a user resizes a window.

For a simple (very simple) example of a program that scales rather than scrolls when its window is resized, look at the Reversi game program that comes with Windows. When you resize its window, the program scales the grid and the dots that occupy it to fit within the new window. Geometrical forms like these are said to be *resolution-independent,* meaning that they can be mathematically scaled up or down without a loss of precision (see Figure 1-14).

Programs that rely heavily on bitmapped graphics are considerably more difficult to scale with accuracy. Bitmaps are inherently *resolution-dependent.* In other words, you can't scale them up or down without some loss of precision, and usually at a considerable computational cost, as well. This means that a bitmap-based game program is going to run slower if it's scaled to resolutions different than those of the original bitmaps. As we'll learn later, Windows *does* provide functions for automatically scaling bitmaps to fit within any size window. Only the game developer can determine whether the benefits of scalability outweigh the attendant performance penalty.

Pixel Replication vs. Resampling

We'll talk about this subject in greater detail in Chapter 7, but it's worth a mention here. There are several methods by which you can scale bitmapped images, depending on the performance vs. accuracy tradeoffs you are willing to make. At one end of the scale, you can use various *resampling* methods to create new pixels for or delete unwanted pixels of a bitmap based on the colors of neighboring pixels. This can be quite computationally expensive, since the color of each new pixel is based on some form of averaging over some neighborhood distance. And the greater the distance, the better the resulting image will typically look.

The simplest scaling algorithm uses *pixel replication,* which just duplicates neighboring pixels to scale up, and deletes neighboring pixels (a process called pixel *decimation*) to scale down (see Figure 1-15). Pixel replication can be quite fast, since there's very little computational overhead required to simply duplicate a pixel. This

FIGURE 1-15

Pixel replication

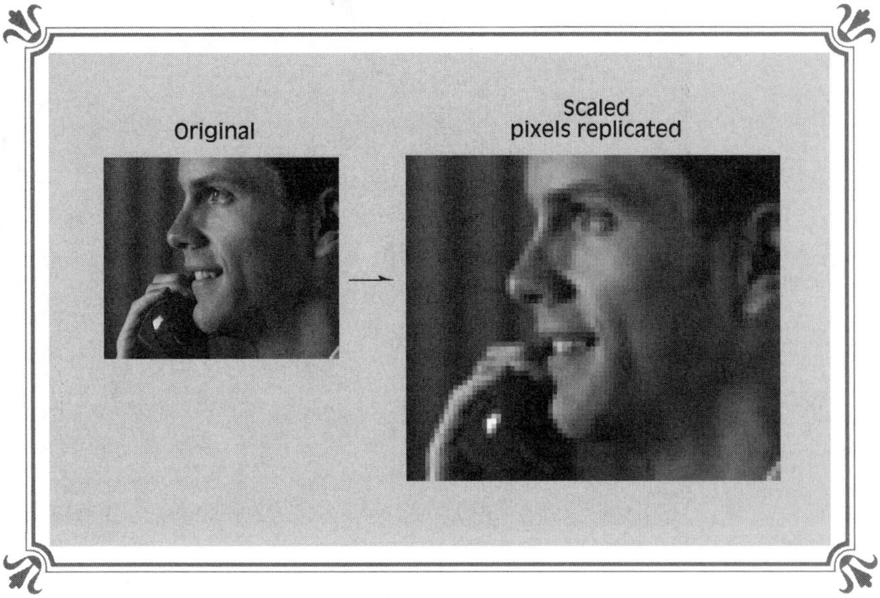

is the type of automatic scaling that Windows provides, and it can be quite useful for many types of applications, especially games.

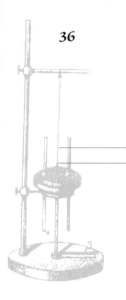

Full-Screen Games and Screen Resolution

The issue of scalability isn't restricted to windowed games. Because screen resolutions can differ under Windows, choosing to develop a full-screen game probably doesn't exempt you from having to select a fixed target resolution in order to get adequate performance. Display resolutions under Windows vary from a low end of 640x480 pixels up to 1024x768 pixels, or even more (though this is less typical). Even if a given display card supports multiple resolutions, changing modes under Windows is an excruciatingly slow process that requires restarting Windows completely (although Windows 95 makes it considerably less painful). Changing display modes in order to play your game is probably more than most users are willing to do.

As a result, many full-screen games actually work at a fixed resolution, with the active part of the game occupying only the central portion of the screen (see Figure 1-16). The rest of the screen is often just plain black, although more creative game developers fill the space with scenery or "props" that aren't really an active part of the game but help add to the overall experience.

Some game programs actually provide two complete sets of graphics: one for low resolution and one for high resolution. Naturally, this is more prevalent on CD-based

FIGURE 1-16

A full-screen game

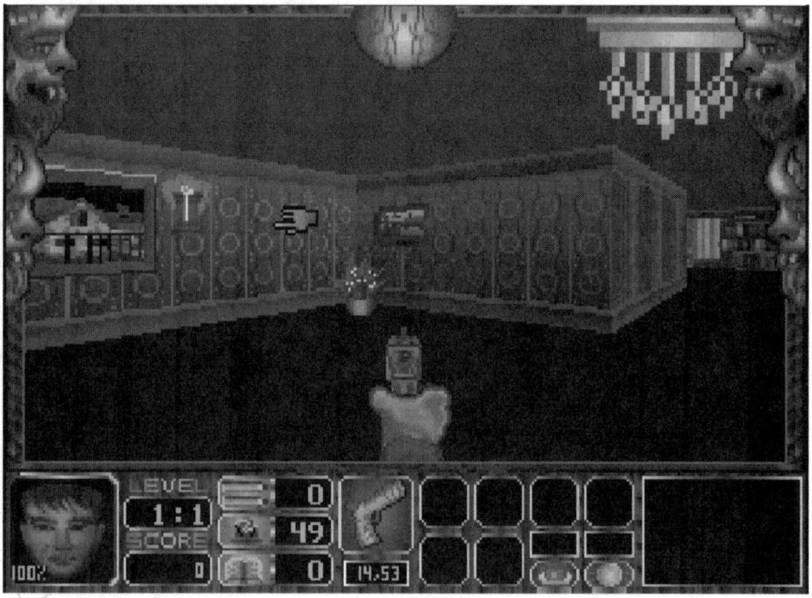

games that can afford the necessary space requirements. A classic scrolling-type game (like the seminal Space Invaders) could just increase the available playing space to consume the whole screen, although a resulting increase of the number of moving elements would certainly have some associated performance penalty.

Using pixel replication may be the most sensible way to adapt a full-screen Windows game to multiple screen resolutions, for several reasons. First, since Windows provides routines for automatically replicating pixels, it's naturally quite easy to do. Second, depending on the target resolution of the game, pixel replication may give results that look like those you would expect if the same game were running in a lower-resolution screen mode under DOS. I'll explain why this is so.

Many DOS games are designed to run in the 320x200x256-color screen resolution mode (so-called "mode 13") supported by all VGA adapters. This mode has many advantages. First, it's the only 256-color mode guaranteed to be supported by *every* VGA adapter on the market, because it is part of the original VGA specification. Second, a 320x200-pixel screen at 256 colors consumes only 64,000 bytes of memory, making it relatively easy to do things like double buffering with meager RAM requirements.

When the VGA adapter is put into mode 13, the *full-screen* resolution is 320x200 pixels. Each pixel actually appears bigger on the screen than when the VGA is in, say, a 640x480-pixel resolution mode. Suppose we were running Windows in a 640x480 resolution mode. If we were to put our game on the display without replicating any pixels, the game would consume the upper left quarter of the screen (320x200 is about one fourth the number of pixels of 640x480). Suppose now that we were to pixel-replicate the game by a factor of two in each direction. The game would fill the screen with a relatively small loss of computational overhead. Of course, the pixels would look twice as "blocky" as the originals—*but* they'd look exactly the same as they would running in mode 13 under DOS, because they would now fill the whole screen!

The choice of target resolution and how much to scale depends on many factors, of course. Many 3D games, for example, are resolution-independent and spend most of their time rendering pixels rather than actually displaying them on the screen. Sprite-based games, on the other hand, typically spend very little time computing pixels compared to the time these games take to actually display them. We'll learn more about these performance tradeoffs in later chapters, but as a game developer you probably already understand many of them. The important thing to remember is that the key to achieving the highest possible performance for your game under Windows is to choose the optimum target resolution combined with the optimum scaling technique—if, in fact, you choose to allow the game to be scaled to different display resolutions at all.

Multiple Windows

Windows has a robust system for dealing with overlapping windows, and there's certainly nothing wrong with taking advantage of this capability in a game context. Performing efficient updates into a window that is partially covered by another window is one of the things Windows does best, and you could put it to good use in a game. Imagine, for example, a "plan-view" window that the user could pop up and drag around the screen while the main window (whether full-screen or not) is continually updated. Updating a window that is partially covered by another window is naturally slower than updating the window when it's unobscured, but at least *you* don't have to write the code to do it—it's one of the most fundamental things that Windows does.

There's also nothing to stop you from using standard Windows controls, like buttons, scrollbars, and so forth, on such pop-up windows (see Figure 1-17). In fact, if your game needs controls that are similar in function to standard Windows controls, it's probably a good idea to use the Windows controls to ensure maximum consumer acceptance.

FIGURE 1-17

Standard Windows controls in a game

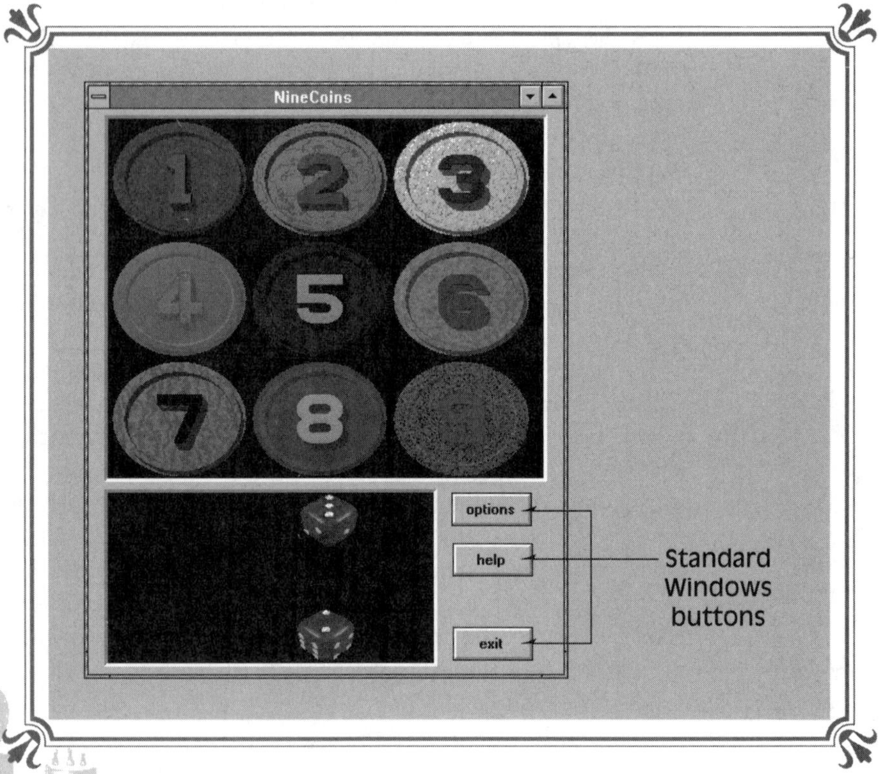

Multitasking and Windows Games

As we learned earlier, Windows is a cooperatively multitasking system, which means that it's possible for any one application to completely steal the machine away from all other running applications. As we also learned, programs that do this generally suffer poor market acceptance, because they effectively nullify multitasking as a benefit. Even full-screen games under Windows typically behave nicely to the rest of the system—they still allow you to press ALT-TAB to cycle through all the running applications, for example. In Chapter 2, we'll learn that it's really not difficult to create an application that's "nice" in terms of multitasking, because of the event-driven nature of Windows.

Summary

By now, you should have some understanding of how Windows works from the user's perspective. You have also learned that users have quite different expectations of how a game vs. a productivity application should work under Windows. Fortunately for you, the game programmer, not all Windows games need to look like productivity applications—running in resizable windows, with menus and dialog boxes and all the other accouterments that are standard parts of a mainstream application. Windows games can take over the screen without remorse, giving the user the same immersing experience associated with DOS-based games.

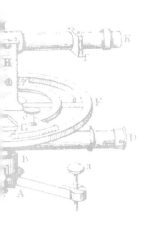

2

Windows—The Programmer's Perspective

Come si debbe fare le manovelle [illegible] le quali si movono e [illegible]
e [illegible] [illegible]
[illegible] manovella [illegible]
la forza e [illegible] l'omo [illegible]

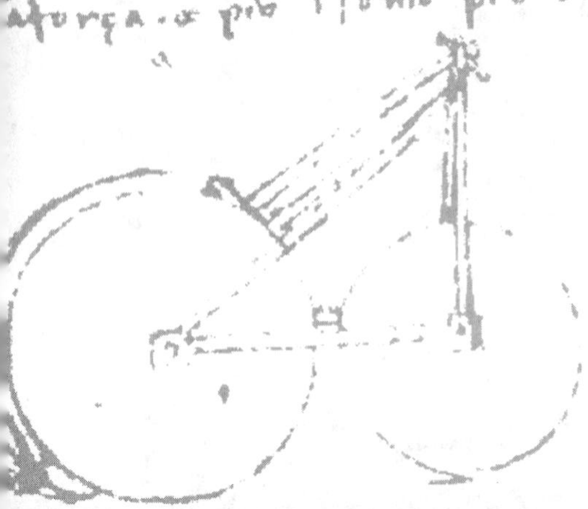

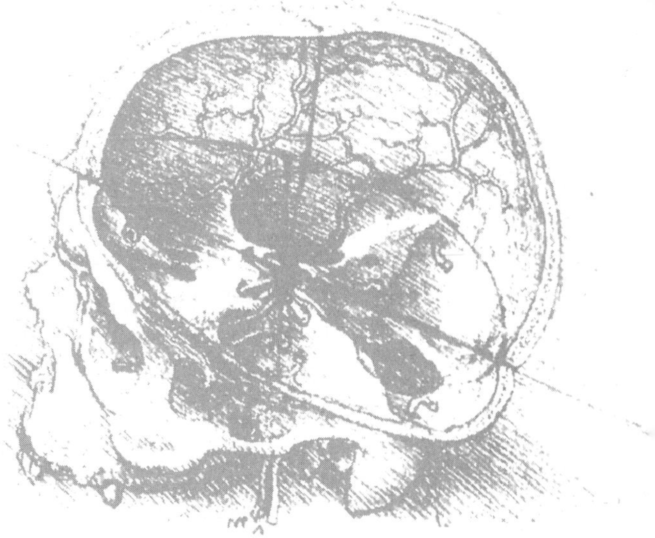

2

Windows—The Programmer's Perspective

Now that you've seen Windows from the outside, it's time to peer into it from the inside. In this chapter, you'll learn about all the basic elements that constitute a Windows program and—finally—actually put something on the screen.

Event-Driven Programming

The first important thing to learn about Windows is that it, like many other GUI systems, is an *event-driven* operating system. The term "event-driven" describes the way in which the program receives input from the user. The counterparts to event-driven programs are *polling* programs; before the advent of event-driven programming, virtually all programs were polling programs. The two differ primarily in how they handle their "inner loops": those parts of the code where a program spends most of its time.

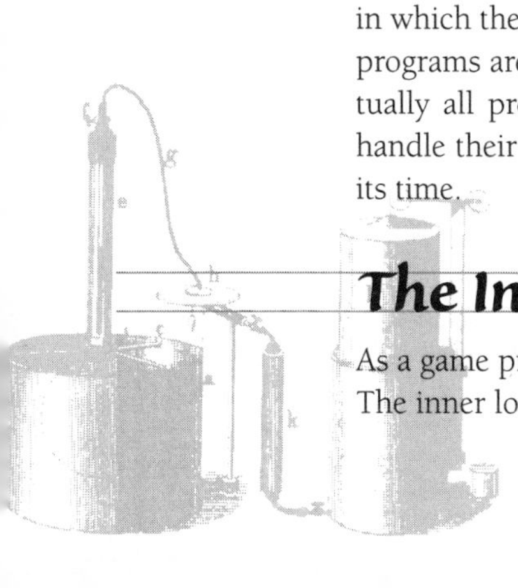

The Inner Loop

As a game programmer, you probably already know what the term *inner loop* means. The inner loop of all interactive programs does essentially two things:

- Gets input from the user
- Processes the input

When the inner loop finishes processing the current input, the program eventually loops back for more input. If this description doesn't look quite right to you, try this variation:

- *If* there's some user input, then
- Process it,
- Redraw the screen, and
- Repeat.

Figure 2-1 illustrates the concept of the inner loop.

This describes the inner loop typical of many programs, including games. The test for user input could be something as simple as a call to **`kbhit()`**, a test of the current position of the joystick, or a combination of different tests. Usually, if the user input hasn't changed, then the program just keeps doing whatever it was doing before. In a flight simulator game, for example, if the joystick position hasn't changed and the user hasn't pressed any keys on the keyboard, the plane keeps flying according to the last input.

An event-driven program is fundamentally different from a polling program in that an event-driven program generally isn't responsible for soliciting user input—it's the

FIGURE 2-1

The inner loop

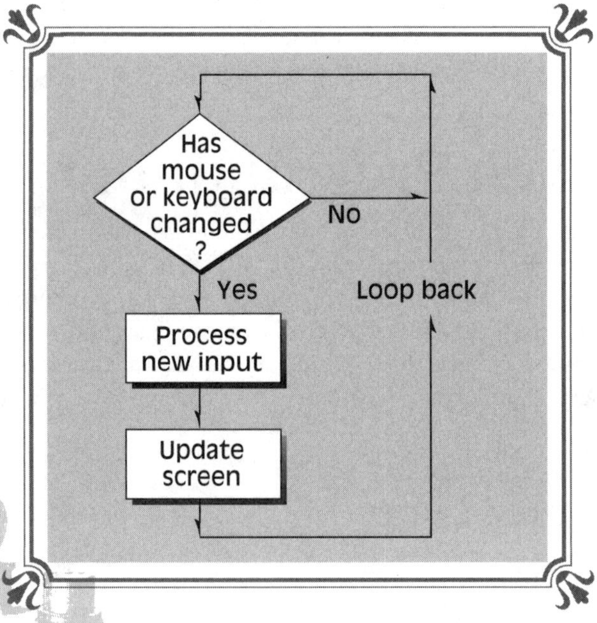

operating system itself that performs that task. The operating system then tells a running application about the input by sending it a *message*. Messages are an inherent part of event-driven programming.

Don't Call Us, We'll Call You

Here's another way to think of event-driven programming: Instead of having the program call various system functions to check for input (as it would for a polling program), the system gathers up all forms of input and calls *your* program, informing it of the type of input, its various parameters, and so on (see Figure 2-2).

This distinction between event-driven and polling programming may at first seem relatively trivial, but depending on how you're used to programming, the effects can be profound. For example, many programs don't have one centralized inner loop: Instead, one loop may switch off to run yet another loop that polls for user input, which eventually may return to the original loop. More importantly, if you're used to the standard C library functions for input and output—like **getch()**, **putch()**, **gets()**, and so on—you might be quite disconcerted to learn that they don't exist in an event-driven system. But don't feel too bad: Compared with everything else you have to learn in order to understand Windows, learning to live with the loss of **getch()** is easy. In fact, very few of the standard C library functions exist or are even useful under Windows. Fortunately, the Windows API (applications programming interface—you knew that) provides equivalent functions where necessary.

FIGURE 2-2

Polling vs. event-driven programs

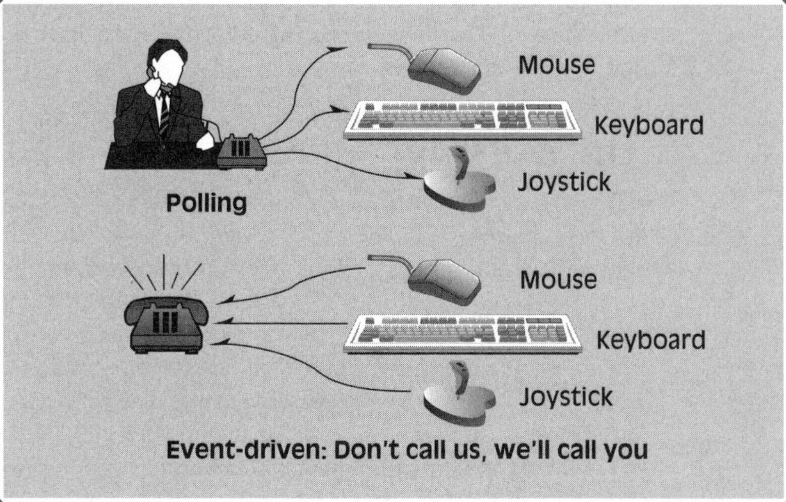

The Main Event

Let's take a look at the Windows equivalent to the standard C **main()** function. The function is called **WinMain()**, and it is the entry point for all Windows programs. Most Windows programs' **WinMain** functions look very similar, something like this:

```
int PASCAL WinMain(HINSTANCE hInstance,
                   HINSTANCE hPrevInstance,
                   LPSTR lpCmdLine,
                   int nCmdShow)
{
     MSG msg;

     // Perform some initialization.
     InitOurProgram ();

     // Process messages.
     while (GetMessage(&msg, NULL, 0, 0)) {
           TranslateMessage(&msg);
           DispatchMessage(&msg);
     }

     // Clean up our stuff.
     CleanUpOurProgram ();

     // Return the wParam of the message to Windows.
     return (msg.wParam);
}
```

Notice that the core of every Windows program is nothing more than a polling loop! How can this be? Where do the messages go? How does all this work? To understand the workings of the **WinMain** function, you first have to understand what Windows does with messages.

The Message Queue

When the user initiates some event—by pressing a key or moving the mouse—Windows places a message in the system message queue as shown in Figure 2-3. When an application actually asks for a message by using **GetMessage**, Windows checks to see if there are any messages in the queue that are intended for that particular application and, if so, stuffs the **msg** parameter with the first such message. If there *aren't* any messages in the queue intended for your application, **GetMessage** yields control to Windows, which can then do things like process messages for other applications.

Calling **GetMessage** is a very important thing for a Windows program to do. The reason is that **GetMessage** is one of the few functions that return control to Windows, thus letting other applications run (there are actually two other functions that

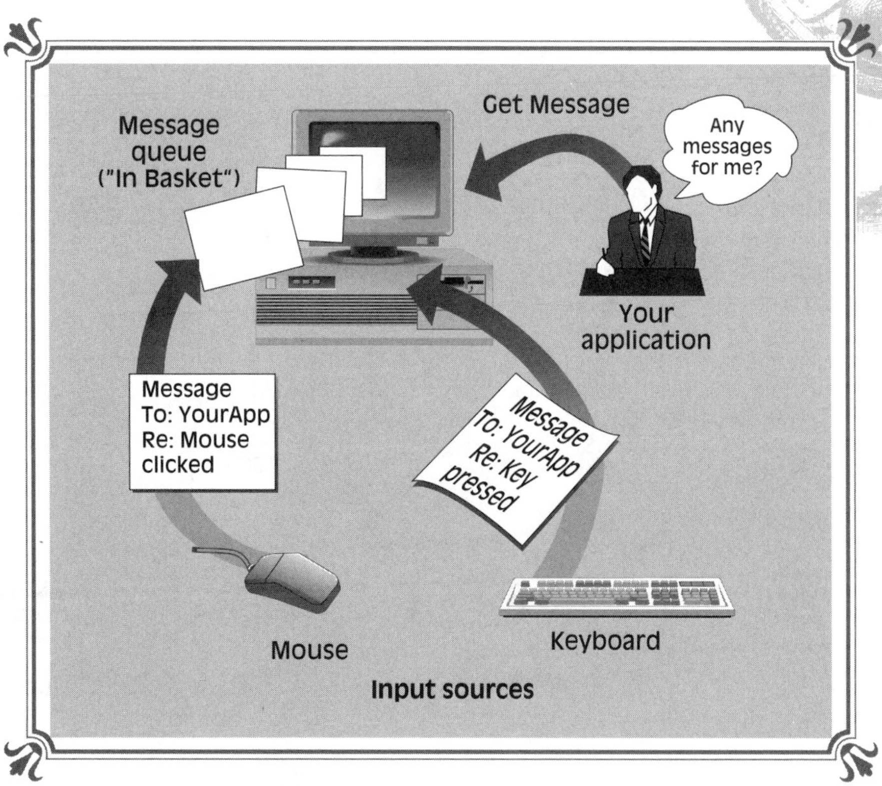

FIGURE 2-3

Each input event becomes a message to Windows

yield control to Windows, both of which I'll cover later). If a program never yields control to Windows, then no other programs are allowed to run. Naturally, this is a very bad thing to do to Windows.

The **GetMessage** function returns zero only in one specific case: when it finds the WM_QUIT message in its message queue, telling the program to quit. Otherwise, it always returns nonzero and the program in turn calls two other Windows functions, **TranslateMessage** followed by **DispatchMessage**.

TranslateMessage calls the Windows keyboard driver to convert raw keystrokes into cooked ASCII values that you can use more easily. The real meat is in **DispatchMessage**. Figure 2-4 shows how this function looks at the message, decides which of the application's windows it corresponds to, and calls that window's *callback function*—the "we'll call you" part of Figure 2-2. So it's not strictly true that Windows is a "don't call us, we'll call you" type of event-driven system; it's more like an "I'll call you first, then let you decide whether to call me" sort of affair. In GUI technical parlance, Windows is a unique combination of *pull-model* and *push-model* processing. Push-model processing uses only the "we'll call you" method—it sends (pushes) messages into some callback function by calling that function directly from

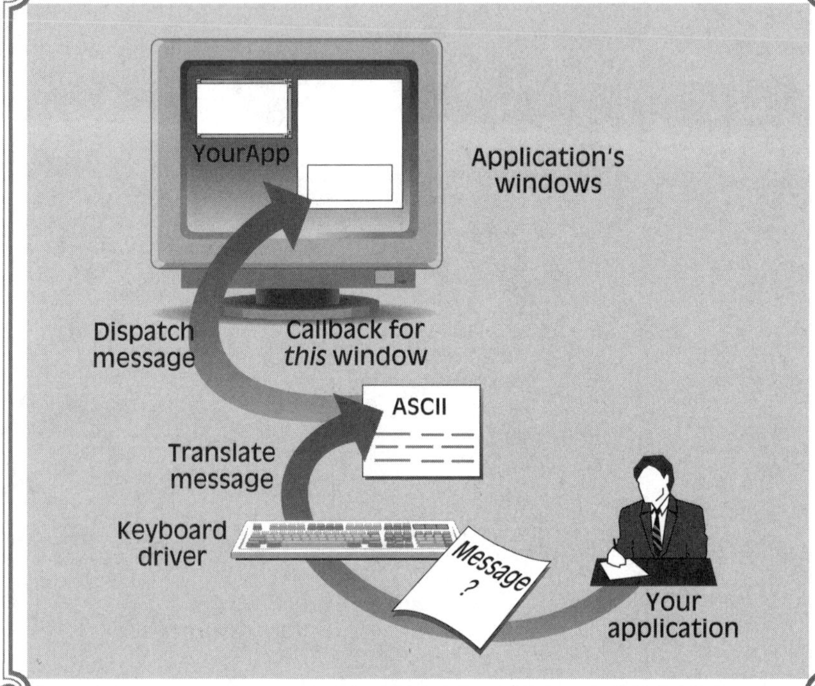

FIGURE 2-4

The application has the message translated and dispatched to the appropriate window

the operating system. Pull-model processing takes messages from a queue and processes them. This is what **GetMessage** does.

The obvious thing to ask is why Windows makes you write a polling loop inside the application—why can't it just call your window's callback function directly? The answer is that the polling loop gives you a certain amount of flexibility. You can look at certain messages and decide *universally* whether you want your program to process them.

The polling-loop requirement also solves a very difficult technical problem for Microsoft, having to do with how to handle very asynchronous events like key presses and mouse movement. By putting these events in a queue and processing them later, the system avoids having to do all the processing during a hardware interrupt, which would shut out all other running programs until the interrupt returned. Finally, the polling loop provides game programmers with a very convenient place to put a screen-updating function, as you'll see later.

Before we take a look at callback functions, let's explore the meanings of those parameters to **WinMain**, and see what some of those strange data types are all about.

Instances and Handles

You'll notice that the first parameter to **WinMain** is an *HINSTANCE.* An HINSTANCE is a handle (I'll talk about these in a moment) to what Windows refers to as a module's *instance.* Remember that Windows is a multitasking system, in which multiple programs can be running at the same time. In fact, not only can different programs be running, but *more than one copy* of any given program can be running, as well. For example, it's possible to run more than one copy of Notepad, each copy displaying a different file. Each copy of a program is an instance of that program.

Instances are significant because Microsoft, in the original design of Windows, implemented the memory-saving idea of allowing instances of the same program to share certain resources. This means that each instance does not require its own copy of the entire program. Multiple instances of a program share the same executable code, since this doesn't change from one copy of the program to another (self-modifying code is a definite no-no under Windows). Obviously, each instance accesses different data, but only one copy of the code need be in memory at any given time. An instance handle identifies a particular instance of a program and, therefore, its data.

There are some programs (many, in fact) that allow you only *one* instance because of their resource requirements or other factors. Whether you want to allow a user to run multiple instances of your game depends on several factors—for example, if yours is a full-screen game, it's very unlikely you'd want to have multiple copies of it running at the same time, because the result would be very confusing to the user.

Programmers use the first HINSTANCE parameter to **WinMain** very widely in Windows API calls, because it identifies the running program to Windows. In general, you'll probably want to tuck this value away in a global somewhere, because it truly *is* a global parameter to the currently running program.

An HINSTANCE is one example (the first I've discussed) of Windows' extensive use of *handles.* A handle is an indirect reference to some sort of memory object within Windows. For example, an HINSTANCE is a handle for a whole instance of a program. Another important type of handle is the window handle, or HWND, that uniquely identifies any given window on the screen. Handles aren't pointers—you can't cast them in some magical way to reference a value. Their values are arbitrary; only Windows knows the relevance of a particular handle. You see handles all throughout Windows code. Most every data type that starts with a capital *H* is a Windows handle of one form or another. Which leads to the next topic: unusual naming conventions you'll encounter in most Windows code examples.

Strange Windows Programming Conventions

If there are two things that are sure to throw off any newcomer to Windows programming, they are the strange variable names and the seemingly infinite variety of data types you'll encounter in example code. For example, what's all this `hInstance` stuff, anyway? Why do all these variables begin with some lowercase letter or letters that make the names unreadable?

These odd variable names and data types are the results of *Hungarian notation,* a common Microsoft naming convention named in honor of the heritage of its Microsoft inventor, Charles Simonyi. Hungarian notation represents a compromise between the practice of giving very long, descriptive names to variables and the practice of giving brief, but incomprehensible names to variables. In Hungarian notation, a variable name is preceded by lowercase letters that identify the variable's data type. This makes it easier for the programmer to avoid accidentally assigning a value to a variable of the wrong data type—an important safeguard, considering that Windows has many data types of the same size, so compilers don't always catch errors.

Hungarian notation can seem completely absurd to the uninitiated, like some sort of horrible language extension that makes variable names longer and more unreadable. This is an understandable reaction. The good thing about Hungarian notation is this: You don't have to use it. Granted, virtually every example of Windows code you'll ever see—and every single structure member that's defined in WINDOWS.H—uses it extensively, and it becomes rather ingrained in your subconscious after a while, but it's completely optional.

Table 2-1 lists and defines some of the more common Hungarian notation prefixes.

WINDOWS.H is the 5,300-line header file that you must include in every Windows programming module that you create. It defines every Windows data type, along with the function definitions (prototypes) for almost every API call (there are some feature-specific definitions that are in other .H files). Note that there's nothing really special about WINDOWS.H; it's a regular C header file. It contains many Windows-specific data types and function definitions, but it's still all C, with no special compiler-specific extensions.

NEAR and FAR Keywords

Windows was originally designed to run on 16-bit microprocessors, and consequently it brings with it all manner of atrocities that are part of the great heritage of Intel microprocessors and the languages that support them. I'm talking here about those little modifiers that all C language compilers use (fortunately, in a consistent way) to distinguish between 16-bit pointers and 32-bit pointers.

TABLE 2-1

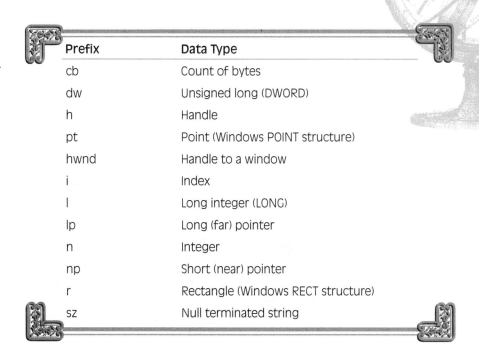

Hungarian notation prefixes

Prefix	Data Type
cb	Count of bytes
dw	Unsigned long (DWORD)
h	Handle
pt	Point (Windows POINT structure)
hwnd	Handle to a window
i	Index
l	Long integer (LONG)
lp	Long (far) pointer
n	Integer
np	Short (near) pointer
r	Rectangle (Windows RECT structure)
sz	Null terminated string

In every 16-bit C environment for Intel-based microprocessors, the two pointer sizes are declared using the **near** and **far** modifiers (or some variation thereof, like **_far**) before the data type. For example,

```
char far *string;
```

identifies a 32-bit pointer to an 8-bit byte (a **char**). None of this should be particularly new to DOS-based programmers, since most DOS programming environments suffer from the same 16-bit heritage. Windows, however, provides you with many new data-type definitions, each of which comes with a full complement of definitions for pointers, both near and far. For example, Windows defines a data type called LPSTR (popularly pronounced "lipstir"), which is, in its Hungarian way, a long pointer to a string. In WINDOWS.H, you'll find LPSTR (and its partner, NPSTR) defined like this:

```
typedef char _far *LPSTR;
typedef char _near *NPSTR;
```

Most every Windows-defined data type has at least two pointer data types defined for it in this way in WINDOWS.H. Certain data types have other pointer types defined, as well. The various pointer types, their sizes, and why you need them will all be covered in great detail in Chapter 3.

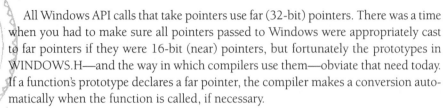

All Windows API calls that take pointers use far (32-bit) pointers. There was a time when you had to make sure all pointers passed to Windows were appropriately cast to far pointers if they were 16-bit (near) pointers, but fortunately the prototypes in WINDOWS.H—and the way in which compilers use them—obviate that need today. If a function's prototype declares a far pointer, the compiler makes a conversion automatically when the function is called, if necessary.

It's good practice to use the data types exactly as they are defined in WINDOWS.H for at least one very important reason: 32-bit compatibility.

Win32

It's possible to write programs for Windows using 32-bit rather than 16-bit programming. There are performance benefits that usually come with 32-bit programming, but it also helps you get around all the nastiness of dealing with the variations of 16- and 32-bit pointers: All pointers become 32-bit ones. Microsoft calls the programming environment for creating 32-bit Windows programs *Win32*. Win32 defines many new Windows API calls, and it provides the functionality to allow your program to automatically call the 16-bit parts of Windows 95 or Windows 3.1 without having to think much about it. If you are diligent in your coding practices, it's quite easy to create programs that will compile and run using *either* a 16-bit programming environment or Win32.

In a 32-bit environment, NEAR and FAR declarations are unnecessary. Most 32-bit compilers just "eat" those declarations if they exist, generating no code, since all data and code are accessed with 32-bit pointers. Some liken this to programming in so-called Intel Large model, wherein the default pointer size is 32 bits. It's actually more like programming in Small model, only with all pointers (and ints) being 32 bits instead of 16.

Pascal vs. C Calling Conventions

You'll notice that `WinMain`, the Windows entry point, is defined with the PASCAL modifier keyword. If you're not familiar with Pascal calling convention, this may look very strange indeed. The PASCAL keyword before a function definition modifies the way that arguments are passed to that function when it is called. In standard C, arguments are pushed on the stack from left to right; when the function returns, the caller must pop the arguments off the stack. In Pascal calling, the arguments are pushed on the stack from right to left, and the "callee" (the function itself) pops the stack before it returns.

What's the big deal, you ask? Why bother with Pascal at all? Well, on Intel microprocessors, Pascal calling generates smaller and faster code than does standard C calling convention. For this reason, Windows uses Pascal calling for almost all its API functions. Most of the time, you don't need to know or care whether Pascal is being used: The function prototypes in WINDOWS.H handle everything for you, making the compiler generate the right code.

To speed up your own code, you can use Pascal calling in your own functions if you like. The only restriction with Pascal calling convention is that it works only with functions that have a fixed number of parameters; a function like `sprintf` can't use Pascal, because it has a variable number of parameters.

The only time you *must* use the PASCAL keyword in your code is when you define a Windows callback function (as I mentioned earlier in the chapter, a callback function is a function you define that is called *from* Windows). `WinMain` is the archetypal callback function—it's called by Windows when your program is started.

Now that you've seen what `WinMain` looks like, it's time to venture on with the rest of Windows programming and see how to actually get a window on the screen.

Everything's a Window

If there's any one phrase that best describes the architecture of the Windows operating system, I'd have to say it is this: *Everything's* a window. I remember when I first began Windows programming and a friend of mine (who had about a year's worth of Windows programming experience) told me those three simple words. Somehow it registered, and a huge mess of muddled concepts that had been dancing around in my mind jelled into a (nearly) cohesive whole.

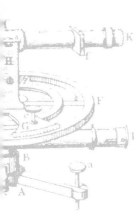

Windows was implemented with an object-oriented model, and one of the most fundamental objects is the window. The system is designed so that creating, destroying, and modifying windows is as inexpensive—in terms of memory and computational overhead—as possible. In keeping with that mission, the underlying structure of a window—its base class, if you like—is nothing more than a rectangular area of the screen.

Windows can, of course, overlap, and have an inherent front-to-back order, called the Z-order. Windows that are overlapped by other windows have their contents automatically clipped to the overlapping windows. They can also have a hierarchical structure: One window can "own" another. When the owner, or *parent,* window is destroyed, all its children are destroyed, as well. A *child* window can automatically have its contents clipped to the boundaries of its parent, too.

Almost every screen object you see in a typical Windows application is some kind of window. Buttons, scrollbars, list boxes, text boxes, and all the other standard Windows controls are really just windows themselves, each with its own special look and behavior. A Windows program isn't really a program unless it has at least *one* window. Figure 2-5 shows some different kinds of Windows windows.

FIGURE 2-5(a)

Examples of different kinds of windows

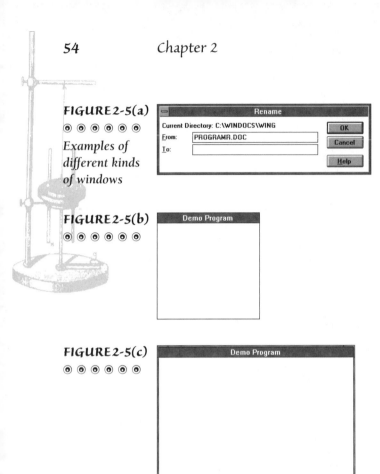

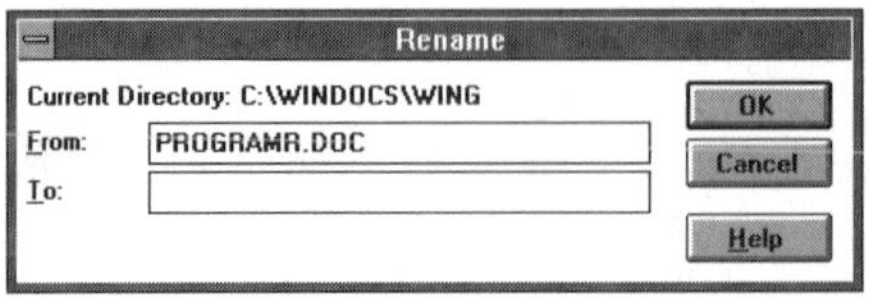

FIGURE 2-5(b)

FIGURE 2-5(c)

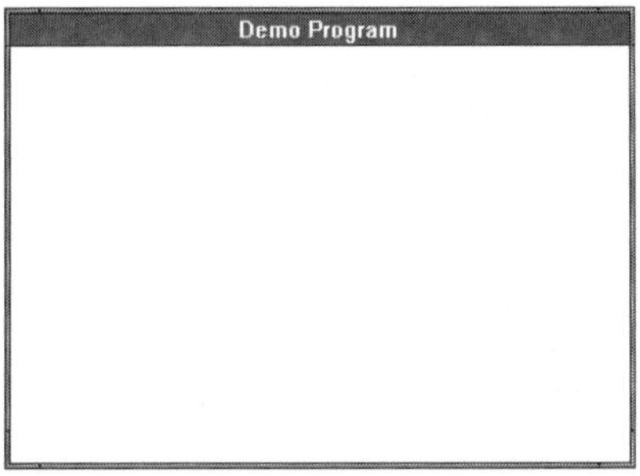

Earlier in this chapter, you learned that Windows is an event-driven system—the operating system sends events to your program in response to changing input devices and so on. But where does Windows send these events? What operating system "object" receives them?

The Window Callback Function

The reason the phrase "everything's a window" is true is that the window is the thing that receives all messages from the operating system. Unless it has a window, your program will never "see" messages like mouse movement, key presses, or much else, for that matter. The operating system (I'll try to use that term instead of "Windows" to lessen the obvious potential for confusion) sends these messages to a window's callback function when **`WinMain`** calls **`DispatchMessage`**, if there are any events waiting in the application's queue. Despite the fact that **`WinMain`** is the program's entry point, it's really in the callback function for a given window where most of a program's work gets done.

Let's take a look at exactly what this callback function thing is. A window's callback function definition looks like this:

```
LRESULT CALLBACK WndProc (HWND hwnd,
                          UINT msg,
                          WPARAM wParam,
                          LPARAM lParam)
```

I'll take this definition apart carefully, because it is the most fundamental of all Windows functions.

The function returns a result called an *LRESULT*. LRESULT is defined in WINDOWS.H as a LONG, which in turn is defined as a `signed long`, or 32-bit signed value (this is true under both 16-bit Windows and Win32). CALLBACK is defined as FAR PASCAL in WINDOWS.H, meaning that this function uses the Pascal calling convention (like all Windows API functions) and can be accessed with a 32-bit pointer. Everything that is called from the operating system uses this CALLBACK declaration (except `WinMain`).

Next, the parameters. The first parameter is an HWND, or handle to a window. This is the system-unique identifier that tells the function which particular window the system is talking about—necessary information, because different windows can share the same callback function. HWNDs are one of the most basic kinds of handles. They're used whenever you want to address a particular window.

The second parameter, `msg`, is defined as a UINT, which, in WINDOWS.H, is in turn defined as an `unsigned int`. (Note that this is a 16-bit value under 16-bit Windows and a 32-bit value under Win32.) This parameter contains the actual Windows message value, of which there are hundreds. A callback function is sent *window* messages; these are the ones in WINDOWS.H that start with *WM_*. There are messages that correspond to input events, like WM_MOUSEMOVE and WM_LBUTTONDOWN, as we'll learn in Chapter 4. There are also internally generated messages like WM_CREATE, which is sent to a window's callback function when the window is first created, and WM_DESTROY, which is sent to a window when it's being destroyed.

The last two parameters are called `wParam` and `lParam`, for "word parameter" and "long parameter." WPARAM is defined in WINDOWS.H as a UINT, which is 2 bytes under 16-bit Windows and 4 bytes under Win32. LPARAM is defined as LONG, which is a 4-byte value under both 16-bit Windows and Win32. WPARAM and LPARAM are two generic data types for passing so-called *polymorphic* values; that is, values whose meanings vary. You can think of them as sort of generic placeholders for values that typically are cast into a *specific* data type within the callback function.

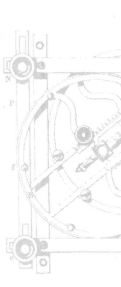

In light of Win32, `wParam` and `lParam` are sort of unfortunate names for these parameters. When Windows was originally designed, the `wParam` parameter was strictly a 16-bit value, or WORD, as defined in WINDOWS.H, while `lParam` was a DWORD, or 32-bit value. When Win32 came along, both `wParam` and `lParam` became the same size—namely, 32 bits (a DWORD). (The WORD and DWORD definitions are designed to have consistent sizes between 16-bit Windows and Win32: 2

and 4 bytes, respectively.) This is a problem during code conversion from 16-bit Windows to Win32 if the programmer has defined **wParam** as a WORD instead of as a WPARAM, which handles both sizes.

The data in **wParam** and **lParam** vary, depending on the message in **msg**. For example, if **msg** is WM_PAINT (the message sent to a window by the operating system when it determines it's time to have the window paint itself), then the data in **wParam** and **lParam** aren't used at all. In this case, WM_PAINT is said to have no parameters. On the other hand, if **msg** is WM_CHAR (the message sent to a window to indicate that the user pressed a key), then the value in **wParam** is the virtual key code of the character whose key was pressed, and **lParam** holds a whole passel of data about the state of the key, whether certain other keys were pressed, and so on, as a bit-encoded 32-bit value.

If a message requires more than just two simple parameters, sometimes the value in **lParam** is a far pointer to some Windows-defined structure that has to do with the particular message being sent. For example, for the WM_CREATE message that is sent to a window when it's first created, **lParam** contains a far pointer to a CREATESTRUCT structure, which contains information about how the window was created. In still other cases, **lParam** may be divided into two 16-bit values that you can unpack using the HIWORD and LOWORD macros. The WM_MOVE message, which informs the callback function when a window has been moved, packs the new location of the window as two WORDs in **lParam**.

Handling Messages

The basic method for handling messages from a callback function is to have a giant C **switch** statement for each message you want to handle. Here's what part of that function might look like for handling WM_CREATE and WM_CHAR:

```
LRESULT CALLBACK WndProc (HWND hwnd,
                          UINT msg,
                          WPARAM wParam,
                          LPARAM lParam)
{
     LPCREATESTRUCT *cs;
     int vkey;
     DWORD dwKeyFlags;

     switch (msg) {
          case WM_CREATE:
               cs = (LPCREATESTRUCT) lParam;
               // Do various things...
               .
               .
               .
```

```
            return 0;

      case WM_CHAR:
            vkey = (int)wParam;
            dwKeyFlags = lParam;
            // Process the key...
            .
            .
            .
            return TRUE;
```

So for each message, there's a corresponding case statement, followed by code that casts the values in **wParam** and **lParam** into variables that have meaning for the particular message, followed by a **return** statement that returns a value whose meaning also varies according to the particular message. If you've looked at a lot of Windows code written before about 1992 (including examples from the vast number of Windows programming books available), this is undoubtedly the style you've seen. To find out what **wParam** and **lParam** mean for a given message, you look in the Windows Messages Reference manual (or, if you're smart, the online help file) and then create variables that correspond to their values, add the **case** statement to the callback function's **switch** statement, and do whatever it is that you need to do for that particular message.

The problem is, this method not only makes for quite messy code, but also is prone to many errors (for example, **lParam** can be too easily cast to the wrong kind of pointer). It's also very easy to use either **wParam** or **lParam** in ways that would break under Win32; in other words, in ways that aren't 32-bit "safe." To overcome this problem, the busy bees at Microsoft came up with a system of message "crackers" that safely crack apart both **wParam** and **lParam** into their proper values, then call a function you define with those values as parameters (see Figure 2-6).

WINDOWSX.H, Crackers, and Message Forwarders

The whole system for "cracking out" the various message parameters from **wParam** and **lParam** is contained in one header file, unimaginatively called WINDOWSX.H. You should include WINDOWSX.H after WINDOWS.H in every file that has a callback function. The powerful macros WINDOWSX.H provides make handling window messages *much* easier.

Instead of having a giant **switch** statement in your callback function with a **case** for each message and a pile of code for taking apart **wParam** and **lParam**, you can rely on WINDOWSX.H's message-cracker macros to handle all the dirty work. You just implement a function for each message you want to handle.

FIGURE 2-6

Message cracking and forwarding

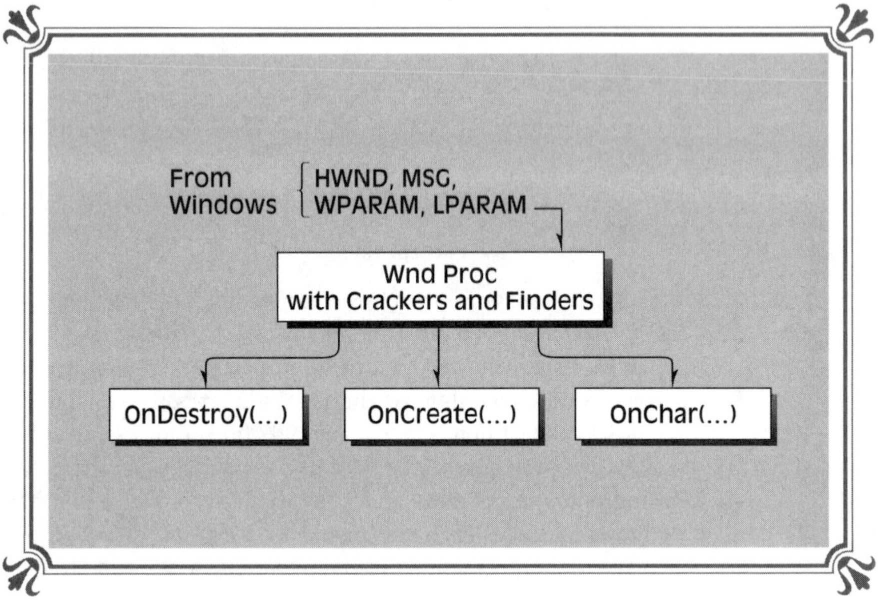

Here's what a corresponding callback function would look like using message-cracker macros:

```
LRESULT CALLBACK WndProc (HWND hwnd,
                          UINT msg,
                          WPARAM wParam,
                          LPARAM lParam)
{

     switch (msg) {
           HANDLE_MSG (hwnd, WM_CREATE, OnCreate);
           HANDLE_MSG (hwnd, WM_CHAR, OnChar);
           // More handlers for other messages...
           .
           .
           .
```

For each message you wanted to handle, you would then implement a function that would be called by the HANDLE_MSG macro. The parameters to the function would be the cracked-out values from `wParam` and `lParam`. To find out what the parameters for the function would be, you would look up the message in WINDOWSX.H—the comment above the macro shows the parameters. Here's what the prototype in WINDOWSX.H would look like for WM_CREATE:

```
BOOL OnCreate(HWND hwnd,
              CREATESTRUCT FAR* lpCreateStruct)
```

This is what our function prototype should look like: It returns a BOOL, has an HWND as its first parameter, and an LPCREATESTRUCT (note that this is the same as saying CREATESTRUCT FAR *) as its second and only other parameter.

The message-cracker macros are actually a sophisticated combination of a couple of macros. The HANDLE_MSG macro looks like this:

```
#define HANDLE_MSG(hwnd, message, fn)    \
    case (message): return HANDLE_##message((hwnd), \
                         (wParam), (lParam), (fn))
```

As you can see, HANDLE_MSG incorporates the **case** statement. The little HANDLE_##**message** hack tells the C preprocessor to append whatever **message** is to HANDLE_. So for WM_CREATE, the macro expands to

```
case WM_CREATE: return HANDLE_WM_CREATE ((hwnd),\
                         (wParam), (lParam), (fn))
```

If you look up the HANDLE_WM_CREATE macro in WINDOWSX.H, you'll find

```
((fn)((hwnd), (CREATESTRUCT FAR*)(lParam))
              ? 0L : (LRESULT)-1L)
```

If we expanded all the macros, the code generated for the WM_CREATE message example would look like this:

```
case WM_CREATE:
     return OnCreate (hwnd,
                         (CREATESTRUCT FAR *)lParam)
                    ? 0 : (LRESULT)-1L;
```

The ternary operator (? 0 : (LRESULT)...) at the end of this macro expansion might look confusing. What it says is, "If **OnCreate** returns nonzero, then return zero out of the **switch** statement; otherwise (if **OnCreate** returns zero), return -1." This strange twist of return values has to do with the fact that the actual return value from the callback function for the WM_CREATE message is very significant: If the value is zero, this tells Windows that everything went fine, and it should continue processing messages for that window. A value of -1 tells Windows that something didn't go well (like maybe you couldn't allocate memory or some such) and that Windows should not create the window (the create request is said to have failed). The little twist in the macro makes it simple for your **OnCreate** function to simply return TRUE if everything is fine or FALSE if it's not, to be more consistent with typical C programming practice.

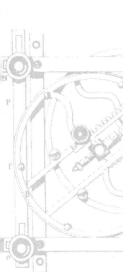

The message-cracker and forwarding macros do many things for you. First, they provide you with a way to process messages that is much easier to look at and understand than a huge **switch** statement. Using the message crackers can make it seem almost like you have callback functions for every Windows message (although you're calling the functions yourself, from your own *real* callback function). They also automatically typecast **wParam** and **lParam** for you into exactly the data types these parameters are meant to represent, and rationalize the return value of the callback function for all messages. WINDOWSX.H also provides you with function prototypes for the message functions you create.

One of the most important characteristics of the message-cracker macros is that they are all 32-bit "safe": They typecast **wParam** and **lParam** in ways that work for both 16-bit Windows and Win32. This means that if you're using the message-cracker macros and WINDOWSX.H, all your code will compile and run without any modification under Win32 as a native 32-bit application. This is a major benefit and one that is difficult to get if you're *not* using WINDOWSX.H.

We'll finish our message-cracker example by filling out the **OnCreate** call:

```
static BOOL OnCreate(HWND hwnd,

                     CREATESTRUCT FAR* lpCreateStruct)
{
    char *stringbuf;
    /*
       Allocate some memory. If no memory
       is available, report that the create request has failed.
    */
    stringbuf = (char *)LocalAlloc (LPTR, 1000);
    if (!stringbuf)
        return FALSE;
    .
    .
    .
    // Return TRUE; create the window.
    return TRUE;
}
```

This trivial example of WM_CREATE handling shows how you can cause creation of a window to succeed or fail, depending on the return value of the function. Later, you'll see some more useful actions you can perform as part of WM_CREATE message handling.

One important note on WINDOWSX.H and its message-cracker macros: They rely on the callback function to define **wParam** and **lParam** exactly as they're spelled in the examples I've included in this book. (This is the only place you're likely ever to see them referenced, so consistency shouldn't be a problem.)

Default Message Handling

Since a window's callback function is called for every single message that goes to that window, what do you do with the messages you're not interested in? You've seen that WINDOWSX.H's message-cracker macros still use a **switch** statement to call the message-handler functions. What should the **default** case of this **switch** do?

The answer is that it should call the standard Windows function known as **DefWindowProc**. This is the default handler for all messages that you don't process. Standard WINDOWSX.H coding practice is to make a **#define** for **DefWindowProc** so that you can change it to some other handler easily, since you might want to call it in places other than the **default** case of the callback function's **switch** statement.

DefWindowProc provides much of the continuity between Windows applications. Really, what distinguishes one Windows program from another is what each does with the various messages that come through the callback function. Messages that aren't handled by the program are handled in a consistent way by Windows itself through **DefWindowProc**.

Assuming that the header file for the callback function's source file has **DefProc** defined as **DefWindowProc**, here's what the callback function should look like now:

```
LRESULT CALLBACK WndProc (HWND hwnd,
                          UINT msg,
                          WPARAM wParam,
                          LPARAM lParam)
{

     switch (msg) {
            HANDLE_MSG (hwnd, WM_CREATE, OnCreate);
            HANDLE_MSG (hwnd, WM_CHAR, OnChar);
            // More handlers for other messages...
            .
            .
            .
            default:
                   return DefProc (hwnd, msg,
                                   wParam, lParam);
     }
}
```

Due to the magic of WINDOWSX.H, the callback function becomes little more than a simple dispatcher of messages to message-specific handler functions, which do the actual work of responding to the message.

SendMessage and PostMessage

You now know that messages are pulled out of an application's message queue by calls to **GetMessage**, and sent to our window callback function by **DispatchMessage**. You might imagine that it would be useful to send messages to callback functions from your own code. It would be simple enough to call the function yourself with the desired window handle, message, and values in **wParam** and **lParam**. Simple, but disastrous.

An explanation of the reason why such a call would be disastrous to your program is beyond the scope of this book, but suffice it to say that it has to do with the way

16-bit Windows was designed. But of course, there's still a way to send messages to your own callback functions; in fact, there are two ways.

The **SendMessage** function has parameters with types identical to the callback function: HWND, UINT, WPARAM, LPARAM, and a return value of LRESULT. Calling **SendMessage** with a valid HWND actually *does* perform a direct function call to the window's callback function. Because of this, you have to be a little careful when using **SendMessage** to avoid getting into a recursive loop (by sending a message, processing that message, sending another message, and so on, without ever calling **DefWindowProc**).

An alternative to **SendMessage** is **PostMessage**, which, instead of calling the callback function directly, just places the message in the application's message queue, where it will soon be plucked out by **GetMessage**. Most of the time you'll want to use **PostMessage** to send messages to your callback functions, though you may find there are certain circumstances under which you'll want to avoid the message loop and make a direct function call.

Now that you know how a window's callback function works, how do you tell Windows the function's name and therefore how to call it? Window callback functions are part of a structure that defines a window class. Window classes are then registered to Windows with the **RegisterClass** function.

Registering Window Classes

A window's callback function is called for every message sent to *any* window from a given window class. Just as you can run multiple instances of a single program, you can run multiple instances of a *class* of windows. A given window is said to be an instance of that window's class. Typically, window classes for windows that you want to create in your program are registered at initialization time, near the beginning of **WinMain**. A window's class *must* be registered before you call **GetMessage/DispatchMessage** or Windows won't find any of your windows to dispatch to.

You register a window class by filling in the members of a WNDCLASS structure, which is defined in WINDOWS.H like so:

```
typedef struct tagWNDCLASS
{
    UINT         style;
    WNDPROC      lpfnWndProc;
    int          cbClsExtra;
    int          cbWndExtra;
    HINSTANCE    hInstance;
    HICON        hIcon;
    HCURSOR      hCursor;
    HBRUSH       hbrBackground;
    LPCSTR       lpszMenuName;
    LPCSTR       lpszClassName;
} WNDCLASS;
```

Note the second member of the WNDCLASS structure—something called a *WNDPROC*. In WINDOWS.H, you'll find that a WNDPROC is defined as a pointer to a function whose parameters are exactly that of a window callback function. You assign this member the address of your callback function.

Let's examine each of the members of the WNDCLASS structure individually to understand what constitutes a window class.

The **style** member of the structure should be filled with flag values that determine certain characteristics of all the windows that will be created from the class. The flag values, which are listed in Table 2-2, are connected by the logical operator OR.

For now, let's just choose a plain-vanilla class style and simply set **style** to zero. Later, you'll learn which CS_ settings are most useful to a game program.

You already know about the **lpfnWndProc** member of the structure; this points to the window's callback function. The next member is called **cbClsExtra**. Assigning a

TABLE 2-2

Settings of the **style** *WNDCLASS member*

Value	Meaning
CS_BYTEALIGNCLIENT	Aligns the client area of a window to a byte boundary (in the *x* direction).
CS_BYTEALIGNWINDOW	Aligns a window on a byte boundary (in the *x* direction).
CS_CLASSDC	Gives the window its own display context, shared by instances.
CS_DBLCLKS	Sends double-click messages to a window.
CS_GLOBALCLASS	Specifies that the window class is an application-global class: The class is available to all applications in the system.
CS_HREDRAW	Redraws the entire window if the horizontal size changes.
CS_VREDRAW	Redraws the entire window if the vertical size changes.
CS_NOCLOSE	Inhibits the Close option on the system menu.
CS_OWNDC	Gives each window instance its own display context.
CS_PARENTDC	Gives the display context of the parent window to the window class.

value to this member causes Windows to allocate that number of extra bytes when the class is allocated. You can access these extra bytes by calling **GetClassWord** or **GetClassLong** with an index value that specifies which 2-byte or 4-byte value, respectively, you want to access. Telling Windows to create some extra bytes with each class provides a convenient mechanism for associating some class-global data with the class, data that can then be accessed by any function that has an HWND to a window that is an instance of that class.

Likewise, the **cbWndExtra** member of the WNDCLASS structure allows us to specify some extra bytes that are associated with each individual *window* that is created from the class. You'll see a little later how you might want to use this feature to stuff a pointer to your own window-specific structure there and access it from within the window's callback function. For example, you might want to store the *x* and *y* coordinates of the mouse position in this window-specific structure so that you can access them across messages, instead of declaring static or global variables in the module.

The next structure member should be set to the HINSTANCE of the program instance that is registering the class. This is important because it tells Windows which application "owns" the window-class definition. It's possible to register a class whose definition is global to the system (by using the CS_GLOBALCLASS setting in the **style** member), in which case any running program can create windows from the class. The important thing about the **hInstance** member is that the class is destroyed whenever its owner—the program module associated with **hInstance**—exits.

The sixth structure member is something called an *HICON,* or handle to an icon resource. (I'll cover icons in greater detail in this chapter's section on resources.) A window class' icon is the thing the user sees on the desktop whenever the user minimizes a window created from that class. If this member is set to NULL, then you have to detect when the window is minimized and draw your own picture as the icon. You've probably seen nifty programs with little icons that are animated when the program is minimized; this is how those programs do it.

The seventh structure member, **hCursor**, should be set to the handle of another type of resource: a *cursor.* A cursor is, of course, the thing that moves around on the screen when you move the mouse. Although the operating system has only one cursor at any given time, what that cursor looks like is defined by the window under it. If you set **hCursor** in the WNDCLASS structure to an HCURSOR resource, every window created from that class will use that cursor whenever the mouse passes over the window. You can use one of the predefined cursors that Windows provides for your class, or you can create your own, add it to your resource file, and set it here to be used for all windows of the given window class.

If you set the **hCursor** member to NULL, then no cursor is defined for windows created from the class. In this case, you need to set the cursor manually by calling **SetCursor** every time you get a WM_MOUSEMOVE message (in WINDOWSX.H parlance, you'd set it in your **OnMouseMove** message-handler function). It may seem like a lot of overhead to call a function that sets the cursor every time the mouse moves, but the **SetCursor** function is designed to return very quickly if it finds you setting the cursor to the last one set. If the **hCursor** member of the WNDCLASS structure isn't NULL, the operating system calls **SetCursor** for you on every mouse move, anyway. The trick is to remember *not* to set **hCursor** to the handle of a cursor resource *and* call **SetCursor** in your mouse-move handler, or the cursor will flicker horribly as first you set the cursor and then the operating system does it.

It's likely that you'd want your game program to have full control over the cursor, and so your program would set **hCursor** to NULL and call **SetCursor** in a window's **OnMouseMove** function. This would also give you the freedom to set the cursor differently for different windows of the same class, since you can identify the window by its HWND in the message handler. Also, calling **SetCursor** with a NULL parameter turns the cursor off, which can be important for some games.

The next member of the WNDCLASS structure, **hbrBackground**,defines the *brush* used to paint the background of windows created from the class. (I cover brushes extensively in Chapter 5.) Basically, a brush defines a pattern that can be drawn in a window. If you set **hbrBackground** to either a brush you've created or one of Windows' so-called stock brushes, the window will fill its background with that brush whenever necessary. A brush can also define a solid color, of course. For example, if you wanted all the windows of your class to have their background automatically cleared to black whenever the window needed updating, you'd set **hbrBackground** like this:

```
WNDCLASS wc;

wc.hbrBackground = GetStockObject (BLACK_BRUSH);
// Other settings of the WNDCLASS structure follow.
.
.
.
RegisterClass (&wc);
```

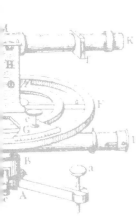

You can also use one of the 20 system colors as the background for your class' windows. Windows allows a user to customize the look of windows by setting these 20 colors in the Colors section of the Control Panel application. To set the window class' background color to one of the 20 system colors, you add the system color to one of the following constants and cast it as an HBRUSH:

COLOR_ACTIVEBORDER	COLOR_ACTIVECAPTION
COLOR_APPWORKSPACE	COLOR_BACKGROUND
COLOR_BTNFACE	COLOR_BTNSHADOW
COLOR_HIGHLIGHTTEXT	COLOR_INACTIVEBORDER
COLOR_INACTIVECAPTION	COLOR_INACTIVECAPTIONTEXT
COLOR_MENU	COLOR_MENUTEXT

COLOR_BTNTEXT	COLOR_CAPTIONTEXT
COLOR_GRAYTEXT	COLOR_HIGHLIGHT
COLOR_SCROLLBAR	COLOR_WINDOW
COLOR_WINDOWFRAME	COLOR_WINDOWTEXT

For example, to use the COLOR_BACKGROUND color (in Control Panel, Desktop), you'd set **hbrBackground** like this:

```
WNDCLASS wc;

wc.hbrBackground = (HBRUSH)(COLOR_BACKGROUND + 1);
// Other settings of the WNDCLASS structure follow.
.
.
.
RegisterClass (&wc);
```

The penultimate member of the WNDCLASS structure is a string that names the menu resource in the resource file associated with the module's **hInstance**. (Again, you'll learn about menus and other resources shortly.) Oddly enough, this parameter specifies a pointer to a string containing the name as it appears in the resource file, rather than to a handle to the resource, as **hIcon** and **hCursor** do. Reason: That's the way Microsoft did it. Note the funky string data type, LPCSTR. In WINDOWS.H, you'll find that an LPCSTR is

```
typedef const char FAR* LPCSTR;
```

Finally, the last parameter defines the actual name of the class, as another LPCSTR. You use the name of the class whenever you want to create a window from that class. It must be unique within a given program (or unique to *all* programs, if the CS_GLOBALCLASS flag is set). Registering a class with the same name as that of an existing class will cause the **RegisterClass** function to fail and return zero.

FIGURE 2-7

Appearance of the example window

There are a number of predefined global class names that you probably shouldn't register yourself. These are the classes for the various Windows controls, like buttons, dialog boxes, edit controls, list boxes, and so on. (Actually, you *can* register a class under one of these predefined names—it's called *subclassing* and it's a little beyond the scope of this discussion. You may have noticed certain programs that have different-looking buttons, check boxes, and so on; these effects were probably obtained by subclassing the controls and giving them new drawing routines.)

Now that you understand all the members of the WNDCLASS structure, let's create a function that fills one completely and registers the class it defines. Figure 2-7 shows the resulting example window.

```
static BOOL InitClass (HINSTANCE hInstance)
{
     WNDCLASS  wc;

     // A basic style
     wc.style = 0;
     wc.lpfnWndProc = WndProc;
     wc.cbClsExtra = 0;
     wc.cbWndExtra = 0;
     wc.hInstance = hInstance;
     // The default application icon
     wc.hIcon = LoadIcon(NULL, IDI_APPLICATION);
     // The standard cursor
     wc.hCursor = LoadCursor(NULL, IDC_ARROW);
     wc.hbrBackground = GetStockObject(BLACK_BRUSH);
     // No menu for this class
     wc.lpszMenuName =  NULL;
     wc.lpszClassName = "DemoClass";

     return RegisterClass(&wc);
}
```

This registers a window's class under the name DemoClass (incidentally, case is ignored in class definitions), with no defined menu and a black background. It also defines a standard arrow cursor for the class (**LoadCursor (NULL, IDC_ARROW)** loads the standard Windows cursor from the system), and a default icon (likewise for the **LoadIcon** call). The **style** member defines a basic style, and the **lpfnWndProc** member gets the address of the window callback function, **WndProc**. No extra bytes are to be added to our class or the windows created from it. The **hInstance** that comes in as a parameter to our function tells Windows what instance owns the class definition.

This little **InitClass** function should be called sometime before you start processing messages for your windows, of course, and its return value should be checked to determine whether to continue. If the call to **RegisterClass** fails, then there's no point trying to create windows from that class!

Note that **InitClass** should be performed only for the first instance of the program (if you allow multiple instances). A window class, once registered, is available to all instances of the program.

The Components of a Windows Program

Before we start creating windows and putting pictures on the screen, let's get a little background on what, exactly, makes up a Windows program. Building a Windows program isn't all that different from building a DOS program, but there are a few extra files you need to create.

In the earliest days of Windows programming, you were responsible for creating all the various files that make up a Windows program (including the make file), and all the tools you had to work with ran only under DOS. Today, if you're using one of the modern Windows-based development environments, like Microsoft Visual C++, Borland C/C++, or even Microsoft Quick C for Windows, the development system automatically takes care of a lot of those files for you.

At a minimum, a Windows program consists of the following three components:

- A module definition file (.DEF file)
- A resource script file (.RC file)
- Source files (.C files, .H files, and so on)

(Strictly speaking, the resource script file is optional, but almost all Windows programs have one.)

The linker uses a program's module definition file to determine the structure and organization of the program. The .DEF file contains statements about the code and data segments for your program, descriptive information that gets embedded in the .EXE file, and a list of the functions that are exported from your program. Here's what a minimum .DEF file for a program might look like:

```
NAME                WinGame
DESCRIPTION         'Game Demo Program'
EXETYPE             WINDOWS

CODE         PRELOAD MOVEABLE DISCARDABLE
DATA         PRELOAD MOVEABLE MULTIPLE

HEAPSIZE     25600

EXPORTS
     WndProc
```

Much of the information in the .DEF is optional, some of it is actually outdated and useless, and some of it is critical to making a program link and run properly.

For example, the DESCRIPTION line of the .DEF file has no useful purpose anymore. Its information, which gets buried in the executable file, could be used for version numbering or some such, but Windows now has much more powerful version-numbering capabilities. The NAME statement is optional for programs; if it isn't there, the executable's file name (less the .EXE portion) is used instead. The EXETYPE statement, though, is important; the linker (Microsoft linkers, anyway) can build both Windows and OS/2 applications, so you need to specify which kind you want.

The CODE and DATA statements are also important. These give Windows vital information about what the operating system can do with the code and data segments of a program, respectively. The attributes you can use in these statements are listed in Table 2-3.

In the bad old days, careful management of code-segment attributes, and the dynamic loading of code segments themselves were critical to optimizing the performance of a Windows program running in low-memory situations. Indeed, sometimes they were critical to getting a program to run *at all*. However, in those days, "low-memory situations" often as not meant real-mode Windows—a long-gone version of Windows that could actually run in *640k of memory!* Fortunately, real-mode Windows died with Windows 3.1, and even Standard-mode Windows (designed to run on Intel 80286 processors) died with Windows for Workgroups version 3.11. Windows 95 will run only in so-called Enhanced mode, which runs only on 80386 and higher processors. This means that many of the programmer's memory-management responsibilities simply go away.

TABLE 2-3

CODE Attributes

Attribute	Meaning
FIXED	The code segments remain in a fixed memory location.
MOVEABLE	The code segments can be moved around in memory by Windows in order to compact memory.
DISCARDABLE	The code segments can be discarded when no longer needed.
PRELOAD	The code segments are loaded when the module is loaded.
LOADONCALL	The code segments are loaded when it is called.

With virtual memory, the attributes MOVEABLE and DISCARDABLE become almost meaningless; the virtual memory manager handles swapping code to and from disk in a way that's quite different than the one their original meanings dictated. There are a few exceptions: Certain interrupt-handling code must be declared as FIXED or the interrupt will be very displeased to find code missing from its original location. This is rarely an issue—generally, you need worry about it only when handling incoming MIDI and audio waveform data using the Multimedia Extensions. Otherwise, you can safely declare your code to be both MOVEABLE and DISCARDABLE and not give it any further thought.

The LOADONCALL attribute is almost completely obsolete, partly because the virtual memory manager decides when code segments will be loaded and partly because the resource compiler (which you'll learn about shortly) can override this attribute to optimize segment loading.

The long and short of this is that unless you're doing something very weird and know otherwise, the attributes listed in the example—namely PRELOAD, MOVEABLE, and DISCARDABLE—are all you need to put on the CODE line of your .DEF file.

The DATA attributes, listed in Table 2-4, are no less straightforward.

Again, except under very special circumstances, your program can use the DATA statement in the example—PRELOAD, MOVEABLE, and MULTIPLE.

Our .DEF file has a statement called HEAPSIZE that defines what Windows calls the *local heap*. The local heap in a Windows program is a section of memory that you access using the `LocalAlloc` function call. The local heap resides in a single 64K segment (under Windows 3.1, that is; in Win32, the local heap is the same as the global heap and can be up to 4 gigabytes in size) and is shared with the program's stack and static data. The HEAPSIZE statement is required in a .DEF file because it

TABLE 2-4

DATA attributes

Attribute	Meaning
NONE	There is no data segment for this module. This attribute is valid only for DLL modules.
SINGLE	One data segment is shared across all instances of the module. This is valid only for DLL modules.
MULTIPLE	Each instance of the module has a separate data segment. This is valid only for executable modules.
PRELOAD	Same as for CODE.
FIXED	Same as for CODE.
MOVEABLE	Same as for CODE.

tells Windows how much of the 64K segment to leave for your program's local heap. There is also a corresponding STACKSIZE statement, but this parameter is usually specified somewhere else as part of whatever integrated development environment you're using. Since this value overrides what you'd put in the STACKSIZE statement, it's seldom used in the .DEF file anymore.

How big should a program's local heap be? This is a sort of "how long is a rope" question, because only the programmer knows how many calls are made to **LocalAlloc**, how much static data the program has, and how big its stack should be. Actually, it's pretty rare that the programmer really *knows* these values, so the setting of HEAPSIZE is generally just an educated guess. Windows programs can be quite stack-intensive, and since stack-overflow problems can be hard to detect, it's prudent to leave plenty of stack space: As huge as it may seem to an experienced programmer, 15K isn't necessarily too much stack space for a Windows program. Consequently, setting HEAPSIZE to 25K or more leaves plenty of room for static variables (especially given the modern practice of exorcising global variables from programs). It's usually easier to find errors where **LocalAlloc** fails than when there's a stack overflow, and the linker will always let you know if there's not enough room for static data.

There's only one statement left in our .DEF file: the EXPORTS statement. EXPORTS tells the linker which functions are exportable, or accessible directly as Windows callback functions. The function names for every callback function in your program should appear in a list under the EXPORTS line in the .DEF file, exactly as they appear in the source code. The only exception is **WinMain** itself, which Windows already expects for executable programs.

The EXPORTS statement in the .DEF file can be a real pain. If you miss a callback function, there's a good chance either your program will crash with an obscure message or some window-creation function will fail at run time, leaving you scratching your head and staring at the code for hours on end. Callback functions run rampant throughout Windows code. They not only perform as window message-handling functions, but serve many other purposes, also. Missing just one can send you on a wild-goose chase for hours.

Fortunately, there's a simple solution to this problem (provided your compiler environment supports it) that doesn't involve touching the .DEF file at all. The Microsoft compilers all support a keyword, **_export**, that can appear in front of a function definition to declare it as an exported function to the linker. So, by declaring our earlier example of a window callback function like this

```
LRESULT CALLBACK _export WndProc (HWND hwnd,
                                  UINT msg,
                                  WPARAM wParam,
                                  LPARAM lParam)
```

we avoid having to list the function in the .DEF file in the EXPORTS section. The examples in this book use **_export**; if your compiler doesn't support this feature, you'll have to remember to put the exports in your .DEF file.

There are several other statements that you can declare in a .DEF file, but they're all optional, and in most cases, the example I've given here will work fine. The linker is the program that reads the .DEF file, and it will usually complain if you do something really wrong (with the exception of the aforementioned EXPORTS nastiness).

Besides the actual source files—.C, .H, .CPP, or whatever—the only other Windows-specific file that your program will have is the *resource script,* or .RC file. It's possible to create a program with no resource file, but such programs are the exception rather than the rule. The resource file, as you might expect, contains what Windows calls *resources:* static data objects that get loaded when you need them. For example, an icon is a resource that usually (and most conveniently) is declared in the resource file and is loaded with **LoadIcon**, which returns a handle to that resource (an HICON).

There are many kinds of resources, including ones that you can define yourself. I'll cover resources in greater detail near the end of this chapter. But by now you must be sick of looking at benign examples, and are probably wondering when we'll ever get down to writing our first Windows program. Get on with it, already!

Getting It on the Screen

It's about time to put together what you've learned thus far and get a canonical "Hello, Windows" program up and running, in classic hacker fashion. You know what the main message loop looks like, how to register a window class, and how to handle messages intended for that window. Still missing is the function that actually puts a window on the screen, which is a fundamental requirement for most Windows programs: Not much of interest happens unless there is at least *one* window for it to happen in.

Creating Windows

The function for creating a window is unsurprisingly called **CreateWindow** and it looks like this:

```
HWND CreateWindow (LPCSTR lpszClassName,
                   LPCSTR lpszWindowName,
                   DWORD dwStyle,
                   int x, int y,
                   int width, int height,
                   HWND hwndParent,
                   HMENU hMenu,
                   HINSTANCE hInst,
                   void FAR *lpvParam)
```

Yes, that's 11 parameters. Let's pick them apart.

First off, **CreateWindow** returns an HWND, or handle to a window, as you might expect. The first parameter to the function specifies the name of the class from which it will be derived. This is the same string as appears in the `lpszClassName` member of the WNDCLASS structure.

The second parameter is another string that defines a name for the window. If the window has a caption bar, this is the string that will be displayed there when the window is first displayed.

The third parameter, **`dwStyle`**, is the most complex of the bunch; I'll cover it a little later.

The next four parameters define the *x* and *y* coordinates of the screen location of the upper left corner of the window and the window's width and height, respectively, in pixels.

The eighth parameter can be an HWND that is the parent window to the window you're creating. If you supply a valid HWND as this parameter (meaning it's an HWND of a window that still exists), then the window being created is said to be either a *child* window or an *owned* window, depending on certain settings of the **`dwStyle`** parameter. A child window is one that cannot stray from the boundaries of its parent; it is displayed within the parent window's client area. In a game program, an example of a child window might be a control panel at the bottom of the main window. An owned window can overlap its parent, but otherwise behaves like the child window—it is minimized and destroyed with its parent. You might imagine an owned window in a game program as a floating information panel that the user can place anywhere within the main window.

If the parent-window parameter is set to the constant HWND_DESKTOP (which is defined in WINDOWS.H as **`((HWND)0)`**), then the window is said to be a *top-level window;* its parent is the whole desktop, which never gets minimized and is destroyed only when the user exits Windows. Every program has at least one top-level window.

The HMENU parameter is usually just what you might think it is—except, of course, when it's not. The meaning depends on the setting of the **`dwStyle`** parameter. If **`dwStyle`** specifies a "pop-up" or "overlapped" window, the HMENU parameter can be either a handle to a menu that will be displayed at the top of the window, or NULL, indicating that the parameter should use the menu defined by the window's class (in the **`lpszMenuName`** member of the WNDCLASS structure). This is very logical. However, if this is a child window, this parameter should be an integer that uniquely identifies the child window to the parent window. Got it? In practice, this usually isn't as difficult to understand as it sounds, but the polymorphic nature of this parameter makes for some confusion until you understand the whole picture of how child windows work. They're most commonly used as controls in dialog boxes, where you don't even have to worry about how they're created, because Windows does it for you.

The HINSTANCE parameter is, fortunately, just what you think it is: an instance handle to the module that owns the window. This tells Windows who's ultimately responsible for this window.

The last parameter, called **`lpvParam`** here, is a FAR pointer to a void data type, meaning it can point to anything. The idea behind this parameter is to let you pass a pointer to your own data to the **CreateWindow** function, which will in turn pass this pointer on with the WM_CREATE message when it is sent to your window's callback function. This allows you to send some initialization data to your callback function without having to store it in an icky global somewhere. In the WM_CREATE message-handler function (**OnCreate**), you can cast your pointer back to whatever it originally pointed to.

Remember that the WINDOWSX.H message-cracker macro for WM_CREATE does a little twist on the return value of the callback function, so that the message handler can simply return TRUE or FALSE, depending on whether you want the window-create request to succeed or fail. If you return FALSE from the handler, the return value of **CreateWindow** will be NULL, and the window will never be created. WM_CREATE actually gets sent before the window is displayed on the screen, so you can "noiselessly" fail in **OnCreate**. Usually, the **OnCreate** handler for the top-most window of an application does lots of initialization stuff, including creating other windows that the application needs in order to start. This design is strictly up to the programmer, of course. A game program might load some startup picture, for example, or initialize some memory, all before the **OnCreate** handler returns.

Provided the callback function doesn't fail in WM_CREATE, the **CreateWindow** function will return the handle to the window so created, and you can begin doing things with the window.

The dwStyle Parameter

The **dwStyle** parameter to **CreateWindow** is a bit-encoded DWORD, or 32-bit value. You can use the logical operator OR to link about 20 of its bits in different ways to create windows of different styles. Some of the bits are mutually exclusive, and some combinations of them don't make a lot of sense. There are bits that add features like caption bars, Minimize and Maximize buttons, and scrollbars. There are bits that specify whether the window is a child window or a "pop-up" window. There are even bits that give the window either a thin border, or a thick border that enables the user to resize the window with the mouse. All these bits have predefined constant names in WINDOWS.H that start with *WS_*.

Probably the most common top-level window you see in most productivity applications is the WS_OVERLAPPEDWINDOW style, which is loaded with pretty much everything: thick (resizable) borders, a system menu, both Minimize and Maximize buttons, and a caption bar. Figure 2-8 shows window features controlled by the **dwStyle** parameter to **CreateWindow**.

The choice of top-level window style naturally has a significant impact on how the program works. For example, if your window has resizable borders, well, your users are going to expect something useful to happen if they resize it. Incidentally, just

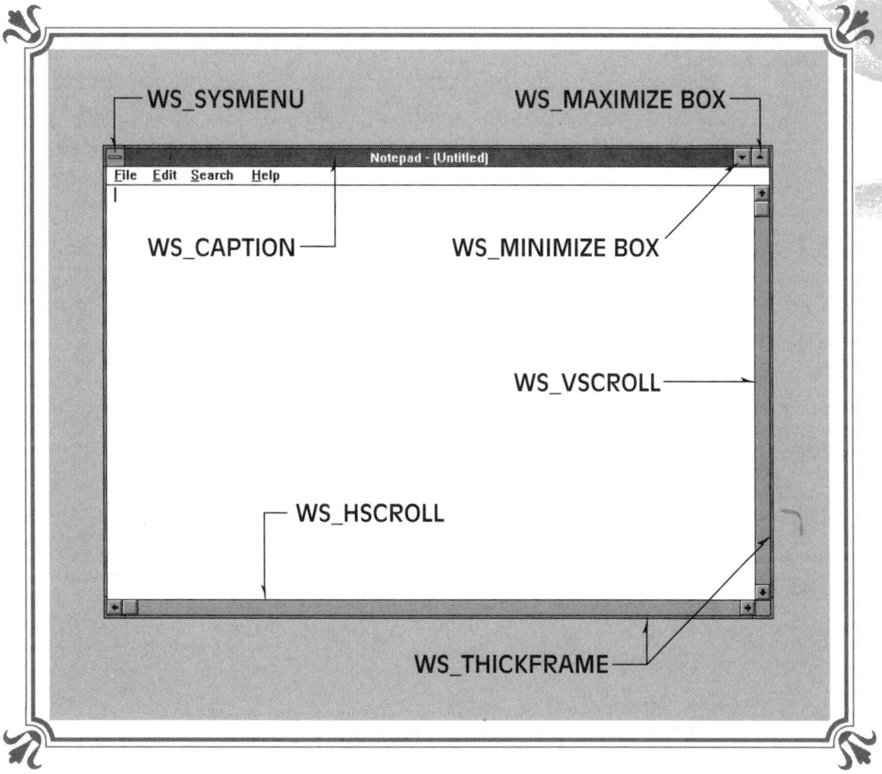

FIGURE 2-8

Various window features

because a feature doesn't appear as part of the window style doesn't mean that you can't use that feature from your own code easily enough. For example, even if you create a window that has no Minimize button, you can still minimize that window by calling `ShowWindow` with the SW_MINIMIZE parameter. Of course, the general principle of Windows is that all applications share a common method for performing certain tasks, but the usual caveat about games applies here—you're creating an experience that may have little to do with having an interface that's consistent with your user's favorite spreadsheet program. You need to think carefully about what features you enable with the `dwStyle` parameter. If you're creating a full-screen game, you'll probably want to go with the most ordinary window you can get: a WS_POPUP window, which has no border, no caption bar, and (thus) no buttons. Since it doesn't have thick borders, it can't be resized with the mouse like a WS_OVERLAPPEDWINDOW can. It also can't be dragged around the screen by its caption bar, since it doesn't have one.

In this, our first Windows program, you can change `CreateWindow`'s `dwStyle` parameter to see how the different windows behave.

The Code

Our first Windows program, out of respect for Kernighan and Ritchie, will simply display a message in the middle of its window. As I mentioned, we'll start with a main window of the WS_OVERLAPPEDWINDOW style, then we'll change it to WS_POPUP to see the difference. Here's the code for MAIN.C:

```
#include <windows.h>
#include <windowsx.h>

#define DefProc DefWindowProc

// Forward declarations
static BOOL InitClass (HINSTANCE hInst);
static HWND Init (HINSTANCE hInst, int nCmdShow);
LRESULT CALLBACK _export WndProc(HWND hwnd, UINT msg,
            WPARAM wParam, LPARAM lParam);

static BOOL OnCreate(HWND hwnd,
                   CREATESTRUCT FAR* lpCreateStruct);
static void OnDestroy (HWND hwnd);
static void OnPaint (HWND hwnd);
static void OnSize(HWND hwnd, UINT state,
                   int cx, int cy);

// Windows entry point
int PASCAL WinMain(HINSTANCE hInstance,
                   HINSTANCE hPrevInstance,
                   LPSTR lpCmdLine, int nCmdShow)
{
    MSG msg;

    // Register the class if this is not the first instance.
    if (!hPrevInstance && !InitClass (hInstance))
        return FALSE;

    if (!Init (hInstance, nCmdShow))
        return FALSE;

    while (GetMessage(&msg, NULL, NULL, NULL)) {
            TranslateMessage(&msg);
            DispatchMessage(&msg);
    }
    return (msg.wParam);
}

static BOOL InitClass (HINSTANCE hInstance)
{
    WNDCLASS  wc;

    // Vanilla style
```

```
    wc.style = 0;
    wc.lpfnWndProc = WndProc;
    wc.cbClsExtra = 0;
    wc.cbWndExtra = 0;
    wc.hInstance = hInstance;
    wc.hIcon = LoadIcon(NULL, IDI_APPLICATION);
    wc.hCursor = LoadCursor(NULL, IDC_ARROW);
    wc.hbrBackground = GetStockObject(BLACK_BRUSH);
    wc.lpszMenuName =  NULL;
    wc.lpszClassName = "OurDemoClass";

    return RegisterClass(&wc);
}

static HWND Init (HINSTANCE hInstance, int show)
{
    int x, y;

    // Get the size of the full screen.
    x = GetSystemMetrics (SM_CXSCREEN);
    y = GetSystemMetrics (SM_CYSCREEN);

    // Create the main window.
    // That's all this init does here;
    // window-specific stuff happens in OnCreate.
    return CreateWindow(
                "OurDemoClass",
                "Demo Program",
                // Standard resizable window
                WS_OVERLAPPEDWINDOW,
                0,
                0,
                x,
                y,
                // No parent, no menu,
                // no parameters to WM_CREATE
                HWND_DESKTOP,
                NULL,
                hInstance,
                // Send the WM_CREATE message
                // WinMain's nCmdShow parameter.
                &show
            );
}

LRESULT CALLBACK _export WndProc(HWND hwnd, UINT msg,
                  WPARAM wParam, LPARAM lParam)
{
    switch (msg) {

        HANDLE_MSG(hwnd, WM_CREATE, OnCreate);
```

continued on next page

continued from previous page

```
        HANDLE_MSG(hwnd, WM_DESTROY, OnDestroy);
        HANDLE_MSG(hwnd, WM_PAINT, OnPaint);
        HANDLE_MSG(hwnd, WM_SIZE, OnSize);
    default:
        return DefProc(hwnd, msg, wParam, lParam);
    }
}

static BOOL OnCreate(HWND hwnd,
                  CREATESTRUCT FAR* lpCreateStruct)
{

    // Show the window according to WinMain's
    // nCmdShow parameter.
    ShowWindow (hwnd,
              *(LPINT)lpCreateStruct->lpCreateParams);
    return TRUE;
}

static void OnDestroy (HWND hwnd)
{
    PostQuitMessage (0);
}

static void OnPaint (HWND hwnd)
{
    PAINTSTRUCT ps;
    HDC hdc;
    RECT r;
    SIZE sz;
    int start_x, start_y;
    char hw[] = "Hello, Windows.";

    hdc = BeginPaint (hwnd, &ps);
    SetBkColor (hdc, RGB (0,0,0));
    SetTextColor (hdc, RGB (255, 0, 0));
    GetClientRect (hwnd, &r);

    GetTextExtentPoint (hdc, hw, lstrlen(hw), &sz);
    start_x = (r.right - sz.cx) / 2;
    start_y = (r.bottom - sz.cy) / 2;

    TextOut (hdc, start_x, start_y, hw, lstrlen(hw));

    EndPaint (hwnd, &ps);
}

static void OnSize(HWND hwnd, UINT state,
                  int cx, int cy)
{
    InvalidateRect (hwnd, NULL, TRUE);
}
```

There it is. Figure 2-9 shows the flow of events of MAIN.C. Several parts of the program still need explanation—namely, the stuff that actually puts text on the window. All in good time. Let's begin by taking apart `WinMain`.

The first thing `WinMain` does (after declaring an MSG structure to hold the program's messages) is test `hPrevInstance` to see if this is the first instance of the program being run. If it is (ANSI C will not continue to evaluate a logical AND once it finds the first FALSE), then `WinMain` tries to register a window class with `InitClass`, which returns what `RegisterClass` returns. The program's main window class is a plain-vanilla class, with a standard icon and cursor: Both `LoadIcon` and `LoadCursor` with a NULL first argument load icons and cursors from a predefined set that Windows provides. Any windows you create from the class will have a black background, and no menu. The class is named OurDemoClass.

After successfully registering the window class, the program calls the `Init` function, which does little more than create the top-level window and return its handle. Looking at `Init`, you'll see two calls to a Windows function called `GetSystemMetrics`. This call returns the value of one of several system constants; there are about 36 in all. All the constants are, of course, defined in WINDOWS.H. In typical Hungarian notation

FIGURE 2-9

Flow of events in MAIN.C

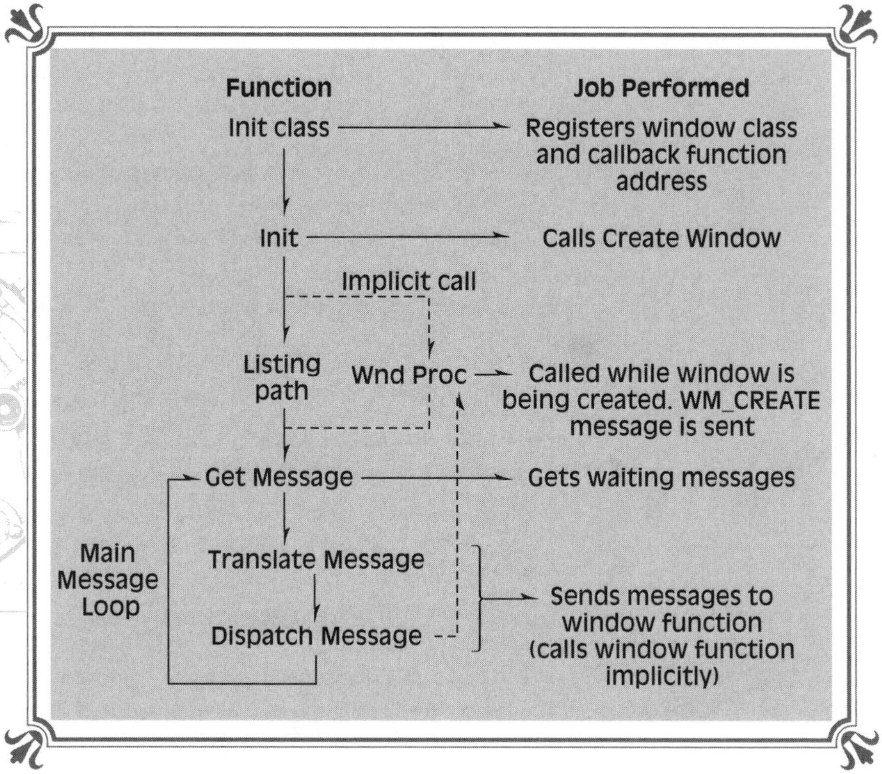

fashion, all start with *SM_*. Two that are of interest for this window are the *x* and *y* dimensions of the full screen, which are found in SM_CXSCREEN and SM_CYSCREEN, respectively. It's usually a good idea to know the screen's resolution before creating your first top-level window, even if it's not a full-screen like this one.

The actual **CreateWindow** call looks just like you might expect: a string that defines our window class; a string for the caption bar; and a **dwStyle** setting of WS_OVERLAPPEDWINDOW, the full-featured style. To make this window consume the whole screen, we set its origin at 0,0 (screen coordinates start at 0,0 and extend to SM_CXSCREEN-1,SM_CYSCREEN-1) and specify that the width and height be taken from the calls to **GetSystemMetrics**. Note that the two former parameters are *width* and *height,* and not the *coordinates* of the lower right corner. This is an area where new (and old) Windows programmers continually trip up—mistaking *dimensions* for *coordinates.* It's an easy mistake to make, and I promise you that you'll make it several times while writing Windows programs.

The window's parent window is the desktop (thus making it a top-level window), and it has no menu that overrides the class definition. You're already familiar with **hInstance**, which was passed in to the **Init** function.

The final parameter to **CreateWindow** is a user-defined pointer. Whatever is put here will be passed in to the **OnCreate** function when the callback function receives the WM_CREATE message. As a simple example, a pointer to the **int show** parameter of the **Init** function is passed to **CreateWindow**. This integer value originally came from **WinMain** itself, and its purpose is to tell the initial window of a program something about the desired initial state of the window. If you're familiar with the Run command that you can select from the File menu of either Program Manager or File Manager, you'll recall that it has a little check box that allows you to start a program in its minimized state. This is what the **nCmdShow** parameter to **WinMain** represents. You'll see how it's used in **OnCreate** in a moment.

Next comes the actual callback function, **WndProc**. From the **switch** statement, you can see that the callback function handles only four messages: WM_CREATE, WM_DESTROY, WM_PAINT, and WM_SIZE. A full explanation of the latter two will have to wait until Chapter 5, and you're already familiar with WM_CREATE, which is sent when the window is first created. Here, let's examine WM_DESTROY and its handler, **OnDestroy**.

```
static void OnDestroy (HWND hwnd)
{
    PostQuitMessage (0);
}
```

The first thing to know about **OnDestroy**—and, in fact, all the message handlers that you'll see defined in this book—is that they'll all be declared with the **static** keyword. As you know, this keyword tells the compiler (and the linker) that this function isn't to be exported; its scope is strictly limited to the source file in which it appears. I'm a real stickler for declaring static functions when they're called only from within the module. If you look in WINDOWSX.H, you'll notice that each message-cracker prototype has a name in the form **Cls_OnDestroy**, where **Cls** is meant to be a placeholder for the window's class name. I've done away with those and shortened the handler's name to its bare essentials; if you do this, however, it means that you *must* use the **static** keyword in order to avoid an external naming conflict when linking.

WM_DESTROY Handling

The WM_DESTROY message is sent to a window just before it gets destroyed. Trapping the WM_DESTROY message for a top-level window turns out to be rather important—required, in fact—because if the window is destroyed, the **GetMessage** loop will carry on merrily forever. Never receiving messages and never terminating, it will be an orphaned program with nowhere to go. Recall that there's only one message that will cause **GetMessage** to return zero: WM_QUIT. This is exactly what the **PostQuitMessage** function does—it puts a WM_QUIT message into an application's message queue. You can think of **PostQuitMessage(0)** as a shorthand for

```
PostMessage (hwnd, WM_QUIT, (WPARAM)0, 0L);
```

where **wParam** is the return value of the program (the same as the single argument to **PostQuitMessage**) and the **hwnd** parameter is the handle of a top-level window.

The program's WM_CREATE handler is very straightforward, as well. It makes one Windows API call, to **ShowWindow**. This function displays, hides, minimizes, or maxmizes a window. The important thing to note here is that **CreateWindow** does not necessarily create a window that is visible (it does so only if the WS_VISIBLE bit is set in its **dwStyle** parameter). Therefore, **ShowWindow** must be called sometime after the window is created in order to make the window visible. If it is not, the result will be much the same as the result of destroying a window without **PostQuitMessage**—a program that hangs in **GetMessage** forever. You could just as easily put the call to **ShowWindow** in the **Init** function, like this:

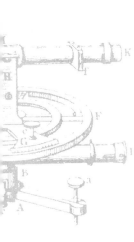

```
static HWND Init (HINSTANCE hInstance, int show)
{
    HWND hwnd;
    int x, y;

    // Get the size of the full screen.
    x = GetSystemMetrics (SM_CXSCREEN);
    y = GetSystemMetrics (SM_CYSCREEN);

    // Create the main window.
    hwnd = CreateWindow(
```

continued on next page

continued from previous page

```
                        "OurDemoClass",
                        "Demo Program",
                        // Standard resizable window
                        WS_OVERLAPPEDWINDOW,
                        0,
                        0,
                        x,
                        y,
                        // No parent, no menu,
                        // no parameters to WM_CREATE
                        HWND_DESKTOP,
                        NULL,
                        hInstance,
                        NULL,
                    );
    if (!hwnd)
        return NULL;
    ShowWindow (hwnd, show);
    return hwnd;
}
```

and leave it out of the WM_CREATE handler.

Passing Parameters to OnCreate

Notice that the eleventh parameter to **CreateWindow** is defined as a **void FAR ***, meaning a long (far) pointer to anything. Here, **&show** is passed in, which is the address of the **int** that was in turn passed in to our **Init** function. How does the program know that the address of **show** will be a far pointer? It doesn't matter; the compiler takes care of it, because of **CreateWindow**'s function prototype in WINDOWS.H.

You can find the value passed in via the eleventh parameter to the **OnCreate** function's **CreateWindow** in the **lpCreateParams** member of the CREATESTRUCT pointer. Here's what CREATESTRUCT looks like in its entirety:

```
typedef struct tagCREATESTRUCT
{
    void FAR* lpCreateParams;
    HINSTANCE hInstance;
    HMENU     hMenu;
    HWND      hwndParent;
    int       cy;
    int       cx;
    int       y;
    int       x;
    LONG      style;
    LPCSTR    lpszName;
    LPCSTR    lpszClass;
    DWORD     dwExStyle;
} CREATESTRUCT;
```

As you can see, a CREATESTRUCT contains 12 elements, one more than the number of parameters to `CreateWindow`. The last element, `dwExStyle`, is the extra one. This element exists because `CreateWindow` isn't the only way to create a window—there's also `CreateWindowEx`, of course! The only reason that `CreateWindowEx` was invented was because Microsoft ran out of bits in the `style` parameter of `CreateWindow`, so they invented a new function to add a few more options. (I won't go into `CreateWindowEx` here; you can look it up in your favorite Windows API reference.) The other 11 members of the CREATESTRUCT correspond directly to the parameters of `CreateWindow`. In the example, I dereferenced `lpCreateParams` and cast it as an integer for the parameter to `ShowWindow`.

Although this example, in which I pass the `nCmdShow` parameter from `WinMain` all the way in through `CreateWindow` and catch it in the `OnCreate` handler, is a very simple one, you can imagine instead passing something more useful, like the address of some user-defined structure that has been initialized in `Init` and whose values are to be used in the `OnCreate` function. A game program might, for example, pass in the address of a structure that defines some settings from the last time the game was run so that the window's display can show those settings.

Actually, you might specifically *not* want your game program to pass `nCmdShow` on to `ShowWindow`. Remember that `nCmdShow` tells the program whether it should be run as initially minimized, and it's possible that you might not want your game program to be minimized at all, or perhaps not *started* minimized. In this case, the thing to do in `OnCreate` (or `Init`—the choice is immaterial in this case) is to call `ShowWindow` like this:

```
ShowWindow (hwnd, SW_SHOW);
```

This will show the window in its normal state, as seen in Figure 2-10.

FIGURE 2-10

The running MAIN.C program

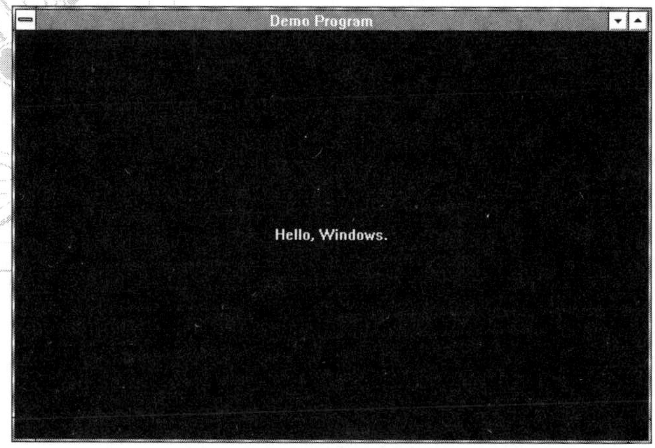

Experimenting with "Hello, Windows"

This is a good point for you to experiment with our minimal program a little. Try to change the window style from WS_OVERLAPPEDWINDOW to WS_POPUP. You'll get a full-screen window that has no borders, no caption bar, no system menu, and no Minimize or Maximize button. Because of this, the only way you'll be able to terminate the program will be to press ALT-F4.

Note that when you resize the WS_OVERLAPPEDWINDOW-style window, the program's text message stays centered in the window. This obviously has something to do with the code that's in the WM_PAINT handler function, **OnPaint**. Without giving too much of Chapter 5 away, I can tell you that the WM_PAINT message is the message that a window receives when the operating system determines that some part of the window needs repainting. For example, when a window has been overlapped by another window, then is popped to the top by the user, some portion of that window must be repainted. It's the program's job to repaint that portion, and the code that does it goes into the WM_PAINT handler. However, when you resize a window by tugging on one of its borders with the mouse, Windows doesn't necessarily send the window a WM_PAINT message, because some portion of the window hasn't changed and therefore doesn't need repainting.

Now take a look at the WM_SIZE handler, **OnSize**. Whenever a window gets resized, Windows kindly sends it a WM_SIZE message. This program's WM_SIZE handler does one thing: It calls **InvalidateRect**. This function tells Windows that some or all of the window specified in its first parameter needs repainting; in other words, it *forces* a WM_PAINT message to be generated. So the effect here is that every time the window changes size, it forces a WM_PAINT message, which in turn draws the text in the middle of the window again.

You can experiment with some of the other parameters in our minimum program, as well. Try setting the **hCursor** member of the WNDCLASS structure to NULL instead of using a "canned" cursor (IDC_ARROW). You'll notice that the window's cursor remains the cursor of the last window the mouse passed over before entering the program's window. Remember, if you don't define a cursor for the window's class, you have to set it yourself at every mouse move, and there is no handler defined for WM_MOUSEMOVE yet.

Another thing you can try is to attach a menu to your window. There are two ways to do this: either by giving the ninth parameter to **CreateWindow** the handle to some menu you've created in code (via a host of Windows menu-creation functions), or by specifying a resource name to the **lpszMenuName** member of the WNDCLASS function. Of course, for the latter to work, you must have a menu resource in your module's resource file.

Right. What's a resource file?

Resources and Resource Files

Earlier, you learned that a "minimum" Windows program consists of three parts: source files, a .DEF file, and a resource script file. Resource files aren't actually required, as it turns out, but they make for a much more interesting program.

Resources are static data objects that are stored as part of a program's executable file. Resources are described in a resource script (or .RC) file, compiled with the resource compiler, and then tacked onto the executable file by the resource compiler as a separate step.

There are nine types of resources that can be described in the .RC file:

- Icons
- Cursors
- Menus
- Dialog boxes
- Bitmaps
- Fonts
- Strings
- Accelerators
- User-defined resources

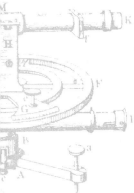

One way to think of a resource is simply as a data file for holding objects that are loaded into memory when they're needed. As a game programmer, you're no doubt familiar with creating data files stuffed with graphics objects, static parameters, and other data that you load as needed. This is one function of resources.

Most of the nine resource types listed here have Windows-specific purposes. Dialog box resources, for example, contain the description of all the controls that make up a Windows dialog box, which is put on the screen with the `DialogBox` function. The Menu resource contains a static description of a menu that can be loaded and attached to a window—either as part of that window's class or in the `CreateWindow` function.

The user-defined resource type can be used to store raw data of any type. It can even be used to completely replace whole files with whatever contents you choose. In this way, you can consolidate all your data files in the executable file, if you like.

An .RC file is an ASCII description of resources, and you can create it with any text editor. Most of the modern, integrated Windows development environments have programs for automatically generating .RC files from a more convenient interface, however. For example, Microsoft's Visual C++ comes with something called AppStudio (see Figure 2-11) that lets you create menus, dialog boxes, and other resources

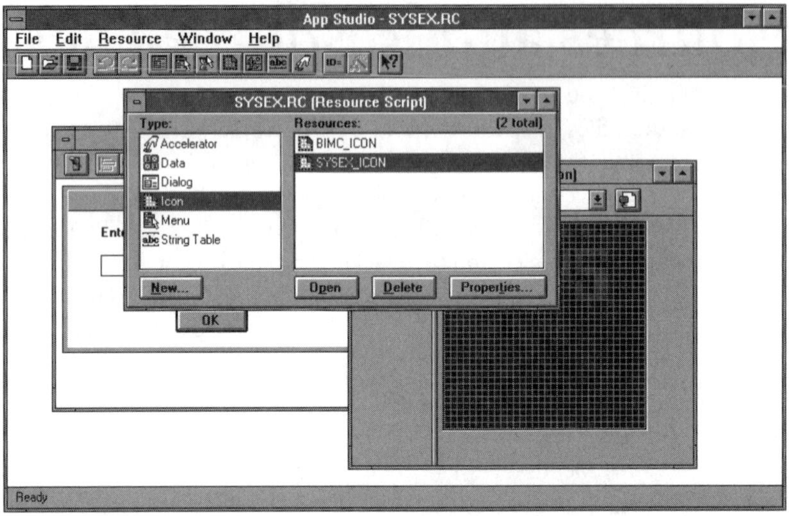

FIGURE 2-11

The AppStudio resource editor

without having to use a text editor. If you're lucky, you might not even have to *look* at an .RC file. Because of this, I won't spend a lot of time talking about the actual structure of the .RC file; you can find ample documentation in your favorite reference manual.

An .RC file's contents are one thing; *using* resources is another. Let's analyze each resource type and how it's used, spending a little more time on user-definable resources, since they are of particular interest to game programmers.

Icons

An *icon* is a special type of graphic element used almost exclusively for one purpose in Windows: to represent a minimized window. Icons are typically 32x32-pixel, 16-color bitmaps (there are a few other icon formats, but this is the most common).

By far the most common place to use an icon is in the class definition for a window. You use the **LoadIcon** function to load icons from the resource file that is attached to the module identified by the instance handle that is **LoadIcon**'s first argument. The definition of **LoadIcon** looks like this:

```
HICON LoadIcon (HINSTANCE hInst,
               LPCSTR lpszIcon);
```

As I mentioned, the **hInst** parameter tells Windows in which file the icon actually resides. Remember that resources are tacked onto our executable file by the resource compiler. Normally, this **hInst** parameter is the handle to our program's currently running instance, which Windows knows corresponds to a specific .EXE file.

The second parameter to **LoadIcon** is a pointer to a string that identifies the particular icon resource. All resources have a unique identifier that can either be a string or a number. Such numbers are called *resource IDs* in Windows parlance, and are generally a little more common than strings. An integrated resource editor like AppStudio produces IDs for you, along with a header file of **#define** statements for them. For icons (and other resources) that are identified by a resource ID rather than a string, you use the MAKEINTRESOURCE macro to identify the resource, like so:

```
// Resource ID header file
#define IDI_ICON1 101
.
.
.

// C Source file
wc.hIcon = LoadIcon (hInstance,
                     MAKEINTRESOURCE(IDI_ICON1));
```

The MAKEINTRESOURCE macro makes the integer value identified by **IDI_ICON1** compatible with the LPCSTR data type that **LoadIcon** expects.

You can use icons for other purposes, but they're not particularly flexible. Chances are, you'll have only one icon defined for your game: the one that represents your game's application on the desktop when that application is minimized. If your application can't ever be minimized, you might not even have *that* icon!

The sample program uses one of Windows' built-in icons. Note the line of code in **InitClass** that specifies the application's icon:

```
wc.hIcon = LoadIcon (NULL, IDI_APPLICATION);
```

The **hInst** parameter is NULL—what module does this identify? As it turns out, it identifies the internal Windows module USER.EXE, where a heck of a lot of Windows itself resides, along with a few icon and cursor resources. The **IDI_APPLICATION** constant identifies the boring default icon that looks like the Windows logo.

Once an icon is loaded with **LoadIcon**, it must eventually be deleted with **DestroyIcon**, which takes an HICON as its single argument. This is *not* true of default icons (those loaded with NULL for the **hInst** parameter); those should never be destroyed.

Cursors

A *cursor* is, of course, the marker that tracks the mouse's movements. Windows cursors have a few limitations: They're monochrome (with transparency and an XOR color), and they can be only 32x32 pixels in size. You create cursors in your favorite resource editor, and they are loaded with the **LoadCursor** function, which looks virtually identical to **LoadIcon**:

```
HCURSOR LoadCursor (HINSTANCE hInst,
                    LPCSTR lpszCursor);
```

In fact, the only difference between **LoadIcon** and **LoadCursor** is that the latter returns a handle to a cursor, or HCURSOR.

There are a number of functions for controlling the Windows cursor. Probably the most important one is **SetCursor**:

```
HCURSOR SetCursor (HCURSOR hcur);
```

which sets the current cursor, returning the value of the previous cursor. Recall that a window whose class doesn't define a cursor (in other words, the **hCursor** member of the WNDCLASS structure is set to NULL) must set the cursor itself, at every WM_MOUSEMOVE message. You do this by using **SetCursor**. You'll see how to set a custom cursor for your main window in Chapter 4, when I cover mouse input.

Another interesting cursor function is **ClipCursor**, which constrains the cursor to a rectangle. This can be quite useful, but if your program uses it you must be careful, because the cursor is, naturally, a shared resource. The cursor must be freed from clipping before a user switches applications.

As you do with icons, you should delete cursors with **DestroyCursor** when you're finished with them.

Menus

Menus are those ubiquitous things that usually hang just above the client area of a window. There are some 24 functions in the Windows API for working with menus. You can load menus from the resource file, and also construct or modify them in code. Menus are typically attached across the top of a window, but they can also be displayed vertically as "floating" menus.

There are three ways to attach a menu to a window:

- Specify the name of the menu resource item in the **lpszMenuName** member of the WNDCLASS structure when the window's class is registered.
- Use **LoadMenu** to load the menu from the resource file, then specify the menu's handle in the **hMenu** parameter of the **CreateWindow** function when the window is created.
- Use **LoadMenu** and then use **SetMenu** with the menu's handle and the window's handle.

The first method, in which you specify the menu in the WNDCLASS structure, makes any window created from that class have that particular menu attached to it. Note that the **lpszMenuName** member of WNDCLASS is a *string*, not a handle to a menu. The string should identify the menu's resource name, or you can use MAKEINTRESOURCE if the menu has a resource ID instead of a string name.

The latter two methods use **LoadMenu**, which, not surprisingly, looks just like **LoadIcon** and **LoadCursor**, except that **LoadMenu** returns a handle to a menu:

```
HMENU LoadMenu (HINSTANCE hInst,
                LPCSTR lpszMenu);
```

SetMenu takes both a window handle and a menu handle

```
BOOL SetMenu (HWND hwnd, HMENU hmenu);
```

and returns TRUE if it's successful (or FALSE, if it's not). Calling **SetMenu** with NULL in the **hmenu** parameter removes the current menu from the window.

Menus are a little different from the other resources I've discussed so far, because they generate *commands* to the window to which they're attached. When you create a menu resource in the .RC file (either "manually" or with your favorite resource editor), each menu item must have a command ID: a number that is sent to the window as a parameter to the WM_COMMAND message whenever a menu item is selected. This is how a program finds out about menu selection—the callback function for the window to which the menu is attached gets a WM_COMMAND message, with the command's ID sent as a parameter.

In Chapter 4, you'll learn more about menus and processing WM_COMMAND messages. If yours is a full-screen game, you might not use Windows menus at all.

Dialog Boxes

Dialog boxes (as shown in Figure 2-12) are windows that appear for the purpose of getting information from the user (you knew that). Typically, a dialog box contains a set of *controls:* things like buttons, list boxes, and so on that get pecked at by the user. After the user has supplied the needed information, he or she removes the dialog box by pushing some command button.

You create the controls and layout of dialog boxes in a dialog editor or other resource editor. The description of a dialog box is just another entry in the .RC file; a name or resource ID identifies it.

Bitmaps

I dedicate a good portion of the remainder of this book to *bitmaps,* since they are so intrinsic to most game programs. For this reason, I'll treat them relatively lightly here. If you're an old-time raster master, you might object to my using the word "bitmap" for the type of object described here. To many people, that term can mean only a strictly monochrome array of pixels—each bit representing a state of on or off. In Windows, "bitmap" can also mean a color image, with a varying number of bits per pixel.

Bitmaps in resource files must be in Windows .BMP format—the various resource handlers work only with this type. As you might expect, the function for loading a

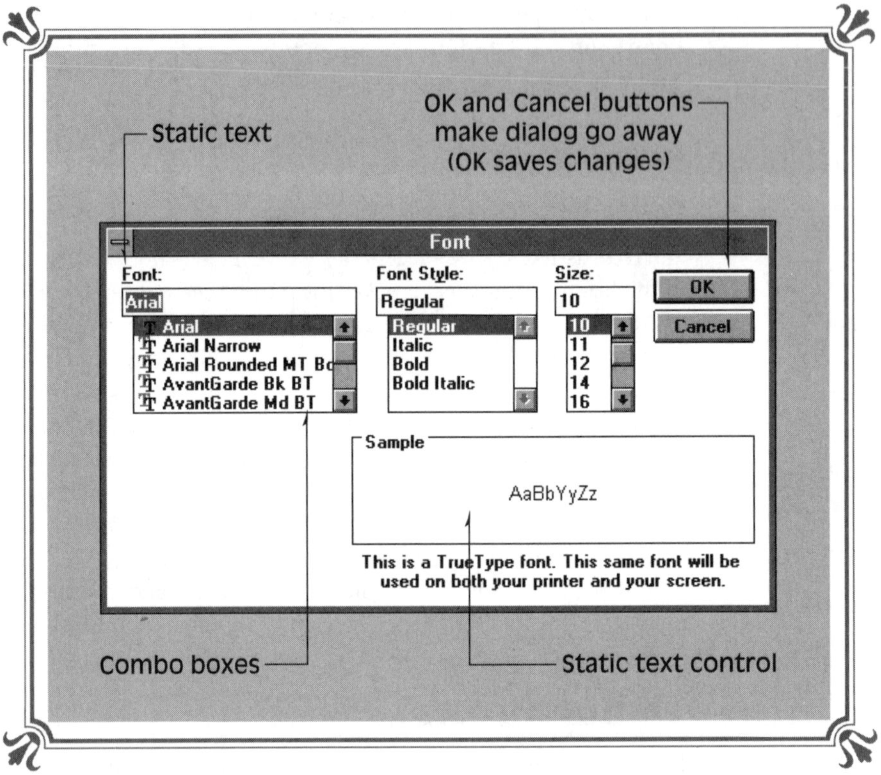

FIGURE 2-12

Parts of a typical dialog box

Windows bitmap from a resource file is **LoadBitmap**, with parameters just like **LoadIcon**, **LoadCursor**, and **LoadMenu**. It returns a handle to a bitmap, or HBITMAP. Bitmaps are deleted with **DeleteObject**—for some reason, there is no **DestroyBitmap** function, as there is for the other resource types.

Fonts

Font resources describe a Windows text font. Windows font definitions are very complex beasts, and usually not within the domain of game programming anyway. Since the advent of TrueType fonts, font resources have become more or less obsolete.

Strings

String resources are simply variable-length, C-style text strings. Strings are loaded with the **LoadString** function:

```
int LoadString (HINSTANCE hInst, UINT id,
                LPSTR buffer, int bufsize);
```

Note that **LoadString** uses an ID, not a string name. Each .RC file has only one string table, containing all strings and their IDs. Because of this, string IDs don't have to be unique among all the resource IDs in the .RC file. Again, most resource editors automatically generate IDs and symbolic constants for them, so you don't really have to think about it.

The **buffer** argument to **LoadString** is the actual text buffer into which the string will be loaded, and **bufsize** specifies the length of this buffer. String resources longer than **bufsize** are truncated. Strings in the resource file's string table are limited to 255 characters. The return value of the function specifies the number of actual characters in the string. The **LoadString** function has no corresponding **DestroyString**, since the buffer being supplied must be preallocated.

If your game is rich with text strings, it's a smart idea to use the resource file and **LoadString**. Not only does it move the strings out of the limited static data segment of the program, but it makes them much easier to change—and you can change them without modifying program code or recompiling a single source module.

A typical way in which to work with resource file strings is to define a couple of functions that make using them a little easier. Here's an example:

```
// Function for allocating and loading a string
// from the resource file
LPSTR GetString (HINSTANCE hInst, UINT id)
{
    LPSTR s;
    // Allocate a suitable buffer.
    if (!s = (LPSTR)LocalAlloc (LPTR, 256))
        return NULL;
    // Load the string. Fail if it has 0 length.
    if (!LoadString (hInst, id, s, 255))
        return NULL;
    // Return the buffer.
    return s;
}
```

This **GetString** function takes an instance handle (you can see why this could rationally be a global now, no?) and the ID of the string in the resource file's string table. It allocates some memory (from the local heap; see Chapter 3) and tries to load the string. When you're done using the string, you can free the memory with a call to **LocalFree**.

Accelerators

Accelerators (sometimes called *keyboard accelerators*) are single-keystroke shortcuts that generate WM_COMMAND messages in exactly the same way selecting a menu item does. To implement accelerators, you need to add a couple of lines of extra code to the **GetMessage** loop to translate the raw keystrokes into their corresponding

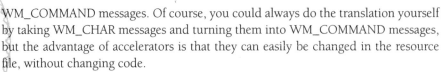

WM_COMMAND messages. Of course, you could always do the translation yourself by taking WM_CHAR messages and turning them into WM_COMMAND messages, but the advantage of accelerators is that they can easily be changed in the resource file, without changing code.

The examples in this book don't use accelerators at all; their application to games is minimal.

User-Defined Resources

The people at Microsoft had the foresight to understand that the preceding eight types of resources aren't necessarily the only static data objects that you might want in a given program. Accordingly, they built the resource compiler so that it would just "suck up" any file you might give it and embed it into the resource file (and consequently, the .EXE file).

Suppose, for example, you have a data file that contains lists of objects that you use in your game. Perhaps it's an ASCII file that you parse out at run time, and from which you build the environment for the game. You'd like to keep it as a separate file, because that makes it easy to edit the ASCII file's contents without changing the program code. But when it comes time to actually ship your game around, you'd just as soon embed the file into your .EXE file for reasons of both convenience and security: You don't want players mucking with its parameters, because they're not "user-safe." You could include this file as part of your resource file as a single, monolithic resource that you could access with `LoadResource`.

To access a user-defined resource object, you need a combination of Windows API calls. User-defined resources are identified by a type and a name in the resource file. Some resource editors don't allow you to specify a user-defined resource type; if yours is such a resource editor, you must key the type into the .RC file. For example, AppStudio doesn't let you create a user-defined resource directly from its interface. If it finds one in an .RC file, however, it handles it just fine. You simply have to enter the type and name (along with the file name to which it refers) yourself, once, in the .RC file. This is the .RC file syntax for a user-defined resource:

```
Name Type Filename.ext
```

As you can see, it's a single line with three parts: the name of the resource, the type of the resource, and the file name and extension that are the actual contents of the resource. The `Name` and `Type` identifiers are used to find the resource in the resource file with the `FindResource` function, which looks like this:

```
HRSRC FindResource (HINSTANCE hInst,
                    LPCSTR lpszName, LPCSTR lpszType);
```

This function returns a handle to a resource object, which is used in only a couple of other Windows functions. One of them is `LoadResource`, the call that actually allocates memory for the resource and loads it:

```
HGLOBAL LoadResource (HINSTANCE hInst, HRSRC hrsrc);
```

The **LoadResource** function returns something called an *HGLOBAL*, which is a handle to a chunk of globally allocated memory, something you'll learn about in the next chapter. An HGLOBAL isn't a pointer quite yet, so you need to make the following call to turn it into one and "lock" it in memory:

```
void FAR *LockResource (HGLOBAL hglb);
```

If you pass the result from **LoadResource** to **LockResource**, you finally end up with a pointer to a resource object.

Another Windows call that takes an HRSRC as an argument is **SizeofResource**, which returns the size, in bytes, of the given resource. The size returned by **SizeofResource** may not be perfectly accurate, because of the way Windows aligns resource objects in memory, but the resource won't be any *larger* than the value it returns.

Let's create a single function that loads a resource and locks it into memory—we'll simply pass it an HINSTANCE and two strings that define its type and name. We'll also pass it a pointer to a LONG in which the function will return the size of the resource.

```
LPSTR GetUserResource (HINSTANCE hInst,
                       LPCSTR type,
                       LPCSTR name,
                       LONG *size)
{
    HRSRC res;
    HGLOBAL hglb;

    // First, find the resource in the file.
    if (!res = FindResource (hInst, name, type))
        return NULL;
    // Return the size of the resource.
    *size = SizeofResource (hInst, res);
    if (!hglb = LoadResource (hInst, res))
        return NULL;
    // The resource has been successfully
    // loaded. Lock it in memory...
    return (LPSTR)LockResource (hInst, hglb);
}
```

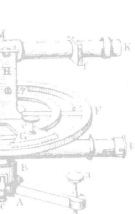

This function finds the resouce, returns its size in **size**, loads the resource, and locks it in memory, returning a pointer to the resource object. The only problem with the function becomes apparent if we try to write its inverse, **FreeUserResource**. This is because you free a resource object with **FreeResource**, a function that takes an HGLOBAL as an argument. Unfortunately, **GetUserResource** didn't save the HGLOBAL, so there's no way to free it. Fortunately, resources are automatically freed when the HINSTANCE module they're associated with exits. If you want to free a resource before the program ends, you need to keep around the HGLOBAL memory handle associated with it. We could rewrite **GetUserResource** to include a pointer to an HGLOBAL, like so:

```
LPSTR GetUserResource (HINSTANCE hInst,
                       LPCSTR type,
                       LPCSTR name,
                       LONG *size
                       HGLOBAL *memhandle)
{
    HRSRC res;

    // First, find the resource in the file.
    if (!res = FindResource (hInst, name, type))
        return NULL;
    // Return the size of the resource.
    *size = SizeofResource (hInst, res);
    if (!*memhandle = LoadResource (hInst, res))
        return NULL;
    // The resource has been successfully
    // loaded. Lock it in memory...
    return (LPSTR)LockResource (hInst, *memhandle);
}
```

Then, we could write **FreeUserResource** like so:

```
BOOL FreeUserResource (HGLOBAL memhandle)
{
    // Unlock the resource. If the function
    // returns nonzero, it's not unlocked.
    if (UnlockResource (memhandle))
        return FALSE;
    // FreeResource returns nonzero
    // on failure, too.
    if (FreeResource (memhandle))
        return FALSE;
    else
        return TRUE;
}
```

Having to keep around a separate memory handle for each user resource is a bit of a hassle. The bad news is that *all* global memory objects require handles in order to be freed. This means that every time you allocate memory, you have to keep around a handle to that memory in order to free it later! If you're used simply to using pointers and standard C library functions like **malloc** and **free**, this can be disconcerting, to say the least.

Lucky for you that in the next chapter, you'll learn how to avoid this hassle completely.

Summary

Well, you've written your first Windows program. You also have some fundamental understanding of how Windows works—how messages are sent, what a callback function does, what a window class is, and how to use resources. Digest for a while—there's a lot there to absorb. With the framework we've built in this chapter, you should have some idea of how to get a window up in which to run your game. Next, we'll delve into the vagaries of Windows memory managment.

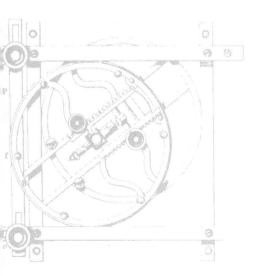

3

Windows Memory Management

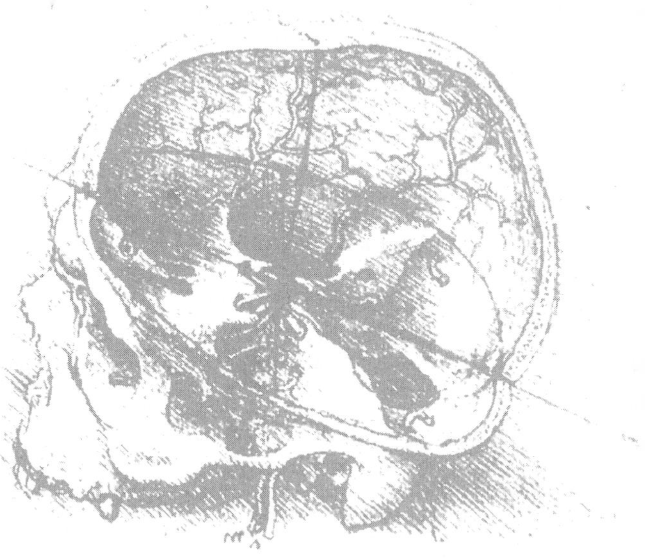

3

Windows Memory Management

Managing memory in a DOS-based program can be a bummer. Not only is there not enough of it—real-mode DOS programs have access to a maximum of only 640K—there's the joy of dealing with the Intel segmented-memory model, in which accessing more than 64K directly is either slow or unduly difficult. Many ambitious DOS programmers have opted to bypass the whole mess by using a 32-bit compiler and so-called DOS Extender, which runs programs in Protected mode and provides access to megabytes of extended memory. But DOS Extenders are no panacea either, and have their own share of problems with managing real-mode resources like DOS files and interrupts.

While Windows memory management isn't a cure-all for these problems, it does offer access to megabytes of extended memory. It also comes with its own share of *new* problems, of course. In this chapter, you'll learn how to avoid some of the common pitfalls associated with Windows memory management and, very importantly, learn how to use memory in a way that's compatible with both 16-bit and 32-bit Windows.

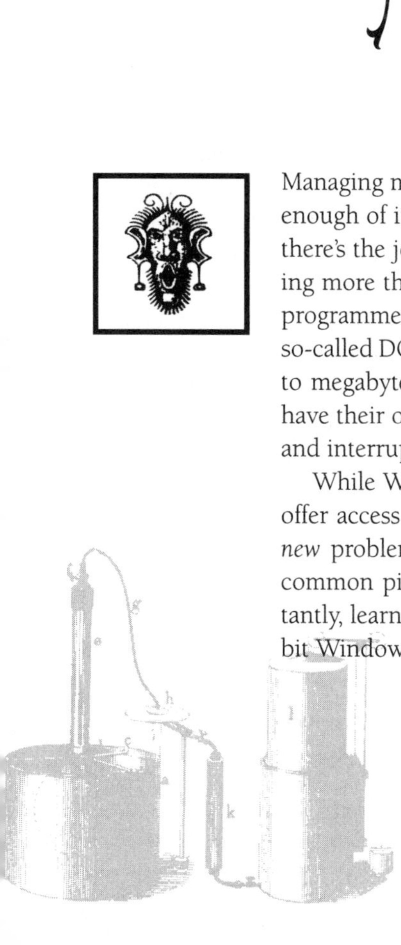

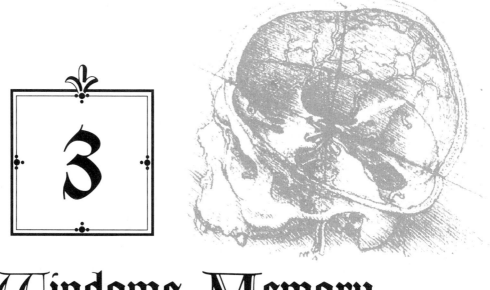

Windows' Operating Modes

When Windows was first designed, lowly Intel 8086-based systems were the only game in town. When the 80286 came along, Windows was modified to take advantage of the greater memory addressability the processor afforded. Then, when the 80386 was created, Windows was modified again to take advantage of that processor's many additional features, including virtual memory management and 32-bit addressability. When Windows 3.0 first came out, it supported all three classes of processors through three different operating modes: Real mode, Standard mode, and Enhanced mode. Windows 3.1 dropped support of the 8086 and supported only Standard and Enhanced modes, and Windows for Workgroups (and Windows 95) dropped support of Standard mode and the 80286. Because of Enhanced-mode Windows' advantages and popularity, I address this book to those using that platform.

Intel Memory Architecture Refresher Course

Since Windows was originally designed to run on 16-bit Intel microprocessors, its memory-management architecture is deeply steeped in Intel *segmented-memory* arcana, even when running in Enhanced mode. In pre-80386 Intel microprocessors, memory was accessed in 64K-small blocks called segments, and spanning segments required extra logic by the programmer. Because of this segmented architecture, you can compile a program by using one of four different memory models, which are distinguished from one another by the number of separate code and data segments each supports. All 16-bit Windows development environments support all four memory models, but most programs use only one of two: Small model or Medium model.

As an experienced DOS programmer, you'll recall that Small-model programs use two 64K segments: one for code, and one for data. The data segment is used not only for static data, but also for the stack (the place where automatic variables, function parameters, and return addresses come from) and the heap (memory allocated by the standard C library function `malloc`). Like Small-model programs, Medium-model programs also have a single 64K segment for the stack and heap, but they can have multiple 64K segments for code.

Windows programs can be compiled using Large model, as well (which allows multiple 64K code *and* data segments), but such a program has some limitations. For one, a Large-model program can have only one running instance under Windows. For this reason, most Windows programs are created using Medium model.

"But wait," you say, "do you really expect me to write a reasonable game program with only *64K* of heap, stack, and static data?" Not at all. As it turns out, it's taboo to use the standard C library **malloc** function in a Windows program anyway. It's replaced by not one but *two* Windows API functions: **LocalAlloc** and **GlobalAlloc**.

The Local and Global Heaps

You can allocate memory under Windows from two places: the local heap or the global heap (see Figure 3-1).

Under 16-bit Windows, the local heap comes from a single 64K segment that is also used for stack space and static data. In other words, the local heap of a Medium-model program under Windows is just like the heap accessed by **malloc** in a conventional DOS Medium-model program. You allocate memory from the local heap with **LocalAlloc**, which is defined as follows:

```
HLOCAL LocalAlloc (UINT flags, UINT size)
```

The first parameter to **LocalAlloc** specifies how to allocate memory, and can be a combination of the constants listed in Table 3-1.

The second parameter, a UINT, is 16 bits under 16-bit Windows and 32 bits under Win32. This makes sense, because 16 bits are all that are needed to allocate up to 64K of memory, which is the maximum size of the local heap.

FIGURE 3-1

Local and global heaps

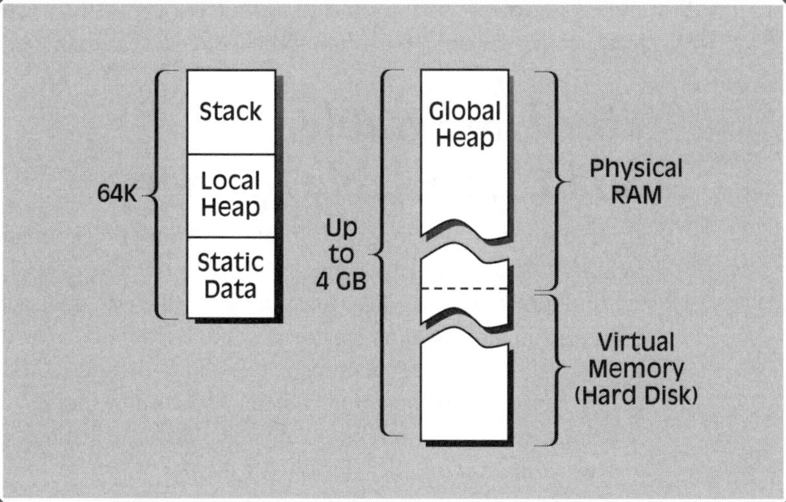

TABLE 3-1
LocalAlloc flag settings

Value	Meaning
LMEM_DISCARDABLE	Allocates discardable memory. Unlocked blocks can be discarded by Windows.
LMEM_FIXED	Allocates fixed memory; Windows cannot move it around.
LMEM_MOVEABLE	Allows the memory blocks to be moved by Windows.
LMEM_NOCOMPACT	Doesn't attempt to compact the local heap before allocating.
LMEM_NODISCARD	Doesn't discard memory to satisfy the request.
LMEM_ZEROINIT	Initializes the memory to zero.
LPTR	Combines the LMEM_ZEROINIT and LMEM_FIXED flags.

Fortunately for you, most of the settings in Table 3-1 are obsolete for a program running exclusively in Windows Enhanced mode. In the bad old days of Windows programming, there was a mantra about memory allocation that programmers were told to repeat constantly to themselves: Keep your memory allocations as *few* as possible, as *small* as possible, and as *discardable* as possible. Yikes! The first two are at least comprehensible, but what in the world is discardable memory?

Fixed, Moveable, and Discardable Memory

Under Windows, dynamically allocated memory blocks come in three forms: fixed, moveable, and discardable. Figure 3-2 shows the three types. *Fixed* memory blocks are undoubtedly what you're most used to—they're equivalent to what the standard C library function **malloc** creates. *Discardable* memory is memory that Windows can reclaim in order to free memory space, and is therefore the type of memory that is most generous to the operating system. *Moveable* memory is somewhere in between: Windows won't throw out its contents like discardable memory, but Windows is free to move it around in order to compact memory.

To deal with discardable and moveable memory, Windows memory-allocation functions don't return a pointer to a block of memory the way **malloc** does. Instead,

FIGURE 3-2

Three different types of memory

they return a handle, which must be *locked* in order to access the memory. The lock functions return a pointer to the actual memory, which, in the case of discardable and moveable memory, may not be the same value between successive locks. When the pointer is no longer needed, you *unlock* the memory so that Windows can move it or discard it if necessary.

You can imagine what a pain it is to manage memory this way. First off, every allocation you make requires not only a pointer to access the physical memory, but also a handle for locking and unlocking it. Then you have to carefully plan exactly when you need a pointer to the memory and for how long, so that you can lock and unlock the block. Of course, a program could always allocate a fixed block of memory and keep it locked until it's time to free it, but this is the most resource-hungry way to use memory, and on memory-scarce machines it could cause Windows to run out of memory rather quickly. A good portion of popular Windows programming books have large sections dedicated to managing discardable and moveable memory, because it is so important to the efficient running of a program on memory-scarce machines.

The good news is that the practice of creating discardable and moveable blocks of memory is useful only when computers have very little memory and no virtual memory; in other words, it was a valuable practice when Windows ran only in real mode or Standard mode. Enhanced mode makes the whole principle of discardable and moveable memory, well, outmoded.

Vive la Fixed Memory!

When Windows is running in Enhanced mode (which requires an 80386 processor or better), the system takes advantage of the memory-management functions built into the CPU itself. This includes the ability to use disk space to extend the amount RAM that appears available to the system—so-called *virtual memory*. The processor does all the work of determining which blocks of memory should be swapped to disk and when, and generally it does it more efficiently than the old model of using discardable and moveable memory, the scope of which is determined by the programmer. Because of this, and the fact that all future versions of Windows will run only in Enhanced mode, you can feel free to allocate fixed memory exclusively and ignore all the logic surrounding discardable and moveable memory.

Going back to the **LocalAlloc** function and Table 3-1, to allocate fixed memory, you use either the LMEM_FIXED flag or the LPTR flag, the latter of which also initializes all the memory to zero before returning the handle. But for it to be useful, you still need a pointer to the memory. Normally, you'd obtain a pointer from the HLOCAL handle returned by **LocalAlloc** by calling **LocalLock**, like so:

```
void NEAR *LocalLock (HLOCAL hloc)
```

LocalLock takes a handle and returns a NEAR pointer to **void**, which you can cast into any data type you'd like. However, if the call to **LocalAlloc** uses the LMEM_FIXED (or LPTR) flags, then you can skip using **LocalLock** altogether and just cast the return value of **LocalAlloc** into the desired data type. For example, suppose we want to allocate 1,000 bytes of **char** via **LocalAlloc**.

```
char *s;

s = (char *)LocalAlloc (LPTR, 1000);
```

You free a block of locally allocated memory with **LocalFree**, which normally takes an HLOCAL. But you can reverse this process and cast a local pointer back to a handle to free it:

```
LocalFree ((HLOCAL)s);
```

You'll notice that the return value of **LocalLock** is a NEAR pointer, or 16-bit pointer. This is because the local heap comes from a single 64K segment, which can be addressed with a NEAR pointer. It's possible to use the local heap with FAR pointers, of course—the compiler will take care of the cast for you. The previous example could also be written like this:

```
LPSTR s;

s = (LPSTR)LocalAlloc (LPTR, 1000);
```

In this case, **s** is a FAR, or 32-bit, pointer (a LPSTR, you'll recall, is a long pointer to a string). The cast takes care of filling out all 32 bits properly. However, different compilers handle this conversion in different ways, and most compilers will generate a warning message when they see a 16-bit quantity being promoted to a 32-bit quantity with a cast, even if they do it properly. You can use a NEAR pointer as a parameter to Windows API calls because all Windows APIs have prototypes that cast them to FAR pointers as necessary, but in this case, it's done at the time of the call.

Generally, you use the local heap for relatively small memory allocations. The local heap has a low *overhead* per allocation of only 2 bytes. (The overhead of any allocation function is the number of bytes that are invisibly added to the requested size so that the system can manage the block of memory.)

Since the size of the local heap is relatively small, and (in Medium model) is shared with the stack and static data of the program, Windows provides another set of functions for allocating larger blocks of memory.

The Global Heap

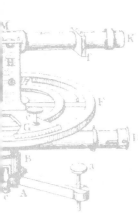

In Enhanced mode, Windows can address up to 4 GB of memory. Even on a modestly configured machine with only 4 MB of RAM, virtual memory can transparently provide running programs with access to huge volumes of memory. All this memory is part of what Windows calls the *global heap,* the big pool of memory that Windows uses to load programs into and from which it creates dynamically allocated memory segments. The global heap includes not only all physical memory, but the virtual memory that comes from the hard disk. As the saying in the old beer commercial has it, when you're out of global heap, you're out of memory.

You allocate memory from the global heap for use by a program by using the **GlobalAlloc** function like so:

```
HGLOBAL GlobalAlloc (UINT flags, DWORD size)
```

Notice first of all that the **size** parameter to **GlobalAlloc** is defined as a DWORD, or 4-byte value. Because **GlobalAlloc** can allocate blocks of memory greater than 64K, it needs a DWORD to specify the size. A single call to **GlobalAlloc** could allocate many megabytes of memory; under Windows 3.1, it can actually allocate up to 16 MB of memory.

The **flags** parameter to **GlobalAlloc** is very similar to the one used in **LocalAlloc**, except that the constants start with *G* instead of *L* (there are also a couple of additions that I'll discuss later). Note, too, that, like **LocalAlloc**, **GlobalAlloc** returns a handle, called an HGLOBAL in this case. There's also an equivalent lock function, **GlobalLock**, which takes the HGLOBAL and returns a FAR pointer to the allocated block of memory:

```
void FAR *GlobalLock (HGLOBAL hglb)
```

However, you can't use the GMEM_FIXED flag as you did with **LocalAlloc**, simply casting the handle returned by **GlobalAlloc** to a pointer to the data type you want and beginning using the memory; you must call **GlobalLock** to access the memory. Likewise, **GlobalFree** won't take a pointer that's been cast as an HGLOBAL to free the memory. You must supply the real handle.

Fortunately, there are a couple of macros provided in WINDOWSX.H that make allocating and freeing global memory blocks virtually as easy as using **malloc**. The first is **GlobalAllocPtr**:

```
void FAR *GlobalAllocPtr (UINT flags, DWORD size)
```

Calling **GlobalAllocPtr** with GMEM_FIXED or GPTR (the latter tells the function to initialize the memory to zero) and the number of bytes to allocate returns a pointer to the block of memory. Its corresponding free macro is

```
GlobalFreePtr (void FAR *ptr)
```

which does some magic to free the memory associated with the given pointer without specifying the HGLOBAL handle.

Using **GlobalAllocPtr** and **GlobalFreePtr** make memory management *much* easier than the old-style alternative of keeping handles, locking and unlocking memory, and all that other nonsense. Resist the temptation to **#define GlobalAllocPtr** to **malloc** if you can, but you might wrap your favorite memory-managment function library around **GlobalAllocPtr**.

There's also a reallocation function, and WINDOWSX.H provides a convenient macro for using it with a pointer:

```
void FAR *GlobalReAllocPtr (void FAR *ptr,
                            DWORD newsize,
                            UINT newflags);
```

This function (macro, really) takes the old pointer allocated with **GlobalAllocPtr**; a new size to which to adjust it; and another **newflags** parameter, which should be either zero or GMEM_ZEROINIT. In the latter case, if the new size is larger than the old size of the buffer, the new bytes will be initialized to zero. Note that like the standard C library function **realloc**, **GlobalReAllocPtr** may not return the same value as the pointer being resized if the size of the block is increasing.

There are a couple of things to note about allocating memory from the global heap in Windows. First, every allocation has an overhead of 32 bytes, so you shouldn't use **GlobalAllocPtr** for very small blocks of memory. Also, **GlobalAlloc** is, by most accounts, notoriously slow. Therefore, if you have many small allocations to make, you might be best off allocating larger chunks with **GlobalAlloc** and suballocating smaller chunks from the large chunks. There are many public domain as well as commercial "heap managers" that can perform this duty for you; designing one is beyond the scope of this book.

Pointers and the Standard C Library

One of the most frustrating problems you'll encounter when creating Windows programs is the dilemma of how to use the standard C function library. Most C programmers are used to having functions like **sprintf**, **sscanf**, **strcat**, and the other (now ANSI-) standard library functions available to them. These functions almost seem like a standard feature of the C language (Kernighan and Ritchie's definitions notwithstanding). While most Windows-compatible compilers do, in fact, provide a standard C function library, mixing its contents with Windows API functions can have nasty results. The reason: The standard C library functions are *model-dependent,* meaning that parameters passed as pointers *must* match the default pointer size for the model being used. Because Windows programs often have data elements that aren't in the default data segment, this can easily cause problems.

Take, for example, a function like **sscanf**, the standard C library function for formatting the contents of a string into a series of variables. Suppose we have the following code:

```
char buf[] = "30";
int i;

sscanf (buf, "%d", &i);
```

This code will put the value 30 into the integer variable **i**, and will work in any memory model. All the arguments to **sscanf** are defined in the default data segment, because they have no explicit NEAR or FAR declarations.

Assume that this example is being used in a Medium-model program, where data pointers are 16 bits by default:

```
char buf[] = "30";
static int FAR i;              // Must be a static declaration.

sscanf (buf, "%d", &i);
```

The problem with this code is that the address of the integer into which the value from **buf** will be stored is no longer in the default data segment. It is now in a FAR segment and its pointer, **&i**, isn't a 16-bit pointer anymore but a 32-bit pointer (note here that the declaration of **i** must be **static**, because an automatic variable in a Medium-model program will always be NEAR). Because the **sscanf** function takes a variable number of arguments, the compiler won't properly check this argument's size and generate an error, and the code will generate some run-time error instead. Just to be really fun, the error doesn't usually occur right away, but perhaps later when something else accesses the stack or when a function tries to return to its caller. What's really happening is that the first 16 bits of the value of **&i** are passed on the stack to the standard library's **sscanf** function, which expects the data to be in the default data segment. In this particular case, the *segment* of the pointer gets passed instead (the first 16 bits of the 32-bit address), and poor **sscanf** tries to format it, probably screwing up the stack in the process. At some point in the future, the stack will be found corrupt and the program might generate a run-time general protection fault error (or something worse). In any case, **i** will never receive the right value.

What makes this error particularly nasty is that the stack is in the same default segment as all the static data and the local heap. So the program might fail on the next **LocalAlloc** call. Or it might just trash a static variable somewhere, unbeknownst to you. Or it might hang the machine at some later point, when it could be difficult to track the problem to the **sscanf** call.

The problem in this simple example is pretty easy to catch, because the definition is right there, close to the **sscanf** function. Most of the time, errors associated with the standard C library functions aren't so readily discovered. You can stare at the code for hours without noticing that *one little argument* to a standard library function isn't in the default data segment—maybe it's a member of a **GlobalAlloc**'d structure and therefore has a 32-bit address. Try this slightly more obscure (but very common) example:

```
typedef struct {
    int a;
    LPSTR s;
} STUFF, FAR *LPSTUFF;
.
.
.
// Create structure pointer and allocate structure.
LPSTUFF stuff = (LPSTUFF)GlobalAllocPtr (GPTR,
                                       sizeof(STUFF));
.
.
.
char buf[40];
// Format the string in stuff.
sprintf (buf, "stuff->s = %s", stuff->s);
```

It's not at all obvious that there's a problem here, and it's unlikely that the compiler would report one. But really there are two: **stuff** is a 32-bit pointer, and the member **s** is also a 32-bit pointer. Poor **sprintf** is going to get a totally wrong address as a last argument, and sooner or later something very bad may happen to the program.

There are two ways to avoid the problems caused by using standard C library functions in Windows programs. The first is just to be very careful whenever you find yourself typing a function name like `sscanf`, `sprintf`, `strlen`, `strcpy`, or any other standard library function name. Check the declarations of the arguments used, and make sure that they correspond to the memory model of the program. This can be very difficult to do if you're used to having these functions readily available.

The other way to avoid problems is simply not to use the standard C library functions in a Windows program, or to use model-independent versions of the functions, if your library supplies them (Microsoft's model-independent versions of functions often start with *_f*, like `_fmemcpy`, which works only with FAR pointers, casting near pointers automatically if necessary). Certain model-independent functions are provided as part of the Windows library itself. These functions all start with *l*, like `lstrcat`, `lstrlen`, `lstrcmp`, and so on (except the equivalent to `sprintf`, which, for some reason, is `wsprintf`).

There are a couple of caveats to keep in mind when using model-independent functions, however. First, although they're "model-independent," functions like `wsprintf` have a variable number of arguments, and if pointers are used, such a function expects them all to be FAR pointers. This means that you must use casts to make sure `wsprintf` gets what it expects:

```
char buf[30];
char *stuff = "Various stuff.";

wsprintf (buf, "%s", (LPSTR)stuff);
```

Without the last cast of `stuff` to `LPSTR`, `wsprintf` would be expecting a 32-bit pointer when in fact it was going to get a 16-bit one. This would probably result in a general protection fault as `wsprintf` tried to reach into some random data segment. Note that the *first* argument to `wsprintf` doesn't need the cast–the function's prototype casts it automatically. But the third and subsequent arguments (if any) *must* all be of the same length (32 bits) or must be converted by casts.

Unfortunately, `wsprintf` isn't quite as general as the standard C library function `sprintf`. For example, `wsprintf` won't format floating-point numbers. It may be hard to totally avoid using the standard C library functions, but use them only with extreme caution and make *sure* you know the size and type of all the arguments.

Using Huge Pointers

Most of the problems discussed in the previous several paragraphs aren't really unique to Windows. Any 16-bit DOS-based program could find itself in many of the same situations. But even more problems await us when we start working with blocks of memory larger than 64K.

While it's absolutely no problem to allocate a block of memory larger than 64K, working with it is another matter entirely. The problem, as you know, is that incrementing pointers beyond the end of a 64K segment—even if they're 32-bit pointers—

simply doesn't work. The pointers "wrap around" back to zero. To help alleviate this problem, most 16-bit Windows compilers support the **_huge** keyword. A huge pointer is more than just a far pointer—it's a 32-bit pointer that can be incremented beyond a 64K-segment boundary. It does so at some performance cost, because extra logic is necessary to keep track of the segment boundaries. Figure 3-3 demonstrates the problem with incrementing FAR pointers and how huge pointers work.

The Windows library supplies one function specifically for copying blocks of memory using huge pointers, **hmemcpy**:

```
void hmemcpy (void _huge *dest,
              const void _huge *src,
              long len)
```

While it would be nice to avoid having to think about such atrocities as the **_huge** keyword, it's unavoidable in certain places in 16-bit Windows.

Memory Allocation Under Win32

As you might expect, Win32 programs are free from all the memory-management strangeness associated with 16-bit Windows. All pointers are 32-bit ones, and the NEAR, FAR, and **_huge** keywords are ignored. Win32 has a new and particularly groovy set of memory-allocation functions that allow more flexibility than do the relatively simple

FIGURE 3-3

Huge- vs. far-pointer arithmetic

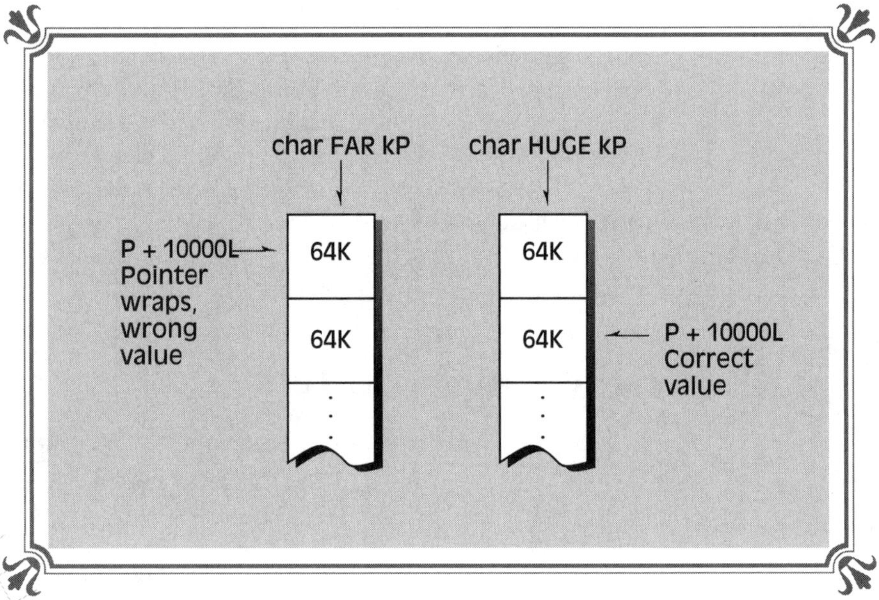

LocalAlloc and GlobalAlloc. Under Win32, a program can allocate up to 2 GB of memory, providing the virtual memory manager has access to enough hard disk space.

The function definitions for LocalAlloc and GlobalAlloc remain the same under Win32. The difference is that a UINT is 32 bits, so LocalAlloc's size parameter isn't limited to 64K. Since DWORDs remain 32 bits long, the same is true for the size parameter to GlobalAlloc. All the examples in this book are Win32-safe and will work under either 16-bit or 32-bit development environments.

Examples of Memory-Allocation Functions

Let's move on to some practical suggestions for using Windows memory-allocation functions.

In Chapter 2, we learned about WINDOWSX.H's message-cracker functions and how they simplify message handling. By combining the message-cracker functions and the LocalAlloc function, a program can cleanly construct a window-specific structure in which to house all the data concerning the window, without creating any icky global variables. This method encapsulates all the data about a window cleanly, and makes the data available to all the message-handler functions. Some might recognize this as an object-oriented methodology for handling the data associated with a window, but of course this can't be true, because it doesn't use C++ (ha).

You first must create a window-specific structure that will contain elements that are commonly accessed across different message-handler functions. For example, the HWND of the window itself is the most obvious parameter that may be used across different messages. Another example might be the handle to the window's menu. Here's an example of a structure for the main window of the program from Chapter 2:

```
/* Main window structure definition
 */

typedef struct MAINtag {
    HWND hwnd;              // This window
    HMENU menu;             // Our window's menu handle
} MAIN;
```

Admittedly a trivial example, it will get filled out as the main window needs more and more information to store across messages.

To store and retrieve a pointer to this window structure, two macros are defined in the header file after the structure definition. These macros have a standard 16-bit Windows definition, and a Win32 definition for portability.

```
// Instance data pointer access functions

#if (defined(M_I86SM) || defined(M_I86MM)) && \
    !defined(WIN32)
#define GetPtr(hwnd) (MAIN*)GetWindowWord((hwnd), 0)
#define SetPtr(hwnd, pfrm)\
        (MAIN*)SetWindowWord((hwnd), 0, (WORD)(pfrm))
#else
#define GetPtr(hwnd) (MAIN*)GetWindowLong((hwnd), 0)
#define SetPtr(hwnd, pfrm)\
        (MAIN*)SetWindowLong((hwnd), 0, (LONG)(pfrm))
#endif
```

To understand these macros, you need to remember something about the WNDCLASS structure from Chapter 2. One member of the WNDCLASS structure is **cbWndExtra**, which specifies a number of "extra" bytes that are allocated with each window when it's created. These extra bytes are accessed with **SetWindowWord** and **GetWindowWord** (under 16-bit Windows) and **SetWindowLong** and **GetWindowLong** (under Win32). The above macros stuff and retrieve a pointer to the MAIN structure in those extra bytes. Consequently, the **InitClass** function should be modified as follows:

```
static BOOL InitClass (HINSTANCE hInstance)
{
    WNDCLASS  wc;

    // Vanilla style
    wc.style = 0;
    wc.lpfnWndProc = WndProc;
    wc.cbClsExtra = 0;
    wc.cbWndExtra = sizeof (MAIN *);
    wc.hInstance = hInstance;
    wc.hIcon = LoadIcon(NULL, IDI_APPLICATION);
    wc.hCursor = LoadCursor(NULL, IDC_ARROW);
    wc.hbrBackground = GetStockObject(BLACK_BRUSH);
    wc.lpszMenuName =  NULL;
    wc.lpszClassName = "OurDemoClass";

    return RegisterClass(&wc);
}
```

Note the portable use of **sizeof(MAIN*)** here. Under 16-bit Windows in Medium model, this will evaluate to 2 bytes, whereas under Win32 it will evaluate to 4 bytes. As long as we consistently use **sizeof** rather than hard-coding the size of a pointer, the code will work properly in either environment.

Now that there's a place to stuff the pointer and macros to do it, we need to modify the window callback function to allocate the structure and set up the access. The technique is to change the HWND parameter that is passed to each message-handler function to the pointer to the MAIN structure, which contains the HWND. This pointer becomes the first parameter to every message handler, so they can access all the members of the structure easily.

Here's what the new window callback function looks like in its entirety:

```
LRESULT CALLBACK _export WndProc(HWND hwnd,
                                         UINT msg,
                                         WPARAM wParam,
                                         LPARAM lParam)
{
    MAIN *main = GetPtr(hwnd);

    if (main == NULL) {
          // Create the structure pointer.
        if (msg == WM_NCCREATE) {
            main = (MAIN*)LocalAlloc(LPTR,
                                     sizeof(MAIN));
            if (main == NULL)
                    // Fail the create request if we can't
                  // get memory.
                return 0L;
                // Set the hwnd member to our window's
                // handle.
            main->hwnd = hwnd;
            SetPtr(hwnd, main);
        } else {
            // Process messages other than WM_NCCREATE
                // while main == NULL.
            return DefProc(hwnd, msg, wParam, lParam);
        }
    }

    if (msg == WM_NCDESTROY) {
          // Free the structure.
        LocalFree((HLOCAL)main);
        main = NULL;
        SetPtr(hwnd, NULL);
    }

    // Handle our messages.
    switch (msg) {

        HANDLE_MSG(main, WM_CREATE, OnCreate);
        HANDLE_MSG(main, WM_DESTROY, OnDestroy);
        HANDLE_MSG(main, WM_PAINT, OnPaint);
        HANDLE_MSG(main, WM_SIZE, OnSize);

    default:
        return DefProc(hwnd, msg, wParam, lParam);
    }
}
```

Here's how it all works: First off, a pointer to the structure of type MAIN is declared as an automatic (stack) variable, and the access macro (**`GetPtr`**) pulls the pointer from the extra bytes associated with the window. If this pointer is NULL, then the structure hasn't been allocated yet. The structure is allocated when the callback function receives the WM_NCCREATE (non-client create) message, which is among the first messages sent to the callback function. Note that after intercepting WM_NCCREATE, the function falls through to the **`default`** case of the **`switch`** statement, which sends the message to **`DefProc`** (which is, of course, defined as **`DefWindowProc`**). The **`hwnd`** member of the structure is set to the **`hwnd`** parameter in the callback function, and the pointer is stuffed into the extra bytes associated with that particular window.

Once the structure is created and a pointer to it stuffed away, the **`main`** pointer is set every time the callback function is called by Windows to process a message, and is in turn passed as an argument to every message-handler function. The message-handler functions need to be modified so that they take a pointer to a MAIN structure as their first argument rather than an HWND. For example, **`OnCreate`** should be changed to look like this

```
static BOOL OnCreate(MAIN* main,
                     CREATESTRUCT FAR* lpCreateStruct)
```

and to use the window's handle within **`OnCreate`**, you would now use the handle stored in the MAIN structure, as **`main->hwnd`**.

For each window class—and therefore, for each different callback function you write—you should create a structure definition unique to that class and copy this method of creating, accessing, and deleting it from within the callback function.

Summary

In this chapter, you've learned the basics of Windows memory management: how to use the local and global heaps and the **`LocalAlloc`** and **`GlobalAlloc`** functions, and about certain parts of Windows memory-management history that you are lucky enough to be able to totally ignore. You've also seen an object-oriented method for using **`LocalAlloc`** and a window's extra bytes for storing and accessing instance data about a window that conveniently encapsulates the data and exposes it to the "methods"—the message handlers—that work with the window.

In the next chapter, you'll learn more about using this window structure to store data about the window across different messages. You'll also get to use the mouse in a meaningful way for the first time, as we cover a topic that is all-important to game programs: *handling user input.*

4

Input Systems

come [illegible] fare le manovelle [illegible] le quali si movano e si alza
e i gran pesi [illegible]
[illegible] manovella [illegible]
forza e più [illegible]

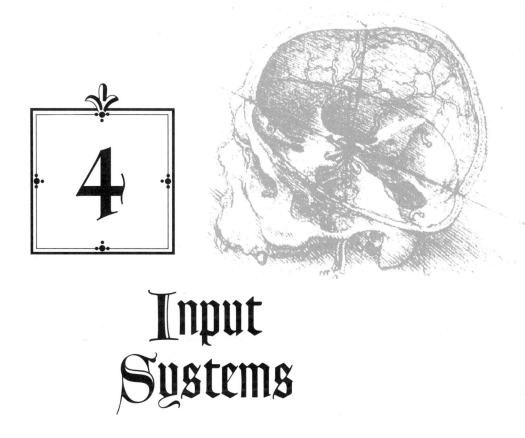

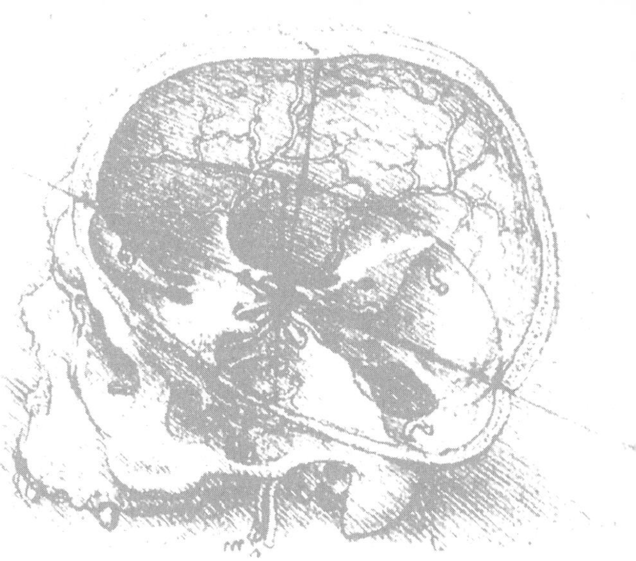

4

Input Systems

In Chapter 1, you learned the basics of how Windows creates windows and displays things on the screen. In the last chapter, you learned about the all-important topic of memory management under Windows. Now it's time to learn how Windows handles user events through various input devices.

A game programmer might assume that input can come from only a few sources: either the keyboard, the mouse, or the joystick. But under Windows, "input" can come from many different places, including Windows itself.

Input and Messages

In Chapter 2, you learned that Windows communicates with a program through *messages,* which are sent to a window's callback function. You learned a few basic window messages, like WM_CREATE and WM_DESTROY, which tell a window when it's being created and destroyed. As it turns out, all forms of input come to the callback function as messages.

A message might tell the program something about a physical device connected to the system, like the WM_MOUSEMOVE message that tells a callback function where the mouse is whenever the user moves it. But a message might also tell us something about the state of Windows itself. An example of this would be the WM_SIZE message that is sent to the callback function whenever a window's size changes. WM_SIZE is sent not only when the user resizes a window with the mouse, but it can also be sent when Windows initiates some action that results in a resizing of the window, like minimizing or maximizing.

Trapping messages and responding to them is essentially all a Windows program does. In the DOS-only programming world, programs typically handled input from either the mouse, keyboard, or joystick, and that was pretty much it. Suddenly, though, there's now the potential for hundreds of different input messages—what's a programmer to do? Let's start by looking at the devices that have familiar counterparts under DOS and the messages they generate.

Standard Windows Devices

Windows supports a wide range of input devices, though it supports some better than others. The two most common are, of course, the keyboard and the mouse. There was a time when Microsoft would tell you to develop applications without assuming the existence of a mouse, but fortunately those days are gone. You can safely assume that if the machine is running Windows, it has a mouse.

Windows also supports the joystick, though it does so through a device driver that the user must install separately.

Another standard Windows "device" is the timer. Windows provides several functions for starting, stopping, and receiving messages from the PC's built-in timer.

Let's start by understanding the mouse messages, then move on to the other standard hardware input devices that Windows supports.

Mouse Messages

There are 20 different messages that the mouse can generate under Windows, and they fall into two classes: client-area messages and non-client-area messages. Recall from Chapter 2 that a window's client area is the place where the program displays information, and the non-client area is everything else, including the caption bar, borders, menu bar, and so on. Most of the time, you'll be interested only in the client-area messages, because that's where the action is. The ten client-area messages and their meanings are summarized in Table 4-1.

Since Windows supports a mouse that has up to three buttons, there is a separate trio of messages for each button. You can't rely on the user having a three-button mouse (Microsoft's, for example, only has two), so it's best to use the middle button as a shortcut for a function that's accessible elsewhere. There are virtually no one-button mice available for the PC, so you *can* rely on there being at least two buttons.

TABLE 4-1
Mouse messages

Message	Meaning
WM_LBUTTONDOWN	Left button down
WM_LBUTTONUP	Left button up
WM_LBUTTONDBLCLK	Left button double-click
WM_MBUTTONDOWN	Middle button down
WM_MBUTTONUP	Middle button up
WM_MBUTTONDBLCLK	Middle button double-click
WM_RBUTTONDOWN	Right button down
WM_RBUTTONUP	Right button up
WM_RBUTTONDBLCLK	Right button double-click
WM_MOUSEMOVE	Mouse move

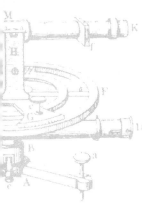

Notice that there is a double-click mouse message for each mouse button. Double-click messages are sent to a window only if the CS_DBLCLKS style is defined for that window's class. Keep in mind, though, that a double click should be used only where a single click performed twice has no ill effect. The reason: A double-click message is always preceded by *two* separate button-down messages. If you think about this for a moment, you'll understand why this side effect is completely unavoidable. General wisdom these days is that a double click should be an optional shortcut anyway, because (believe it or not) many people just plain can't double-click very well. It's important to remember that just because Windows (or any other user interface system, for that matter) supports a particular event, like right-clicking the mouse, doesn't mean you should use it. The key is to keep interaction as intuitive as possible.

Each of the mouse messages comes with several parameters packed in **`wParam`** and **`lParam`**. As usual, by using the message crackers, we can handily break these out into real parameters for our message-handler functions.

Starting with WM_MOUSEMOVE, here's what the message-handler function prototypes look like:

```
void OnMouseMove (HWND hwnd,
                  int x, int y,
                  UINT keyFlags)
```

Figure 4-1 shows the parameters of the **`OnMouseMove`** function. The first parameter is, of course, the window handle over which the mouse is moving. The next two parameters are the *x* and *y* coordinates of the mouse. The last parameter is a UINT that holds a set of flags about the state of various buttons. The different flags are listed in Table 4-2.

FIGURE 4-1

Receiving information about the mouse

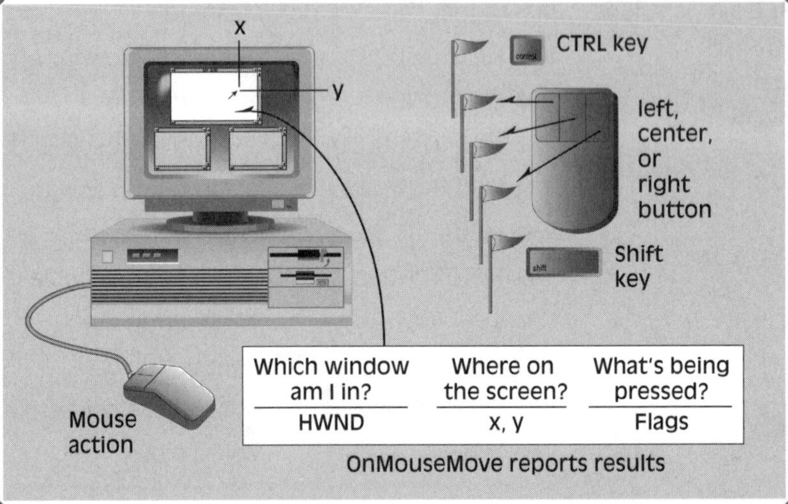

TABLE 4-2

`keyFlags` *values*

Value	Meaning
MK_CONTROL	Set if CTRL is down
MK_LBUTTON	Set if the left mouse button is down
MK_MBUTTON	Set if the middle mouse button is down
MK_RBUTTON	Set if the right mouse button is down
MK_SHIFT	Set if SHIFT is down

To test if CTRL is being held down during mouse movement, for example, you would logically-AND the MK_CONTROL value with **keyFlags**, like so:

```
// Test for CTRL held down
if (keyFlags & MK_CONTROL)
    // CTRL held...
    .
    .
    .
```

The function prototype for the WM_LBUTTONDOWN (or RBUTTONDOWN or MBUTTONDOWN, for that matter) looks like this:

```
void OnLButtonDown (HWND hwnd,
                    BOOL fDoubleClick,
                    int x, int y, UINT keyFlags);
```

Here, the **hwnd**, **x**, **y**, and **keyFlags** parameters are the same as in WM_MOUSEMOVE. The new parameter, **fDoubleClick**, is TRUE if the mouse was double-clicked, but *only* if the handler was called by processing the WM_LBUTTONDBLCLK message (and if the window supports double-clicks in its style definition). To perform this trick, the message handler must be called by *two* different messages in the callback function's **switch** statement, like so:

```
HANDLE_MSG(hwnd, WM_LBUTTONDOWN, OnLButtonDown);
HANDLE_MSG(hwnd, WM_LBUTTONDBLCLK, OnLButtonDown);
```

The last mouse message is WM_LBUTTONUP (or WM_MBUTTONUP or WM_RBUTTONUP), which is sent when the user releases the left (or middle or right) mouse button. Its message-handler function prototype looks like this:

```
void OnLButtonUp(HWND hwnd,
                 int x, int y,
                 UINT keyFlags)
```

Note that this looks just like the handler for WM_LBUTTONDOWN.

Using Mouse Messages

In most programs, the mouse is used for two purposes: selecting things and dragging things. To enable the user to select an object, the program handles WM_LBUTTONDOWN messages, then "hit tests" them with the all the possible objects that the mouse may be over. To enable the user to drag, the program first hit tests an object when the WM_LBUTTONDOWN message is sent to the window. Then, if the program finds that the object was selected, it drags that object on subsequent WM_MOUSEMOVE messages until a WM_LBUTTONUP message is received.

Game programs vary widely in their use of the mouse. Often, it is permanently "attached" to some central character or object on the screen. If this is the case, WM_MOUSEMOVE messages are used to drag the object around on the screen, while WM_LBUTTONDOWN might be used to do something like fire the weapon or jump to hyperspace or grab the sumo wrestler. The use of the left mouse button in productivity applications is pretty standardized, but its use in games is still very much open to the creativity of the game developer.

Figure 4-2 gives an example of how mouse keys can be assigned to game actions. In an archery game, the left mouse button might move the character when held down. The right button, held down, aims the bow. Releasing the right button fires the arrow.

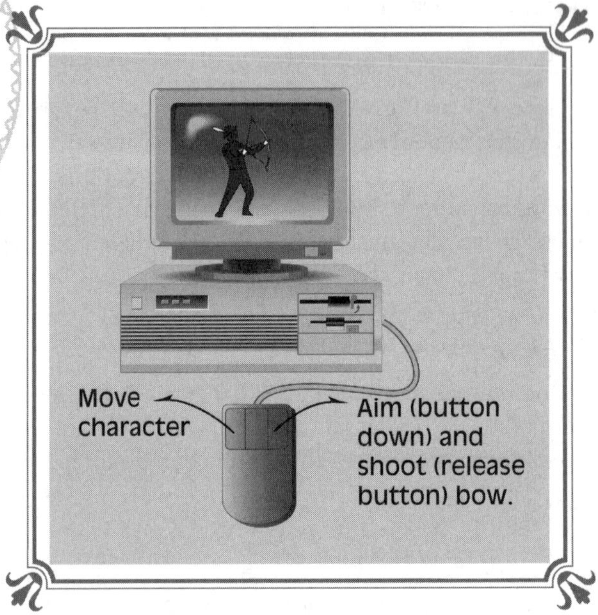

FIGURE 4-2

Assigning mouse keys to game actions

In another part of the game, the right button might control the sword instead of a bow, or perhaps be used to cast a magic spell.

The mouse messages and the cursor are closely related. Recall from Chapter 2 that if a cursor is defined in the **hCursor** member of the WNDCLASS structure used to register the window's class, that cursor is set every time the mouse moves in a window derived from that class. Conversely, if there is no cursor defined for the class, then the callback function *must* set the cursor at every mouse move.

Suppose you're developing a classic arcade game, like Space Invaders. You want the mouse to be attached to your spacecraft, and you want mouse movements to be translated into movements of the craft in some indirect way. In this case, you really don't want a visible cursor in your window at all, or maybe only under certain circumstances, like when the game is paused. To do this, you'd set the **hCursor** member of the WNDCLASS structure for the window's class to NULL, and also set the cursor to NULL at every mouse move. Here's what part of the window's WM_MOUSEMOVE handler would look like:

```
static void OnMouseMove (MAIN *main, int x, int y,
                                 UINT keyFlags)
{
    if (Paused)
        SetCursor (main->cursor);
    else
        SetCursor (NULL);
        .
        .
        .
```

This function assumes that the MAIN structure for our window contains a **`cursor`** member that has been set to some cursor handle (loaded with **`LoadCursor`**), probably at WM_CREATE time. It also assumes that there's a **`Paused`** variable that is set to TRUE when the game is paused, in order to display the cursor. The rest of the function would process the mouse-move message to determine the position and/or orientation of the spacecraft.

Limitations of Mouse Messages

The mouse messages that Windows generates have a couple of shortcomings. The first is that the *x* and *y* coordinates passed to the message handler, although already adjusted to the client area of our window, are in *screen coordinates,* meaning that they "hit the wall" at the edges of the screen or window, whichever comes first. For some programmers this doesn't present a problem, but if you're used to getting mouse coordinates in terms of "mickeys"—an encoding of the physical pulses that the mouse sends to the mouse driver—then you're in for a surprise. The problem with the Windows method of handling mouse input is that it throws away the resolution inherent in the mouse and reduces it to screen resolution. For programs that map mouse movement directly to the movement of things on the screen this works fine, but if you're mapping mouse movement into something like rotation or direction vectors, you'll lose some of the resolution that you would have had if you were using DOS calls to get mouse movement. Unfortunately, there's no reasonable way of getting around this limitation, so you'll just have to live with it.

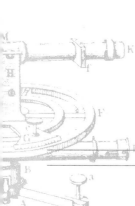

A side effect of the same problem is that mouse movement stops at the edges of the screen or window. Suppose, for example, that you have a full-screen game running on a screen of 800x600 pixel resolution. When the mouse cursor—whether it's visible or not—hits the right side of the screen, the *x* coordinate sent to the WM_MOUSEMOVE handler will be 799—and will never get any larger, no matter how far the user moves the mouse to the right. Again, this isn't a problem if you're moving something in the window in a 1:1 relationship with the mouse.

Using SetCapture and ReleaseCapture

Windows will send the WM_MOUSEMOVE, WM_xBUTTONDOWN, and WM_xBUTTONUP messages to a window only when the cursor is over that window. When the user moves the mouse outside the window, Windows sends WM_MOUSEMOVE messages to the new window over which the cursor currently lies. If your game is in a full-screen window, this isn't a problem: The cursor is, by definition, *always* over your window (as long as it's the active window). But if your game runs in a moveable pop-up window smaller than the whole screen, there may be times when you'd still like to be getting mouse messages even though the cursor has fallen outside your window.

Consider what happens when you are dragging something around on the screen when the left mouse button is down. If you receive messages only when the cursor is in your window, moving off the edge of the window—even if it's just by a little—and then reentering the window will cause the object you're dragging to jump from spot to spot along the edge.

For this reason, Windows provides two functions for capturing and releasing mouse input, ones that work even when the cursor isn't over your window. The first is **SetCapture**:

```
HWND SetCapture (HWND hwnd)
```

This function tells Windows to keep sending mouse messages to the window whose handle is the function's single parameter. Windows does this until you call the **ReleaseCapture** function:

```
void ReleaseCapture ()
```

The typical procedure is to call **SetCapture** at WM_LBUTTONDOWN time, and then call **ReleaseCapture** when a WM_LBUTTONUP message is received. In between, all the mouse-move messages will go to the designated window. Generally speaking, **SetCapture** and **ReleaseCapture** are needed only for dragging objects.

Now that you know a little about the mouse messages, let's see some action on the screen. Keeping it simple, let's create a WM_MOUSEMOVE handler that displays the coordinates of the mouse in the main window's title bar whenever the mouse is down. Figure 4-3 shows the results.

```
static void OnMouseMove (MAIN *main, int x, int y,
                               UINT keyFlags)
{
    char buf[30];
```

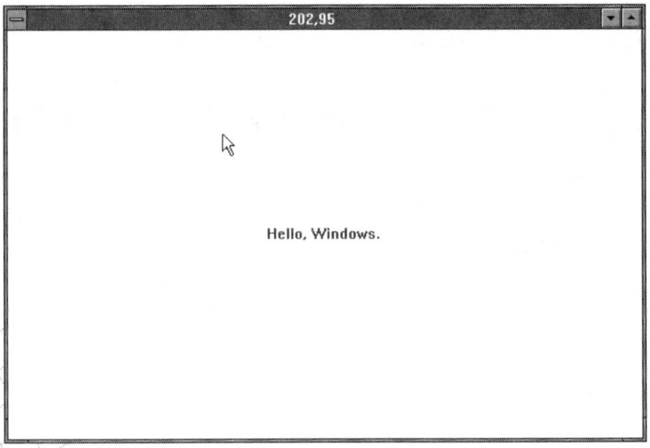

FIGURE 4-3

This OnMouseMove function puts the current mouse coordinates in the window's title bar

```
    // If the mouse is down, display the coords.
    if (keyFlags & MK_LBUTTON) {
        // Format the coords into a buffer.
        wsprintf (buf, "%d,%d", x, y);
        // Set the title-bar text.
        SetWindowText (main->hwnd, buf);
    }
}
```

The function checks **keyFlags** to see if the left mouse button is down; if it is, the function then formats the *x* and *y* coordinates of the mouse position into a local buffer. The **wsprintf** function is the Windows version of **sprintf** and although it's more restrictive (it doesn't handle floating-point formatting, for example), it's very fast and also model-independent. The **SetWindowText** call sets the title bar of a window to the text specified as its second argument.

Keyboard Messages

Handling keyboard input in a Windows program is no less difficult than handling mouse movement. There are eight standard keyboard messages, as shown in Table 4-3:

TABLE 4-3
Keyboard messages

Message	Meaning
WM_CHAR	Character input
WM_DEADCHAR	Dead character (umlaut, accent, etc.)
WM_KEYDOWN	Key has been depressed
WM_KEYUP	Key has been released
WM_SYSCHAR	System character input
WM_SYSDEADCHAR	System dead character
WM_SYSKEYDOWN	System key has been depressed
WM_SYSKEYUP	System key has been released

Hey, whoa—what are these "dead" key things? You can pretty much ignore them; they're special cases used primarily for creating multiple-keystroke characters.

The WM_SYS* messages are not very interesting—they're used to trap characters destined for the window's system menu. These messages are sent when ALT is held down and another key is pressed. ALT presses are generally reserved for Windows-menu shortcut-key operations, so your program shouldn't use them directly (although it has been done in certain cases).

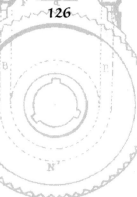

The interesting messages are WM_CHAR, WM_KEYDOWN, and WM_KEYUP. You can think of the WM_CHAR message as the "cooked" version of WM_KEYDOWN and WM_KEYUP: It represents translated key values, while WM_KEYDOWN and WM_KEYUP send "raw" values.

In other words, WM_CHAR messages are sent only for valid ASCII characters—the normal keys you can type on any keyboard. Certain keys are sent *only* as WM_KEYDOWN and WM_KEYUP messages. These include the cursor keys, function keys, and other key combinations that don't have valid ASCII values. Here's the handler definition for WM_CHAR messages:

```
void OnChar(HWND hwnd, UINT ch, int cRepeat)
```

The second argument is the actual ASCII key value. For example, if the user presses s on the keyboard, the value in `ch` will be hex 73. If the user presses S (the uppercase version), `ch` will be hex 53 (the ASCII value of the character). The PC has a feature that repeatedly sends keystrokes for keys held down on the keyboard. The `cRepeat` argument keeps a count of these repeated keys. The `cRepeat` value will be greater than 1 only if your message-processing function isn't able to process the keys fast enough. Otherwise, Windows sends just one WM_CHAR message each time the key is repeated.

You could write a simple handler similar to the previous mouse-move handler to display each key as it's pressed.

```
static void OnChar(MAIN *main, UINT ch, int cRepeat)
{
    static char buf[30];
    static int n = 0;

    // Display up to 29 characters, then start over.
    if (n == 29)
        n = 0;
    buf[n++] = (char) ch;
    buf[n] = 0;
    // Set the title-bar text.
    SetWindowText (main->hwnd, buf);

}
```

The results are shown in Figure 4-4. Note that certain keys correspond to nondisplayable ASCII characters that will look funny in the title bar.

You must use the WM_KEYDOWN and WM_KEYUP messages to handle certain keys that don't have translatable ASCII values. As their names suggest, these two messages are sent at the transition of *every* key on the keyboard, regardless of whether that transition might result in a subsequent WM_CHAR message. The keys in Table 4-4 are available only as WM_KEYUP and WM_KEYDOWN messages; they have no ASCII equivalents and therefore don't get "cooked" into a WM_CHAR message.

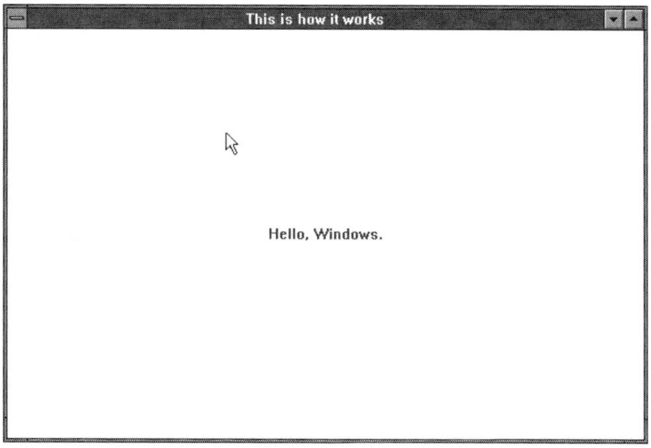

FIGURE 4-4
This OnMouseMove function reports the characters being typed at the keyboard in the window's title bar

The WM_KEYDOWN and WM_KEYUP messages are handled by a single function definition in WINDOWSX.H:

```
void OnKey (HWND hwnd, UINT vk, BOOL fDown,
            int cRepeat, UINT flags)
```

Like WM_*x*BUTTONDBLCLK and WM_*x*BUTTONDOWN, this message handler should be called for both WM_KEYUP and WM_KEYDOWN messages, like so:

```
HANDLE_MSG(main, WM_KEYUP, OnKey);
HANDLE_MSG(main, WM_KEYDOWN, OnKey);
```

The `BOOL fDown` parameter is used to indicate that the key has been depressed (if TRUE) or released (if FALSE). The `cRepeat` parameter is the same as in `OnChar`. The `flags` parameter is a bit-encoded UINT.

For most purposes, the bit definitions in Table 4-5 aren't used. Sometimes it's important to distinguish whether a cursor key is coming from the numeric keypad or the inverted *T* extended keys, but in general it's better *not* to distinguish between these keys, to prevent confusion.

The `vk` parameter to the function specifies the virtual key code for the key being depressed or released. There is a virtual key code for every key on the standard 101-key IBM keyboard; a table of these keys would be too lengthy to put here, but can be found in your favorite Windows programming reference. Virtual-key-code constants are defined in WINDOWS.H and they all begin with VK_. For example, VK_CAPITAL corresponds to [CAPS LOCK]. There are, of course, virtual-key-code constants defined for all the "normal" keys on the keyboard, as well. These are the ones that get turned into "cooked" ASCII and sent as WM_CHAR messages. For example, VK_K is [K] on the keyboard. Since the WM_KEYUP and WM_KEYDOWN messages handle only raw keystrokes, only single-key depressions and releases

TABLE 4-4
Keystrokes available only through WM_KEYUP and WM_KEYDOWN

Keystroke	Description
F1-F9, F11-F16	Function keys. F10 is reserved for Windows use as the menu select hot key (not all keyboards have F13-F16).
SHIFT, CTRL, ALT	Shift keys. ALT is a reserved key and does not generate WM_KEYDOWN or WM_KEYUP messages unless CTRL is down. Normally, it generates only WM_SYSKEYDOWN and WM_SYSKEYUP messages.
CAPS LOCK, NUM LOCK, SCROLL LOCK	Toggle keys.
PRINT SCREEN	Reserved for copying screen to Clipboard (PRINT SCREEN alone), or for copying the active window to the Clipboard (ALT-PRINT SCREEN). Windows eats the WM_KEYDOWN message, and sends only WM_KEYUP.
PAUSE	Pause key.
INSERT, DELETE, HOME, END, PAGEUP, PAGEDOWN	Text-editing keys. Although there are two sets of these keys on the 101-key IBM keyboard, they send the same virtual key code. They can be distinguished with the Extend flag.
UP, DOWN, LEFT, RIGHT	Direction keys. Like the text-editing keys, the two sets found on the 101-key IBM keyboard can be distinguished with the Extend flag.

count—combinations of keys have to be decoded separately. For example, if you wanted to decode a key combination like CTRL-RIGHT, the code would look like this:

```
static void OnKey (MAIN *main, UINT vk, BOOL fDown,
                   int cRepeat, UINT flags)
{
    // Variable to hold the Control key state,
    // Down = TRUE
    static BOOL CtrlState = FALSE;

    // Set CtrlState according to whether the
```

TABLE 4-5
Bits of the `flags` *parameter to* `OnKey`

Bit	Description
0–7	Scan code. This is the actual hardware scan code from the keyboard, and is dependent on the keyboard manufacturer.
8	Specifies whether the key is an extended key, such as a function key or a key on the numeric keypad.
9–10	Not used.
11–12	Used internally by Windows.
13	Context code. The value is 1 if ALT is held down; otherwise, the value is 0.
14	Specifies the previous key state. The value is 1 if the key is down before the message is sent, 0 if the key is up.
15	Specifies the key transition state. The value is 1 if the key is being released, 0 if the key is being pressed.

```
// the Control key is up or down.
if (vk == VK_CONTROL)
    CtrlState = fDown ? TRUE : FALSE;

// Detect the VK_RIGHT key, see if Control
// is being held down.
if (vk == VK_RIGHT && fDown && CtrlState)
    HandleCtrlRightArrow (...
.
.
.
```

Note how the last **`if`** statement makes sure that the VK_RIGHT key is detected as a WM_KEYDOWN event (only when the **`fDown`** parameter is TRUE). Otherwise, the **`HandleCtrlRightArrow`** function would be called on both WM_KEYDOWN *and* WM_KEYUP.

For most keystrokes, you need to detect really only WM_KEYDOWN (for example, when **`fDown`** is TRUE) and ignore WM_KEYUP messages. Remember also that CTRL-*letter* (CTRL-A, CTRL-B, and so on) all have ASCII definitions and therefore send WM_CHAR messages, so no multiple-key decoding is necessary via WM_KEYDOWN and WM_KEYUP.

So much for the mouse and keyboard. On to the messages that Windows generates to keep things in sync on the screen.

Window-Maintenance Messages

Besides the basic hardware-device messages, there are messages that Windows generates to keep windows in shape. Although these are internally generated messages, almost all of them are generated as a direct or indirect result of the user doing something on the screen.

The window-maintenance messages fall into three categories:

- Notifications
- Requests for action
- Queries

Window-Notification Messages

Not all the 11 window-maintenance messages are necessarily of interest to game programmers. Table 4-6 and Figure 4-5 show only the five particularly interesting ones; you can find a complete list in your favorite Windows programming reference.

You've already learned about the WM_CREATE and WM_DESTROY messages, which are sent when a window's being created and destroyed.

The WM_ACTIVATEAPP message is particularly useful for game programs. This message is sent to the main window of an application when that application becomes (and again when it ceases being) the current application. There can be only one cur-

TABLE 4-6
Select window-notification messages

Message	Meaning
WM_ACTIVATEAPP	The application is becoming the current application, or it is no longer the current application.
WM_CREATE	The window is being created.
WM_DESTROY	The window is being destroyed.
WM_MOVE	The window has been moved.
WM_SIZE	The window has been resized.
WM_WINDOWPOSCHANGING	The window's position or size is changing.

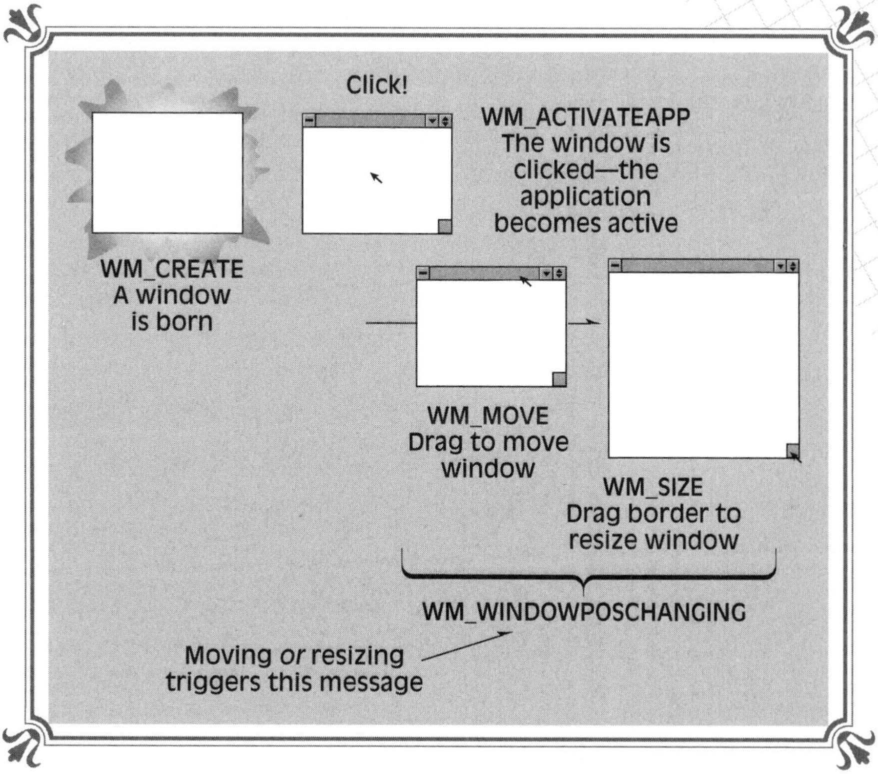

FIGURE 4-5

A day in the life of a window

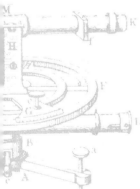

rent application under Windows; it's the one whose window shows the active caption style (if the window has a caption). Generally, the current application's window is on top (though not always). A game program might use the information from the WM_ACTIVATEAPP message to suspend or resume activity—this is especially true for a full-screen game, which could waste a lot of cycles in the background if it weren't suspended. Also, if the game you are programming uses sound—and there aren't many that don't—you will probably want it to stop making noise when it's not the active application.

Here's what the WINDOWSX.H message-handler definition for WM_ACTIVATEAPP looks like:

```
void OnActivateApp(HWND hwnd, BOOL fActivate,
                   HTASK htaskActDeact)
```

The first parameter is the usual window handle. The **fActivate** parameter is TRUE if the application associated with the window handle is becoming active, and FALSE if the application is about to cease being active. This is the parameter you would use to suspend or resume game activity. The HTASK parameter is a handle to the task being deactivated; I won't go into its use here.

WM_MOVE is sent to a window when that window has been moved (for example, when the user drags the window by its caption bar). Users can't move most windows that do not have caption bars, and a full-screen game window, by definition, can't be moved.

The WM_SIZE message is sent whenever a window is resized, either because the user is tugging on the borders of the window or because the window is being

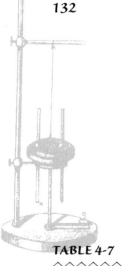

TABLE 4-7

State parameters for WM_SIZE

Value	Meaning
SIZE_MAXIMIZED	The window has been maximized.
SIZE_MINIMIZED	The window has been minimized.
SIZE_RESTORED	The window has been resized, but neither SIZE_MAXIMIZED nor SIZE_MINIMIZED applies.
SIZE_MAXHIDE	This message is sent to all top-level windows when some other window is maximized.
SIZE_MAXSHOW	This message is sent to all top-level windows when some other window has been restored to its former size.

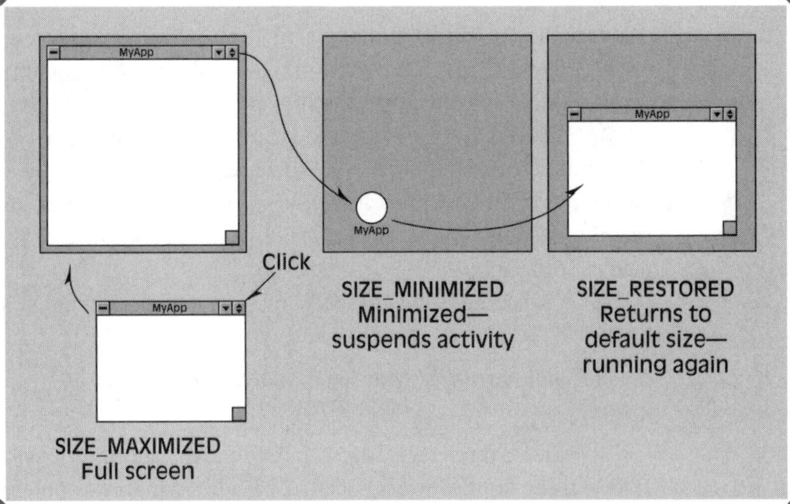

FIGURE 4-6

Effects of maximizing, minimizing, and restoring a window

minimized or maximized. It's also sent to a window when that window is first created, sometime after WM_CREATE.

The WM_SIZE message handler in WINDOWSX.H comes with two parameters that tell the size of the new window, along with a parameter that tells us something about the way it's been sized:

```
OnSize (HWND hwnd, UINT state, int x, int y)
```

The **state** parameter holds one of the values shown in Table 4-7. Figure 4-6 shows the effects of maximizing, minimizing, and restoring a window.

If a full-screen game can be minimized, it should definitely catch the WM_SIZE message and do something appropriate, like suspend activity if it's being minimized and resume activity if it's being maximized. The two size parameters (**x** and **y**) sent with the WM_SIZE message indicate the new size of the window. Note that this isn't necessarily the size of the *client area* of the window, but the size of the whole window (on a window with no borders, menu bar, or caption bar, the two are the same). Later, you'll learn how to use **GetClientRect** to get the size of the client area of the window.

The WM_WINDOWPOSCHANGING message was new to Windows 3.1 and allows a window to finely control its size and position. Its handler's prototype looks like this:

```
OnWindowPosChanging (HWND hwnd, LPWINDOWPOS lpwpos)
```

A WINDOWPOS structure, to which a pointer is passed as the second argument, looks like this:

```
typedef struct tagWINDOWPOS
{
    HWND    hwnd;
    HWND    hwndInsertAfter;
    int     x;
    int     y;
    int     cx;
    int     cy;
    UINT    flags;
} WINDOWPOS;
```

By modifying the members of the WINDOWPOS structure, a program can override the size and position of a window as it's being changed. Why would someone want his or her program to do this? Probably the most common reason is to keep the client area of a window DWORD-aligned for speed. As we'll learn in Chapter 7, some bitmap objects work at optimum speed when Windows can assume that their destination rectangles—typically the client area of a window—are aligned to 4-byte (DWORD) boundaries. The user can stretch a resizable window to any size, but the WM_WINDOWPOSCHANGING message gives the program a chance to modify the

TABLE 4-8
Request-for-action messages

Message	Meaning
WM_CLOSE	The window is closing.
WM_ERASEBKGND	Erase the background.
WM_PAINT	Redraw the client area.

user's resizing request and DWORD-align it. We'll cover this method of alignment in Chapter 7.

Request-for-Action Messages

Of the 12 messages in this group, 3 are worthy of note. They are listed here in Table 4-8.

The WM_CLOSE message is sent just before a window is closed. This gives the program a chance to let the user confirm that he or she wants the window destroyed. If WM_CLOSE is processed by a callback function, the WM_DESTROY message won't be sent—the WM_CLOSE handler must "manually" call **DestroyWindow** instead, which generates the WM_DESTROY message. This is standard practice for productivity applications: The WM_CLOSE handler checks the state of a flag that indicates whether the user has unsaved changes, and prompts the user to save them. If the user cancels the message box, the WM_DESTROY message is never sent and the window stays put. If the user chooses to save the changes or ignore them, the program eventually calls **DestroyWindow**, which sends the WM_DESTROY message. The WM_DESTROY handler for the top-level window is where **PostQuitMessage**, which finally terminates the program, normally resides.

A game program may or may not process WM_CLOSE messages, depending on whether the unsaved-data scenario I've just mentioned applies.

WM_ERASEBKGND is sent to a window whenever its background needs to be erased. If a background brush is specified in the **hbrBackground** member of the WNDCLASS structure of the class from which the window is derived (are you getting used to that phrase yet?), then the callback function doesn't need to process the WM_ERASEBKGND message—Windows will dutifully erase the background with the designated brush. If, however, the **hbrBackground** member is NULL *or* you want to erase the background with something other than the class brush, specify your instructions in the WM_ERASEBKGND handler. Its WINDOWSX.H prototype looks like this:

```
void OnEraseBkgnd (HWND hwnd, HDC hdc)
```

The second parameter, **hdc**, is a handle to a *device context*. It is necessary if you want the program to do any drawing whatsoever in the window. (Device contexts and drawing are covered extensively in Chapter 5.) Normally, it's easiest just to specify the background brush in the WNDCLASS structure and skip handling the WM_ERASEBKGND message.

It's hard to say that there's any one *most* important message to handle in Windows, but if the matter were brought to a vote, WM_PAINT would probably win. The WM_PAINT message is sent to a window when its client area needs redrawing. In other words, the WM_PAINT message handler is the place where everything having to do with redrawing the window's contents resides. Usually, the WM_PAINT handler just calls a function that repaints the window's contents completely. WM_PAINT handling is also covered extensively in Chapter 5, where you'll learn all about drawing things in the window's client area.

Query Messages

Of this group of seven messages, only two are very interesting. They appear in Table 4-9.

TABLE 4-9

Select window-query messages

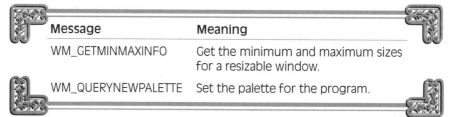

Message	Meaning
WM_GETMINMAXINFO	Get the minimum and maximum sizes for a resizable window.
WM_QUERYNEWPALETTE	Set the palette for the program.

If you want to restrict the size of a resizable window, use the first message, WM_GETMINMAXINFO. Normally, a user can change a window with resizable borders to any size by dragging the borders with the mouse. Often, you will want to restrict this so that only a certain minimum or maximum size is possible. The WINDOWSX.H handler for WM_GETMINMAXINFO looks like this:

```
void OnGetMinMaxInfo(HWND hwnd,
                     MINMAXINFO FAR* lpMinMaxInfo)
```

The MINMAXINFO structure, to which a pointer is passed to the message handler, in turn looks like this:

```
typedef struct tagMINMAXINFO
{
    POINT ptReserved;
    POINT ptMaxSize;
    POINT ptMaxPosition;
    POINT ptMinTrackSize;
    POINT ptMaxTrackSize;
} MINMAXINFO;
```

The WM_GETMINMAXINFO message is sent to a window whenever Windows needs the maximized position or dimensions of the window or needs the maximum or minimum tracking size of the window. The maximized size of a window is the size of the window when its borders are fully extended. The maximum tracking size of a window is the largest window size that can be achieved by using the borders to size the window. The minimum tracking size of a window is the smallest window size that can be achieved by using the borders to size the window. Windows fills in a MINMAXINFO data structure, specifying default values for the various positions and dimensions. Changing the values in the structure will restrict the size of the window correspondingly. Figure 4-7 shows how a window's size is restricted by handling the WM_GETMINMAXINFO message.

This the first time you've seen the Windows POINT structure, which is simply defined as:

```
typedef struct tagPOINT
{
    int x;
    int y;
} POINT;
```

To restrict the size of a resizable window to a maximum of 800x600 pixels, the WM_GETMINMAXINFO message handler would look like this:

```
static void OnGetMinMaxInfo(MAIN *main,
              MINMAXINFO FAR* lpMinMaxInfo)
{
    lpMinMaxInfo->ptMaxTrackSize.x = 800;
    lpMinMaxInfo->ptMaxTrackSize.y = 600;
```

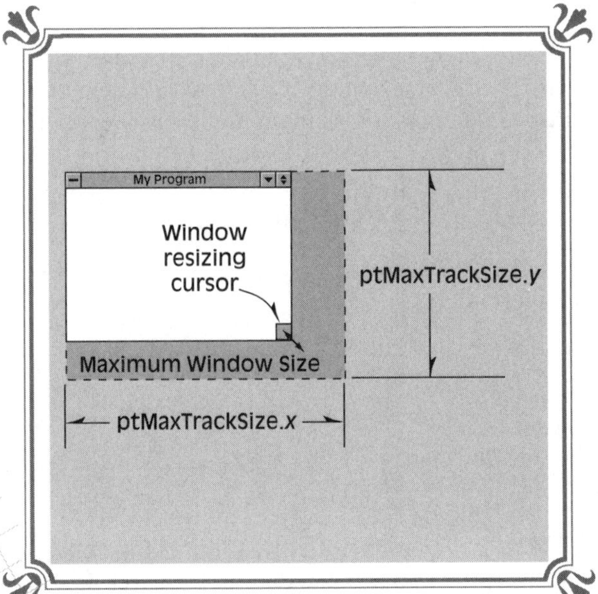

FIGURE 4-7

The MINMAXINFO effect

```
    // Also set the maximum size...
    lpMinMaxInfo->ptMaxSize.x = 800;
    lpMinMaxInfo->ptMaxSize.y = 600;
}
```

The WM_QUERYNEWPALETTE message is sent to a window when the window becomes current. This allows the window to set a new palette if it is needed. Palettes are covered in detail in Chapter 8, where we cover the WM_QUERYNEWPALETTE message, as well.

So much for the window-maintenance messages. The next set of input messages typically comes from actions the user performs on things like menus, controls, and dialog boxes: These are called user interface messages.

User Interface Messages

This set of 35 messages can be divided into six categories:

- Menu messages
- System commands
- Mouse-pointer messages
- Scrollbar messages
- Dialog box and control messages
- MDI messages

Since the Multiple Document Interface doesn't really apply to game programs, we'll thankfully be able to skip the MDI messages. Dialog boxes will be discussed later, so I won't cover them here.

Menus and Menu Messages

Menus can generate up to five messages. Only two are widely used, and are described in Table 4-10.

TABLE 4-10 *Selected menu messages*

Message	Meaning
WM_COMMAND	A menu item has been selected.
WM_INITMENUPOPUP	A pop-up menu has been initialized.

The WM_COMMAND message tells us what menu item has been selected. To understand how WM_COMMAND works, you first need to know how menus in general work under Windows. I'll cover this topic rather briefly; menus aren't very popular in games, because they detract from the immersive nature of these programs. There are games that do use menus extensively, however. The games in the Sim series from Maxis, for example, have a look that is similar to that of a regular productivity application. All the games in the Microsoft Entertainment Packs also use menus and resizable windows.

You can define a menu in one of two ways: either in the resource file or through function calls like **CreateMenu**, **CreatePopupMenu**, and **AppendMenu**. Regardless of how they're created, menus can be modified with calls like **InsertMenu**, **DeleteMenu**, and **ModifyMenu**, which can add items, delete items, and change items. You can do things to a menu item like "gray" it (making it unselectable), give it a check mark, or disable it. Windows menus are very flexible, and an enthusiastic programmer can even create a menu filled with pictures instead of text, although there's a fair amount of programming involved.

Regardless of how a menu is created or what it contains, its function is the same: to present a list of items from which the user can make a selection. The act of selecting a menu item generates a WM_COMMAND message to the window that owns the menu, with a parameter that defines which menu item was selected. Here's what a WM_COMMAND handler looks like in WINDOWSX.H parlance:

```
void OnCommand(HWND hwnd, int id, HWND hwndCtl,
               UINT codeNotify)
```

A typical text-only menu consists of a bunch of menu strings and corresponding IDs, which are 16-bit numbers that are usually associated with some **#define** in a header file somewhere. The **id** parameter sent along with the WM_COMMAND message identifies which menu item is selected.

Menus aren't the only things that generate WM_COMMAND messages. Windows *controls* also generate them. Recall that a control is a user interface object like a button, list box, text field, and so on. When the user clicks on a control, it generates a WM_COMMAND message like a menu; in the case of a control, however, the **hwndCtl** parameter is set to the handle of the actual control sending the message, and the **codeNotify** parameter contains some sort of notification code associated with the control.

There are generally two types of menus: menus that are "attached" to a window and therefore display a menu bar at the top of the window, and pop-up menus that can be displayed anywhere on the screen. Two of the most common examples of these menu types are shown in Figure 4-8.

The easiest way to specify a menu that's attached to a window is to specify its name as part of the WNDCLASS structure that registers the window's class. The name specified in the **lpszMenuName** parameter is the name given to the menu in the resource

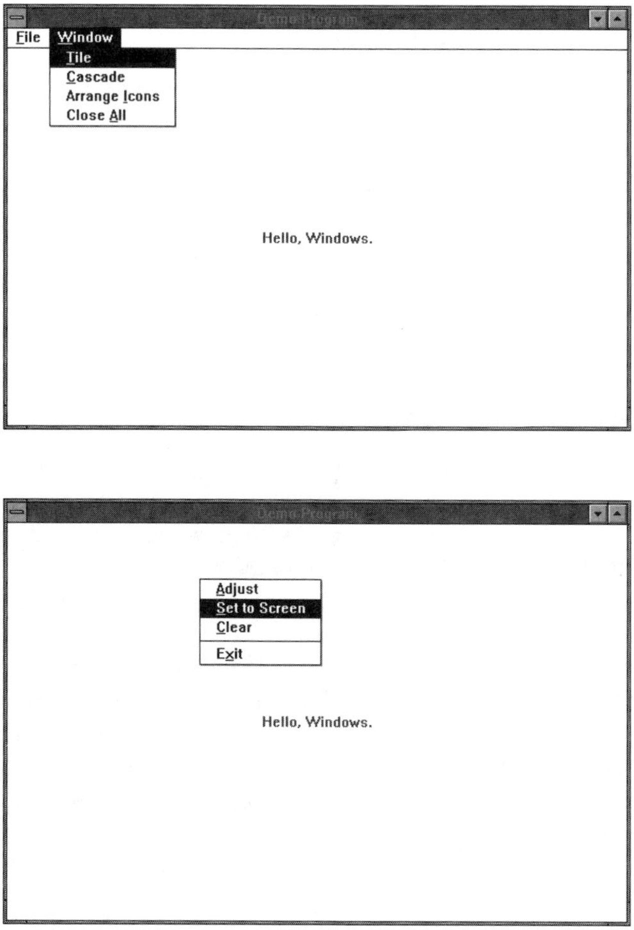

FIGURE 4-8

Menu types

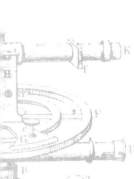

file; this name is specified directly rather than by using a handle returned from the **LoadMenu** function, for some unknown reason.

Of course, any window created from a class registered with a menu name specified will automatically have that menu. For a little more flexibility, Windows also provides the **LoadMenu** and **SetMenu** functions, which load a menu from the resource file and attach it to the specified window, respectively.

The other popular type of menu is one that pops up in response to some mouse action; typically, when the user presses the right mouse button. The **TrackPopupMenu** function brings up a menu anywhere within a window, tracks menu items with the mouse, and sends a WM_COMMAND message to the window when the user selects a menu item.

System Commands

System commands all come from one message: WM_SYSCOMMAND. Ninety percent of the time, you won't care about WM_SYSCOMMAND messages; they just aren't that interesting. They're generated by items on the system menu, which is activated when the user clicks on the system-menu button in the upper left corner of a window (that is, if there is such a button—a full-screen game doesn't have one). Occasionally, WM_SYSCOMMAND messages are useful for reinterpreting what system-menu commands do, but it's usually not a good idea to use them, because they cause the program to behave in very nonstandard ways.

Mouse-Pointer Messages

There are only two mouse-pointer messages: WM_NCHITTEST and WM_SETCURSOR. The first is sent to a window every time the mouse is moved. The return value of the callback message receiving the message tells Windows where the mouse is in the window: whether it's in the client area, over one of the borders, in the caption bar, and so on. If you want to thoroughly confuse Windows, you can use WM_NCHITTEST to tell it that the cursor is over some part of the window that it really isn't. If confusion is not your goal, though, it's best to just let it be passed to **`DefWindowProc`**.

WM_SETCURSOR can be equally fun. It, too, is sent whenever the user moves the mouse within a window. Supposedly, a callback function processing the WM_SETCURSOR message should return TRUE if it sets the cursor itself, or FALSE if it wants Windows to set the cursor. Unfortunately, this doesn't quite seem to work, so you need to pass the message to **`DefWindowProc`** in the WM_SETCURSOR message handler if you actually want Windows to display its choice of cursor. By trapping the WM_SETCURSOR message, a program can set a nonstandard cursor for things like Windows' resizable borders and so on.

Scrollbar Messages

Scrollbars are those ubiquitous little things along the edges of a window that allow the window's contents to be scrolled into and out of view. Depending on their orientation, they generate one of two messages: WM_HSCROLL or WM_VSCROLL (for horizontal and vertical bars, respectively). The scrollbar messages come complete with a parameter that provides information on the position and movement of the scrollbar. Scrollbars also have functions that set their range and position directly. Because of their relative rarity in games, I won't discuss them in any detail here. If you'd like further information, look up the scrollbar functions and notification codes in your favorite Windows programming reference.

Timer Messages

Timing and games go hand in hand. Timers have literally dozens of uses in games, from simply measuring play time to providing a system-independent way of controlling the speed of action. Timers are often less important in DOS-based games than in games that run under Windows, because a DOS program can always loop until some event happens. A hard loop under Windows is a definite no-no, since it steals the machine away from all other running applications. Fortunately, Windows provides a number of useful timer functions to help you cope.

For simply measuring elapsed time, you can call **GetCurrentTime()**, which returns a count of the number of milliseconds that have passed since the system was started, as a DWORD. This function is useful mostly for making run-time measurements, especially for performance tuning.

Windows also provides for the creation of up to 16 timers that run for specified intervals, then send a window or callback function the WM_TIMER message. You can create timers with the **SetTimer** function:

```
UINT SetTimer (HWND hwnd, UINT timerid, UINT timeout,
                    TIMERPROC tmprc)
```

If the first parameter to the **SetTimer** function is a valid window handle, the timer will send WM_TIMER messages to that window every **timeout** milliseconds. The second parameter is a nonzero identifier for this timer, and is returned by the function if it is successful. Because timers are a global resource and Windows allows only 16 of them at any one time, the return value should always be checked. The last parameter can specify the address of a function to receive timer messages, in which case the HWND parameter should be null. I won't cover this case, because it's seldom necessary to create a separate timer procedure; the window callback function can handle WM_TIMER timer messages and call a function instead.

A timer created with **SetTimer** is a so-called *periodic* timer because it keeps going off every **timeout** milliseconds. To shut the timer off (and free the resource), you call **KillTimer**.

```
BOOL KillTimer (HWND hwnd, UINT timerid)
```

KillTimer takes the window handle and the ID that was returned by **SetTimer** and returns TRUE if it is successful. To create a one-shot timer, you'd call **SetTimer** to start it, then call **KillTimer** when the WM_TIMER message to stop it was received. The WM_TIMER handler prototype looks like this:

```
OnTimer (HWND hwnd, UINT timerid,
          LPTIMERPROC tmprc)
```

The **timerid** parameter identifies the particular timer. The **tmprc** parameter will be NULL if this timer is associated only with a window.

Here's some code that creates a one-shot timer that waits 1 second after the user presses any key, and then causes the speaker to beep.

```
static void OnKey (MAIN *main, UINT vk, BOOL fDown,
                         int cRepeat, UINT flags)
{
    // Any key starts timer.
    main->timerid = SetTimer (main->hwnd, 1,
                                        1000, NULL);
    if (!main->timerid)
        // Error condition, notify user.
        .
        .
        .
}

static void OnTimer (MAIN *main, UINT timerid,
                          LPTIMERPROC tp)
{
    // Make sure this is our timer.
    if (timerid == 1) {
        KillTimer (main->hwnd, timerid);
    }
    MessageBeep (0);
}
```

This code assumes that there's a UINT in the MAIN structure for the window to hold the timer ID, since it's needed later to kill the timer. The **MessageBeep** function just instructs the speaker of the PC to beep. If a timer can't be created with **SetTimer**, you probably should either put up some critical-error message (if the timer is, in fact, critical to the execution of the game), or gracefully handle the condition as best you can. It's rare for all 16 timers to be in use at any given moment in Windows, but it has happened.

Timer Resolution

The Windows timer functions just covered rely on the PC's built-in timer, which has a period of about 55 milliseconds. This means that measurements made using **GetCurrentTime**—or intervals set with **SetTimer**—are going to be accurate to, *at most,* only 55ms. This is fine for many purposes, especially when the interval is large; say, several seconds. But what's this "at most" part mean? Well, as it turns out, the WM_TIMER message is sent to a callback function via the program's message queue, and only when Windows finds there's no other message in the queue. What this really means is that the **SetTimer** function actually sets the *minimum* time before the WM_TIMER message will be received; it could be longer. It usually isn't *much* longer, but again, these functions are mostly useful for specifying either long events or short ones whose accuracy isn't critical.

What if we want better accuracy than **SetTimer** provides? When Microsoft created the Multimedia Extensions and added them to Windows 3.1, they included a set of functions for working with a high-resolution timer. The high-res timer available through the MME is accurate to within 1 millisecond—considerably better than the system default timer. You can also vary the resolution of the timer to fit your application.

Unfortunately, using the MME's high-res timer as a periodic or one-shot timer is considerably more difficult than using the simple **SetTimer/KillTimer**. You need to create a DLL, put a callback function there, and do a whole lot of other work. It's worth it if your application needs to create very accurate timed events, but if all you're looking for is more accurate *measurement* of time, you can use one simple MME function: **timeGetTime()**. This function is identical to **GetCurrentTime** in that it returns the number of milliseconds since the system was started as a DWORD. The difference is that it's 55 times more accurate.

To use **timeGetTime**, you need to include MMSYSTEM.H, and also link with the MMSYSTEM.LIB import library so that you can have access to the Multimedia Extensions.

The Joystick

Windows provides support for standard analog joysticks through the IBMJOY.DRV driver. This driver is installed with the Control Panel program; it isn't installed automatically when Windows is installed. Some joysticks come with the IBMJOY.DRV driver, but it's on the Windows installation disks as well. If your game program requires IBMJOY.DRV, you'll need either to have the user install it or to have your program install it for the user automatically, as part of the game's installation.

All the functions that deal with the joystick are part of the MME and reside in MMSYSTEM.DLL. Therefore, to use the IBMJOY.DRV driver, you must link MMSYSTEM.LIB with your program (and include MMSYSTEM.H).

Since the joystick is a strictly optional piece of hardware, a game program should first find out if one is connected. If one is, the program should then find out a little about the joystick's capabilities. The call for doing this is **joyGetDevCaps**:

```
UINT joyGetDevCaps (UINT joyid, LPJOYCAPS jc,
                    UINT wsize)
```

The first parameter to this function identifies which joystick you're asking about; the PC is capable of handling up to two standard joysticks. The manifest constants JOYSTICKID1 and JOYSTICKID2 are defined in MMSYSTEM.H. The second parameter is a pointer to a JOYCAPS structure, which is defined as follows:

```
typedef struct joycaps_tag {
    UINT wMid;
    UINT wPid;
```

continued on next page

continued from previous page

```
    char szPname[MAXPNAMELEN];
    UINT wXmin;
    UINT wXmax;
    UINT wYmin;
    UINT wYmax;
    UINT wZmin;
    UINT wZmax;
    UINT wNumButtons;
    UINT wPeriodMin;
    UINT wPeriodMax;
    } JOYCAPS;
```

Figure 4-9 shows a typical Windows joystick.

The designers of the Multimedia Extensions really went nuts with the various capabilities structures that are defined in MMSYSTEM.H. This particular structure has only a few really important members. The **wXmin**, **wXmax**, **wYmin**, **wYmax**, **wZmin**, **wZmax**, and **wNumButtons** members are pretty much what you'd expect: the minimum and maximum values sent by the joystick's three axes (most joysticks support only two, however), and the number of buttons on the joystick. Standard IBM-compatible joysticks should all have minimum and maximum values of 0 and 65,535, respectively, but you should use the values returned in the JOYCAPS structure just to be on the safe side.

The **wPeriodMin** structure member is important. It's used in conjunction with the next joystick function we'll explore, **joySetCapture**:

```
UINT joySetCapture (HWND hwnd, UINT joyid,
                    UINT period, BOOL changed)
```

To understand **joySetCapture**, you must first know something about the way PC joysticks work. The joystick hardware on the PC is a very minimalist implementation and doesn't generate an interrupt when the joystick changes position. As a result, the *only* way to read a joystick's position is to poll the joystick port whenever you need its position. This doesn't fit well within the Windows event model that sends events to a window callback function whenever the state of some input hardware changes. So the **joySetCapture** function creates a timer and polls the joystick for us at the interval specified in **period** (in milliseconds). Naturally, setting this to a very low value (say, 5) creates an unnecessarily fast timer that consumes more resources than necessary. The minimum value for the timer can be as low as the **wPeriodMin** value in the JOYCAPS structure filled in by **joyGetDevCaps**. The minimum value a game actually *needs* is about half the time of the fastest event that requires joystick input in order to perform. For example, if your game is a flight simulator that can display 15 frames per second on the fastest of PCs, then 33ms is the fastest speed you'll ever need to poll the joystick. By the time a frame has been rendered, it's guaranteed that there'll be a new joystick value at your disposal. Since you

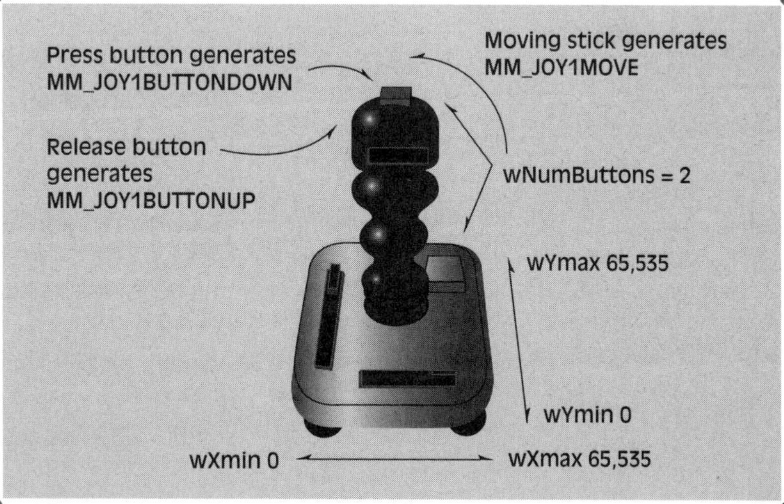

FIGURE 4-9

A typical joystick as defined by Windows

may not readily know this value, try using **wPeriodMin** and see if it actually slows down the game.

The second parameter to **joySetCapture** is the joystick ID, either JOYSTICKID1 or JOYSTICKID2. The last parameter, **changed**, is used in conjunction with **joySetThreshold**, which sets a movement threshold for the joystick:

```
UINT joySetThreshold (UINT joyid, UINT threshold)
```

The value **threshold** is the minimum distance the joystick has to move in order to generate a new message by **joySetCapture**, if the **changed** parameter to **joySetCapture** is TRUE. If it's FALSE, the **threshold** value is ignored.

By supplying a window handle to **e**, MM_JOY* messages are sent to the window at the interval specified. The joystick messages are described in Table 4-11.

Unfortunately, there are no message-cracker macros defined in WINDOWSX.H for the joystick messages, so we'll either have to define them ourselves or just have to use the old method of cracking apart **wParam** and **lParam** into their constituent parts.

For each of these messages, the *x* and *y* coordinates of the joystick are stuffed into the high and low word of **lParam**, respectively (except the *z*-axis messages, which stuff the single value into the low word). **wParam** contains information about the state of the buttons for each of the messages. Some joysticks have up to four buttons, and the settings of **wParam** are a combination of four flag values: JOY_BUTTON1 through

TABLE 4-11
Joystick messages

Message	Meaning
MM_JOY1MOVE	Joystick 1's position has changed.
MM_JOY2MOVE	Joystick 2's position has changed.
MM_JOY1BUTTONDOWN	One of joystick 1's buttons has been pressed.
MM_JOY2BUTTONDOWN	One of joystick 2's buttons has been pressed.
MM_JOY1BUTTONUP	One of joystick 1's buttons has been released.
MM_JOY2BUTTONUP	One of joystick 2's buttons has been released.
MM_JOY1ZMOVE	Joystick 1's z-axis position has changed.
MM_JOY2ZMOVE	Joystick 2's z-axis position has changed.

JOY_BUTTON4. So if you wanted to test if the joystick had buttons 3 and 4 held down while it was moving, the code would look like this:

```
POINT p1;
.
.
.
case MM_JOY1MOVE:
        // Get the position from lParam.
        p = MAKEPOINT (lParam);
        if ((wParam & JOY_BUTTON3) &&
           wParam & JOY_BUTTON4))
            // Both buttons 3 & 4 held down...
            .
            .
            .
```

Since **joySetCapture** uses a timer to poll the joystick for movement, there's a corresponding function that frees the timer and releases capture:

```
UINT joyReleaseCapture (UINT joyid)
```

It's important to call **joyReleaseCapture** when joystick input is finished, or chances are the next time you call **joySetCapture** it will fail. Supposedly, when the window associated with the **joySetCapture** call is destroyed, capture is released, but that's not been my experience. I've found that the best way to handle making sure the joystick is released is to do so just prior to calling **joySetCapture**, like so:

```
joyReleaseCapture (JOYSTICKID1);
if (joySetCapture (main->hwnd, JOYSTICKID1,
                        jc.wMinPeriod, FALSE)
    != JOYERR_NOERROR) {
    // Couldn't get the joystick for some reason.
    .
    .
    .
```

Look in your favorite Windows programming reference for the definitions of the various error conditions returned by **joySetCapture**.

As you can see, joystick input is not all that different from mouse input, except that there are a few additional steps required.

Summary

You've learned how Windows handles input from devices like the keyboard and mouse, and also a lot about how it sends messages for events that are indirectly affected by the mouse and/or keyboard. There's much more here than the old DOS standbys **kbhit** and **mousepos**, isn't there? Still, it's not all that difficult to comprehend once you understand the model.

Now that you understand input, it might be nice to know something about *output* and how to actually put pictures on the screen. In the next chapter, you'll learn all about that complicated beast that controls all output to the screen: the Graphical Device Interface.

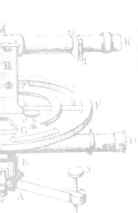

5

Graphical Device Interface

5

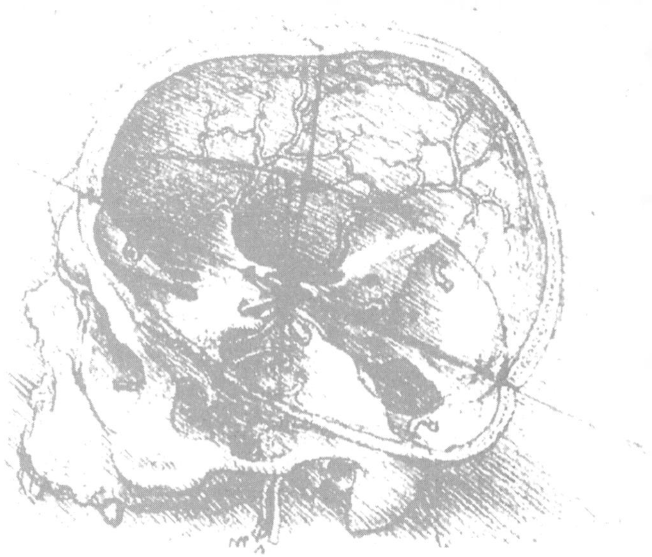

The Graphical Device Interface

The Graphical Device Interface (GDI) is the part of Windows that controls the display of graphical objects on the screen. As you can imagine, this is a large piece of the overall Windows programming pie. You've learned about messages, memory, and input devices. Now it's time to learn how to put those all to use and actually *draw* on the screen.

Understanding and using the Windows GDI could be the most difficult part of Windows programming. The GDI has hundreds of functions and messages, many with complex side effects and interfunction interactions. As if that weren't bad enough, any run-time errors in the GDI usually result in wholly unfriendly crashes of your program and, often as not, Windows itself. Because the GDI is shared among all running applications, one application's error can cause the whole system to lose its balance, bringing everything spiraling to the ground. (Although GDI is an abbreviation for Graphical Device Interface, beginning Windows programmers often find a more suitable set of (frequently expletive) meanings for those letters, usually after the first seven or eight hours of hunting down a "GP Fault in Module GDI.EXE.")

Regardless of its complexities, the GDI is fundamental to all Windows applications, governing every single drawing operation on every device supported by Windows.

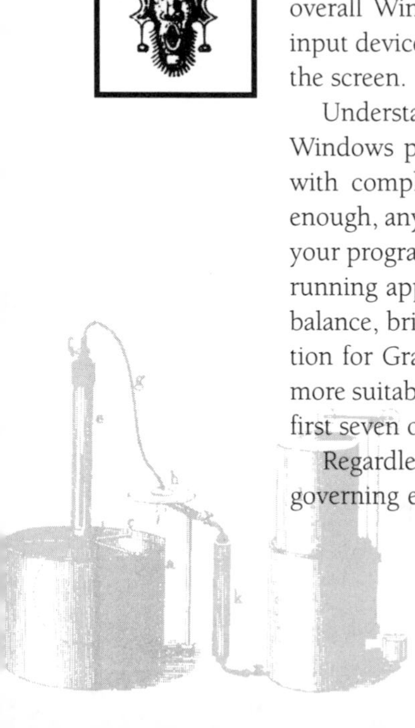

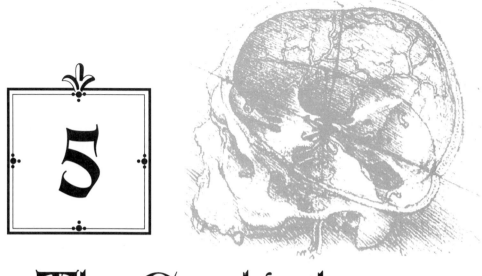

As we will learn, it is through the GDI that Windows achieves its whole method of device independence. To the DOS-based game programmer, the GDI replaces the VGA-specific (and/or chipset-specific) code for putting things on the screen. Besides insulating the programmer from the hardware specifics of the particular display device, it also offers the advantage of being able to support printing with (potentially) very little additional code, although this benefit may not be of particular significance to most games.

In this chapter, we'll learn all we need to know about the GDI: its basic architecture, the calls that make it up, and how we use it to draw graphics on the screen. We'll also learn which nasty traps to avoid, and about certain parts of the GDI that, as game programmers, we can ignore altogether.

GDI Devices

The GDI actually represents four devices, or more properly, two devices and two *metadevices* (see Figure 5-1). Metadevices are things that aren't physical devices but otherwise share similar characteristics with real devices.

The first device and the one probably most important to the game programmer is, naturally, the *display*. A second device (which may or may not be of importance to you) is the *printer*. The two metadevices are the *bitmap* (also very significant to the

FIGURE 5-1

GDI devices

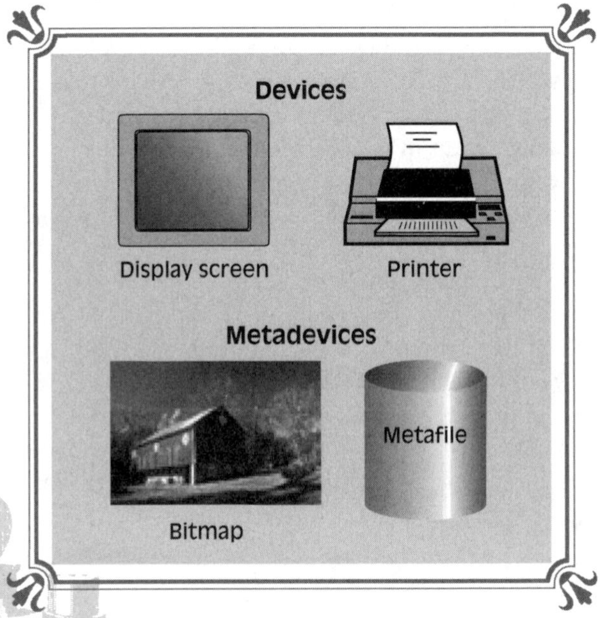

game programmer) and the *metafile*, which is like a tape recording of GDI commands that can be saved and recalled or passed to other applications through the Clipboard. It's unlikely you'll have much to do with metafiles, so we won't spend any time on them in this chapter.

Display Drivers and the GDI

GDI devices are supported through *drivers* that are typically the responsibility of the manufacturer of the particular hardware device in question to create. Although Microsoft graciously provides drivers for a small range of generic devices (the generic, 16-color VGA driver, for example), most Windows users install drivers that have been optimized to some degree by their hardware manufacturers. (When you go out and buy that new Speedmaster TurboMatic LocalBus Ultra+ Super VGA card, it's a given that it will come with a set of drivers for Microsoft Windows for you to install in order to gain access to all its special high-speed characteristics.) This is, after all, one of the primary reasons for writing games for Windows: *You* don't have to write all the drivers for every display card on earth. Because of Windows' incredible market presence, display-card manufacturers are compelled to ship Windows drivers with their hardware or they're out of the market. In fact, because of the architecture of the GDI, the drivers themselves have a huge impact on overall Windows performance and consequently manufacturers spend a lot of time optimizing them. Driver optimization is so important that when magazines review and rate video cards, they often give the date or version number of the display driver because it changes so frequently.

The truth is, the GDI is largely just a thinly disguised set of routines that are implemented almost *directly* in the display driver. This has the advantage of offering the display-driver writer with the most leeway for optimizing performance, although at the cost of a fair amount of complexity. Microsoft, of course, provides plenty of sample code for driver developers to draw from to help ease the load. From these examples, the driver developers can then optimize the parts that their particular hardware does best.

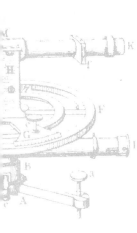

Why is all this important to you, the game developer? For several reasons, actually. First of all, the quality of a particular display driver will directly affect the quality and performance of your game. Some drivers are good at certain GDI operations (text and pattern fills, say) and terrible at others (maybe block transfers and line drawing). The display-card manufacturers have typically been driven by the market for business applications, and have consequently tuned their drivers to perform best under benchmarks specific to these applications (sometimes via highly dubious methods). In fact, it's for precisely these reasons that Microsoft developed WinG: to provide performance across *all* display drivers for operations that games rely on most; notably bit block transfers, or *Blts* (pronounced "blits"). A Blt is a transfer of a section of a bitmap from one area of memory to another, and often from internal memory to the screen. Since most games do lots of Blting, and since Blts have traditionally been the area most ignored by driver manufacturers, this was an eminently reasonable approach.

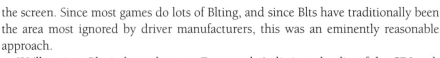

We'll get into Blts in later chapters. For now, let's dig into the dirt of the GDI and, in particular, see how we get stuff on the screen.

Device Contexts

As I mentioned, there are hundreds of calls in the GDI. There are also lots of calls that more or less relate to graphics that aren't strictly part of the GDI. We could specifically define the GDI as all functions that take a handle to a *device context* as their first parameter. What's a device context, you ask? Basically, it's shorthand for a pile of settings for a particular device: 20 settings, to be precise. These settings are used as a default whenever you make a call to a graphics function, avoiding the need for the function to have 20 additional parameters. You can think of the device context as a sort of set of "environment" variables for the GDI. You can change the settings by calling certain GDI functions with the handle of the device context as the first parameter.

Table 5-1 shows the 20 settings (Windows calls them attributes) that are part of a device context (I'll call it a DC, for short), their defaults, and the Windows functions you can use to change them.

A combination of all these settings constitutes a DC. To change the default setting, you call the corresponding function. The new setting will be used for all subsequent GDI operations on that DC. I'll cover each of the 20 attributes in detail later in this chapter.

You now know all the attributes that make up a DC, but where, exactly, does a DC come from? Device contexts come from the device *driver* of the particular device we want to draw on. The device driver and the device context are, as you might guess, highly related concepts. In fact, it's easy to think of the DC as a sort of conduit we use to address the device driver. DCs are referenced by a handle that's returned with a call to a function like **CreateDC**, **GetDC**, or **BeginPaint**, and it is this handle that is passed as the first parameter to all the GDI's drawing functions.

With luck, it's becoming clear how the DC abstracts the physical devices that it represents. Whether drawing a line on a printer, the screen, or into a bitmap, for example, you use the same function (**LineTo**, in this case), but you pass it the handle to the DC associated with that particular device (or metadevice, in the case of the bitmap).

For the moment, let's talk specifically about the display device, since it's the device games deal with most. Just to make things confusing, you may find that some Windows documentation (including Microsoft's) refers to a DC as, interchangeably, either a device context or a *display context*. This rather nasty ambiguity undoubtedly results

TABLE 5-1
The GDI attributes

Attribute	Default	Function
Background color	*white*	`SetBkColor`
Background mode	OPAQUE	`SetBkMode`
Bitmap	*none**	`SelectObject`
Brush	WHITE_BRUSH	`SelectObject`
Brush origin	(0,0)	`SetBrushOrg`
Clipping region	*entire surface*	`SelectClipRgn`
Color palette	DEFAULT_PALETTE	`SelectPalette`
Current pen position	(0,0)	`LineTo`, `MoveTo...`
Drawing mode	R2_COPYPEN	`SetROP2`
Font	SYSTEM_FONT	`SelectObject`
Intercharacter spacing	0	`SetTextCharacter-Extra`
Mapping mode	MM_TEXT	`SetMapMode`
Pen	BLACK_PEN	`SelectObject`
Polygon-filling mode	ALTERNATE	`SetPolyFillMode`
Stretching mode	STRETCH_ANDSCANS	`SetStretchBltMode`
Text color	*black*	`SetTextColor`
Viewport extent	(1,1)	`SetViewportExt`
Viewport origin	(0,0)	`SetViewportOrg`
Window extent	(1,1)	`SetWindowExt`
Window origin	(0,0)	`SetWindowOrg`

from the fact that by far the most oft-used device context is the video display. Indeed, since DCs are associated not only with actual video displays but printers, as well, it's not too much of a stretch to consider a printer some perverse type of display device. Since we won't be talking much about printing, it's perfectly safe to call our DCs display contexts, as well.

Display Contexts

Since DCs come from device drivers, it would be logical for the DC for the screen to come from the display driver. Windows, however, makes it a little easier for you to retrieve a handle to the display driver's DC, since it's the one you deal with the most. In fact, a Windows program doesn't usually draw on the whole screen, but rather into a particular *window* that's floating around somewhere *on* the screen. This is, after all, what makes Windows *Windows*. So to encourage programmers to draw only into their application's window, the GDI provides a couple of calls that return a handle to a particular window's DC. When we use that DC's handle in GDI drawing calls, Windows kindly restricts all our drawing operations to fit within that window's client area.

Figure 5-2 illustrates all the various components of a standard Windows window: the title bar (often referred to as the caption), the system-menu box, the Minimize and Maximize buttons, the border, and the client area. This is a standard, "overlapped" window in Windows parlance.

We can get a handle to a DC quite simply with the following call:

```
HDC hdc;        // Handle to the display (device) context

hdc = GetDC (hwnd);
```

where **hwnd** is the handle to the particular window whose client area we want to draw on.

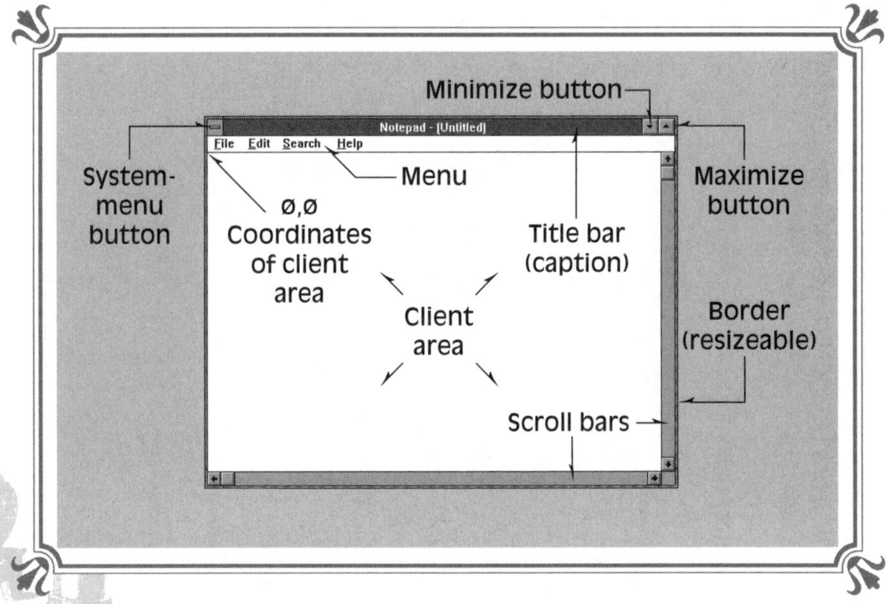

FIGURE 5-2

The parts of a window

The DC is associated with the window's client area, regardless of where the window might be on the screen. As shown in the figure, the client area's origin is the upper left corner of the main part of the window, below the caption bar and menu, and within the border of the window. When we draw using the DC of a given window, Windows kindly offsets all our coordinates and clips the things we draw so that they appear within the client area of the window; we don't have to compute where the window is ourselves.

It's possible to create windows that don't have caption bars, menus, or even borders, and in fact, a game programmer might elect to create a full-screen window without these elements. It's also possible to get a DC for the whole screen, by calling **`GetDC`** with a **`NULL`** parameter. This gives you the DC for the so-called *desktop*, which is the parent window of all windows. You usually won't want to draw on the desktop, because that would result in scribbles over the top of *everything* on the screen (of course, it's possible that might be part of the design of your game).

There are four standard types of DCs you can use, plus the new WinG type. They vary in the way their defaults are handled and how long they remain "in scope." (I'll save discussion of the WinG DC for later, when I talk about bitmaps.) The four standard types of display contexts are:

- Common
- Class
- Private
- Window

The DC type is specified when the window is created and when the window's class is created and registered.

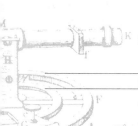

Common Display Contexts

The *common DC* is the default type for all windows, and it has all the default attributes listed in Table 5-1. As its name implies, this is the type most often used. It's also the DC type that is the kindest to Windows in terms of resource use.

Most of the examples of Windows code you'll see floating around the Microsoft universe assume the use of a common display context. For windows that use a common DC, you get a handle to the DC using **`GetDC`** or **`BeginPaint`**. After you scribble around in the window, you must release the DC back to the system by using either **`ReleaseDC`** or **`EndPaint`**.

When you ask for a common DC with **`GetDC`** or **`BeginPaint`**, the DC is actually retrieved from a small cache of DCs that Windows reserves. Because there are five DCs in this cache, if a common DC isn't released back to the system by **`ReleaseDC`** or **`EndPaint`**, very unfortunate things start to happen to your application (and soon thereafter, to Windows itself). One of the most common causes of GDI problems for beginning Windows programmers is failure to release DCs after use. (Why the cache of common DCs is fixed at five is only one of the many mysteries of Windows generally attributable to its history of running on memory-scarce machines.)

Another unfortunate property of common DCs is that they must be released back to the system in the same default state in which you got them. This means that if you've changed the settings by selecting new fonts, brushes, and so on, you have to change them back to the defaults before releasing the DC. If you don't, again, very bad things will happen—often not until your application has been running for a while.

Class Display Contexts

In Chapter 2, we learned that all windows are created from a specific class that has been registered with RegisterClass. A *class display context,* as you might guess, has *one* DC that's shared by all windows of that particular class. Like the common display context, the class display context has the defaults listed in Table 5-1 when Windows first retrieves the DC.

You specify that you want a class DC by using the CS_CLASSDC style flag when you declare the window class. A class display context is not part of the display-context cache. Instead, Windows specifically allocates a DC for the sole use of the window class.

As with the common display context, a handle to a class DC is retrieved with **GetDC** or **BeginPaint**, but it does *not* have to be released after use (the **ReleaseDC** and **EndPaint** functions have no effect and, in fact, are optional). If your program creates only one window of this class (this is probably the most common situation for game programs), then you can save the DC and reuse it whenever you need to draw on the window.

There are a couple of side effects of having a class display context—like goofiness if you change the mapping mode and have a special background pattern defined—but if you use brushes carefully, you can usually ignore these minor irritations.

Private Display Contexts

The *private display context* is one that's attached to a specific window, not all windows of a given class. Windows allocates a separate DC for each window (instance) of the class; like the class DC, the private DC doesn't come from the common DC cache. If you create only one window of a specified class, there's really no difference between the private DC type and the class DC type.

You specify the private DC type by using the CS_OWNDC style flag when creating the window class. It's a little humorous to note the caution that often accompanies the description of private display contexts in Microsoft's documentation: "A private display context should be used with discretion because each display context uses 800 bytes of memory." Lest you think 800 bytes is trivial overhead, remember that these 800 bytes come from the GDI's heap, which is a total of 64K. Nonetheless, unless you're creating a great many windows from a class declared with CS_OWNDC, it's very little memory indeed.

Window Display Contexts

A *window display context* is a special case that's very similar to the common DC type, except that *(a)* you get it using **GetWindowDC** and *(b)* its coordinates (and display "surface") are that of the entire *window*, not just the client area. This allows you to scribble around on the borders, caption bar, and all the parts of the window, if you want. This special DC was designed as a sort of escape mechanism so that you can make special windows that have custom borders and things that differ from "standard issue" window elements.

Like a common DC, a window DC comes from the internal cache of five, and must be released with **ReleaseDC** or **EndPaint**. In general, the use of window DCs is discouraged, especially since you can always create a window without captions, borders, and so on and treat it any way you like.

Which DC Type Is Right for Games?

Simply put, the private DC type is probably the most convenient for game programmers to use. You can retrieve it with **GetDC** when the window is created and store it off for use in all the places that draw on the given window. If your game primarily uses one main window and you're used to managing the whole screen under DOS, using a private DC will feel the most familiar.

Drawing with the Display Context

Now that you know how to get a DC, let's see how you start putting stuff on the screen with one. We'll use an example that's independent of the type of DC we want to use, which is generally good practice anyway. Never one to believe there's such a thing as a too-trivial example, I'll create a function that draws a diagonal line and a line of text in the client area of our window. The basic procedure goes something like this:

- Get a handle to the device context for the window.
- Call whatever GDI drawing functions you want to use, passing the handle to each.
- Release the DC.

Here's the code:

```
void DrawStuff (HWND hwnd)
{
        char buf[] = "Hello, Windows.";
        // Get the device context for this window.
        HDC hdc = GetDC (hwnd);

        // Draw a line from 100,100 to 200,200.
        MoveTo (hdc, 100, 100);
        LineTo (hdc, 200, 200);

        // Display our text at the end of that line
        // using the default font.
        TextOut (hdc, 200, 200, buf, lstrlen(buf));

        // Release the DC.
        ReleaseDC (hwnd, hdc);
}
```

Simple enough. The output looks something like that shown in Figure 5-3.

And so goes drawing in our window with the GDI. Our line is created with the default pen (BLACK_PEN), which has a width of 1 pixel. Note that the starting position of text in Windows is the upper left corner of the text box; in our example, this is right at the end of the line we drew (at coordinates 200,200). The text is drawn in the default color (black) and in the default drawing mode, which is OPAQUE (though it's hard to tell in this simple example).

Straightforward enough, right? Well, maybe. If there's any one thing about the GDI that is hard for most new programmers to understand, it's the fact that GDI drawing routines *don't draw the last coordinate of the object specified*. For example, the line we just drew supposedly went from 100,100 to 200,200. However, the GDI didn't actually draw the pixel at 200,200: It updated the current position, but left that pixel alone. If we drew another line from 200,200 to, say, 300,100, the pixel at 200,200

FIGURE 5-3

Drawing with a DC

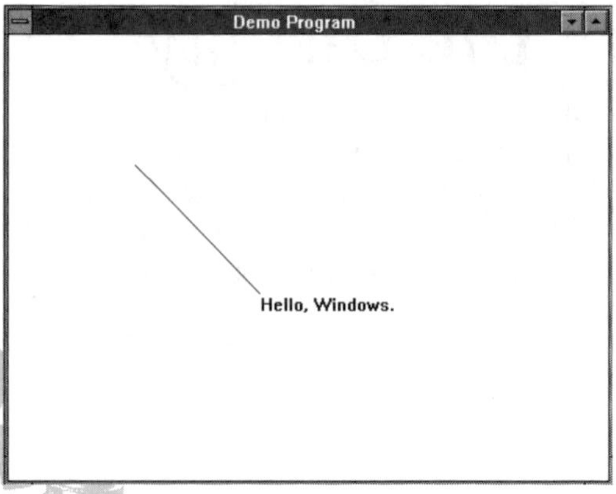

would be filled by the starting point of the line, but again, 300,100 would not be drawn.

The **Rectangle** function has a similar attitude: It considers the lower right corner of the rectangle specified to be the *outside edge* of the rectangle. For example, guess what pixel coordinates the rectangle drawn by this code will occupy (assuming the current pen is 1 pixel wide):

```
RECT r;
r.left   = 0;
r.top    = 0;
r.right  = 100;
r.bottom = 100;
Rectangle (hdc, r.left, r.top, r.right, r.bottom);
```

You might think that the rectangle would extend from 0,0 to 100,100. Wrong! The pixel coordinates that have the pen color in them will go from 0,0 to 99,99. In other words, the equivalent function using **LineTo** and **MoveTo** would look like this:

```
MoveTo (hdc, r.left, r.top);
LineTo (hdc, r.right-1, r.top);
LineTo (hdc, r.right-1, r.bottom-1);
LineTo (hdc, r.left, r.bottom-1);
LineTo (hdc, r.left, r.top);
```

Another way of putting it is that the coordinates supplied to the **Rectangle** function specify the rectangle's starting point and *extents,* not the starting and ending *coordinates*. You can think of the extents as the *count* of the pixels, whereas coordinates start at 0,0.

It would be nice if we could just go on from here, happily drawing game graphics into our window, blissfully ignorant of the rest of Windows programming. Ah, if only life under Windows were so simple. But our game program, monumental as it may be, is still only one lowly application floating in a sea of applications, each of which must behave according to the same set of rules in order to stay afloat—indeed, in order for *all* to stay afloat.

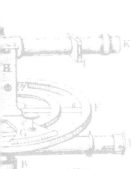

So at this point we'll take some time out to talk about how Windows tells us *when* to update our DCs and what *parts* of a given window need updating.

Repainting and the WM_PAINT Message

Previously, we learned that whenever a window changes position or size, all the windows that intersect it need to be updated. For example, when a window that has been partially obscured by another window gets popped to the top, the previously covered part of that window needs *repainting,* in Windows parlance. Windows keeps good track of exactly what portion of any given window is in need of updating, and notifies that window via the WM_PAINT message.

WM_PAINT handling is often a central part of any program's display system. In our usual WINDOWSX.H programming style, we'll build a handler for the WM_PAINT message. In our window's callback function, we add WM_PAINT to the list of messages we handle, like so:

```
LRESULT CALLBACK _export
OurWindow(HWND hwnd, UINT msg, WPARAM wParam,
            LPARAM lParam)
{
        // Switch on the given message, call the handler.
        switch (msg){
                HANDLE_MSG (hwnd, WM_CREATE, OnCreate);
                HANDLE_MSG (hwnd, WM_COMMAND,OnCommand);
                ...
                HANDLE_MSG (hwnd, WM_PAINT, OnPaint);
                ...
        // If we don't handle the message, pass it
        // on to DefWindowProc.
        default:
                return
                DefWindowProc (hwnd, msg, wParam, lParam);
        }
}
```

The first thing a WM_PAINT handler must do is call **BeginPaint**. **BeginPaint** takes a handle to the window and the address of a PAINTSTRUCT structure that Windows fills with information about the area of the window that needs painting, and it returns a handle to the DC (I'll call such handles HDCs from here out). Once we have the HDC, the handler can make any GDI calls it needs in order to paint on the client area of the window and update it. The PAINTSTRUCT is defined in WINDOWS.H like this:

```
/* BeginPaint() return structure */
typedef struct tagPAINTSTRUCT
{
        HDC     hdc;
        BOOL    fErase;
        RECT    rcPaint;
        BOOL    fRestore;
        BOOL    fIncUpdate;
        BYTE    rgbReserved[16];
} PAINTSTRUCT;
```

The **hdc** member is the same thing that **BeginPaint** returns. The **fErase** flag tells our program whether we should redraw the background; this flag is set only if our window was created from a class with no background brush defined (we'll learn more about brushes later). The **rcPaint** member is a rectangle that tells us exactly what part of the window needs repainting. The other three members of the structure are reserved for internal use by Windows.

After calling **BeginPaint** and doing the necessary drawing on the window, you must call **EndPaint** to finish handling the WM_PAINT message.

Here are the steps required for handling the update of a window via the WM_PAINT message:

- Create an HDC and a PAINTSTRUCT.
- Call **BeginPaint** with the address of the PAINTSTRUCT, and assign what it returns to the HDC.
- Use the HDC to draw everything needed in order to update the window using GDI functions.
- Release the HDC with **EndPaint**.

We can turn our simple drawing example into a WM_PAINT handler easily:

```
void OnPaint(HWND hwnd)
{
        // Declare a PAINTSTRUCT, text buffer, and HDC.
        PAINTSTRUCT ps;
        char buf[] = "Hello, World.";
        HDC hdc;

        // Call BeginPaint and assign the HDC.
        hdc = BeginPaint (hwnd, &ps);

        // Draw a line from 100,100 to 200,200.
        MoveTo (hdc, 100, 100);
        LineTo (hdc, 200, 200);

        // Put up some text at the end of that line,
        // using the default font.
        TextOut (hdc, 200, 200, buf, lstrlen(buf));

        // Release the DC back to Windows with EndPaint.
        EndPaint(hwnd, &ps);
}
```

Now, whenever our window needs updating, Windows will send a WM_PAINT message to our window's callback function, and our window will update itself by painting the diagonal line and line of text.

Note that the PAINTSTRUCT we passed to **BeginPaint** isn't really used within our function. In particular, we ignore the **rcPaint** RECT element of the structure that contains the rectangle of the specific area of the window that needs repainting; we just go ahead and update the whole thing, even if only the tiniest corner of our window was the part that had been obstructed. You could imagine cases where this might be inefficient—when our window consumes all or most of the screen and yet only a tiny portion is obscured, we end up painting the whole screen. In practice, this hardly makes much difference, especially with games. With games, quite often we're updating the whole window anyway, so the extra logic required to update just a portion isn't worth the effort. However, because WM_PAINT handling is so central to the way Windows works, I'll talk a little more about its innards; in particular, the concept of the invalid rectangle.

Invalid Rectangles

Whenever a Windows window changes position on the screen, it reveals something—either the background or other windows—behind it. The portion being revealed needs updating, and that portion of the window or windows is called the *invalid rectangle*. A simple-minded and inefficient algorithm (the so-called "Painter's Algorithm") could simply ask every window in the system to update itself when any one window changes. A better algorithm would compute the rectangle (provided, of course, that all windows are rectangles, which, in the case of Windows, is true) being revealed, and tell every window that intersects it to update that particular rectangular portion of itself. This is the concept behind the invalid rectangle.

Windows has a complete set of functions for adding and subtracting rectangles to and from the list of invalid rectangles to be updated at the next WM_PAINT message. By the time a window receives a WM_PAINT message, all the rectangles are collected into the minimum rectangle that contains them all, much in the same way a "dirty rectangle" animation package works.

It turns out the invalid rectangle concept probably has little relevance to game programmers, because of the frequency of screen updates in games. If your game is running in a window that covers the whole screen, the only other time that you'll get a WM_PAINT message is when the user switches to another application, then back to yours. You can just repaint the whole screen (window) in that instance. Doesn't it feel good to know that there's one more whole Windows complex that you don't need to care about?

Device-Context Attributes

Now that we've done some basic drawing on our window using a device (display) context, let's look into some of the components of the DC, including those 20 attributes.

Color

The concept of color in Windows is based on the RGB model, as it is in virtually all display cards used in PCs. The Windows color model is quite flexible, and is able to support both *palettized* and *true-color* devices easily. I'll talk a little about each here; even if you're completely familiar with the difference between true-color and palettized devices, this is a good opportunity to review this topic. The way Windows handles color isn't quite what a DOS-based game programmer is used to.

True-Color Devices

A true-color device is one that supports separate, discrete values for the red, green, and blue components of a pixel, usually allowing 8 bits of color resolution per component. This is also called *24-bit color,* because it allows a single pixel to have one of 16.7 million different colors (2^{24}), which is considerably more than the eye can distinguish (it's also more than any display device can display). With a true-color display, one screen at 640x480 resolution consumes 921,600 bytes of memory (640 * 480 * 3), because each pixel uses 3 bytes to store.

True-color devices are used mainly in publishing and photo-editing applications, where color resolution (often called color *depth*) is critical to achieving a high-quality output. Because a single screen consumes so much memory, most game programmers don't use displays (or display modes) that support true-color.

Palettized Devices

A palettized display doesn't store the actual RGB color values at every pixel, but rather stores a number that is an index into a *color table* that defines the actual RGB color. Color tables are often also called lookup tables, especially if you're from IBM, or palettes, referring to the artist's palette that holds a limited number of colors.

Typical palettized devices store 4 or 8 bits per pixel, for a total of 16 or 256 independent colors. Although a palettized device can display relatively few colors, the colors are chosen from a set that is determined by the overall size of the palette, which often supports color resolutions up to 24 bits. For example, the standard VGA display has a mode that supports 256 colors, and the colors can be chosen from a palette that uses 6 bits per RGB channel. So the 256 colors are chosen from a palette of 262,144 colors ($2^{6 * 3}$). Because each pixel occupies only 1 byte, an 8-bit display at 640x480 resolution consumes only 307,200 bytes of memory.

Windows Display Cards and Color Resolution

When you install and configure Windows, you must choose a resolution and color depth for your display. Unfortunately, in current versions of Windows, this resolution and color depth is fixed for the duration of your Windows session. To change resolution or color depth, you must run the SETUP program, choose another display driver for your card, and restart Windows. To the DOS-based game programmer, this may seem a little inflexible—after all, under DOS you can program the display card's chipset directly, changing video modes to your heart's content. But remember, Windows supports multiple applications at any one time, and you can imagine that it could be seriously annoying to have your display resolution switched out from underneath you by some wayward game.

Having said that, not being able to switch resolutions on the fly isn't usually much of a limitation for game programs under Windows. Every Super VGA card sold on the market today supports 256 colors at resolutions usually up to 1024x768. The WinG extensions assume the use of an 8-bit (256-color) palettized display, and most games are written for 8-bit modes of the VGA, as well. I'll talk more about palettized devices in later chapters.

15- and 16-Bit Color

I'd like to take a brief turn down a side road on this trip through the wonders of Windows color management. In recent years, most Super VGA cards have offered some new color modes, the so-called *high-color* modes. This designation is used to distinguish them from true-color cards, because they typically use either 15 or 16 bits of color depth rather than 24. So instead of 16.7 million colors, it's possible to display 32,768 or 65,536 discrete colors in high-color mode. This has the advantage of having one-third fewer calories—I mean *bytes*—than true-color, while still supporting enough colors to display startlingly realistic images. Great looking, less filling (sorry). What it allows display-card manufacturers to do is support a resolution of 800x600 in 64K colors (65,536) and do it with only 1 MB of memory on the card (800 * 600 * 2 = 960,000 bytes).

The display driver actually tells Windows that the display is a true-color (paletteless) device, then just lops 3 bits off each channel of the actual 24-bit color Windows tells it to display on the screen (the 16-bit cards typically lop only 2 bits off the blue channel, because blue generally needs more dynamic range). To the programmer, a VGA card running in this mode looks like a true-color device. I mention this because virtually all VGAs now on the market support high-color modes, and the game programmer must be aware of this fact, because it's not possible to set the palette on a device running in this mode. Also, it's slower to refresh a screen at a given resolution in high-color mode than it is in 8-bit mode; there are twice as many bits to move.

Back to Windows Color

The predefined **COLORREF** data type is used for specifying a color, which is defined in WINDOWS.H as a **DWORD**, or 32-bit value. A **COLORREF** contains the red, green, and blue components of a specified color in the 3 lowest-order bytes of the **DWORD**.

The high-order byte specifies whether the values are to be interpreted as an actual RGB color, as an RGB color relative to the current palette, or as an index into the current palette. (See Figure 5-4.) I cover palette-relative colors later, in Chapter 8.

There are many GDI functions that take a **COLORREF** as a parameter. For example, to set the current background color for the DC, you call:

```
SetBkColor (HDC hdc, COLORREF color);
```

Likewise, to set the current text color, the call is:

```
SetTextColor (HDC hdc, COLORREF color);
```

Windows provides several macros for creating a color with a **COLORREF**, including the ever-popular **RGB(r,g,b)**, which creates a **DWORD** with the **r**, **g**, and **b** values cast into the lower 3 bytes. Other popular macros are **PALETTEINDEX(index)**, which creates a **COLORREF** that indicates a specific palette index color, and **PALETTERGB(r,g,b)**, which tells Windows to find a palette index that is closest to the given RGB color (I'll talk about palettes in Chapter 8).

Here are three ways to specify the same color to Windows using a **COLORREF**:

```
COLORREF red;
// Absolute red
red = RGB(255, 0, 0);
// The palette entry closest to absolute red
red = PALETTERGB(255, 0, 0);
// Palette index 10 (red in this palette)
red = PALETTEINDEX(10);
```

In this example, it's assumed that the actual display device is a palettized device, and that index 10 of the current palette is mapped to full red.

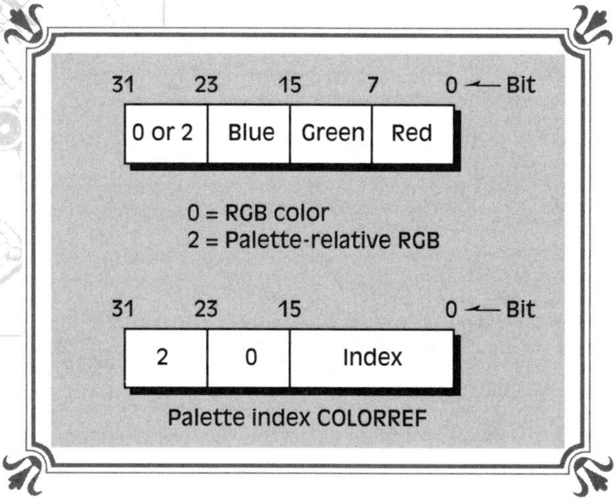

FIGURE 5-4

COLORREF byte layout

FIGURE 5-5

The color-scheme selector

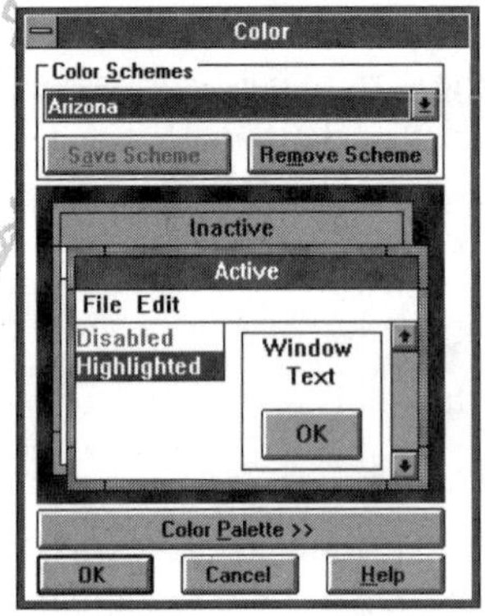

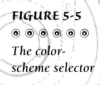

Windows also uses several system-defined colors for various standard interface elements, like button faces or the caption part of an active window. The user customizes these colors in the Control Panel application via the Color selection. Figure 5-5 shows the color-scheme selector from Control Panel.

Windows manages 19 system colors. You can retrieve a **COLORREF** for any one of these 19 colors via

```
GetSysColor (index);
```

where **index** is one of the values shown in Table 5-2.

You can also use **COLORREF**s when creating brushes and pens, our next subject.

Pens

Certain game programs rely a lot on line drawing. For example, the classic vector arcade games, like Space Invaders and Tank, were essentially line-drawing games. In the Windows GDI, a *pen* is a GDI *object* that is used for drawing lines. Every DC has one—and only one—pen defined for it at any given time.

Like all GDI objects, pens must be *selected into* a DC to make them current. This is in contrast to something like the background color, which you set simply through a function call. I'll cover selection in a moment; for now, let's concentrate on how pens work.

You create a pen with

```
CreatePen (int style, int width, COLORREF color)
```

which returns a handle to a pen, or **HPEN**. The possible values for the **style** parameter are listed in Table 5-3.

The **width** parameter defines the width in *logical units* of the pen. Logical units are turned into physical, or *device,* units according to the current mapping mode of the DC; we'll get into mapping modes in a moment.

TABLE 5-2

System colors

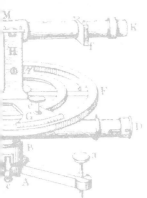

Value	Meaning
COLOR_ACTIVEBORDER	The active window border.
COLOR_ACTIVECAPTION	The active window caption.
COLOR_APPWORKSPACE	The background color of Multiple Document Interface (MDI) applications.
COLOR_BACKGROUND	The desktop.
COLOR_BTNFACE	The face shading on push buttons.
COLOR_BTNHIGHLIGHT	Selected button in a control.
COLOR_BTNSHADOW	The edge shading on push buttons.
COLOR_BTNTEXT	The text on push buttons.
COLOR_CAPTIONTEXT	The text in caption, size box, and scrollbar arrow box.
COLOR_GRAYTEXT	Grayed (disabled) text. This color is set to 0 if the current display driver does not support a solid gray color.
COLOR_HIGHLIGHT	Highlights selected item in a control.
COLOR_HIGHLIGHTTEXT	The text of the item selected in a control.
COLOR_INACTIVEBORDER	The inactive window's border.
COLOR_INACTIVECAPTION	The inactive window's caption.
COLOR_INACTIVECAPTIONTEXT	Color of text in an inactive title.
COLOR_MENU	The menu background.
COLOR_MENUTEXT	The text in menus.
COLOR_SCROLLBAR	The scrollbar's gray area.
COLOR_WINDOW	The window's background.
COLOR_WINDOWFRAME	The window's frame.
COLOR_WINDOWTEXT	The text in windows.

TABLE 5-3

Values for the `style` *parameter of* `CreatePen`

Value	Meaning
PS_SOLID	Creates a solid pen.
PS_DASH	Creates a dashed pen (valid only when **`width`** is 1).
PS_DOT	Creates a dotted pen (valid only when **`width`** is 1).
PS_DASHDOT	Creates a pen with alternating dashes and dots (valid only when **`width`** is 1).
PS_DASHDOTDOT	Creates a pen with alternating dashes and double dots (valid only when **`width`** is 1).
PS_NULL	Creates a null pen.
PS_INSIDEFRAME	Creates a pen that draws a line inside the frame of closed shapes produced by GDI output functions that specify a bounding rectangle (for example, the **`Ellipse`**, **`Rectangle`**, **`RoundRect`**, **`Pie`**, and **`Chord`** functions). When this style is used with GDI output functions that do not specify a bounding rectangle (for example, the **`LineTo`** function), the drawing area of the pen is not limited by a frame.

TABLE 5-4

Pen functions

Function	Description
LineTo	Draws a line from the current position to the position specified. The last pixel of the line is not drawn.
Polyline	Draws a set of line segments.
Arc	Draws an arc.

The **`color`** parameter is a **`COLORREF`** that defines the color for the pen. Yes, it's true: Every time you want to draw a line in a different color, you need to create a different pen for it.

Pens are used in virtually every GDI call that draws a line, either directly or indirectly. Table 5-4 lists GDI drawing functions that use the current pen.

FIGURE 5-6

Pen styles

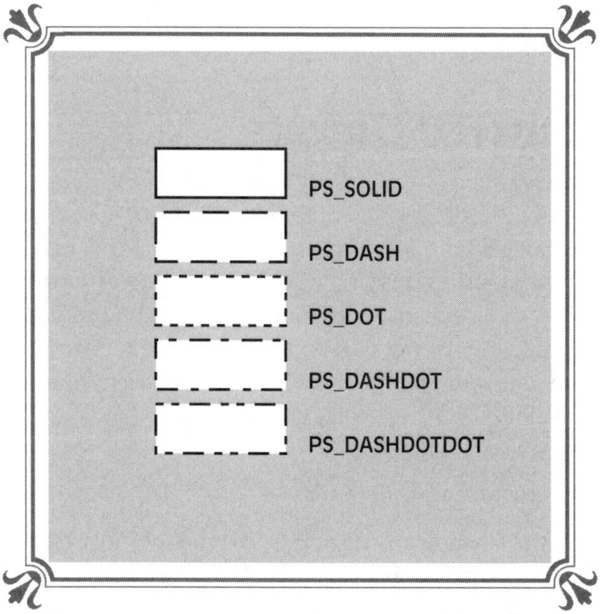

Figure 5-6 shows examples of the different pen styles.

You can also create pens with **CreatePenIndirect**—which takes a pointer to a LOGPEN structure that contains elements for style, width, and color—instead of passing the parameters to **CreatePen** directly.

Later, we'll talk about the performance of the Windows GDI line-drawing routines and try to determine when you should and shouldn't use them in games.

GDI Objects

Now that you know how to create your first GDI object, the pen, let's learn how GDI objects work in general. A *GDI object* is an internal Windows data structure that's created with a call to the appropriate **Create** function, like the previously illustrated **CreatePen**. GDI objects are referenced by handles, which have object-specific types in WINDOWS.H, like **HPEN**, **HBRUSH**, **HBITMAP**, and so on. There are five kinds of GDI objects that you can create: pens, brushes, fonts, regions, and bitmaps.

Just creating a GDI object doesn't actually let you use it on the DC. To make a GDI object current for a given DC, you must select it into the DC with:

```
SelectObject (HDC hdc, HGDIOBJ object);
```

HGDIOBJ is a general-purpose object handle cast; the **SelectObject** function is used for selecting all five types of objects. The **SelectObject** function returns an

HGDIOBJ that is a handle to the object being replaced, since only one object of a given type can be active in a DC at one time.

Deleting GDI Objects

Although GDI objects are dynamically allocated by the various **Create** functions, in Windows 3.1 they're all allocated from the precious GDI heap, which is both limited and shared among all running applications. Once the GDI heap has been exceeded, further **Create** calls stop creating objects and the display starts looking rather...shall we say, *plain* all of a sudden. Sadly, there's nothing you can do about this condition except to limit the number of GDI objects you create to the absolute minimum necessary to carry out your graphics functions, and to delete all unreferenced objects as quickly as possible.

You delete GDI objects with

```
DeleteObject (HGDIOBJ object);
```

where **object** is a handle to one of the five types of GDI objects.

Keep in mind one very important caution when using **DeleteObject**: *Never* delete an object that is currently selected into a DC. If you do, you can expect typical GDI-error results—very bad things happen, often resulting in a crash of your (or some other) program. Because of this, GDI "leaks"—an accumulation of orphaned GDI objects—are a common problem among novice (and expert!) GDI programmers.

Deselecting GDI Objects

How do you deselect a GDI object that you created from a DC? You select in the original object whose handle was given to you by the initial call to **SelectObject**. Thus, the steps for drawing a red rectangle would look something like this:

- Create a red pen object.
- Select it into the DC, saving the old pen.
- Draw the rectangle.
- Select the old pen back into the DC.
- Delete the red pen object.

In code, our example would look like this:

```
HPEN mypen, oldpen;

// Create a red pen.
mypen = CreatePen (PS_SOLID, 1, RGB(255, 0, 0));

// Select it into the DC.
oldpen = SelectObject (hdc, mypen);
```

```
// Draw a rectangle with this pen.
Rectangle (hdc, 10, 10, 100, 100);

// Select the old pen back into the DC.
SelectObject (hdc, oldpen);

// Now we can delete it.
DeleteObject (mypen);
```

Selecting a GDI object into the DC is like a carpenter selecting a tool from a drawerful and putting it into a tool belt. There can be only one hammer in the carpenter's belt at a time, but it's one chosen from a large selection of hammers in the drawer (see Figure 5-7).

GDI Objects, Memory, and Performance

There is a question of when to create and delete GDI objects based on performance and resource use. Unfortunately, there aren't any simple answers to the equation—it all depends on how many objects you need to create and how often you need to use them. Certainly, the slowest way to use GDI objects is to create, select, use, and then delete them each time you want to draw something. It is, however, the most resource-friendly way, since you'll have only one new GDI object created at a time. It's difficult to say what the best trade-off is, but if you run out of GDI heap space because you've

FIGURE 5-7

GDI objects and selection

created too many objects, the performance increase isn't going to do much for you. In Windows 3.1, the GDI heap space is fixed at 64K and it's not unusual for Windows itself to take upward of 40 percent of that space. GDI objects vary in size, with pens taking 1k and fonts taking 5k. You can use these figures to roughly budget your resource usage.

Because GDI-resource management has a strong effect on how many applications you can run at once, Windows users generally *hate* programs that are resource hogs. Some programs are worse than others; Microsoft Word 6.0, for example, is pretty demanding on system resources. I think that it's quite reasonable for a game program to be demanding on GDI resources, because game programs are typically demanding on every other part of the machine, and it's not likely your users will want to have many of these running at once.

Because there are certain objects that are pretty common to many programs, Windows provides them in a set of so-called *stock* objects; using them doesn't affect the GDI heap space. You get a handle to a stock object with the call:

```
GetStockObject (index);
```

Table 5-5 lists the possible values of **index**.

So, for example, to select a white pen into a given device context, you'd use:

```
HPEN hOldPen;
hOldPen = SelectObject (hdc, GetStockObject (WHITE_PEN));
```

It follows that you should *never* delete a stock object—for all but the most egregious games, I suppose…

Brushes

A *brush* is a GDI object that defines the color and pattern used for solid filled areas. As with the pen, there is only one current brush in a DC at any given time. It is created with one of several **Create** calls that specify its color and pattern. Since it is a GDI object, like the current pen, you select it into a DC to use it and must select it out of the DC (by restoring the original brush) before the DC is released and before the object is deleted.

Here are all the functions that create brushes:

```
CreateBrushIndirect (LOGPEN *logpen);
CreateHatchBrush (int style, COLORREF color);
CreatePatternBrush (HBITMAP bitmap);
CreateSolidBrush (COLORREF color);
```

The first function, **CreateBrushIndirect**, uses the address of a LOGPEN structure that holds the information about the style, color, and pattern for the brush. A LOGPEN structure looks like this:

```
typedef struct tagLOGPEN {
        UINT            lbStyle;                // Brush style
        COLORREF        lbColor;                // Brush color
        int             lbHatch;                // Hatching info
} LOGPEN;
```

TABLE 5-5

Stock objects

Value	Meaning
BLACK_BRUSH	Black brush.
DKGRAY_BRUSH	Dark gray brush.
GRAY_BRUSH	Gray brush.
HOLLOW_BRUSH	Hollow brush.
LTGRAY_BRUSH	Light gray brush.
NULL_BRUSH	Null brush.
WHITE_BRUSH	White brush.
BLACK_PEN	Black pen.
NULL_PEN	Null pen.
WHITE_PEN	White pen.
ANSI_FIXED_FONT	ANSI fixed system font.
ANSI_VAR_FONT	ANSI variable system font.
DEVICE_DEFAULT_FONT	Device-dependent font.
OEM_FIXED_FONT	OEM-dependent fixed font.
SYSTEM_FONT	The system font. By default, Windows uses the system font to draw menus, dialog box controls, and other text. In Windows 3.0 and later, the system font is a proportional-width font; earlier versions of Windows use a fixed-width system font.
SYSTEM_FIXED_FONT	The fixed-width system font used in versions of Windows earlier than 3.0. This stock object is available for compatibility purposes.
DEFAULT_PALETTE	Default color palette. This palette consists of the 20 static colors always present in the system palette for matching colors in the logical palettes of background windows.

TABLE 5-6 `lbStyle` *settings*

Value	Meaning
BS_DIBPATTERN	Specifies a pattern brush defined by a device-independent bitmap (DIB) specification.
BS_HATCHED	Specifies a hatched brush.
BS_HOLLOW	Specifies a hollow brush.
BS_PATTERN	Specifies a pattern brush defined by a memory bitmap.
BS_SOLID	Specifies a solid brush.

TABLE 5-7 `lbHatch` *values*

Value	Meaning
HS_BDIAGONAL	45-degree upward hatch (left to right)
HS_CROSS	Horizontal and vertical crosshatch
HS_DIAGCROSS	45-degree crosshatch
HS_FDIAGONAL	45-degree downward hatch (left to right)
HS_HORIZONTAL	Horizontal hatch
HS_VERTICAL	Vertical hatch

Table 5-6 lists the possible values for the **`lbStyle`** member of the structure.

As you can see, brushes can have very complex patterns. The BS_DIBPATTERN style of brush can actually use a bitmap to define its pattern; the bitmap is tiled across the surface being painted by the brush. Using the BS_HATCHED style, you specify the hatch pattern with the **`lbHatch`** member of the structure. Table 5-7 lists the possible values for **`lbHatch`**.

The simplest brush pattern is the solid brush. This is, of course, a brush that "paints" filled areas using a solid color, like a real paint brush would. You can create a solid brush by setting the **`lbStyle`** member to BS_SOLID and the **`lbColor`** member to the COLORREF of the color you want, ignoring the **`lbHatch`** member in this case. Of course, it's easier just to use **`CreateSolidBrush`**, if that's what you want to do.

Let's create a rectangle with a red outline (pen) and a filled green, crosshatched interior:

```
HPEN mypen, oldpen;
HBRUSH mybrush, oldbrush;
LOGBRUSH lb;

// Create a red pen.
mypen = CreatePen (PS_SOLID, 1, RGB(255, 0, 0));
// Set up the LOGBRUSH structure.
lb.lbStyle = BS_HATCHED;
lb.lbColor = RGB(0, 255, 0);
lb.lbHatch = HS_CROSS;
// Create the brush.
mybrush = CreateBrushIndirect (&lb);

// Select them into the DC.
oldpen = SelectObject (hdc, mypen);
oldbrush = SelectObject (hdc, mybrush);

// Draw a rectangle with this pen and brush.
Rectangle (hdc, 10, 10, 100, 100);

// Select the old ones back into the DC.
SelectObject (hdc, oldpen);
SelectObject (hdc, oldbrush);

// Now we can delete them.
DeleteObject (mypen);
DeleteObject (mybrush);
```

Figure 5-8 shows what the output looks like. Satisfying, no?

As I mentioned earlier, all functions that create solid, filled objects use the current brush. The outline of the object is drawn in the current pen. These functions are listed in Table 5-8.

There's one other important reason to use a brush: to paint the *background* of a window. You'll recall (from Chapter 2) that when we declare a new window class, one of the WNDCLASS structure members is **hbrBackground**. This defines the brush used for redrawing the background of the window. If this member is NULL, then you're responsible for redrawing the background—when Windows sends you a

FIGURE 5-8

Crosshatched brush

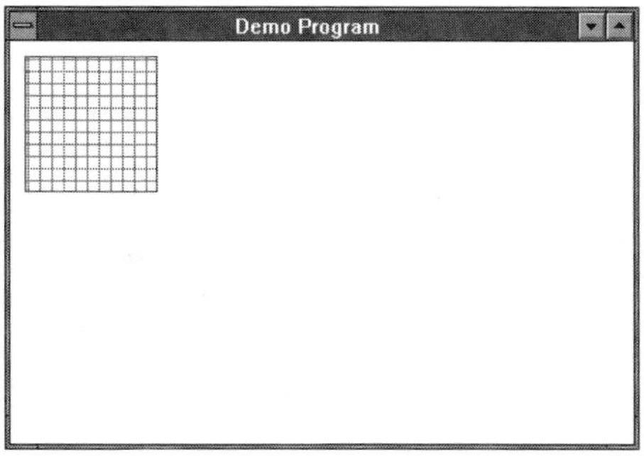

TABLE 5-8
Brush functions

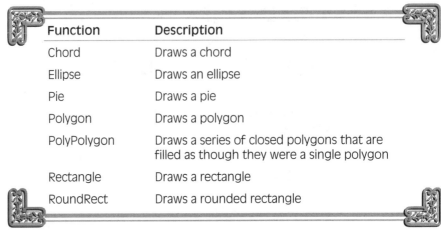

Function	Description
Chord	Draws a chord
Ellipse	Draws an ellipse
Pie	Draws a pie
Polygon	Draws a polygon
PolyPolygon	Draws a series of closed polygons that are filled as though they were a single polygon
Rectangle	Draws a rectangle
RoundRect	Draws a rounded rectangle

WM_PAINT message, it'll always have the **fErase** flag set. You can set this member to a stock brush, like so:

```
WNDCLASS wc;

// Declare the background as black.
wc.hbrBackground = (HBRUSH)
                        GetStockObject (BLACK_BRUSH);
```

You can also use one of the system colors for a window's background brush. Windows provides a convenient hack for this; you don't have to create a brush specially for this purpose. You just add one to the constant from Table 5-2 and assign it to the structure member, as follows:

```
WNDCLASS wc;

// Declare the class background
// as the system background color.
wc.hbrBackground = (HBRUSH)COLOR_BACKGROUND + 1;
```

Fonts

The Windows GDI provides a very rich set of text-drawing functions. Of all the GDI drawing functions, those for text drawing are probably the ones you're most likely to use for game programs, primarily because text drawing is quite easy to do—so long as you stick to the basics. As you'll see here, text drawing relies on Windows *fonts,* and understanding fonts is easily *the* most complex part of the GDI.

The term "font" has some ambiguous meanings in the context of Windows. To a user, a font is the thing that comes on a disk, gets installed with the Control Panel application, and defines what a particular text face looks like. Since Windows 3.1, TrueType has been the standard for Windows fonts. TrueType fonts are *scalable,* meaning that one font—in the Control Panel sense of the word, anyway—can generate multiple sizes.

From a programming point of view, a font is a GDI object, like a pen or a brush. You create a font by calling **CreateFont** with a set of 14 parameters that define the height, style, spacing, and so on, including the face name, which is the name that corresponds to what the user thinks of as a font (that is, the name that the user sees in Control Panel). Once it is created, you can select a font into a DC with **SelectObject** just like you would a pen or brush. Similarly, you delete a GDI font with **DeleteObject**, but only after you've selected it back out of a DC by calling **SelectObject** with the handle of the original font. Deleting the GDI font object has no effect on what the user sees in Control Panel. If it seems easier, you can think of what the user installs as, perhaps, a font *class,* and what you've "created" in the GDI as an instance of that class.

Games and Fonts

It's possible that a game program might use a wide variety of fonts for different purposes. In the interest of simplification, however, we'll limit ourselves to the fonts easiest to use—the precreated ones, or *stock fonts.* Stock fonts are like all stock GDI objects, and you can access them with **GetStockObject (index);** where index is one of the font entries listed in Table 5-5—Stock Objects.

Note in Table 5-1 that SYSTEM_FONT is the default font you get with a DC. This is the font programmers normally use to draw menu text and other common text in Windows. It is a *proportional* font, meaning different characters have different widths. This is generally nicer to look at than its alternative, the fixed font, but it creates complications if you need to position the text exactly. We'll learn in a moment how to find out the exact dimensions of a text string with **GetTextExtentPoint**.

Drawing Text

We learned in our first example that using the **TextOut** function is one easy way to display a line of text. **TextOut** uses, naturally, the DC's current font—that is, the last font selected into the DC with **SelectObject**. There are a total of four text-drawing GDI functions:

- TextOut
- ExtTextOut
- DrawText
- TabbedTextOut

We'll learn about each here, starting with **TextOut**:

```
BOOL TextOut (hdc, x, y, string, length)
HDC hdc;               // Handle to DC
int x, y;              // Starting coordinates
LPCSTR string;  // Pointer to text string
int length;            // Length of string
```

This is the most basic of the text-drawing functions. It simply draws a string starting at coordinates **X,Y**, which specify the upper left corner of the starting *character cell* of the string (see Figure 5-9). A character cell is an imaginary box that surrounds each character of a text string. All character cells from a given font are of the same height. For monospaced fonts, the character cell's width is also fixed; for proportionally spaced fonts, the character cell's width varies, depending on the character.

It's possible to change the starting position of text by using the **SetTextAlign** function to specify centered or left- or right-aligned text. You can also use it to update the current pen position for functions like **LineTo**.

A slight variation on **TextOut** is offered in **ExtTextOut** (for extended **TextOut**—very clever).

```
BOOL ExtTextOut (hdc, x, y, options, rc, string,
length, spacing)
HDC hdc;               // Handle to DC
int x, y;              // Starting position
UINT options;   // Text options
LPRECT rc;             // Pointer to formatting RECTangle
LPCSTR string;  // Text string
UINT length;    // String length
LPINT spacing;  // Array of ints for char spacing
```

As you can see, this function adds several parameters to **TextOut**. The pointer to a **RECT** structure defines a rectangle that can be used to clip the text, depending on the setting of **options**, which can be one of, both, or neither **ETO_CLIPPED** and **ETO_OPAQUE**. If **options** is set to **ETO_CLIPPED**, then the text string will be clipped at the boundaries of the rectangle. With **ETO_OPAQUE**, the current background color (the one set with **SetBkColor**) fills the rectangle around the text. The first option is obviously useful for clipping text into a specific rectangle—in other words, to make sure the text doesn't "bleed" off onto other parts of the area on which you want to draw. The second option is useful primarily for clearing a rectangle to the background color as you are drawing the text.

For example, suppose you're continuously updating a text field somewhere on the DC. If you don't use **ETO_OPAQUE**, then the first time you draw a line of text that's shorter than the previous one, you'll get little bits left over on the end where the old line of text was. This is because **ExtTextOut** and the other text-drawing functions stop drawing right at the end of the line of text. Using **ETO_OPAQUE** with a rectangle that's at least as long as the longest line of text you plan to display (like maybe the width of the whole field) will ensure that the whole area gets cleared to the background color each time you update the field. (See Figure 5-10.)

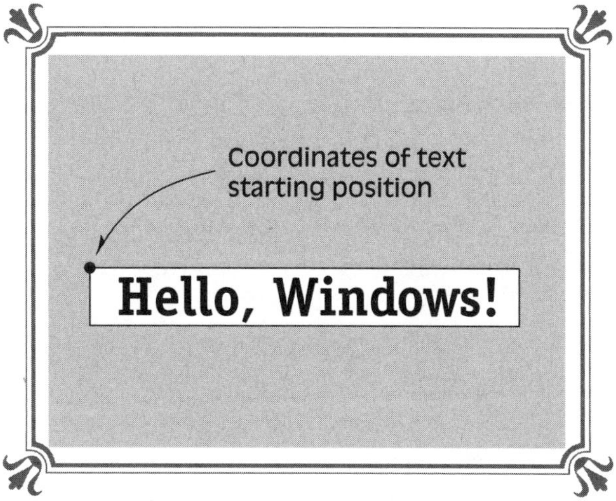

FIGURE 5-9

The text starting position

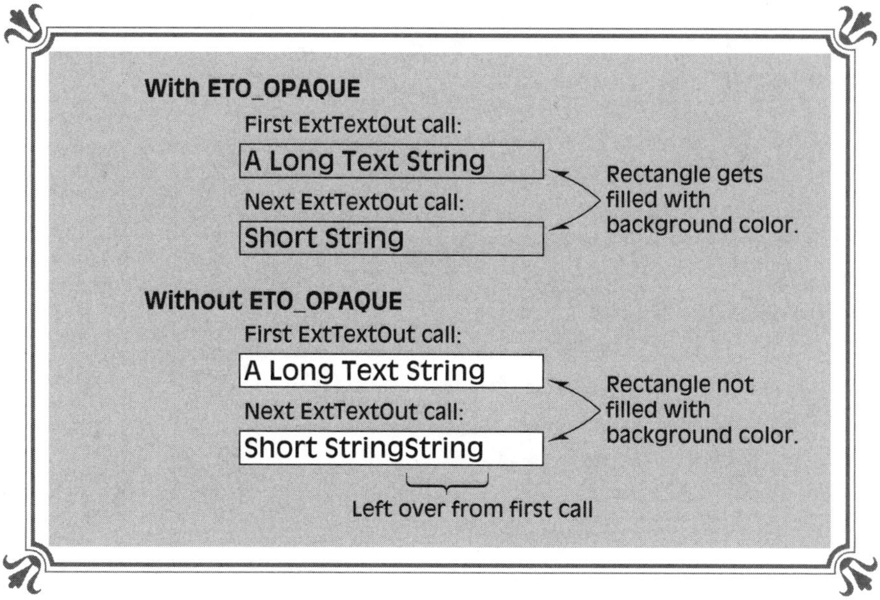

FIGURE 5-10

Using ETO_OPAQUE

Warning: The Background Isn't Always What It Seems

Note that the text-drawing functions—all of them—use the current background color to fill in the background of the text area. A common error is assuming that the background color is the same as the color of the background *brush*, which generally isn't the case.

You'll recall that when you register a window class with **RegisterClass**, the **hbrBackground** member of the **WNDCLASS** structure gets set to the brush you want to use to paint the background. Suppose you set it to the stock object **BLACK_BRUSH**

```
wc.hbrBackground = GetStockObject (BLACK_BRUSH);
```

when you register the window class. The background of all the instances of that window will now be automatically drawn with a solid black background. However, black is *not* the default background *color*. The default background color for a DC is always *white*, as described in Table 5-1. To make sure that the background color is black, you have to call

```
SetBkColor (hdc, RGB(0,0,0));
```

with the handle to the DC in **hdc**, of course. If you don't, the text will look like that shown in Figure 5-11.

Incidentally, the **LPRECT** parameter that defines the box for drawing the background can be **NULL**, in which case only the actual extents of the text box are used. Likewise, the **LPINT** parameter can point to an array of **int**s (one for each

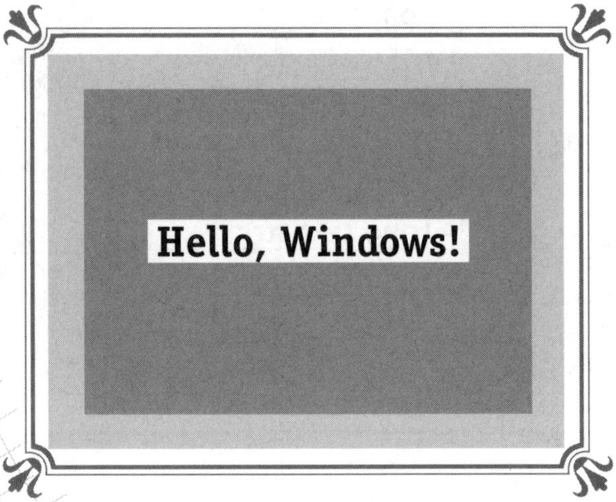

FIGURE 5-11

The wrong background color

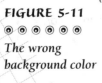

character in the string) that define the distance in pixels between the origins of adjacent character cells. If this parameter is **NULL**, then the function uses the default character spacing.

TextOut and **ExtTextOut** are the two fastest text-drawing routines in the GDI. Windows also supplies a function—**DrawText**—for automatically formatting text into a rectangle using a large pile of formatting options. I'll leave it to you to look up the parameters of **DrawText** in your favorite Windows API reference document if your game relies heavily on text input and display.

The remaining text-drawing function is **TabbedTextOut**, which, as you might surmise, draws text with embedded tab characters at specific tab stops that you can define with an array. Again, I'll leave it to you to find its description if you need it. **TabbedTextOut** is primarily designed to make it easier for word processing and other text-intensive applications to format text.

How Big Is That Text String?

Regardless of which text function you use, it's often important to know the exact dimensions of a given string of text. Since the most common Windows font—the **SYSTEM_FONT**—is proportional, you can't just ask for a character cell's width and multiply it by the number of characters in the string. Fortunately, Windows provides a function to give you the dimensions of a string as it would be drawn on the DC with one of the text output functions:

```
BOOL GetTextExtentPoint (hdc, string, length, size)
HDC hdc;                          // Handle to DC
LPCSTR string;              // String to measure
int length;                       // Length of string
LPSIZE size;                // Address of result buffer
```

This function takes a handle to the DC, the string you want to measure, the length of that string, and a pointer to a **SIZE** structure that gets filled with the result. A Windows **SIZE** structure's definition is:

```
typedef struct tagSIZE {
        int cx;
        int cy;
} SIZE;
```

You would think a function named **GetTextExtentPoint** would take, say, a pointer to a Windows **POINT** structure, but that would be too logical. **GetTextExtentPoint** computes the width and height of the string using the font that's currently selected in the DC, and returns that width and height in the **cx** and **cy** members of the supplied **SIZE** structure. This width and height represent the minimum extents of a box, starting at the text-drawing position, that will completely enclose the text string as it would be drawn on the DC.

Putting our text-drawing and text-extent functions together, let's create a WM_PAINT handler that draws a line of text centered in a window's client area:

```
void OnPaint(HWND hwnd)
{
        RECT r;
        HDC hdc;
        PAINTSTRUCT ps;
        SIZE sz;
        char buf[] = "Hello, Windows."
        int start_x, start_y, len;

        // Call BeginPaint.
        hdc = BeginPaint (hwnd, &ps);

        // Get the size of the client area.
        GetClientRect (hwnd, &r);

        len = lstrlen (buf);
        // Get the extents of the text string.
        GetTextExtentPoint (hdc, buf, len, &sz);

        // Compute the starting position.
        start_x = (r.right - sz.cx) / 2;
        start_y = (r.bottom - sz.cy) / 2;

        // Draw the text there, using the
        // SYSTEM_FONT (default).
        TextOut (hdc, start_x, start_y, buf, len);

        // End painting.
        EndPaint(hwnd, &ps);
}
```

This function will draw the string of text exactly in the center of the rectangle that represents the given window's client area. Note the use of **GetClientRect** here: This function takes the handle to a window and a pointer to a **RECT** in which to store the coordinates of the four corners of the window's client area.

You'll also note that there is what would appear to be a bug in the code example—you might think the formula for finding the starting *x* coordinate would look more like this:

```
        start_x = ((r.right - r.left) - sz.cx) / 2;
```

that is to say, the width of the rectangle, minus the width of the text, divided by 2. As it turns out, **GetClientRect** returns the extents of the client-area rectangle in—what else?—*client* coordinates, which start at the upper left corner of the client area. Therefore, the **left** and **top** members of the **RECT** passed to **GetClientRect** will always be initialized to zero, and the **right** and **bottom** members represent the *extents* of the client area, not the actual coordinates themselves.

One might ask about the usefulness of a function that takes a pointer to a rectangle structure, yet always fills two members of the structure with zero. "Why," asks the curious Windows programmer, "didn't they use a `SIZE` structure instead?"

"Good question," replies the Master Coder.

Good question, indeed. One reason might be that the results returned from `GetClientRect` are in suitable form for passing to `Rectangle` in order to draw a rectangle around the entire client area. Maybe.

Clipping Regions

The penultimate GDI object we'll talk about here is the *clipping region*. A clipping region defines an area of the DC outside of which nothing will be drawn, regardless of what GDI drawing functions you use. The "area" can be more than just a simple rectangle—in fact, it can be quite a complex combination of intersecting shapes. You can create a region from a combination of rectangles, ellipses, and polygons. Once you've created a region, you select it into the DC just like you would any other DC object.

I'm not going to go into more detail on this subject, for two reasons. First, clipping regions slow down GDI drawing considerably (depending on the complexity of the region). Once you select a clipping region into the DC, every GDI drawing operation has to clip itself to that region, and clipping takes time. Note that the default clipping region is the entire "surface" of the DC, which corresponds to the window from which the DC came. In this case, the GDI has to clip only at the rectangular boundaries of the window, which doesn't consume much time.

Second, creating complex shapes by using clipping regions probably isn't a common aspect of most games. Chances are that if you need to create a complex shape, you can draw it using the other GDI functions. If you're porting a DOS game to Windows, it's doubtful you're using a set of drawing functions that support clipping regions. The usual caveat applies: If you think clipping regions are important to your game program, by all means look into using them.

Bitmaps

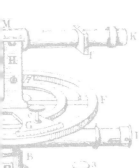

Bitmaps are the only remaining GDI object. Since I'll cover them extensively in the next few chapters, I'll mention just a few basics here.

As with all GDI objects, you select bitmaps into the DC with `SelectObject` and delete them with `DeleteObject` after you've selected them back out (as usual, by selecting in the original bitmap object). But bitmaps have a fundamental importance to the DC that goes a little beyond that of the other GDI objects: A DC's currently selected bitmap is the thing in which all the actual drawing takes place! In other words, when you draw a line with **LineTo**, the line is actually drawn by the GDI *into* the currently selected bitmap object. This is why, early in this chapter, I referred to the bitmap as one of the GDI's metadevices.

Note in Table 5-1 that by default, a DC has no bitmap. For a DC obtained from a window handle, the default bitmap is actually the physical bitmap of the display device—that is to say, the actual bitmap represented by the memory on the display card. This makes good sense, of course. When you get a DC with **GetDC** or **BeginPaint**, the thing you want to draw on is the screen, and it's only logical that the bitmap for the screen is already "selected" into a DC so obtained.

An important thing to note about the bitmap that comes with the screen DC is that you should never select it *out* of that DC by trying to select in another bitmap. This would be the logical equivalent of unplugging the display card and plugging in another one; an operation that, sadly, the GDI explicitly doesn't support.

Bitmaps *really* become useful when we create DCs that don't represent the actual, physical screen: so-called *memory DCs*. As I mentioned, we'll learn about these DCs and the bitmaps they use in the following chapters. We'll also learn about the stretching-mode DC attribute so intrinsically related to bitmaps.

So much for the GDI objects that are part of a device context. Next come some of the attributes—mode settings that govern the way coordinates and drawing operations are interpreted by the GDI—associated with a DC.

Mapping Modes, Viewports, and Window Extents

Often, it is convenient to specify *x* and *y* positions using a coordinate system that more closely corresponds to a particular application's data set. For example, a CAD system might have a native coordinate system in which one unit equals 1 inch, or a desktop publishing system might choose one in which one unit equals 1 point (a unit of text height). Likewise, it is common to shift (translate) these coordinate systems in *x* and *y* in order to achieve certain coordinate transforms.

Windows, in an effort to offer a robust GDI, provides functions to automatically transform coordinates specified in drawing functions into one of several coordinate systems. Together, mapping modes, viewports, and window extents provide a flexible set of two-dimensional transformations.

Given all this, my advice to the game programmer is to *completely ignore* everything having to do with mapping modes and viewports in Windows. The default mapping mode for a display context, MM_TEXT, maps one logical unit (the value specified in GDI calls) into 1 pixel (the device unit), an eminently reasonable default. Likewise, the default viewport origin and extent map to the whole of the DC. This mapping mode probably corresponds most closely to what a DOS-based game programmer is used to—doing everything in pixels. Another important reason to use MM_TEXT (don't ask me why they didn't call it MM_PIXELS) is that the WinG extensions work fully only with that mapping mode.

If your game program requires calculation of coordinates in some space other than the display's pixel coordinates, you should probably do the calculation within your own code rather than relying on Windows. Mapping modes, viewports, and window extents are yet another chunk of programming overhead you can live without.

Drawing Modes

The *drawing mode* attribute specifies how the colors of the pen and the interior of filled objects are combined with the color already on the screen surface. The drawing mode is specified via

```
int SetROP2 (HDC hdc, int drawmode);
```

where **drawmode** is one of 16 constants that represent the complete set of so-called *raster operations* (also called rasterops or ROPs). The 16 combinations come from combining AND, OR, XOR, and NOT with a source and destination pixel (that's why there's a "2" at the end).

I haven't listed all 16 constants you can use here, because you'll typically use only two: **R2_COPYPEN** (the default) and **R2_NOTXORPEN**. The first one (which is the default drawing mode) is simply a basic copy operation: It overwrites existing pixels with new pixels. The latter rasterop is the ever-popular *XOR draw* used for nondestructively drawing things that the user can drag across the screen, like a rubber-band line.

Using the XOR draw raster operation is the easiest and typically fastest way to nondestructively draw things like cursors and rubber-band lines. The only disadvantage to XOR drawing is that it doesn't use a specific color—the color is the XOR of the drawing color and whatever color is in the background that you're drawing over. The only alternative for nondestructively drawing something over a background is to save the actual bits of the background; draw the thing; and then when it moves, draw the old background back in. Needless to say, this can take a lot of time and it requires a buffer in which to hold the background. It *does* look better, and this is why some graphical elements—like the Windows cursor, for example—use this method rather than XOR. But for most simple dragging operations, XOR is probably the best way to go.

When you use XOR draw to create a rubber-band line, this is what happens: The first time you draw the line using XOR, the raster operation creates a line on the display by XORing all the pixels along the line. Then, when you draw the line in exactly the same place again, the raster operation XORs the XORed pixels, which, by definition, restores the original pixels. Isn't logic wonderful?

I'll demonstrate how XOR drawing works with an example of a rubber-band box, something that is useful for specifying a rectangular selection. This example will use handlers for the WM_LBUTTONDOWN, WM_MOUSEMOVE, and WM_LBUTTONUP messages that we learned in Chapter 4 for tracking the mouse movements.

The steps for creating a rubber-band selection box go like this:

On WM_LBUTTONDOWN:

- Capture the mouse (from Chapter 4).
- Store the mouse coordinates into static **POINT** variable **start**.
- Store the mouse coordinates into static **POINT last**.
- Set **dragflag** to TRUE.

On WM_MOUSEMOVE:

- Store the current mouse coordinates into **POINT** variable **new**.
- Set the drawing mode to **R2_NOTXORPEN**, and save the old drawing mode.
- Draw the box from **start.x,start.y** to **last.x,last.y** using **MoveTo** and **LineTo**.
- Draw the box *again* from **start.x,start.y** to **new.x,new.y**.
- Copy **new** into **last**.
- Reset the old drawing mode.

On WM_LBUTTONUP:

- Release mouse capture.
- Set **dragflag** to FALSE.
- "Undraw" the selection box by drawing it again using **R2_NOTXORPEN**.

First, we'll create the handlers for the mouse functions:

```
LRESULT CALLBACK _export
OurWindow(HWND hwnd, UINT msg, WPARAM wParam,
               LPARAM lParam)
{
       // Switch on the given message and call the handler.
       switch (msg){
               HANDLE_MSG (main, WM_CREATE, OnCreate);
               HANDLE_MSG (main, WM_COMMAND, OnCommand);
               HANDLE_MSG (main, WM_PAINT, OnPaint);
```

```
                ...
                HANDLE_MSG (main, WM_LBUTTONDOWN,
                                        OnLButtonDown);
                HANDLE_MSG (main, WM_MOUSEMOVE,
                                        OnMouseMove);
                HANDLE_MSG (main, WM_LBUTTONUP,
                                        OnLButtonUp);
                ...
        // If we don't handle the message, pass it
        // on to DefWindowProc.
        default:
                return
                DefWindowProc (hwnd, msg, wParam, lParam);
        }
}
```

Now we'll add a couple of **POINT** variables to the main window structure:

```
typedef struct tagMAIN {
        HWND hwnd;              // This window
        HDC  hdc;               // DC for our window
        int command;    // Current command
        POINT start;    // Selection start point
        POINT last;             // Selection end point
        BOOL dragflag;  // Dragging selection?
} MAIN;
```

Now we'll look at the function definitions for `OnLButtonDown`, `OnMouseMove`, and `OnLButtonUp`:

```
static void OnLButtonDown (MAIN *main, BOOL fDblClk,
                                int x, int y, UINT flags)
{
        // Capture the mouse so we get all moves.
        SetCapture (main->hwnd);
        // Store away the point.
        main->start.x = x; main->start.y = y;
        // Copy it into the last point, as well.
        main->last = main->start;
        main->dragflag = TRUE;
}

static void OnMouseMove (MAIN *main, int x, int y,
                                UINT flags)
{
        // If we're dragging...
        if (main->dragflag) {
                POINT new;
                // Save these new points.
                new.x = x; new.y = y;
                // Draw the previous box (erase).
                DrawBox (main->hdc, &main->start,
```

continued on next page

continued from previous page

```
                                        &main->last);
                // Draw the new box.
                DrawBox (main->hdc, &main->start,
                                        &new);
                // Update the new point.
                main->last = new;
        }
}
```

Note here that we let a function called **DrawBox** do all the actual drawing work. **DrawBox** looks like this:

```
static void DrawBox (HDC hdc, LPPOINT p1, LPPOINT p2)
{
        int oldrop;

        // Save the old ROP, and set to XOR.
        oldrop = SetROP2 (hdc, R2_NOTXORPEN);
        // Draw lines for four box sides.
        MoveTo (hdc, p1->x, p1->y);
        LineTo (hdc, p2->x, p1->y);
        LineTo (hdc, p2->x, p2->y);
        LineTo (hdc, p1->x, p2->y);
        LineTo (hdc, p1->x, p1->y);
        // Reset the ROP.
        SetROP2 (hdc, oldrop);
}
```

Finally, there's **OnLButtonUp**:

```
static void OnLButtonUp (MAIN *main,
                                int x, int y, UINT flags)
{
        if (main->dragflag) {
                // Release the mouse.
                ReleaseCapture ();
                // Erase the last box.
                DrawBox (main->hdc, &main->start,
                                        &main->last);
                // Reset the flag.
                main->dragflag = FALSE;
        }
}
```

This example represents the basics of XOR drawing for things like a selection box. You may want to experiment with the other drawing modes using this example to see how they work.

You may wonder why we use **R2_NOTXORPEN** rather than **R2_XORPEN** in the drawing function. The example assumes that the current pen is black (the default). If the current pen is white, then you should use **R2_XORPEN**. I'll leave the math to you.

The Other DC Attributes

I'll briefly explain the few remaining attributes from Table 5-1 here.

Brush Origin

The brush origin is used to determine from what point a brush starts drawing. For solid brushes, the brush origin has no effect, but for hatched or pattern brushes it obviously does, and it determines where within the hatch or pattern the brush will start.

Color Palette

Color palettes are a topic unto themselves, and I'll cover them in Chapter 8.

Current Pen Position

You update the current pen position automatically whenever you use **MoveTo** or **LineTo**. The text output functions can also change it if the **TA_UPDATECP** flag has been supplied to **SetTextAlign**. If for some reason you lose track, you can get the current position at any time by using

```
BOOL GetCurrentPositionEx (HDC hdc, LPPOINT p);
```

which fills the **POINT** pointed to by **p** with the coordinates of the current pen position. There's also an older, simplified function called **GetCurrentPosition** that returns the position packed into a **DWORD**, but this is not portable to Win32 and thus its use is highly inadvisable.

Intercharacter Spacing

This attribute overrides the default setting for the spacing between characters when you are using the various text output functions. You set it with:

```
int SetTextCharacterExtra (HDC hdc, int extra);
```

This adds the number of pixels specified in **extra** to the space between characters on a text string.

Polygon-Filling Mode

You use this attribute primarily to draw polygons with "holes" or unfilled sections in them. You set it with:

```
int SetPolyFillMode (HDC hdc, int mode);
```

where **mode** is either **ALTERNATE** (the default) or **WINDING**. In alternate mode, the system fills the area between odd-numbered and even-numbered polygon sides on each scan line. That is, the system fills the area between the first and second sides, the area between the third and fourth sides, and so on.

When the polygon-filling mode is winding, the system uses the direction in which you drew the figure to determine whether to fill an area. Each line segment in a polygon is drawn in either a clockwise or a counterclockwise direction. Whenever an imaginary line drawn from an enclosed area to the outside of a figure passes through a clockwise line segment, a count is *incremented* (increased by one); when the line passes through a counterclockwise line segment, the count is *decremented* (decreased by one). The system fills the area if the count is nonzero when the line reaches the outside of the figure. Using this mode and the function **PolyPolygon** (which draws multiple polygons in one call), you can create nested polygons in which the inner polygons aren't filled (or vice versa).

Summary

Take a minute to relax—that was a lot to digest. As you've probably gathered, the GDI is huge and complex. No doubt, you now comprehend why I warned you at the beginning of this chapter that understanding and using the Windows GDI could be the most difficult part of Windows programming. In the interest of making things as painless as possible, I glossed over a number of functions here—functions for drawing ellipses, polygons, arcs, and so on. You can find a listing of all the various GDI drawing functions in your favorite Windows API reference manual.

Now that we know all this stuff about the GDI, this might be a good time to ask whether we'll actually need to use any of it. The answer depends on how much graphics-primitive drawing your game does; whether you've already got functions for doing all of it; and if so, how fast they are (and need to be).

As I mentioned early on, most of the GDI is really implemented in the display driver. While display-card manufacturers have a vested interest in making their drivers the fastest possible, GDI performance also depends a lot on how you're using the calls, not just on the speed of the calls themselves. While a given display driver might be very fast at line drawing, if your game draws lots of lines of widely varying colors (requiring separate pens), using the GDI might not be the fastest way to draw them.

If you already have a passel of line-drawing code that you've used for DOS games, you might be better off using it instead of GDI calls. Unfortunately, the only way to tell for sure whether your code or the GDI's (in other words, the display driver's) is faster is to test them both, which is sort of an ugly proposition.

The big question is how much your game uses two-dimensional graphics primitives. If it's a sprite-based game, you might not use any of the GDI line-drawing primitives, or you might want to use them to draw into the background bitmap only at startup time. If it's a vector-based game, GDI line drawing might be reasonable, but if you have some absolutely unbeatable line-drawing code—say, written in 32-bit assembly code—then yours may be faster. If you are writing a 3D simulation game (like a flight simulator or maze game), then two-dimensional primitives probably aren't your bag at all; you're more interested in the following chapters on bitmaps and Blting.

Regardless of what type of game you're writing, understanding how the GDI works is fundamental to getting your program running under Windows. In the following chapters, we'll build on our understanding of display contexts and the GDI in general as we work with bitmaps.

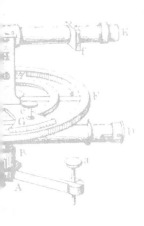

6

Windows Bitmaps—The Device-Dependent Bitmap

come tutte le manovelle ... le quali si movano e s'alza
e gra pesi ... le quali ... saranno ...
... nella ... manovella pegi ...
forza e più ... più ...

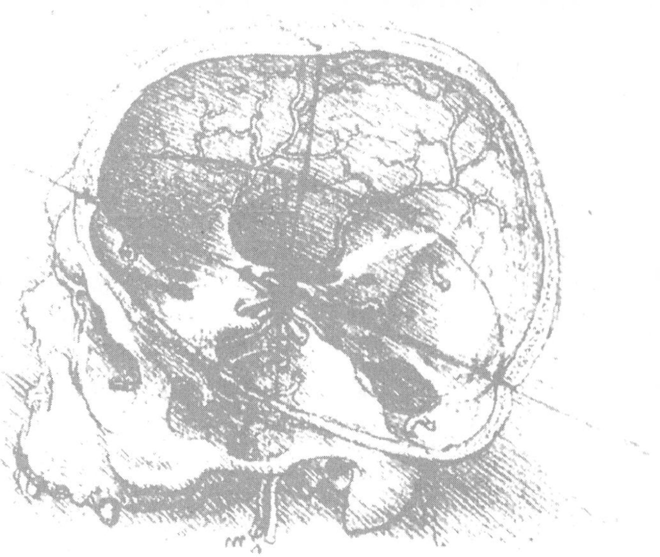

6

Windows Bitmaps—The Device-Dependent Bitmap

The previous chapter touched on Windows' use of bitmaps, but this is where we'll really dig into it. Bitmaps are an important part of virtually every game, and understanding the variations of bitmaps and their use under Windows is critical to making your game work.

What Are Bitmaps?

Let's start with a little review of what constitutes a bitmap. If you're an old-time bitmap hacker, this will be familiar territory, so you have permission to skip ahead to the next section if you like.

Bitmaps, at least in the Windows programming universe, are rectangular arrays of pixels, represented in memory as one contiguous array of bytes. The actual value of each byte—and the corresponding color of the pixel on the screen—is a product of many factors.

A bitmap comes in one of three forms: monochrome, grayscale, or color. The monochrome bitmap is the simplest—every pixel is represented by 1 bit, representing either black or white (the actual color depends on the display device, of course). A grayscale bitmap can display roughly continuous shades of gray by using groups of bits—often 1 byte for 256 levels—to represent different levels of gray. Typically, 0 is used to represent black and 255 is used to represent full white.

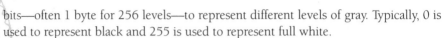

Color bitmaps use groups of bits to represent either discrete or continuous color values, depending on the number of bits used. At one end of the scale is the so-called *true-color bitmap,* which uses 24 bits (3 bytes) for each pixel. Each byte represents one of 256 levels of red, green, or blue, which are combined by the display hardware and monitor to display a single color. They're called true-color bitmaps because the number of colors resulting from using 24 bits is 16,777,216—considerably more than the human eye can distinguish (although most display devices aren't capable of differentiating anywhere near 16 million colors). True-color bitmaps naturally consume large chunks of memory: A 640x480 pixel true-color bitmap is 921,600 bytes. Because of their size (and hence, slow speed), true-color bitmaps are seldom used in games.

It's possible to use any number of bits to represent a color bitmap, but it's typical to use only three or four values. Windows supports three: 4 bits per pixel, 8 bits per pixel, and 24 bits per pixel. Doing the math, you can see that these *pixel depths* represent 16, 256, and 16,000,000 colors, respectively. Besides pixel depth, the actual organization of the pixels can vary between two common types: planar and chunky. Planar bitmaps are organized such that all the red values come first, then all the blue values, then all the green. The actual value of a single pixel is therefore a combination of bits in three disparate locations in memory. Chunky bitmaps place the color values next to each other, so each pixel is represented by a contiguous set of bits. Figure 6-1 illustrates the two types of bitmaps.

It's easy to understand the variations of pixel depth and planar vs. chunky format for 24-bit pixels, but what about the other two? Exactly *which* 16 or 256 colors do these bitmaps represent?

The colors of a 16-color bitmap were originally those from the fixed set that was part of the design of the first color-display card for the PC, the mighty CGA. The colors were simply binary combinations of the red, green, and blue primary colors (that's eight), with high-intensity versions thrown in as well (making 16). So you had black, red, yellow, blue, magenta, green, cyan, and white, plus a high-intensity version of each. Yuk, to say the least. There was a day when 16 colors were all games had to work with. Fortunately, the VGA introduced the PC world to 256-color capability, and as a rule, games have used 256 colors ever since.

The Layout of the 256-Color Bitmap

You'll note that 256 colors can be neatly represented as 1 byte (8 bits) per pixel, and fortunately this is the way most 256-color (often also called *8bpp* for 8 bits per pixel, or simply 8-bit) bitmaps are laid out. Each byte represents 1 pixel, with the array of bytes typically going from the upper left-most pixel, progressing rightward across the display's width in what's called a *scan line,* and then wrapping back around to the next lower scan line (see Figure 6-2).

FIGURE 6-1

Planar vs. chunky bitmaps

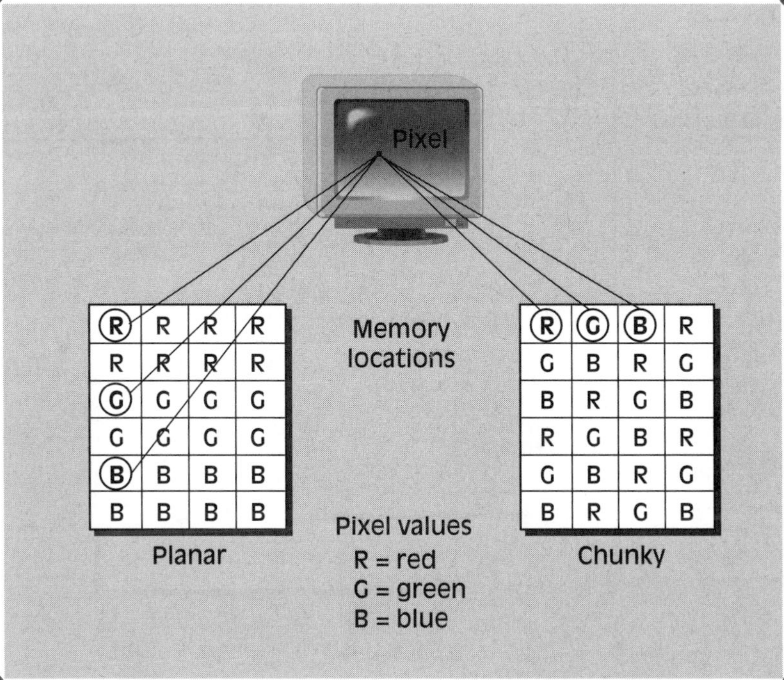

Since each pixel is represented by 1 byte and since each scan line is the same length, the address of a particular pixel can be found with the following formula: char * pixel = bitmap[y * ScanWidth + x]; where **bitmap** is the array of pixels (as 8-bit **char**s); **ScanWidth** is the width of the scan line; and **x** and **y** are the zero-based row and column, respectively, of the pixel you want. You can see how simple and fast this algorithm is: One multiplication operation and one addition operation, and you've got the address of the pixel, which is conveniently represented as a **char**. But what color does the actual value of the **char** (to be proper, it really should be an **unsigned char**) represent?

You could imagine a scheme where the 8-bit byte that represents a pixel was divided into red, green, and blue components: say, 3 bits for red; 3 bits for green; and 2 bits for blue. That's certainly a valid scheme, but the resulting range of colors would leave a lot to be desired. There are several colors that just plain wouldn't be there. No matter how you allocate the bits, a range of 256 fixed colors just isn't different enough from a range of 16 to be interesting.

Another alternative to using a fixed set of 256 colors is to use the value of the pixel as an index to a *color table* containing 256 entries, each of which represents a unique color derived from a much larger color space. Such a color table is variously

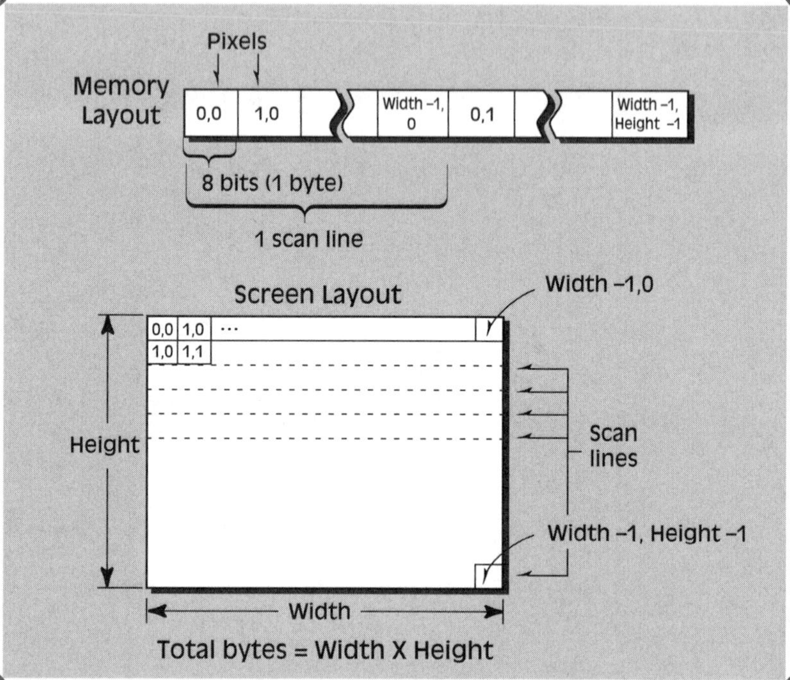

FIGURE 6-2

Scan lines and pixels in memory

called a lookup table, or a palette (as in "artist's palette"). The palette is physically implemented in hardware on the display card, which turns an 8-bit index into a real RGB value that goes out to the monitor. The color depths of palettes vary with the hardware implementations of those palettes; they typically use up to 8 bits per red, green, and blue primary. This means that the 256 simultaneous colors to which an 8-bit bitmap is limited can be chosen from a set as large as 16 million. The standard VGA card that's in virtually every PC has a color resolution of 6 bits per primary, resulting in a palette of 262,144 possible colors (2^{18}). Many VGA cards have a full 8 bits per primary these days, so the color range is even greater.

Figure 6-3 shows how the hardware translates the pixel value into an actual color that's displayed on the monitor through the palette or lookup table. Basically, the idea of using a palettized bitmap is a sort of "more colors, less filling" approach. It has only one-third the memory requirement of true color, yet can display a very wide range of colors—so long as there are only 256 of them at once.

You've undoubtedly seen many 256-color images. It can be startling how good a 256-color image can look. Part of the reason is that many types of images—particularly computer-generated 3D scenes—often have very few source colors. If an image

FIGURE 6-3

How a color lookup table works

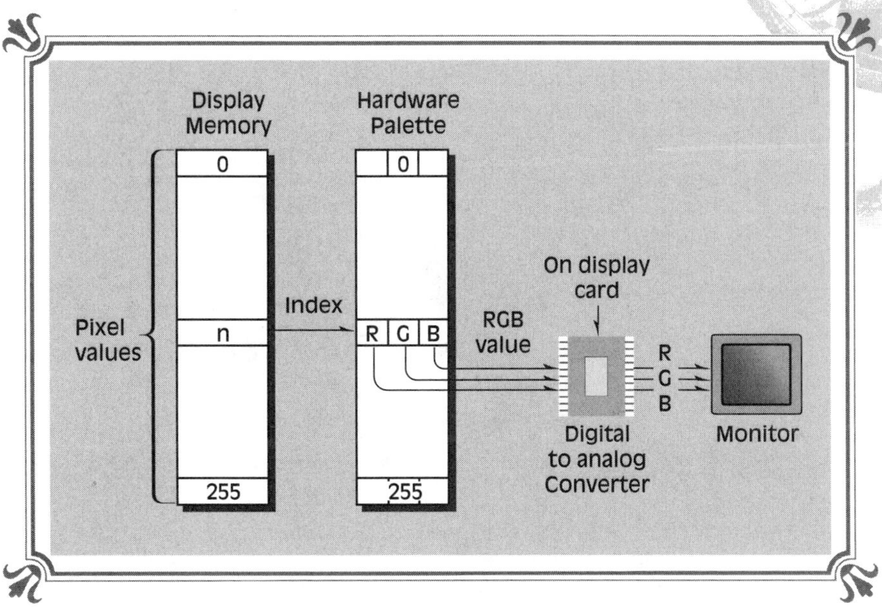

has, say, only 10 actual source colors, then the remaining 246 palette "slots" can be used for different *shades* of those colors, making the image appear very realistic.

Enough about the layout of bitmaps—let's dive into how Windows works with them.

Bitmaps and Device Contexts

In Chapter 5, you learned that a device context is a pile of settings that govern all the drawing operations that the GDI can perform. You also learned that one component of a device context is the bitmap on which the drawing activity actually takes place. For device contexts obtained through the **GetDC** call, the bitmap is that of the physical display—drawing operations are displayed in a window on the screen directly.

It's also possible to create device contexts that aren't associated directly with the screen; these are called *memory DCs*. In order to do anything useful, a memory DC must have a bitmap associated with it—it's the bitmap that actually gets drawn on, after all. The inverse is also true—if it is to be useful in any way, a bitmap requires an associated DC. You might think of the DC's bitmap as one of the essential components of an artist's toolbox, along with brushes and paint. Figure 6-4 illustrates this relationship.

Before you get started creating memory DCs and bitmaps for them, you might ask, "Why do we need them?" Ah. Good question.

FIGURE 6-4

Bitmaps and DCs

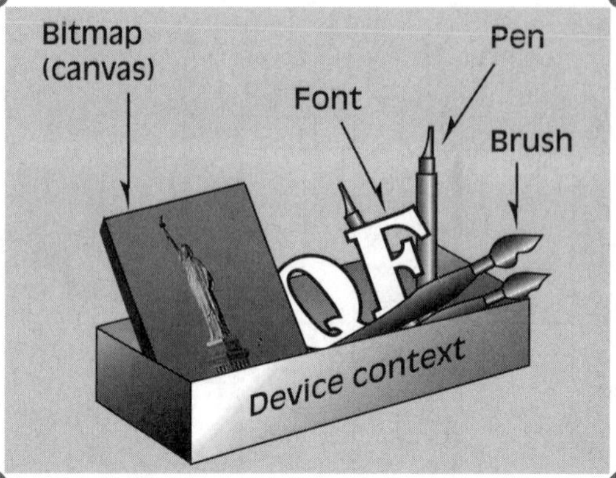

Only two Windows functions are used to display bitmaps on the screen: **BitBlt** and **StretchBlt**. Both functions actually copy bitmaps from one device context to another; the source and destination DCs are parameters to the functions. It's not possible to directly copy bits from one bitmap into another bitmap—at least, not with the device-dependent bitmaps that are the subject of this chapter. Consequently, to do *anything* useful with a bitmap, you must select it into some device context. Here's what the **BitBlt** function looks like:

```
BOOL BitBlt (HDC dest, int Xdest, int Ydest,
             int width, int height,
             HDC source, int Xsource, int Ysource,
             DWORD rop)
```

The two **HDC** parameters are handles to the destination and source device contexts that have the bitmaps that are to be copied from and to. The other parameters specify the size and location for the destination and source bitmaps.

To use the **BitBlt** function, you must first create a couple of bitmaps to Blt from and to. Let's assume a common destination bitmap: a window on the screen.

Creating Memory DCs

There are two calls that create memory-based device contexts: **CreateDC** and **CreateCompatibleDC**. The first creates a device context given the name of an actual device driver, like the printer driver or even the screen driver. The second offers a sort of shorthand: It creates a device context in memory that's compatible with an already existing device context, the screen's DC being the most typical. You can create such a memory DC as follows:

```
HDC memDC;

memDC = CreateCompatibleDC (NULL);
```

The single argument to **CreateCompatibleDC** is a handle to the device context from which you want a compatible one to be created. NULL is shorthand for the screen's DC.

A memory DC consumes semiprecious GDI memory and must be deleted with **DeleteDC** when it's no longer needed. Also, remember that deleting objects that are currently selected into a DC wounds, and eventually even kills (your program, that is).

Creating Bitmaps

Recall from Chapter 5 that there is no default bitmap for a device context. Well, this isn't exactly true. A DC created with **CreateCompatibleDC** actually *does* have a default bitmap associated with it—it's a 1x1 pixel monochrome bitmap, in fact. You're more clever than I am if you can figure out something useful to do with a 1x1 pixel monochrome bitmap. In order to get something done, you have to have a larger and more interesting bitmap to select *into* the DC—remember that a bitmap is akin to the pens, brushes, and other objects that you select into a DC to make them available.

There are generally two ways to create a bitmap that can be selected into a memory DC. The first is to use one of the Windows functions that create bitmaps, like **CreateBitmap** or **CreateCompatibleBitmap**. These functions create a bitmap of the specified dimensions and layout, and return a handle to a bitmap (HBITMAP) that can be selected into a DC. The other way is to load a bitmap from the program's resource file with **LoadBitmap**, which also returns a handle with which to select the bitmap into a DC. A bitmap resource can be created with your favorite resource editor, like AppStudio or the Borland Resource Workshop. The bitmap is then loaded like so

```
HBITMAP hbmp;

hbmp = LoadBitmap (hinst, "picture");
```

where **picture** is the string name of the resource (you can also use the MAKEINTRESOURCE macro if the bitmap resource is identified by an ID instead of a string), and **hinst** is the instance handle for the program.

Using the BitBlt Function

Now that you know something about creating a memory device context and a bitmap, let's put the two together and—with **BitBlt**—display a bitmap in a window.

The first question is where to put the code for displaying the bitmap. It could go in the **OnPaint** handler, but that's pretty boring—it would simply display the bitmap in the window when the window needed painting. A more interesting (and slightly more gamelike) way to display the bitmap might be to attach it to the mouse, like in **OnMouseMove**, perhaps letting the user drag the bitmap around when the left button is down. Here's a new WM_MOUSEMOVE handler:

```
static void OnMouseMove (MAIN *main, int x, int y,
                                 UINT keyFlags)
{
    HDC memDC;
    BITMAP bmp;

    if (keyFlags & MK_LBUTTON) {
        // Create a memory DC compatible with
        // the screen.
        memDC = CreateCompatibleDC (NULL);

        // Select the previously loaded bitmap
        // resource into the memory DC.
          SelectObject (memDC,  main->bmp);

        // Get the bitmap's dimensions.
        GetObject (main->bmp, sizeof(BITMAP), &bmp);

          // Blt the bitmap to the screen.
        BitBlt (main->hdc, x, y,
                    bmp.bmWidth, bmp.bmHeight,
                memDC, 0, 0, SRCCOPY);

        // Clean up.
        DeleteDC (memDC);
    }
}
```

Whoa, hey, there's some new stuff here. The first thing the function does is create some temporary variables to hold a handle to the memory DC and a handle to the default bitmap (the 1x1 monochrome) of the memory DC so that it can be selected back in before the DC is deleted. The function also creates a temporary BITMAP structure, which is used to hold the dimensions (and other information) about the bitmap (I'll get to that in a moment).

The **if** statement checks to see if the left mouse button is down. The statement will permit the user to drag the bitmap around on the screen only if it is.

The **CreateCompatibleDC** call, as I explained earlier, creates a DC compatible with the screen. The next thing the function does is select the *previously loaded* bitmap into the memory DC. This assumes that there is an HBITMAP member of the window's instance data structure (**main**) called **bmp** that has previously been set to the handle of the loaded resource. The likely place to set the handle is somewhere like **OnCreate**, when the window is first created:

```
BOOL OnCreate (MAIN *main,
               CREATESTRUCT FAR* lpCreateStruct)
{
    .
    .
    .
    // Load the bitmap resource identified
    // as "picture".
    main->bmp = LoadBitmap (hInst, "picture");

    // Get the DC for the window once; it must
    // be registered with the CS_OWNDC flag set
    // in the WNDCLASS structure for this to work.
    main->hdc = GetDC (main->hwnd);
    .
    .
    .
```

There's something else here, as well. As you'll recall from Chapter 5, it's possible to create a window from a class registered with the CS_OWNDC flag set—a window that has its own device context. Once you've retrieved the device context with **GetDC**, you don't have to release it until just before the window is destroyed. This is a convenient way to work with a main window, since you don't always have to remember to release the DC after using it (it's also a tiny bit faster).

Getting back to the **OnMouseMove** example, the **SelectObject** function returns the handle of the previously selected object (HBITMAP, in this case), which is stored into **holdbmp** so that it can be selected back into the DC before the DC is deleted.

The next call, **GetObject**, is new. The **GetObject** function fills a buffer with information about the object whose handle is given as the first argument. The function itself figures out what kind of GDI object the handle refers to—all you have to do is supply the address of a buffer (the third argument) and the buffer's size (the second argument). The buffer is the structure that defines the object you're inquiring about—in this case, a BITMAP structure. The BITMAP structure (from WINDOWS.H) looks like this:

```
typedef struct tagBITMAP
{
    int       bmType;
    int       bmWidth;
    int       bmHeight;
    int       bmWidthBytes;
    BYTE      bmPlanes;
    BYTE      bmBitsPixel;
    void FAR* bmBits;
} BITMAP;
```

In particular, the parts that are interesting are the width and height of the bitmap, stored in **bmWidth** and **bmHeight**, respectively. The last member of the function,

bmBits, is used as a pointer to the actual bits of the bitmap, but only when the structure is used to *create* a bitmap; using **GetObject** sets this member to NULL. To get the bits of a bitmap, you must use **GetBitmapBits**, which, as we'll learn by the end of this chapter, is one of the big problems with these device-dependent bitmaps.

The **bmPlanes** and **bmBitsPixel** members of the structure define the number of planes and bits per pixel of the bitmap, respectively. However, bitmaps loaded with **LoadBitmap** will *always* have the same organization (in other words, number of planes and bits per pixel) as the current display screen device. The **LoadBitmap** function does the translation for you automatically (except for monochrome bitmaps, which always have 1 plane and 1 bit per pixel). So the value of these members isn't all that important, in this case.

The **bmWidth** and **bmHeight** members of the **bmp** structure are used in the next call, **BitBlt**. This nine-parameter function is where all the action is: It copies a rectangular region from the source DC into an equal-size rectangular region in the destination DC. What it actually does is copy the bits of the bitmaps that are currently selected in the two respective DCs. A handle to the destination DC is the first argument; in this case, it's the screen's DC that came from a member of the window's instance data structure, as set in **OnCreate**. The next two parameters are the *x* and *y* coordinates of the point in the destination DC where the upper left corner of the bitmap will be placed; in this case, the *x* and *y* coordinates of the mouse position. Following these are the dimensions of the source area of the rectangle to be transferred. The full dimensions of the bitmap, obtained from the **GetObject** call, are used here, meaning that the whole bitmap will be copied. The next three parameters define the

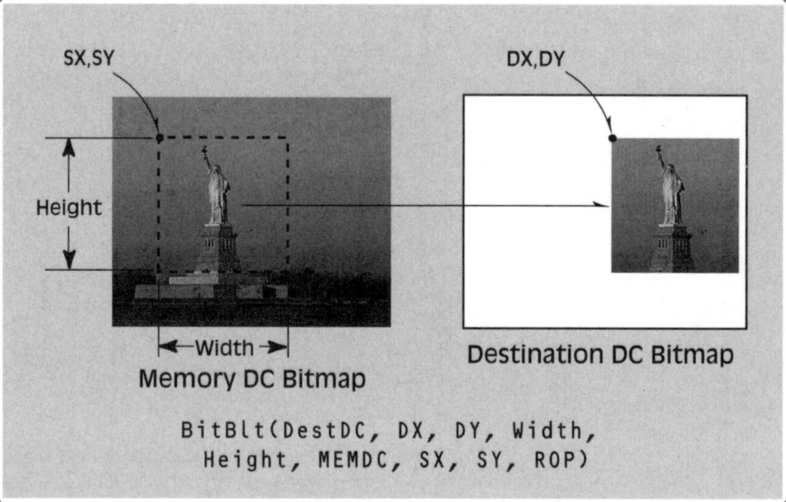

FIGURE 6-5

Coordinates for BitBlt

source DC and its starting coordinates. A handle to the memory DC is passed in, along with 0,0 to denote the upper left corner of the source bitmap.

Figure 6-5 illustrates the relationship between the source and destination coordinates in `BitBlt`.

TABLE 6-1

Raster operations for `BitBlt`

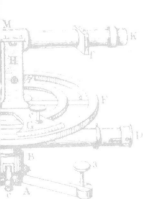

Setting	Meaning
BLACKNESS	Turns all output black.
DSTINVERT	Inverts the destination bitmap.
MERGECOPY	Combines the pattern and source bitmap with the Boolean AND function.
MERGEPAINT	Combines the inverted source bitmap with the destination bitmap using the Boolean OR function.
NOTSRCCOPY	Copies the inverted source bitmap to the destination.
NOTSRCERASE	Inverts the result of combining the source and destination bitmaps with the Boolean OR function.
PATCOPY	Copies the pattern to the destination bitmap.
PATINVERT	Combines the destination bitmap with the pattern using the Boolean XOR function.
PATPAINT	Combines the inverted source bitmap with the pattern by using the Boolean OR operator. Combines the result of this operation with the destination bitmap by using the Boolean OR function.
SRCAND	Combines pixels of the destination and source bitmaps by using the Boolean AND operator.
SRCCOPY	Copies the source bitmap to the destination bitmap.
SRCERASE	Inverts the destination bitmap and combines the result with the source bitmap by using the Boolean AND operator.
SRCINVERT	Combines pixels of the destination and source bitmaps by using the Boolean XOR operator.
SRCPAINT	Combines pixels of the destination and source bitmaps by using the Boolean OR operator.
WHITENESS	Turns all output white.

The last parameter to **BitBlt** is the raster operation to be used for the transfer. In Chapter 5, you learned that there are 16 possible raster operations that can take place between a source and a destination pixel. The **SetROP2** function is used to set the raster operation for GDI drawing; however, **BitBlt** *doesn't* use this setting but rather has a specific parameter for it. There are 15 raster operations defined for **BitBlt** (Microsoft opted to leave out the NOP operation for this one). The 15 settings can be found in Table 6-1.

The example uses the most common raster operation, SRCCOPY, which simply copies the bitmap from the source to the destination, overwriting whatever's in the destination.

After the **BitBlt** call, the function cleans up by selecting the old 1x1 monochrome bitmap back into the memory DC, then safely deleting it.

Running the program (seen in Figure 6-6), you'll see the bitmap from the resource file with the name **picture** getting dragged around on the screen when you move the mouse while holding down the left button. You'll also notice that the bitmap just gets copied over the background at each new mouse position, eventually leaving "trails," or copies of itself, all over the destination window. While this is an interesting effect, it's hardly ever what you'd like to see in a game (or much of anything else, for that matter). Typically, you want to drag an object around the screen, *leaving the background intact.* In the next example, we'll take a look at one way to do this.

Nondestructive Bitmap Animation

The most obvious way to move a bitmap around on the screen without destroying the background is to keep a copy of the background, and restore it before moving the

FIGURE 6-6

The BitBlt *program in operation*

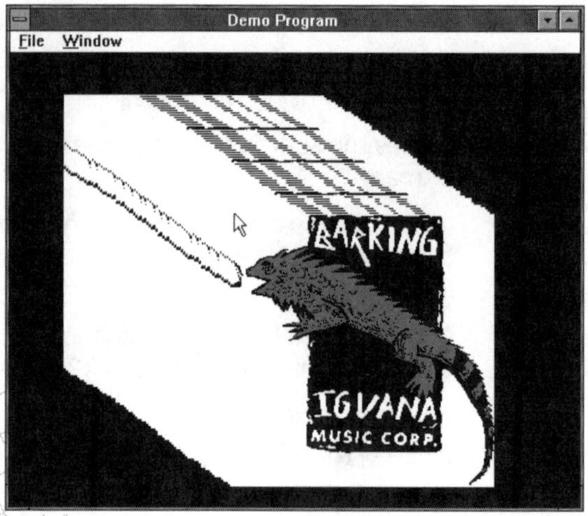

bitmap. To do this, the program will need a little more than just a WM_MOUSEMOVE handler—it'll also need handlers for the mouse-button-down and mouse-button-up messages. I'll call the bitmap to be dragged around the screen the *source* bitmap, and the saved background bitmap the *background* bitmap for clarity.

Here are the steps (illustrated in Figure 6-7) that the WM_LBUTTONDOWN message handler (called **`OnLButtonDown`** in the usual WINDOWSX.H fashion) needs to perform:

- Use **`BitBlt`** to save the screen background into a bitmap buffer the same size as the source bitmap at the current mouse position.
- Use **`BitBlt`** again, this time to copy the source bitmap to the screen.
- Save the current position of the mouse.

Then, at each WM_MOUSEMOVE message, the program does the following:

- Using **`BitBlt`**, the program copies the previously stored background bitmap to the screen at the last saved position.
- It then copies the screen background at the *new* position into the bitmap buffer by using **`BitBlt`**.
- It again copies the source bitmap to the screen with **`BitBlt`**, at the new position.
- The program updates the current position of the mouse.

FIGURE 6-7

Using memory buffering for animation

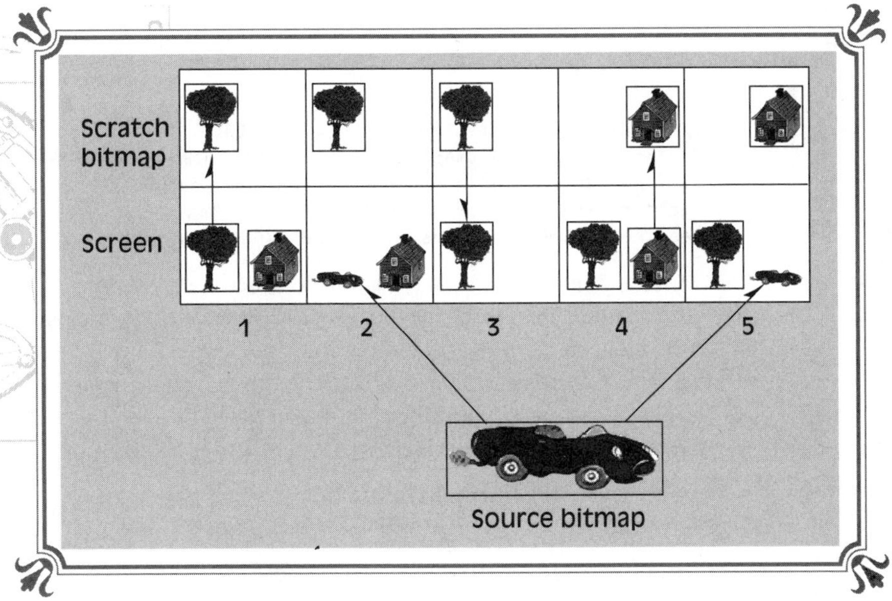

Finally, at WM_LBUTTONUP time, the program just copies the background bitmap onto the screen again, clearing the source bitmap and leaving the screen as it was before the user pressed the mouse button.

It's a good idea for your program to capture the mouse with **SetCapture** when the mouse button goes down and release it with **ReleaseCapture** when the mouse button comes back up, to ensure that the window gets all the mouse messages.

The buffer for the background bitmap could be created and destroyed within each handler, but it would obviously be faster to create the buffer once, when the window is created, and destroy it when the window is destroyed. The background bitmap also needs a memory device context in order to be useful—remember that **BitBlt** transfers pixels from the bitmaps that are selected into a source and a destination DC. To handle the two DCs, two bitmaps, and related items, I'll add a little nested structure to the window's instance data structure, like so:

```
typedef struct tagMAIN {
    HWND hwnd;                  // This window
    HDC  hdc;                   // DC for our window

    struct {
        struct {
            HBITMAP bmp;        // Bitmap
            HDC memDC;          // Memory DC
        } bmpdata[2];           // Source, background
        int width, height;      // Size of bitmap
        int oldx, oldy;         // Previous position
    } bitmaps;
} MAIN;

#define SOURCE  0
#define BACKGND 1

// Access macros for the bitmaps structure.
#define SRC_DC   bitmaps.bmpdata[SOURCE].memDC
#define BK_DC    bitmaps.bmpdata[BACKGND].memDC
#define SRC_BMP  bitmaps.bmpdata[SOURCE].bmp
#define BK_BMP   bitmaps.bmpdata[BACKGND].bmp
```

The nested array of two **bmpdata** structures contains a handle for the actual bitmap, and a handle for the memory DC. There are also members to hold the width and height of the bitmaps and their last positions. I like to define macros to access nested structures to save myself from typing the whole name.

Now let's take a look at the code that needs to be added to the **OnCreate** handler to create the bitmaps and memory DCs the program needs:

```
static BOOL OnCreate (MAIN *main,
                  CREATESTRUCT FAR* lpCreateStruct)
{
    BITMAP b;
    .
    .
```

```
    .
    // Get the DC for the window once; it must
    // be registered with the CS_OWNDC flag set
    // for this to work.
    main->hdc = GetDC (main->hwnd);

    // Load the bitmap resource identified
    // as "picture".
    main->SRC_BMP = LoadBitmap (hInst, "picture");

    // Find out the size of the bitmap and save it.
    GetObject (main->SRC_BMP, sizeof(BITMAP), &b);
    main->bitmaps.width = b.bmWidth;
    main->bitmaps.height = b.bmHeight;

    // Create a bitmap in which to store the
    // background, same size as the source.
    main->BK_BMP = CreateCompatibleBitmap (main->hdc,
                                main->bitmaps.width,
                                main->bitmaps.height);

    // Create memory DCs for both the source and
    // background bitmaps and select them in.
    main->SRC_DC = CreateCompatibleDC (main->hdc);
    main->BK_DC  = CreateCompatibleDC (main->hdc);
    SelectObject (main->SRC_DC, main->SRC_BMP);
    SelectObject (main->BK_DC, main->BK_BMP);
    .
    .
```

Note the **CreateCompatibleBitmap** call here. This function creates a bitmap whose layout is the same as that of the DC it's given as its first argument, of the dimensions specified in the second and third arguments. This is a very handy function for creating bitmaps that will have screen contents copied into them with **BitBlt**.

Now that all the DCs and bitmaps are created and stored, we'll move on to the mouse handlers. The first is the left-button-down handler:

```
static void OnLButtonDown (MAIN *main,
                                    BOOL fDoubleClick,
                                    int x, int y,
                                    UINT keyFlags)
{
    SetCapture (main->hwnd);

    // Get the background for the current position.
    BitBlt (main->BK_DC, 0, 0,
            main->bitmaps.width, main->bitmaps.height,
            main->hdc, x, y,
            SRCCOPY);

    // Put the source bitmap here.
```

continued on next page

continued from previous page

```
    BitBlt (main->hdc, x, y,
            main->bitmaps.width, main->bitmaps.height,
            main->SRC_DC, 0, 0,
            SRCCOPY);

    // Set the old position to this position.
    main->bitmaps.oldx = x; main->bitmaps.oldy = y;
}
```

The first **BitBlt** copies an area the size of the source bitmap from the screen DC to the background memory DC. Remember, what this does is copy the actual *bits* of the screen into the actual bits of the bitmap that has been selected into the memory DC (which, in this case, is the bitmap created with **CreateCompatibleBitmap**). The second **BitBlt** copies the bits from the source bitmap's DC (the thing to be displayed) into the screen DC, thus displaying the bitmap. The function then sets the position passed in via *x* and *y* into the **bitmaps** structure.

Next, the **OnMouseMove** handler. This one does three different Blts:

```
static void OnMouseMove (MAIN *main, int x, int y,
                                    UINT keyFlags)
{
    // Do something only if the button is down.
    if (keyFlags & MK_LBUTTON) {

        // Restore the background at the old position.
        BitBlt (main->hdc,
                    main->bitmaps.oldx,
                    main->bitmaps.oldy,
                main->bitmaps.width,
                    main->bitmaps.height,
                main->BK_DC, 0, 0,
                SRCCOPY);

        // Get the background at the new position.
        BitBlt (main->BK_DC, 0, 0,
                main->bitmaps.width,
                    main->bitmaps.height,
                main->hdc, x, y,
                SRCCOPY);

        // Blt the source to the screen at
          // the new position.
        BitBlt (main->hdc, x, y,
                main->bitmaps.width,
                    main->bitmaps.height,
                main->SRC_DC, 0, 0,
                SRCCOPY);
        // Save the new position as the old position.
        main->bitmaps.oldx = x;
        main->bitmaps.oldy = y;
    }
}
```

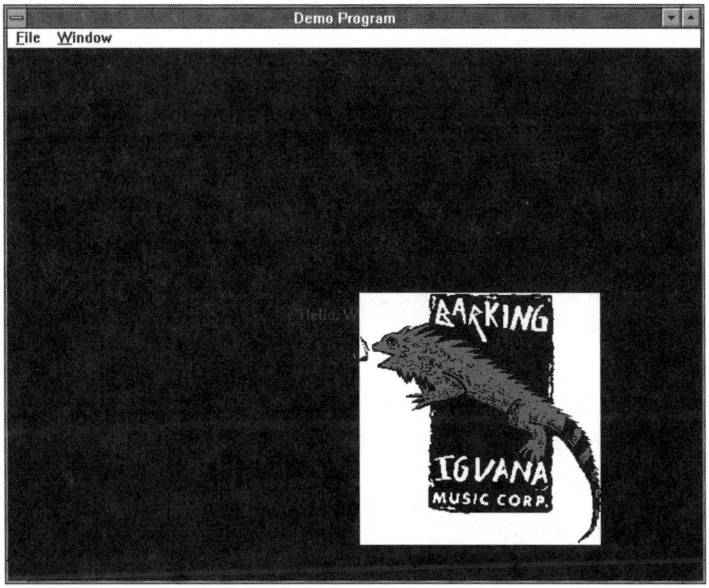

FIGURE 6-8
`BitBlt` *animation*

This should be straightforward enough to follow. First, where the bitmap had been placed by **`OnLButtonDown`**, the old background is restored. Then, the background is saved again, this time at the *new* (intended) position of the bitmap. Finally, the bitmap is Blted into place at the new position and the position is saved. Figure 6-8 shows the animation program in action.

The **`OnLButtonUp`** handler is even more trivial:

```
static void OnLButtonUp (MAIN *main, int x, int y,
                                UINT keyFlags)
{
    // Release mouse capture.
    ReleaseCapture ();

    // Blt the background back.
    BitBlt (main->hdc, x, y,
            main->bitmaps.width, main->bitmaps.height,
            main->BK_DC, 0, 0,
            SRCCOPY);
}
```

This handler just cleans up by copying the background at the position where the user released the mouse button.

Speaking of cleaning up, the bitmaps and memory device contexts that we created back in **`OnCreate`** should be deleted at some point. A good place to do so would be in **`OnDestroy`**:

```
static void OnDestroy (MAIN *main)
{
    // Release the screen DC.
    ReleaseDC (main->hwnd, main->hdc);

    // Delete DCs, objects.
    DeleteDC (main->SRC_DC);
    DeleteObject (main->SRC_BMP);

    DeleteDC (main->BK_DC);
    DeleteObject (main->BK_BMP);

    PostQuitMessage (0);
}
```

Notice the first call, to **ReleaseDC**. This is made here because we created the window with the CS_OWNDC style so that the program could hold onto the screen DC throughout its execution, rather than having to retrieve and release it whenever it was needed. Next, the DCs are deleted with **DeleteDC** and the bitmaps are deleted with **DeleteObject**. Remember that performing these operations in the wrong order—first deleting the bitmap, then deleting the DC—would probably cause GDI to crash at some point.

Now you can drag the bitmap nondestructively around the window by using memory device contexts and **BitBlt**, but you'll notice something rather unpleasant when you actually run the program—the bitmap flickers horribly as you drag it. Yikes! What's the problem? All the logic makes sense, and the program does what we wanted: Namely, it preserves the background. But the flicker—ugh! It might be unnoticeable for very small bitmaps, but for anything reasonably large, it's unbearable.

Animation Without Flicker

Before you can eliminate the flicker, you need to understand what causes it. If you think about it for a moment, it should be clear why there's so much flicker. Even if you move the mouse only a few pixels, the program copies the background back over the old position of the source bitmap before it copies the background into the new position. Even the fastest computer is going to show some kind of blink as the rectangular area under the bitmap's position first goes black, and then is replaced with the source bitmap.

Note, though, that the problem occurs only when the movement of the mouse is smaller than the bitmap being moved (which, of course, is most of the time). What the program needs is some way of restoring the background *and* copying in the source bitmap without writing to the screen twice.

The solution, if you haven't guessed by now, is to create an additional offscreen bitmap into which the program first restores the background and then copies the source bitmap. *Then* the program can copy the whole thing to the screen once. This simple double-buffering technique (though that term is often used to mean many different things) is at the heart of all animation—and hence, game—programs.

Here, then, are the new steps (illustrated in Figure 6-9) the **OnMouseMove** function needs to perform in order to eliminate flicker:

- Create a "scratch" bitmap for holding the composite screen update.
- Copy (with **BitBlt**) the affected area of the screen into the scratch bitmap. This area will contain the source bitmap that has been placed there by **OnLButtonDown**.
- Blt the background into the scratch bitmap, clearing the old position of the source bitmap.
- Blt *from* the scratch bitmap into the background bitmap at the new position to get a new background bitmap for the next time around.
- Blt the source bitmap into the scratch bitmap at the new position.
- Blt the scratch bitmap—which now contains the source bitmap in its new position—to the screen.

Note that only the last step actually writes something to the screen. This is what eliminates flicker—the screen update happens only once. Unfortunately, the cost of eliminating flicker is two Blts that we didn't have before, which certainly slows performance. Such is life; the flicker simply isn't acceptable.

FIGURE 6-9

Double-buffering for flicker-free animation

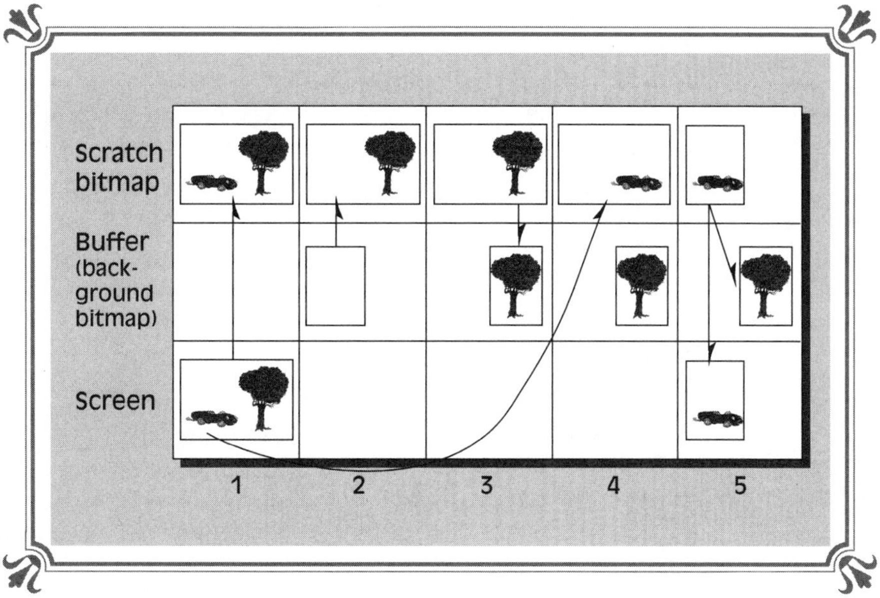

FIGURE 6-10

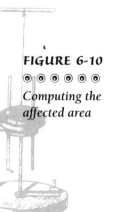

Computing the affected area

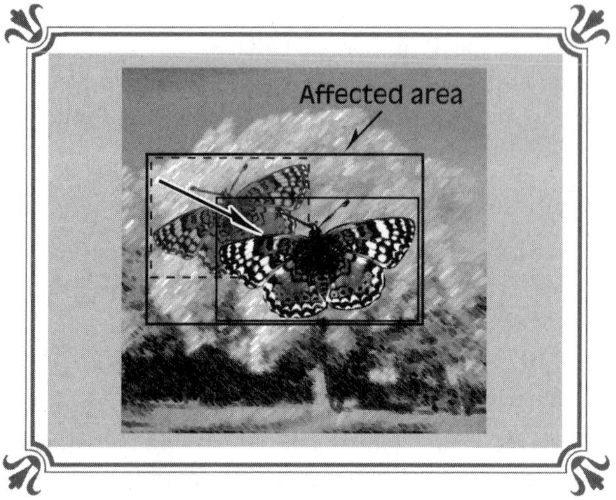

The Affected Area

In this discussion, you may have noted the little part about the *affected area* of the screen. What exactly *is* the affected area? It's the smallest part of the screen that contains both the old and new positions of the source bitmap. It's easy to compute the affected area by using Windows' various rectangle functions.

Looking at Figure 6-10, you can see that the affected area is simply the union of two rectangles: the rectangle containing the original position of the source bitmap, and the rectangle containing its new position. This is how big the scratch bitmap needs to be, and also the size of the portion of the screen that will actually be Blted to in the last step.

To help calculate this rectangle, Windows has a passel of functions that work with the RECT structure, defined in WINDOWS.H as follows:

```
typedef struct tagRECT
{
    int left;
    int top;
    int right;
    int bottom;
} RECT;
```

To compute the affected area of the screen, we can use the `UnionRect` function, which takes pointers to three rectangles: the two source rectangles, and the rectangle into which it will put the union of the two. Now, computing the union of two rectangles isn't a particularly difficult task, and you could certainly write your own code to do it. But as it turns out, many of Windows' rectangle functions are written in optimized assembler code, so it's doubtful you could write one that's any faster. Besides, the computation time for the union rectangle is but a tiny drop in the big bit bucket compared to the time it takes to perform the five Blts that follow it.

Here's the beginning of the function, rewritten to include the computation of the affected area (I'll add to it as we go):

```
static void OnMouseMove (MAIN *main, int x, int y,
                                UINT keyFlags)
{
    RECT Newrect, Oldrect, Unionrect;
    SIZE UnionSize;
    HBITMAP workBMP;
    HDC workDC;

    if (!(keyFlags & MK_LBUTTON))
        return;

    // Create rectangles for the old and new positions.
    Oldrect.left = main->bitmaps.oldx;
    Oldrect.top = main->bitmaps.oldy;
    Oldrect.right = Oldrect.left +
                        main->bitmaps.width;
    Oldrect.bottom = Oldrect.top +
                        main->bitmaps.height;

    // The rectangle of the new position of the source
    // bitmap
    Newrect.left = x; Newrect.top = y;
    Newrect.right = x + main->bitmaps.width;
    Newrect.bottom = y + main->bitmaps.height;

    // Compute the affected area, and store it in Unionrect.
    UnionRect (&Unionrect, &Newrect, &Oldrect);

    // Save the size of the union rectangle.
    UnionSize.cx = Unionrect.right - Unionrect.left;
    UnionSize.cy = Unionrect.bottom - Unionrect.top;
    .
    .
    .
```

The function declares three RECT structures to hold the old and new positions of the source bitmap and their union. It also declares a SIZE structure, which is a simple two-element structure:

```
typedef struct tagSIZE
{
    int cx;
    int cy;
} SIZE;
```

A Windows POINT structure would work, too, but the SIZE structure is custom-designed for such an application. The function also declares handles for a bitmap and a DC, which we will use later.

The process of filling out the members of the old and new rectangles should be obvious enough. The **Oldrect** rectangle starts at the old position of the source bitmap and extends through its full size, and the **Newrect** rectangle starts at the new position (which comes in through the **x** and **y** parameters to **OnMouseMove**) and also extends through its full size. The **UnionRect** function then computes the union of the two rectangles, storing the result in **Unionrect**. Later, the function will need to know the size of the union rectangle, so it's stored in **UnionSize** for convenience.

Creating the Scratch Bitmap

The next step is to create the scratch bitmap—and its associated device context—in which the update will take place. Since the affected area can vary depending on how much the mouse moves between updates, the function will create the bitmap on the fly. Three calls are needed:

```
.
.
.
scratchDC = CreateCompatibleDC (main->hdc);
scratchBMP = CreateCompatibleBitmap (main->hdc,
                                UnionSize.cx,
                                UnionSize.cy);
SelectObject (scratchDC, scratchBMP);
.
.
.
```

These calls should all be familiar by now. The program creates a scratch DC, then creates a bitmap that's the size of the affected area of the screen, and then selects the bitmap into the scratch DC. Next comes the five **BitBlt**s that transfer the bits around:

```
// Copy a Unionrect's worth of the screen
// to the scratchBMP.
BitBlt (scratchDC, 0, 0,
        UnionSize.cx, UnionSize.cy,
        main->hdc, Unionrect.left, Unionrect.top,
        SRCCOPY);

// Copy the background into the scratchDC,
// clearing the old source bitmap.
BitBlt (scratchDC, main->bitmaps.oldx -
                        Unionrect.left,
                  main->bitmaps.oldy -
                        Unionrect.top,
```

```
                main->bitmaps.width, main->bitmaps.height,
                main->BK_DC, 0, 0,
                SRCCOPY);

        // Copy a bitmap's worth of the scratchDC into the
        // background DC at the new position. This
        // saves the background for the next pass.
        BitBlt (main->BK_DC, 0, 0,
                main->bitmaps.width, main->bitmaps.height,
                scratchDC, Newrect.left - Unionrect.left,
                        Newrect.top - Unionrect.top,
                SRCCOPY);

        // Copy the source bitmap into the scratchDC.
        BitBlt (scratchDC, Newrect.left - Unionrect.left,
                        Newrect.top - Unionrect.top,
                main->bitmaps.width, main->bitmaps.height,
                main->SRC_DC, 0, 0,
                SRCCOPY);

        // Finally, copy the scratchDC to the screen.
        BitBlt (main->hdc, Unionrect.left, Unionrect.top,
                UnionSize.cx, UnionSize.cy,
                scratchDC, 0, 0,
                SRCCOPY);
```

You have to understand the significance of the coordinates to the **BitBlt** functions to know what's going on here. The Blts come in two sizes: One type of Blt is the same size as the affected area (the first and last Blts are of this size), and the other Blt type is the size of the source bitmap (the other three Blts are of this size). Refer again to Figure 6-10 and the code, and you'll get the idea.

After all the Blting is done, the function needs to clean up by deleting the scratch DC and bitmap:

```
        .
        .
        .
        // Delete the DC and bitmap.
        DeleteDC (scratchDC);
        DeleteObject (scratchBMP);

        // Update the current position of the source.
        main->bitmaps.oldx = x;
        main->bitmaps.oldy = y;
```

The last thing the function does is update the current position of the source bitmap. Here's the new, flicker-free **OnMouseMove** function in its entirety:

```
static void OnMouseMove (MAIN *main, int x, int y,
                                UINT keyFlags)
{
```

continued on next page

continued from previous page

```
RECT Newrect, Oldrect, Unionrect;
SIZE UnionSize;
HBITMAP workBMP;
HDC workDC;

if (!(keyFlags & MK_LBUTTON))
    return;

// Create rectangles for the old and new positions.
Oldrect.left = main->bitmaps.oldx;
Oldrect.top = main->bitmaps.oldy;
Oldrect.right = Oldrect.left +
                     main->bitmaps.width;
Oldrect.bottom = Oldrect.top +
                      main->bitmaps.height;

// The rectangle of the new position of the source
// bitmap
Newrect.left = x; Newrect.top = y;
Newrect.right = x + main->bitmaps.width;
Newrect.bottom = y + main->bitmaps.height;

// Compute the affected area, and store it in Unionrect.
UnionRect (&Unionrect, &Newrect, &Oldrect);

// Save the size of the union rectangle.
UnionSize.cx = Unionrect.right - Unionrect.left;
UnionSize.cy = Unionrect.bottom - Unionrect.top;

scratchDC = CreateCompatibleDC (main->hdc);
scratchBMP = CreateCompatibleBitmap (main->hdc,
                                 UnionSize.cx,
                                 UnionSize.cy);
SelectObject (scratchDC, scratchBMP);

// Copy a Unionrect's worth of the screen
// to the scratchBMP.
BitBlt (scratchDC, 0, 0,
        UnionSize.cx, UnionSize.cy,
        main->hdc, Unionrect.left, Unionrect.top,
        SRCCOPY);

// Copy the background into the scratchDC,
// clearing the old source bitmap.
BitBlt (scratchDC, main->bitmaps.oldx -
                              Unionrect.left,
                   main->bitmaps.oldy -
                                Unionrect.top,
        main->bitmaps.width, main->bitmaps.height,
        main->BK_DC, 0, 0,
        SRCCOPY);

// Copy a bitmap's worth of the scratchDC into the
```

```
    // background DC at the new position. This
    // saves the background for the next pass.
    BitBlt (main->BK_DC, 0, 0,
            main->bitmaps.width, main->bitmaps.height,
            scratchDC, Newrect.left - Unionrect.left,
                    Newrect.top - Unionrect.top,
            SRCCOPY);

    // Copy the source bitmap into the scratchDC.
    BitBlt (scratchDC, Newrect.left - Unionrect.left,
                    Newrect.top - Unionrect.top,
            main->bitmaps.width, main->bitmaps.height,
            main->SRC_DC, 0, 0,
            SRCCOPY);

    // Finally, copy the scratchDC to the screen.
    BitBlt (main->hdc, Unionrect.left, Unionrect.top,
            UnionSize.cx, UnionSize.cy,
            scratchDC, 0, 0,
            SRCCOPY);

    // Delete the DC and bitmap.
    DeleteDC (scratchDC);
    DeleteObject (scratchBMP);

    // Update the current position of the source.
    main->bitmaps.oldx = x; main->bitmaps.oldy = y;
}
```

Well, it's a little slower and slightly more complicated, but the results are *much* better than the alternative, especially for reasonably large source bitmaps.

Flicker vs. Tear

Depending on how fast your computer and display card are, you might notice one little nasty effect as you drag the bitmap around the window: It might look as though one part of the bitmap is just a bit ahead of or a bit behind the other part. This is a condition called *tear.* Tear is a result of how video-display hardware physically works. The electron beam traces across the monitor from top to bottom at a certain speed, regardless of what's happening on the screen. If the electron beam traces part of the bitmap as the bitmap is moving, but doesn't paint the rest of the bitmap until the beam's next pass, the two parts (or more, if it's a very large bitmap on a very slow machine) will look like they're out of sync with each other—which they are.

Unfortunately, the only way to completely eliminate tear is to synchronize screen painting with the vertical retracing of the monitor, something that is generally not practical under Windows, because of the wide variety of display-driver implementations. Tear isn't nearly as bad as flicker, however, and on fast machines (or with small bitmaps) it may not even be noticeable.

Optimizations

If you're a quick study, you might see a few relatively easy ways to make up some of the speed lost to the extra Blts that eliminated flicker. For example, creating the scratch bitmap on the fly is somewhat time-consuming. Instead, you could do that once in the beginning, as with the background bitmap. The problem is that you won't know how big the bitmap needs to be until you have the mouse-move information. Well, you might also deduce that if the new and old rectangles don't intersect each other, then you really don't need the scratch bitmap; the flicker isn't going to happen unless the new position and old position overlap at least a little. You could go back to using three Blts in that case, and test for it by using the Windows function **`IntersectRect`**, which returns NULL if there's no intersection. This also means that the maximum size of the scratch rectangle is going to be twice the size of the source bitmap in each dimension (in other words, four times larger than the source bitmap). You could allocate this bitmap (and its DC) at **`OnCreate`** time and delete it at **`OnDestroy`** time, and probably pick up a few percentage points' worth of time.

But before you start optimizing this code, I should point out several shortcomings of the device-dependent bitmap that will probably make such optimization plans moot.

The Drawbacks of DDBs

Device-dependent bitmaps (or DDBs, as they're often called) have many shortcomings, especially for game programs. To begin with, it's impractical to perform operations based on the actual *bits* of a DDB, because your code never really has access to the bits. You can use **`GetBitmapBits`** to *copy* the bits into a buffer, modify them, and copy them back with **`SetBitmapBits`**, but the speed overhead (not to mention memory overhead) makes it completely impractical to do this in an interactive application like a game. For this reason, DDBs are useless in flight simulation or other 3D games, where the entire picture changes every frame.

Even in sprite-based animation, where the moving objects are often just static bitmaps (or combinations of static bitmaps), DDBs aren't the perfect solution. First of all, sprite-based animation requires bitmaps with *transparent* portions in order to be useful, and DDBs don't support transparency. It's possible to create transparency by using a combination of masks and raster operations, but there is a significant performance penalty, as each object must be Blted twice (at least) to make it work.

Summary

So if DDBs don't work well for games, what does? And why did we even spend time on them? Well, back around the time when Windows 3.0 was being created,

Microsoft and its then-partner, IBM, decided to fix the device-dependency problems with bitmaps. They created the device-*independent* bitmap—or DIB, as it's usually called—which, although it has its own function calls and data structures, shares many characteristics and some of the general principles associated with the DDB. Knowing DDBs well is a prerequisite to understanding DIBs, and in particular the WinG bitmaps that are the focus of Chapter 9.

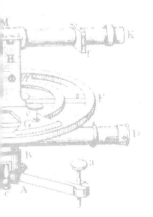

Now, on to DIBs.

7

Windows Bitmaps—The Device-Dependent Bitmap

[illegible]

o, ome tutte fare le manovelle ... le quali si movano e ...
... grandi pesi ... le ... ...
orzare nella ... ... alla manovella per ... ...
la forza ... più ... omo più ...

[illegible]

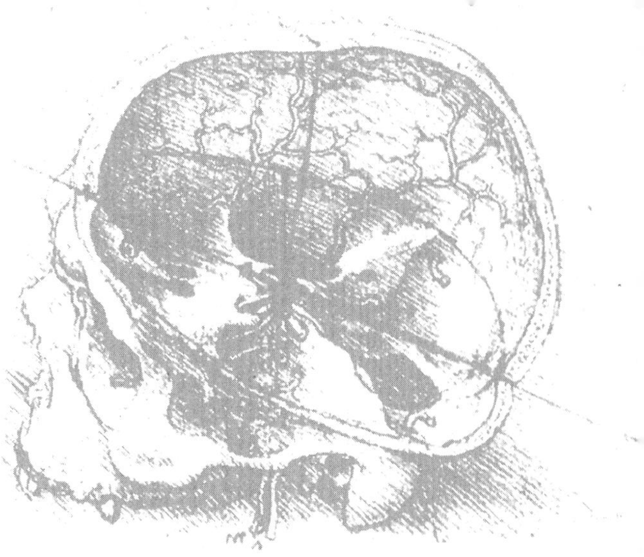

7

Windows Bitmaps—The Device-Independent Bitmap

The *device-independent bitmap*—or DIB—was designed to get around all the limitations of its predecessor, the device-dependent bitmap (DDB). In particular, DDBs don't let you directly access the bits that make them up. In fact, the bits of a DDB don't really even belong to the application that's using them; they belong to the *display driver,* because only the display driver really knows how to interpret the bits. That's why DDBs are accessed through a handle, and the memory created for them isn't directly addressable. The result is that the only way to change the actual bits of a DDB—that is to say, the image it represents—is by using the GDI. And while the GDI is a reasonably robust and complete system for drawing stuff, its performance is completely in the hands of the display-driver supplier instead of the game programmer.

DIBs are different. Not only do they allow you to access the actual bits that make them up, but they also contain information about the actual *colors* that the bits represent. (This is another aspect that's missing from DDBs.) Because of this flexibility, it's much more logical to use DIBs for game programming than it is to use DDBs.

Why Device-Independent?

Besides providing direct access to their bits, DIBs provide other benefits. One is the fact that they are transportable between platforms, whereas DDBs technically are not. Every Windows .BMP file you'll find that's been created since about 1989 is in DIB format. DIBs stored in a file include not only the bits that make up the image but a *color table* that defines what colors are used in the image. You can use the color table to set a palette on a physical display device. If a color table wasn't included, it would be impossible to consistently display the image on a variety of Windows configurations.

There is a DIB format for virtually every popular pixel depth—1, 4, 8, 16, 24, and even 32 bits per pixel. Although a color table can be specified for any of these depths, it's usually not used with 16, 24, or 32 bits per pixel, because these are generally considered *paletteless* depths—the number of colors per pixel is large enough that a palette is virtually never needed. As you learned in Chapter 6, by far the most common pixel depth used for games is 8 bits per pixel, or 256 colors, with a palette. (From this point on, I'll refer to pixel depth as simply "8-bit" or "24-bit" rather than adding the unwieldy "per pixel" designation.)

Although DIBs accommodate several pixel depths, they come in chunky flavor only. That is, the actual *layout* of the pixels is as a single plane, with the red, green, and blue components sitting next to each other in memory. If you think about it, this is relevant only for 24-bit (or 32-bit) DIBs, since 8-bit (and lower) formats use a color table to define the actual red, green, and blue values.

Even though DIBs are portable across Windows machines and display devices, they perform no miracles: A 24-bit image displayed on an 8-bit device doesn't look very good. It's also a painfully slow process to display an image this way, as Windows has to find some color match for every single pixel in the image. DIBs work fastest when the source pixel depth—that is, the depth specified in the DIB itself—either matches or is lower than the pixel depth of the display.

Using DIBs is superior to using device-dependent bitmaps, with two exceptions. First, DIBs are considerably slower than DDBs, as the display driver has to convert a DIB into a DDB before it can display it. Second, the GDI doesn't work natively with a DIB, so you can't use the GDI's line-, text-, and pattern-drawing functions. In Chapter 9, you'll learn how WinG fixes both of these restrictions, however, making DIBs the obvious choice for game development.

DIB Structure

The structure of a DIB on disk and in memory is nearly identical, fortunately. Figure 7-1 shows the structure of a DIB file.

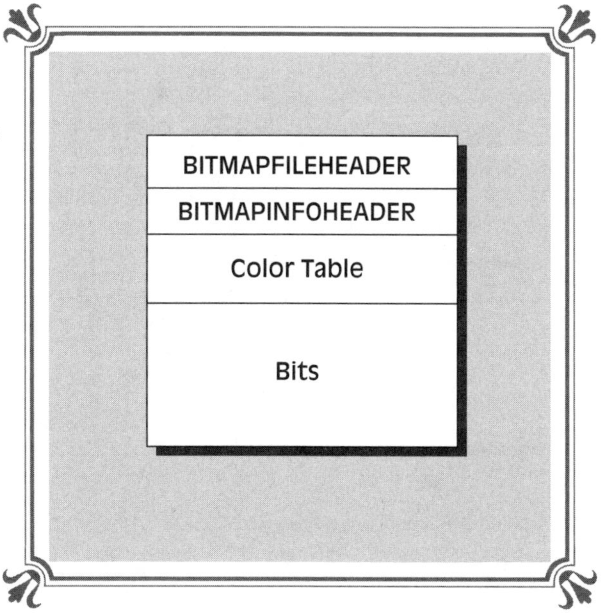

FIGURE 7-1

DIB file structure

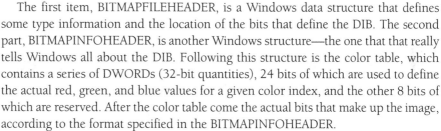

The first item, BITMAPFILEHEADER, is a Windows data structure that defines some type information and the location of the bits that define the DIB. The second part, BITMAPINFOHEADER, is another Windows structure—the one that that really tells Windows all about the DIB. Following this structure is the color table, which contains a series of DWORDs (32-bit quantities), 24 bits of which are used to define the actual red, green, and blue values for a given color index, and the other 8 bits of which are reserved. After the color table come the actual bits that make up the image, according to the format specified in the BITMAPINFOHEADER.

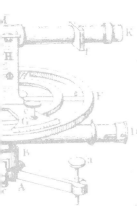

Although this structure looks relatively simple and straightforward, the truth is there are actually *two* kinds of DIBs—Windows DIBs and Presentation Manager (OS/2) DIBs. They vary in that an OS/2 DIB uses a BITMAPCOREHEADER structure instead of a BITMAPINFOHEADER, and the color table is specified in 24-bit values rather than 32-bit values. Later, we'll develop a .BMP-file loader that catches this difference, loads either OS/2 or Windows DIBs, and creates a Windows DIB in memory from them.

As I've mentioned, the format of a DIB in memory is very much like that of a DIB file. The main differences are that it doesn't require a BITMAPFILEHEADER, and the location of the actual bits is separate from the BITMAPINFOHEADER (although the color table still follows the BITMAPINFOHEADER in memory). Figure 7-2 shows the structure of a DIB in memory.

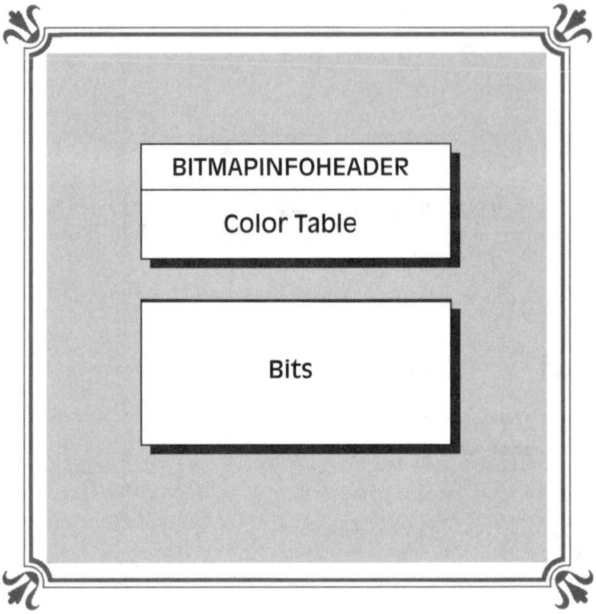

FIGURE 7-2

DIB memory structure

Let's take a look at the BITMAPINFOHEADER and see how it defines all the information about a DIB.

Picking Apart the BITMAPINFOHEADER

The BITMAPINFOHEADER structure is defined in WINDOWS.H like so:

```
typedef struct tagBITMAPINFOHEADER
{
    DWORD   biSize;
    LONG    biWidth;
    LONG    biHeight;
    WORD    biPlanes;
    WORD    biBitCount;
    DWORD   biCompression;
    DWORD   biSizeImage;
    LONG    biXPelsPerMeter;
    LONG    biYPelsPerMeter;
    DWORD   biClrUsed;
    DWORD   biClrImportant;
} BITMAPINFOHEADER;
```

The first structure member, **biSize**, isn't the size of the DIB but actually the *size of the structure itself*. In other words, this member should always be set like so:

```
BITMAPINFOHEADER bihdr;

bihdr.biSize = sizeof (BITMAPINFOHEADER);
.
.
.
```

Back around 1990, Microsoft started to realize that with all the various structure definitions that are part of Windows, and all the revisions to those structures that could possibly take place—not to mention the fact that OS/2 uses a BITMAPCOREHEADER structure for DIBs—that there probably ought to be some reasonably reliable way to tell if a structure is really the one you think it is, especially if that structure might come from a file. If you put the size of the structure as its first member (and always make the size a DWORD), your code can compare the size of the structure as it appears in a file with the size of the structure in memory. If they are not the same, then either something is wrong with the file or it contains a structure that you don't know about. For example, since a BITMAPINFOHEADER and a BITMAPCOREHEADER are different sizes, you can tell which kind of file you're dealing with by testing this value. It's not necessarily the best possible way to determine a file's type, but it's the only way you've got for DIBs and .BMP files.

The next two members—**biWidth** and **biHeight**—define the width and height of the DIB, respectively, in pixels. The next member, **biPlanes**, defines the number of planes for the target device. As I mentioned previously, since Windows supports only the chunky (single-plane) format, this member must always be set to 1.

The **biBitCount** member can be either 1, 4, 8, or 24 in Windows 3.1 and earlier, and can also be 16 or 32 for later versions of Windows. All the code in this book (and, as you'll learn in Chapter 9, all code that works with WinG) uses 8-bit bitmaps; therefore, this member will always be set to 8.

The **biCompression** member of the structure can specify one of three compression types that Windows' DIB functions support: **BI_RLE4**, **BI_RLE8**, or **BI_RGB**. The latter isn't really a compression type at all but specifies that the bits are, in fact, uncompressed. The other two define run-length encoded formats for either 4-bit or 8-bit bitmaps. I won't go into the format of the run-length encoded bitmaps because they're seldom used, they leave decompression up to the display driver, and they're hard to use in game programming where you frequently need direct, fast access to a pixel value.

The next structure member, **biSizeImage**, defines the size of the image in bytes. If you set **biCompression** to **BI_RGB**, you can set this member to zero; Windows can do the math itself.

The next two members, **biXPelsPerMeter** and **biYPelsPerMeter**, have funny names that betray their origin. If you know much about IBM, you probably know that they seem to have their own language for all things in computerdom. (For example, hard disks aren't called hard disks, they're called *DASDs* (that's *daz-dees*), for direct-access storage devices; memory isn't called RAM, but rather *program store;* and pixels are called *pels,* for picture elements.) DIBs came into being about the same time that Microsoft and IBM were working together on OS/2 Presentation Manager, and IBM had a lot to say about how things worked. The **biXPelsPerMeter** and **biYPelsPerMeter** structure members define the *x* and *y* resolution, in pixels per meter, of the target device for the bitmap. The idea here is that you could choose from a variety of bitmap resources to find one that most closely matched the resolution of the target device. It's very common for these values to be set to zero, meaning the target resolution is either arbitrary or unknown.

The **biClrUsed** member defines how many colors are in the color table. Just to make more work for you, this value can either be the actual number (like 256 for 8-bit DIBs) or zero, meaning that it's the maximum number of colors corresponding to the value in the **biBitCount** member. It's very common for this value to be zero, in fact, which makes it necessary to actually compute the number of colors in a DIB (okay, it's a simple shift operation, admittedly), rather than just reading a value in the structure. Note that this number should never be higher than the number of colors represented by **biBitCount**, but it could be lower, which would mean that only certain colors were defined.

The **biClrImportant** member tells Windows which colors in the color table are, well, considered important to the display of the bitmap. Now, it's pretty hard to imagine that there would be unimportant colors in your bitmap: "Oh, gee, I don't *really* need all 256—only 15 or 20 are *important* to me." The reason this member exists is so that Windows can attempt to optimize palette matching to get the "important" colors first. Most DIBs set this value to that used for **biClrUsed**.

Notice that the actual color table is not part of the BITMAPINFOHEADER structure, even though I mentioned earlier that it directly follows the structure in memory. This is handled by yet another structure, BITMAPINFO, defined in WINDOWS.H as follows:

```
typedef struct tagBITMAPINFO
{
    BITMAPINFOHEADER bmiHeader;
    RGBQUAD          bmiColors[1];
} BITMAPINFO;
```

As you can see, a BITMAPINFO is nothing more than a BITMAPINFOHEADER followed by an array of RGBQUADs exactly one element long. The principle here is to allocate a chunk of memory the size of a BITMAPINFOHEADER plus the size of an RGBQUAD *multiplied* by the number of colors in the color table. Why the color table must exactly follow the BITMAPINFOHEADER in memory—as opposed just to having a pointer to it as part of the structure itself—is a mystery, but probably has something to do with performance. The result is that code for allocating and accessing the memory for these structures can be a little convoluted. The BITMAPINFO structure is used in the calls that copy a DIB to the screen's device context, because those calls need to know the color table of the DIB, not just the layout information. Most programs just use casts to specify a BITMAPINFO structure vs. a BITMAPINFOHEADER structure, since one is just a superset of the other. This is a perfectly reasonable approach, and you could take it one step further by allocating enough memory to hold the *bits* for the DIB as well, making the whole DIB one contiguous piece of memory. As you'll learn later in this chapter, that's exactly the technique I use to load and manipulate .BMP files (which are, of course, DIBs).

This leads to the obvious question of where the actual bits are used, and how.

Using DIBs

Now that you know what a DIB is made of, let's discuss how it's displayed on the screen. Since a DIB isn't a DDB, and therefore can't be selected into a device context, how do you blt it? There are several possible solutions.

One way around the problem is to use **`CreateDIBitmap`**, which, despite its name, does *not* create a DIB at all, but creates a DDB *from* a DIB. The function returns an HBITMAP, which can be treated like any normal device-dependent bitmap—it can be selected into a memory DC, and hence, blted to and from. The problem with **`CreateDIBitmap`** is that it requires twice the memory size of the bitmap to work: one chunk to hold the DIB's bits that you loaded or created, and one chunk (that's created automatically by the function) to hold the bits of the DDB. Another problem is that there is no real control over how the colors in the DIB's color table are used in the DDB.

Another alternative is to use **`SetDIBits`**, which copies scan lines of the DIB into a device-dependent bitmap. But this is hardly different from the previous example: It still requires that you have a DDB whose bits will be set, and thus requires twice the memory.

Fortunately, Windows provides a few more functions for working with DIBs. The roughly equivalent function to the device-dependent **`BitBlt`** for DIBs is **`SetDIBitsToDevice`**, which copies bits from a DIB directly to a device surface represented by a device context, usually the screen. Rather than list all the parameters to **`SetDIBitsToDevice`**, I'll follow the Microsoft party line and tell you that the function is obsolete. You should instead use its more generalized parent, **`StretchDIBits`**, which is to DIBs roughly what **`StretchBlt`** is to DDBs. Although **`StretchDIBits`** offers the ability to scale the bitmap as well, Microsoft assures us that if the source and destination rectangles are 1:1, there is no performance advantage over **`SetDIBitsToDevice`**—they undoubtedly end up in the same place inside the display driver.

Now that we know that **`StretchDIBits`** is our man, let's take a look at how it works.

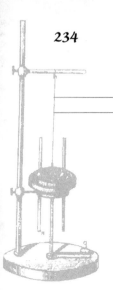

The `StretchDIBits` Function

The function's prototype looks like this:

```
int StretchDIBits(HDC hdc, int XDest, int YDest,
                        int cxDest, int cyDest,
                        int XSrc, int YSrc,
                        int cxSrc, int cySrc,
                        const void FAR *lpvBits,
                        LPBITMAPINFO lpbmi,
                        UINT fuColorUse, DWORD fdwRop)
```

In typical C convention, the first set of parameters define the destination of the copy, and the rest define the source. The first parameter, of course, is a handle to the device context into which the bits of the DIB will be copied; typically, this is the DC of the destination window. The next two parameters, **XDest** and **YDest**, are the starting coordinates of the destination rectangle—in other words, where, in the destination DC, the copy will start.

The next two parameters, **cxDest** and **cyDest**, define the dimensions of the destination rectangle, and **XSrc** and **YSrc** define the starting coordinates of the source rectangle. The **cxSrc** and **cySrc** parameters in turn define the dimensions of the source rectangle. You can optimize performance by making **cxSrc** equal to **cxDest** and **cySrc** equal to **cyDest**; this is a 1:1 blt.

Before I go on to the last few parameters, I should introduce you to a particularly, uh, shall we say interesting artifact of DIBs. All the parameters described so far seem perfectly normal and generally similar to those used in **StretchBlt**. But there's one little difference: *DIBs are generally upside down.*

By upside down, I mean that the 0,0 pixel in a DIB is at the *lower left* corner of the bitmap, rather than the upper left corner that is the origin of a DDB and also of a normal device context (see Figure 7-3). Why? Well, again, when Microsoft and IBM were designing Presentation Manager for OS/2, IBM decided that PM should address the screen using a regular, right-hand Cartesian coordinate system, and that means that origins are in the lower left corner. Consequently, DIBs were designed to comply with this orientation. The problem with DIBs being upside down isn't that it's difficult to rectify mathematically—after all, subtracting the *y* coordinate from the overall height isn't a difficult or even slow operation—but that most display hardware organizes its memory the other way, with the origin in the upper left corner and successive scan lines growing *down* the display, not *up*. Because of this, most display drivers have to invert the scan lines as they copy them to the screen, often with some loss of performance.

The "upside-downness" of DIBs was a thorn in Microsoft's side for some time. It's one of the reasons that display-driver writers have more or less ignored the performance of DIBs and haven't taken the time to optimize them.

FIGURE 7-3

Upside-down DIBs

Fortunately, Microsoft decided to fix the problem, starting with WinG. You can now create DIBs in a normal, right-side-up configuration. Although they won't work with **StretchDIBits**, they'll work with the WinG functions that are described in Chapter 9. For now, assume the orientation isn't a problem and that you can work either way.

The next parameter to **StretchDIBits** is a pointer to the actual bits that make up the image. Since the bits aren't part of the BITMAPINFO (or BITMAPINFO-HEADER) structure, they must be specified separately here.

The next parameter is a pointer to the BITMAPINFO structure that defines the size and other parameters of the DIB, along with the color table. Recall that a BITMAP-INFO structure is nothing more than a BITMAPINFOHEADER structure directly followed by enough RGBQUAD data structures to define the DIB's color table. As it turns out, the color table that's part of the BITMAPINFO structure can actually be one of two kinds, identified by the next parameter to **StretchDIBits**, **fuColorUse**. If **fuColorUse** is set to DIB_RGB_COLORS, then the color table is indeed an array of RGBQUAD structures that define the actual red, green, and blue components of the color index, and the values in **lpvBits** form an index to that color table.

If, on the other hand, **fuColorUse** is set to DIB_PAL_COLORS, then instead of an array of RGBQUADs following the BITMAPINFOHEADER, an array of WORDs (16-bit values) the size of the palette (256, in the case of 8-bit DIBs) is expected instead. The value of each WORD in the array is not an actual RGB value in this case, but an index value into the current logical palette. You'll learn all about logical palettes in Chapter 8, but consider this a little preview.

When DIB_RGB_COLORS is used in the twelfth parameter to **StretchDIBits**, the values in the color table may or may not (most likely *not*) match the colors in the current logical palette. Windows kindly creates a translation table that maps all the DIBs' colors into the closest ones in the current logical palette, a time-consuming process that Windows does on every call to **StretchDIBits**.

The idea behind DIB_PAL_COLORS is that if you already know that the DIB you're going to display with **StretchDIBits** has a color table that contains the same colors as the current system palette, then you don't have to define all the RGB values for it—they're already in the palette. The 256 WORDs in the color-table part of the BITMAPINFO structure (again, we're talking 8-bit images here) then just define a translation table into the current logical palette and Windows doesn't have to do any color matching.

Bottom line: DIB_PAL_COLORS is much faster than DIB_RGB_COLORS, which should be avoided at all costs. You can save Windows even more time by making the DIB_PAL_COLORS color table what's called an *identity table,* meaning that the 256 WORDs are just a count from 0 to 255. Then Windows doesn't even have to index through the color table: The value of a pixel is a real index to the current palette. Personally, I think they should have had another setting for this (like DIB_IDENTITY_COLORS or something) so that it would be explicit, but this is hardly the worst part about DIB color handling.

FIGURE 7-4

DIB_RGB_COLORS vs. DIB_PAL_COLORS

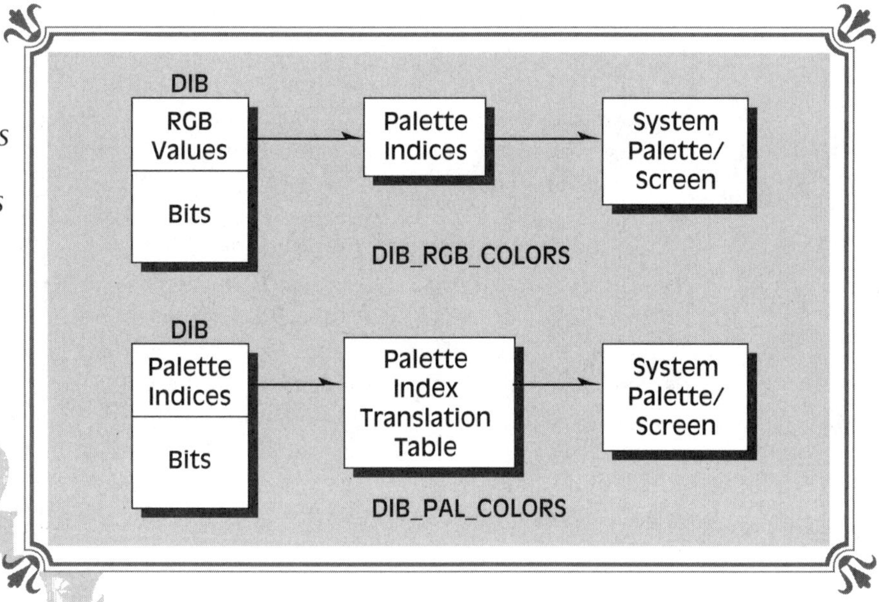

The use of the color table will become clearer as we explore palettes in Chapter 8, but Figure 7-4 illustrates the difference between the DIB_RGB_COLORS and DIB_PAL_COLORS settings of **fuColorUse** in the **StretchDIBits** call.

Finally, the last parameter to **StretchDIBits** is a DWORD that defines the raster operation to be used. This parameter (**fdwRop**) can have any value that the **BitBlt** function's **dwRop** parameter can have. Ninety percent of the time it will be SRCCOPY, which simply copies the bits of the source into the destination.

Creating and Displaying a DIB

Let's get down to coding an example how to display a DIB on the screen. Building on what we did in Chapter 6, the code will construct and display a DIB at the current cursor location when the user presses the right mouse button; the old DDB will still be dragged around with the left mouse button.

The first task is to construct the DIB. In Chapter 6, a device-dependent bitmap was simply loaded from the resource file with **LoadBitmap**, which returns a handle to a DDB. Clearly, that won't work for DIBs. (Actually, it *is* possible to load a DIB from the resource file, and later I'll show the magic trick that makes it simple. But instead of loading a DIB from a file here, let's construct one in memory by creating the color table and bits that make it up. After all, that's one thing we simply couldn't do with a DDB—we had to use the GDI to actually modify the bits, which we could never directly access.)

The easy way to proceed is to create a function that creates a DIB for us of a specified width and height, with an uninitialized color table and bits. Later, we'll set the color table and bits.

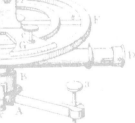

DIB-Access Macros

Since a DIB is really nothing more than a BITMAPINFO structure, a color table, and an array of pixel values, it would be convenient to have some macros that let us access the parts of the DIB. We can use such macros only if the DIB is in so-called *packed-DIB* format, which simply means that the bits of the DIB follow the BITMAPINFO structure and color table in memory. This is a very useful format, as it keeps things all together and makes it easy, for example, to read and write DIBs from and to files. Following are a set of macros for accessing various parts of a packed DIB:

```
//
// macros to access the fields in a BITMAPINFO struct
// field_value = macro(pBitmapInfo)
//

#define BI_WIDTH(pBI) \
                (int)((pBI)->bmiHeader.biWidth)
```

continued on next page

continued from previous page

```
#define BI_HEIGHT(pBI) \
              (int)((pBI)->bmiHeader.biHeight)
#define BI_PLANES(pBI) \
              ((pBI)->bmiHeader.biPlanes)
#define BI_BITCOUNT(pBI) \
              ((pBI)->bmiHeader.biBitCount)
#define BI_CLRUSED(pBI) \
              ((pBI)->bmiHeader.biClrUsed)

//
// macros to access BITMAPINFO fields in a DIB
// field_value = macro(pDIB)
//

#define DIB_WIDTH(pDIB) \
        (BI_WIDTH((LPBITMAPINFO)(pDIB)))

#define DIB_HEIGHT(pDIB) \
        (BI_HEIGHT((LPBITMAPINFO)(pDIB)))

#define DIB_PLANES(pDIB) \
        (BI_PLANES((LPBITMAPINFO)(pDIB)))

#define DIB_BITCOUNT(pDIB) \
        (BI_BITCOUNT((LPBITMAPINFO)(pDIB)))

#define DIB_CLRUSED(pDIB) \
        (BI_CLRUSED((LPBITMAPINFO)(pDIB)))

#define DIB_COLORS(pDIB) \
        ((BI_CLRUSED(pDIB)) ? (BI_CLRUSED(pDIB)) : \
        (1<<(BI_BITCOUNT(pDIB))))

#define DIB_PCLRTAB(pDIB) \
        ((LPRGBQUAD)(((LPSTR)((LPBITMAPINFO)(pDIB))) \
        + sizeof(BITMAPINFOHEADER)))

#define DIB_BISIZE(pDIB) \
        (sizeof(BITMAPINFOHEADER) \
        + DIB_COLORS(pDIB) * sizeof(RGBQUAD))

#define DIB_PBITS(pDIB) \
        (((LPSTR)((LPBITMAPINFO)(pDIB))) \
        + DIB_BISIZE(pDIB))

#define DIB_PBI(pDIB)   ((LPBITMAPINFO)(pDIB))

#define DIB_STORAGEWIDTH(pDIB) \
        ((DIB_WIDTH(pDIB) + 3) & ~3)
```

Each of the macros takes a pointer to a packed DIB, which is really a pointer to its BITMAPINFO structure, since the color table and bits follow it in memory. In fact, it would be convenient to define a data type as a pointer to a packed DIB, like so:

```
typedef LPBITMAPINFO PDIB
```

Using the macros and that data type, you can easily access all the parameters of a DIB without having to keep a bunch of independent variables floating around.

Most of these macros should be easy to follow. There are a couple, however, that deserve further explanation. The DIB_COLORS macro computes the number of colors, depending on whether **biClrUsed** is zero or not. If it is, then it's based on the **biBitCount** field.

The DIB_PCLRTAB macro returns a pointer to the color table, which can be found after the BITMAPINFOHEADER.

The DIB_STORAGEWIDTH macro betrays an important point about DIBs: Their scan-line widths must all be *DWORD-aligned.* This is done to optimize access to the bits on 32-bit computers. As a result, all the inner loops that compute on the scan lines of a DIB will need to use DIB_STORAGEWIDTH to determine where scan lines end.

DIB_BISIZE returns the size of the BITMAPINFOHEADER *and* the color table. Another way to think of it is as the size of the whole packed DIB, less the actual bits.

Note all the various casts to different data types. These rely on the fact that a BITMAPINFO structure has a BITMAPINFOHEADER structure as its first element, so that they can be treated identically.

Using these macros and the packed-DIB format greatly simplifies DIB handling and eliminates many of the errors commonly associated with working with DIBs. There are a couple of cases where you can't use the packed-DIB format, but they're rare and can be handled easily. We'll learn more about them in Chapter 9.

Now on to the function that creates an "empty" 8-bit DIB:

```
PDIB CreateDIB (int width, int height)
{
    LPBITMAPINFOHEADER new;
    long storage;

    // Compute the size. Remember that
    // the width is DWORD-aligned.
    storage = sizeof(BITMAPINFOHEADER) +
                 256 * sizeof(RGBQUAD) +
                 (long)((width + 3) & ~3) * height;

    // Allocate a chunk of memory, cast
    // as a BITMAPINFOHEADER struct for
    // easy initializing.
    new = (LPBITMAPINFOHEADER)
             GlobalAllocPtr (GPTR, storage);
    if (!new)
        return NULL;

    new->biSize = sizeof(BITMAPINFOHEADER);
    new->biWidth = width;
```

continued on next page

continued from previous page

```
    new->biHeight = height;
    new->biPlanes = 1;          // Always 1
    new->biBitCount = 8;
    new->biCompression = BI_RGB;
    new->biSizeImage = 0;       // Not needed for BI_RGB
    new->biXPelsPerMeter = 0;
    new->biYPelsPerMeter = 0;   // These are arbitrary.
    new->biClrUsed = 0;         // Use biBitCount.
    new->biClrImportant = 0;    // Not important

    // Return the PDIB.
    return (PDIB)new;
}
```

Now it's easy to access the bits and color table from the PDIB returned by **CreateDIB** with the DIB macros. The first thing to do is to create a color table. Simplicity rules in this example: This color table will be just a red ramp going from 0 to 255. You can have any color you want as long as it's a shade of red. (This is for purposes of illustration only; you'll usually get a color table from a file, which we'll examine in detail in the next chapter.)

```
void RedRamp (PDIB pDIB)
{
    int n;
    LPRGBQUAD pQ = DIB_PCLRTAB (pDIB);

    // Set the entries to a red ramp.
    for (n = 0; n < 256; n++) {
        pQ->rgbRed = (BYTE)n;
        pQ->rgbGreen = 0;
        pQ->rgbBlue = 0;
        pQ++;
    }
}
```

Simple enough. Now that there's a color table, it's time to set the actual bits that make up the image. To best illustrate the ramp, the next function will set the bits of a DIB such that the pixels of each line are set to one of the color table's values. The DIB should be at least 256 lines high in order to use all the color table's values.

```
void SetDIBtoColorMap (pDIB)
{
    int n;
    char huge *p;
    int linelength;

    // A huge pointer is needed here in order to
    // properly increment past 64k, if necessary.
    p = (char huge *)DIB_PBITS(pDIB);

    // Get the storage length of a single line
    // into a variable that can be used to increment
```

```
    // the pointer.
    linelength = DIB_STORAGEWIDTH(pDIB);

    // Loop through the lines of the DIB.
    for (n = 0; n < DIB_HEIGHT(pDIB); n++) {
        // Set the bits of the current line
        // to one of the 256 colors in the map
        // (works only for 256-color DIBs).
        _fmemset (p, n%256, linelength);
        // Increment the pointer.
        p += linelength;
    }
}
```

To display the bitmap, we'll add code to the example developed in Chapter 6 so that it's displayed at the current mouse position when the user presses the right mouse button. We need to modify the MAIN structure in MAIN.H to include a PDIB:

```
typedef struct MAINtag {
    HWND hwnd;                  // This window
    HDC  hdc;                   // DC for our window

    struct {
        struct {
            HBITMAP bmp;        // Bitmap
            HDC memDC;          // Memory DC
        } bmpdata[2];           // Source, background
        int width, height;      // size of bitmap
        int oldx, oldy;         // previous position
    } bitmaps;
    PDIB pDIB;
} MAIN;
```

Then, the initialization code should be added to **OnCreate**, listed here in its entirety:

```
static BOOL OnCreate(MAIN* main,
                            CREATESTRUCT FAR* lpCreateStruct)
{
    BITMAP b;
    int i;
    long scanwidth, height;
    char huge *p;

    // We get the DC once, and save it away.
    // This works only because we use CS_OWNDC.
    main->hdc = GetDC (main->hwnd);

    SetBkColor (main->hdc, RGB (0,0,0));
    SetTextColor (main->hdc, RGB (255, 0, 0));
    SelectObject (main->hdc,
                        GetStockObject (GRAY_BRUSH));
```

continued on next page

continued from previous page

```
    // Get a cursor.
    main->cursor = LoadCursor (NULL, IDC_ARROW);
    // and a bitmap.
    main->SRC_BMP = LoadBitmap (G_app.hinst,
                                      "picture");

    if (!main->SRC_BMP)
        return FALSE;

    // Create the source memory DC and
    // select the bitmap into it.
    main->SRC_DC = CreateCompatibleDC (main->hdc);
    main->OLD_SRC_BMP  = SelectBitmap (main->SRC_DC,
                                     main->SRC_BMP);

    // Create the backing-store memory DC
    // and a bitmap for it.
    main->BK_DC = CreateCompatibleDC (main->hdc);
    // How big?
    GetObject (main->SRC_BMP, sizeof(BITMAP), &b);
    main->bitmaps.width = b.bmWidth;
    main->bitmaps.height = b.bmHeight;
    main->BK_BMP = CreateCompatibleBitmap (main->hdc,
                           main->bitmaps.width,
                           main->bitmaps.height);
    // Select it.
    main->OLD_BK_BMP = SelectBitmap (main->BK_DC,
                                   main->BK_BMP);

    // Create a DIB.
    main->pDIB = CreateDIB (256, 256);
    // Make sure we got it.
    if (!main->pDIB)
        return FALSE;

    // Initialize the color table to a red ramp.
    RedRamp (main->pDIB);

    // Now initialize the bits, showing the
    // red ramp on each line.
    scanwidth = DIB_STORAGEWIDTH(main->pDIB);
    height = DIB_HEIGHT(main->pDIB);
    p = DIB_PBITS(main->pDIB);
    for (i = 0; i < (int)height; i++) {
        _fmemset (p, i, scanwidth);
        p += scanwidth;
    }

    main->menu = LoadMenu (G_app.hinst, "MainMenu");
    ShowWindow (main->hwnd, G_app.cmdShow);
    return TRUE;
}
```

There's a certain simplicity to DIBs: Since the GDI can't draw on them, it isn't necessary to create a memory-device context to get them on the screen. All that's needed is a call to **StretchDIBits**. All the memory used by the DIB is owned by the application, so we don't need any mysterious functions (like **GetObject**) to find out valuable information about the bitmap, like its dimensions. They're all right there in the BITMAPINFO structure. If you use the packed-DIB format and access macros, it is very easy to manipulate a DIB.

Now let's get it on the screen with **StretchDIBits** in the **OnRButtonDown** handler function:

```
static void OnRButtonDown (MAIN *main,
                                   BOOL fDoubleClick,
                           int x, int y,
                           UINT keyFlags)
{
    int cx = DIB_WIDTH (main->pDIB);
    int cy = DIB_HEIGHT(main->pDIB);

    StretchDIBits (main->hdc, x, y,
                   cx, cy,
                   0, 0,
                   cx, cy,
                   DIB_PBITS(main->pDIB),
                   main->pDIB,
                   DIB_RGB_COLORS,
                   SRCCOPY);
}
```

Examining the function closely, you'll see that the destination size (the fourth and fifth parameters) is the size of the full DIB, and that the whole DIB is copied (the same values are in the eighth and ninth parameters). If the fourth and fifth parameters had different values than the eighth and ninth, **StretchDIBits** would stretch (or shrink) the bitmap to fit, with an associated loss of speed.

The pointer to the bits is obtained with the DIB_PBITS macro, and since a PDIB is nothing more than an LPBITMAPINFO anyway, it's just passed in straight to the eleventh parameter. The thirteenth parameter specifies a source copy, overwriting whatever was in the destination DC.

The twelfth parameter specifies that the DIB contains a color table with actual RGB values (DIB_RGB_COLORS), rather than indices to the current logical palette. This means that Windows has to do a color match on each pixel with the current palette, at some considerable loss of speed compared to DIB_PAL_COLORS. But since the code hasn't set the current palette, this is the only way to get a result with colors that are somewhat like what we want.

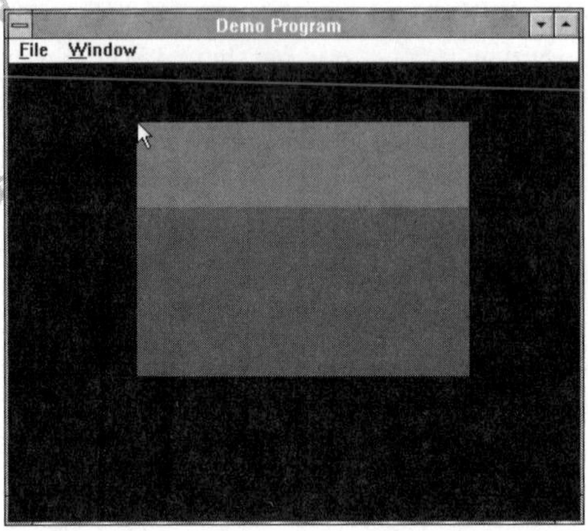

FIGURE 7-5
Displaying the red ramp—there's a problem!

Running the Program

Time to compile and run the program, and press the right mouse button somewhere. If you're lazy, just run the executable file found in this chapter's directory on the CD-ROM. See Figure 7-5 for the results.

Hey! What's *that?* It sure doesn't look like a square with 256 levels of red in it! In fact, it looks like it has about *three* levels of red: really red, sort of red, and no red—like *black!* What's happening here?

Recall what **StretchDIBits** does when given the DIB_RGB_COLORS flag: It tries to find the closest match in the current palette for the specified DC for each pixel in the image. Unfortunately, the stock Windows palette on a 256-color display has only 20 colors defined, and only two of those are red. Thus **StretchDIBits**, in an attempt to find the closest match, finds only red, redder, and black to match the 256 red levels specified in the DIB's color table.

Summary

After taking you through the ins and outs of DIBs, I've left you with a program that obviously isn't going to work, and to fix it you'll have learn about one of the nastiest beasts in Windows graphics programming: the Palette Manager, which is the subject of the next chapter.

8

Palette Management Under Windows

[illegible]

Come tu debbi fare le manovelle [illegible] le quali si movano e l'alza
no i gran pesi [illegible]
forzare nella mano [illegible] alla manovella perchè [illegible]
la forza [illegible] più [illegible] più [illegible]

[illegible]

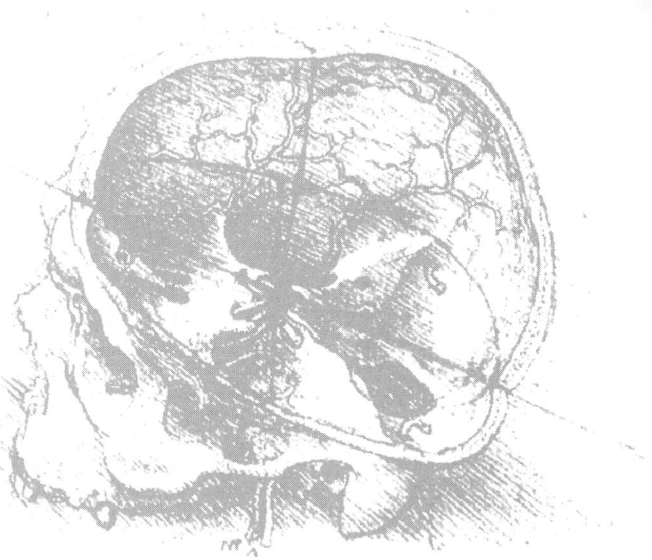

8

Palette Management Under Windows

The internal workings of the Windows Palette Manager are as complex as anything in Windows gets. If you're an old hand at DOS games programming, you know how simple working with the palette can be: With one call you can blast the entire palette of the VGA, and *wham*—256 of your favorite colors get displayed in their full splendor, no questions asked.

But in the sharing, caring world of Windows, there's only one palette, and it must be shared among many applications. Since the palette controls how every color looks on the display, sharing it improperly can be disastrous. The Palette Manager (which is an integral part of the GDI, rather than a complete subsystem proper) attempts to make sharing the palette possible, with certain unavoidable compromises.

Let's begin with an overview of palettes and Windows.

Windows Palettes and Multitasking

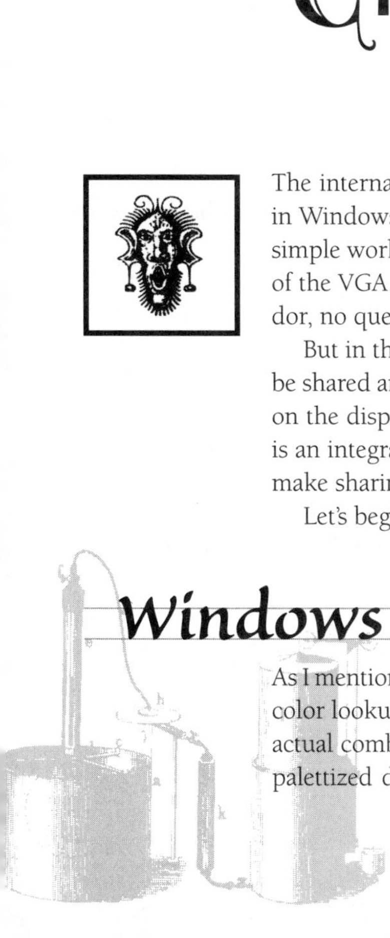

As I mentioned in Chapter 5, a *palettized* display is characterized by having an on-board color lookup table or palette whose function is to decode the value of a pixel into the actual combination of red, green, and blue values that will be sent to the monitor. A palettized display is a compromise design that allows for reasonable color richness without the memory (and thus, performance) overhead of a true-color display, where each pixel contains separate values for red, green, and blue. Typical pixel depths for palettized displays are 4 and 8 bits per pixel, representing 16 and 256 colors, respectively. Since 16 colors are generally too few for an interesting game, most game programs use 256 colors. Because of this (and the fact that there are very few palettized displays that support more than 256 colors), this chapter will be dedicated to the discussion of managing a palette of 256 colors.

Given the multitasking nature of Windows and the fact that there is only *one* physical hardware palette for the display, there are a limited number of approaches to sharing the palette. At one extreme, you could give full control of the hardware palette to the foreground application, allowing it to update and change the palette in whatever way it sees fit—other applications be damned. In fact it *is* possible for the Windows Palette Manager to operate in this way, but it requires a lot of careful management and you should avoid it if at all possible.

At the other extreme, Windows could have created a generic system palette for all applications to use, not allowing any one application to actually set the palette directly. The limitations of this approach are obvious—no application really would get the colors it wanted, so everyone would suffer equally. This is clearly too limiting for most applications, especially game programs.

The approach that the Palette Manager takes is a compromise somewhere in between these two extremes. It provides a small set of colors (20) that all applications can use consistently, and a larger set (the remaining 236) that it gives the foreground application priority to set. In other words, the foreground application has first pick of the 236 definable colors of the system palette, while background applications get their colors squeezed in wherever possible.

The System Palette

You can think of the system palette as a copy of the physical hardware palette. Windows maintains the system palette in sync with the hardware palette at all times. It isn't *really* a bit-for-bit copy of the hardware palette, because the hardware palette doesn't necessarily use all the bits that Windows maintains for the system palette. On Super VGA hardware, for example, the hardware palette supports only 18 bits of resolution (6 bits per red, green, and blue channel), while the Windows system palette always contains a full 8 bits per channel.

The 20 constant colors that Windows reserves for all applications to use are called the *static* colors, while the remaining 236 are creatively called the *nonstatic* colors. In actuality, there may be more or fewer than 20 static colors; it's the display-device driver that determines this. In practice, however, virtually all conventional Super VGA-type drivers reserve exactly 20 static colors.

The 20 static colors aren't a contiguous lot in the palette; rather, there are 10 contiguous slots at either end, as illustrated in Figure 8-1.

The 20 static colors of the system palette are shown in Table 8-1.

Looking at the colors represented in this table, you'll notice a few oddities. For example, why is Medium Gray not quite gray? Who knows—somebody probably thought it looked better on their monitor with a little more blue in it. Also notice the names "Sky" Blue and "Money" Green: These are rumored to be derived from the desires of a certain large corporation that once had a codevelopment relationship with Microsoft.

Note that the first eight entries (0–7) and the last eight (248–255) are essentially the original 16 VGA (and EGA, for that matter) colors. The original EGA had *digital* outputs, where the red, green, and blue guns were either on or off, with one more bit for the so-called "high-intensity" colors.

The reason that the 20 static colors appear at either end of the system palette is to allow the commonly used XOR raster operation to do something similar to what it would do on a regular 16-color VGA display. These 20 static colors are relatively constant among display drivers, though the 4 non-VGA colors may be slightly different from driver to driver. When you learn about creating an identity palette later in this chapter, you'll see how to ask the system for the actual values in the 20 static entries.

There are many applications, of course, that aren't really very color-intensive and so don't require more than the 20 system colors. These applications don't require any of the Palette Manager features at all; they just select colors from the system set.

Let's take a look at how a program changes any of the remaining 236 colors in the system palette.

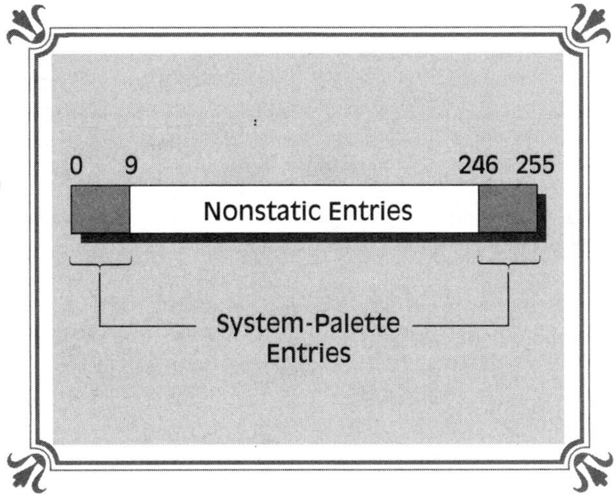

FIGURE 8-1

Layout of the system palette

TABLE 8-1

The static colors

Index	Red	Green	Blue	Color
0	0	0	0	Black
1	128	0	0	Dark Red
2	0	128	0	Dark Green
3	128	128	0	Dark Yellow
4	0	0	128	Dark Blue
5	128	0	128	Dark Magenta
6	0	128	128	Dark Cyan
7	192	192	192	Light Gray
8	192	220	192	"Money" Green
9	166	202	240	"Sky" Blue
246	255	251	240	Cream
247	160	160	164	Medium Gray
248	128	128	128	Dark Gray
249	255	0	0	Red
250	0	255	0	Green
251	255	255	0	Yellow
252	0	0	255	Blue
253	255	0	255	Magenta
254	0	255	255	Cyan
255	255	255	255	White

Logical Palettes

The system palette can be thought of as the actual, physical hardware palette, but programs specify what entries they want to change through the use of *logical palettes*. You can create a logical palette by using the LOGPALETTE data type, defined in WINDOWS.H as follows:

```
typedef struct tagLOGPALETTE
{
    WORD    palVersion;
```

```
    WORD    palNumEntries;
    PALETTEENTRY palPalEntry[1];
} LOGPALETTE;
```

Notice that the last member of the LOGPALETTE structure, **palPalEntry**, is an array only one element long. This is very similar to the **bmiColors** entry in the BITMAPINFO structure used to maintain DIBs. The idea is that you allocate enough memory to hold a PALETTEENTRY structure for each color you need. The PALETTEENTRY structure, in turn, is defined like so:

```
typedef struct tagPALETTEENTRY
{
    BYTE    peRed;
    BYTE    peGreen;
    BYTE    peBlue;
    BYTE    peFlags;
} PALETTEENTRY;
```

This looks a lot like an RGBQUAD, except that the order of the red, green, and blue entries is exactly backward for some reason. The setting of the **peFlags** member will be covered a little later in this chapter; for now, I'll use its default setting of zero.

A LOGPALETTE doesn't actually represent the actual palette. The GDI palette object is created with a call to **CreatePalette**, which returns a handle to a palette or an HPALETTE. The code below illustrates the creation of a palette, with the entries representing a red ramp.

```
HPALETTE CreateRedRampPalette (int numentries)
{
    LOGPALETTE *pLogPal;
    HPALETTE hPal;
    BYTE red;
    int n;

    // Allocate a LOGPALETTE of numentries size
    pLogPal = (LOGPALETTE *)LocalAlloc (LPTR,
                                   sizeof(LOGPALETTE)+
                                   sizeof(PALETTEENTRY)*
                                   // One there already...
                                   numentries-1);
    if (!pLogPal)
        return NULL;

    // Palette version is currently always the same.
    pLogPal->palVersion = 0x300;
    pLogPal->palNumEntries = numentries;

    // Create a ramp.  Put the high-intensity values
    // at the beginning.
    for (red = 255, n = 0;
```

continued on next page

continued from previous page

```
         n < numentries;
         red -= 256 / numentries, n++) {
        pLogPal->palPalEntry[n].peBlue =
        pLogPal->palPalEntry[n].peGreen =
        pLogPal->palPalEntry[n].peFlags = 0;
        pLogPal->palPalEntry[n].peRed = red;
    }
    hPal = CreatePalette (pLogPal);
    LocalFree (pLogPal);
    return hPal;
}
```

Figure 8-2 shows the results.

Notice that the LOGPALETTE structure really isn't needed after you have created the palette object with **CreatePalette**; its memory is therefore tossed at the end.

Once you've created a palette, it's selected into a device context with **SelectPalette**, whose definition is:

```
HPALETTE SelectPalette (HDC hdc, HPALETTE hPal,
                                  BOOL fPalBack);
```

Note that **SelectPalette** has one more parameter than **SelectObject**, which is why the latter isn't used. The **fPalBack** parameter tells **SelectPalette** whether the specified palette is to be considered a *background palette*. You'll hardly ever need to specify a background palette, so this argument is customarily set to FALSE.

FIGURE 8-2

Creating a palette object from a logical palette

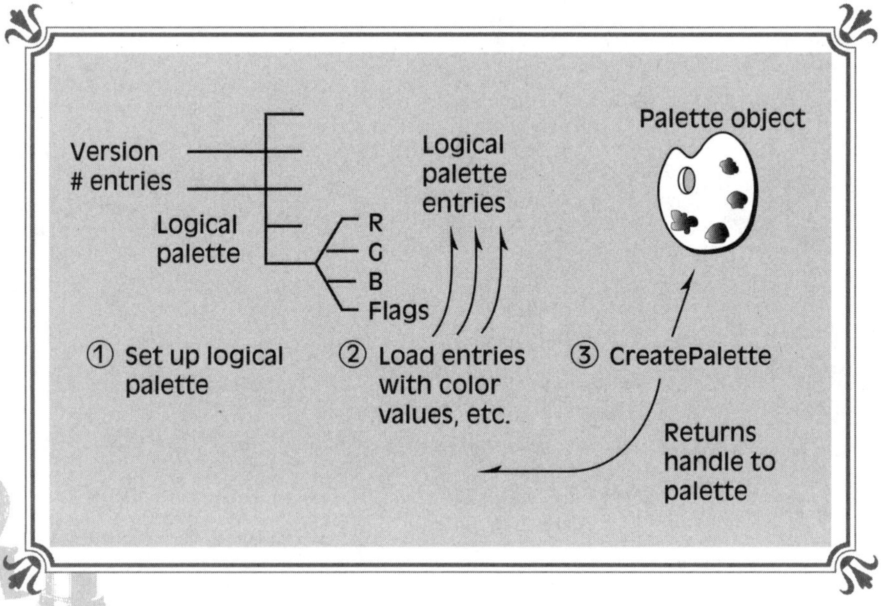

You can delete a palette object in the usual GDI way, with **DeleteObject**. All the usual GDI rules apply: The palette must not be selected into any DC when it's deleted, and the old palette returned by **SelectPalette** should be selected back into the DC before the DC is released or deleted.

Simply selecting a palette into a device context doesn't, however, change the way colors are displayed. There's one more call you'll need in order to get the selected palette copied into the system palette (and, therefore, the hardware palette). This call is **RealizePalette**:

```
UINT RealizePalette (HDC hdc);
```

SelectPalette and **RealizePalette** are frequently called in direct succession, typically from within the WM_PAINT handler function (**OnPaint**). The return value from **RealizePalette** indicates how many entries in the palette last selected into the DC (with **SelectPalette**) were mapped into actual entries in the system palette as shown in Figure 8-3. To understand the meaning of this value, we have to dig into the grungy details of what **RealizePalette** actually does.

Realizing a Logical Palette

The **RealizePalette** function doesn't just blast entries from the logical palette into the system palette and call it a day. Actually, it *can* do that, and that's often what we'd

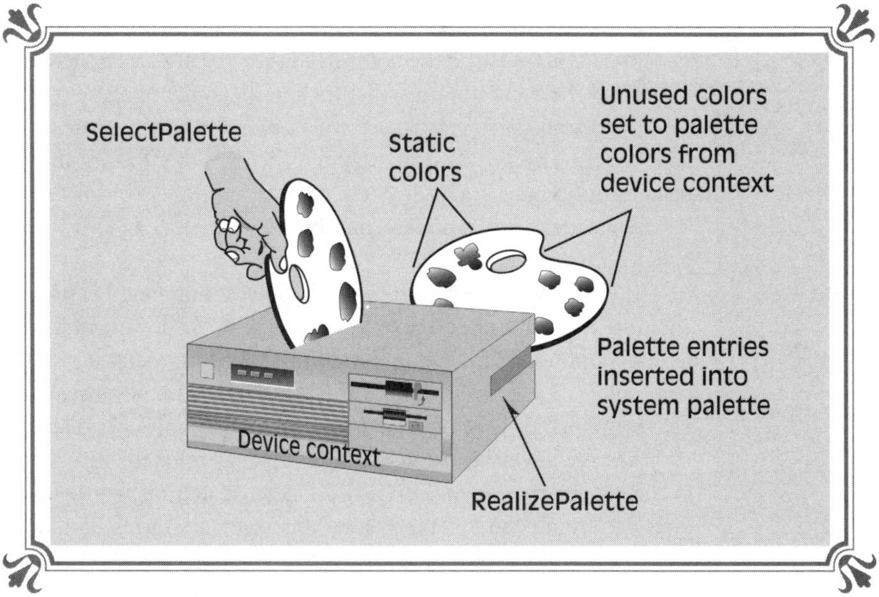

FIGURE 8-3

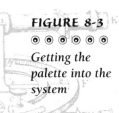

Getting the palette into the system

like to have happen. But to get it to do so requires that we understand all the actions that take place when **RealizePalette** is called. This process is complex, and varies depending on the setting of the **peFlags** entries of the LOGPALETTE that was used to create the palette being realized, so I'll deal with the simpler cases first.

Each entry in the system palette has one of three states: static, used, or unused. **RealizePalette** doesn't overwrite static entries: These entries are, in effect, permanently used by the system (they are the 20 static colors). Unused entries can be set as part of the realization process; once they're set, they become used entries. The difference between a used entry and an unused entry has to do with whether the application currently realizing the palette is a foreground application or a background application.

A foreground application is, of course, the application that is currently selected. It's the one with its window typically on top of all other windows. All the others are background applications (this should come as no surprise). When a foreground application calls **RealizePalette**, all but the static entries in the system palette can be overwritten. The Palette Manager does this by first marking all system-palette entries that are not static as unused at the start of the realization process. If, on the other hand, **RealizePalette** is being called by a background application, the Palette Manager doesn't change the state of any of the palette entries. Thus, a background application can modify only those entries that are marked as unused.

The realization process continues by color matching every entry in the logical palette (the one last selected into the DC) with every entry in the system palette. If an exact match for a color in the logical palette is found in the system palette, the entry in the system palette is marked as used, and color matching continues. If an exact match *isn't* found, then the Palette Manager looks for the first unused entry in the system palette, puts the the color from the logical palette there, and marks the entry as used. If there are no unused entries in the system palette (the palette is full), then the color from the logical palette gets mapped to the closest match in the system palette. One artifact of this matching process is that a color in the logical palette can be mapped to a color in the system palette that was set by *another* color from the same logical palette. The value returned by **RealizePalette** is the number of system-palette entries that actually changed.

The mapping process starts with the lowest numbered entries in the logical palette and also scans the system palette starting with the lowest numbered entries. For this reason, common Windows-programming wisdom dictates putting the most "important" colors of a logical palette at the beginning. (I've never really understood what an *unimportant* color was, but this mapping process sort of explains the logic behind it.)

In the end, every entry in the logical palette ends up with a mapping to one entry in the system palette, whether it's an exact match or just the closest one the Palette Manager could find. The Palette Manager performs this mapping every time **RealizePalette** is called with a palette that's never been realized before. To save time, the Palette Manager keeps a *foreground mapping* for each palette that's been created and realized into a device context. This mapping is unique for a given palette and is used whenever that palette is realized into the DC again. In general, you don't need to worry about how this is done, except to know that it means the very first time a palette is realized into a DC it can take significantly longer than subsequent times. This usually isn't a problem for a game program, because it happens only the first time the screen is painted, provided that the game doesn't change palettes often.

The Color-Matching Algorithm

What do I mean when I say the "closest match" to a given color? The Palette Manager uses a closest-Pythagorean-distance algorithm in RGB space to find the closest color. It tries to find the minimum number using the formula

$$deltaRed^2 + deltaGreen^2 + deltaBlue^2$$

where the deltas are just the differences between the red, green, and blue component values. This isn't the best algorithm in the world, but it's the one that Windows uses. Any color-matching algorithm has various subjective qualities, and this one has the advantage of yielding relatively good results at decent speed.

Note that when a palette is realized, the color entries can end up pretty much anywhere within the system palette, depending on how the Palette Manager finds matches. How, then, does one specify a color without knowing where that color is in the palette?

Recall from Chapter 5 that there are three ways to specify a color to the GDI. The PALETTEINDEX macro is one way that, in fact, *does* require that you know what the color values of the system-palette entries are, since it specifies an index directly. However, the PALETTERGB macro tells the GDI to find the *nearest* color in the currently realized system palette, using the color-matching algorithm. This tends to work okay when you're looking just for a near match, particularly for solid colors that will most likely match one of the static colors anyway.

The last method for specifying a color to the GDI is the RGB macro. Unlike PALETTERGB, however, the RGB macro doesn't match colors in the currently realized system palette, but rather returns a dithered version of one of the static colors in the palette.

Palette Messages

Windows defines three palette-related messages: WM_QUERYNEWPALETTE, WM_PALETTECHANGED, and WM_PALETTEISCHANGING. The third message is obsolete and shouldn't be used in modern Windows applications.

The WM_QUERYNEWPALETTE message tells an application that it is being activated, at the ideal time to select and realize its palette. The WM_PALETTECHANGED message is sent to all applications to inform them that the system palette has changed. It's sent with the handle of the window that was responsible for changing the palette, and you should compare this handle to the handle of the receiving application's window to make sure a recursive condition doesn't occur.

The simplest way of handling palette messages is illustrated in the following code. Although WINDOWSX.H defines message crackers for both WM_QUERYNEWPALETTE and WM_PALETTECHANGED, the handling of one is just a single test different than the handling of the other, so it's easiest just to deal with this fact in the main window handler's **`switch`** statement:

```
HANDLE_MSG(main, WM_PAINT, OnPaint);
.
.
.
case WM_PALETTECHANGED:
    if (wParam == hwnd)
        // It's from our window, break.
        break;
    // else, fall through...
HANDLE_MSG(main, WM_QUERYNEWPALETTE,
                  OnQueryNewPalette);
.
.
.
```

The **`OnQueryNewPalette`** handler code looks like this:

```
static BOOL OnQueryNewPalette (MAIN *main)
{
    HPALETTE hOldPal;
    UINT i;

    // Select our palette as a foreground palette
    // and realize it.
    hOldPal = SelectPalette (main->hdc,
                             main->hPalette,
                             FALSE);
    i = RealizePalette (main->hdc);

    // If entries were changed, repaint the window.
    if (i)
        InvalidateRect (main->hwnd, NULL, TRUE);

    // Select the old palette back, as a background
    // palette, and realize it.
    SelectPalette (main->hdc, hOldPal, TRUE);
    RealizePalette (main->hdc);
    return i ? TRUE : FALSE;
}
```

The function relies on the **main** window instance structure having a valid handle to a device context in its **hdc** member, presumably through the use of an CS_OWNDC window class style, as I illustrated in Chapter 5. Also, **main** should have a valid HPALETTE in its **hPalette** member, created previously with **CreatePalette**.

Note that the function realizes the palette twice: once as a foreground palette, and once again with the DC's old palette as a background palette. This ensures that if the application is a background application, it behaves and restores the original palette.

Palette messages are easy to handle. Let's move on to the more difficult subject of actually using a palette in combination with a device-independent bitmap (DIB).

Palettes and DIBs

It should be pretty obvious by now that to fix last chapter's problem of displaying the 256-color DIB, you must construct a palette from the DIB's color table. Creating such a palette is quite easy, of course: You simply fill in the PALETTEENTRY structures of a LOGPAL with the RGBQUAD values in the color table, create the palette, and voila! Select and realize the palette into the DC, and call **StretchDIBits** to display the image.

Indeed, it is pretty much that simple, provided you don't care much about performance (and not too much about what colors you actually get). The easy method for creating a palette from a DIB's color table goes something like this:

```
HPALETTE CreatePaletteFromDIB (PDIB pDIB)
{
    LPRGBQUAD pQ;
    int I;
    // A quick LOGPAL structure complete with
    // an array of PALETTEENTRYs
    struct {
        WORD Version;
        WORD NumberOfEntries;
        PALETTEENTRY aEntries[256];
    } Palette =
    {
        0x300,
        256
    };

    // Get the address of the color table in the DIB
    // using one of the DIB macros.
    pQ = DIB_PCLRTAB(pDIB);
    // Set aEntries to the values in the color table.
    for (i = 0; i < DIB_COLORS(pDIB); i++) {
```

continued on next page

continued from previous page

```
        Palette.aEntries[i].peRed   = pQ[i].rgbRed;
        Palette.aEntries[i].peGreen = pQ[i].rgbGreen;
        Palette.aEntries[i].peBlue  = pQ[i].rgbBlue;
        // Set peFlags to zero (default)
        Palette.aEntries[i].peFlags = 0;
    }
    // Set any unused entries' peFlags.
    for (; i < 256; i++)
        Palette.aEntries[i].peFlags = 0;

    // Return a handle to the created palette.
    return CreatePalette ((LOGPALETTE *)&Palette);
}
```

The function declares a structure that looks a lot like a LOGPALETTE, with 256 PALETTEENTRY structures in just the right place. The red, green, and blue members of the structure get set to the corresponding entries in the color table of the DIB passed in (using the PDIB definition from Chapter 7). If there were fewer than 256 entries in the color table, then the last **for** loop makes sure the **peFlags** structure members get initialized properly. The function ends by returning a handle to a palette created with **CreatePalette**.

The only problem is that it's very unlikely you'll get all 256 colors that are in the DIB's color table into the final system palette—not just unlikely, in fact, but impossible. Remember, there are 20 reserved (static) colors that can't be changed, so when the palette is realized, 20 of the colors are going to be dropped and substituted with the static colors.

DIB_RGB_COLORS and DIB_PAL_COLORS

What happens when you use **StretchDIBits** to copy the DIB to the screen? After all, who knows where it may have put those 236 remaining entries in the palette? What happens to the colors in the DIB that reference the first and last ten palette entries, anyway?

Well, recall from Chapter 7 the meaning of the twelfth parameter to **StretchDIBits**, **fuColorUse**. This parameter can have one of two settings: DIB_RGB_COLORS or DIB_PAL_COLORS. If it's the former, then **StretchDIBits** knows that it can find the DIB's color table attached to the BITMAPINFO structure. All it has to do then is create a table that matches a color in the DIB's color table with the nearest color in the system palette. In 236 of 256 cases, there'll be an exact match, because the entries came from the DIB in the first place. For the other 20 colors, well, there's probably a color close enough elsewhere in the palette to make the picture look reasonable.

Figure 8-4 illustrates the process that **StretchDIBits** goes through as it builds a match for each color in the DIB's color table.

The big bummer is that **StretchDIBits** not only has to build the translation table on every call, but it has to translate *every pixel* in the DIB through it. This is, as you might surmise, less than optimal.

The alternative is to use DIB_PAL_COLORS in the **fuColorUse** parameter to **StretchDIBits**. In this case, instead of an actual color table at the end of the BITMAPINFO structure, **StretchDIBits** expects to find the translation table that it would otherwise have to build itself as an array of WORDs (16-bit values). In the case of 8-bit DIBs, this is an array of 256 WORDs, with the value of each being the entry in the system palette that corresponds to the color in the DIB.

Since using DIB_PAL_COLORS saves **StretchDIBits** the trouble of creating the translation table on every call—and since it's unlikely that the table is going to change on every call—it's obvious that DIB_PAL_COLORS is the way to go whenever possible. But how do you know where the Palette Manager put all the colors in the palette? And what about the colors that got dropped—how do you find the closest ones so you can do the equivalent of what DIB_RGB_COLORS does?

While it might be an amusing exercise to build a table of WORDs that contain the actual palette entries for each of the colors in a DIB's color table, it turns out there's an even better way to use DIB_PAL_COLORS. You've probably intuited that it would be even faster for **StretchDIBits** to copy bits to the screen if it needed no translation table whatsoever—that is, if the color indices in the DIB were a

FIGURE 8-4

DIB_RGB_COLORS color mapping

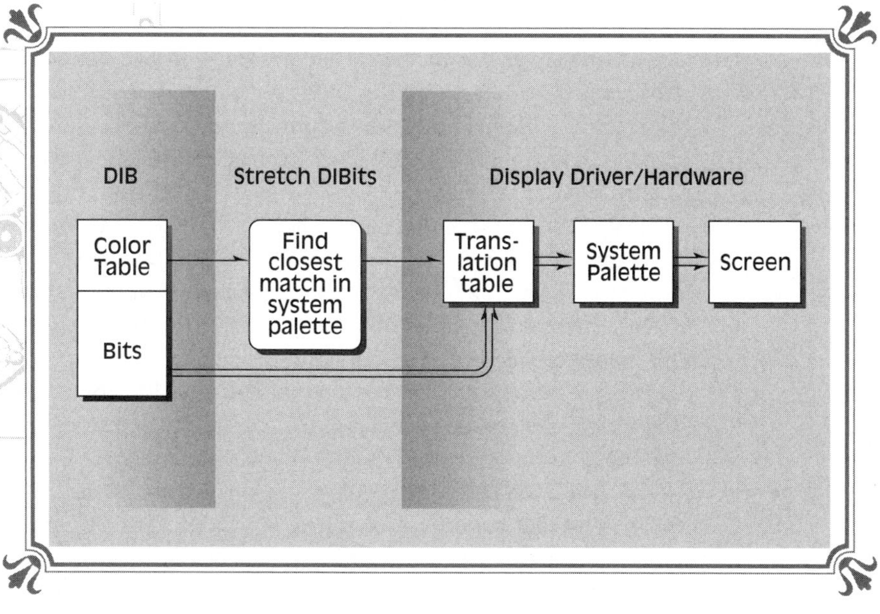

one-to-one match with the colors in the current system palette. We'd somehow tell **StretchDIBits**, "Hey, just copy the bits, dude!" and it wouldn't bother with a translation table at all.

Well, as I mentioned in Chapter 7, it would indeed be nice if there were a DIB_IDENTITY_COLORS option, but there isn't. Instead, display drivers are supposed to implement code that *detects* if the DIB_PAL_COLORS translation table sent to **StretchDIBits** is identical; that is, if it contains an array of WORDs counting up from 0 to 255. If so, then it can conclude that the pixel values in the DIB don't require any translation at all and it can just blast the pixels into display memory.

At least, that's what's *supposed* to happen. Unfortunately, many Windows display drivers don't implement the code that checks the table for identity mapping, so you get a translation no matter what. Still, it's a good idea to try to use DIB_PAL_COLORS with an identity table to get maximum performance on displays that do the right thing, and it's critical when you're using WinG, as you'll learn in the next chapter.

Identity Palettes

In order to use DIB_PAL_COLORS effectively (in other words, with a 1:1 mapping table), a program must have a way of creating a reliable palette—that is, a logical palette that will end up being 1:1 with the system palette when it's realized. Since the realization process does some unavoidable color matching, creating an identity palette is largely a matter of reverse-engineering the Palette Manager's realization process and constructing a palette that will always get realized the same way. Once you reali…um, grasp all this, it gets a lot easier (sorry, I can't help myself).

An *identity palette* is the beast that performs this trick. An identity palette is a logical palette that is characterized by two attributes: It has the static, system-palette colors already in place at either end (the upper and lower ten slots), and the slots in between have the PC_NOCOLLAPSE (or PC_RESERVED) flag set in all the logical palette's PALETTEENTRY **peFlags** members.

Figure 8-5 illustrates this idea.

To understand how the identity palette works, first remember what happens during the realization process. The logical palette's entries are color matched into the system palette, starting at entry 0 and proceding through entry 255. If an exact match for the logical-palette color is found in the system palette, that color is mapped and the process moves on to the next logical-palette color. So, if a logical palette has the same exact values as the system palette in the lower ten (static) positions, it will always map those 1:1.

The next 236 entries are a little trickier. Normally (that is, when **peFlags** is set to 0), each color of the logical palette is matched against each color of the system palette that's being built—meaning that if there are duplicate colors in the logical palette, the duplicate colors will get "collapsed" into the index of the first one. The

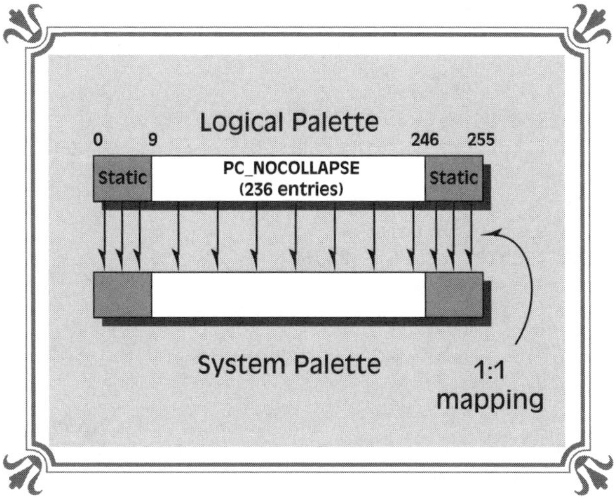

FIGURE 8-5

An identity palette

PC_NOCOLLAPSE flag prevents this from happening. Thus, if the next 236 entries have the PC_NOCOLLAPSE flag set, they will very likely get mapped into slots 10–245.

The last ten static slots, like the first ten, should be filled with the system colors that appear in the logical palette. There's one catch, however. If the logical palette contains an exact duplicate of one of the high-intensity (upper ten) colors anywhere in postions 10–245, then the Palette Manager will want to collapse that entry into the existing high-intensity color, ruining our identity match. The way to fix this is to mark any duplicate of the high-intensity colors as PC_RESERVED, whose function is to keep that entry from collapsing into any other, in addition to not allowing any other entry to collapse into it.

Alternatively, instead of checking for a duplicate color, you could just mark all the entries from 10 to 245 as PC_RESERVED. The consequence of this would be that when your application went to the background, all its palette entries would be reserved and the Palette Manager, left with little alternative, would map them all to black. For a full-screen game program, this might not be such a bad thing. However, if you really intend to share the screen with other applications and be fair to them, then you'll have to check for duplicates and use PC_NOCOLLAPSE.

Creating an identity palette isn't very difficult once you understand all this. The following function takes an array of RGBQUAD structures and builds an identity palette from them, returning an HPALETTE. When this HPALETTE is selected into a device context and realized, its 256 entries will be mapped directly into the 256 entries of the system palette, thus enabling the application to use DIB_PAL_COLORS reliably.

```
HPALETTE CreateIdentityPalette (LPRGBQUAD aRGB,
                                          int nColors)
{
    int i;
    int nStaticColors;
    int nUsableColors;
    struct {
        WORD Version;
        WORD NumberOfEntries;
        PALETTEENTRY aEntries[256];
    } Palette =
    {
        0x300,
        256
    };

    // Just use the screen DC where we need it.
    HDC hdc = GetDC(NULL);

    // Get the static colors from the system palette.
    nStaticColors = GetDeviceCaps(hdc, NUMCOLORS);
    GetSystemPaletteEntries(hdc, 0, 256,
    `                                       Palette.aEntries);

    // Set the peFlags of the lower static colors
    // to zero.
    nStaticColors = nStaticColors / 2;

    for (i=0; i<nStaticColors; i++)
        Palette.aEntries[i].peFlags = 0;

    // Fill in the entries from the given color table.
    nUsableColors = nColors - nStaticColors;
    for (; i<nUsableColors; i++) {
        int n, copy_high = FALSE;

        // Start the color table index
        // at 0.
        Palette.aEntries[i].peRed =
                        aRGB[i-nStaticColors].rgbRed;
        Palette.aEntries[i].peGreen =
                        aRGB[i-nStaticColors].rgbGreen;
        Palette.aEntries[i].peBlue =
                        aRGB[i-nStaticColors].rgbBlue;

        // Check for a duplicate of the "upper ten,"
        // mark it PC_RESERVED.
        for (n = 256-nStaticColors; n < 256; n++) {
            if (Palette.aEntries[n].peRed ==
                        aRGB[i-nStaticColors].rgbRed &&
                Palette.aEntries[n].peGreen ==
```

```
                        aRGB[i-nStaticColors].rgbGreen &&
                Palette.aEntries[n].peBlue ==
                        aRGB[i-nStaticColors].rgbBlue) {

                    // It matches.
                Palette.aEntries[i].peFlags =
                                PC_RESERVED;
                copy_high = TRUE;
                break;
            }
        }

        if (!copy_high)
            Palette.aEntries[i].peFlags =
                        PC_NOCOLLAPSE;
    }

    // Mark any empty entries as PC_NOCOLLAPSE.

    for (; i<256 - nStaticColors; i++)
        Palette.aEntries[i].peFlags = PC_NOCOLLAPSE;

    // Set the peFlags of the upper static colors
    // to zero.
    for (i = 256 - nStaticColors; i<256; i++)
        Palette.aEntries[i].peFlags = 0;

    // Remember to release the DC!
    ReleaseDC(NULL, hdc);

    // Return the palette.
    return CreatePalette((LOGPALETTE *)&Palette);
}
```

Note the call to **GetDeviceCaps (hdc, NUMCOLORS)**. Contrary to what intuition might tell you, this does not return the number of colors the device supports, but rather the number of *reserved* colors, which is typically 20 on a 256-color (8-bit) display. It is possible that there are drivers out there with more than 20 colors, but because they'd be so nonstandard, it's highly unlikely. Also, the function assumes that the display device (whose device context is retrieved with **GetDC(NULL)**) is a 256-color device; if it isn't, you shouldn't be here.

The **GetSystemPaletteEntries** function does just what it sounds like it does: fills an array of PALETTEENTRY structures with the colors found in the current system palette. This is how the function knows exactly what those entries are in order to create an identity palette.

The little inner loop compares the current color table entry with all the high-intensity (upper ten) palette entries to check for a duplicate and mark it PC_RESERVED instead of PC_NOCOLLAPSE.

Finally, look at the loop that actually sets the palette entries for colors 10–245. The color table index (**aRGB** in the code) is started at zero instead of **nStaticColors** (note the highlighted section), assuming that the color table has entries down there that it needs to have plugged into the palette. The alternative is to create 236-color DIBs that use only pixel values in the range 10–245. This can range from difficult to impossible, so this function assumes that the table is from a regular, 256-color DIB that uses all 256 colors. The result of this assumption is that the pixel values in the DIB will no longer match up with the new identity palette. The pixel values in the range 0–9 are now mapped to the lower static colors, the upper ten colors are mapped to the day-glo high-intensity colors, and the original upper ten color table entries are simply ignored. How, then, can you fix the DIB to overcome this problem?

Remapping the DIB

The technique I'm about to describe is a compromise for 256-color DIBs, because it uses only the 236 nonstatic colors of the palette. A lot of images can easily stand losing 20 colors out of 256, but if your game uses images that simply cannot afford to lose these colors, then you'll have no choice but to use the considerably more complex method of palette management that frees up 18 of the 20 static colors for your use (black and white remain static). I outline this technique at the end of the chapter, but you should avoid using it if at all possible—the Palette Manager behaves even more ungracefully than it does normally if you use this method.

Unless you've created DIBs that accommodate the 20 static palette entries, the only other way to get the right picture is to remap the actual pixels of the DIB at some convenient time, like when they're being loaded. This results in a read-modify-write operation for every pixel in the image, but the overhead is considerably less than that for reading the image from disk and has to be done only once, so it's generally quite tolerable—usually a lot more tolerable than trying to create images that don't use the upper and lower ten palette slots.

Remember from Chapter 7 that DIB color table entries are meant to be stored in order of the color's importance. The meaning of the term "importance" becomes evident when the DIB goes through this remapping process—there are 256 pegs for 236 holes, so 20 pegs have to go, and it's the *upper* 20 that are heaved out. If your DIB has a critical (say, background) color in color table position 250, you won't be very happy with the result, unless there's another color very close to it elsewhere in the color table or in one of the 20 static colors. With that caveat, I recommend the following **MapDIBits** function:

```
void MapDIBits (HPALETTE hPal, PDIB pDIB)
{
    BYTE imap[256];
    LPRGBQUAD pQ;
    int i;
```

```
    long length;
    unsigned char huge *p;

    pQ = DIB_PCLRTAB(pDIB);
    for (i = 0; i < 256; i++) {
        imap[i] = (BYTE)GetNearestPaletteIndex (hPal,
                    RGB(pQ->rgbRed,
                        pQ->rgbGreen,
                        pQ->rgbBlue));
        pQ++;
    }

    // Map the bits.
    p = DIB_PBITS(pDIB);
    length = (long)DIB_STORAGEWIDTH(pDIB) *
                (long)DIB_HEIGHT(pDIB);
    while (length--) {
        *p = imap[*p];
        p++;
    }
}
```

The function creates a mapping table the size of the palette (which should be 256 entries long). The table is created by using **GetNearestPaletteIndex** to find the entry in the palette whose color most closely matches that of the specified DIB color table entry. This is a Windows function that does exactly what it says—it finds either an exact match in the specified palette for the specified RGB color, or the closest match using the color-matching algorithm. Once the table is built, all the pixels of the DIB are remapped with it. Note the use of the **huge** pointer to access the bits; this is necessary because the DIB's bits could span a 64k memory boundary.

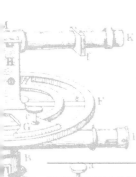

Once a DIB has been remapped through **MapDIBits**, the color table associated with it is no longer meaningful. You could, of course, go through the steps of remapping the color table as well, but most game programs use one palette and match all bitmaps to it, either when the bitmaps are created or through a technique like **MapDIBits**. So the original color table is no longer important, just the palette that was derived from it.

Displaying It All

Now we can pick up where we left off in Chapter 7 and actually display a color DIB wherever the user clicks the right mouse button. To do so, we should add the **CreateIdentityPalette** function to the **OnCreate** function, along with **MapDIBits**.

Rather than displaying a boring red ramp, let's do something a little more interesting, like display a DIB loaded from a file. As a bonus, you get to learn one of the many Stupid DIB Tricks that makes loading a DIB file out of the resource file incredibly easy.

Recall from Chapter 2 that you can embed a Windows .BMP file into the resource file with the BITMAP directive, and load it with **LoadBitmap**. The only problem is that **LoadBitmap** returns a handle to a device-dependent bitmap, which isn't useful to DIB functions like **StretchDIBits**. Still, the .BMP file as it exists in the resource file is a DIB. Here's how you can get to it:

Windows provides the **LoadResource** call for loading "raw" resources out of the resource file. **LoadResource** must first have the resource identified for it by **FindResource**. Once the resource is loaded, a direct pointer to its block of memory can be obtained with **LockResource**. The big trick is that a loaded and locked resource can be freed with **GlobalFreePtr** as though it were a regular global memory block (which, in fact, it is). So, to pull a .BMP file out of the resource file, use the following code:

```
// Load a bitmap resource as a DIB.
main->pDIB = (PDIB)LockResource(
                         LoadResource(G_app.hinst,
                              FindResource(G_app.hinst,
                        MAKEINTRESOURCE(IDB_BITMAP3),
                              RT_BITMAP
                         )
                           )
                       );
```

The **pDIB** member of the **main** structure here is defined as a **PDIB**, which is nothing more than an LPBITMAPINFO. You see, Windows kindly dumps the BITMAPFILEHEADER that's part of the .BMP file when it's embedded in the .EXE file by the resource compiler. Neat, huh?

The MAKEINTRESOURCE macro identifies a bitmap in the resource file called **IDB_BITMAP3**, which is of type **RT_BITMAP** (which means just that it was declared in the resource file with the BITMAP type identifier).

Okay, given the previous code, here's what the modified **OnCreate** handler should look like in order to load the DIB, create an identity palette from its color table, and remap its bits to fit:

```
static BOOL OnCreate(MAIN* main,
                          CREATESTRUCT FAR* lpCreateStruct)
{
    BITMAP b;
    int i;
    long scanwidth, height;
    char huge *p;

    // We get the DC once, and save it away.
    // This works only because we use CS_OWNDC.
    main->hdc = GetDC (main->hwnd);

    SetBkColor (main->hdc, RGB (0,0,0));
    SetTextColor (main->hdc, RGB (255, 0, 0));
```

```
SelectObject (main->hdc,
                    GetStockObject (GRAY_BRUSH));

// Get a cursor.
main->cursor = LoadCursor (NULL, IDC_ARROW);
// and a bitmap.
main->SRC_BMP = LoadBitmap (G_app.hinst,
                                       "picture");

if (!main->SRC_BMP)
    return FALSE;

// Create the source memory DC and
// select the bitmap into it.
main->SRC_DC = CreateCompatibleDC (main->hdc);
main->OLD_SRC_BMP  = SelectBitmap (main->SRC_DC,
                                     main->SRC_BMP);

// Create the backing-store memory DC
// and a bitmap for it.
main->BK_DC = CreateCompatibleDC (main->hdc);
// How big?
GetObject (main->SRC_BMP, sizeof(BITMAP), &b);
main->bitmaps.width = b.bmWidth;
main->bitmaps.height = b.bmHeight;
main->BK_BMP = CreateCompatibleBitmap (main->hdc,
                             main->bitmaps.width,
                             main->bitmaps.height);
// Select it.
main->OLD_BK_BMP = SelectBitmap (main->BK_DC,
                                   main->BK_BMP);

// Load the DIB from the resource file and lock
// it in memory.
main->pDIB = (PDIB)LockResource(
                       LoadResource(G_app.hinst,
                         FindResource(G_app.hinst,
                    MAKEINTRESOURCE(IDB_BITMAP3),
                                     RT_BITMAP)));
// Die if it didn t happen.
if (!main->pDIB)
    return FALSE;

// Create an identity palette from the DIB s
// color table.
main->hPalette = CreateIdentityPalette (
                     (LPRGBQUAD)DIB_PCLRTAB(main->pDIB),
                     256);
// Make sure we got a palette.
if (!main->hPalette)
    return FALSE;
```

continued on next page

continued from previous page

```
    // Remap the bits to fit the palette.
    MapDIBits (main->hPalette, main->pDIB);

    // One last thing: Clear the system palette.
    ClearSystemPalette ();

    main->menu = LoadMenu (G_app.hinst, "MainMenu");
    ShowWindow (main->hwnd, G_app.cmdShow);
    return TRUE;
}
```

Note the call to **ClearSystemPalette** that comes after the DIB's bits are remapped. This isn't a Windows function, though it probably should be. The function is necessary because of the way palette realization happens if your application isn't the first to start using entries in the system palette. If you don't call **ClearSystemPalette** before realizing a palette for the first time, there's a chance you won't get an identity mapping (which would, of course, screw up the whole thing). Here's what **ClearSystemPalette** does:

```
void ClearSystemPalette(void)
{
    // A dummy palette setup
    struct
    {
        WORD Version;
        WORD NumberOfEntries;
        PALETTEENTRY aEntries[256];
    } Palette =
    {
        0x300,
        256
    };

    HPALETTE BlackPal, OldPal;
    HDC hdc;
    int Counter;

    // Reset everything in the system palette to black.
    for(Counter = 0; Counter < 256; Counter++) {

        Palette.aEntries[Counter].peRed = 0;
        Palette.aEntries[Counter].peGreen = 0;
        Palette.aEntries[Counter].peBlue = 0;


        Palette.aEntries[Counter].peFlags =
                                    PC_NOCOLLAPSE;
    }

    // Create, select, realize, deselect, and
```

```
    // delete the palette.
    hdc = GetDC(NULL);
    BlackPal = CreatePalette(
                     (LOGPALETTE *)&Palette);
    if (BlackPal) {
        OldPal = SelectPalette(hdc,BlackPal,FALSE);
        RealizePalette(hdc);
        SelectPalette(hdc,OldPal,FALSE);
        DeleteObject(BlackPal);
    }
    ReleaseDC(NULL, hdc);
}
```

As you can see, the function creates an all-black palette, with each entry set to PC_NOCOLLAPSE; selects it; realizes it; deselects it; and deletes it. It has to do this because of something ugly in the way the Palette Manager marks palette entries, but you really don't need to worry about it. Using this function helps guarantee that the palette you select and realize will be an identity palette.

You also need to add the palette selection and realization to the `OnRButtonDown` handler:

```
static void OnRButtonDown (MAIN *main,
                                  BOOL fDoubleClick,
                           int x, int y,
                           UINT keyFlags)
{
    HPALETTE OldPal;
    int cx = DIB_WIDTH (main->pDIB);
    int cy = DIB_HEIGHT(main->pDIB);

    // Select and realize our palette.
    OldPal = SelectPalette (main->hdc, main->hPalette,
                                   FALSE);
    RealizePalette (main->hdc);

    StretchDIBits (main->hdc, x, y,
                   cx, cy,
                   0, 0,
                   cx, cy,
                   DIB_PBITS(main->pDIB),
                   main->pDIB,
                   DIB_PAL_COLORS,
                   SRCCOPY);
    // Select the palette back out.
    SelectPalette (main->hdc, OldPal, FALSE);
}
```

There it is. If you compile and run the sample program, you'll see a 256-color DIB copied to the screen in all its splendor every time you press the right mouse button. Figure 8-6 shows the final palette realization program.

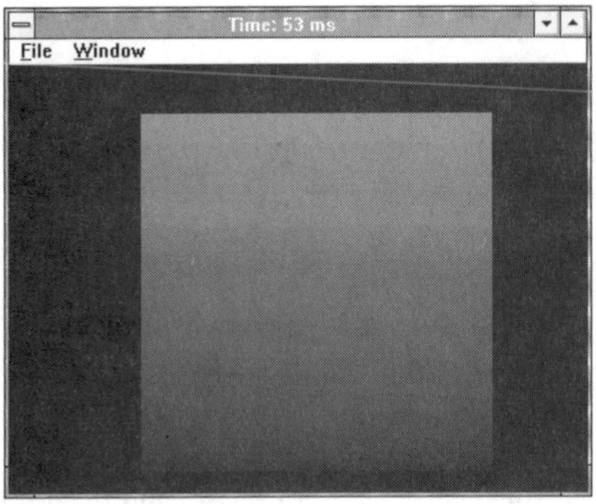

FIGURE 8-6

The final palette realization program

When You Just Gotta Have 256 Colors

Because the technique for accessing all 256 colors of the palette is fraught with considerable peril (and besides, you actually get only 254 colors for all your trouble), I'll only outline it here. If you really have to use this technique, you can fill in the blanks with some standard Windows reference documentation.

The Windows function **SetSystemPaletteUse** allows a program to free up 18 of the 20 static colors. Black and white remain static at positions 0 and 255, respectively. While this may sound like a good thing, the fact is that the Palette Manager and other parts of the system don't handle this condition very gracefully. Your program will have to do a lot of maintenance work to keeps things from getting generally trashed (especially other running applications). Here are a few guidelines to using the SYSPAL_NOSTATIC option of **SetSystemPaletteUse**:

- Use SYSPAL_NOSTATIC only when your program is the active (foreground) *full-screen* program.
- Save all the current system colors (0–9 and 246–255).
- Send the WM_SYSCOLORCHANGE message to Windows to tell all running applications that the system colors have changed.
- Any palette being realized while using SYSPAL_NOSTATIC must first be unrealized with **UnrealizeObject**.

When your program becomes inactive (or terminates), you need to do the following to restore the system:

- Call **SetSystemPaletteUse** with the SYSPAL_STATIC option.
- Restore all the old system colors, and realize them.
- Unrealize any palette used under SYSPAL_NOSTATIC before realizing it again.

The biggest problem with using SYSPAL_NOSTATIC is that the Palette Manager does not remap the default palette to use only black and white, and the display driver isn't made aware of the lack of static colors. Therefore, whenever another application starts drawing with what were the static colors, it gets whatever's in the palette, which can be total garbage to things like menu bars, title bars, and so on. Nonetheless, if yours is a full-screen game, and you're nice about giving up control when you must (try using ALT-TAB to get to another application while you're in the SYSPAL_NOSTATIC state!), then it's possible to make use of this feature. If yours is *not* a full-screen game, you just can't do it—use 236 colors.

Summary

As nasty as palette manipulation is under Windows, if you stick to the basics outlined in this chapter, you'll get both maximum speed and maximum convenience. It's a shame that it takes so much reverse engineering of the Palette Manager to achieve maximum performance, but the whole thing was designed more for convenience and easy sharing of the palette among several applications than for high performance.

You learned how to use a 256-color DIB even though you have only 236 colors to work with. You also learned one of the Stupid DIB Tricks for loading a Windows .BMP file from the resource file. Congratulations! Learning how to deal with Windows palettes is something to celebrate.

Now, on to the *real* high-performance stuff. WinG was designed to get the highest speed possible out of a wide range of Windows display drivers. It's all based on the information you've learned already—DIBs, palettes, and the GDI. So get ready to dive in . . .

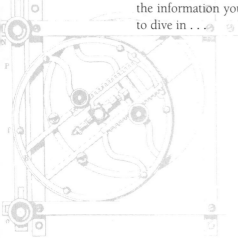

9

Fast Windows Bitmaps—The WinG Bitmap

[illegible] le manovelle [illegible] le quali si movano e l'alza
e i grā pesi [illegible]
[illegible] nella mano [illegible] alla manovella perchè [illegible]
la forza e più l'omo più vale.

[illegible]

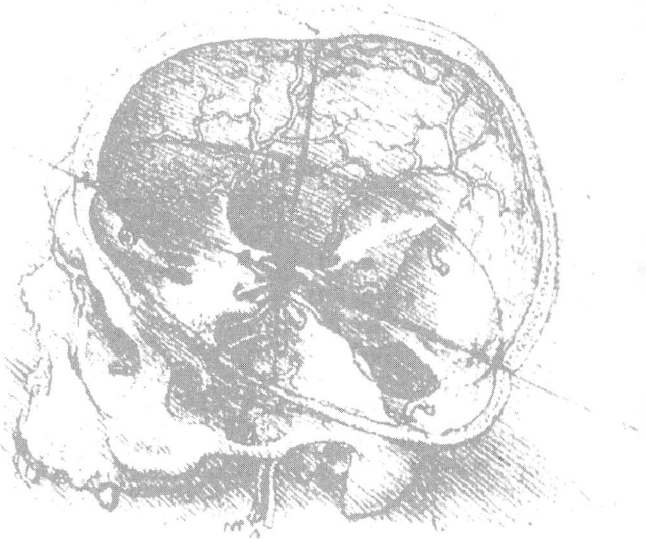

9

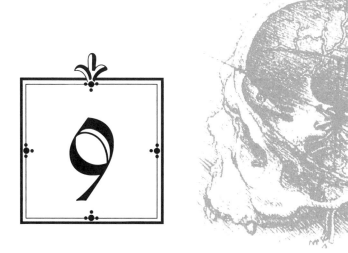

Fast Windows Bitmaps—The WinG Bitmap

If there's a game programmer's battle cry, it's probably speed, *speed,* SPEED! Even the most technically or visually interesting game in the world isn't a lot of fun to play if it's as slow as a slug. Of course, some games rely on speed more than others–a role-playing game, for example, may not require the same blazing graphics speed that a simulation game needs.

Part of the reason that there are fewer Windows-based games than DOS-based ones on the market is that Windows has never really been perceived as a lightning-fast graphics environment. Affectionately dubbed "Windoze" by many developers, all the versions to date just haven't been fast enough to be able to afford to give up speed for ease of installation, device independence, and sound support.

WinG was created for the specific purpose of bringing more games to Windows by getting rid of its biggest obstacle—slow speed. The goal was to come as close as possible to matching the performance of DOS games that interface directly to the display hardware (typically, 8-bit Super VGA-class devices) under Windows, and to do it across all *existing* Windows devices and device drivers. This was no small feat, and the degree to which it succeeds is based partly on the quality of some of those existing Windows display-device drivers. The bottom line, however, is that WinG can

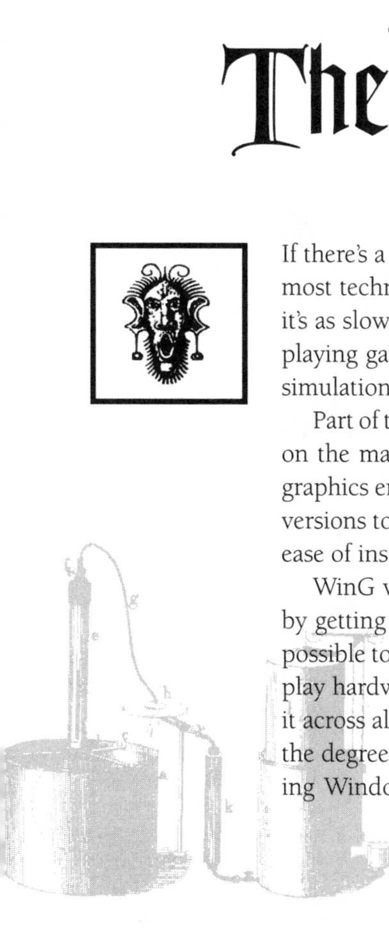

improve Blt speed across a wide variety of hardware by a factor of two to as much as ten. In other words, it really works.

Before diving into the workings of WinG, let's step back and review some game programming techniques and how they're affected by Blt speed.

Game Programming Techniques

As diverse as computer games are, you can divide them largely into a couple of broad categories based on the primary methods they use for computing and displaying graphics. I'll call one class the *sprite-based* games, and another *rendering-based.* Still other games use a combination of both sprite and rendering techniques.

Sprite-based games are typified by the traditional arcade style (as shown in Figure 9-1). The display usually consists of a two-dimensional background picture, with any number of nonrectangular moving images darting to and fro across the screen (how's that for simplification?). Most of the games available for dedicated game machines (like Nintendo and Sega) are sprite-based games. These games have relatively low processing requirements by comparison to rendering-based games.

Rendering-based games are usually (though not necessarily always) 3D simulations of one form or another. Figure 9-2 gives an example of a typical rendering-based

FIGURE 9-1

Sprite-based game

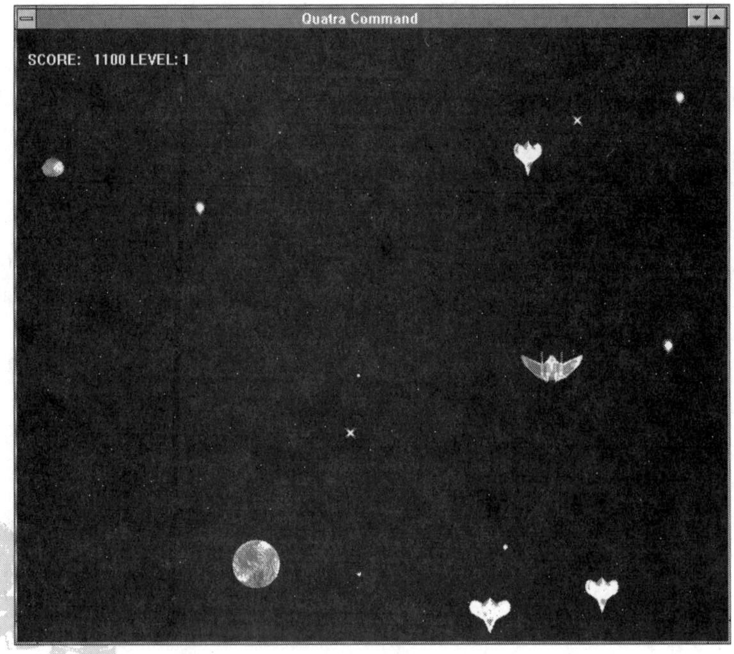

FIGURE 9-2

Rendering-based game

game. Instead of a constant, two-dimensional background, a rendering-based game features a displayed image that it must recompute in its entirety at each game cycle. Many rendering-based games have a sprite-based component, as well. For example, Nitemare-3D (see Figure 9-3) uses rendering for the buildings and other stationary objects, but the creatures themselves are sprites.

There are significantly different performance issues for the two types of games. While both make heavy use of bit Blt operations, the rendering-based game usually

FIGURE 9-3

Mixing sprites and rendering

updates the *entire screen* with every move of the player, while a sprite-based game need update only those areas of the screen where objects are actually moving. The speed of either type of game depends on how quickly the game can compute the screen update, and how quickly the screen can actually be updated. A game that can compute much faster than it can display (this arrangement is most common for sprite-based games) is said to be *pixel-bound,* whereas one that spends more time computing the screen update than displaying it (an arrangement common for rendering-based games) is called *compute-bound.* A compute-bound game can become pixel-bound if the display is slow enough. In other words, with a slow display, a formerly compute-bound game may end up taking longer to display a single pixel than to compute what its color should be. Whether compute- or pixel-bound, the amount of time a game takes to display the updated picture on the screen is almost always somewhere near the critical path, since that job typically must be done by the same processor that does the compute. Here's another way to think about this: If a rendering-based game on a given hardware configuration spends half its time computing the value of a pixel and the other half displaying it, then it could run twice as fast if the display time went to zero. Since the time it takes to display an image isn't often easy to minimize (because it relies on hardware capabilities, device drivers, and other things outside the programmer's direct control), a lot of the magic in game design is figuring out how to minimize the compute time.

Another important performance factor for both types of games is the fact that reading and writing pixels to and from the actual display device is considerably slower than doing it in regular RAM—by a factor of 10 to 100. Therefore, minimizing the number of reads and writes to the display device—updating as few pixels as possible—is the most direct way to improve display speed. This generally leads to the use of an *offscreen bitmap*—a RAM-based copy of exactly what should appear on the screen during any given game cycle. The pixels of the offscreen bitmap are computed and updated, and then the results are copied to the screen via a bit Blt operation. For a rendering-based game, the Blt is often 1:1—the whole of the offscreen bitmap is simply copied to the screen at every cycle. However, a sprite-based game might copy only the portions of the offscreen bitmap that needed updating during the cycle, an area which could often be considerably smaller than the whole offscreen bitmap, unless the background image were moving at the same time.

WinG is designed to maximize the process of copying an offscreen bitmap to the display device, pure and simple. It comprises surprisingly few function calls—eight, to be exact; a testament to its simplicity. WinG is based completely on DIBs, which is why the previous few chapters are required reading if you are to understand WinG. In fact, the easiest way to describe WinG is to say that it gives DIBs all the same capabilities and qualities of device-dependent bitmaps—including, most importantly, their speed.

WinG and Profiling

You can think of WinG (with all due respect to its authors) as a big set of hacks that find the fastest shortcuts around, over, and through a given Windows display driver and display card combination. By empirically testing various alternatives, WinG builds a profile of capabilities that it can dynamically configure at run time to provide the guaranteed fastest route for a pixel from the WinG API calls to the hardware.

The WinG profiling step happens the first time you run a WinG application, and every time you run one after changing display drivers or modes. Profiling is completely automatic. After you've installed WinG from the CD-ROM included with this book, run one of the sample applications, like DOGGIE. You'll see a dialog box come up and display various and sundry bizarre patterns, like a Rorschach test gone awry. The profiler can take up to a couple of minutes to run, but it needs to be run only once for a given display configuration. After the profiling finishes, the application executes.

The DOGGIE program has a red "balloon dog" that you can drag around on the screen. Yes, those trails it leaves are intended and are not caused by a bug; the program doesn't save or clear the background after each move.

Once you've gotten the DOGGIE sample program running, try running TIMEWING. The TIMEWING program performs a benchmark that compares the relative speeds of bit Blt operations for various types of bitmaps: device-dependent, device-independent, and WinG. The goal is for the WinG bitmap performance to be as close as possible to the device-dependent bitmap performance, which will almost always be substantially faster than the device-independent bitmap Blt time. (If there is a wide disparity between the WinG Blt time and the DDB Blt time, Microsoft would be interested in hearing about it in the form of a bug report! Since the performance speed of WinG is pretty much its *raison d'être,* they want to know details about configurations that aren't performing up to snuff. The WinG distribution notes explain how to submit bug reports to Microsoft, and there's even a program that creates a bug report for you automatically.)

Using WinG

While the whole of WinG consists of only eight function calls, using it effectively requires many carefully planned steps. First off, WinG has a few restrictions. The first is that (under Windows 3.x, anyway) it supports only 8-bit (256-color) source DCs. Effectively, this means that your game should be created for 8-bit color. WinG does support greater than 8-bit *destination* DCs; that is, a game that uses WinG will work fine on 16-bit or even 24-bit displays, though it might not gain all the performance advantages. Under Windows 95 and Windows NT, other color depths are supported, as well. Consider carefully the target market for your game before choosing a color depth greater than 8 bits per pixel.

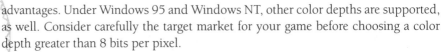

As I mentioned previously, WinG is based entirely on device-independent bitmaps. Recall from Chapter 7 that DIBs have certain restrictions: DIBs aren't fully recognized by the GDI, so you can't draw on them like you can a DDB. WinG solves this problem—a WinG bitmap can be selected into a DC just like a device-dependent bitmap, but it also offers a direct pointer to the image "surface" like a DIB. You get the best of both worlds.

Also recall that DIBs are upside down with respect to most of the imaging graphics world—the origin of the bitmap is in the lower left corner instead of in the upper left corner. The good news is that WinG bitmaps can be what's termed *top-down,* with the origin in the upper left corner. The bad news is that they can also be what's now called bottom-up, like a traditional DIB. The reason it's bad news is because the orientation of a WinG bitmap isn't determined until run time, so you must write your code to handle either case in the event that one format is faster than the other on a particular configuration. In most cases, fortunately, this really isn't very difficult.

Getting Started

Once you've installed WinG, your first step should be to include the WinG header file, WING.H, in all the source modules that make WinG calls. Beyond that, you must include the WinG import library, WING.LIB, in your program's make file or project definition, in whatever manner is necessary for your development environment (for native 32-bit development environments like Windows 95 and Windows NT, use WING32.LIB instead). A little tip: One of the mistakes people often make when creating their first WinG program is to name it WING.EXE or declare the name in the .DEF file as WING. This results in a global naming conflict and prevents the program from running, although WinG gives little clue as to why.

Before getting started with code, I'll outline the process that's used to maximize speed with WinG. This technique consists of creating an offscreen WinG bitmap that will contain a copy of whatever the program needs to display on the screen, then Blting from that offscreen bitmap to the screen. Figure 9-4 illustrates the basic concept.

The image that the program ultimately needs to display on the screen is composed into the WinG bitmap—which starts life as an ordinary DIB, except that it may be top-down—and the result is then Blted to the screen via one of two calls, either **`WinGBitBlt`** or **`WinGStretchBlt`**.

Unlike an ordinary DIB, for which the program allocates the bits, a WinG DIB's bits are allocated by a call to WinG: **`WinGCreateBitmap`**. The reason for this has to do with ownership of the memory—WinG maximizes the speed of Blts by letting the display driver, rather than the program's process, have ownership of the bits. This really isn't of much consequence, because **`WinGCreateBitmap`** assigns a pointer to

FIGURE 9-4

WinG and the screen

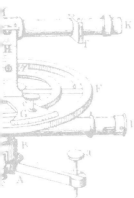

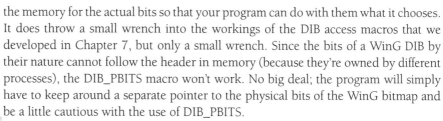

the memory for the actual bits so that your program can do with them what it chooses. It does throw a small wrench into the workings of the DIB access macros that we developed in Chapter 7, but only a small wrench. Since the bits of a WinG DIB by their nature cannot follow the header in memory (because they're owned by different processes), the DIB_PBITS macro won't work. No big deal; the program will simply have to keep around a separate pointer to the physical bits of the WinG bitmap and be a little cautious with the use of DIB_PBITS.

Before calling **WinGCreateBitmap** to create a WinG DIB, there are a few prerequisite steps you need to perform to get things ready. The first call a program should make to WinG is to **WinGRecommendDIBFormat**, whose definition follows:

```
BOOL WINGAPI WinGRecommendDIBFormat
                                (BITMAPINFO FAR *pFormat );
```

The WINGAPI calling convention definition is the same as that for WINAPI, which is FAR PASCAL. The function returns TRUE or FALSE on success or failure. The single argument is a pointer to a BITMAPINFO structure. Recall that a BITMAPINFO structure contains a BITMAPINFOHEADER structure and a unit-sized array of RGBQUAD entries. **WinGRecommendDIBFormat** requires a buffer a little larger; it must have an array of at least three DWORDs' (same size as RGBQUAD) worth of memory after the BITMAPINFOHEADER. Typically, you'll pass it a BITMAPINFO structure that has a whole color table derived from, say, a background image.

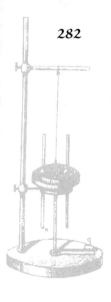

The function of **`WinGRecommendDIBFormat`** is to fill the BITMAPINFO structure with information about which DIB format to use to get maximum speed from WinG. It may be possible to create a WinG DIB in other formats, but doing so may sacrifice all or most of the speed advantages of WinG. Since speed is the sole reason you're using WinG in the first place, it's a pretty good idea to create a WinG DIB in the format that **`WinGRecommendDIBFormat`** specifies.

`WinGRecommendDIBFormat` optimizes its recommendation based on doing 1:1 (nonstretched) Blts from memory to the screen with an identity palette. If this isn't what your game is going to be doing most of the time, **`WinGRecommendDIBFormat`** may not actually recommend the fastest format, and you'll have to do your own timing profile to find the best choice. However, if you're not doing 1:1 Blts from memory to the screen with an identity palette, you're sacrificing speed and probably should consider another method that ensures 1:1 Blts.

One of the things that the WinG profiling steps determines is whether top-down DIBs are faster than bottom-up DIBs. The answer is returned to you in the **`bmiHeader.biHeight`** member of the BITMAPINFO structure passed in to **`WinGRecommendDIBFormat`**. If the value of **`biHeight`** is -1, then a top-down DIB will be faster. If the value is 1, then a bottom-up DIB (the traditional orientation) will be faster. The sign of this member is used by **`WinGCreateBitmap`** to construct a WinG DIB of the designated orientation.

WinG and the WinG DC

Recall from Chapter 6 that in order to draw on the "surface" of a device-dependent bitmap, you must select the bitmap into a memory device context. You do this by calling **`SelectObject`** with the handle of the DDB loaded from the resource file or created with **`CreateBitmap`**. Also recall from Chapter 7 that one of the limitations of DIBs is that they can't be selected into device contexts: DIB functions don't return handles. Consequently, you can't use the GDI to draw on the surface of a DIB.

Lifting this limitation is one of the many great things that WinG does for you. **`WinGCreateBitmap`** returns an HBITMAP that not only *can* be selected into a memory DC (and used with all the GDI functions), but *must* be selected into one in order for you to do anything useful with the bitmap. WinG has a special call just for creating DCs that are compatible with the screen: **`WinGCreateDC`**, which takes no arguments and returns an HDC.

Here's a summary of the steps necessary to create and use WinG bitmaps:

- Get the recommended DIB format from **`WinGRecommendDIBFormat`** into a BITMAPINFO structure.

- Create a WinG memory device context with **WinGCreateDC** and save it somewhere.
- Create a bitmap of the desired dimensions and orientation (top-down or bottom-up) with **WinGCreateBitmap**; store the handle and the pointer to the bits that it returns.
- Select the bitmap into the WinG DC with **SelectObject**; save the old (1x1 monochrome) bitmap that **SelectObject** returns for cleanup at termination time.
- Use **WinGBitBlt** to copy the bitmap's bits from the WinG DC to the screen.

There are a couple of caveats having to do with WinG DCs that you need to know about. The first is that **WinGCreateDC** has a fairly high memory and speed overhead. Normally, your program should create only one WinG DC somewhere around initialization time, then select different bitmaps created with **WinGCreateBitmap** as needed (like when the destination window changes size). Another important point is that a WinG DC represents a paletteless device, even though it generally works only with 8-bit images. This means two things: You don't have to use functions like **SelectPalette** and **RealizePalette** on the WinG DC, and the color table of the WinG bitmap that's selected into the DC had better be a one-to-one (identity) mapping with the logical palette that's selected into the screen DC into which WinG is going to Blt. (More on setting up an identity color table and palette in a moment.)

Time to look at some code. An obvious thing to do is to modify the DIB code from Chapter 8 to work with a WinG DIB, and demonstrate the (let's hope substantial) performance gain. You can put most of the code in the WM_CREATE handler, **OnCreate**. You need to add some new variables to the instance structure for the window (MAIN) to hold the WinG DC handle, old bitmap handle, a pointer to the bits of the WinG DIB, and a new PDIB for the WinG DIB. The reason for a separate PDIB for the WinG DIB will become clear as we go through the code. First, the new MAIN structure, defined in MAIN.H:

```
typedef struct MAINtag {
    HWND hwnd;                 // This window
    HDC  hdc;                  // DC for our window
    HCURSOR hCursor;
    PDIB pDIB;                 // For the resfile DIB
    PDIB pWinG;                // WinG bitmap; NOT packed
    LPSTR pBits;               // WinG bits
    HBITMAP hOldWinGBitmap;    // Old one
    HDC hdcWinG;               // WinG HDC
    BOOL topdown;              // Top-down flag
    HPALETTE hPalette;         // Identity palette
} MAIN;
```

I've deleted all the old junk that had to do with DDBs (we're on to The New Way now). Note the **topdown** flag, used to inform certain functions that the bits in the WinG DIB are top-down in orientation.

The WM_CREATE handler now looks like this:

```
static BOOL OnCreate(MAIN* main,
                     CREATESTRUCT FAR* lpCreateStruct)
{
    HBITMAP hBitmap;

    // We get the DC once, and save it away.
    // This works only because we use CS_OWNDC.
    main->hdc = GetDC (main->hwnd);

    // Get a cursor.
    main->cursor = LoadCursor (NULL, IDC_ARROW);

    // Load a bitmap resource as a DIB.
    main->pDIB = (PDIB)LockResource(
                    LoadResource(G_app.hinst,
                    FindResource(G_app.hinst,
                    MAKEINTRESOURCE(IDB_BITMAP3),
                         RT_BITMAP)));

    // Create a new DIB header that's a copy
    // of the original.
    main->pWinG = CopyDIBHeader (main->pDIB);

    // Recommend a format, create a compatible DIB.
    if (WinGRecommendDIBFormat (main->pWinG)) {
        main->pWinG->bmiHeader.biCompression = BI_RGB;
        main->pWinG->bmiHeader.biBitCount = 8;
        main->topdown =
               main->pWinG->bmiHeader.biHeight == -1 ?
                            TRUE : FALSE;
    } else {
        main->pWinG->bmiHeader.biSize =
                            sizeof(BITMAPINFOHEADER);
        main->pWinG->bmiHeader.biPlanes = 1;
        main->pWinG->bmiHeader.biBitCount = 8;
        main->pWinG->bmiHeader.biCompression = BI_RGB;
        main->pWinG->bmiHeader.biSizeImage = 0;
        main->pWinG->bmiHeader.biClrUsed = 0;
        main->pWinG->bmiHeader.biClrImportant = 0;
        // Bottom-up default.
        main->pWinG->bmiHeader.biHeight = 1;
    }

    // Copy the width of the resfile DIB.
```

```
    main->pWinG->bmiHeader.biWidth =
                    main->pDIB->bmiHeader.biWidth;
    // Copy height; retain orientation.
    main->pWinG->bmiHeader.biHeight *=
                    main->pDIB->bmiHeader.biHeight;

    // This must be done before WinGCreateBitmap.
    main->hPalette = CreateIdentityPalette
            (DIB_PCLRTAB(main->pWinG), 256, TRUE);

    // Create the WinG DC.
    main->hdcWinG = WinGCreateDC ();
    // Create the WinG bitmap, select it in,
    // save the old one.
    hBitmap = WinGCreateBitmap(main->hdcWinG,
                        main->pWinG, &main->pBits);
    main->hOldWinGBitmap = SelectBitmap(main->hdcWinG,
                              hBitmap);

    // Make sure the height is positive from
    // this point on.
    main->pWinG->bmiHeader.biHeight =
            abs(main->pWinG->bmiHeader.biHeight);

    // Copy the bits into the WinG bitmap.
    hmemcpy (main->pBits, DIB_PBITS(main->pDIB),
           (long)DIB_STORAGEWIDTH(main->pDIB)*
           (long)DIB_HEIGHT(main->pDIB));

    // Problem is, the picture's all messed up now.
    // Remap the colors so that it looks right again,
    // but use the color table from the ORIGINAL
    // bitmap.
    MapDIBits (main->hPalette, main->pDIB,
            main->pBits, main->topdown);

    ShowWindow (main->hwnd, G_app.cmdShow);
    return TRUE;
}
```

There's a fair amount of new stuff there, so let's start at the beginning. After loading the DIB from the resource file into **main->pDIB**, a call to a new function, **CopyDIBHeader**, allocates a BITMAPINFO structure and color table to match the one passed in to it, and copies the source PDIB data into it. Note here that there are two separate PDIBs: one for the original resource-file DIB, and one for the WinG DIB. It's possible that the code could use the same header and color table from the resource-file DIB for the WinG DIB, but it would require a fair amount of shuffling, as you'll see shortly.

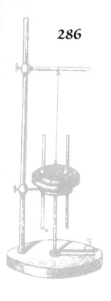

For reference, the code for **CopyDIBHeader** looks like this:

```
static PDIB CopyDIBHeader (PDIB pDIB)
{
    PDIB pRet;
    long hdrsize;

    // Don't copy null PDIBs.
    if (!pDIB)
        return NULL;

    // Allocate a header and full color table.
    hdrsize = sizeof(BITMAPINFOHEADER) +
                  DIB_COLORS(pDIB) * sizeof(RGBQUAD);

    pRet = (PDIB)GlobalAllocPtr (GPTR, hdrsize);

    if (!pRet)
        return NULL;

    // Copy the source into the new PDIB.
    _fmemcpy (pRet, pDIB, hdrsize);

    return pRet;
}
```

The next call is to **WinGRecommendDIBFormat**. The WinG documentation says that the call may, in fact, fail to determine an optimum DIB format, and so the code handles both the success and fail cases. If the call succeeds, the code just makes sure the bit depth is 8 bits per pixel, uncompressed. It also sets the flag indicating whether the recommended format is top-down or not (that is, bottom-up). All the other members of the BITMAPINFO structure are set by the call, or by the **else** code if the call fails.

Next, the function sets the width and height of the WinG DIB header to match that of the resource-file DIB. Note the multiplication operation for the **biHeight** member—this retains the sign that came from **WinGRecommendDIBFormat**. The reason is that the **WinGCreateBitmap** call uses the sign of the **biHeight** member to determine whether to create a top-down DIB: If it's positive, it's bottom-up (the traditional DIB orientation).

The next call is to the function I defined in Chapter 8, **CreateIdentityPalette**. Note, however, the one additional flag parameter, in this case set to TRUE. The purpose of this flag is to tell the function whether to reset the values of the color table passed as its first parameter to match the palette it creates. This additional step is very important—the color table of the WinG DIB *must* exactly match the palette to be realized in the screen's DC and ensure an identity palette. Recall from Chapter 8 that because the DIB loaded from the resource file has a full 256-color color table, 20 colors have to be dropped and the DIB's pixels have to be remapped. Here's the portion of **CreateIdentityPalette** that copies the palette colors into the color table:

```
HPALETTE CreateIdentityPalette(LPRGBQUAD aRGB, int nColors, BOOL
copy_table)
{
    .
    .
    .
    // Set the color table to be identical with the
    // logical palette's entries if this flag is set.
    if (copy_table) {
        for (i = 0; i < nColors; i++) {
            aRGB[i].rgbRed   =
                    Palette.aEntries[i].peRed;
            aRGB[i].rgbGreen =
                    Palette.aEntries[i].peGreen;
            aRGB[i].rgbBlue  =
                    Palette.aEntries[i].peBlue;
        }
    }

    // Return the palette.
    return CreatePalette((LOGPALETTE *)&Palette);
}
```

If you happen to know for sure that the color table of the DIB from which you want to create a palette doesn't have colors in the first and last ten entries (and that the pixels in the DIB don't use values in the range 0–9 and 246–255), then you can set this flag to FALSE. This would be true only if you had very tight control over the way the images were created, which might be the case, for example, if the images were rendered from 3D models and the renderer *knew* which palette entries couldn't be used.

It's also important to note that you must call **CreateIdentityPalette** prior to calling **WinGCreateBitmap**. The bitmap that is selected into the WinG DC *must* have a color table that identity-maps to the palette that will be realized in the screen DC. Otherwise, the colors of the DIB will map instead of match, considerably slowing the Blt process.

Next, the WinG DC is created with **WinGCreateDC**, and saved into a new window instance structure member. This will be the source DC used later in the call to **WinGBitBlt**. Then, the WinG bitmap is created with **WinGCreateBitmap**. Note the last argument, which is the address of the pointer to the actual bits that will be created by the call. Because a WinG bitmap's bits aren't created by the program itself, the bitmap can't be deleted with a call to **GlobalFreePtr** like a conventional DIB. You delete it by calling **DeleteObject** with its handle.

Once created, the WinG bitmap is selected into it and the old bitmap's handle is retained for use later, when the program terminates. The old bitmap is selected back into the WinG DC, and the bitmap it displaces (the WinG bitmap created with **WinGCreateBitmap**) is deleted. You could just as easily save a handle to the WinG bitmap rather than to the one it displaces in the DC, and do it the other way around.

After the WinG bitmap is created, the **biHeight** member of its BITMAPINFO structure is returned to a normal, positive value. This is done so that subsequent functions that use the DIB_HEIGHT macro never get a negative value. The sole purpose of the (potentially) negative value in **biHeight** is to allow **WinGCreateBitmap** to create a top-down DIB. Once the **biHeight** value has been set to a positive value again, code that needs to know whether the DIB is top-down will have to look at **main->topdown** instead.

The next step is to copy the actual bits of the source DIB—the one that came from the resource file—into the bits of the WinG DIB. The **WinGCreateBitmap** call just creates the memory for the bits and initializes it all to zero. The library function **hmemcpy** is used to copy the bits from the original DIB. The function **hmemcpy** is like the C Standard Library function **memcpy**, except that it knows how to handle memory-to-memory copies that can span 64k boundaries. All Windows C development environments have something akin to **hmemcpy**; check your documentation if it doesn't link properly.

After copying the bits, you must remap them so that they match the identity palette created by **CreateIdentityPalette**. The **MapDIBits** function from Chapter 8 doesn't *quite* serve the purpose here. For one, the old **MapDIBits** relied on packed-DIB format (the bits follow the header and color table), so another parameter needed to be added in case the bits were specified separately from the header. Also, note that the new version is called with the color table from the *original* DIB and the bits of the WinG DIB. This is because the color table for the WinG DIB has already been modified (by **CreateIdentityPalette**) to identity-map into the palette. This is the reason that the original DIB's header and color table were kept around. **MapDIBits** is also a logical place to turn the bitmap "upside down" if the WinG bitmap is of the top-down variety. Here's what the slightly modified **MapDIBits** function looks like:

```
void MapDIBits (HPALETTE hPal, PDIB pDIB,
                LPSTR pBits, BOOL top_down)
{
    BYTE imap[256];
    LPRGBQUAD pQ;
    int i;
    long length;
    unsigned char huge *p;

    pQ = DIB_PCLRTAB(pDIB);
    // Create the mapping table from the palette.
    for (i = 0; i < 256; i++) {
        imap[i] = (BYTE)GetNearestPaletteIndex (hPal,
                    RGB(pQ->rgbRed,
                        pQ->rgbGreen,
                        pQ->rgbBlue));
        pQ++;
    }

    // Get the pointer to the bits.
```

```
    if (!pBits)
        p = DIB_PBITS(pDIB);
    else
        p = (unsigned char huge *)pBits;

    // If this is a top-down bitmap, flip the scan
    // lines accordingly.
    if (top_down) {
        long height = DIB_HEIGHT(pDIB);
        long scanline = DIB_STORAGEWIDTH(pDIB);
        long n;
        unsigned char huge *ps, huge *pd;
        // We need a single scan-line buffer to flip.
        unsigned char huge *ptemp =
                        (unsigned char huge *)
                        GlobalAllocPtr (GPTR, scanline);

        for (n = 0; n < (height-1)/2; n++) {
            ps = p + n * scanline;
            pd = p + (height - 1 - n) * scanline;
            _fmemcpy (ptemp, ps, scanline);
            _fmemcpy (ps, pd, scanline);
            _fmemcpy (pd, ptemp, scanline);
        }
        GlobalFreePtr (ptemp);
    }

    // Map the bits.
    length = (long)DIB_STORAGEWIDTH(pDIB) *
                (long)DIB_HEIGHT(pDIB);
    while (length--) {
        *p = imap[*p];
        p++;
    }
}
```

The main change to **MapDIBits** is the addition of a loop that optionally swaps scan lines from top to bottom. Use the **_fmemcpy** function here to copy the memory from one scan line to another. You need a scan-line-size buffer to do the swap; allocate it with **GlobalAllocPtr** and free it with **GlobalFreePtr**.

Blting to the WinG DC

Now that the WinG bitmap has been created and selected into the WinG DC, you can Blt it from there to the screen's DC with **WinGBitBlt** or **WinGStretchBlt**. To do so via the right mouse button, use this handler:

```
static void OnRButtonDown (MAIN *main,
                           BOOL fDoubleClick,
                           int x, int y,
```

continued on next page

continued from previous page

```
                              UINT keyFlags)
{
    HPALETTE hOldPal;

    // Make sure the palette's been initialized.
    if (!main->hPalette)
        return;

    // Select the palette in and realize it.
    hOldPal = SelectPalette (main->hdc,
                              main->hPalette, FALSE);
    RealizePalette (main->hdc);

    // Blt the image at 1:1.
    WinGBitBlt (main->hdc, x, y,
                DIB_WIDTH(main->pWinG),
                DIB_HEIGHT(main->pWinG),
                main->hdcWinG, 0, 0);

    SelectPalette (main->hdc, hOldPal, FALSE);
}
```

Again, the beauty of WinG is in the simplicity of using **WinGBitBlt** to quickly copy bits from the WinG DC to the screen. If you've done everything correctly, there's no faster way to get the picture on the screen. See Figure 9-5 for a summary. To prove it, let's do some timing of the two methods—using **StretchDIBits** and using **WinGBitBlt**.

First, a little cleaning up is necessary. The new **OnClose** WM_CLOSE handler function looks like this:

```
static void OnClose (MAIN *main)
{
    HBITMAP hold;

    // Here's where we release the window's
    // DC.
    ReleaseDC (main->hwnd, main->hdc);

    // Free the source DIB, loaded
    // from the resource file.
    GlobalFreePtr (main->pDIB);

    // Free the header of the WinG PDIB...
    GlobalFreePtr (main->pWinG);
    // ...and delete its bitmap.
    hold = SelectBitmap (main->hdcWinG,
                         main->hOldWinGBitmap);
    DeleteObject (hold);

    // Delete the WinG DC.
    DeleteDC (main->hdcWinG);
```

```
    // Delete the palette we created.
    DeleteObject (main->hPalette);

    // End the program.
    PostQuitMessage (0);
}
```

Ah, that feels good. You can see why it's easy to have memory leaks in Windows programs—there are so many things to delete at the end.

Timing WinGBitBlt vs. StretchDIBits

To prove the performance difference between **WinGBitBlt** and **StretchDIBits**, the easiest thing to do is call one of Windows time functions. Windows has two simple ones: **GetTickCount** and the Multimedia Extensions function **timeGetTime**. Both functions return a DWORD containing the number of milliseconds elapsed since Windows was started. The difference between the two is that **timeGetTime** uses the high-resolution multimedia timer, which is accurate to within about a millisecond,

FIGURE 9-5

Creating and displaying a WinG bitmap

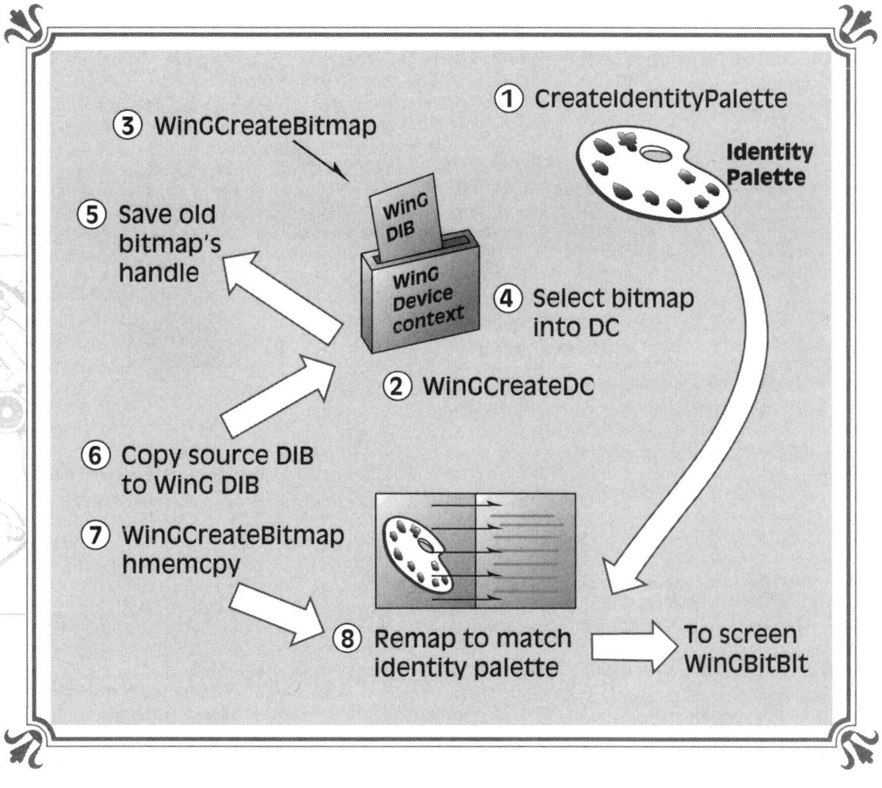

whereas **GetTickCount** uses the PC's standard timer, which is accurate only to within about 18 milliseconds. Since 18 milliseconds really isn't very good resolution, by and large you should use **timeGetTime**. In order to use it, you must include MMSYSTEM.H in your source file and link with MMSYSTEM.LIB in the project.

To make it simple, this WM_RBUTTONDOWN handler will use **WinGBitBlt** normally, but use **StretchDIBits** if SHIFT is held down at the same time. You can easily display the time in the title bar of the window.

```
static void OnRButtonDown (MAIN *main,
                           BOOL fDoubleClick,
                           int x, int y,
                           UINT keyFlags)
{
    HPALETTE hOldPal;
    int cx = DIB_WIDTH (main->pWinG);
    int cy = DIB_HEIGHT(main->pWinG);
    DWORD start, end, i;
    char buf[20];

    // Make sure the palette's been initialized.
    if (!main->hPalette)
        return;

    // Select the palette in.
    hOldPal = SelectPalette (main->hdc,
                             main->hPalette, FALSE);
    RealizePalette (main->hdc);

    // Get the time.
    start = timeGetTime ();

    // Use StretchDIBits if SHIFT is held down;
    // otherwise, use WinGBitBlt.
    if (keyFlags & MK_SHIFT)
        StretchDIBits (main->hdc, x, y,
                       cx, cy,
                       0, 0,
                       cx, cy,
                       DIB_PBITS(main->pDIB),
                       main->pDIB,
                       DIB_PAL_COLORS,
                       SRCCOPY);
    else
        WinGBitBlt (main->hdc, x, y, cx, cy,
                    main->hdcWinG, 0, 0);

    // Get the end time.
    end = timeGetTime();
```

```
    SelectPalette (main->hdc, hOldPal, FALSE);
    // Format the time and display it in the caption.
    wsprintf (buf, "Time: %ld ms", end-start);
    SetWindowText (main->hwnd, buf);
}
```

Note that the **StretchDIBits** call uses DIB_PAL_COLORS, which means that the color table that's part of **main->pDIB** should be an identity table for maximum speed. Also, the actual bits of **main->pDIB** need to be remapped so that they come out correctly with the given palette; the code as it now stands remaps only the WinG DIB's bits. Adding the following to the **OnCreate** function accomplishes the task:

```
    .
    .
    .
    // Add a couple of variables to the function.
    int i;
    LPWORD pword;
    .
    .
    .
    // Remap the bits of the original DIB, as well.
    MapDIBits (main->hPalette, main->pDIB,
               NULL, FALSE);
    // Set the color table of the original DIB
    // to an identity table for DIB_PAL_COLORS.
    pword = (LPWORD)DIB_PCLRTAB(main->pDIB);
    for (i = 0; i < 256; i++)
        *pword++ = i;
    .
    .
    .
```

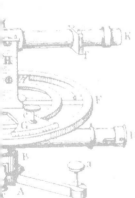

Now run the program and see the speed difference. Figure 9-6 gives an example of the program in action. The percentage difference should be about the same as the results you get from running TIMEWING. If it isn't, something's wrong. Depending on your display hardware and driver, this difference could be a factor of five or more, or it may be as little as a few percentage points. In any case, **WinGBitBlt** should always be faster than **StretchDIBits**.

At this point, you can experiment with different settings to see how it affects performance. For example, you might deliberately mess up an entry in the WinG DIB's color table to see the performance hit when there isn't an identity palette (it's significant). You could also force **WinGCreateBitmap** to create a bottom-up (or top-down) bitmap instead of the type that **WinGRecommendDIBFormat** recommends, and then measure the difference. Be aware, however, that the performance differences you measure on your machine might not correspond very closely with the performance differences that might exist on machines with different display cards and drivers. Still, it should be obvious that WinG improves things substantially.

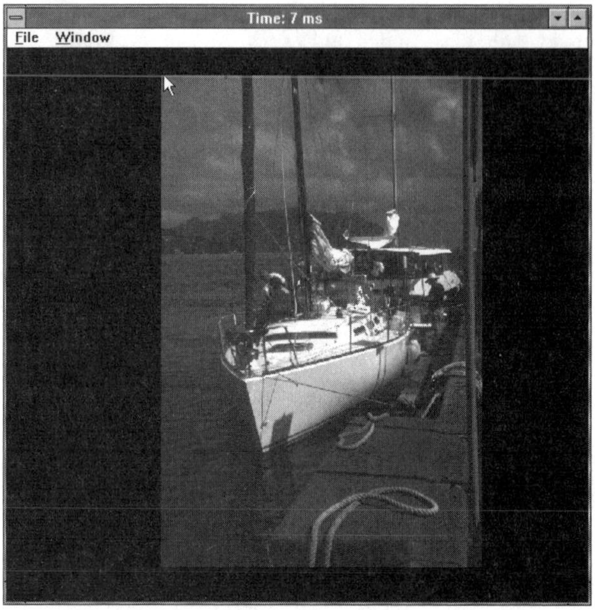

FIGURE 9-6

Example of running the timing program

Debugging with WinG

In case you *haven't* done everything correctly, you can take advantage of the debugging settings that WinG provides to help out. To display WinG's debugging information, you need to run a program like DBWIN.EXE (from the Windows SDK) that displays output from the Windows function **`OutputDebugString`**. All development environments supply something like DBWIN for this purpose.

To turn on WinG debugging, edit your WIN.INI file and look for the section labeled [WinG]. Under that section, add the following two lines:

```
Debug=1
DebugPalette=1
```

The first setting turns on some general WinG debugging information, and the second turns on messages dealing specifically with palettes that are selected into a DC into which WinG is Blting.

Easily the most common performance mistake is creating a nonidentity palette. The code works fine, but there's a significant performance hit. Turning on DebugPalette will cause WinG to display information about palette mapping whenever **`WinGBitBlt`** or **`WinGStretchBlt`** is called.

Another common performance mistake is using GDI functions to copy bits *into* the WinG DC (and hence, its bitmap). The advantage of using a WinG bitmap in the first place is that you get a pointer to the actual bits of the image, which you can modify directly with your own code. Memory-to-memory copies are always going to be faster than whatever GDI does, so just use the pointer. There's a good chance that your code is faster than GDI at a great many things, in fact, including line drawing. About the only thing that's really handy in GDI is text drawing, especially if you want to use fancy TrueType fonts.

Summary

Congratulations, you now know about all there is to know about Windows bitmap handling! As you can see, you had to learn all about the GDI, DDBs, DIBs, and palettes in order to make effective use of WinG. Now that you've got it all tucked under your belt, writing programs that use WinG is really quite simple. Here is a summary of the steps for using WinG effectively:

- Create a WinG offscreen bitmap and DC using **WinGRecommendDIB-Format**, **WinGCreateDC**, and **WinGCreateBitmap**.
- Select the bitmap into the WinG DC with **SelectObject**.
- Set the bits in the WinG bitmap with your own code and/or using the GDI.
- Blt the WinG bitmap to the screen with **WinGBitBlt**.

Most of the code you've seen up to this point in this book has been designed to express the use of Windows calls as simply as possible, often with somewhat generic examples. In the next chapter, everything you've learned will be applied to the task of creating an actual sprite engine based on DIBs and WinG. You could use the sprite engine as the basis for an entire game (such as BugBots—see Appendix A) or rip out appropriate bits of it and use them in other game programs. In either case, the sprite engine brings together all that you've learned about Windows, as well as some of the concepts of sprite animation that I've touched on in earlier chapters.

10

Bringing It All Together—Sprite Animation

Ogni [illegible] le manovelle [illegible] le quali si movano e l'alza
e i gran pesi [illegible] [illegible] faceβero [illegible]
sforzare nella [illegible] alla manovella [illegible]
la forza e più [illegible] omo più vale.

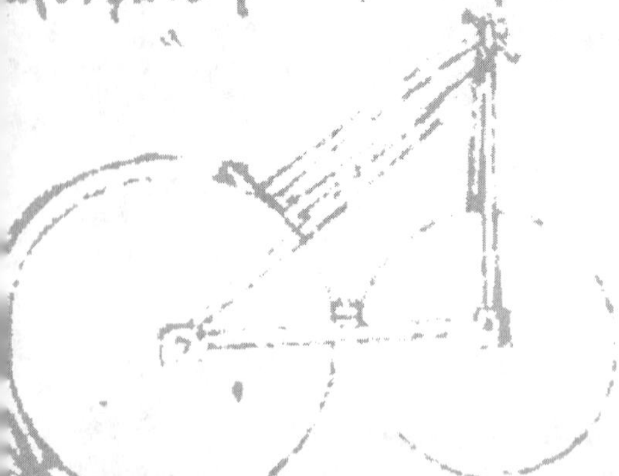

[illegible]

10

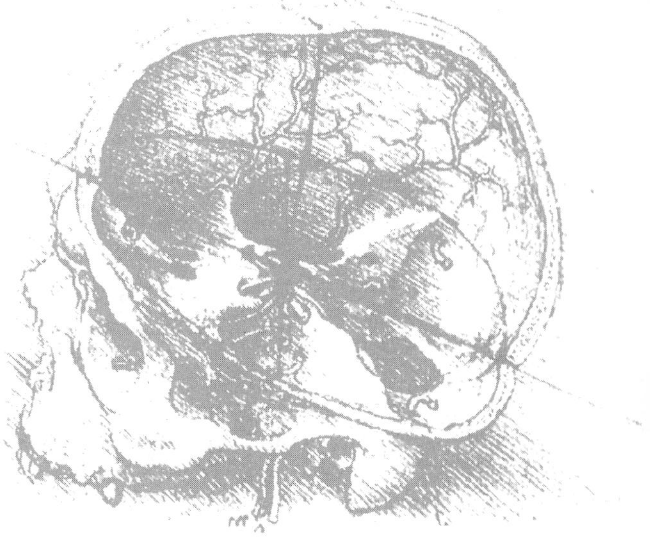

Bringing It All Together—Sprite Animation

Now that you know all this great stuff about programming under Windows, it's time to put it into action. In this chapter, you'll do that by developing a simple sprite engine for Windows. The sprite engine incorporates everything you've learned so far, along with a few new tricks, like handling transparency and efficient updating.

Before diving into the code, let's take a look at exactly what's required to do sprite animation, particularly under Windows.

Sprite Animation Basics

A *sprite* is an irregularly shaped (nonrectangular, that is) picture that can be moved nondestructively (without changing the background image) anywhere on the screen. Because images in memory are always rectangular arrays of pixels, sprites make use of *transparent pixels* in order to achieve an irregular shape. A transparent pixel is one that reveals whatever's underneath it instead of its own inherent color. There are two ways to achieve transparency: by using *masks* or by the convention of making one pixel value the so-called *transparent color.* Figure 10-1 illustrates the concept of transparency in sprites.

FIGURE 10-1

Transparency in sprites

A mask is simply a 1-bit-per-pixel bitmap (which is, incidentally, the true meaning of the word "bitmap") of exactly the same dimensions as the sprite image. If a bit in the mask is set, the corresponding pixel in the sprite is transparent. Using a transparent color is even simpler—any pixel of a certain color (or index, in the case of palettized images) is transparent. This approach saves you from having to keep a separate bitmap for each sprite image, but at the cost of the use of one color (out of 236, in the case of Windows' 8-bit images).

But how is the transparency of pixels in a sprite actually computed? The process of displaying an image with a background and one or more sprites is usually called *rendering*, a term borrowed from the process of turning a 3D model into an image. Rendering sprites involves looking at each pixel of the sprite image (and mask, if that method is used) and deciding whether to copy the sprite pixel or the corresponding background pixel to the screen. On dedicated game hardware systems, rendering can happen very quickly—the hardware is optimized to do just that. On PCs (whether running Windows or not), rendering must take place in software and its speed is tied to the cleverness of the rendering algorithm. Most often, the inner rendering loop that copies either the sprite's or the background's pixels to the screen is written in assembly language for speed. In the sprite engine I develop in this chapter, the inner rendering loop is written in 32-bit Intel assembly language for the best possible performance.

Z-Order

Sprites can pass over each other, and hence have an implicit *z-order*—a stack position relative to the background image. The rendering algorithm must take into account the fact that any number of sprites may be intersecting a given displayed pixel. The pixel to be displayed is the topmost, nontransparent one. The easiest way to do this is via the so-called *Painter's Algorithm*—sprites are rendered onto the display from the bottom up, starting with the background image. Figure 10-2 illustrates the idea of z-order.

Page Flipping with Hardware

You learned back in Chapter 6 that to create animation without flicker requires making changes to an offscreen buffer that is then copied to the screen. One really excellent way to accomplish this (provided the hardware supports it) is to use *page flipping*. In a video card that supports page flipping, there's enough memory to support two full screens. The hardware can flip between these screens virtually instantaneously by just plugging a register that determines which page to display.

To use page flipping, you render one scene into a buffer while displaying the other, and then you tell the hardware to do the flip. The flip can even be synchronized (usually) to the vertical retracing so that there's no tear. Figure 10-3 illustrates this technique.

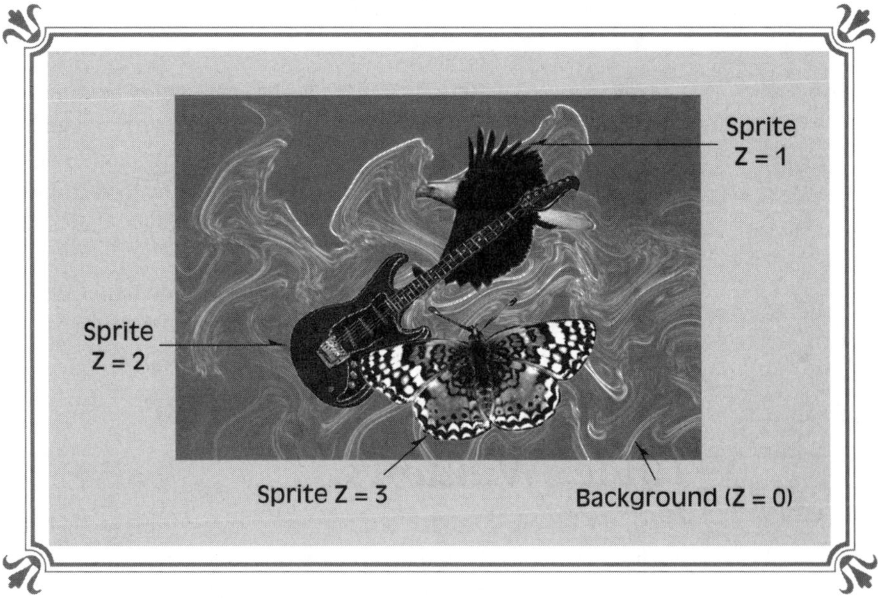

FIGURE 10-2

Z-order

FIGURE 10-3

Page flipping

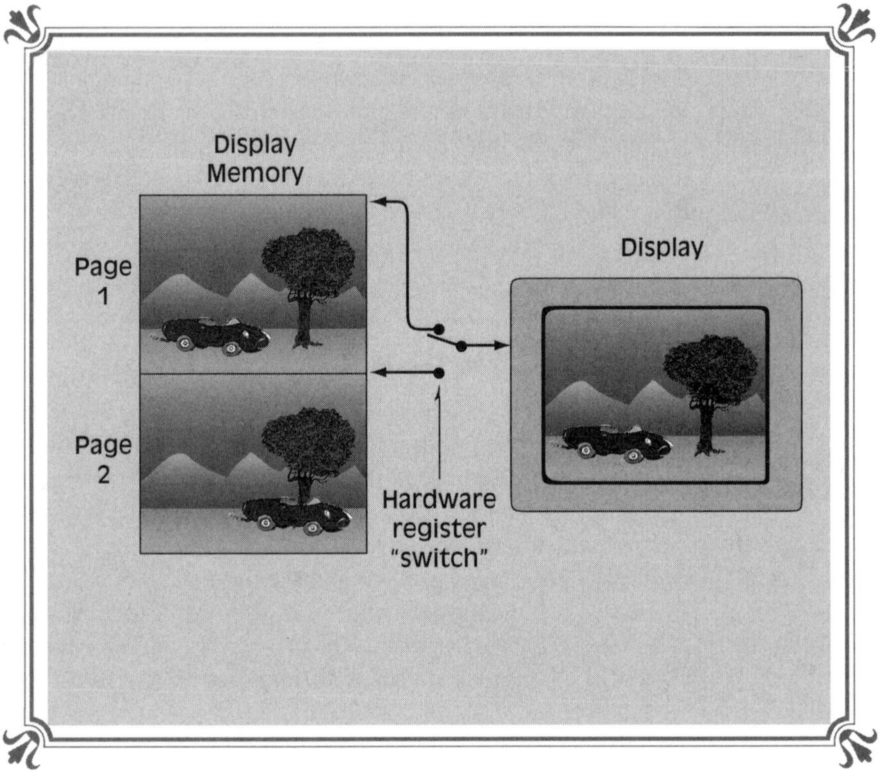

Unfortunately, Windows doesn't allow such handy manipulations, partly because it isn't supported across a wide range of display hardware and resolution combinations. Besides, sometimes page flipping doesn't really pay, because what time you gain during the process of changing the picture you may lose in the time it takes to write to the undisplayed page (due to the aforementioned slowness of writing to video memory).

Under Windows, the only practical way to render and display animation is to use an offscreen buffer.

Using an Offscreen Buffer Under Windows

Using an offscreen buffer accomplishes three things. First, it eliminates flicker, because the screen is updated only when all the necessary changes are already rendered to the offscreen buffer. Second, it eliminates the slow operation of reading pixels from the screen—pixels are only *written* to the screen from the offscreen buffer. Third, it makes it possible to update only *portions* of the screen in order to get optimum performance. This third benefit may not always be available if the entire screen changes between updates (as happens in the case of a flight simulator game), but in a sprite-based game, it's often the case that only certain areas of the screen change.

An offscreen buffer is simply a bitmap the same size and format as the client area of the game's window. You might have surmised from the previous chapter that a WinG bitmap is ideally suited to this purpose, because it gives you full access to the bits without having to go through the GDI. This makes it possible for you to write your own, optimized, rendering routine for combining sprites with the background image.

To do sprite animation with an offscreen buffer, three things must be kept in memory:

- The offscreen buffer
- The background image
- The sprite images

It's possible to copy the background image into the offscreen buffer only once and then free the background image from memory, but to then update the offscreen buffer, you first need to save portions of it into temporary buffers, which usually doesn't pay. In the old days of low-memory machines, there wasn't much choice, but even a modestly configured Windows machine today can generally afford the overhead of one more screen-size (or smaller) buffer.

If you're thinking about how much memory all this takes, think in terms of your target resolution. It's possible to do real-time scaling of the background image and bitmaps, but it's not very fast. Consequently, you need to pick a resolution and stick to it. Typically, this will be 640x480, since it's the most widely available resolution. If yours is a full-screen game and someone is running a higher resolution, your only reasonable choice is to center the game on an otherwise blank (or possibly cleverly painted) screen.

Let's have a step-by-step look at the process of rendering the background image and the sprites moving across it, and see how it all gets displayed on the screen.

Step 1: Copy the background. The first thing the rendering algorithm has to do is copy the background image into the offscreen buffer so sprites can then be rendered on top of the background. Later, you'll learn how to optimize this so that only portions of the background are copied.

Step 2: Render the sprites. The rendering algorithm walks the list of sprites from back to front, copying nontransparent pixels into the offscreen buffer and skipping over transparent pixels. When the algorithm reaches the end of the sprite list, rendering is done.

Step 3: Display the buffer. The offscreen buffer is copied to the screen with a Blt. As with Step 1, this step can be optimized to copy only a portion of the offscreen buffer. Figure 10-4 shows the results.

After each of the three steps is performed, the algorithms that govern sprite movement compute the new positions of the sprites and repeat the process I've just described. Obviously, sprite movement is a major component of the game's overall design. The game engine you'll develop in this chapter uses a very simple routine that moves the sprites by simply changing their coordinates along a position vector, wrapping them from one side of the screen to the other. Once you understand how it all works, you can substitute other, more interesting, algorithms. I'll throw in a couple more examples once I've covered the basics.

Optimizing Sprite Animation

It should be clear that there are some straightforward ways to optimize all the steps I've outlined here. The most obvious thing to do is to render only the portions of the picture that change between updates. Figuring out what portions change isn't too difficult—for each sprite, you simply track the old and new positions, create a rectangle that is the union of two, and then render and redraw that rectangle. This technique

FIGURE 10-4

Sprite animation using an offscreen buffer

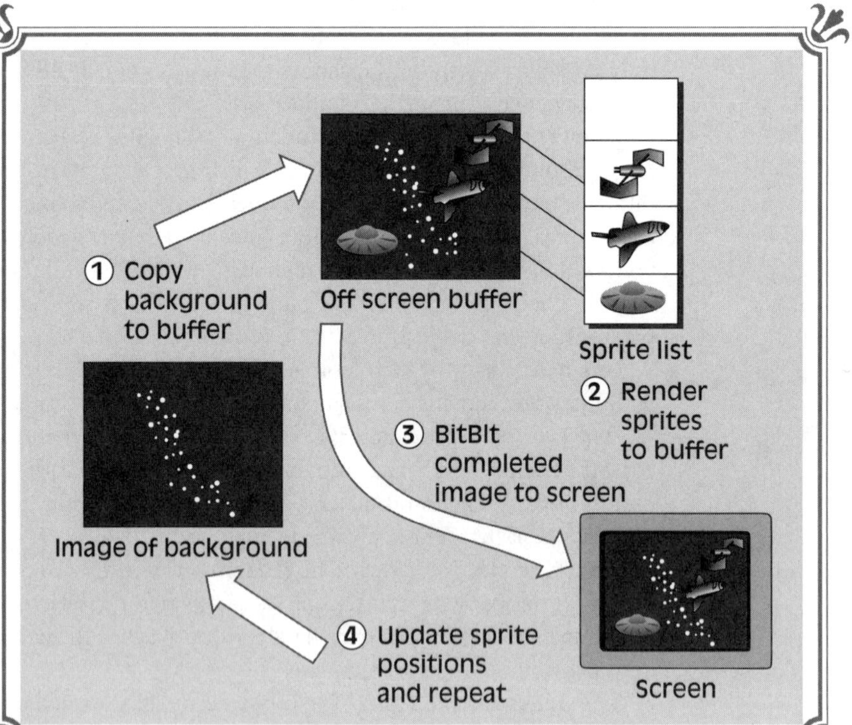

is called *dirty-rectangle* updating. To make it really efficient, however, you can perform a few other simple optimizations.

Dirty-Rectangle Updating

Figures 10-5 and 10-6 show the basic idea behind dirty-rectangle updating. The controlling algorithms compute a list of update rectangles that contain all the areas of the screen that have changed—the "dirty" areas. Then, the algorithms perform each of the three steps—copying, rendering, and displaying—for each rectangle.

A quick study would find an obvious shortcoming in this simple scheme. If any of the dirty rectangles intersect, the algorithms will copy, render, and display the overlapping areas multiple times. A simple way to eliminate this redundancy is to find all the intersecting rectangles and merge them into one rectangle before the copy/render/display steps are performed. This ensures that the code will modify the fewest pixels possible, which is usually the key to the highest performance. It also takes care of the case where a sprite's position changes enough between updates that the rectangles around its old and new positions don't intersect, by simply leaving the two rectangles independent.

The key assumption in dirty-rectangle updating is that writing pixels is slower than computing intersecting rectangles. If this weren't true, then it would be faster to simply Blt all the update rectangles or possibly to update the whole picture. As it turns out, this assumption is virtually always true on today's hardware configurations—it's cheaper to compute rectangles than to Blt pixels. Of course, there's some threshold where Blting the pixels takes as much time as the overhead required to do the Blt, but this threshold number of pixels is usually very small. If your game has lots of

FIGURE 10-5

Starting sprite positions

FIGURE 10-6

Ending sprite positions

single-pixel (or very small) sprites, then dirty-rectangle updating may not be efficient. In the code you'll develop in this chapter, you can experiment by timing sprites of different sizes, with and without the dirty-rectangle merging step.

Before diving into the code, I need to give credit where it's due. I based my sprite engine on code found on Microsoft's Multimedia Jumpstart CD-ROM, written by multimedia guru Herman Rodent at Microsoft. (I've modified it to work with WinG and made a number of other changes, as well.) Many thanks to Microsoft for allowing the use of this code.

The Sprite-Engine Code

A good place to start is with data structures. The sprite-engine code uses one large header file, GLOBAL.H, that defines most of the common data structures I've used throughout the program. It's too large and boring to print in its entirety here, but I'll cover all the interesting parts as needed.

To start, there's one global structure that holds variables that are used throughout the program:

```
//
// global data
//
```

```
struct {
    char *szAppName;            // App name
    HINSTANCE hAppInstance;     // App instance
    HWND hwndMain;              // Main window handle
    PSPRITE pSpriteList;        // Pointer to sprite list
    PDIB pdibBkGnd;             // Background DIB
    PDIB pdibWinG;              // Offscreen WinG DIB
    HDC hdcWinG;                // Main offscreen WinG DC
    HBITMAP hWinGBitmap;        // WinG bitmap handle
    LPVOID pOffScreenBits;      // WinG bitmap bits pointer
    UINT uiTimer;               // Update timer
    HPALETTE hpalCurrent;       // Current palette
    BOOL bShowUpdateRects;      // Show the updated rectangles
    BOOL bCaptured;             // Is the sprite captured?
    char szIniFile[_MAX_PATH]; // INI file name
    BOOL bAutoUpdate;           // Move sprites flag.
} G;
```

The meaning of most of the members of the structure should be obvious. The **bShowUpdateRects** member triggers the display of the dirty rectangles so that you can see how they're being merged. The **bAutoUpdate** flag turns on and off the main animation loop. The **bCaptured** flag indicates whether a sprite has been captured by the mouse (and is therefore being dragged around the screen). The **pSpriteList** member is a pointer to the list of sprites. The sprite structure is defined in GLOBAL.H, as well:

```
typedef struct _SPRITE {
    struct _SPRITE FAR *pNext; // Pointer to next item
    struct _SPRITE FAR *pPrev; // Pointer to prev item
    PDIB pDIB;                 // Sprite's DIB
    int x;                     // X coordinate of top-left corner
    int y;                     // Y coordinate of top-left corner
    int z;                     // Z-order for sprite
    int vx;                    // X velocity
    int vy;                    // Y velocity
    int width;                 // Width of bounding rectangle
    int height;                // Height of bounding rectangle
    BYTE bTopLeft;             // Top-left pixel value
    COLORREF rgbTopLeft;       // Top-left pixel color
    BOOL bSelectable;          // TRUE if sprite is selectable
} SPRITE, FAR *PSPRITE;
```

This sprite structure contains only the basics: location, size, z-order, a PDIB to hold the actual sprite image, and forward- and back-pointers so that the list can be walked in either direction. There's also a couple of variables to hold the color and index value of the top-left pixel—this is how the transparent color is determined. This scheme allows each sprite to have its own transparent color rather than having a fixed index value or color used for transparency. The **bSelectable** flag is used to indicate whether the sprite is selectable by the mouse.

We need another set of structures to keep track of the dirty rectangles:

```
//
// Define a structure used to maintain rectangle lists.
// Note: These are allocated on the local heap
// and we use near pointers deliberately for speed.
//

typedef struct _DRAWRECT {
    struct _DRAWRECT *pPrev;     // Previous
    struct _DRAWRECT *pNext;     // Next
    RECT rc;                     // Data item
} DRAWRECT, *PDRAWRECT;

typedef struct _DRAWRECTLIST {
    PDRAWRECT pHead;       // Pointer to first item
} DRAWRECTLIST, FAR *PDRAWRECTLIST;
```

Note that the DRAWRECTLIST structure contains nothing more than a pointer to a **DRAWRECT**, making it easy to create multiple dirty-rectangle lists, if needed. Also note that **PDRAWRECT** doesn't have a memory classification before it, which means that under Medium model it's a near (16-bit) pointer. As the comment says, I've done this for speed—near pointers are inherently faster than far pointers. As a result, you must do all the allocation of the dirty rectangles with **LocalAlloc**. (If you're using a 32-bit environment, you get to ignore all this nonsense, of course.)

I've defined all the function prototypes for the various code modules in GLOBAL.H, as well. (I usually define them in separate header files for each module, but this isn't really a big enough piece of code to justify that practice.) Besides the prototypes, the only other things worthy of note in GLOBAL.H are the **#define** statements for memory allocation and freeing:

```
//
// Memory allocation macros
//

#define ALLOCATE(s) (GlobalAllocPtr (GPTR, s))
#define FREE(p) (GlobalFreePtr (p))
```

Again, if you're using a 32-bit development environment, you can substitute **malloc** and **free** for these calls. There are also some clever debugging-support macros and function prototypes in GLOBAL.H. I will cover these as I unfold their use later in the chapter.

I think the best way to analyze the code is to look at it from the inside out, starting with the main animation loop. You'll find this in MAIN.C, right where you might expect—as part of the main message loop. After you've done some standard initialization things, the loop looks like this:

```
    .
    .
    .
    //
    // Check for messages from Windows and process.
    // If we have nothing else to do,
    // move the sprites.
    //

    do {
        if (PeekMessage(&msg, NULL, 0, 0, PM_REMOVE)) {

            //
            // Got a message to process
            //

            if (msg.message == WM_QUIT) break;

            TranslateMessage(&msg);
            DispatchMessage(&msg);

        } else {

            //
            // Perform the update routine or just
            // give up so Windows can run until our
            // next message.
            //

            if (G.bAutoUpdate && !G.bCaptured) {
                UpdatePositions();
            } else {
                WaitMessage();
            }
        }
    } while (1);
```

In Chapter 2, you learned about the **GetMessage** function that removes a message from the application's message queue and returns FALSE when the message is WM_QUIT. **PeekMessage** is a little different—it returns TRUE whenever there's a message waiting, and FALSE if there's no message. With the PM_REMOVE option, **PeekMessage** also removes the waiting message from the queue. You can see why you'd want to use **PeekMessage** for the animation loop here—it allows the loop to do something useful if there's no message in the queue for the program, while still allowing normal processing of Windows messages. The **WaitMessage** function just gives time back to Windows so that it can do its thing. Using **PeekMessage** and **WaitMessage** in this way lets the program be a well-behaved Windows application while maintaining a continuous update loop.

An alternative to using **PeekMessage** and **WaitMessage** in the main event loop is to create a Windows timer, which sends WM_TIMER messages directly to the window handler function. One advantage of using a timer is that you can create a relatively reliable update time on machines of different speeds—so long as the timer interval is guaranteed to be no shorter than the total update time required on the *slowest* machine. Using the **PeekMessage/WaitMessage** method allows the engine to run at the highest possible speed on any machine.

The real action happens in **UpdatePositions**, which can be found in DRAW.C:

```
//
// Update sprite positions
// (main animation function).
//

void UpdatePositions()
{
    PSPRITE pSprite;
    BOOL bChanged = FALSE;
    RECT rcPos;

    pSprite = G.pSpriteList;
    while (pSprite) {

        if (pSprite->vx || pSprite->vy) {

            //
            // Add the old (current) position
            // of the sprite to the redraw-rectangle list.
            //
            GetSpriteRect(pSprite, &rcPos);
            Render(&rcPos, NO_UPDATE);

            pSprite->x += pSprite->vx;

            // Wrap sprites around one edge to the other.
            if ((pSprite->vx < 0) &&
                (pSprite->x + pSprite->width < 0)) {

                pSprite->x = DIB_WIDTH(G.pdibBkGnd);

            } else if ((pSprite->vx > 0) &&
              (pSprite->x > DIB_WIDTH(G.pdibBkGnd))) {

                pSprite->x = - (int)pSprite->width;

            }

            pSprite->y += pSprite->vy;

            if ((pSprite->vy < 0) &&
```

```
                (pSprite->y + pSprite->height < 0)) {

                pSprite->y = DIB_HEIGHT(G.pdibBkGnd);

            } else if ((pSprite->vy > 0) &&
             (pSprite->y > DIB_HEIGHT(G.pdibBkGnd))) {

                pSprite->y = - (int) pSprite->height;

            }

            //
            // Add the new position of the sprite
            // to the redraw-rectangle list.
            //
            GetSpriteRect(pSprite, &rcPos);
            Render(&rcPos, NO_UPDATE);

            bChanged = TRUE;
        }

        pSprite = pSprite->pNext;
    }

    //
    // Render (with screen update)
    // if anyone changed position.
    //
    if (bChanged)
        // Ask for the last one again.
        Render(&rcPos, UPDATE_SCREEN);
}
```

Understanding how **UpdatePositions** works is half of understanding how the whole sprite engine works, and it's not all that hard to understand. The function walks the sprite list (**G.pSpriteList**), first getting the rectangle that surrounds each sprite in its current position and adding the rectangle to the redraw list. (The purpose of the **Render** function is a bit deceptive in this context—if it's called with the **NO_UPDATE** flag, all it really does is copy the rectangle passed in as the first argument onto the redraw list.) Next, **UpdatePositions** moves the sprite by incrementing its **x** and **y** structure members by the values in **vx** and **vy**, which represent nothing more than a distance vector (in pixels) for each trip through the loop. The bulk of the code in **UpdatePositions** then does nothing more than wrap the position of the sprite around from one side of the screen to the other by computing when a sprite passes beyond the width and height of the background image (**G.pdibBkGnd**).

After the sprite is moved, its new position is grabbed with **GetSpriteRect** again, and this new position is added to the redraw list. The loop then proceeds to the next sprite until it reaches the end of the list.

At this point, if any of the sprites changed postion (**bChanged == TRUE**), the last rectangle is added to the list again, but this time the results are actually computed and displayed, as specified by the **UPDATE_SCREEN** flag.

Obviously, all the real work happens in **Render**. The **Render** function really does three things. First, it adds dirty rectangles to the redraw list. In fact, this is the *only* thing it does if the value of its second argument is **NO_UPDATE**. If instead the second argument is set to **UPDATE_SCREEN**, then **Render** first merges all the dirty rectangles into the minimum set of union rectangle. Then, the function takes the portions of the background image and sprite images that intersect the resulting list of dirty rectangles and renders them to the offscreen buffer. Finally, **Render** displays the redraw list on the screen. Here's the listing for **Render**:

```
void Render(LPRECT prcClip, BOOL bUpdate)
{
    PSPRITE pSprite, pLastSprite;
    HDC hDC;
    PDRAWRECT pDrawRect;
    RECT rcAll;

    //
    // Add the rectangle to the list.
    //

    if (prcClip) {
        AddDrawRectItem(&DrawList, prcClip);
    } else {

        //
        // If we have a background defined,
        // add a rectangle to cover it.
        //

        if (G.pdibBkGnd) {
            rcAll.left = rcAll.top = 0;
            rcAll.right = DIB_WIDTH(G.pdibBkGnd);
            rcAll.bottom = DIB_HEIGHT(G.pdibBkGnd);
            AddDrawRectItem(&DrawList, &rcAll);
        }
    }

    //
    // If no update is requested, that's all there is.
    //

    if (bUpdate == NO_UPDATE) return;

    //
    // Make sure there is a background DIB and DC.
    //

    if (!G.pdibBkGnd || !G.hdcWinG) return;
```

```
//
// Merge the draw-rectangle list and walk it, doing renders.
//

MergeDrawRectList(&DrawList);

//
// Find the end of the sprite list.
//

pLastSprite = G.pSpriteList;
if (pLastSprite) {
    while (pLastSprite->pNext)
        pLastSprite = pLastSprite->pNext;
}

if (bUpdate == UPDATE_SCREEN) {
    hDC = GetDC(G.hwndMain);
}

//
// Walk the draw-rectangle list.
//

pDrawRect = DrawList.pHead;

while (pDrawRect) {

    //
    // Render the background DIB to the offscreen DC.
    //

    RenderDIBBitsOffScreen(G.pdibBkGnd,
                           0, 0,
                           &(pDrawRect->rc),
                           0,
                           FALSE);

    //
    // Draw the sprites.
    // Walk the list from the bottom (back) to the top (front).
    //

    pSprite = pLastSprite;
    while (pSprite) {
        RenderSpriteOffScreen(pSprite, &(pDrawRect->rc));
        pSprite = pSprite->pPrev;
    }

    //
    // See if we need to repaint.
    //
```

continued on next page

continued from previous page

```
        if (bUpdate == UPDATE_SCREEN) {

            Paint(hDC, &(pDrawRect->rc));
        }


        pDrawRect = pDrawRect->pNext;
    }

    if (bUpdate == UPDATE_SCREEN) {
        ReleaseDC(G.hwndMain, hDC);
    }

    //
    // Empty the redraw list.
    //

    EmptyDrawRectList(&DrawList);

}
```

Taking the function step by step, you'll see that the first thing it does is add the rectangle passed in as its first argument (if non-NULL) to a globally defined redraw-rectangle list called **DrawList**. The **AddDrawRectItem** helper function does this. (I'll give its definition in a moment.) If the first argument to **Render** is NULL, then it adds a rectangle for the whole background image to the redraw list. If the second parameter is **NO_UPDATE**, then the function is done and just returns.

The good stuff happens after we reach the last rectangle, when the second parameter to **Redraw** is **UPDATE_SCREEN**. After a safety check for an existing background and WinG DC object, **MergeDrawRectList** is called with a pointer to the global **DrawList**. This helper function merges all the intersecting rectangles of the redraw list.

Next, the end of the sprite list (whose head is held in **G.pSpriteList**) is found. (Yes, **Render** would be faster if the tail of the sprite list were held in a separate variable, but finding the end of the list takes a tiny fraction of the time required by the rest of **Render**'s activities.) Then, a DC handle for the window is retrieved (this code doesn't require the use of a CS_OWNDC window class), and the function begins walking the redraw-rectangle list.

The main loop of **Render** first renders a portion of the background image to the offscreen bitmap with **RenderDIBBitsOffScreen**. This helper function is the key function for copying bits from a PDIB to the offscreen (WinG) bitmap, so let's take a look at its definition here:

```
void RenderDIBBitsOffScreen(PDIB pDIB, int x, int y,
                            LPRECT prcClip,
                            BYTE bTranClr, BOOL bTrans)
{
```

```
RECT rcDraw, rcDIB;
HPBYTE pStartS;
// Destination 48-bit pointer
WORD DestSegment;
DWORD DestOffset;
long lScanS, lScanD;
BOOL TopDown = (DIB_HEIGHT(G.pdibWinG) < 0) ? TRUE : FALSE;

//
// Intersect the clip rectangle with the offscreen DIB to make
// sure we don't try to draw to any invalid coordinates.
//

rcDraw.top = rcDraw.left = 0;
rcDraw.right = DIB_WIDTH(G.pdibWinG) - 1;
// DIB_HEIGHT could be negative for a top-down DIB.
rcDraw.bottom = abs(DIB_HEIGHT(G.pdibWinG)) - 1;

if (prcClip) {
    if (!IntersectRect(&rcDraw, &rcDraw, prcClip))
        return;
}

//
// Intersect the clip rectangle with the DIB rectangle.
//

rcDIB.left = x;
rcDIB.right = x + DIB_WIDTH(pDIB) - 1;
rcDIB.top = y;
rcDIB.bottom = y + DIB_HEIGHT(pDIB) - 1;

if (!IntersectRect(&rcDraw, &rcDraw, &rcDIB))
    return;

//
// We have a sprite that is at least partially visible in
// the clip rectangle.
// Calculate the address of the first pixel of the bottom
// scan line.
//
pStartS = GetDIBPixelAddress(pDIB,
                             rcDraw.left - x,
                             rcDraw.bottom - y);

ASSERT(pStartS);

//
// Calculate the address of the offscreen DIB.
// This function returns its value as a 48-bit (16:32)
// pointer: 16 bits in DestSegment, 32 bits in DestOffset.
```

continued on next page

continued from previous page

```
    // The reason for this is that passing a normal FAR
    // pointer (32-bits) will fail in the assembly routines,
    // because the offset part of the pointer (the lower 16 bits)
    // will wrap when it goes below 0 (when using top-down DIBs).
    // Therefore, we compute the offset as a 32-bit value, which
    // will decrement to 0 only.
    //
    // This is necessary only for the destination address (the
    // WinG bitmap), because the source bitmaps are all bottom-up
    // DIBs that come from files and are in packed-DIB format.
    //

    GetWinGPixelAddress(G.pdibWinG,
                        rcDraw.left,
                        rcDraw.bottom,
                        G.pOffScreenBits,
                        &DestSegment,
                        &DestOffset);

    //
    // Calculate the scan-line width of the DIBs.
    //

    lScanS = DIB_STORAGEWIDTH(pDIB);
    lScanD = DIB_STORAGEWIDTH(G.pdibWinG);

    if (!bTrans) {

        //
        // Copy the bits without transparency.
        //
        CopyDIBBits(DestSegment,
                    DestOffset,
                    pStartS,
                    rcDraw.right - rcDraw.left + 1,
                    rcDraw.bottom - rcDraw.top + 1,
                    // Negative scan width if top-down dest...
                    TopDown ? -lScanD : lScanD,
                    lScanS);

    } else {

        TransCopyDIBBits(DestSegment,
                         DestOffset,
                         pStartS,
                         rcDraw.right - rcDraw.left + 1,
                         rcDraw.bottom - rcDraw.top + 1,
                         // Negative scan width if top-down dest...
                         TopDown ? -lScanD : lScanD,
                         lScanS,
                         bTranClr);

    }
```

```
    if (G.bShowUpdateRects) {
        DrawRect(G.hdcWinG,
                 rcDraw.left+1,
                 rcDraw.top+1,
                 rcDraw.right,
                 rcDraw.bottom,
                 CYAN);
    }
}
```

This is the big, nasty function where the program spends most of its time. The whole point of the dirty-rectangle scheme is to call this time-consuming function as infrequently as possible. Speeding up the function itself will also directly affect the speed of the whole program, so optimizing `RenderDIBBitsOffScreen` really pays off. Let's examine how it works.

The first argument to the function is the PDIB whose bits are to be copied to the offscreen buffer. Next come the destination coordinates for the PDIB—these tell the function where the PDIB will be rendered onto the offscreen buffer by identifying the upper left corner's coordinates. The size of the destination rectangle is governed by the size of the PDIB (that is, its `DIB_HEIGHT` and `DIB_WIDTH`) and the clipping rectangle passed in as the next argument to the function. This rectangle—which always comes from the redraw list—tells `RenderDIBBitsOffScreen` to write into only the bits of the offscreen buffer that lie within it. The last two arguments are used for rendering sprites to the offscreen buffer—one defines the index for the transparent color, and the last argument is a flag that tells the function to actually use the index and do a "transparent" copy (in other words, to copy only the bits in the PDIB that are *not* set to the specified index value).

If you refer again to the listing of the `Render` function, you'll see that the call to `RenderDIBBitsOffScreen` simply tells it to copy the background DIB—without transparency—to the offscreen bitmap within the redraw rectangle. Back to `RenderDIBBitsOffScreen`.

The first thing that the function does is check to see if the specified rectangle is within the coordinates of the offscreen bitmap (`G.pdibWinG`) so that it doesn't try to render into nonexistent bits. The Windows library function `IntersectRect` does this, placing the results in its first argument (`rcDraw`) and returning FALSE if the rectangles don't intersect. In this case, the function would just return. You could save a little time by making sure invalid coordinates are never passed into the function, but you might have to perform the same test elsewhere anyway.

If the redraw rectangle and the offscreen bitmap do intersect, then `RenderDIBBitsOffScreen` creates yet another clipping rectangle based on the source PDIB's dimensions and the previous clipping rectangle. If, in turn, *these* two rectangles don't intersect, then it means the caller is asking `RenderDIBBitsOffScreen` to render a DIB onto the background in a position that's neither within the redraw rectangle nor within the dimensions of the offscreen bitmap, so there's nothing to do. The function returns.

Next, the function sets out to get the address of the first pixel on the bottommost scan line within the intersecting (redraw) rectangle. Note that it always looks for the *bottommost* scan line, because the function always assumes that the source PDIB is a top-down DIB; in other words, one that came from a file versus one that was created by **WinGCreateBitmap**. This is a reasonable assumption, because the only WinG bitmap in the program is the one used as the offscreen buffer, and all other DIBs must come from files (or be created on the fly, and had better be of the traditional bottom-up type). The **ASSERT** statement brings up a dialog box if the condition that is its single argument resolves to FALSE (or NULL, in this case).

The next call, to **GetWinGPixelAddress**, is basically the same as **GetDIB-PixelAddress**, with two exceptions. First, it can handle both top-down and bottom-up DIBs (by looking at the sign of the **biHeight** member of the PDIB that is its first argument). Secondly, it doesn't return its argument as a huge pointer to an **unsigned char**, as the former function does. The comments explain why—it has to do with the way the 32-bit assembly language functions that are called next work with pointers. (The comments in the code explain the complexities of using a 16-bit segment and 32-bit offset address in the assembly language functions.)

Next, the scan-line width of the two DIBs is stored into a couple of local variables, and the function calls either **CopyDIBBits** or **TransCopyDIBBits**, depending on whether this is a transparent copy. The latter two functions are 32-bit assembly language routines defined in FAST32.ASM. Their sole function is to copy a rectangle's worth of pixels (bytes, in this case, because both functions assume 8-bit images) from one starting memory address to another. It's within these two functions that the program *really* spends most of its time, even though these functions are written in assembly code. It's just the nature of the beast that the process of copying pixels—especially transparent ones, where there's a potential branch at *each pixel*—takes time. If you've worked on imaging software before, you know that it's in the code that actually touches pixels where you have to do all the optimization. Unless you're working with very small images, it's always where all the time goes. The reason is simple: A 640x480 screen has 307,200 pixels, and copying them from one place to another takes a lot more time than doing even a whole heck of a lot of math. I won't go into the guts of **CopyDIBBits** and **TransCopyDIBBits**, but if you're an Intel 32-bit assembly guru, feel free to optimize the assembly code to your heart's content.

The last thing the **RenderDIBBitsOffScreen** function does is test a global flag that makes the function draw a rectangle on the offscreen bitmap so you can see where all the redraw rectangles are created, for debugging purposes.

Now that you know how **RenderDIBBitsOffScreen** works, we can go back to **Render** and continue where we left off. After rendering a portion of the background DIB to the offscreen bitmap, **Render** walks the sprite list, rendering each sprite to the offscreen bitmap with **RenderSpriteOffScreen**. The latter function is quite simple:

```
void RenderSpriteOffScreen(PSPRITE pSprite, LPRECT prcClip)
{
    RECT rc;

    if (!G.hdcWinG) return;

    dprintf4("RenderSprite()");

    //
    // See if the sprite rectangle is visible in the clip rectangle.
    //

    if (prcClip) {
        GetSpriteRect(pSprite, &rc);
        if (!IntersectRect(&rc, &rc, prcClip)) {
            return;
        }
    }

    RenderDIBBitsOffScreen(pSprite->pDIB,
                           pSprite->x,
                           pSprite->y,
                           prcClip,
                           pSprite->bTopLeft,
                           TRUE); // Transparent

}
```

As you can see, all **RenderSpriteOffScreen** does is intersect the sprite's rectangle with the passed-in redraw rectangle, and tell **RenderDIBBitsOffScreen** to copy that portion of the sprite's bitmap (**pSprite->pDIB**) to the offscreen bitmap, with transparency. Since the sprite list is walked from back to front, each sprite is rendered onto the offscreen bitmap without regard for where it may have intersected previous sprites or what's underneath it (this is the Painter's Algorithm).

Once all the sprites have been rendered to the offscreen buffer, **Render** calls **Paint** to actually update the screen (if the **UPDATE_SCREEN** flag is used), at whatever position the current redraw rectangle defines. When it's done walking the entire redraw-rectangle list, it releases the DC for the destination window and empties the redraw list in preparation for next time.

Redraw-List Functions

The **Render** function is the main feature of the sprite engine, and now you know most of its inner workings. The remaining three helper functions used in **Render** are for managing the redraw-rectangle list: **AddDrawRectItem**, **MergeDrawRectList**, and **EmptyDrawRectList**. All three function definitions are in DRAW.C. The first, **AddDrawRectItem**, looks like this:

```
void AddDrawRectItem(PDRAWRECTLIST pList, LPRECT pRect)
{
    PDRAWRECT pItem;

    pItem = (PDRAWRECT) LocalAlloc(LPTR, sizeof(DRAWRECT));
    if (!pItem) {
        dprintf1("No memory for draw rect");
    } else {
        pItem->rc = *pRect;
        pItem->pNext = pList->pHead;
        pItem->pPrev = NULL;
        pList->pHead = pItem;
        if (pItem->pNext) {
            pItem->pNext->pPrev = pItem;
        }
    }
}
```

The first parameter to the function is a pointer to a **DRAWRECTLIST** item, which, as you'll recall from the definition in the header file, is nothing more than a pointer to a **DRAWRECT**—which itself is a doubly linked list of Windows **RECT** structures. The function simply adds the rectangle pointed to by **pRect** (the second argument) to the head of the list. It does this by allocating memory for a **RECT** from the local heap, copying **pRect** into it, and then linking it into the list.

Note the **dprintf1** statement used if the memory allocation fails. This is part of the debugging system that prints out statements to a currently active Windows debugging window. (More on this system at the end of this chapter.)

The **MergeDrawRectList** function examines the whole redraw-rectangle list and merges any intersecting rectangles into a single rectangle that is the union of all the rectangles. Here's what it looks like:

```
void MergeDrawRectList(PDRAWRECTLIST pList)
{
    PDRAWRECT pItem1, pItem2;
    BOOL bChanged;
    RECT rcNew;

    if (!pList || !pList->pHead) return;

    do {
        bChanged = FALSE;

        pItem1 = pList->pHead;
        while (pItem1) {

            pItem2 = pItem1->pNext;
            while (pItem2) {

                if (IntersectRect(&rcNew, &(pItem1->rc),
```

```
                                         &(pItem2->rc))) {

                    UnionRect(&(pItem1->rc), &(pItem1->rc),
                                            &(pItem2->rc));
                    DeleteDrawRectListItem(pList, pItem2);
                    bChanged = TRUE;
                    break;
                }
                pItem2 = pItem2->pNext;
            }
            if (bChanged)
                break;
            pItem1 = pItem1->pNext;
        }
    } while (bChanged);
}
```

This code simply walks the redraw list, intersecting each rectangle with every other rectangle. If two rectangles intersect, the code merges the two (with the Windows function **UnionRect**), deletes one of the items, and restarts the walk. This continues until no intersecting rectangles are found. It isn't necessarily the best way to walk the list, and finding intersections may not even be fruitful if sprites seldom intersect. There are many optimizations possible here, depending on the actual characteristics of your sprite-based game.

The **DeleteDrawRectListItem** function simply unlinks and frees a rectangle item from the list:

```
void DeleteDrawRectListItem(PDRAWRECTLIST pList, PDRAWRECT pItem)
{
    PDRAWRECT pPrev, pNext;

    pPrev = pItem->pPrev;
    pNext = pItem->pNext;

    if (pNext) {
        pNext->pPrev = pPrev;
    }

    if (pPrev) {
        pPrev->pNext = pNext;
    } else {
        pList->pHead = pNext;
    }

    LocalFree((HANDLE)(pItem));
}
```

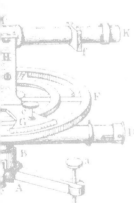

The last thing **Redraw** does is to call **EmptyDrawRectList**, which simply deletes all the rectangles:

```
void EmptyDrawRectList(PDRAWRECTLIST pList)
{
    while (pList->pHead)
        DeleteDrawRectListItem(pList, pList->pHead);
}
```

The only thing left unexplained in the **Render** function (and in DRAW.C) is **Paint**.

Painting the Screen

The **Render** function adds redraw rectangles to the redraw list, renders the background and sprite objects to the offscreen buffer, and then calls **Paint** for every redraw rectangle. The **Paint** function is where all writing to the screen occurs, making it ideal as a handler for the main window's WM_PAINT messages, as well:

```
void Paint(HDC hDC, LPRECT prcClip)
{
    int w, h, xs, ys, xd, yd;
    HPALETTE hOldPal;

    if (prcClip) {
        dprintf2("Paint(%d,%d,%d,%d)",
                 prcClip->left,
                 prcClip->top,
                 prcClip->right,
                 prcClip->bottom);
    } else {
        dprintf2("Paint(NULL)");
    }

    if (!G.hdcWinG) {
        dprintf1("No offscreen DC to paint from");
        return;
    }

    //
    // Copy the update rectangle from the offscreen DC
    // to the window DC.
    //

    if (prcClip) {
        //
        // Set the destination rectangle for the Blt.
        // Note that the WinG DIB coordinates are
        // "normal" top-down format, regardless of the
        // orientation of the bitmap.
        //
        w = prcClip->right - prcClip->left+1;
        h = prcClip->bottom - prcClip->top+1;
        xs = xd = prcClip->left;
```

```
        yd = ys = prcClip->top;

    } else {
        // No clip rectangle; Blt the whole offscreen bitmap.
        w = DIB_WIDTH(G.pdibWinG);
        h = abs(DIB_HEIGHT(G.pdibWinG));
        xs = xd = ys = yd = 0;
    }

    if (G.hpalCurrent) {
        hOldPal = SelectPalette(hDC, G.hpalCurrent, 0);
        RealizePalette(hDC);
    }

    // Do the Blt!
    WinGBitBlt (hDC, xd, yd, w, h, G.hdcWinG, xs, ys);

    if (G.bShowUpdateRects)
        DrawRect(hDC, xd, yd, xd+w, yd+h, MAGENTA);

    if (hOldPal) SelectPalette(hDC, hOldPal, 0);
}
```

The **Paint** function Blts the entire offscreen bitmap either to the screen or to a portion of it, depending on whether **prcClip** is NULL. If it's not, **Paint** computes the size of the rectangle being Blted, and passes these as parameters to **WinGBitBlt**. The current palette is selected and realized before the **WinGBitBlt** call in order to establish the palette. (Remember that realizing a palette that's been realized before doesn't really take much time.) After doing the Blt, the function optionally draws a rectangle around the area, selects the old palette back, and returns.

Summary of Drawing and Rendering Functions

You now know how the core of the sprite engine functions. The main animation loop is handled by **UpdatePositions**, which is called in the main Windows message loop when there's nothing else to do. This simple function moves sprites according to a vector that's part of the sprite structure definition.

The real work is done in the **Render** function. Here, the background and sprite objects are rendered (via **RenderDIBBitsOffScreen**) to the offscreen buffer, and a dirty-rectangle display list is created. Once the display list has been merged into the minimum number of intersecting rectangles, the **Render** function calls **Paint**, which actually Blts the offscreen buffer to the screen.

There are a number of other helper functions in the sprite code. I'll cover a few of the interesting ones here; you can peruse the code for the rest.

BKGND.C

This file contains function definitions for loading the background DIB from a file, as well as for creating the offscreen WinG bitmap and DC. Each time a new background is loaded, the old offscreen bitmap and DC are deleted and new ones are created. There's only one function in BKGND.C, **LoadBackground**:

```
void LoadBackground(LPSTR pszPath, BOOL bUpdateScreen)
{
    RECT rcWnd;

    dprintf2("LoadBackground(%s)", pszPath ? pszPath : "NULL");

    //
    // Delete the current sprite set.
    //

    DeleteSpriteList();

    //
    // Nuke any old DIB.
    //

    DeleteDIB(G.pdibBkGnd);

    //
    // Try to load the new DIB.
    //

    G.pdibBkGnd = LoadDIB(pszPath);
    if (!G.pdibBkGnd) {
        return;
    }

    //
    // Adjust the window to fit the new background,
    // but don't make it too small overall.
    //

    rcWnd.top = 0;
    rcWnd.left = 0;
    rcWnd.right = max (DIB_WIDTH(G.pdibBkGnd), 150);
    rcWnd.bottom = max(DIB_HEIGHT(G.pdibBkGnd), 100);
    AdjustWindowRect(&rcWnd, WS_OVERLAPPEDWINDOW, TRUE);
    SetWindowPos(G.hwndMain,
                 NULL,
                 0,
                 0,
                 rcWnd.right-rcWnd.left,
                 rcWnd.bottom-rcWnd.top,
```

```
                SWP_NOACTIVATE | SWP_NOMOVE);

//
// Delete the old WinG DC and bitmap
// if they exist.
//

if (G.hdcWinG) {
    DeleteDC (G.hdcWinG);
    DeleteObject (G.hWinGBitmap);
    G.hdcWinG = NULL;
}

// Create a WinG DC.

G.hdcWinG = WinGCreateDC ();

//
// Create a PDIB for the offscreen WinG bitmap.
// Note that the bits are created elsewhere and
// can't be accessed with the DIB_PBITS macro.
// The header and color table are there as normal.
// Free the old one (if it exists) first.
//

if (G.pdibWinG) {
    FREE (G.pdibWinG);
    G.pdibWinG = NULL;
}

// Create header and color table for the WinG bitmap, and
// copy contents into it from the background DIB.
//
G.pdibWinG = (PDIB) ALLOCATE (DIB_BISIZE(G.pdibBkGnd));
if (!G.pdibWinG) {
    dprintf1("Couldn't allocate offscreen bitmap header");
    return;
}
_fmemcpy (G.pdibWinG, G.pdibBkGnd,
          (UINT)DIB_BISIZE(G.pdibBkGnd));

//
// Create a new palette based on the background DIB.
//

if (G.hpalCurrent) DeleteObject(G.hpalCurrent);
G.hpalCurrent = CreateIdentityPalette(G.pdibWinG);

// Map the bits of the background DIB to match
// the identity palette.
```

continued on next page

continued from previous page

```
    MapDIBits (G.hpalCurrent, G.pdibBkGnd, DIB_PBITS(G.pdibBkGnd));

    // Find out what the best WinG DIB format is.
    WinGRecommendDIBFormat ((LPBITMAPINFO)G.pdibWinG);

    // Set height and width according to the recommended format
    // (the multiplication operation retains the top-down/bottom-up sense).
    // Minimum size = 150x100
    G.pdibWinG->bmiHeader.biHeight *= max (DIB_HEIGHT(G.pdibBkGnd),
                                           100);
    G.pdibWinG->bmiHeader.biWidth   = max (DIB_WIDTH(G.pdibBkGnd),
                                           150);

    // Create the bitmap; get the pointer to the bits.
    G.hWinGBitmap = WinGCreateBitmap (G.hdcWinG,
                                      (LPBITMAPINFO)G.pdibWinG,
                                      &G.pOffScreenBits);

    if (G.hWinGBitmap) {
        // Select it in. I don't save the old bitmap.
        SelectObject (G.hdcWinG, G.hWinGBitmap);
    } else {
        // Fail...
        DeleteDC (G.hdcWinG);
        G.hdcWinG = NULL;
        FREE (G.pdibWinG);
        G.pdibWinG = NULL;
    }

    //
    // Draw the background to the offscreen DIB
    // and update the screen, if required.
    //

    Render(NULL, bUpdateScreen);

}
```

All the code in **LoadBackground** should look familiar to you by now. The background image is loaded with **LoadDIB**, whose definition can be found in DIB.C. Once the background image is loaded, a WinG DIB header is created and the contents of the background DIB's header are copied into it. Then **CreateIdentityPalette** is called (found in PALETTE.C), which both creates the identity palette and sets the entries in the color table of **G.pdibWinG** to the necessary system color values. Since this undoubtedly rearranges the indices of the background DIB, that DIB must be remapped with **MapDIBits** (DIB.C). Note that after calling **MapDIBits**, the color table of **G.pdibBkGnd** no longer represents the actual colors and isn't used elsewhere in the code. Figures 10-7(a) through 10-7(c) show the sprite animation engine in action.

FIGURE 10-7(a)

Sprite animation engine in action, part 1

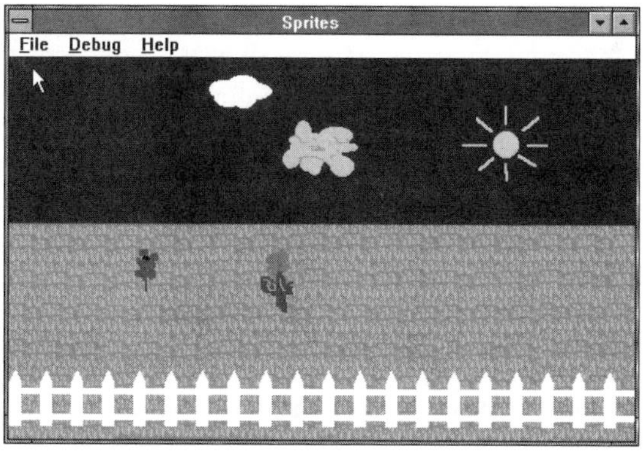

FIGURE 10-7(b)

Sprite animation engine in action, part 2

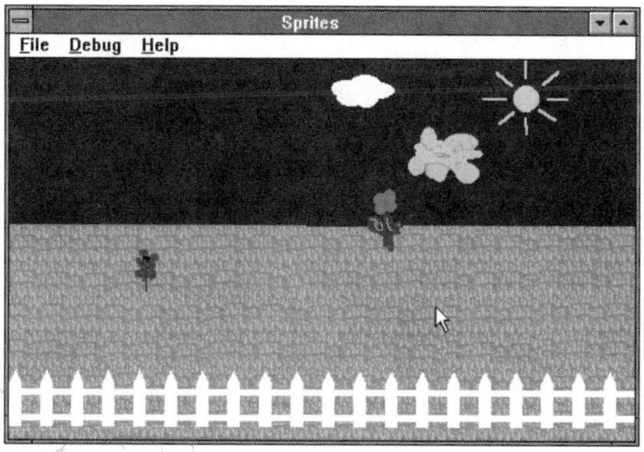

FIGURE 10-7(c)

Sprite animation engine in action, part 3

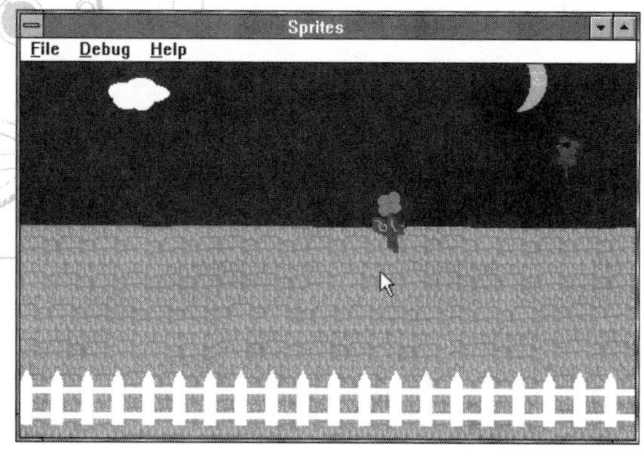

SPRITE.C

This module contains code for loading and maintaining the list of sprites. The head of the global sprite list is held in **G.pSpriteList**. You can follow the code for loading and deleting sprites from the file; I won't bore you with it here.

Recall that the **Render** function called **GetSpriteRect** to fill a rectangle with the sprite's current position:

```
void GetSpriteRect(PSPRITE pSprite, LPRECT prcSprite)
{
    prcSprite->left = pSprite->x;
    prcSprite->right = pSprite->x + pSprite->width-1;
    prcSprite->top = pSprite->y;
    prcSprite->bottom = pSprite->y + pSprite->height-1;
}
```

The code in **UpdatePositions** moved sprites by directly incrementing their coordinates, but there's a helper function in SPRITE.C for moving sprites. This helper function is **SetSpritePosition**:

```
void SetSpritePosition(PSPRITE pSprite, int x, int y, BOOL bUpdate)
{
    RECT rcOld, rcNew, rcChange;


    dprintf4("SetSpritePosition(%u,%u)", x, y);

    ASSERT(pSprite);

    //
    // Get the current sprite position.
    //

    GetSpriteRect(pSprite, &rcOld);

    //
    // Update the position and get the new rectangle.
    //

    pSprite->x = x;
    pSprite->y = y;
    GetSpriteRect(pSprite, &rcNew);

    //
    // Update the change rectangle to include the old and the new
    // positions of the sprite.
    //

    CopyRect(&rcChange, &rcOld);
    UnionRect(&rcChange, &rcChange, &rcNew);
```

```
    //
    // Render the changes, if required.
    //

    if (bUpdate != NO_UPDATE) {
        Render(&rcChange, bUpdate);
    }
}
```

This function updates the position of the sprite and adds a rectangle to the redraw list that contains the union of the sprite's old and new position rectangles. It updates the screen if the **bUpdate** parameter is **UPDATE_SCREEN**. You can use this function to drag a sprite's position around with the mouse—look at the **OnMouseMove** handler in MAIN.C.

The z-order of the sprites is represented by an arbitrary number stored in the **z** member of the sprite's structure. The **SetSpriteZOrder** function changes a sprite's z-order:

```
void SetSpriteZOrder(PSPRITE pSprite, WORD z, BOOL bUpdate)
{
    RECT rcChange;
    PSPRITE pNew, pLast;

    dprintf4("SetSpriteZOrder(%u)", z);

    ASSERT(pSprite);
    ASSERT(G.pSpriteList);

    pSprite->z = z;

    //
    // Get the current sprite position.
    //

    GetSpriteRect(pSprite, &rcChange);

    //
    // Unlink the sprite from the list.
    //

    if (pSprite->pPrev) {
        pSprite->pPrev->pNext = pSprite->pNext;
    } else {
        G.pSpriteList = pSprite->pNext;
    }
    if (pSprite->pNext) {
        pSprite->pNext->pPrev = pSprite->pPrev;
    }
    pSprite->pNext = pSprite->pPrev = NULL;
```

continued on next page

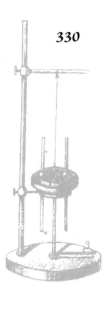

continued from previous page

```
    //
    // Walk down the list from the top (front) until we find
    // a sprite with higher z-order or the end of the list.
    //

    pNew = pLast = G.pSpriteList;
    while (pNew) {
        if (pNew->z > pSprite->z) break;
        pLast = pNew;
        pNew = pNew->pNext;
    }

    if (!pNew) {

        //
        // There is no sprite further back than this, so put
        // this one on the end.
        //

        if (pLast) {
            pLast->pNext = pSprite;
        } else {
            G.pSpriteList = pSprite;
        }
        pSprite->pPrev = pLast;

    } else {

        //
        // pNew points to the one we want after this one,
        // so insert the new sprite before it.
        //

        if (pNew->pPrev) {
            pSprite->pNext = pNew;
            pSprite->pPrev = pNew->pPrev;
            pNew->pPrev->pNext = pSprite;
            pNew->pPrev = pSprite;
        } else {
            pSprite->pNext = pNew;
            G.pSpriteList = pSprite;
            pNew->pPrev = pSprite;
        }

    }

    //
    // Render the changes, if required.
    //

    if (bUpdate != NO_UPDATE) {
```

```
        Render(&rcChange, bUpdate);
    }
}
```

The sprite engine allows the user to select and move sprites by simply clicking on them and dragging. In order to determine which sprite is selected, use the **SpriteHitTest** function:

```
PSPRITE SpriteHitTest(int x, int y)
{
    PSPRITE pSprite;
    int dx, dy;

    pSprite = G.pSpriteList;
    while (pSprite) {

        //
        // Test to find if the click is inside the sprite rectangle.
        //

        if ((x > pSprite->x)
        && (x < pSprite->x + (int) pSprite->width)
        && (y > pSprite->y)
        && (y < pSprite->y + (int) pSprite->height)) {

            dprintf4("Hit is in sprite rect");

            //
            // See if this point is transparent by testing to
            // see if the pixel value is the same as the top-
            // left corner's value.  Note that top left of the
            // image is in the bottom left of the DIB.
            //

            dx = x - pSprite->x;
            dy = y - pSprite->y;

            if (GetDIBPixelValue(pSprite->pDIB, dx, dy)
               != pSprite->bTopLeft) {
                break;
            }
        }

        pSprite = pSprite->pNext;
    }

    return pSprite;
}
```

Look at the **OnLButtonDown** handler in MAIN.C to see how to use **SpriteHitTest**.

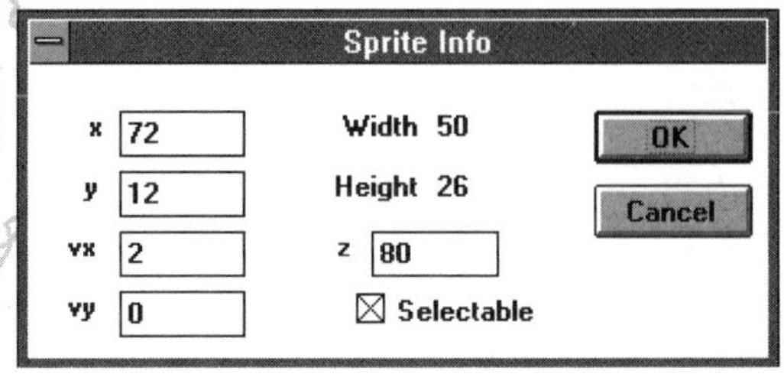

FIGURE 10-8

Setting sprite parameters

Setting Sprite Parameters

If you double-click on a sprite, you will bring up a dialog box that allows you to set the sprite's parameters—the values that are in the **SPRITE** structure as shown in Figure 10-8. You can look in the **OnLButtonDown** handler (which handles double clicks, as well) in MAIN.C, along with the dialog box handler in SPRITE.C, to see how it all works. If you change the *vx* and *vy* settings, you need to turn on Auto Update (from the Debug menu) to make the sprites move.

Debugging Functions

While every modern programming environment (even under Windows) comes equipped with a source-level debugger, there always seems to be a place for good old-fashioned "printf"-style debugging statements. Of course, under Windows there's no such animal as **stdout**, so what's a poor programmer to do?

Fortunately, Windows provides the debugging window tool: DBWIN.EXE in Microsoft SDKs. The primary purpose of DBWIN is to display the output from the Windows function **OutputDebugString**. The function takes a LPSTR as its only argument, and the output is directed to wherever debugging output is aimed, which is normally a program like DBWIN.

By wrapping a few functions and macros around **OutputDebugString**, you can create a simple and effective debugging system. That's exactly what you'll find in GLOBAL.H and DEBUG.C. The debugging system dissolves into nothingness if DEBUG isn't defined by the compiler; in other words, no code is generated for the debugging printing statements.

It's often useful to print different levels of debugging information and to determine the debugging level at run time. The macros in GLOBAL.H support this idea:

```
#ifdef DEBUG

    DWORD    __dwEval;
    int __iDebugLevel;

    extern void SetDebugLevel(int i);
```

```
    extern void __AssertMsg(LPSTR exp ,LPSTR file, int line);
    extern void cdecl DbgOut(LPSTR lpFormat, ...);

    #define ASSERT(exp) \
        ((exp) ? (void)0 : __AssertMsg((LPSTR)(#exp), \
(LPSTR)__FILE__, __LINE__))
    #define EVAL(exp) \
        (__dwEval=(DWORD)(exp), (__dwEval) ? (void)0 :\
__AssertMsg((LPSTR)(#exp), (LPSTR)__FILE__, __LINE__), __dwEval)

    #define dprintf                              DbgOut
    #define dprintf1 if (__iDebugLevel >= 1) DbgOut
    #define dprintf2 if (__iDebugLevel >= 2) DbgOut
    #define dprintf3 if (__iDebugLevel >= 3) DbgOut
    #define dprintf4 if (__iDebugLevel >= 4) DbgOut

#else // not DEBUG

    #define ASSERT(exp) 0
    #define EVAL(exp) (exp)

    #define dprintf  if (0) ((int (*)(char *, ...)) 0)
    #define dprintf1 if (0) ((int (*)(char *, ...)) 0)
    #define dprintf2 if (0) ((int (*)(char *, ...)) 0)
    #define dprintf3 if (0) ((int (*)(char *, ...)) 0)
    #define dprintf4 if (0) ((int (*)(char *, ...)) 0)

#endif // DEBUG
```

The macros create two kinds of debugging support. The various **dprintf** statements simply check the global **__iDebugLevel** and call **DbgOut** which is just a formatter for **OutputDebugString**. The **ASSERT** function evaluates a logical expression and, if the result of that evaluation is FALSE, calls **__AssertMsg**, which brings up a dialog box displaying the source-file name and the line number of the **ASSERT**. Here's the code (from DEBUG.C) that supports the macros:

```
#ifdef DEBUG

//
// Set the current debugging level.
//

void SetDebugLevel(int i)
{
    HMENU hMenu;
    int m;

    hMenu = GetMenu(G.hwndMain);
    for (m=IDM_DEBUG0; m<=IDM_DEBUG4; m++) {
        CheckMenuItem(hMenu, m, MF_UNCHECKED);
    }
```

continued on next page

continued from previous page

```
    CheckMenuItem(hMenu, i + IDM_DEBUG0, MF_CHECKED);
    __iDebugLevel = i;
}

//
// Show a message box with assertion failure information in it.
//

void __AssertMsg(LPSTR exp, LPSTR file, int line)
{
    char buf[256];
    int i;

    wsprintf(buf,
             "Exp: %s\nFile: %s, Line %d",
             (LPSTR)exp,
             (LPSTR)file,
             line);
    i = MessageBox(G.hwndMain,
                   buf,
                   "Assertion failure",
                   MB_OK | MB_ICONEXCLAMATION);
}

//
// Function to print a debug string
//

void cdecl DbgOut(LPSTR lpFormat, ...)
{
    int i;
    char buf[256];

    //
    // Format the string.
    //

    wvsprintf(buf, lpFormat, (LPSTR)(&lpFormat+1));
    lstrcat (buf, "\r");
    OutputDebugString (buf);
}
#endif
```

The **SetDebugLevel** function simply sets the global **__iDebugLevel** and tries to check a menu item from a menu associated with the main window. You can turn on and off this menu item in the resource file by using **#ifdef DEBUG** statements so that the whole thing works in sync. The **__AssertMsg** function just formats its parameters into a message box. The **DbgOut** function formats its parameters into a buffer that's passed to **OutputDebugString**.

The **dprintf** statements take a "printf"-like format string and set of variables and output the string to the debugging window according to the debugging level. This simple little system is particularly handy when you're using **timeGetTime** to get rough timing information about your program.

The best part about the system is that if DEBUG isn't defined (by the compiler or, say, in GLOBAL.H), then *no code is generated*—and you don't have to surround the debugging statements themselves with **#ifdef DEBUG/#ENDIF** statements.

Automated Sprite Loading

The sprite engine is really intended as a starting point for a sprite-based game. As such, the functions available on the menus are designed primarily for the purpose of testing the engine.

A simple mechanism is used to load a background image and a set of sprites (and their parameters) from a single file. Windows provides a set of functions for reading and writing text strings to files according to a certain format. This format is commonly used in profile or initialization files; usually, these files have an .INI extension. In Chapter 12, you'll learn all about how the mechanism works; for now, I'll just explain a little about what's used in the sprite engine.

The Load Scene item from the File menu displays a list of files with the .INI extension. If you use Notepad to look at the sample file, SPRITES.INI, it should be obvious how the file is constructed. First, there's a section (sections are the parts of the file that follow a line enclosed in brackets) called Background that lists the file name of the background image. Then there's a section called Sprites that lists each sprite's name. (The value on the right side of the equal sign is meaningless; it's just a placeholder that's needed in order for the reader code to work correctly.) Finally, there's a section for each sprite's name (sprite names are case-insensitive) that defines the DIB used for the sprites, its initial *x* and *y* positions, and the other parameters that are stored in the SPRITE structure. All the code for reading the INI file can be found in INIT.C.

A game based on the sprite engine would probably use an entirely different method for initializing the program; this approach mainly serves the purpose of making testing easier. For example, a game would probably load the DIBs for the background and sprite objects directly from the resource file. This even obviates the need for the DIB file-reading code in DIB.C. By storing the initialization settings and image files in the resource file, you give yourself the ability to change those parts without recompiling the actual program code—all it takes is a resource compile and link.

Summary

The sprite engine developed in this chapter demonstrates many important principles of Windows game programming. You learned how to use a WinG bitmap as an off-screen buffer, and how dirty rectangles can be used to speed up display on the screen.

You learned how to render sprites quickly—and without resorting to the GDI—by using 32-bit assembly language functions.

You can use this sprite engine as the basis for a sprite-based game, easily enhancing it to include collision detection, multi-image sprites, or other game requirements. The most important thing that the base sprite engine provides is the fastest possible method for moving 256-color sprites across a Windows screen. The rest is up to your imagination.

In the next several chapters, you'll learn about some other parts of Windows important to game programmers: the sound subsystem, file handling, and some optimization and 32-bit programming techniques.

11

Using Sound Under Windows

come trabe fare le manovelle ... le quali si movano e s'alza
[illegible] ... sagrano ...
[illegible] ... della manovella perchè ...
la forza e più ... omo più ...

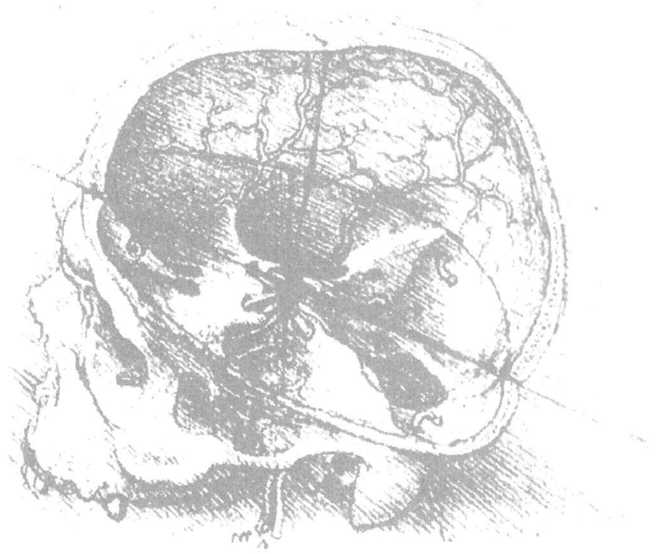

11

Using Sound Under Windows

No modern PC game is complete without accompanying noises. Sound is more than just an audible enhancement to a game; it's often the most important cue you can give the player about certain events, like two objects colliding. Fortunately, Windows provides a robust set of functions for making sound: the Multimedia Extensions that Microsoft introduced as a standard part of Windows 3.1.

Sound comes in a few flavors under Windows, and in this chapter you'll learn about all of them.

Three Kinds of Audio

There are three basic types of audio that the Windows Multimedia Extensions can produce—MIDI, waveform, and CD audio. These represent completely different data types.

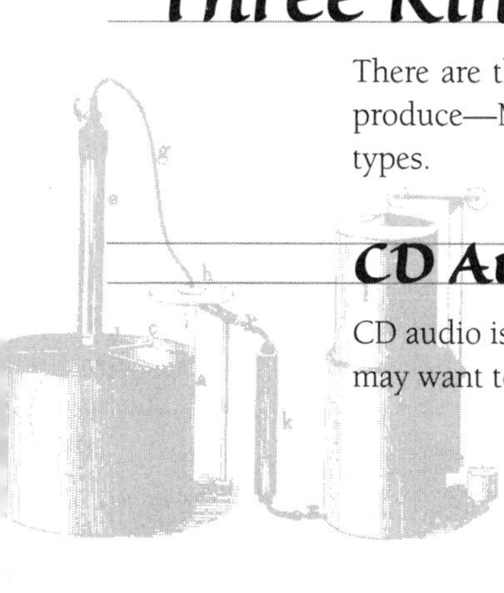

CD Audio

CD audio is probably the *least* useful audio type for game programming, though you may want to use it for some games that are heavily music-based. CD audio is exactly what it would appear to be—actual music coming from an actual music CD. This is often referred to as Red Book audio, after the color of the Sony/Philips standards book that defined the format.

To use CD audio, the user must have a music CD in the CD-ROM drive. That means that your game can't use the CD-ROM drive for anything else (actually, there *is* a method for combining CD-ROM data and Red Book data on the same CD, but making use of it requires highly devious code that's beyond the scope of this book). The Multimedia Extensions provide a very generalized mechanism for controlling the drive in order to play CD audio: the *Media Control Interface* (MCI). Functions that mimic a standard CD player's remote-control options—Play, Skip, Pause, Stop, and so on—are available through the MCI.

If your game is somehow tied to the music recorded on an audio CD, then the MCI is for you. I cover the MCI later in this chapter.

MIDI Audio

MIDI (Musical Instrument Digital Interface) began life as a hardware/software specification that allowed you to connect electronic musical instruments—synthesizers, drum machines, and the like—to each other and to computers. Today, of course, an entire music synthesizer can exist on a single sound card inside the PC. In an effort to help standardize the software that drives the many sound cards available, Microsoft chose to use MIDI data to control these music cards.

From a software point of view, MIDI represents *performance* data; that is, a set of instructions that mimic what a person would play on an instrument. You can think of MIDI data as being comparable to the instructions imparted to a musician by a musical score.

The simplest and most common type of MIDI data are Note On and Note Off messages, which tell a sound device to play a specific musical note and to stop playing a musical note, respectively (see Figure 11-1). Each note is identified by a number in the standard Western equal-tempered scale. While the MIDI data stream itself doesn't contain timing information about *when* the sound device should play and stop notes, the Standard MIDI File (SMF) format allows you to embed timing information along with the data so that a program can properly time the events. All MIDI hardware can play multiple notes at once (called *polyphony*), though the number of notes you can play is completely up to the hardware manufacturer. The notes don't have to sound the same, however—MIDI can accommodate up to 128 different instrument sounds.

Windows can play Standard MIDI Files (which often have an extension of .MID) through the MCI, much like it plays CD audio. The Multimedia Extensions also permit low-level access for playing (and recording) MIDI data. Using the low-level functions, you gain access to the actual MIDI messages. Of course, this control comes

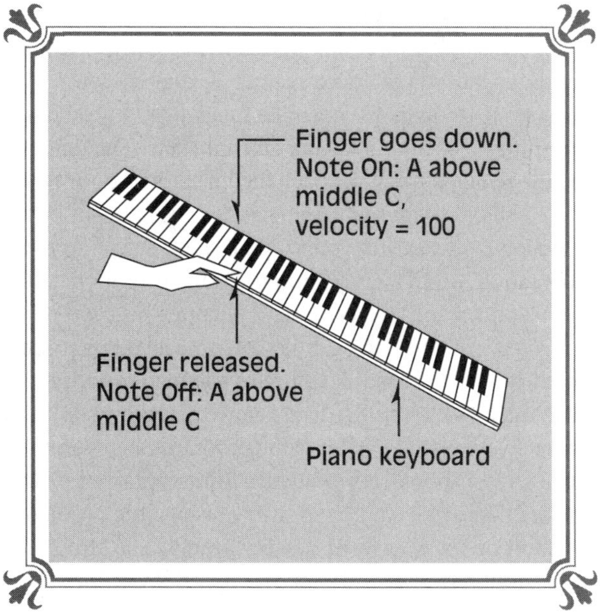

FIGURE 11-1

MIDI as performance data

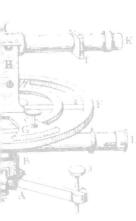

at a cost: Using Multimedia Extensions is considerably more complex than simply using the MCI. I'll cover playing MIDI data via the MCI later in this chapter.

Using MIDI has several advantages and several drawbacks. One advantage is size—you can represent a whole song in only a few kilobytes of MIDI data, because all you store is the note information. You can also play back music at any speed, which may or may not be an advantage for a game program. Among its drawbacks is the fact that although the note information itself is quite standardized, what a note actually *sounds* like is completely dependent on the sound device's implementation. In other words, what sounds like a piano on one card or instrument might sound like a saxophone on another.

Actually, it's not quite that bad. Recognizing this limitation, the MIDI Manufacturer's Association came up with what they call *General MIDI*—essentially a set of reliable instrument definitions. The definition doesn't specify the quality of the sound that comes out of a device, just a common set of terms for labeling the sounds. If you specify a piano on a General MIDI device, you'll get something that sounds more or less like a piano, for example. Unfortunately, the General MIDI specification assumes a level of sound device that's often quite a bit more than what your average PC sound card can handle. To help bridge the gap, Microsoft adopted a slightly scaled-down subset specification for sound-card manufacturers to follow.

Because MIDI is designed for playing music, it doesn't handle many of the sounds that games use most—sound effects and speech, for example. Playing these requires waveform audio.

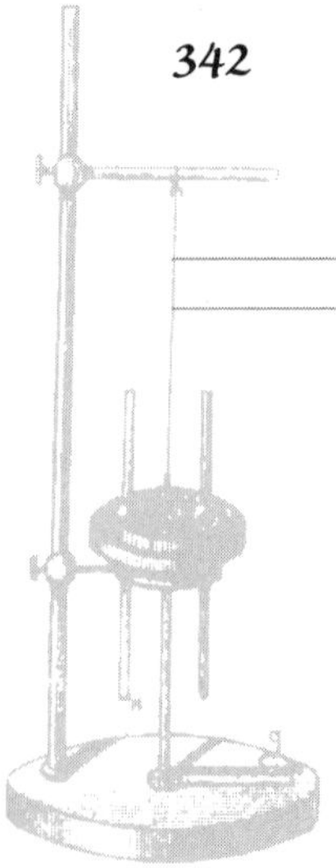

Waveform Audio

Waveform audio is literally digitized sound. To digitize sound, you *sample* an analog audio signal at some frequency (called the *sampling rate*), yielding a number that represents the amplitude of the signal at a given instant. The range that the number can hold is called the *resolution*. Playing back digital audio is done by converting the stored numbers (called *samples*) into an analog audio signal again by feeding the numbers through an analog-to-digital converter at the same sampling rate.

The data on an audio CD is stored in the same way, with a sampling rate of about 44 kHz and a resolution of 16 bits (times 2 channels), as you probably know. You can see that this takes almost 10 megabytes of storage per recorded minute of sound. While CD-quality audio is capable of pretty adequately addressing the entire human hearing range, most PC sound hardware can't reproduce sound that's anywhere near that comprehensive. Fortunately for game programmers, sampling rates of 22 kHz or even 11 kHz at a resolution of 8 bits are usually acceptable for the kinds of explosions and other noises that games make, so storage isn't a big problem.

Windows supports a waveform device through the Multimedia Extensions, and can control it through the MCI as well as through lower-level functions, much like it does with MIDI. For waveform audio, the MCI offers the same sort of Play, Pause, and Stop controls as it does for the MIDI and CD-audio devices. For game programs, though, this isn't usually enough control, because the waveform-audio device allows only *one* sound to be played at a time. Games often have many sounds that need to be played more or less simultaneously. The Multimedia Extensions do support a mixer device, but this device mixes the sound coming from the CD-audio, MIDI, and waveform devices, and will not mix several waveforms together. Mixing multiple waveform-audio streams is really a signal-processing task—you have to group the samples and normalize them in more or less real time.

Fortunately, Microsoft has done all this work for us in the form of the Wavemix DLL. This little gem of a library allows you to play up to eight independent waveform files simultaneously, and automatically takes care of the problems of mixing and of sample-rate and resolution conversion. Since sound effects are the staple of game sound (and since the Wavemix DLL simplifies waveform-sound programming considerably), I'll cover the use of the Wavemix DLL extensively in this chapter.

But first, let's take a look at the MCI and how it works.

The Media Control Interface

The MCI was designed to provide a simple method for controlling all manner of "linear" playback media. The programming interface is styled after the way many consumer electronics devices, such as VCRs, work—with functions like Play, Stop, Pause, and so on. The MCI specification defines a basic set of commands that all devices must support, and an extended set of commands that vary depending on the device type (see Figure 11-2). For example, not all devices can record, so the record function isn't available on all MCI devices.

MCI devices can be classified as either *simple devices* or *compound devices*. Simple devices do not require a data file for playback, while compound devices do. For example, CD-audio players are simple devices. A MIDI player (conventionally called a *sequencer*, after its early electronic-music predecessor) is a compound device—the MIDI data comes from a file.

MCI Programming Interfaces: Command-String vs. Command-Message

There are two ways to send commands to the MCI. You can send them as ASCII strings, through the `mciSendString` function, or as messages through the `mciSendCommand` function. The command-string interface is primarily designed to be used with high-level multimedia programming and authoring tools, like Microsoft Visual Basic and Asymetrix ToolBook. The command-message interface is designed for C-based applications programmers, like you, the game programmer. Of course, there's nothing stopping you from using the command-string interface if it works for you, but the command-message interface offers slightly more control.

FIGURE 11-2

MCI device commands

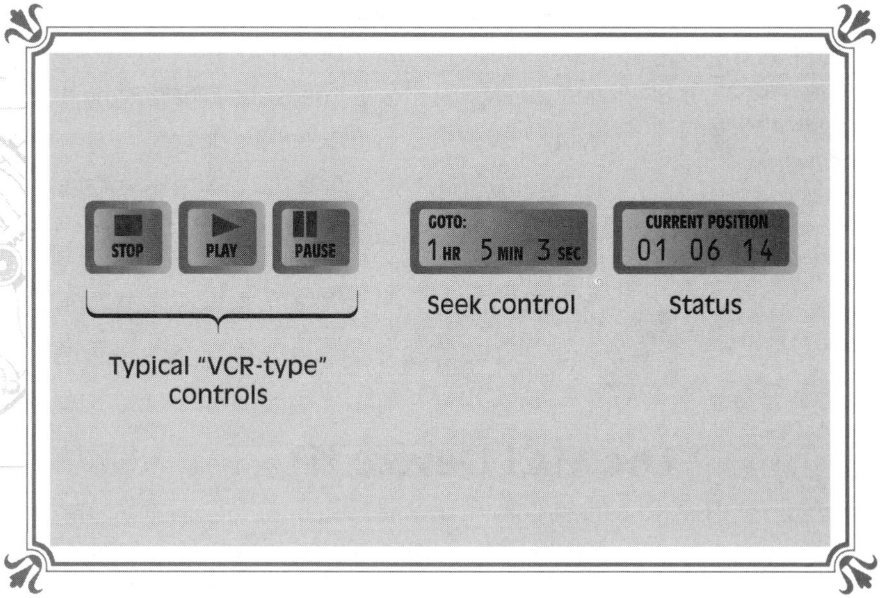

For example, to begin playing a MIDI file called SONG.MID using the command-string interface, you'd use the **mciSendString** function like this:

```
DWORD mciError;

mciError = mciSendString ("play song.mid", NULL, 0, NULL);
```

The same thing using the command-message interface would look like this:

```
MCI_PLAY_PARMS mciPlayParms;
DWORD mciError;

mciError = mciSendCommand (wDeviceID, MCI_PLAY, 0,
                           (DWORD)(LPVOID)&mciPlayParms);
```

While the command-string interface will work for applications that don't require much control—for example, simple start/stop functionality—it's really much better to use the command-message interface if you're programming in C. There are certain functions for which the command-string interface just isn't practical, like obtaining real-time status information from a device. For this reason, I'll discuss only the command-message interface here.

MCI devices must support a certain set of commands. These are summarized in Table 11-1.

A device may also support certain basic commands. These are summarized in Table 11-2.

TABLE 11-1

Required MCI commands

Command	Description
MCI_OPEN	Opens and initializes the device
MCI_CLOSE	Closes the device
MCI_GETDEVCAPS	Gets the capabilities of the device
MCI_INFO	Gets certain textual information about the device (driver name, manufacturer, etc.)
MCI_STATUS	Obtains status information about the device

The MCI Device ID

MCI returns a device ID when you open a device using the MCI_OPEN command. The system uses this ID to identify the opened device when sending subsequent commands. A special constant, MCI_ALL_DEVICE_ID, indicates a command that should

TABLE 11-2 *Basic MCI commands*

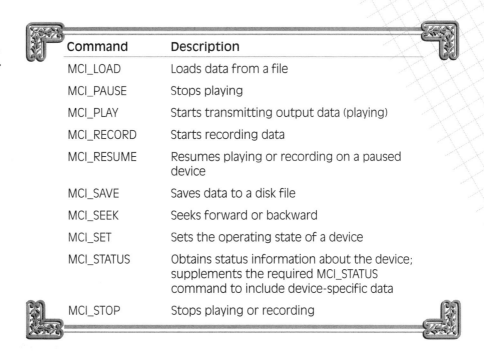

Command	Description
MCI_LOAD	Loads data from a file
MCI_PAUSE	Stops playing
MCI_PLAY	Starts transmitting output data (playing)
MCI_RECORD	Starts recording data
MCI_RESUME	Resumes playing or recording on a paused device
MCI_SAVE	Saves data to a disk file
MCI_SEEK	Seeks forward or backward
MCI_SET	Sets the operating state of a device
MCI_STATUS	Obtains status information about the device; supplements the required MCI_STATUS command to include device-specific data
MCI_STOP	Stops playing or recording

be sent to all devices that an application has opened. Typically, you might use this constant to close all devices:

```
DWORD dwReturn;

// Close all previously opened MCI devices, wait for completion.
dwReturn = mciSendCommand (MCI_ALL_DEVICE_ID, MCI_CLOSE, MCI_WAIT, NULL);
```

Every MCI message has a corresponding data structure and set of flags that identify what parts of the data structure are used. For example, the data structure for the MCI_OPEN message is called MCI_OPEN_PARMS and looks like this:

```
typedef struct  {
    DWORD dwCallback;
    UINT wDeviceID;
    UINT wReserved0;
    LPCSTR lpstrDeviceType;
    LPCSTR lpstrElementName;
    LPCSTR lpstrAlias;
} MCI_OPEN_PARMS;
```

This is the minimum structure for opening a device. Associated with the structure is also a set of flags that is passed as the third parameter to **mciSendCommand**. Table 11-3 shows the flags you use for all devices.

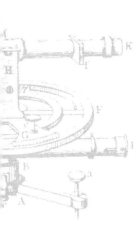

TABLE 11-3

MCI_OPEN flags

Flag	Meaning
MCI_NOTIFY	Specifies that MCI should post the MM_MCINOTIFY message to the application when the command finishes. The message is sent to the window whose handle is specified in the **dwCallback** member of the MCI_OPEN_PARMS structure.
MCI_WAIT	Specifies that the open operation should finish before MCI returns control to the operation.
MCI_OPEN_ALIAS	Specifies that an alias name is included in the **lpstrAlias** member of the MCI_OPEN_PARMS structure.
MCI_OPEN_SHAREABLE	Specifies that the device or device element should be opened as shareable.
MCI_OPEN_TYPE	Specifies that a type name or constant is included in the **lpstrDeviceType** member of the MCI_OPEN_PARMS structure.
MCI_OPEN_TYPE_ID	Specifies that the low-order word of the **lpstrDeviceType** member of the MCI_OPEN_PARMS structure contains a standard MCI device-type ID and that the high-order word contains the ordinal index for the device. Used in conjunction with MCI_OPEN_TYPE.

Using aliases from the command-message interface isn't particularly useful, so just ignore the **lpstrAlias** structure member and MCI_OPEN_ALIAS flag.

But wait, there's more! As if *those* flags weren't enough, there are two more that you use for compound devices, like the MIDI sequencer. The first is MCI_OPEN_ELEMENT, which specifies that there's a file name in the **lpstrElementName** member of the MCI_OPEN_PARMS data structure (for some reason, the file associated with a compound device is called an *element* in MCI parlance). The other is MCI_OPEN_ELEMENT_ID. It tells the driver to interpret the value in **lpstrElementName** as a DWORD; its meaning is internal to the particular driver. In other words, you use MCI_OPEN_ELEMENT_ID when you know exactly which device driver you're dealing with and the meaning of this DWORD—it's a device-specific "escape."

Some of the MCI commands have message-specific data structures associated with them. For example, the MCI_PLAY command uses the MCI_PLAY_PARMS structure. Some other MCI commands use a generic structure—MCI_GENERIC_PARMS—for data associated with the command. The MCI_GENERIC_PARMS structure looks like this:

```
typedef struct  {
    DWORD dwCallback;
} MCI_GENERIC_PARMS;
```

This structure's only purpose is to identify the window that will be sent the MM_MCINOTIFY message when the command finishes (the MCI_NOTIFY flag must be specified with the command). If you don't care about sending a message to the window, you can pass NULL instead of a pointer to an MCI_GENERIC_PARMS in the **mciSendCommand** call.

Sound complicated? Well, it sort of is. Fortunately, as a game programmer, you're likely to be interested in only a very small subset of all the commands and devices that MCI supports. Let's explore these by looking at a very common task—playing a standard MIDI file from MCI.

MIDI via MCI

The following function will play the standard MIDI file specified in its second argument, and will notify the window passed as its first argument when it's done. Any error condition returned by **mciSendCommand** is passed to another function, **ShowMCIError**, which displays the error in a message box.

```
BOOL PlayMIDIFile (HWND hwndNotify, LPSTR filename)
{
    UINT DeviceID;
    DWORD dwReturn;
    MCI_OPEN_PARMS mciOpenParms;
    MCI_PLAY_PARMS mciPlayParms;

    // Open the device with both device name and device element (file).
    // The first parameter to mciSendCommand is NULL, of course, since
    // there's no device ID yet.
    // It's opened with MCI_WAIT, because we want it to finish before we
    // continue.
    mciOpenParms.lpstrDeviceType = "sequencer";
    mciOpenParms.lpstrElementName = filename;
    if (dwReturn = mciSendCommand (NULL, MCI_OPEN,
                                   MCI_OPEN_TYPE | MCI_OPEN_ELEMENT |
                                   MCI_WAIT,
(DWORD)(LPVOID)&mciOpenParms)) {
        // Error. Call ShowMCIError.
        ShowMCIError (hwndNotify, dwReturn);
```

continued on next page

continued from previous page

```
        return FALSE;
    }
    // Device opened successfully. Get the device ID.
    DeviceID = mciOpenParms.wDeviceID;

    // Begin playback. Specify the window to which the MM_MCINOTIFY
    // message will be sent when it finishes; the message handler
    // should close the device when it gets it.
    mciPlayParms.dwCallback = (DWORD)hwndNotify;
    if (dwReturn = mciSendCommand (DeviceID, MCI_PLAY,
                                   MCI_NOTIFY,
                                   (DWORD)(LPVOID)&mciPlayParms)) {
        // Failed. Display the error and close the device.
        ShowMCIError (hwndNotify, dwReturn);
        mciSendCommand (DeviceID, MCI_CLOSE, 0, NULL);
        return FALSE;
    }
    return TRUE;
}

// Display the MCI error using mciGetErrorString.
void ShowMCIError (HWND parent, DWORD error)
{
    char buf[100];

    mciGetErrorString (error, buf, sizeof(buf));
    MessageBox (parent, buf, "MCI Error", MB_OK|MB_ICONEXCLAMATION);
}
```

Not so bad, really. You'll want to have message-handler and message-forwarder macros for the MM_MCINOTIFY message so that your window handler can close the device when it's done. The macros aren't in WINDOWSX.H, so you'll have to write your own. Here's what they look like:

```
/* void OnMCINotify(HWND hwnd, UINT deviceID, UINT message); */
#define HANDLE_MM_MCINOTIFY(hwnd, wParam, lParam, fn) \
    ((fn)((hwnd), (UINT)LOWORD(lParam), (UINT)(wParam)), 0L)
#define FORWARD_MM_MCINOTIFY(hwnd, deviceID, message, fn) \
    (void)(fn)((hwnd), MM_MCINOTIFY, message,
MAKELPARAM((UINT)(deviceID), 0))
```

The message-handler function should look something like this:

```
void OnMCINotify (HWND hwnd, UINT deviceID, UINT message)
{
    DWORD dwRet;

    // Close the device.
    dwRet = mciSendCommand (deviceID, MCI_CLOSE, 0, NULL);
    if (dwRet)
        ShowMCIError (hwnd, dwRet);
}
```

Of course, you may want to do something fancier. Later in this chapter, I'll show you how to handle playing a MIDI file in a loop while waveform audio is playing for effects (a common game-sound architecture).

Playing MIDI audio is one thing—creating MIDI files that can be played across a wide variety of hardware is another.

Authoring MIDI Files

To understand how to author MIDI files, you need to know a little more about what they contain. As I mentioned previously, MIDI files represent performance data—the actual notes of a piece of music. Timing information for each note is included in the file so that the sequencer—the device that usually plays back MIDI audio—knows when the note starts and for how long it lasts.

MIDI Messages

A MIDI file consists of a collection of MIDI messages along with timing information for each message. The most common messages are Note On and Note Off, which start and stop sounds on a device. Another common message is Program Change, which selects a specific sound for notes on a given channel.

MIDI messages are short and sweet. They're between 1 and 3 bytes in length (except for a sort of device-specific "escape" message that can be any length). There's a good reason for the brevity of MIDI messages. MIDI was created as a way of interconnecting electronic musical instruments and computers, and the physical connection between the devices is a fast serial line (it runs at about 31k baud). Because MIDI messages are sent serially—even if two or more notes are intended to be played simultaneously—there's a slight propagation delay that is a factor of both the transmission speed and the length of the message. Because of the short message length and the speed of the serial line, two Note On or Off messages can be spaced as closely as 1 millisecond (or even closer, if you use Running Status—a form of MIDI compression).

While MIDI Note On and Note Off messages cause a MIDI device to make or stop making sound, the Program Change message tells the device what sort of sound to make on a given channel.

Channels and Patches

There are 16 independent *channels*, each of which typically has the sound of a different instrument. To accommodate the sound of more than one instrument, you can play notes on more than one of these channels.

You select instrument sounds by using *patches*—a term that is a holdover from the days when electronic music synthesizers were "programmed" through the use of patch cords that connected parts of the synthesizer. In a modern MIDI synthesizer, you create patches through software or via knobs on the synthesizer's front panel, if it has one. This process is dependent on the architecture of the synthesizer—for example, the method for creating a piano patch for a Yamaha DX7 synthesizer is completely different than the method for creating a piano patch for a Korg M1.

Once you've created and stored a patch, you can access it by sending a *Program Change* message to the synthesizer. The Program Change MIDI message is a lot like the Note On and Note Off messages, except that it only selects a patch on a given channel—it doesn't cause any sound to be generated. The MIDI specification allows you to access up to 128 patches via the Program Change message. So, for each of the 16 channels, you can choose one of 128 patches (see Figure 11-3).

The actual *sound* of a certain patch is also completely determined by the implementation of the synthesizer. Patch 1 of a Roland LAPC-1 might be piano, while patch 1 of an Emu Proteus sound module might be church organ. This means that standard MIDI files aren't completely device-independent—the Program Change messages embedded in a file may have little or no bearing on what sounds are generated on a given device. Pianos can become electric guitars, and tubas can turn into piccolos.

The situation is even worse for percussion instruments. You implement drums via MIDI by using Note On and Note Off messages to trigger the different sounds from a drum kit, since drum components are generally pitchless. So middle C might trigger the bass drum on a given drum patch or instrument, but might trigger a cymbal crash on another (see Figure 11-4).

FIGURE 11-3

MIDI channels and patches

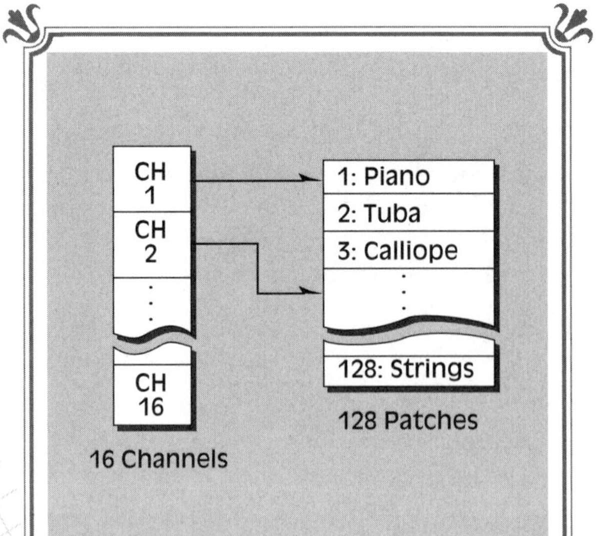

FIGURE 11-4

Percussion instruments via MIDI

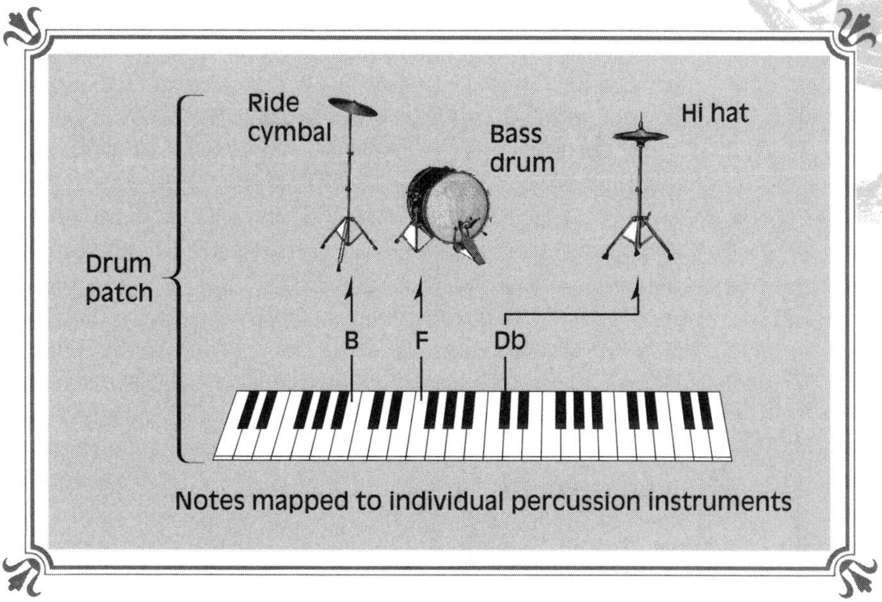

From a computer-sound point of view, it would seem absurd to have such a "standard" as MIDI—it's like having a language where the words are well-defined, but their actual meanings are left completely to the reader's interpretation. But MIDI wasn't invented to serve computer types; it was created to serve musicians. A standard that would have defined how every instrument *sounds* would have been far too limiting for musicians—for one thing, it would take the art and craft of designing instrument sounds away from them. Still, because MIDI was so useful in other applications, it became necessary to define an instrument standard that people could rely on, especially for computer-based applications.

General MIDI

The standard that was created by the MIDI Manufacturers Association (in conjunction with several MIDI hardware manufacturers) to solve the MIDI device-dependence problem is called General MIDI. Among other things, General MIDI defines 128 instrument sounds that correspond to each patch addressable by the Program Change message. If a device conforms to General MIDI, patch 0 will always be acoustic grand piano. Of course, an acoustic grand piano on an inexpensive FM-based synthesizer most certainly isn't going to sound the same as an acoustic grand piano on a $3,000 sampling synthesizer, but if they're General MIDI-compatible, you'll get something that sounds more or less like a piano on both of them.

The actual interpretation or quality of the instruments that General MIDI specifies isn't part of the specification, making it possible to implement General MIDI over a wide variety of hardware. Certain instrument names—take patch 103, sci-fi, for example—aren't much more than labels for whatever sound the particular device's manufacturer wanted to put there. Others—like patch 56, trumpet—are more or less expected to sound like what their names imply.

General MIDI is a great way to standardize MIDI data, especially for computer-based applications like games. But it comes with two shortcomings. First, like all standards, it can't take into account the hundreds of sound modules and sound cards already on the market. Second, to be able to claim full General MIDI compatibility requires a fairly capable synthesizer; most FM-synthesis-based PC cards would never be able to make full compatibility. To compensate for this, Microsoft did two very smart things. They created the MIDI Mapper for existing MIDI devices, and defined a Base-level and an Extended-level synthesizer specification to accommodate a range of device capabilities.

The MIDI Mapper

If you have a sound card that supports MIDI, you'll find a MIDI Mapper icon in the Control Panel application. The MIDI Mapper is nothing more than a big set of lookup tables that map channels, patches, and notes from one place to another.

To a game program, the MIDI Mapper looks like another MIDI output device. In fact, it's the default output device for the sequencer device, if the MIDI Mapper is available. The MIDI Mapper can have one of several *setups* active. A setup consists of a combination of the following types of maps:

- Channel map
- Patch map
- Key map

To understand how the three maps work, look at Figure 11-5.

A *channel map* affects all MIDI messages by mapping them from their incoming channel to an outgoing channel. It's rare to have a channel map that's not 1:1, because, for most devices, all channels are created equal. The difference between channels is defined by the current patch for the channel.

A *patch map* is a translation table that works with the Program Change message. For each of the 128 possible program-change values, the patch map specifies the following:

- A destination program-change value
- A volume-scalar value
- An optional key map

With a patch map, you can often make a MIDI device that doesn't conform to the General MIDI specification look like a General MIDI device to the application. For

FIGURE 11-5

The MIDI Mapper architecture

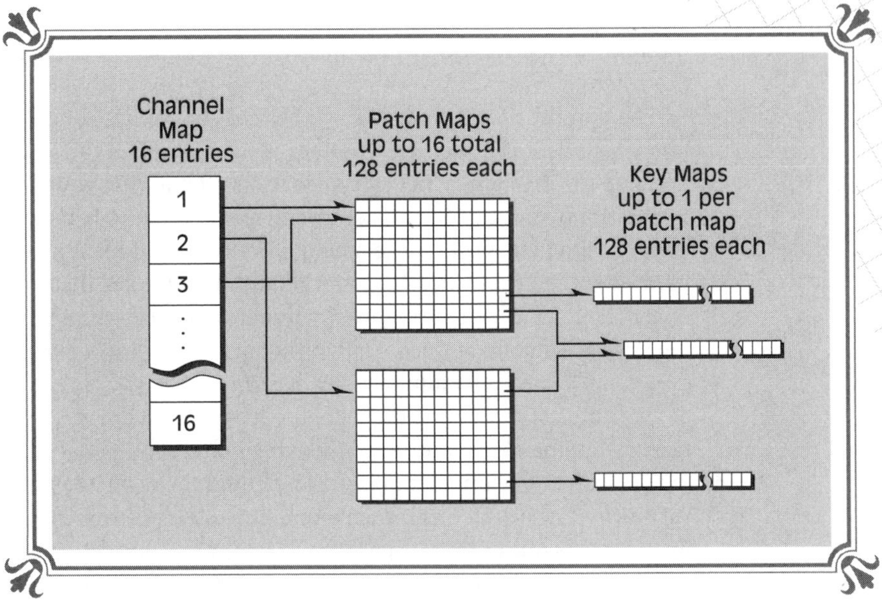

example, the Roland MT32 device isn't a General MIDI device—its electric guitar is patch 61 instead of patch 28. By specifying a destination program-change value of 61 for patch 28 (and by creating a map for the other 127 General MIDI sounds), you can make the MT32 look a lot like a General MIDI device.

You use the volume-scalar value to equalize the volume of different patches. Most of the time it's set to 100 percent, meaning there is no compensation for the volume of the patch.

The key map generally is necessary only for the percussion channel because percussion instrument sounds are activated by actual Note On and Note Off (sometimes called key) messages. General MIDI defines only 47 percussion sounds, so this map isn't too difficult to set up.

The MIDI Mapper is great if you have a MIDI synthesizer that isn't General MIDI-compatible but still has a wide range of instrument sounds. With a Mapper setup (often available from the manufacturer of the device), you can emulate a General MIDI device. But certain synthesizers just aren't capable of all General MIDI requires. For these devices, Microsoft has defined the Base-level and Extended-level synthesizer standards.

Base-Level and Extended-Level Synthesizers

Today, your average $100 sound card just isn't going to be capable of emulating a full General MIDI synthesizer, no matter how ambitious your MIDI Mapper setup. This

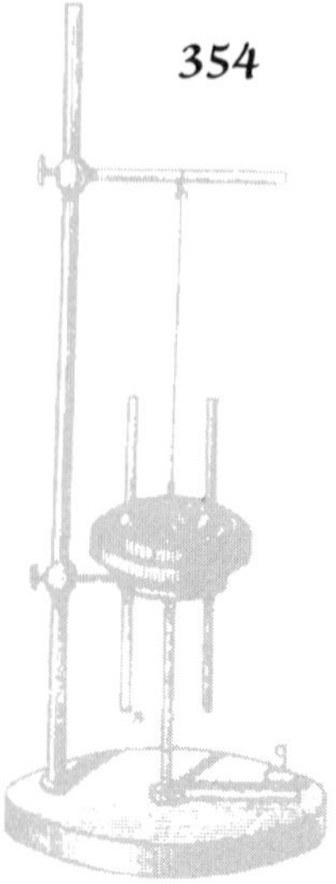

is because there are two general characteristics that govern the capabilities of a synthesizer (independent of sound quality): total number of instruments (patches) and polyphony.

The number of instruments a synthesizer supports is equal to the number of different sounds it can produce. In other words, although the MIDI specification supports up to 128 sounds, not all synthesizers offer all 128 sounds.

Polyphony (at least in this context) refers to the number of notes the synthesizer can play simultaneously. Since sound is constructed in real time by the synthesizer's hardware, there's always a limit to the number of notes that the device can play at once. The General MIDI specification requires that the synthesizer be capable of playing at least 16 notes at once. Many inexpensive synthesizers and sound cards, however, can play only a handful of notes at a time; when you try to exceed the polyphony of a synthesizer by playing one note too many, the synthesizer responds by automatically stopping one of the already-playing notes.

Quite often, the number of instruments and the polyphony on a given synthesizer vary between *melodic* instruments and *percussive* instruments. Because percussive instruments (at least in this sense) don't have pitch and because an "instrument" like a drum kit is really a combination of sounds, percussive instruments are mapped to notes within a given patch (refer again to Figure 11-4). Melodic instruments are simply the pitched instruments whose notes correspond to the notes of the equal-tempered scale (the black and white keys on a piano). The two types of instruments are often synthesized differently—even on the same device. The specifications for the Base-level and Extended-level synthesizers under the Multimedia Extensions, therefore, are divided into requirements for both melodic instruments and percussive instruments. Table 11-4 lists the requirements for number of instruments and polyphony of Base-level and Extended-level synthesizers.

All multimedia PCs (that is, PCs sold with the MPC logo) have at least a Base-level synthesizer. The Base-level synthesizer was designed to fit the capabilities of the Yamaha FM chipset that is used on all basic SoundBlaster cards and their compatibles. This provides what was at one time considered to be good computer sound, but today, the products of a Base-level synthesizer seem like just some extended bleeps and blorps.

TABLE 11-4

Base-level and Extended-level synthesizer specifications

Synthesizer	Melodic Instruments		Percussive Instruments	
	Instruments	Polyphony	Instruments	Polyphony
Base-level	3	6 notes	3	3 notes
Extended-level	9	16 notes	8	16 notes

There are sound cards that produce results somewhere between those of a Base-level synthesizer and those of an Extended-level synthesizer, of course.

The key to authoring MIDI files for use under Windows is to prioritize the use of instrument voicing. This way, you can ensure that it will be the less-important instrument sounds that will be dropped as the capabilities of the synthesizer degrade. But how, exactly, can you determine which instruments will be dropped?

In addition to the instruments/polyphony specification, Base-level and Extended-level synthesizers use certain preassigned MIDI channels. These assignments aren't part of the MIDI specification or even part of General MIDI—they're just what Microsoft chose in order to be able to use Base-level and Extended-level synthesizers easily. Since Base-level synthesizers can have only 3 melodic instruments, that level needs only 3 of the 16 possible MIDI channels, plus 1 channel for the percussive instruments (remember, these instruments use notes rather than patches to trigger the actual sounds). Microsoft chose to use channels 13 through 15 for the Base-level synthesizer's melodic parts, and channel 16 for its percussion parts. The Extended-level synthesizer uses channels 1 through 9 for melodic parts and channel 10 for percussion parts (channels 11 and 12 are unused in the specification). Figure 11-6 shows how the channels, parts, and polyphony relate for the Base-level and Extended-level synthesizers.

By prioritizing the melodic sounds in the lower-numbered channels, you can take advantage of synthesizers offering capabilities between those of the Base-level and Extended-level devices. This technique also allows you to take advantage of

FIGURE 11-6

Channel mapping for Base-level and Extended-level synthesizers

Base-Level and Extended-Level Synthesizers

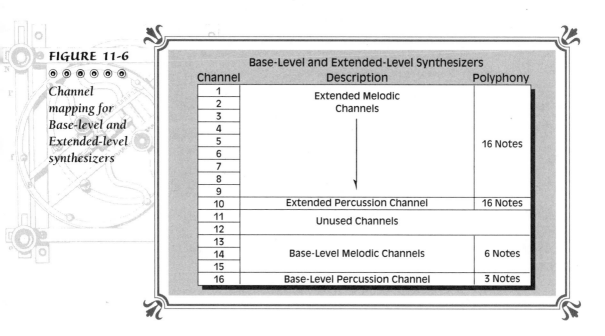

Channel	Description	Polyphony
1	Extended Melodic Channels	16 Notes
2		
3		
4		
5		
6		
7		
8		
9		
10	Extended Percussion Channel	16 Notes
11	Unused Channels	
12		
13	Base-Level Melodic Channels	6 Notes
14		
15		
16	Base-Level Percussion Channel	3 Notes

synthesizers offering features better than those provided by Extended-level devices. For example, although such lines wouldn't play on a strictly Extended-level synthesizer, you could create melodic lines on channels 11 and 12 for synthesizers that offered more than nine melodic voices.

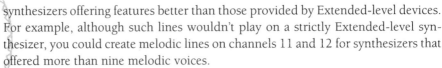

It's possible (and generally smart) to create MIDI files that contain the same music for *both* Base-level and Extended-level synthesizers. Since the data are on different channels, the driver and hardware will play only those channels that match the capabilities of the synthesizer.

If you have a MIDI file that follows all the guidelines for working on both Base-level and Extended-level synthesizers, you should mark your MIDI file with the MARKMIDI utility program (included in the Windows SDK from most vendors). MARKMIDI simply puts some data in a standard tag in the MIDI file so that when the sequencer device loads the file, it can tell that the file was authored for Windows. If you don't mark your files in this way, a dialog box will come up and inform the user that the selected MIDI file may not play properly (or at all!) on the hardware.

Summary

The following list summarizes everything you should do to create MIDI files that maximize compatibility with various Windows hardware setups:

- Author your files for both Base-level and Extended-level synthesizer setups.
- Use MIDI channels 13 through 16 for Base-level synthesizer data, with percussive instruments on channel 16.
- Use MIDI channels 1 through 10 for Extended-level synthesizer data, with percussive instruments on channel 10.
- Prioritize MIDI data by putting crucial melodic information in the lower-numbered channels.
- Limit the polyphony of melodic channels to a total of 6 notes for Base-level and 16 notes for Extended-level synthesizers.
- Limit the polyphony of percussive channels to a total of 3 notes for Base-level and 16 notes for Extended-level synthesizers.
- Use the General MIDI patch assignments and key assignments.
- Always send a Program Change message to a channel to select a patch before sending other messages to that channel. For the two percussion channels (10 and 16), always select patch 0.
- Always follow a MIDI Program Change message with a MIDI Main Volume Controller message (controller 7) to set the relative volume of the patch.

- Use a value of 80 for the main-volume controller for normal listening levels.
- Use only the following MIDI messages in MIDI files: Note On (with velocity), Note Off, Program Change, Pitch Bend, Main Volume (controller 7), and Damper Pedal (controller 64). Internal (card-based) synthesizers are required to respond to these messages and virtually all MIDI musical instruments (external) respond to them, as well.
- Use the MARKMIDI utility to mark your MIDI files that follow these guidelines.

If you're the multitalented type and create your own MIDI files for your games, then the terms and workings of MIDI will probably already be familiar to you. If you aren't intimately familiar with MIDI and are getting your MIDI files from someone else, make sure your supplier understands these guidelines or make sure that you have the tools necessary for modifying their files to fit the guidelines. There are many talented folks out there who specialize in sound for games, and there are also lots of public-domain MIDI files that you can use for games. Remember, though, that just because you have a MIDI file in your possession doesn't mean that it's legal for you to use in a commercial game. If you use such a file without permission, you may be infringing on the rights of both the composer of the song and the author of the MIDI file.

Playing CD Audio via MCI

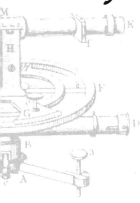

A growing category of entertainment software is tied to the playing of audio CDs on the CD-ROM drive in your computer. Sometimes referred to as *interactive liner notes,* this software enhances the music on the CD with pictures, text, and an interactive interface for exploring it all.

It's possible to combine both data and regular Red Book audio on the same CD in a *mixed-mode* CD. Currently, you must put all the data for a mixed-mode CD in what an ordinary CD player recognizes as the first track of the disc (see Figure 11-7). Play this track on a regular CD player and you can expect some rather nasty noises to come out of your speakers (perhaps as their dying breath). New standards for *multisession* CDs will eliminate this "track 1 problem."

Mixed-mode CDs (even the forthcoming multisession CDs) have one catch: The CD-ROM drive can operate in only one mode at a time. If you're accessing data on the CD, you can't play audio, and vice versa. An easy solution to this problem is to copy the required data from the CD onto the local hard drive, then play the CD as a regular audio CD from that point on.

Playing an audio CD with the MCI is a lot like playing a MIDI file. Unlike the sequencer, the *cdaudio* device is a simple device—one that doesn't require a file. You open it in much the same way as you do the sequencer device, except that it

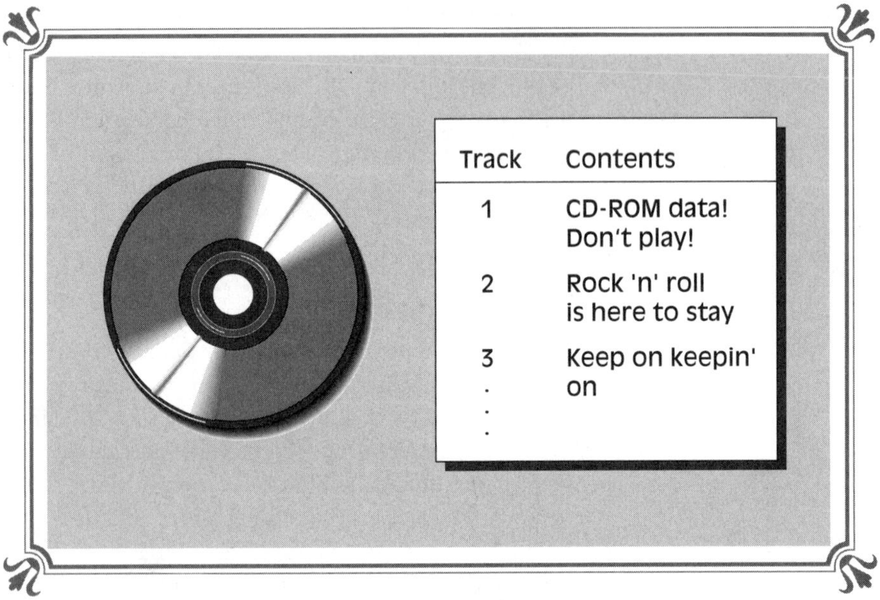

FIGURE 11-7

Current mixed-mode CDs and track 1

isn't necessary to use the MCI_OPEN_ELEMENT flag (and corresponding MC_OPEN_PARMS structure member):

```
DWORD dwReturn;
MCI_PLAY_PARMS mciPlayParms;

mciOpenParms.lpstrDeviceType = "cdaudio";
dwReturn = mciSendCommand (NULL, MCI_OPEN,
                           MCI_OPEN_TYPE | MCI_WAIT,
                           (DWORD)(LPVOID)&mciOpenParms);
```

Usually, you want to have control over (at least) what tracks are played on the CD. You can specify this in the MCI_PLAY_PARMS structure passed with the MCI_PLAY message. The MCI_PLAY_PARMS structure looks like this:

```
typedef struct  {
    DWORD dwCallback;
    DWORD dwFrom;
    DWORD dwTo;
} MCI_PLAY_PARMS;
```

Use the `dwCallback` member in the usual fashion; it should contain the handle of a window to which the MM_MCINOTIFY message will be sent if the MCI_NOTIFY flag is specified in the `mciSendCommand` call. The `dwFrom` and `dwTo` members of the function specify the start and end points of the MCI_PLAY command. But in what units are the values in these DWORDs interpreted, you ask?

You specify the time units for a given device by using the MCI_SET command with the MCI_SET_TIME_FORMAT flag. Except for MCI_FORMAT_MILLISECONDS, which is supported by all devices that support timing information, time units vary depending on the device. For example, the sequencer device can use song-pointer units (a MIDI standard timing unit) by specifying MCI_SEQ_FORMAT_SONGPTR. The cdaudio device supports a device-specific unit called MCI_FORMAT_TMSF for tracks, minutes, seconds, and frames. This is one of the most useful time formats for the cdaudio device, because it's the native format for audio CDs (it's also the cdaudio device's default format). A Red Book CD encodes its data in tracks, minutes, seconds, and frames, where there are 75 frames per second.

There are macros provided in MMSYSTEM.H to pack and unpack a DWORD according to the different time formats. The MCI_MAKE_TMSF macro packs a DWORD like so:

```
DWORD tmsf;

tmsf = MCI_MAKE_TMSF(track, minute, second, frame);
```

There are four macros for extracting the track, minute, second, and frame from a DWORD, as well:

```
MCI_TMSF_TRACK(DWORD tmsf);
MCI_TMSF_MINUTE(DWORD tmsf);
MCI_TMSF_SECOND(DWORD tmsf);
MCI_TMSF_FRAME(DWORD tmsf);
```

Now that you know all this stuff, we can put it together. Here's a function that plays a track of an audio CD in the CD-ROM drive all the way through, then stops and notifies a window with MM_MCINOTIFY:

```
BOOL PlayCDTrack (HWND hwndNotify, UINT track)
{
    DWORD dwReturn;
    MCI_OPEN_PARMS mciOpenParms;
    MCI_PLAY_PARMS mciPlayParms;
    MCI_SET_PARMS mciSetParms;
    UINT DeviceID;

    // Open the cdaudio device (simple) with wait.
    mciOpenParms.lpstrDeviceType = "cdaudio";
    dwReturn = mciSendCommand (NULL, MCI_OPEN,
                               MCI_OPEN_TYPE | MCI_WAIT,
                               (DWORD)(LPVOID)&mciOpenParms);
    if (dwReturn) {
        ShowMCIError (hwndNotify, dwReturn);
        return FALSE;
    }
    // Get the device ID.
```

continued on next page

continued from previous page

```
    DeviceID = mciOpenParms.wDeviceID;

    // Set the current time format to TMSF.
    // This should be the default, but do it anyway.
    mciSetParms.dwTimeFormat = MCI_FORMAT_TMSF;
    dwReturn = mciSendCommand (DeviceID, MCI_SET,
                               MCI_WAIT|MCI_SET_TIME_FORMAT,
                               (DWORD)(LPVOID)&mciSetParms);
    if (dwReturn) {
        ShowMCIError (hwndNotify, dwReturn);
        return FALSE;
    }

    // Set the start and stop positions of the CD.
    mciPlayParms.dwFrom = MCI_MAKE_TMSF(track, 0, 0, 0);
    mciPlayParms.dwTo = MCI_MAKE_TMSF(track+1, 0, 0, 0);
    mciPlayParms.dwCallback = (DWORD)hwndNotify;

    // Send the play command with notification.
    dwReturn = mciSendCommand (DeviceID, MCI_PLAY,
                               MCI_FROM | MCI_TO | MCI_NOTIFY,
                               (DWORD)(LPVOID)&mciPlayParms);
    if (dwReturn) {
        ShowMCIError (hwndNotify, dwReturn);
        return FALSE;
    }

    // Return success.
    return TRUE;
}
```

If you're playing an audio CD and have any hope of synchronizing your program with it, you'll need to get timing information from the CD. There's no way for the MCI to send messages to your program as the time passes on the CD, so the only way to know where you are is to poll the status of the cdaudio device with MCI_STATUS. Here's a function to do just that:

```
DWORD GetCDPosition (UINT DeviceID)
{
    DWORD dwReturn;
    MCI_STATUS_PARMS mciStatParms;

    // The dwItem member of the MCI_STATUS_PARMS structure
    // is set to the status item we want, then the
    // MCI_STATUS_ITEM flag is used in the MCI_STATUS call.
    // Eeesh.
    StatParms.dwItem = MCI_STATUS_POSITION;
    dwReturn= mciSendCommand (DeviceID, MCI_STATUS,
                              MCI_WAIT|MCI_STATUS_ITEM,
                              (DWORD)(LPMCI_STATUS_PARMS)&mciStatParms);
```

```
    // The return value is stored in the dwReturn member
    // of the MCI_STATUS_PARMS structure.
    return mciStatParms.dwReturn;
}
```

By calling **GetCDPosition** on a regular basis (for example, using a Windows timer), you can synchronize the playing of the CD with whatever your program's doing. Remember that the native units for CD audio are tracks, minutes, seconds, and frames (75 per second), so don't expect accuracy better than 1/75 of a second, even if you're using MCI_FORMAT_MILLISECONDS.

Let's move on to the last type of audio supported under the Multimedia Extensions, waveform audio.

Using WAVEMIX.DLL

You also can control waveform audio by using the MCI. However, as I mentioned previously, the *waveaudio* device (where all waveform audio goes) supports only a single stream of waveform audio at any given time, limiting its usefulness for game applications. It's much easier to handle waveform sound for games by using the Wavemix DLL instead.

The device driver for the waveaudio device is installed when you install your sound card. You can access it through the Drivers item in the Control Panel application. The Wavemix DLL uses the waveaudio device for output, so you must install such a device in order for the Wavemix DLL to work.

Because the Wavemix DLL must use the PC's CPU to do all the signal-processing tasks, it has a couple of limitations. First, it can handle only 11 kHz, 8-bit mono files. Also, it can mix a maximum of only 8 separate channels. Neither of these restrictions should pose a problem for most games.

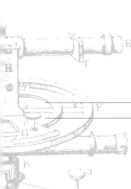

The Wavemix DLL Functions

Since the purpose of the Wavemix DLL is to simplify the process of playing wave files, it would follow that its API specification would be brief. In fact, WAVEMIX.DLL contains only 12 public functions, and you may not even need to use all of them. To begin playing wave files, your program need only perform the following four steps (illustrated in Figure 11-8):

- Initialize the DLL with **WaveMixInit** or **WaveMixConfigureInit**.
- Open one or more wave files with **WaveMixOpenWave**
- Open one or more channels with **WaveMixOpenChannel**.
- Play the file(s) with **WaveMixPlay**.

FIGURE 11-8

Mixing and playing wave files

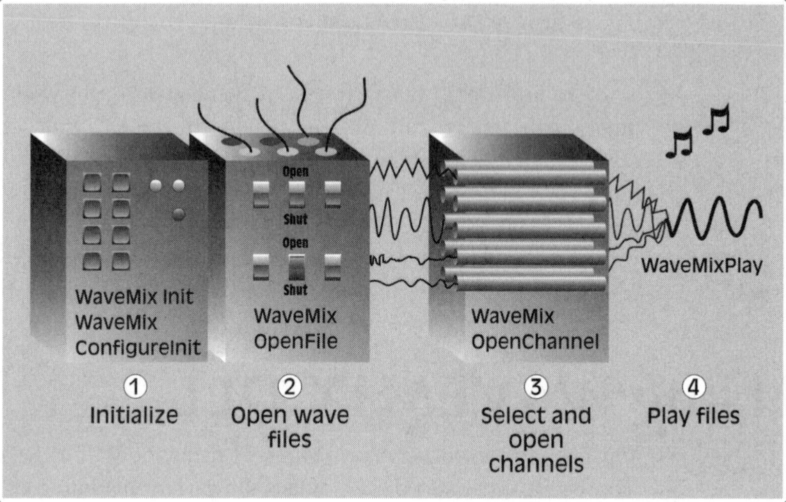

When the program finishes, you must perform the following three steps:

- Close the open channels with **WaveMixCloseChannel**.
- Free the memory for the wave files with **WaveMixFreeWave**.
- End the session with **WaveMixCloseSession**.

The other functions preempt wave playing, activate and deactivate the Wavemix DLL, and so on.

Since the API is so simple, let's take a look at the initialization process as a whole. You could place this code in your game's **Init** function or some other suitable place. In the sample on the CD-ROM that accompanies this book, the initialization code is in the **OnCreate** handler, and the **MAIN** window instance structure has some new members specific to the Wavemix DLL:

```
typedef struct MAINtag {
    HWND hwnd;              // This window
    HDC  hdc;               // DC for our window
    HMENU menu;             // Our window's menu handle
    HCURSOR cursor;         // Our window's cursor
    BOOL down;

    LPMIXWAVE mw[8];        // Pointer to MIXWAVE handles
    HANDLE MixSession;      // Mix Session handle
    int command;
} MAIN;
```

The actual handler has the following code for initializing the Wavemix DLL and opening up to eight channels:

```
    BOOL fErr;
    .
    .
    .
    if (!(main->MixSession = WaveMixInit()))
        return FALSE;

    for (i = 0; i < NUM_WAVS; i++) {
        main->mw[i] = WaveMixOpenWave(main->MixSession,

(LPSTR)MAKEINTRESOURCE(WAVE_START+i),
                                        G_app.hinst, WMIX_RESOURCE);
        if (!main->mw[i]) {
            CloseWaveStuff (main);
            return FALSE;
        }
    }

    fErr=WaveMixOpenChannel(main->MixSession,NUM_WAVS,WMIX_OPENCOUNT);
    if (fErr) {
        CloseWaveStuff (main);
        return FALSE;
    }
```

The **NUM_WAVS** constant is set in a header to the number of wave files that you can play at once. The **WAVE_START** constant defines the resource ID of the first WAVE resource in the resource file; remaining WAVE resources should have sequential IDs. A WAVE resource is defined just like all the other file-based resources, such as icons and bitmaps. A line in the resource file like this

```
1002    WAVE    boom.wav
```

does the job.

The Wavemix DLL is initialized with **WaveMixInit**, which returns a handle to a "mix session." This handle is used in subsequent calls to the Wavemix DLL. Once initialized, wave files are loaded with **WaveMixOpenWave**, which takes the handle to the mix session and either the wave file name, or the resource file ID (suitably massaged by **MAKEINTRESOURCE**). The **WMIX_RESOURCE** flag as the last parameter tells the function to use the latter.

The **CloseWaveStuff()** function is a cleanup function:

```
void CloseWaveStuff(MAIN *main)
{
    int i;

    if (!main->MixSession)
```

continued on next page

continued from previous page

```
        return;

    WaveMixCloseChannel(main->MixSession,0,WMIX_ALL);

    for (i = 0; i < NUM_WAVS; i++) {
        if (main->mw[i]) {
            WaveMixFreeWave (main->MixSession, main->mw[i]);
            main->mw[i] = NULL;
        }
    }

    WaveMixCloseSession(main->MixSession);
    main->MixSession = NULL;
}
```

This function should be called when the window closes and the program terminates. If all went well loading the wave files, **WaveMixOpenChannel** is called to open **NUM_WAVS** channels, and the Wavemix DLL is ready to play wave files.

Playing Wave Files

Playing a wave file with the Wavemix DLL is as simple as plugging a **MIXPLAYPARAMS** structure and calling **WaveMixPlay** with the address of the structure. The **MIXPLAYPARAMS** structure (from WAVEMIX.H) looks like this:

```
typedef struct
{
    WORD wSize;
    HANDLE hMixSession;
    int iChannel;
    LPMIXWAVE lpMixWave;
    HWND hWndNotify;
    DWORD dwFlags;
    WORD wLoops;  /* 0xFFFF means loop forever */
} MIXPLAYPARAMS, * PMIXPLAYPARAM, FAR * LPMIXPLAYPARAMS;
```

The first member, **wSize**, should be set to **sizeof(MIXPLAYPARAMS)** to help identify different versions of the structure. The **hMixSession** member should, of course, be set to the handle returned by **WaveMixInit**. The **iChannel** member identifies which channel to use for playing the previously loaded wave file, depending on the setting of the **dwFlags** member. The **lpMixWave** member is set to the **MIXWAVE** pointer returned from **WaveMixOpenWave**. If the **hWndNotify** member is set to a valid top-level window handle, that window will receive the **MM_WOM_DONE** message when the wave finishes playing. This is the only notification message that the Wavemix DLL uses.

The value of **dwFlags** is a bitwise OR combination of the values listed in Table 11-5.

The **wLoops** member sets a loop count—the sound will play over and over the specified number of times. If **wLoops** is set to 0xFFFF, the wave will loop endlessly, until silenced by **WaveMixFlushChannel** or **WaveMixCloseChannel**.

TABLE 11-5
Settings of **dwFlags**

Value	Meaning
WMIX_QUEUEWAVE	The wave will be placed on the specified channel and played after all waves that are currently waiting to play on that channel.
WMIX_CLEARQUEUE	The wave will preempt any waiting waves on the specified channel. The MM_WOM_DONE message will not be sent for any waves that are preempted. This flag should not be combined with WMIX_QUEUEWAVE.
WMIX_HIGHPRIORITY	Play this wave immediately. This flag will interrupt the data buffered in the wave driver and remix the sound. If this flag is not set, it may take a small amount of time to mix the current wave.
WMIX_USELRUCHANNEL	Play the wave on any available channel (the value in **iChannel** is ignored). You should combine this flag with WMIX_QUEUEWAVE or WMIX_CLEARQUEUE.
WMIX_WAIT	The wave will be put on a "waiting list" of waves to play, so that multiple waves can be played simultaneously without delay. The waves will be played when **WaveMixPlay** is called without this flag set.

To illustrate the use of **WaveMixPlay**, the sample code takes a numeric key press and starts playing the associated wave file. This is done with an **OnChar** handler:

```
static void OnChar (MAIN *main, UINT ch, int cRepeat)
{
    int i;
    MIXPLAYPARAMS MixPlayParams;

    MixPlayParams.wSize = sizeof(MIXPLAYPARAMS);
    MixPlayParams.hMixSession = main->MixSession;
    MixPlayParams.hWndNotify=NULL;
    MixPlayParams.dwFlags=WMIX_CLEARQUEUE;
```

continued on next page

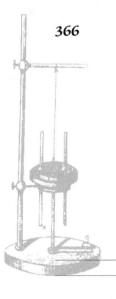

continued from previous page

```
    MixPlayParams.wLoops=0;
    MixPlayParams.iChannel = ch - '1';
    MixPlayParams.lpMixWave=main->mw[ch - '1'];

    WaveMixPlay(&MixPlayParams);


}
```

This example clears the queue for the given channel before playing the wave. You can experiment with different settings of **dwFlags** to see how each behaves.

Suspending the Wavemix DLL

One of the rules for using the Wavemix DLL is that you must call **WaveMixActivate** whenever your application is activated or deactivated. This is simple enough—you create an **OnActivate** handler for the WM_ACTIVATE message that looks like this:

```
static void OnActivate(MAIN *main, UINT state,
                       HWND hwndActDeact, BOOL fMinimized)
{
    BOOL fActivate = (state != WA_INACTIVE && !fMinimized);

    // Activate/deactivate the Wavemix DLL according to state of window.
    WaveMixActivate(main->MixSession, fActivate);
}
```

This suspends all the output from the Wavemix DLL so that other applications can do their thing.

Other Wavemix DLL Functions

There are only four other Wavemix DLL functions: **WaveMixFlushChannel**, **WaveMixGetInfo**, **WaveMixConfigureInit**, and **WaveMixPump**. The **WaveMixFlushChannel** function does just what it says; namely, it flushes one or all channels, killing any sound from those channels. The **WaveMixGetInfo** function takes a pointer to a **WAVEMIXINFO** structure as its only argument. This structure is defined in WAVEMIX.H as follows:

```
typedef struct
{
    WORD wSize;
    BYTE bVersionMajor;
    BYTE bVersionMinor;
    char szDate[12]; /* Mmm dd yyyy */
    DWORD dwFormats;
} WAVEMIXINFO, *PWAVEMIXINFO, FAR * LPWAVEMIXINFO;
```

You should first initialize the **wSize** member of this structure to **sizeof(WAVEMIXINFO)** before you pass a pointer to it to **WaveMixGetInfo**. The other members of the structure are then filled in with version (and other) information about the Wavemix DLL.

You can use the **WaveMixConfigureInit** function in place of **WaveMixInit** to specify certain parameters to the Wavemix DLL. The function takes a pointer to a **MIXCONFIG** structure, which looks like this:

```
typedef struct
{
    WORD wSize;
    DWORD dwFlags;
    WORD wChannels;   /* 1 = MONO, 2 = STEREO */
    WORD wSamplingRate; /* 11,22,44  (11=11025, 22=22050, 44=44100 Hz) */
} MIXCONFIG, *PMIXCONFIG, FAR * LPMIXCONFIG;
```

After the customary initialization of **wSize**, you can set the other structure members to specify an output sampling rate and format, either mono or stereo. You can set the **dwFlags** member to the bitwise OR of **WMIX_CONFIG_CHANNELS** or **WMIX_CONFIG_SAMPLINGRATE**, and set the other members as indicated. Microsoft recommends *not* setting the sampling rate via **WaveMixConfigureInit**, but rather leaving it to the Wavemix DLL to choose the setting based on settings in WAVEMIX.INI.

The last remaining function, **WaveMixPump**, helps the Wavemix DLL along if your program does a lot of processing without calling the main message loop. If output sounds jerky or breaks up, call **WaveMixPump** in your main processing loop to help feed the Wavemix DLL.

The WAVEMIX.INI File

The Wavemix DLL uses settings in the WAVEMIX.INI file to obtain the best performance. In general, you shouldn't have to change the settings in WAVEMIX.INI. If you find you do need to adjust something, however, you can look at the file itself for documentation for the parameters.

WAVEMIX.DLL comes with an import library, WAVEMIX.LIB, for use in linking. You can put WAVEMIX.DLL in the same directory as your executable program, but—and this is important—WAVEMIX.INI *must* reside in the WINDOWS directory (the directory where WIN.COM is) or the Wavemix DLL won't read it properly.

Music and Sound Effects Together

As promised, we'll create a program that uses both music—in the form of a MIDI file—and effects—through the use of the Wavemix DLL—at the same time. The program will play a MIDI file in an endless loop in the background, while responding to mouse and keyboard input with one of four sounds. The program will divide its main window into four quadrants. When you click on the quadrants, each will fire a different waveform sound through the Wavemix DLL. By pressing the numeric keys 1 through 4, you will also be able to activate the sounds.

Let's start with the header file, MAIN.H:

```
/* Main window structure definition
 */

typedef struct MAINtag {
    HWND hwnd;                // This window
    HDC  hdc;                 // DC for our window
    HMENU menu;               // Our window's menu handle
    HCURSOR cursor;           // Our window's cursor.

    LPMIXWAVE mw[8];          // Pointer to MIXWAVE handles
    HANDLE MixSession;        // Mix Session handle
    HANDLE midiID;
    BOOL midiPause;           // MIDI is paused.
    int command;
} MAIN;


#define DefProc  DefWindowProc

// Instance data pointer access functions

#if (defined(M_I86SM) || defined(M_I86MM)) && !defined(WIN32)
#define GetPtr(hwnd)          (MAIN*)GetWindowWord((hwnd), 0)
#define SetPtr(hwnd, pfrm)    (MAIN*)SetWindowWord((hwnd), 0,
(WORD)(pfrm))
#else
#define GetPtr(hwnd)          (MAIN*)GetWindowLong((hwnd), 0)
#define SetPtr(hwnd, pfrm)    (MAIN*)SetWindowLong((hwnd), 0,
(LONG)(pfrm))
#endif

// Message handler for MM_MCINOTIFY
/* void OnMCINotify(HWND hwnd, UINT deviceID, UINT message); */
#define HANDLE_MM_MCINOTIFY(hwnd, wParam, lParam, fn) \
    ((fn)((hwnd), (UINT)LOWORD(lParam), (UINT)(wParam)), 0L)
#define FORWARD_MM_MCINOTIFY(hwnd, deviceID, message, fn) \
    (void)(fn)((hwnd), MM_MCINOTIFY, message,
MAKELPARAM((UINT)(deviceID), 0))
```

In this file, you'll see the window instance structure (MAIN) has an array of eight LPMIXWAVE pointers to hold up to eight Wavemix wave files (we use only four here). There is a handle to the global mix session (**MixSession**) and a handle for the ID of the open MIDI device (**midiID**). The **midiPause** member's function will become clear a little later. Note also the two macros for handling MM_MCINOTIFY messages.

Next, let's look at MAIN.C through the window callback function.

```
/*
 * Play MIDI and waveform audio
 * Eric Lyons 12/12/95
 */

#include <windows.h>
#include <windowsx.h>
#include <mmsystem.h>
#include "wavemix.h"
#include "app.h"
#include "main.h"
#include "id.h"
#include "resource.h"

// Application global structure
APP G_app;

HANDLE PlayMIDIFile (HWND hwndNotify, LPSTR filename);
void ShowMCIError (HWND parent, DWORD error);
BOOL PlayCDTrack (HWND hwndNotify, UINT track);
void CloseWaveStuff(MAIN *main);

// Forward declarations
static BOOL InitClasses (HINSTANCE hInst);
static HWND Init (HINSTANCE hInst);
LRESULT CALLBACK _export WndProc(HWND hwnd, UINT msg, WPARAM wParam,
LPARAM lParam);

static BOOL OnCreate(MAIN* main, CREATESTRUCT FAR* lpCreateStruct);
static void OnClose (MAIN *main);
static void OnPaint (MAIN* main);
static void OnSize(MAIN *main, UINT state, int cx, int cy);
static void OnCommand(MAIN* main, int id, HWND hwndCtl, UINT codeNotify);
static void OnLButtonDown (MAIN *main, BOOL fDoubleClick, int x, int y,
UINT keyFlags);
static void OnLButtonUp (MAIN *main, int x, int y, UINT keyFlags);
static void OnMouseMove (MAIN *main, int x, int y, UINT keyFlags);
static void OnChar (MAIN *main, UINT ch, int cRepeat);
static void OnActivate(MAIN *main, UINT state, HWND hwndActDeact, BOOL
fMinimized);
static void OnMCINotify (MAIN *main, UINT deviceID, UINT message);

// Windows entry point
int PASCAL WinMain(HINSTANCE hInstance, HINSTANCE hPrevInstance,
                   LPSTR lpCmdLine, int nCmdShow)
{
```

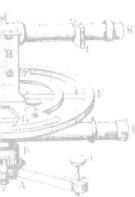

continued on next page

continued from previous page

```
    // Plug the global structure.
    G_app.hinst = hInstance;
    G_app.lpszCmdLine = lpCmdLine;
    G_app.cmdShow = nCmdShow;

    // Register the classes if this is not the first instance.
    if (!hPrevInstance && !InitClasses (hInstance))
        return FALSE;

    G_app.hwndMain = Init (hInstance);
    if (!G_app.hwndMain)
        return (FALSE);

    while (GetMessage(&G_app.msg, NULL, NULL, NULL)) {

    /* Translate the message only if it is not an accelerator message. */

        //if (!TranslateAccelerator(G_app.hwndMain, G_app.accel,
&G_app.msg)) {
            TranslateMessage(&G_app.msg);
            DispatchMessage(&G_app.msg);
        //}
    }
    return (G_app.msg.wParam);
}

static BOOL InitClasses (HINSTANCE hInstance)
{
    WNDCLASS  wc;

    // We register the window class(es) here.
    wc.style = CS_BYTEALIGNWINDOW | CS_OWNDC;    // Window DC type
    wc.lpfnWndProc = WndProc;
    wc.cbClsExtra = 0;
    // Extra bytes for the pointer to the structure.
    wc.cbWndExtra = sizeof (MAIN *);
    wc.hInstance = hInstance;
    wc.hIcon = LoadIcon(NULL, IDI_APPLICATION);
    wc.hCursor = LoadCursor(NULL, IDC_ARROW);
    wc.hbrBackground = GetStockObject(WHITE_BRUSH);
    wc.lpszMenuName =  NULL;
    wc.lpszClassName = "DemoClass";

    return RegisterClass(&wc);
}

static HWND Init (HINSTANCE hInstance)
{
    int x, y;

    x = GetSystemMetrics (SM_CXSCREEN);
```

```
    y = GetSystemMetrics (SM_CYSCREEN);

    // Create the main window.
    // That's all this init does here;
    // window-specific stuff happens in OnCreate.
    return CreateWindow(
                    "DemoClass",
                    "Demo Program",
                    WS_OVERLAPPEDWINDOW,
                    0,
                    0,
                    CW_USEDEFAULT,
                    CW_USEDEFAULT,
                    NULL,
                    NULL,
                    hInstance,
                    NULL
                );
}

LRESULT CALLBACK _export WndProc(HWND hwnd, UINT msg, WPARAM wParam,
LPARAM lParam)
{
    MAIN* main = GetPtr(hwnd);

    if (main == NULL) {

        if (msg == WM_NCCREATE) {
            main = (MAIN*)LocalAlloc(LPTR, sizeof(MAIN));

            if (main == NULL)
                return 0L;

            main->hwnd = hwnd;
            SetPtr(hwnd, main);
        } else {
            return DefProc(hwnd, msg, wParam, lParam);
        }
    }

    if (msg == WM_NCDESTROY) {

        LocalFree((HLOCAL)main);
        main = NULL;
        SetPtr(hwnd, NULL);
    }

    switch (msg) {

        HANDLE_MSG(main, WM_CREATE, OnCreate);
        HANDLE_MSG(main, WM_CLOSE, OnClose);
```

continued on next page

continued from previous page

```
        HANDLE_MSG(main, WM_PAINT, OnPaint);
        HANDLE_MSG(main, WM_COMMAND, OnCommand);
        HANDLE_MSG(main, WM_LBUTTONDOWN, OnLButtonDown);
        HANDLE_MSG(main, WM_MOUSEMOVE, OnMouseMove);
        HANDLE_MSG(main, WM_LBUTTONUP, OnLButtonUp);
        HANDLE_MSG(main, WM_CHAR, OnChar);
        HANDLE_MSG(main, WM_SIZE, OnSize);
        HANDLE_MSG(main, WM_ACTIVATE, OnActivate);
        HANDLE_MSG(main, MM_MCINOTIFY, OnMCINotify);


    default:
        return DefProc(hwnd, msg, wParam, lParam);
    }
}
```

Pretty vanilla stuff. Note the messages being handled, especially WM_ACTIVATE and MM_MCINOTIFY. You need the WM_ACTIVATE message for both Wavemix and MIDI playing so that the program can pause both when it's not active.

Next, the WM_CREATE handler, **OnCreate**:

```
static BOOL OnCreate(MAIN* main, CREATESTRUCT FAR* lpCreateStruct)
{
    BOOL fErr;
    WAVEMIXINFO Info;
    MIXCONFIG MixConfig;
    int i;

    // We get the DC once, and save it away.
    // This works only because we use CS_OWNDC.
    main->hdc = GetDC (main->hwnd);

    //
    // Initialize and set up WAVEMIX.
    //
    Info.wSize = sizeof(WAVEMIXINFO);
    if (WaveMixGetInfo(&Info))
        return FALSE;

    MixConfig.wSize = sizeof(MIXCONFIG);
    MixConfig.dwFlags = WMIX_CONFIG_CHANNELS | WMIX_CONFIG_SAMPLINGRATE;
    MixConfig.wChannels = 2;
    MixConfig.wSamplingRate = 44;
    if (!(main->MixSession = WaveMixConfigureInit(&MixConfig)))
        return FALSE;

    for (i = 0; i < NUM_WAVS; i++) {
        main->mw[i] = WaveMixOpenWave(main->MixSession,

(LPSTR)MAKEINTRESOURCE(WAVE_START+i),
                                          G_app.hinst, WMIX_RESOURCE);
        if (!main->mw[i]) {
```

```
                CloseWaveStuff (main);
                return FALSE;
            }
        }

        fErr=WaveMixOpenChannel(main->MixSession,NUM_WAVS,WMIX_OPENCOUNT);
        if (fErr) {
            CloseWaveStuff (main);
            return FALSE;
        }

        main->midiID = PlayMIDIFile (main->hwnd, "sbach.mid");


        ShowWindow (main->hwnd, G_app.cmdShow);
        return TRUE;
}
```

There are several things to notice here. First, note that you initialize the Wavemix DLL with **WaveMixConfigureInit**, which permits you to set the number of channels and the output sample rate (remember, input is always 22 kHz 8-bit). The **WaveMixOpenWave** call is used with the **WMIX_RESOURCE** flag, meaning that the wave files are actually embedded resources; the **MAKEINTRESOURCE** macro is used to get their IDs. The constant WAVE_START is set to the ID of the first WAVE resource in the resource file, while NUM_WAVS is defined as 4.

There are two helper functions defined later in the file, **CloseWaveStuff** and **PlayMIDIFile**. The former just closes down the Wavemix DLL, and the latter opens the sequencer device and starts playing the specified file. Unfortunately, the MCI doesn't permit you to load MIDI files from a resource, for some reason; they must come from a separate file (SBACH.MID, in this case). The **CloseWaveStuff** function looks like this:

```
void CloseWaveStuff(MAIN *main)
{
    int i;

    if (!main->MixSession)
        return;

    WaveMixCloseChannel(main->MixSession,0,WMIX_ALL);

    for (i = 0; i < NUM_WAVS; i++) {
        if (main->mw[i]) {
            WaveMixFreeWave (main->MixSession, main->mw[i]);
            main->mw[i] = NULL;
        }
    }

    WaveMixCloseSession(main->MixSession);
    main->MixSession = NULL;
}
```

The function just closes all the channels, frees all the wave files, and closes the Wavemix session. The **PlayMIDIFile** function is a little more complex:

```
HANDLE PlayMIDIFile (HWND hwndNotify, LPSTR filename)
{
    UINT DeviceID;
    DWORD dwReturn;
    MCI_OPEN_PARMS mciOpenParms;
    MCI_PLAY_PARMS mciPlayParms;

    // Open the device with both device name and device element (file).
    // The first parameter to mciSendCommand is NULL, of course, since
    // there's no device ID yet.
    // We open itwith MCI_WAIT, because we want it to finish before we
    // continue.
    mciOpenParms.lpstrDeviceType = "sequencer";
    mciOpenParms.lpstrElementName = filename;
    if (dwReturn = mciSendCommand (NULL, MCI_OPEN,
                                MCI_OPEN_TYPE | MCI_OPEN_ELEMENT |
                                MCI_WAIT,
(DWORD)(LPVOID)&mciOpenParms)) {
        // Error. Call ShowMCIError.
        ShowMCIError (hwndNotify, dwReturn);
        return 0;
    }
    // Device opened successfully. Get the device ID.
    DeviceID = mciOpenParms.wDeviceID;

    // Begin playback. Specify the window to which the MM_MCINOTIFY
    // message will be sent when it finishes; the message handler
    // should close the device when it gets it.
    mciPlayParms.dwCallback = (DWORD)hwndNotify;
    if (dwReturn = mciSendCommand (DeviceID, MCI_PLAY,
                                MCI_NOTIFY,
                                (DWORD)(LPVOID)&mciPlayParms)) {
        // Failed. Display the error and close the device.
        ShowMCIError (hwndNotify, dwReturn);
        mciSendCommand (DeviceID, MCI_CLOSE, 0, NULL);
        return 0;
    }
    return DeviceID;
}
```

The function opens the sequencer device (named in the **lpstrDeviceType** member of the **mciOpenParms** structure) with the specified file name as the element. If only Microsoft had included the option for the **lpstrElementName** member to contain a resource file ID or name, with some appropriate flag to indicate it, then we could embed the whole MIDI file in the resource file for the program. Oh well.

Next, the device ID of the successfully opened sequencer device is held for later return by the function in **DeviceID**. Then, the MCI_PLAY command is sent to the device with the MCI_NOTIFY flag so that the specified window (**hwndNotify**, plugged into the **dwCallback** member of the **mciPlayParms** structure) will be notified with the MM_MCINOTIFY message when playback is complete.

The **ShowMCIError** function just looks up the error and displays it in a message box.

```
// Display the MCI error using mciGetErrorString.
void ShowMCIError (HWND parent, DWORD error)
{
    char buf[100];

    mciGetErrorString (error, buf, sizeof(buf));
    MessageBox (parent, buf, "MCI Error", MB_OK|MB_ICONEXCLAMATION);
}
```

So much for **OnCreate**. Let's take a look at the **OnClose** WM_CLOSE handler and see how it wraps things up when we close the window.

```
static void OnClose (MAIN *main)
{
    DWORD retval;

    // Here's where we release the dc...
    ReleaseDC (main->hwnd, main->hdc);

    // And close all MCI devices.
    retval = mciSendCommand (main->midiID, MCI_CLOSE,
                             0, NULL);
    if (retval)
        ShowMCIError (main->hwnd, retval);

    // Kill the MIDI device ID.
    main->midiID = NULL;

    // Close the wavemix stuff.
    CloseWaveStuff (main);

    PostQuitMessage (0);
}
```

The code closes the sequencer device by passing the **main->midiID** handle to the MCI_CLOSE message. The **CloseWaveStuff** function closes down the Wavemix DLL. Also note that the device context for this window is released here. This is because the window was created with the CS_OWNDC class definition flag, which allocates a DC just for the window.

The WM_PAINT handler is simple—it just draws two lines and four numbers on the window. Here's its definition:

```
static void OnPaint (MAIN *main)
{
    PAINTSTRUCT ps;
```

continued on next page

continued from previous page

```
    HDC hdc;
    SIZE sz;
    RECT r;
    int x, y;
    char text[][4] = {"1","2","3","4"};

    hdc = BeginPaint (main->hwnd, &ps);

    // Get the size of the text (use "4").
    GetTextExtentPoint (hdc, text[3], lstrlen(text[3]), &sz);
    GetClientRect (main->hwnd, &r);

    // Divide the window into four zones.
    MoveTo (hdc, r.right/2, r.top);
    LineTo (hdc, r.right/2, r.bottom);
    MoveTo (hdc, r.left, r.bottom/2);
    LineTo (hdc, r.right, r.bottom/2);

    // Put text in the four quadrants.
    x = (r.right/2 - sz.cx) / 2;
    y = (r.bottom/2 - sz.cy) / 2;

    ExtTextOut (hdc, x, y, ETO_OPAQUE, NULL, text[0], lstrlen(text[0]),
NULL);
    ExtTextOut (hdc, x+r.right/2, y, ETO_OPAQUE, NULL,
                text[1], lstrlen(text[1]), NULL);
    ExtTextOut (hdc, x, y+r.bottom/2, ETO_OPAQUE, NULL,
                text[2], lstrlen(text[2]), NULL);
    ExtTextOut (hdc, x+r.right/2, y+r.bottom/2, ETO_OPAQUE, NULL,
                text[3], lstrlen(text[3]), NULL);

    EndPaint (main->hwnd, &ps);

}
```

These quadrants are later hit-tested in the WM_LBUTTONDOWN handler, and the appropriate wave file is played by the Wavemix DLL:

```
static void OnLButtonDown (MAIN *main, BOOL fDoubleClick,
                           int x, int y, UINT keyFlags)
{
    RECT r;
    MIXPLAYPARAMS MixPlayParams;

    int hit = -1;

    GetClientRect (main->hwnd, &r);

    // Hit-test the mouse in one of the four quadrants
    if (x < r.right/2) {
        if (y < r.bottom/2)
            // 1
            hit = 1;
```

```
        else
            // 3
            hit = 3;
    } else {
        if (y < r.bottom/2)
            // 2
            hit = 2;
        else
            // 4
            hit = 4;
    }
    if (hit == -1)
        // error
        return;

    // Play the associated Wavemix sound.
    MixPlayParams.wSize = sizeof(MIXPLAYPARAMS);
    MixPlayParams.hMixSession = main->MixSession;
    MixPlayParams.hWndNotify = NULL;
    MixPlayParams.dwFlags = WMIX_CLEARQUEUE;
    MixPlayParams.wLoops = 0;
    MixPlayParams.iChannel = hit - 1;
    MixPlayParams.lpMixWave = main->mw[hit-1];

    WaveMixPlay(&MixPlayParams);

}
```

Once the quadrant is determined, the appropriate channel and handle to the wave file (held in the **main->mw[]** array) is plugged into the **MixPlayParams** structure and the structure is submitted to **WaveMixPlay**. The WMIX_CLEARQUEUE flag makes any existing wave on the specified channel stop playing.

The WM_CHAR handler does pretty much the same thing, except it uses a numeric key press to determine which wave to play:

```
static void OnChar (MAIN *main, UINT ch, int cRepeat)
{
    MIXPLAYPARAMS MixPlayParams;

    if (ch > '0' && ch < '5') {
        // Play the associated Wavemix sound.
        MixPlayParams.wSize = sizeof(MIXPLAYPARAMS);
        MixPlayParams.hMixSession = main->MixSession;
        MixPlayParams.hWndNotify = NULL;
        MixPlayParams.dwFlags = WMIX_CLEARQUEUE;
        MixPlayParams.wLoops = 0;
        MixPlayParams.iChannel = ch - '0';
        MixPlayParams.lpMixWave = main->mw[ch - '0'];

        WaveMixPlay(&MixPlayParams);
    }
}
```

Things start to get a little trickier with the MM_MCINOTIFY handler, called **OnMCINotify**:

```
static void OnMCINotify (MAIN *main, UINT deviceID, UINT message)
{
    DWORD retval;

    // If it's the MIDI device, loop playback.
    // But only if *NOT* paused...
    if (deviceID == main->midiID && !main->midiPause) {
        MCI_PLAY_PARMS mciPlayParms;

        // Notify us again when playback is complete.
        mciPlayParms.dwCallback = (DWORD)main->hwnd;
        // Start from the beginning.
        mciPlayParms.dwFrom = 0;
        if (retval = mciSendCommand (main->midiID, MCI_PLAY,
                                     MCI_NOTIFY | MCI_FROM,
                                     (DWORD)(LPVOID)&mciPlayParms)) {
            // Failed. Display the error.
            ShowMCIError (main->hwnd, retval);
        }
    }
}
```

First, remember that this function is called when the current MIDI file finishes playing (via the MM_MCINOTIFY message-handler macro). The message includes the handle to the device ID as its second parameter, so that if there is more than one device open and sending MM_MCINOTIFY messages, the function can identify which device is sending the message. The **if** statement checks to make sure that this is indeed the MIDI device, and it also checks the condition of the **main->midiPause** flag. This flag is set in **OnActivate** (whose definition is coming up) when MIDI output is paused; the **OnMCINotify** handler function shouldn't start playing the MIDI file again in this case.

Note that the **dwFrom** member of the **mciPlayParms** structure is set to 0, denoting the beginning of the MIDI file. The MCI_FROM flag is used in the **mciSendCommand** call so the MCI_PLAY message can look at what's in this structure member.

Now comes the complicated part—handling activation. The idea is that if your program isn't the currently active program, it shouldn't play anything. When it becomes active again, it should pick up where it left off. From the Wavemix DLL's point of view, this is simple. You call the **WaveMixActivate** function with the state of the program's window, either activating or deactivating. This is not so easy for MIDI. Here's the WM_ACTIVATE message-handler function:

```
static void OnActivate(MAIN *main, UINT state,
                       HWND hwndActDeact, BOOL fMinimized)
{
```

```
MCI_PLAY_PARMS mciPlayParms;
MCI_STATUS_PARMS mciStatParms;
DWORD retval;
BOOL fActivate = (state != WA_INACTIVE && !fMinimized);

// Activate/deactivate the Wavemix DLL.
WaveMixActivate(main->MixSession, fActivate);

// Stop/start playing the MIDI file.
if (fActivate && main->midiID) {

    mciStatParms.dwItem = MCI_STATUS_MODE;
    if (retval = mciSendCommand (main->midiID, MCI_STATUS,
                                 MCI_STATUS_ITEM,
                                 (DWORD)(LPVOID)&mciStatParms)) {
        // Failed. Display the error.
        ShowMCIError (NULL, retval);
    }

    // If the sequencer is paused, play it.
    if (mciStatParms.dwReturn == MCI_MODE_PAUSE) {

        mciPlayParms.dwCallback = (DWORD)main->hwnd;
        if (retval = mciSendCommand (main->midiID, MCI_PLAY,
                                     MCI_NOTIFY,
                                     (DWORD)(LPVOID)&mciPlayParms)) {
            // Failed. Display the error.
            ShowMCIError (NULL, retval);
        }
        // Tell the looper that it's not paused.
        main->midiPause = FALSE;
    }
} else {
    // Deactivating. See if we're playing.
    mciStatParms.dwItem = MCI_STATUS_MODE;
    if (retval = mciSendCommand (main->midiID, MCI_STATUS,
                                 MCI_STATUS_ITEM,
                                 (DWORD)(LPVOID)&mciStatParms)) {
        // Failed. Display the error.
        ShowMCIError (NULL, retval);
    }

    // If the sequencer is playing, pause it.
    if (mciStatParms.dwReturn == MCI_MODE_PLAY) {

        if (retval = mciSendCommand (main->midiID, MCI_PAUSE,
                                     0, NULL)) {
            // Failed. Display the error.
            ShowMCIError (NULL, retval);
        }
```

continued on next page

continued from previous page

```
            // Make sure it doesn't loop while paused.
            main->midiPause = TRUE;
        }
    }
}
```

The **fActivate** flag is set to TRUE if this window is being activated, and FALSE if it's being deactivated. This flag is passed directly to **WaveMixActivate**; the job is done.

The sequencer, however, demands a little more. First, the **main->midiID** handle is checked along with **fActivate**. As it turns out, the window may actually get a WM_ACTIVATE message just after it's been closed—and it's in the WM_CLOSE handler that the MIDI device is closed. The rest of **OnActivate** would fail in this case, because the device ID would no longer be valid.

Next, we have to determine whether the sequencer is currently playing or currently paused. The safest way to do this is to ask the device with the MCI_STATUS command. The command takes a structure with its **dwItem** member set to the ID of the thing whose status is to be checked. There are several status items supported by the MCI_STATUS command, but the one we want is MCI_STATUS_MODE, which will determine the play/pause/stop state of the sequencer. The result is returned in the **dwReturn** member of the **mciStatParms** structure and is tested for MCI_MODE_PAUSE (if the window is being activated) or MCI_MODE_PLAY (if the window is being deactivated). Finally, the code issues either the MCI_PLAY or the MCI_PAUSE command, depending on the activation state and the results of the status check.

The **main->midiPause** flag is set to TRUE (if paused) or FALSE (if playing) so that it can be checked in the MM_MCINOTIFY handler. If MIDI playback is paused, then the handler won't loop the playing of the file when it receives the message. Also note that when **OnActivate** issues the MCI_PLAY command, it does so with the MCI_NOTIFY flag so that the end can be detected again. Otherwise, after an activation or deactivation the MIDI file wouldn't loop.

When you run the program, you'll hear the MIDI sound right away. Click in the quadrants (or press numeric keys 1 through 4) to activate the Wavemix sound. Note that there's no degradation of one type of sound when another is playing; different hardware handles the different sound types, so there isn't a problem.

Summary

You've seen how the various types of Windows sound—CD audio, MIDI audio, and waveform audio—are all handled by the Multimedia Extensions. You've also had a good overview of the Media Control Interface, which facilitates high-level control of audio (and other) services. You've learned all about how to author MIDI files so that they'll play on a wide range of multimedia PCs.

A little warning: Stay away from the low-level audio services, if at all possible. While conceptually simple, the details of buffers and messages can be quite difficult to manage. The MCI provides a simple and reliable way of playing audio data across three data types, which yields ample coverage for most games.

The Multimedia Extensions really make working with sound under Windows much easier than writing dozens of device drivers under DOS. The MCI handles all the low-level details of getting bytes to the sound card, too. It also provides you with a rich and complete way of adding music to your games via MIDI. Let there be noise!

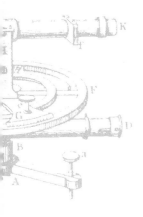

12

Windows and Files

Come si debbe fare le manovelle [illegible] le quali si movono e si alza
e i gran pesi [illegible] s'adoperano [illegible]
sforzare nella mano [illegible] alla manovella perchè quanto
la forza e più [illegible] l'omo più [illegible]

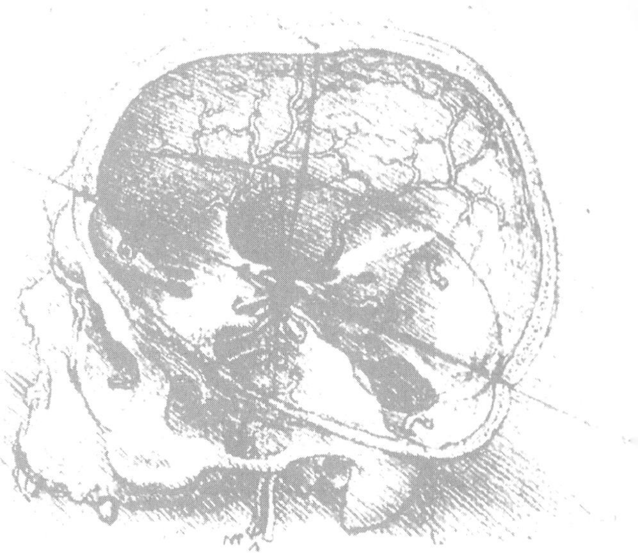

12

Windows and Files

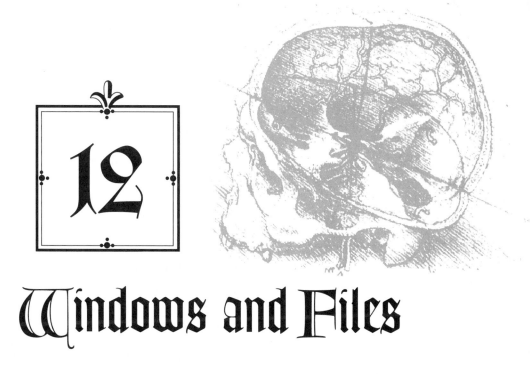

File handling under Windows is not much different than file handling under DOS, with a few notable exceptions. Besides having a special function for opening files, Windows also provides a handy set of functions for reading and writing *profile strings*—settings that are stored in those ubiquitous .INI files you find scattered all over your hard disk. This chapter explores the basics of Windows file handling, as well as the special functions for reading and writing .INI files.

Opening and Closing Files Under Windows

To open and close buffered files under DOS, you typically use the standard I/O library functions **fopen()** and **fclose()**. While it's possible to use these functions from within a Windows program, it's inadvisable for several reasons. First, the standard C library functions for reading and writing files are *model-dependent*. This means that the sizes of the pointers passed as arguments to the functions vary, depending on the memory model of the program. Second, **fopen()** and **fclose()** don't allow all the file-sharing options that the Windows versions of the functions offer; files open in so-called *compatibility mode,* which effectively nullifies sharing. Finally, there are equivalent Windows functions designed specifically for Windows applications.

The Windows function for opening files is called (amazingly enough) **OpenFile**, while the function for closing files is for some reason called **_lclose**.

The OpenFile Function

Here's the prototype for the **OpenFile** function:

```
HFILE WINAPI OpenFile(LPCSTR, OFSTRUCT FAR*, UINT)
```

The return value, an **HFILE**, is defined as an **int** in WINDOWS.H and represents a handle to a file. The second argument, a **LPCSTR**, is a long pointer to a constant C string—in other words, a **const FAR *char**. This argument holds the string containing the name of the file to be opened. The size of the buffer used to hold the string should typically be equal to **_MAX_PATH**, which is defined in STDLIB.H as 260. If the string doesn't contain a fully qualified path name, **OpenFile** looks for the file in five places, listed here in order, before giving up:

- The current directory.
- The Windows directory (where WIN.COM is located). You can get the path of this directory yourself with the **GetWindowsDirectory** function.
- The Windows system directory. You can retrieve the path of this directly with **GetSystemDirectory**.
- The directory containing the executable file for the current task. You can retrieve this directory directly with **GetModuleFileName**.
- The directories listed in the PATH environment variable.

The second argument to the function is a pointer to an **OFSTRUCT** structure, whose definition (from WINDOWS.H) is:

```
typedef struct tagOFSTRUCT
{
    BYTE cBytes;
    BYTE fFixedDisk;
    UINT nErrCode;
    BYTE reserved[4];
    char szPathName[128];
} OFSTRUCT;
```

The members of the **OFSTRUCT** member contain useful information about the opened file or, if the return value from **OpenFile** is **HFILE_ERROR**, about the error condition. The **nErrCode** contains one of several dozen error codes. If the **OpenFile** function doesn't return **HFILE_ERROR**, then the function was successful, the return value is a regular file handle, and the various other members of the **OFSTRUCT** contain information about the file.

If the **fFixedDisk** member is not zero, Windows opened the file on a fixed disk. This information can be useful. It's generally unwise to leave files on a floppy disk open for long periods of time, because of the possibility that the user could physically remove the disk from the drive.

The **szPathName** member contains the fully qualified path name for the file you are opening. The **reserved** member of the structure is, in fact, reserved and you shouldn't use it. The **OpenFile** function sets the **cBytes** member of the structure to **sizeof(OFSTRUCT)**. The function doesn't require you to initialize this member before passing in this particular structure. (Hey, you can't be consistent *all* the time, can you?)

The last argument to **OpenFile** is a **UINT** that contains a bitwise-OR combination of one or more of the values listed in Table 12-1.

TABLE 12-1
OpenFile *flags*

Value	Meaning
OF_CREATE	Creates a new file. If the specified file already exists, it truncates it to 0 length. When this flag is specified, the sharing flags are ignored. If a file must be shared, it should be closed after creation and then reopened with the appropriate sharing flags.
OF_DELETE	Deletes the file. The file handle returned should not be used by other file functions.
OF_EXIST	Opens the file, then closes it. This flag is used to test for file existence. The file handle returned should not be used by other file functions.
OF_READ	Opens the file for reading only.
OF_READWRITE	Opens the file for reading and writing.
OF_WRITE	Opens the file for writing. Note that this function will not create a file if it doesn't exist; use OF_CREATE to create the file first.
OF_SEARCH	Searches all the directories, even when the fully qualified path name is given.

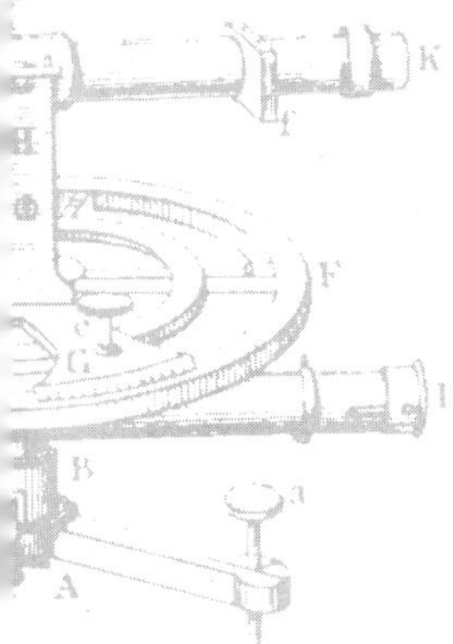

continued on next page

continued from previous page

Value	Meaning
OF_VERIFY	Compares the time and date of the file with the time and date contained in the **OFSTRUCT** (whose values were obtained in a previous **OpenFile** call). **OpenFile** returns **HFILE_ERROR** if the date and time don't match.
OF_SHARE_COMPAT	Opens the file for compatibility mode. Any program can open the file any number of times, unless the file was previously opened with any of the other sharing modes. This is the default mode if no other sharing flags are used.
OF_SHARE_DENY_NONE	Allows any other program to open the file for reading or writing. Fails if the file has been opened with compatibility mode.
OF_SHARE_DENY_WRITE	Opens the file for exclusive write access. Fails if the file was opened by any other program with write access or with compatibility mode.
OF_SHARE_DENY_READ	Opens the file for exclusive read access. Fails if the file was opened by any other program with read access or with compatibility mode.
OF_SHARE_EXCLUSIVE	Denies any other program either read or write access to the file. Fails if the file was opened with any other mode.
OF_REOPEN	Reopens the file with a previously used **OFSTRUCT**.

Obviously, not all the flags can be used in combination with each other. One of the important differences between **OpenFile** and the standard C function **fopen** is that **OpenFile** doesn't create a file if you try to open a nonexistent file for write access. You must first use **OF_CREATE** and then reopen the file, typically reusing the previously filled-in **OFSTRUCT** by using **OF_REOPEN** in conjunction with some other open flag, like **OF_WRITE**.

Note also that you can use—and, in fact, *should* use—**OpenFile** to delete files, as well, by specifying the **OF_DELETE** flag.

The _lcreat Function

There *is* one alternative to **OpenFile**, but it doesn't offer the same flexibility. The **_lcreat** function is useful only for creating new files or overwriting existing files. Here's its prototype:

```
HFILE _lcreat (LPCSTR filename, int attribute)
```

The value of **attribute** can be one of the settings listed in Table 12-2.

TABLE 12-2 *Values of* **attribute**

Value	Meaning
0	Normal. File is opened for reading and writing.
1	Read-only. File is created with the read-only attribute set.
2	Hidden. File is created with the hidden attribute set.
3	System. File is created with the system attribute set.

The **_lcreat** function creates a new file or, if the file exists, truncates the file's size to 0. The file opens for reading and writing, even if the value of **attribute** is 1—in which case, the file will simply have the read-only attribute set.

The most useful thing **_lcreat** can do is create temporary files, typically in conjunction with another handy Windows file I/O function, **GetTempFileName**.

Using GetTempFileName

In most programs, you'll need to create a temporary file once in a while, and the **GetTempFileName** function offers you a standard way to do it. The function's definition looks like this:

```
int GetTempFileName (BYTE DriveLetter, LPCSTR prefix, UINT unique,
                     LPSTR tempfilename)
```

The first argument, **DriveLetter**, suggests a drive on which to create the temporary file. Normally, the value of **DriveLetter** should be zero, which tells the function to use either the first hard disk found or the drive (and directory) toward which the TEMP environment variable points.

The next parameter, **prefix**, should contain a string that will be used as the temporary file name's prefix.

The next argument, if not 0, is a number that will be appended to the temporary file name. If this argument is 0, Windows will attempt to create a unique number based on the current system time. If Windows finds a file of the same name, it will increment the number by 1 and try the name again. It's obviously faster to supply your own number, in which case, Windows makes no test is for the file's existence.

The **tempfilename** argument is a buffer into which the temporary file name will be placed. It should have a size of at least 144 bytes to accommodate the string.

By combining **_lcreat** and **GetTempFileName**, you could create a function for opening a temporary file called **OpenTempFile**:

```
HFILE OpenTempFile (UINT number)
{
    char buf[256];

    GetTempFileName (0, "t", number, buf);
    return _lcreat (buf, 0);
}
```

Now you know how to open a file under Windows, but how do you close one?

The _lclose Function

It might satisfy your sense of symmetry if you could close files under Windows with a function called **CloseFile** but, alas, no such function exists. Instead, you must use the Windows function **_lclose**. Why the underscore? Why the *l*? Another Windows mystery.

The **_lclose** function takes an **HFILE** as its single argument and returns zero if it's successful or **HFILE_ERROR** if it's not.

Reading and Writing Files Under Windows

Windows provides several functions for reading from and writing to files, as well. For files opened with **OpenFile**, you should use these functions rather than their standard C library counterparts.

Reading Files with _lread and _hread

Yet another underscore function, **_lread** reads data from a file into a buffer pointed to by a far pointer. Its prototype is:

```
UINT _lread (HFILE hf, void _huge *buffer, UINT size)
```

The function's first argument is the file handle returned by **OpenFile**. The second argument is the address of the buffer into which the file will be read, and is of type **void _huge ***. You might think that since this is a huge pointer, you could read as many bytes into the buffer as you'd like. Wrong! Although the pointer is a huge type, the function can read a maximum of 65,535 bytes: the maximum value of the **size** parameter. If you'd like to read more than 65,535 bytes of a file, you need to use the **_hread** function:

```
long _hread (HFILE hf, void _huge *buffer, long size)
```

You might ask why you would even care to use the **_lread** function, given that **_hread** can do the same thing and more. The **_hread** function was new in Windows 3.1; prior to that, you had to write your own code for reading files larger than 64k.

Both functions return the actual number of bytes read or **HFILE_ERROR** if there's an error. If the number of bytes read is less than the number of bytes specified in **size**, then you have reached the end of the file.

Writing Files with _lwrite and _hwrite

The file writing functions are, symmetrically enough, **_lwrite** and **_hwrite**. Their prototypes are:

```
UINT _lwrite (HFILE hf, const void _huge *buffer, UINT size)
long _hwrite (HFILE hf, const void _huge *buffer, long size)
```

Like their equivalent reading functions, **_lwrite** and **_hwrite** return the number of bytes written to the file or **HFILE_ERROR**, if there's an error. If the **size** argument is zero, the file is expanded or truncated to the current file-pointer position.

A simple piece of code for copying one file to another using a small buffer would look like this:

```
UINT cbRead;

do {
    cbRead = _lread(hfReadFile, pbBuf, 2048);
    _lwrite(hfTempFile, pbBuf, cbRead);
} while (cbRead != 2048);
```

Using Initialization Files

Most programs need to store certain operating parameters, options, and user preferences in a file so that the program can use them each time it runs. Games are certainly no exception. Windows provides a useful set of functions for storing and retrieving settings from initialization files in a uniform way.

The Structure of an .INI File

The Windows convention for naming the files that are used to store a program's settings is to give them an .INI extension. These files contain simple ASCII data records

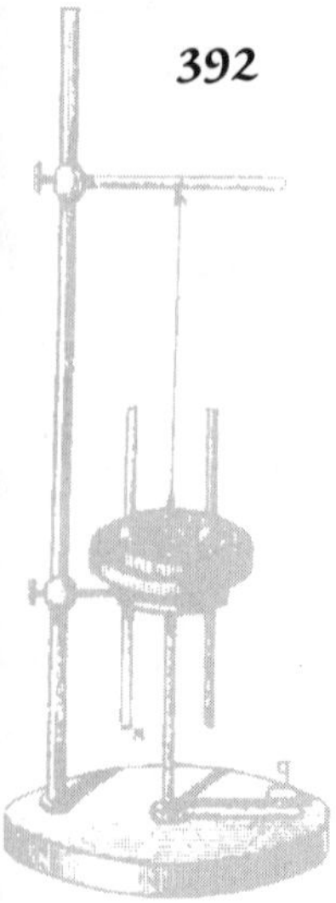

with a structure enforced by the functions used to access them. The structure looks something like this:

```
[Section1]
Entry1=<value>
Entry2=<value>
.
.
.
[Section2]
AnotherEntry=<value>
ThisHereSetting=<value>
.
.
.
```

Sections are delimited by text within square brackets. The entries within a section take the form of a string, an equal sign, and another string (tag/value pairs, if you're a database type). This is a very flexible and simple way to store settings, and has the added advantage of being easily readable by humans because it's an ASCII file.

Windows provides a set of functions for adding sections and entries so that you don't have to write your own parser. These are called the profile functions, presumably because people once called these files *profiles* rather than *initialization* files.

There are two sets of profile functions: one for reading and writing to the user's WIN.INI file only, and one for reading and writing to a file of any specified name.

`GetProfileString` *and* `GetPrivateProfileString`

You use these two functions to get a value from WIN.INI or a specified initialization file, respectively. The only difference between them is that **`GetPrivateProfileString`** has an extra argument in which to specify the file name:

```
int GetProfileString (LPCSTR section, LPCSTR entry, LPCSTR default,
                      LPSTR buf, int size)

int GetPrivateProfileString (LPCSTR section, LPCSTR entry,
                             LPCSTR default, LPSTR buf,
                             int size, LPCSTR filename)
```

The first argument specifies the section of the profile from which the entry will be chosen. This is a case-insensitive string containing the name of the section (no brackets). The next argument is the case-insensitive entry name. If no such entry exists, then Windows will copy the value in the next argument, **`default`**, into **`buf`** instead of whatever appears on the right of the equal sign. The **`size`** argument specifies the size, in bytes, of the buffer so that Windows doesn't overwrite it. The return value of the function is the number of bytes copied into **buf**, including the terminating null character.

For example, if you wanted to retrieve the name of the file in use for the Windows desktop's wallpaper, the call would look like this:

```
char buf[256];

GetProfileString ("desktop", "wallpaper", "", buf, 256);
```

If the **entry** parameter is NULL, the functions retrieve all the entries for a section, placing them in **buf**. Each entry is zero-terminated, and the final entry has a double-zero terminator. This allows entries to be created without the prior knowledge of the reader code. Typically, you use one section as a "master index" to other sections whose names are stored as entries in the master section. Code for reading an .INI file so constructed could look something like this:

```
char buf[1000];
char entrybuf[100];
char *p;
.
.
.
GetPrivateProfileString ("Master", NULL, "", buf, sizeof(buf),
                         "myprog.ini");
p = buf;
while (*p) {
    // Get each entry, use as a section name,
    // and look up known parts of the section.
    GetPrivateProfileString (p, "Entry1", "", entrybuf,
                             sizeof(entrybuf), "myprog.ini");
    // Parse the value.
    .
    .
    .
    GetPrivateProfileString (p, "Entry2", "", entrybuf,
                             sizeof(entrybuf), "myprog.ini");
    .
    .
    .
    // Get the next section name.
    p += lstrlen(p) + 1;
}
// No more entries...
.
.
.
```

Figure 12-1 shows the process of looking up the entries from an .INI file.

FIGURE 12-1

Looking up selected entries from an .INI file

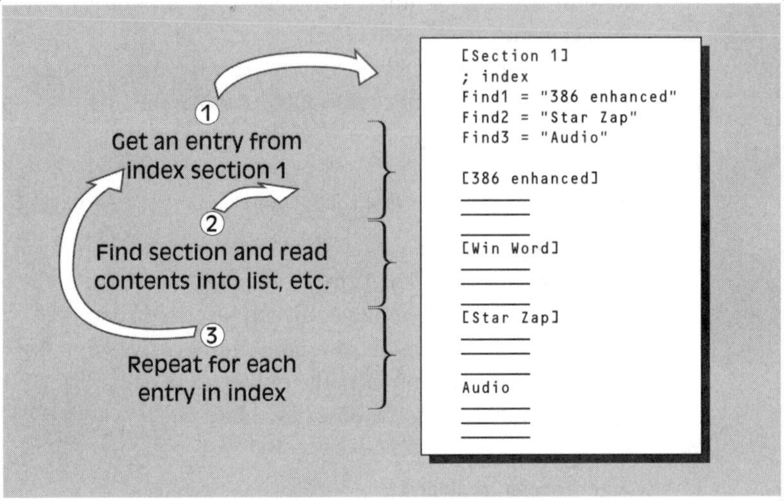

There is an equivalent pair of functions for writing profile strings, as well, of course.

WriteProfileString *and* WritePrivateProfileString

These functions look a lot like their "get" counterparts, but without a return buffer:

```
BOOL WriteProfileString (LPCSTR section, LPCSTR entry,
                         LPCSTR string)

BOOL WritePrivateProfileString (LPCSTR section, LPCSTR entry,
                                LPCSTR string, LPCSTR filename)
```

When writing a profile string, you retain the case of the section, entry, and string. The write functions automatically create a new section if one doesn't exist (remember that the test for existence is case-insensitive) to accommodate a new entry. In fact, the **WritePrivateProfileString** function will create the whole *file* if it doesn't exist on the first call to create a profile string. This is quite useful: If you always use default values for **GetPrivateProfileString** in your code, and then save the .INI file settings whenever they change, you never have to include a "prebuilt" .INI file with your program—the code will create one with all the default values whenever it needs to read and save a value. A good way to do this is to build a string table (or user-defined resource) in the resource file that contains all the entries and their default values so that they can be easily changed if necessary. Then, each time one of the settings is changed, the value should be written back to the .INI file with **WritePrivateProfileString**.

Integer Reading

Just for convenience, Windows includes the **GetProfileInt** and **GetPrivateProfileInt** functions:

```
UINT GetProfileInt (LPCSTR section, LPCSTR entry, int default)
UINT GetPrivateProfileInt (LPCSTR section, LPCSTR entry,
                           int default, LPCSTR filename)
```

These functions return an unsigned integer that represents the number on the right side of the equal sign for the given entry and section. This number must be in the range 0 to 32,767 (for 16-bit Windows); therefore, you cannot use these functions to retrieve negative numbers. There also are no corresponding write functions, so you must do your own formatting to store an integer.

One important note about .INI files you read from and write to with the profile functions: They cannot exceed 64k in total size. This isn't usually a limitation, given the type and quantity of data normally stored in them.

Summary

File handling under Windows is much like file handling under DOS, except that a few names change and there are some additional useful functions. There's a standard way to create temporary files with **GetTempFileName**, and **OpenFile** supports all the sharing attributes supported under various Windows networks.

Windows also supplies functions for reading and writing profile strings with **GetPrivateProfileString** and **WritePrivateProfileString**. These functions provide a uniform way of storing and retrieving program-initialization options and other stored program settings.

Most DOS file I/O functions will work under Windows, but it is important you use the Windows-specific functions to ensure future portability. After all, there's no guarantee that future versions of Windows will run on top of DOS!

13

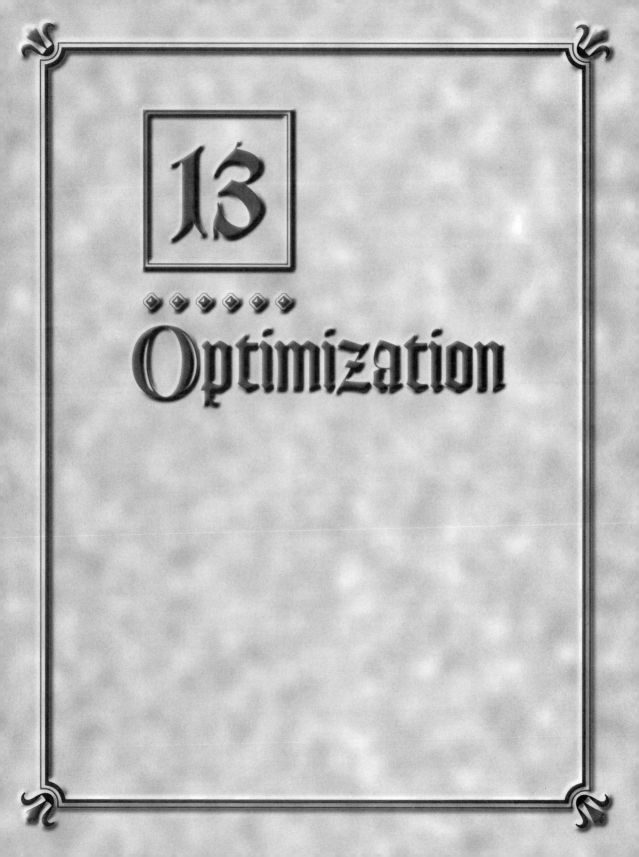

Optimization

come si debbe fare le manovelle le quali si movano e si alza
e i gran pesi [illegible]
[illegible] nella manovella [illegible]
forza e più [illegible]

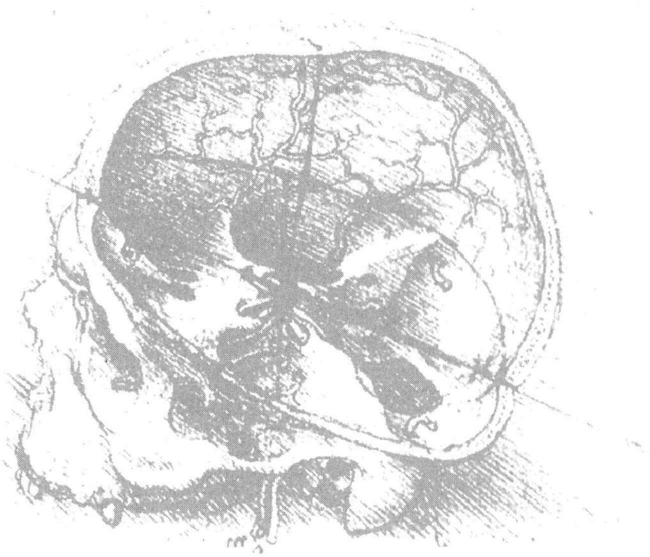

13

Optimization

The process of optimizing a game program can have several dimensions. It can include optimizing the program to work within certain hardware restrictions, like a lack of floating-point processing or low memory configurations. It can also simply mean increasing the speed of the program. Usually, optimization has an inevitable tradeoff: You can often get more speed by using more memory, and you can often make something consume less memory by sacrificing speed.

In this chapter, you'll learn about how to identify the parts of a program that can benefit from optimization, and also a little about how you can sometimes "cheat" by using assembly language functions to gain speed while preserving memory.

Principles of Optimization

In a game program, speed is king. The faster certain key elements of a game run, the better the simulation or experience, generally speaking. Although a game could in theory run *too* fast for the user to keep up, the trend toward complexity and richness guarantees that there will never be enough computer horsepower for this to happen.

The key principle of optimization is knowing exactly what parts of a program consume the most time, and which of those parts matter the most. As simple as it sounds, this understanding can be deceptively difficult to come by. Game programs often have a high degree of variability in the way they handle data, and this variability makes benchmarking hard.

The first task in the optimization process is to create a test case that represents a typical user session—a run of the game (or key parts of it) that is as close as possible to what a user would actually experience. Pressing the limits of the game can give an indication of how linear the optimization problem is. In other words, does the game slow down exponentially with the addition of, say, more sprites, or does it slow down linearly? Often, you can gain insight into these dynamic characteristics only through experimentation.

Once you have a feel for the dynamics of the game and how it handles progressively greater amounts of data, you then need to understand its critical path.

Finding the Critical Path

Games often have very obvious places in which you can begin looking for areas where optimization will yield the most benefits. A computer game does two basic things: It *computes* how the screen should look, and then it *displays* the results. The first thing

FIGURE 13-1

The critical path of a flight simulator

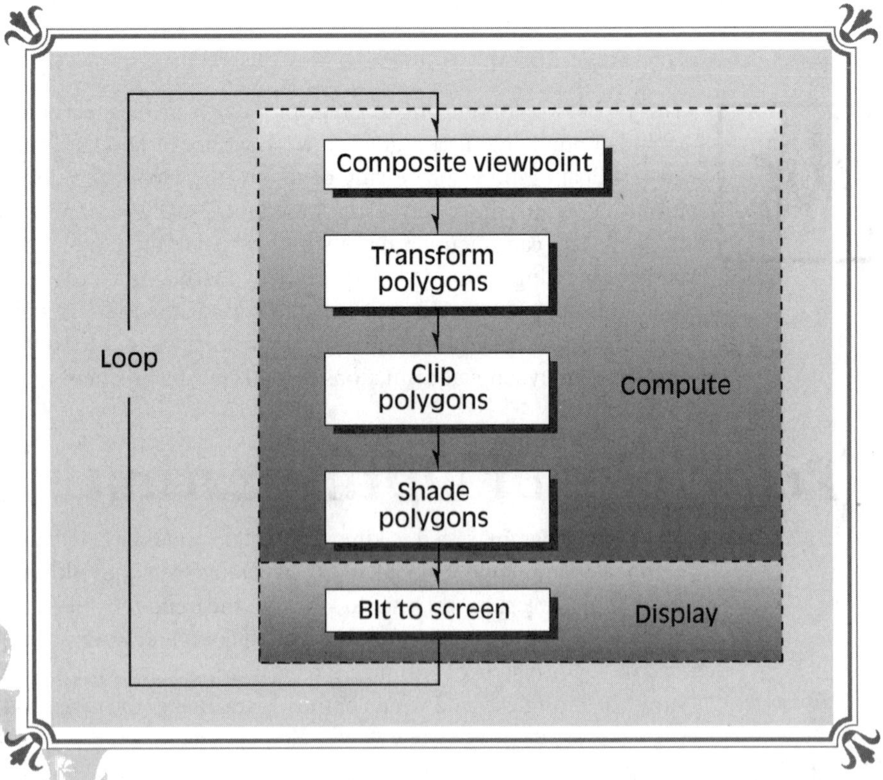

to know about your game is which of those two things takes longer—this is the *critical path.*

In a rendering-based game (like a flight simulator), the compute step is very complex—usually, it must render 3D polygons onto a two-dimensional bitmap, which is Blted to the screen in the display step (see Figure 13-1). If the compute step *always* takes longer than the display step, then that's obviously where you should spend most of your time optimizing.

Of course, there may come a point where the two steps trade places in terms of total processing time. On an extremely slow display device, for example, the rendering step may actually be faster than the display step. This may occur because you've optimized the rendering so much that displaying the results on the screen actually takes longer than computing what the results should be. Or, it may occur because the amount of data being rendered is small, moving the display step onto the critical path. Figure 13-2 illustrates this concept.

When determining the difference between the compute step and the display step, what you're really interested in is the *ratio* between computing and displaying. Suppose, for example, that the display step takes only ten percent of the total time for a given benchmark. This means that if the display step were infinitely faster, your game

FIGURE 13-2

The critical path: from the compute step to the display step

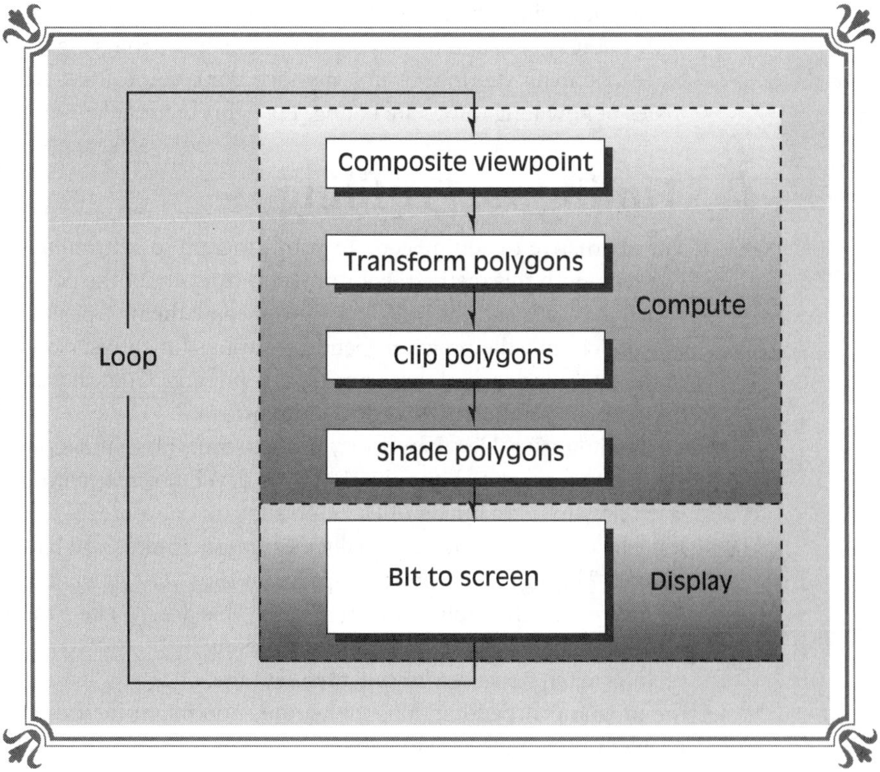

would speed up by only ten percent (see Figure 13-3). Clearly, this would not be a productive way to spend your time.

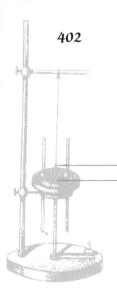

The question is, how do you know where to start?

Gross Timing Estimates

One of the easiest ways to determine how much time a program spends in its displaying vs. computing processes is to time a benchmark of the entire program, then turn off the display step and time the benchmark again. (The display step is usually easy to identify—it starts wherever the final Blt to the screen occurs.) Simply comment out the Blt call.

Even with WinG, there's not a whole lot you can do about the speed of the actual Blt, because it's handled in the display driver and display hardware, over which you have no control. If your game goes ten times faster after you comment out the Blt, then there's only one way to speed up the game. You have to Blt less—either less frequently or to a smaller area. If this is not feasible, then chances are you've reached maximum speed for the given hardware configuration.

You can easily time parts of your program with Windows' timer functions. In Chapter 9, you learned about the **timeGetTime** function that returns the number of milliseconds since the user started Windows. By wrapping key portions of your code with **timeGetTime** and displaying the results in a debugging window (or on the title bar of the main window, or in a message box), you can get some pretty quick estimates of how long things are taking. I use this method later in the chapter.

Timing vs. Profiling

The alternative to adding code to your program to get timing information is to use *profiling*. With this method, your program runs under the control of a profiling tool, which logs calls and the time it takes to execute them. A profile report can show you how much time the program spends in various functions, along with the percentage of the total time each of these functions represents. You can tune a profile to include only certain function calls, or the entire program.

Profiling is trickier than it may at first seem. First, most profiling tools for Windows aren't integrated into the Windows development environment, so you have to learn how to use a bunch of DOS tools for this purpose. Second, the results of profiling an entire program are usually meaningless unless you have some idea of where to look. Third, under a profiler a program runs very slowly because the profiler has to intercept all the profiled function calls. This doesn't affect the accuracy of the profile, but it can make the process rather tedious.

In general, it's easiest to call **timeGetTime**, once you have a rough idea of where the program is spending most of its time. You might then run the program under a profiler to fine-tune certain parts.

FIGURE 13-3

The critical path ratio

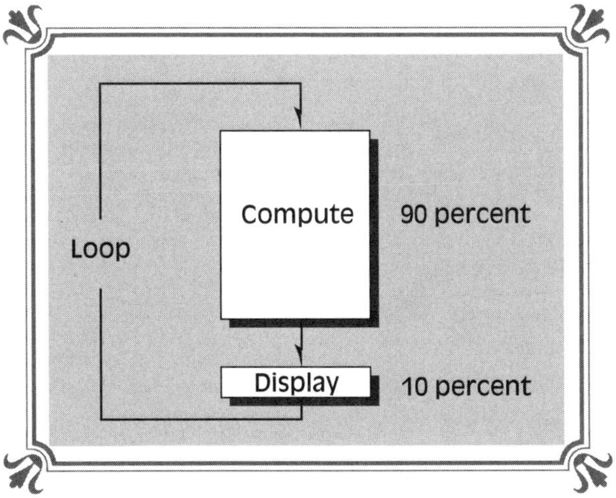

With these basic principles in mind, let's see what you can do to speed up the sprite engine. We'll start with the big time-consumers, then move on to smaller conquests.

Optimizing the Sprite Engine

The sprite engine we developed in Chapter 10 could definitely benefit from optimization. I've done some optimizing already—dirty-rectangle updating is really performance optimization based on the assumption that it is always slower to write pixels than it is to compute intersecting rectangles. To prove this theorem, let's do some gross timing of the sprite engine, then play with various optimization techniques to see the results.

The Benchmark

The first thing that you need in order to get accurate results is a repeatable benchmark. For the sprite engine, you can use Load Scene and load the SPRITES.INI scene that specifies several sprites and their movements.

SPRITES.INI gives us a reliable starting point, so the next thing to do is decide how long the program should run—in "animation cycles"—for the benchmark. Recall that the main animation loop is in **`UpdatePositions`** in DRAW.C. This is a very convenient place to put a timing test, by going through the loop a predetermined number of times, then displaying the time it took to do so. The technique I use here is a little different from what I outlined earlier—we want to know the total time consumed by several iterations of the whole **`UpdatePositions`** function, not just the time consumed by some arbitrary set of functions. The code is a little simpler in this case because it can all be in one place—at the beginning of the **UpdatePositions** function. A couple of static variables and a few lines of code are all we need:

```
//
// Update sprite positions.
// (Main animation function)
//
#define TIMINGS
void UpdatePositions()
{
    PSPRITE pSprite;
    BOOL bChanged = FALSE;
    RECT rcPos;

#ifdef TIMINGS
    static DWORD dwLast=0, iCount=0;

    // Do some gross timings over 500 update cycles.
    if (!dwLast)
        dwLast = timeGetTime();

    if (iCount++ == 500L) {
        Message(0, "Time: %ld", timeGetTime()-dwLast);
        iCount = dwLast = 0;
    }
#endif
    pSprite = G.pSpriteList;
    while (pSprite) {

        if (pSprite->vx || pSprite->vy) {

            //
            // Add the old (current) position
            // of the sprite to the redraw-rectangle list.
            .
            .
            .
```

By defining TIMINGS, the code displays a message box after 500 iterations through the main animation loop. The message box displays the total number of milliseconds required to perform the 500 iterations.

The value 500 should be sufficient for the given data set (in SPRITES.INI) to perform several sprite movements that include intersections; this is, after all, where the dirty-rectangle optimization performs its magic. Don't make the mistake of thinking that a single trip through the loop takes 1/500 of the total time for 500 loops. Although each loop performs the same functions, the data changes, so the loops may take different amounts of time. For this reason, you'll get a much more accurate measurement if you perform the test over a long period of time rather than a short one.

A little helper function for displaying the timing information, **Message**, is defined in MAIN.C as

```
//
// Show a message box.
//

UINT cdecl Message(UINT uiBtns, LPSTR lpFormat, ...)
{
    char buf[256];

    wvsprintf(buf, lpFormat, (LPSTR)(&lpFormat+1));
    MessageBeep(uiBtns ? uiBtns : MB_ICONEXCLAMATION);
    return (UINT) MessageBox(G.hwndMain,
                             buf,
                             G.szAppName,
                             uiBtns ? uiBtns : MB_OK|MB_ICONEXCLAMATION);
}
```

This is a simple function for displaying a formatted string within a message box.

Dirty-Rectangle-Merging Optimization

Let's try a little experiment. In Chapter 10, you learned about dirty-rectangle updating. The assumption was that maintaining a dirty-rectangle list containing all the portions of the window that need updating, merging the rectangles, and displaying the results would save a lot of time because it would minimize the number of pixels being copied to the screen. Let's see exactly how much time it saves.

Run the program a couple of times with TIMINGS defined to make sure the results are relatively consistent. Make sure that the sprite engine is the only program running. Now comment out the piece of code that merges all the dirty rectangles in the **Render** function of DRAW.C and recompile.

```
    .
    .
    .
    if (bUpdate == NO_UPDATE) return;

    //
    // Make sure there is a background DIB and DC.
    //

    if (!G.pdibBkGnd || !G.hdcWinG) return;

    //
    // Merge the draw-rectangle list and walk it, doing renders.
    //

    //MergeDrawRectList(&DrawList);
```

continued on next page

continued from previous page

```
//
// Find the end of the sprite list.
//

pLastSprite = G.pSpriteList;
if (pLastSprite) {
    while (pLastSprite->pNext) pLastSprite = pLastSprite->pNext;
}
.
.
.
```

Now run the benchmark again. Yikes! Big difference. On my 486/66, it took about 11 seconds to run through the 500 iterations of the **UpdatePositions** loop when the redraw list was being merged, and almost 29 seconds when the line was commented out. This shows that combining the dirty rectangles of the redraw list really does save a lot of time, even though the **MergeDrawRectList** function does a more or less n-squared walk of the list.

Of course, the results depend partly on how many sprite intersections occur in the 500 iterations—if the sprites don't intersect much, then the dirty-rectangle merging will have less of an effect. Then again, think about where all those dirty rectangles come from—not only from intersecting sprites, but also from the starting and ending positions of *each* sprite as it moves across the screen. Unless the sprites are moving a distance greater than their size in each loop, the starting and ending sprite positions are going to intersect, which guarantees that the merging operation will at least halve the number of rectangles (Figure 13-4 shows how the starting and ending

FIGURE 13-4

Sprite starting and ending positions

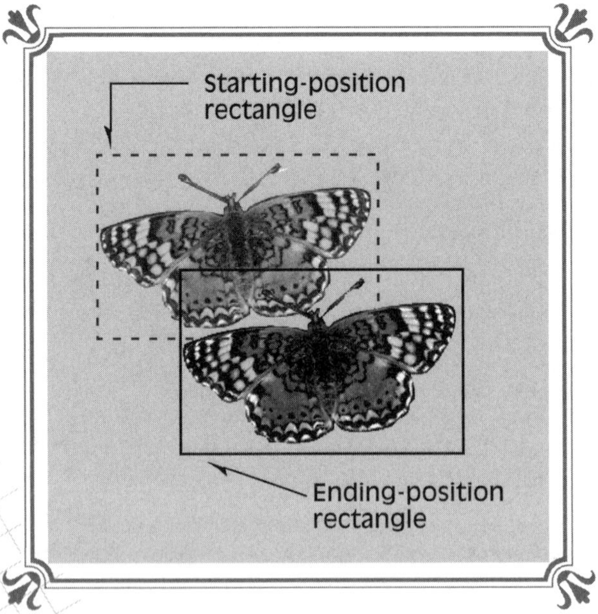

positions intersect). The merging operation speeds things up by a factor of almost three—indicating that there must also be several sprite-to-sprite intersections in the benchmark, as well.

It's nice to know that dirty-rectangle optimization actually works as expected. But now that you have a basic understanding of how to time the `UpdatePositions` loop, let's move on to finding other time-critical parts of the sprite engine. (Don't forget to "uncomment" the `MergeDrawRectList` function first!)

Blt Speed Testing

To find out how much time the sprite engine spends actually writing to the screen, you need only comment out one line of code. In the `Paint` function in DRAW.C, comment out the Blt:

```
.
.
.
if (G.hpalCurrent) {
    hOldPal = SelectPalette(hDC, G.hpalCurrent, 0);
    RealizePalette(hDC);
}

// Do the Blt!
//WinGBitBlt (hDC, xd, yd, w, h, G.hdcWinG, xs, ys);

if (G.bShowUpdateRects)
    DrawRect(hDC, xd, yd, xd+w, yd+h, MAGENTA);
.
.
.
```

Run the benchmark again. Depending on your hardware configuration, you may see the time drop a little bit, but probably not by much. On my 486/66 with a moderately slow display adapter, the original time was about 11 seconds; after removing the Blt, it was a little less than 10 seconds. Not a very big difference.

What does this tell us? Well, we can deduce that the sprite engine doesn't spend most of its time Blting. The time required by `WinGBitBlt` is about 1 second—a little more than 10 percent of the total time. That means that even though we can't optimize `WinGBitBlt`, there is still plenty of room for improvement. Figure 13-5 shows the relationship between `WinGBitBlt` and the rest of the `UpdatePositions` loop.

Finding Where the Time Goes

If `WinGBitBlt` accounts for such a small part of the total time required by `Update-Positions`, the question is, where *is* the time going? There are several ways to approach the problem.

FIGURE 13-5

`WinGBitBlt` *vs. everything else*

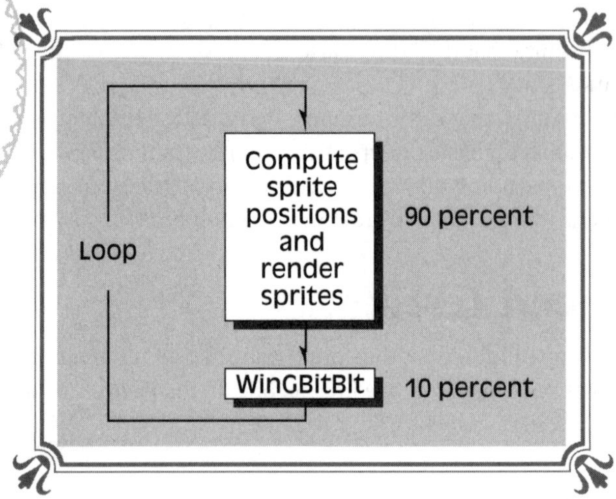

You could run a profile on all the functions in DRAW.C and see what's happening there. However, it's a bit of a painstaking exercise. First of all, the program needs to run a sufficient number of **`UpdatePositions`** cycles for the test to be meaningful, and running the program under the profiler is about ten times slower. Second, the time it takes to set up the profiler's option files—and just to learn about using the profiler!—could be a significant portion of the total time you spend optimizing the sprite engine.

But how will you know where to look if you don't use the profiler? Here's where a little experience can save you lots of time. In bitmapped-graphics programs—including games—the time virtually *always* goes to the code that actually acts on pixels. Pixels are, after all, in abundant supply. Code acting on an individual pixel or even a scan line's worth of pixels is going to consume a lot of time compared to, say, code that intersects a few rectangles or computes the new positions of the sprites. Consequently, programmers usually optimize pixel-oriented graphics in two ways: by minimizing the time spent in pixel loops, and by trying to avoid reaching pixel loops at all. Dirty-rectangle updating falls into this second category, of course.

Look at the **`UpdatePositions`** function. It walks the sprite list, and gets each sprite's rectangle. Then, it computes the new position of the sprite with a few additions and tests so that the sprite wraps around from one side of the window to the other. Finally, it calls **`Render`**, either to simply add the update rectangle or, after walking the entire sprite list, to actually update the screen. The **`Render`** function is called twice for each sprite and once again for the whole list. Obviously, **`UpdatePositions`** spends most of its time in **`Render`**, at least when the **`UPDATE_SCREEN`** flag is used, at the end of the sprite list-walking loop. (If you don't believe this or don't quite see it, try commenting out the **`Render`** at the end of the loop and watch the time drop to about 1 second!)

Now look at the Render function. When the UPDATE_SCREEN flag is set, the function walks the redraw list and copies the background and sprites to the offscreen buffer. The actual copying is done by RenderDIBBitsOffScreen and RenderSpriteOffScreen, the latter of which is a very small wrapper around the former. In turn, RenderDIBBitsOffScreen ends up calling either CopyDIBBits or TransCopyDIBBits, depending on whether the copy is to use transparent pixels (for sprites). These two functions do nothing more than copy bytes from one area of memory to another and are likely to be time-wasters.

To test these assumptions, simply comment out both CopyDIBBits and TransCopyDIBBits and run the timing test again. Suddenly, the time drops by a factor of four or five, even with the WinGBitBlt still there! This means that CopyDIBBits and TransCopyDIBBits take almost five times as long as *everything else* in the UpdatePositions loop does (Figure 13-6 illustrates this). Clearly, anything you can do to improve the speed of those two functions will dramatically affect the overall speed of the sprite engine; improvements will come back to us four- or five-fold.

There are several ways to improve the speed of CopyDIBBits and TransCopyDIBBits. The two functions are very small, so probably the best way to begin is to move them into assembly language.

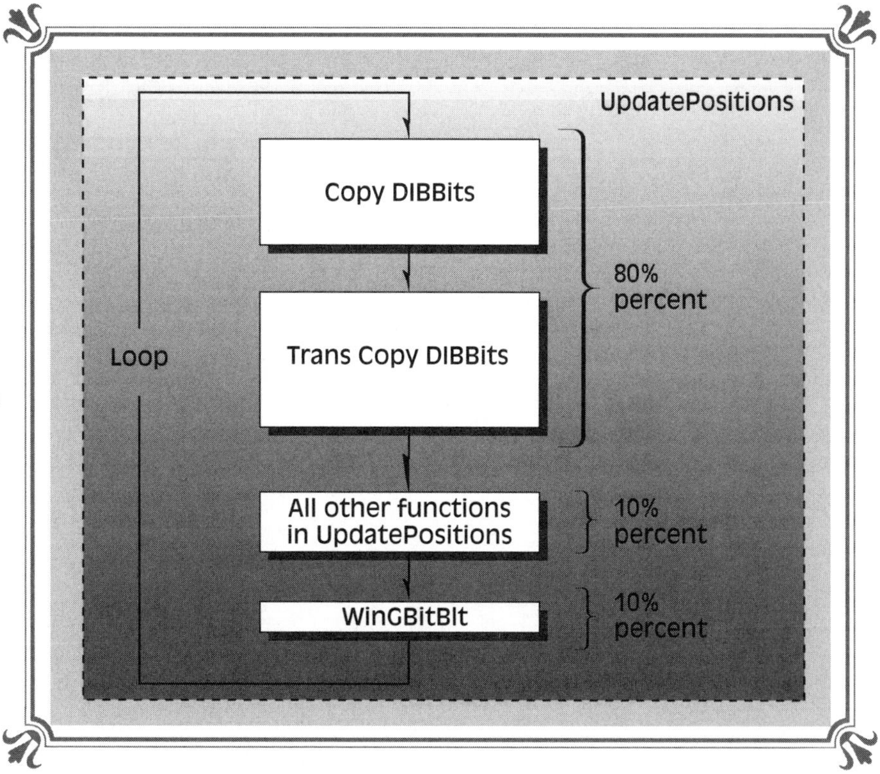

FIGURE 13-6

CopyDIBBits *and* TransCopyDIBBits *time consumption*

Using Assembly Language for the Optimization Process

There was a time when programmers had to write their game programs completely in assembly language in order to get adequate speed. There are still programmers, in fact, who believe that the more assembly language routines they can use in a program, the faster it will perform. But substituting assembly functions for C functions that aren't on the critical path is clearly a waste of time—you should use assembly language only where the code spends the most time.

Programming in Intel assembly language provides some other benefits. If you are willing to restrict your market to 80386 processors or better (this is hardly a restriction these days), then you can take advantage of 32-bit registers and instructions that are especially handy for copying blocks of memory from one place to another.

Optimizing CopyDIBBits and TransCopyDIBBits

Translating **CopyDIBBits** and **TransCopyDIBBits** to assembly language is relatively straightforward. Doing it in 32-bit assembler is a little more difficult, though it helps to use the CMACRO32.INC macro file that Microsoft provides in their SDK (it's also on the CD-ROM that comes with this book, of course).

If you're not an assembly language expert, don't worry. The functions my listings define are eminently usable, regardless of whether you understand their mechanics.

The CMACRO32.INC macro file requires that the following setup information be in the beginning of the assembly language file (FAST32.ASM):

```
;
; 32-bit code segment version of FAST16.ASM
; General technology courtesy of Todd Laney
;
; Note! CMACRO32.INC needs MASM 5.1 (or compatible).
; You would think MASM 6 would be compatible, but it isn't.
;
?PLM=1
?WIN=1
     .xlist
     include cmacro32.inc
     .list
;
; NOTE!!!! Because we are generating USE32 code, this must NOT
; be located in a code segment with USE16 code, so we put it into
; its own little segment....
;
```

```
ifndef SEGNAME
    SEGNAME equ <FAST_TEXT32>
endif

createSeg %SEGNAME, CodeSeg, word, use32, CODE

sBegin Data
sEnd Data

sBegin CodeSeg
        assumes cs,CodeSeg
        assumes ds,nothing
        assumes es,nothing
.
.
.
```

The **ifndef SEGNAME** statement is critical to the functioning of the 32-bit assembly module. As it turns out, you can't combine 32-bit code with 16-bit code in the same code segment, so you must create a separate segment. This is also important at link time (I'll cover this topic later).

The **createSeg** macro is related—it actually names and creates the separate code segment for the module. You would normally declare static data to this module between the **sBegin Data** and **sEnd Data** statements. These are macros that simplify access to the data from C. Since this module has no static data, there's nothing declared between the statements (though there should be, so that the assembler can confirm there's no data).

The **sBegin CodeSeg** macro begins declaring the stuff that goes in the code segment, starting with register assumptions. The CS register holds the address of the code segment, and the program assumes that the DS and ES registers do not point to anything meaningful when the program enters the functions defined in the code segment.

The easiest of the two functions to understand is **CopyDIBBits**, because it simply copies bytes based on a starting address, width, height, and scan-line storage width (remember that all DIBs have 4-byte aligned scan lines). Here's the listing of the function from FAST32.ASM:

```
;---------------------------------------------------------------------;
;
; CopyDIBBits
;
; Copy a block without transparency.
;
;---------------------------------------------------------------------;

cProc CopyDIBBits,<FAR, PASCAL, PUBLIC>,<>
```

continued on next page

continued from previous page

```
        ParmW   DestSelector    ; 16:32 destination pointer
        ParmD   DestOffset

        ParmD   pSource         ; Source pointer (16:16)
        ParmD   dwWidth         ; Width pixels
        ParmD   dwHeight        ; Height pixels
        ParmD   dwScanD         ; Width bytes dest
        ParmD   dwScanS         ; Width bytes source
cBegin
        push ds                 ; Save these registers.
        push esi
        push edi

        mov ecx, dwWidth        ; Width pixels into ecx
        or ecx,ecx
        jz cdb_nomore     ; Test for silly case (width = 0)

        mov edx, dwHeight       ; EDX is line counter
        or edx,edx
        jz cdb_nomore     ; Test for silly case (Height = 0)

        xor esi, esi              ; Clear esi
        lds si, pSource           ; DS:[ESI] points to source

        mov es, DestSelector    ; es:[edi] points to dest
        mov edi, DestOffset     ; as a 16:32 pointer


        sub dwScanD,ecx         ; Bias these--subtract the width
        sub dwScanS,ecx         ; bytes for the last scan line.

        mov ebx,ecx             ; Divide width bytes by 4--
        shr ebx,2               ; we want to move DWORDs for speed.

        mov eax,ecx             ; Keep the remainder in
        and eax,11b             ; eax, move bytes to finish.

        align 4
cdb_loop:
        mov ecx, ebx            ; Do it in DWORDs first.
        rep movs dword ptr es:[edi], dword ptr ds:[esi]
        mov ecx,eax             ; Now remaining bytes
        rep movs byte ptr es:[edi], byte ptr ds:[esi]

        add esi, dwScanS        ; Next scan line - source
        add edi, dwScanD        ; Next scan line - destination
        dec edx                 ; Line counter
        jnz short cdb_loop

cdb_nomore:
        pop edi                 ; Pop saved registers.
```

```
        pop esi
        pop ds
cEnd
```

Even if you don't have a lot of assembly language experience, you should be able to pick up on what's happening in the **CopyDIBBits** function (refer to Figure 13-7 for further clarification). The **ParmW** and **ParmD** statements at the beginning of the function are handy macros that CMACRO32.INC provides for passing parameters from C to the assembly function—the *W* is for WORD-size parameters and the *D* is for DWORD-size ones.

The only confusing parts are the first two parameters, **DestSelector** and **DestOffset**. The first is a WORD-length (16-bit) value, and the second is a DWORD (32-bit) value. They're loaded into **es** and **edi** with the two highlighted instructions. These two parameters represent a single pointer to the destination address—that is, the address of the first pixel of the WinG bitmap into which the source pixels will be copied. Yet the source address requires only one DWORD-length parameter and is loaded with one instruction:

```
lds si, pSource         ; DS:[ESI] point to source
```

FIGURE 13-7

How the `CopyDIBBits` *function works*

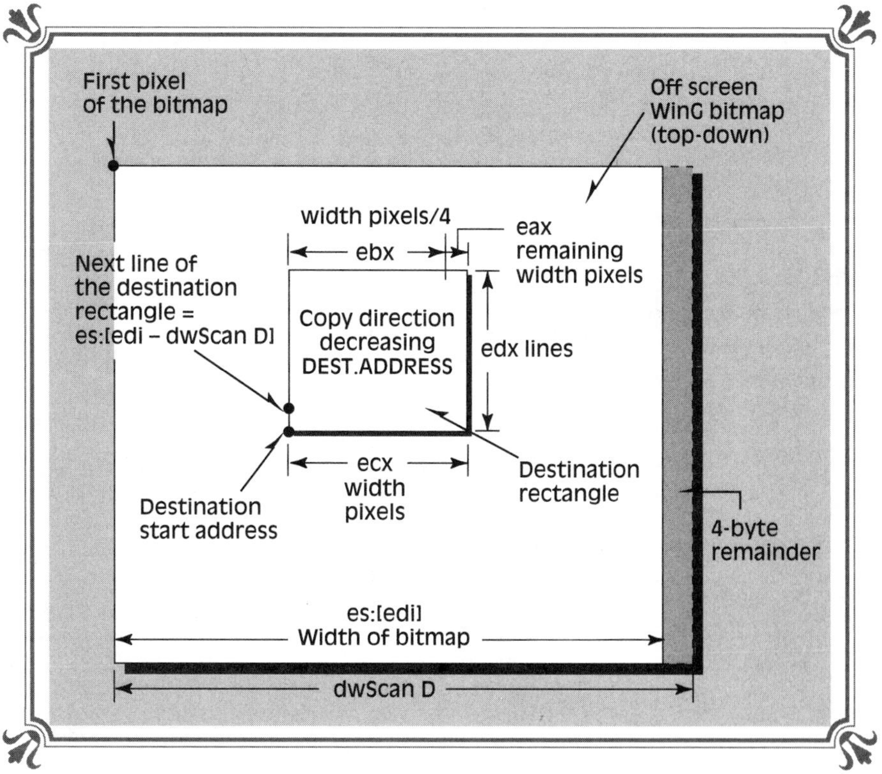

What's the deal here? Why are the source and destination parameters different sizes? The answer lies in the complexities of handling far pointers in 32-bit assembly. (Skip the following section if you've already read enough about Intel segmented memory to last a lifetime.)

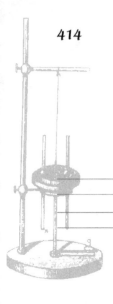

Segments, Pointers, Windows, and "48-Bit Pointers"

A far pointer under 16-bit Windows is, of course, 32 bits long. But the pointer is really two separate objects: a segment address (in the high-order 16 bits) and an offset value (in the low-order 16 bits). Although the pointer can point to a globally allocated area of memory larger than 64k, a far pointer can address really only the *first* 64k of memory—if you increment the pointer so that the offset part goes beyond 65,535, it just wraps around to 0.

Huge pointers in C work a little differently, in that the compiler and run-time environment handle the task of incrementing the segment portion of the pointer to point to the next correct segment. Windows allocates a block of contiguous segments so this all works out. This scheme creates the illusion that you have a "real" 32-bit pointer because you can increment the pointer past 64k and it will still point to the right memory address (see Figure 13-8).

But things get ugly in assembly language. In the 32-bit assembly module, you want to completely avoid changing the 16-bit segment for speed reasons. Consequently,

FIGURE 13-8

Far pointers vs. huge pointers under Windows

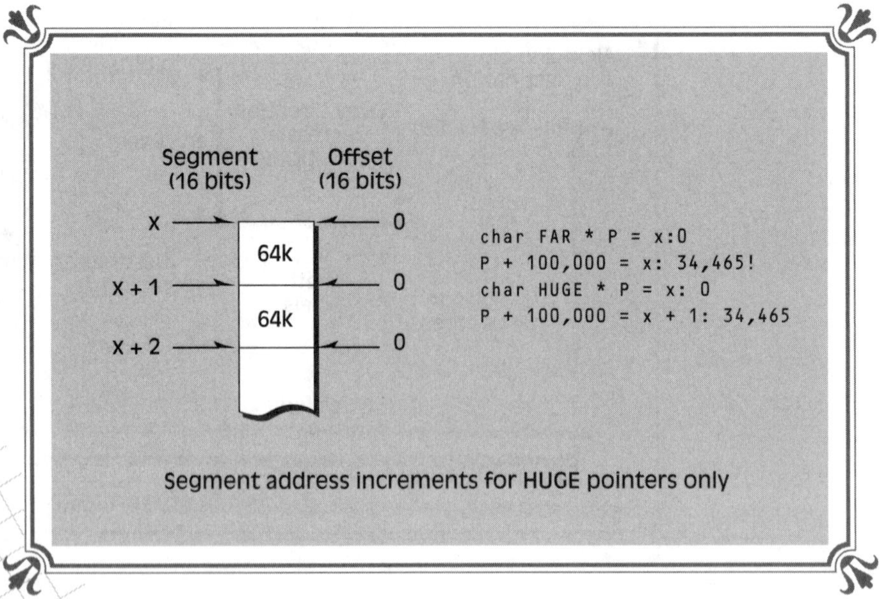

the function uses a 16-bit segment address and a *32-bit* offset value. The `lds si, pSource` statement loads the segment address into the DS register and the 16-bit offset value into the 32-bit ESI register. The rest of the code can then increment this offset value without having to change the segment register—being 32 bits long, ESI can address up to 4 GB of memory.

The problem is with the destination address and the fact that a WinG DIB can be in top-down format. The `CopyDIBBits` function copies scan lines from the *bottom up*—the natural order for bottom-up DIBs. In this case, each pass through the `cdb_loop` increments the source and destination pointers by the `dwScanS` or `dwScanD` (scan-line width) amount. For a top-down DIB, the `dwScanD` value is negative—since it's starting at the bottom scan line of the copy, it needs to *decrement* the destination pointer. If the WinG DIB is larger than 64k (highly likely), then it would also be likely for a starting pixel address to be more than 64k beyond the starting address of the DIB. Loading the start address into ES:[EDI] the same way you loaded the source address (with `les di, pDest`) would result in EDI having a value less than 65,536—the offset portion of a huge pointer is still only 16 bits. When this value is decremented below 0, EDI simply wraps it to 4,294,967,295—leaving the segment value the same and causing the code to generate a protection fault (see Figure 13-9).

A huge pointer handled solely in C would work fine, but the whole point of using 32-bit code is that it enables you to avoid all the segment calculation required in huge pointers. As a result, you must pass in the starting address of the WinG DIB as a separate segment address and offset—the latter of which is held in a 32-bit DWORD.

FIGURE 13-9

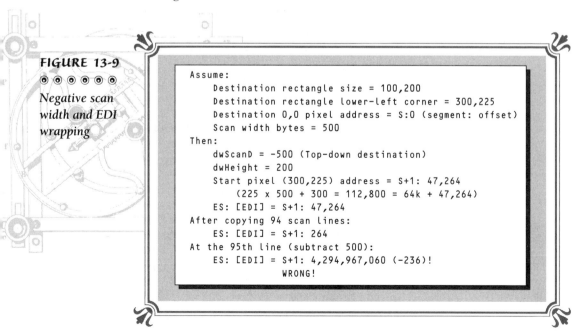

Negative scan width and EDI wrapping

```
Assume:
    Destination rectangle size = 100,200
    Destination rectangle lower-left corner = 300,225
    Destination 0,0 pixel address = S:0 (segment: offset)
    Scan width bytes = 500
Then:
    dwScanD = -500 (Top-down destination)
    dwHeight = 200
    Start pixel (300,225) address = S+1: 47,264
        (225 x 500 + 300 = 112,800 = 64k + 47,264)
    ES: [EDI] = S+1: 47,264
After copying 94 scan lines:
    ES: [EDI] = S+1: 264
At the 95th line (subtract 500):
    ES: [EDI] = S+1: 4,294,967,060 (-236)!
                WRONG!
```

Then the assembly function can happily decrement the offset portion without fear of wrapping.

If you're sitting there scratching your head and thinking, "Is all this really necessary?"—don't worry about it. Just accept that you have to use a "48-bit pointer" (16-bit segment, 32-bit offset) to make it all work out.

There's no problem for the source bitmap, because source bitmaps are *always* bottom-up DIBs—they're DIBs loaded from files, which are always in bottom-up format. Therefore, the value in ESI will always increment, never decrement. Even if the starting pixel address is more than 64k from the starting address of the DIB, the segment value will still be valid and ESI will have no problem incrementing up to the address of the last pixel of the DIB.

The next question is, how do you get a 48-bit pointer from a far or huge pointer? Fortunately, it turns out to be quite easy.

The GetWinGPixelAddress Function

The need for 48-bit pointers arises only for WinG DIBs, so you must create a special function to return a 48-bit pixel address. First, take a look at the vanilla function (in DIB.C) that returns the source pixel address, **GetDIBPixelAddress**:

```
HPSTR GetDIBPixelAddress(PDIB pDIB, int x, int y)
{
    HPSTR p;
    long lWidth;

    //
    // Make sure it's in range. If it is not, return zero.
    //

    if ((x < 0)
    || (y < 0)
    || (x >= DIB_WIDTH(pDIB))
    || (y >= DIB_HEIGHT(pDIB))) {
        dprintf1("Attempt to get out of range pixel addr");
        return NULL;
    }

    //
    // Calculate the scan-line storage width.
    //

    lWidth = DIB_STORAGEWIDTH(pDIB);

    ASSERT(lWidth <= DIB_WIDTH(pDIB) + 3);
    ASSERT(lWidth >= DIB_WIDTH(pDIB));

    p = (HPSTR) DIB_PBITS(pDIB);
    p += (long)(DIB_HEIGHT(pDIB)-y-1) * lWidth + (long)x;
```

```
    return p;
}
```

The essential calculation is the last one, the **p+=** statement. Since **p** is a huge pointer, this works fine in C.

The **GetWinGPixelAddress** function needs to do things a little differently. Here's its definition:

```
void GetWinGPixelAddress(PDIB pDIB, int x, int y,
                         LPVOID pbits, WORD *seg,  DWORD *off)
{
    DWORD off1;
    WORD seg1;
    long lWidth;
    BOOL TopDown = (DIB_HEIGHT(pDIB) < 0) ? TRUE : FALSE;
    int Height = abs(DIB_HEIGHT(pDIB));

    //
    // Make sure it's in range. If it is not, return zero.
    //

    if ((x < 0)
    || (y < 0)
    || (x >= DIB_WIDTH(pDIB))
    || (y >= Height)) {
        dprintf1("Attempt to get out of range pixel addr");
        return;
    }

    //
    // Calculate the scan-line storage width.
    //

    lWidth = DIB_STORAGEWIDTH(pDIB);

    ASSERT(lWidth <= DIB_WIDTH(pDIB) + 3);
    ASSERT(lWidth >= DIB_WIDTH(pDIB));

    *seg = SELECTOROF(pbits);
    *off = (DWORD)OFFSETOF(pbits);

    if (TopDown)
        *off += (long)y * lWidth + (long)x;
    else
        *off += (long)(Height-y-1) * lWidth + (long)x;

}
```

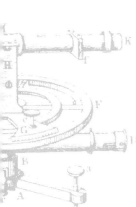

First off, the function doesn't return a value, but assigns the return value to two of the new arguments, the pointers **seg** and **off**. Also note that there's an argument specifically for the bits of the DIB because a WinG bitmap's bits can't follow the header, as you recall from Chapter 9.

The **SELECTOROF** and **OFFSETOF** macros are defined in WINDOWS.H as:

```
#define SELECTOROF(lp)       HIWORD(lp)
#define OFFSETOF(lp)         LOWORD(lp)
```

Note that because a WinG bitmap might have the bottom-up format, the code has to branch in order to perform the correct calculation. As you can see, the calculation affects only the offset portion of the "48-bit pointer." Since this is a DWORD, the numbers will never be out of range (see Figure 13-10).

If you lived through that explanation, congratulations. Understanding the vagaries of Intel segmented-memory addressing is no small feat, and you've just gone through the proverbial initiation by fire. If you still don't get it, you can either reread the whole thing again and again until you do, or forget it all—the important point is that it *works*, and works *fast*.

Back to the assembly language module for a moment. The **TransCopyDIBBits** function is quite a bit more complex, because it has to look at *every single pixel* to determine whether it's transparent. Normally, this would require a test and branch at every pixel, which is a rudely slow operation on virtually every known processor. To optimize things a little further, the assembly language implementation of **TransCopyDIBBits** tests runs of four pixels, then branches only if there's a transition from transparent to opaque or vice versa. Rather than printing the whole listing here, I'll leave it to you to peruse the source in FAST32.ASM (it's on the CD-ROM in the SPRITES directory with the rest of the source). The 48-bit destination pointer stuff is exactly the same as it is for **CopyDIBBits**.

FIGURE 13-10

Bottom-up vs. top-down DIB address calculation

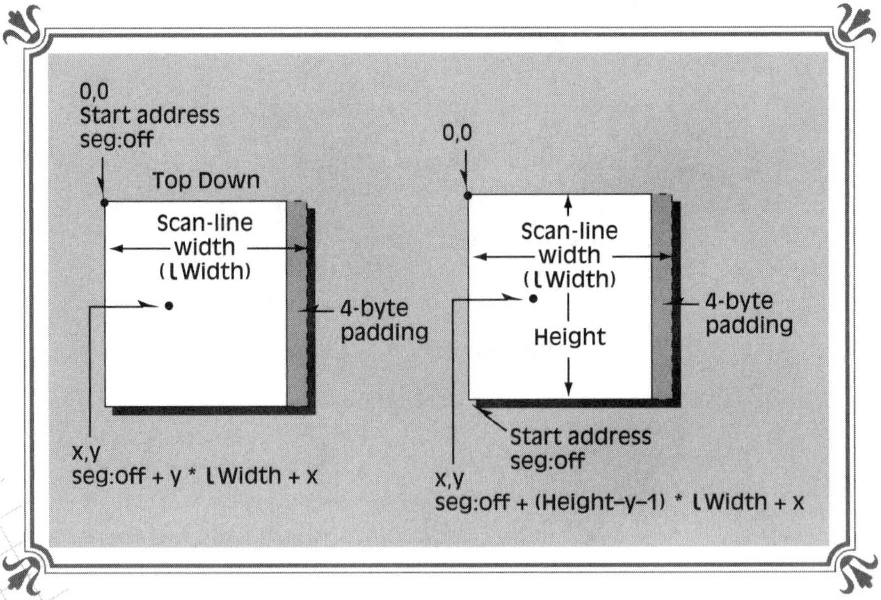

Build It and Go

Besides adding the `GetWinGPixelAddress` function to look up the starting pixel address of the WinG DIB, you must add new function prototypes for the assembly language versions of `CopyDIBBits` and `TransCopyDIBBits`, because their parameters are now different (the destination pointers are 48-bit ones). To make the changes both obvious and easy to compare, I've put them all between `#ifdef FAST32` statements in the source. If `FAST32` is defined, the assembly language functions (and their supporting C counterparts) are used; if not, the slow C functions are used. The changes are all in DRAW.C, DIB.C, and GLOBAL.H. In case you don't have a compatible assembler, I've included the object file FAST32.OBJ. You need to add FAST32.OBJ to your project or make file, depending on your development environment.

The Linking Trick: Avoiding GPF

There's one more change that you must make in order to be able to use the assembly functions in FAST32.ASM. You must tell the linker not to pack multiple code segments together, via the /NOPACKCODE switch (this is the switch for the Microsoft linker; if you are using a different development environment, check your documentation for the appropriate switch). By default, the linker packs multiple code segments into one, which will cause a GP fault in the case of the 32-bit assembly functions. It's not enough just to declare a new code segment in the source; the linker has to be informed, as well. It'll drive you just about crazy if you forget to add this option because the code will cause a GP fault in the assembly module and you'll have no clue as to why.

Timing the Changes

So how do the new functions perform? Run the program with `TIMINGS` and `FAST32` defined, and you should see the speed improve by as much as a factor of four. By commenting out the same parts of the code as you did earlier in the chapter, you'll begin to get a feel for how much room for improvement remains. It's likely you'll find that other optimization targets are much less well-defined than `CopyDIBBits` and `TransCopyDIBBits`, meaning that time is being spent more or less equally across a number of functions. Optimizing any one of these functions will produce only small gains in performance—performance that, as I mentioned earlier, is ultimately limited by the speed of `WinGBitBlt`.

At some point, it becomes necessary to get more exact timing information—how long does it take certain *functions* to perform? An easy way to get approximate times is by using a couple of static DWORDs and the `timeGetTime` function. By bracketing some function calls with the following code, you can get a pretty close estimate of how much time the calls take:

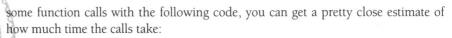

```
static DWORD TS=0, TC=0;
.
.
.
// Get the time.
TS = timeGetTime();

    FunctionCall (....
    .
    .
    .
    AnotherCall (...
    .
    .
    .
// Add up the time.
TC += (timeGetTime()-TS);
.
.
.
```

Let's use this method to find other time "holes" in the sprite engine.

First, we should find out exactly how much more room there is for improvement. The easiest way to do this is to comment out code that we can't do anything about—like `WinGBitBlt`—or that has been pretty well optimized already, like `CopyDIBBits` and `TransCopyDIBBits`. If you comment out all three of those functions, the total time drops from about 4 seconds to a little over 1 second. This means that the `UpdatePositions` loop still spends some 25 percent of its time doing other things. What are they?

At this point, it starts to become impractical to keep commenting out code and taking timings. Up until now, the only code that has been commented out is code that has no side effects—that is, by commenting it out, we won't change the data actually being computed (just the data that is displayed). For example, when we commented out the `MergeDrawRectList` function, the time actually *increased* because a side effect of `MergeDrawRectList` is that it decreases the number of rectangles displayed. But the `MergeDrawRectList` function must take *some* time to do its job. Let's measure it.

Here's how to use the previous method to wrap the `MergeDrawRectList` function with a timer:

```
// Declare a couple of timing statics for the module.
static DWORD TS=0, TC=0;
    .
    .
    .
    //
```

```
    // Merge the draw-rectangle list and walk it, doing renders.
    //
TS = timeGetTime();
    MergeDrawRectList(&DrawList);
TC += (timeGetTime() - TS);
    .
    .
    .
```

By displaying the value of **TC** with the **Message** function after displaying the overall timing information, you'll get an estimate of how much time is spent in **MergeDrawRectList**. The **Message** function should be called right next to the other **Message** function, in **UpdatePositions**:

```
#ifdef TIMINGS
    // Do some gross timings over 500 update cycles.
    if (!dwLast)
        dwLast = timeGetTime();

    if (iCount++ == 500L) {
        Message(0, "Time: %ld", timeGetTime()-dwLast);
        Message(0, "MergeDrawRectList time: %ld", TC);
        iCount = dwLast = TC = 0;
    }
#endif
```

On my machine, **MergeDrawRectList** takes only about 0.25 seconds over 500 loops—less than 25 percent of the time required by functions that we have yet to optimize. So **MergeDrawRectList** probably isn't a very good candidate for optimizing—after all, the function still needs to do its job, and it's going to take *some* time to do it.

It turns out that if you time all the functions in DRAW.C, you'll never find one that takes more than about 250 milliseconds over 500 loops of **UpdatePositions**, and they're all pretty evenly distributed. This means that optimizing any one of them *all the way to 0 seconds* will at most result in a 10 percent gain in speed. This is a worthy target, especially if you can find more than one 10 percent "hole." Unfortunately, you can get 10 percent only if you can optimize the function to do its job in *zero time*—in other words, only if you can completely eliminate it. Most of the functions take considerably less than 250 milliseconds, so this is a maximum achievable percentage. For the given data set and hardware configuration, it's going to be hard to get the sprite engine to run much faster.

Profiling—The Last Frontier

If the basic timing information you obtain from **timeGetTime** points to a widely distributed set of optimizations, then the next step is probably profiling. By this time, you should have a good idea which functions might be optimization targets, even

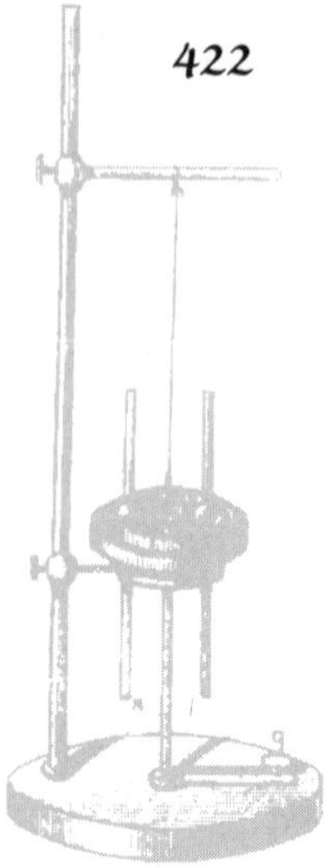

though it may not be clear which is the highest priority. This information is extremely useful when profiling.

The use of profiling tools tends to vary widely among development platforms, so I won't go into specific details on how to profile here. The important thing to remember is that profiling yields the most useful results when you already have some idea of where to look. Many first-time profiler users run the whole program through the profiler, only to be told that most of the time required by the program is spent, say, in the main message loop—clearly, this is not information that is helpful. The more specific you can be when selecting functions to profile, the more useful the resulting information will be—provided, of course, that you're looking in the right places. Many profilers have a source-code line-level resolution, meaning you can get a profile report based on which lines of code in a given source module require the most time.

Remember also that the run-time environment—the CPU, display card, display drivers, memory configuration, and other factors—can greatly affect the performance dynamics of a program. It takes experience to learn which optimizations are universal across a wide range of run-time configurations, and to avoid optimizations that offer increased speed on only a small range of configurations. The bottom line is that you must know your target market, and you should do performance testing on a wide range of popular configurations within that market.

Summary

This chapter touched on some of the basic concepts of optimization, particularly those that apply directly to improving the speed of the sprite engine. Effective optimization focuses on three main areas, listed here in the order of their importance:

- Code that is executed frequently
- Code that consumes a large portion of the program's time
- Code that can be improved; in other words, code that is under the programmer's control

Keep these factors in mind when attacking any optimization problem and you'll spend more time speeding up those functions that, in the long run, really matter.

Credit is due to the developers at Microsoft who wrote FAST32.ASM, including Nigel Thompson and especially Todd Laney, developer of the 32-bit macro package.

14

32-Bit Programming

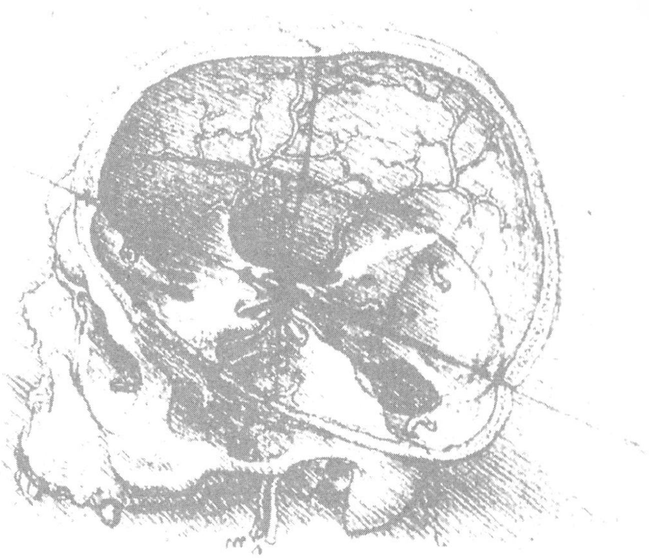

14

32-Bit Programming

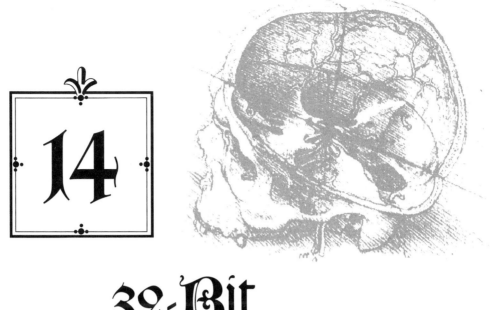

In September of 1986, manufacturers began shipping the first PCs containing the Intel 80386 microprocessor. The 80386 was a breakthrough—it was a true 32-bit microprocessor, meaning that it offered 32-bit memory addressability, 32-bit internal registers, and even some new 32-bit instructions. At the same time, the processor was completely backward-compatible with Intel's previous architectures, the 80286 and venerable 8086.

In the nine years since Intel introduced the 80386, programmers have slowly been moving toward 32-bit computing in order to take advantage of the memory-management and speed improvements it makes possible. The vast majority of the PC's installed base still uses 16-bit operating systems, DOS and Windows 3.1 being the market leaders, but the rate of acceptance for 32-bit operating systems is destined to increase rapidly with the introduction of Windows 95. This user-friendly, compatible 32-bit operating system will prove hard to resist for a large number of Windows users, making it likely that the model Windows NT introduced in 1993 for 32-bit Windows computing will finally be taken up by the masses.

In this chapter, you'll learn about the differences between 16-bit and 32-bit Windows program development, how those differences affect WinG, and how to hedge your bet a little against the projected rapid acceptance of Windows 95.

32-Bit Windows Environments

There are four distinct classes of 32-bit Windows run-time environments:

- Windows NT
- Windows 95
- Win32s
- Non-Microsoft extensions (Watcom, and so on)

Each of these has different development and run-time characteristics.

Windows NT

Windows NT was the first fully 32-bit operating system Microsoft introduced. Written from the ground up as a 32-bit operating system, NT was nonetheless created to be as compatible as possible. As a result, NT can run most 16-bit Windows 3.1 applications (I'll call these Win16 apps from here on) directly, without recompiling or otherwise touching the executable file. And although NT does away with DOS as a foundation, it provides an emulator for those old DOS applications that refuse to die.

Besides providing a full 32-bit programming environment, NT offers many other advanced features, including true preemptive multitasking, threads, better memory protection, and a host of other nifty bells and whistles like enhanced security and a new file system called NTFS. It also supports the Win32 API, which contains almost all the old Win16 calls, plus hundreds of new ones (the few Win16 API calls Microsoft dropped deal mostly with DOS).

The designers of Win32 tried very hard to keep it as compatible as possible with Win16 without sacrificing performance, and they succeeded to a large extent. (Note the subtle distinction between Windows NT, the operating system, and Win32, the API. Win32 programs can run under Windows NT, Windows 95, and Win32s—provided they use only the features supported under the target environment.) There are certain places where the designers couldn't maintain compatibility, however, owing mostly to the fundamental change that occurs in the size of memory objects when you're going from 16 to 32 bits. Still, it's quite straightforward to create Windows programs that compile and run under both environments. You'll find that most of the code in this book does just that.

Windows NT has never caught on as a primary end-user operating system; Microsoft didn't really intend it to. The configuration requirements are high (16 MB RAM is the practical minimum), device-driver support is limited, and not all users actually need everything NT has to offer (especially not at a street price higher than that of Windows 3.1). Because of its advanced networking and security capabilities, NT is well-suited as a network server operating system, though, and works well with

Windows for Workgroups 3.11 clients. It is also a highly stable development environment, since it does away with DOS (and its inherent instabilities) and provides a new and more robust memory-management system. Windows NT is currently the only 32-bit software-development platform offered by Microsoft, regardless of the target run-time operating system.

Windows 95

This soon-to-be-released operating system inherited many of the advanced features of Windows NT, but offers greater compatibility for Win16 applications. Its configuration requirements are also slightly less hungry than those of Windows NT. Microsoft intends it to be a true replacement for Windows 3.1, in the same sense that Microsoft meant for Windows 3.1 to replace Windows 3.0.

One of the biggest advantages of Windows 95 is its completely new user interface, which is much more intuitive to learn and use than that of Windows 3.1. Gone are the endless windows of Program Manager and File Manager, which are now integrated into a much richer desktop-based shell.

Windows 95 also offers preemptive multitasking and threads (for native Windows 95 applications, anyway), and a *mostly* 32-bit environment. To make Windows 95 as compatible as possible with Win16, Microsoft had to sacrifice a fully 32-bit implementation in a few areas, most notably the GDI. For the most part, this shortcoming will go unnoticed by users. Presumably, it will be rectified in a future version of the operating system as applications developers migrate their code to native 32-bit Windows 95 applications.

Currently, the only way to develop a program for Windows 95 is under Windows NT—there are no software development kits available from Microsoft specifically for Windows 95. Of course, because Windows 95 offers *most* of NT's Win32 API, it may be possible to run some of the NT development environments under Windows 95. (It's a little early in the life of Windows 95 to conclude comprehensively what shape all its development environments will take.) However, it's important to note that there are still a few advanced features that remain the exclusive province of NT, like security. Programs written using the Win32 API and compiled under NT run fine under Windows 95, provided they don't use those unique features.

Because of its many other advantages, Windows NT may prove to be the development environment of the future for all Microsoft Windows applications, at least as far as Microsoft development products are concerned.

Win32s

Win32s isn't an operating system, but rather a set of DLLs that make it possible to run programs developed using the Win32 API under Win16. This gives 32-bit programming capabilities to applications that, for whatever reasons, must run under Win16. This is, of course, quite a trick. The underlying operating system is still a fully 16-bit one, but to the programmer, everything looks like it belongs to a 32-bit operating system. Well, almost everything.

The catch is that Win32s can't provide more features than the operating system can actually support—in other words, no preemptive multitasking, threads, or other advanced features. However, you do get genuine 32-bit compiled code, a flat memory model, and the other advantages of a 32-bit programming environment. WinG is also supported under Win32s, making Win32s ideal for games. Figure 14-1 illustrates how Win32 calls Win16 under Windows 3.1.

Non-Microsoft Extensions

Microsoft isn't the only company supplying 32-bit development tools for Windows. Notably, Watcom Corporation has provided a means of running 32-bit applications under Windows for some time. Their product includes a 32-bit compiler and debugging environment. Watcom first provided tools before Win32s existed, using methods of its own creation for handling communications with Win16.

Other 32-bit development environments are becoming available, but most target Win32 binaries—which, through Win32s, can run under Win16. This is a natural trend, because the Win32 API can support three different operating systems with the same binary executable file—Windows NT, Windows 95, and Windows 3.1 with Win32s.

FIGURE 14-1

Win32/Win16 call handling

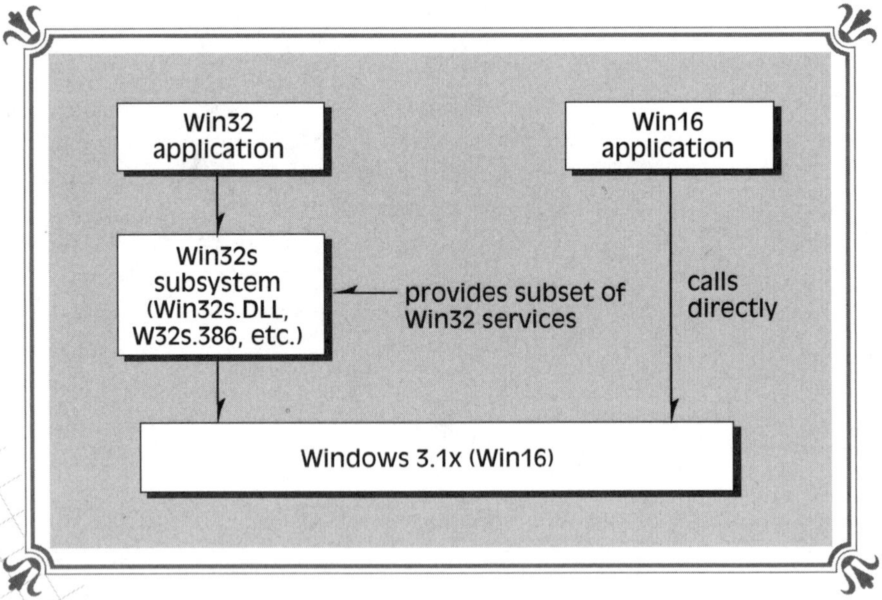

How to Choose an Environment

It should be clear that a smart programmer wanting the advantages of 32-bit programming should probably stick to the Win32 API. It endows programs with the flexibility necessary to run on three different operating systems, and is clearly the path of the future. Microsoft's only current offering for creating 32-bit applications in C is Visual C++ version 2.0 for Windows NT, an integrated development environment that produces Win32 binaries that can run on all three operating systems, although under the constraints I mentioned previously.

All this means is that it is becoming difficult to resist developing your game programs under Windows NT, whether you target Windows 95 or Windows 3.1 as your end-user environment. And why resist? As it turns out, Windows NT is a really *great* development environment—vastly more stable than Windows 3.1, with a better array of tools and very high compatibility with Win16 applications. It's very easy to install Windows NT from a CD-ROM and the current version (3.5) supports nearly all the hardware configurations supported under Windows 3.1. It's even easy to set up your machine in a "dual boot" configuration so that you can choose between Windows NT and DOS/Windows 3.1 at startup. The only caveat: Windows NT *is* resource-hungry and requires at least 16 MB of memory (20 MB is better) for development. Just the operating system takes some 100 MB of disk space, and Visual C++ requires up to another 130 MB or so. So don't jump into NT development with an under-equipped machine.

Microsoft isn't the only game in town, though—Watcom, Borland, Symantec, and others also provide integrated development systems for the Win32 API that produce binaries capable of running under all three operating systems. The proprietary methods developed to enable 32-bit programming under Win16 are quickly vanishing now that Win32 and Windows 95 are here.

The Advantages of 32-Bit Programming

Any programmer who has spent a significant amount of time working with the segmented-memory architecture that Intel introduced with the 8086 microprocessor—architecture that is still the foundation for Win16 today—probably already knows why 32-bit programming is a good thing. The advantages can be summarized in two words: simplicity and speed.

Gone are the 64k segment boundaries that have made life so miserable all these years. The so-called "flat memory model" provides a 4-GB linear address space to the 32-bit program. No longer is there a distinction between a "local" heap and a "global" heap; memory comes from one giant pile that includes all the virtual memory available to the system.

The speed advantage also comes partly from the flat memory model. Since memory isn't segmented, accessing a memory location no longer requires loading or computing a segment address; a 32-bit direct pointer to the memory is all you need. This can often double speed all by itself, though through clever optimization of 16-bit code (by using 32-bit assembly-language functions, for example), you can often provide a similar performance increase. A 32-bit program, however, enjoys the advantage of using 32-bit code everywhere, not just in the critical performance loops.

The Differences Between Win16 and Win32

In the following section, I list some of the important differences between 16-bit and 32-bit Windows programs. In the Win32 API, Microsoft did drop a certain number of Win16 calls that were either obsolete or poorly suited to the 32-bit environment. If you follow the advice I give throughout this book, however, you'll find that many of these losses are inconsequential.

Widened Variable Types

One of the most significant differences between 16-bit programming and 32-bit programming is, of course, that many variables that are 16 bits wide in 16-bit programs are 32 bits wide in 32-bit programs. The C programming language requires that the size of an int be the "natural" size of the processor's data bus. Thus, an int under Win16 is 16 bits, and an int under Win32 is 32 bits. Although this fact is widely known, programmers often make the mistake of counting on the size of an integer or other variable type size.

In an attempt to help porting efforts, Microsoft altered the Windows 3.1 SDK to use more consistent variable types and define a few constant-sized variable types. It also defines some *polymorphic* types: variable types that change size across implementations. For example, a WORD and a DWORD are the same size under both Win16 and Win32: 16 and 32 bits, respectively. However, a UINT is simply defined as an unsigned int—16 bits under Win16 and 32 bits under Win32. Polymorphic type definitions optimize the performance on a given processor: 32-bit ints are faster than 16-bit ints on a 32-bit machine. A BOOL is also polymorphic—yes, it takes 4 bytes to represent a single bit's worth of information efficiently on a 32-bit processor.

Most importantly, all pointers in Win32 are 32 bits long. There is no longer a distinction between near pointers and far or huge pointers; all memory comes from the same address space. The various memory models supported under Win16—Small, Compact, Medium, and Large—all vanish. (In actuality, Win32 uses Intel 32-bit

"Small" model programming. All pointers are near pointers, but now they can address up to 4 GB of memory.) The near, far, and huge keywords used in Win16 programming just get swallowed up by null macros under Win32, making their use unnecessary, although compatible.

All the various Windows data types that have pointers defined still use the *LP* prefix, even though all pointers are the same length. The various Win32 header files (WINDOWS.H is now subdivided into several modular pieces for Win32) consistently define pointers with a *P* prefix as well, for migrating code away from the segmented memory references.

Now that Windows functions have a uniform pointer size, you no longer need certain Windows functions that were designed as model-independent substitutes for standard C library functions. For example, functions like `hmemcpy` and `_fmemcpy` are indistinguishable from their standard C counterpart, `memcpy`. Likewise, you can now safely go back to using the conventional C run-time library routines for string and file handling. There's only one memory model, so you never have to worry about making sure the parameters to these functions are the right size.

Window Callback-Function Parameter Changes

The foundation of Windows programming is the window callback function, the function that Windows directly calls to push messages into an application. The callback function has four parameters: a window handle; a message value; and the polymorphic parameters `wParam` and `lParam`, whose values change depending on the message. Under Win16, the lengths of these parameters are 16, 16, 16, and 32 bits, respectively. Under Win32, all four parameters are 32 bits long.

It probably won't take you long to identify the nasty problem this difference creates. Changing the size of the window handle and message value wouldn't be such a big problem if it weren't for the fact that handles are frequently stuffed into one half of `lParam` under Win16. When the size of a handle increases to 32 bits, as it does in Win32, this doesn't work very well.

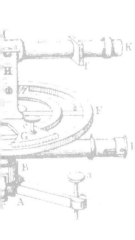

About a dozen Windows messages were affected by the change in parameter lengths. Most have to do with text controls. A dozen or so Windows API functions were also affected, and began doing something dumb like returning a coordinate pair as two WORDs stuffed into a DWORD return value. Programmers new to Windows shouldn't have any trouble as a result, though: New functions, most of them available since Windows 3.1, have replaced the problematic ones.

Let's look at one of the functions Microsoft changed, `GetTextExtent`. Its prototype was:

```
DWORD GetTextExtent(HDC hdc, LPSTR string, int len);
```

In this form, the function returns the x and y extents of the given string of text as it would be rendered into the given device context, with whatever text font is currently selected into the DC. The x extent (width) is returned in the low-order 16 bits of the return value, while the y extents (height) are stuffed into the high-order 16 bits. This obviously would be a problem under Win32, where the coordinate space of the GDI would be a full 32 bits in x and y.

Now look at Microsoft's new, better function, which is portable between Win16 and Win32:

```
BOOL GetTextExtentPoint(HDC hdc, LPSTR string, int len, SIZE FAR* size);
```

The last argument to this function is a pointer to a Windows **SIZE** structure, which is defined thusly in WINDOWS.H:

```
typedef struct tagSIZE
{
    int cx;
    int cy;
} SIZE;
```

Note the use of **int**s in the definition. This type is (appropriately) 16 bits under Win16 and 32 bits under Win32, so the function is compatible with both.

The message crackers and forwarders I introduced in Chapter 2 are designed to completely get around this potential incompatibility nightmare. Not only do they make your code easier to understand, but a version of WINDOWSX.H for Win32 handily disguises the changes in parameter length, making everything work transparently.

GDI Coordinate Space

Another victim of parameter-widening confusion under Win32 was the coordinate space for GDI functions. The coordinate space went from +/-32,767 to +/-2,147,483,648. This doesn't mean much if all your calculations are done in pixels, but it does mean something to several Win16 GDI functions that stuffed coordinate pairs into DWORDs. Again, alternatives to these functions have been available since Windows 3.1; programs, even Win16 ones, written using these new functions won't have any problems.

One difference between Windows NT and Windows 95 is that the latter still has a 16-bit GDI coordinate space. This is not to say that the various GDI functions and structures still use 16-bit integers, but they are truncated to 16 bits by the GDI when they're passed as arguments. Microsoft did this purely for compatibility's sake—not for the benefit of new Win32 applications, but in order to maintain a high level of compatibility for Win16 programs running under Windows 95. As long as you don't use coordinates out of 16-bit range, your newly developed Win32 application should have no problem.

GetWindowWord and GetClassWord Obsolete

These functions, used to retrieve window instance and class data, respectively, still operate, but they no longer return the values you want (gee, how handy!). Microsoft has defined a new set of constants for `GetWindowLong` and `GetClassLong` to solve the problem. (I wouldn't even mention this trivial difference, except that the little system I developed in Chapter 2 for stuffing a pointer to a window's instance structure into a window WORD would break under Win32, were it not for the conditional compiler statement surrounding the `GetPtr` and `SetPtr` macros in all the header files that use them.)

Memory Functions

Under Win16, there were two primary memory-allocation functions: `LocalAlloc` and `GlobalAlloc`. The former allocated memory from the small local heap, part of a 64k data block shared with static variables and the stack (under Medium model, at least). The latter function allocated memory from the global heap, accessible via a far pointer once the handle returned by `GlobalAlloc` was locked with `GlobalLock`. In Chapter 3, you learned how to ignore all the locking/unlocking nonsense by using the `GlobalAllocPtr` macro.

Under Win32, all memory comes from the same place—the global heap—and is accessed via 32-bit pointers. Win32 retains the `LocalAlloc` and `GlobalAlloc` functions for the sake of compatibility, but they both return 32-bit pointers when you use the `GMEM_FIXED` (or `LMEM_FIXED`) flags. These two functions do exactly the same thing as the standard C library function `malloc` under Win32. In fact, it's no longer taboo to use `malloc` in a Windows program under Win32, though the API specifies a large and robust set of memory-management functions that are much more flexible than `malloc`.

I won't go into all the enhanced memory-management functions available under Win32, but they probably deserve your attention in the long run. Using Win32 memory management, you can ensure that a certain block of memory won't get paged to disk, for example. This simply wasn't possible under Win16. It's also possible to create your own optimized heaps for doing small allocations faster. Most of the memory-management functions of Win32 work under Win32s (on Windows 3.1), as well.

Should you use the new memory-management functions of Win32? If you find your game is having performance problems related to memory management, then chances are you can benefit from these new functions. If your game runs fine using the old `GlobalAllocPtr` and `GlobalFreePtr`, then there's probably no need to bother.

"First Instance"

Previously, you learned that Windows allows code sharing between multiple running instances of an application. The first instance of a program is special in that it must do certain initialization tasks (like registering window classes) that shouldn't be done by second and subsequent instances. Win32 programs don't share code, though, so there's nothing special about the first running instance of a program; in fact, the term *instance* no longer has any real meaning. This really isn't a very important distinction for the most part, unless you're writing programs that don't allow multiple instances.

Under Win16, you can prevent the user from running multiple instances by checking the value of the `hPrevInstance` parameter to the `WinMain` function. If it is a value other than zero, you put up a message of some kind indicating that only one instance is allowed, then return to the operating system.

Under Win32, it's a little harder to verify that the currently running program is the *only* one running. The `hPrevInstance` parameter to `WinMain` is always null under Win32, so it's necessary to take other measures if you want to ensure that only a single copy of the program is running. Several methods for doing this are covered in the Win32 SDK; which is best may vary, depending on the specific requirements and design of a given program.

Other Differences

This is hardly a comprehensive list of the differences between Win16 and Win32, although it covers some of the differences that are important for programs that must run on *both* Win16 and Win32. If you are targeting only Windows 95 or Windows NT for your game, you'll be interested in the many enhancements like multiple threads and new interprocess communications functions Win32 provides. However, you can't use any of these advanced features if you want your program to run under Windows 3.1 via Win32s.

Some other differences between Windows 3.1 and either Windows 95 or Windows NT are less important from a programming point of view, but merit mention nonetheless. For example, under Windows 95 and Windows NT, programs run in their own protected address space. Under Windows 3.1, however, all programs run in the *same* protected address space. This makes Windows 95 and Windows NT inherently less prone to system crashes resulting from the activities of a single application, though it's still possible for this to happen.

WinG Under Win32

Microsoft created WinG primarily to solve a speed problem with Windows 3.1 display drivers and to create a migration path to Win32. Part of the WinG distribution is its 32-bit library, WING32.DLL and WING32.LIB. This library must be linked with a Win32 application instead of WING.LIB (the Win16 library), because WING32.LIB is in Common Object File Format, the new format used by Win32 compilers and linkers.

WinG under Win32 isn't quite what it seems. Under Win32, the WinG functions simply pass through to new Win32 functions (as shown in Figure 14-2). In particular, the `WinGCreateBitmap` function passes through to `CreateDIBSection`, a new Win32 call that provides virtually the same functionality.

Under Win32s and Windows 3.1, WinG has to be a little smarter. In these cases, it does all the work necessary to interface with the 16-bit operating system and take advantage of the WinG enhancements just like a WinG-based Win16 application would. The important thing to remember is that all you need to do is link your Win32 application with WING32.DLL and you'll get the full benefits of WinG on all platforms. If you're using Windows NT for development, don't be surprised if this doesn't result in much of a performance increase—WinG wasn't really designed to optimize Windows NT display-driver performance. But running the program under Windows 3.1 using Win32s will give you everything WinG has to offer.

32-Bit to 16-Bit "Thunking"

Win32s really does perform a lot of magic. It not only convinces your Win32 program it's running under Windows NT (with the aforementioned limits), but it does so without making any really fundamental changes to the underlying 16-bit Windows operating system. How can this be? What are the implications for performance?

FIGURE 14-2

WinG under Win16/Win32

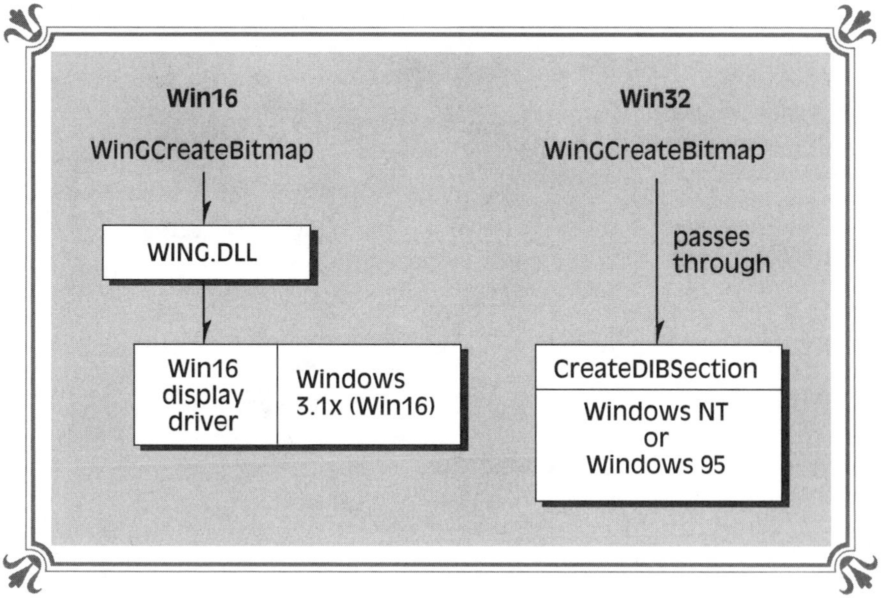

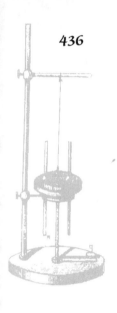

Most of the magic that Win32s performs occurs through a process called *thunking*: calling down to 16-bit functions from a 32-bit application. A little explanation of how Windows works will help you understand thunking.

The architecture of 16-bit Windows is based on the use of DLLs—dynamically loaded libraries that bind to your application at run time. Most of Windows 3.1 (and its predecessors) is really just a bunch of DLLs that go by the slightly unconventional names USER.EXE, GDI.EXE, and KRNL386.EXE. These DLLs supply all the functions in the Windows API. When your Windows program is loaded, all the external function-call references are dynamically patched to call the functions in these DLLs. `GlobalAlloc`, for example, actually resides in KRNL386.EXE. Some Windows API functions are implemented in separate DLLs whose import libraries must be linked with your application before your application can access them; the common dialog library (COMMDLG.DLL) and the multimedia extensions (MMSYSTEM.DLL) are two examples.

Calling a 16-bit DLL from a 16-bit program is quite straightforward. The DLL and program share a common 16-bit stack, and parameter lengths are already matched. Calling a 16-bit DLL from a 32-bit program is another matter entirely. The 32-bit program has a 32-bit stack that must be properly mapped to the DLL's memory space, for one. Also, pointers in the "Small" 32-bit memory model need to be remapped to match the segment:offset model needed by the 16-bit DLLs, as illustrated in Figure 14-3. This is the essence of thunking—remapping all these values before calling down to the DLL, then mapping the results back upon return.

FIGURE 14-3

"Thunking down" to a 16-bit DLL

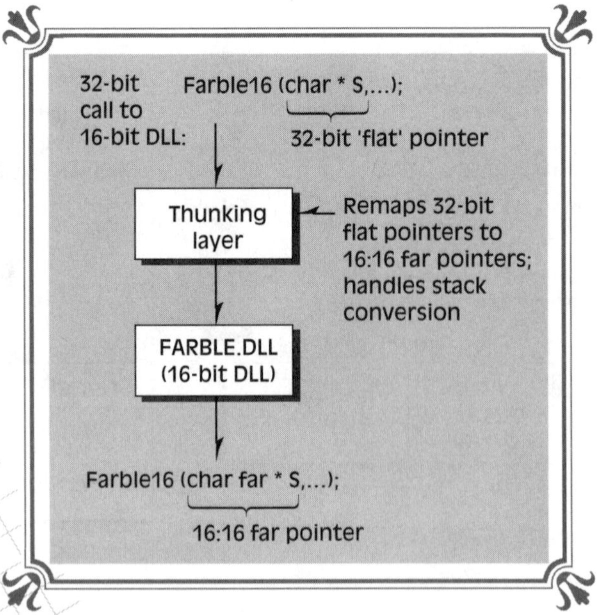

Naturally, all this mapping comes at some performance cost. The performance hit varies with the number of parameters and the way return values are handled. Too, the 16-bit DLL being called is undoubtedly slower than its 32-bit counterpart under a "true" 32-bit operating system like Windows NT or Windows 95 (although this speed difference may not be noticeable, depending on what the calls are actually doing). The net result is that if a Win32 program running under Win32s makes a lot of 16-bit thunks, it's certainly going to run slower than if it were running under Windows NT or Windows 95. In fact, it might even run slower than if it were a strictly *Win16* application!

But how do you know how often your program is thunking? Simple: If it's calling a Windows function, it's almost assuredly thunking. What?! You mean that *every* Windows call must be thunked? Of course—the underlying operating system is still a 16-bit one, remember.

To avoid this problem, you'll want to call Windows as infrequently as possible—except in the main message loop, of course. In practice, this is a pretty natural situation, especially for game programs and especially when using WinG. The whole point of using WinG is to speed up Blting to the screen while simultaneously allowing you to use *your* code, rather than unpredictably slow Windows GDI calls, to manipulate bitmaps.

Win32s takes care of almost all the thunking you'll ever need to do. It's possible you may be stuck with a 16-bit DLL from a third party that you simply must use with your game for one reason or another; if this is the case, you'll have to write your own thunking layer to access the DLL. This is no trivial task, and it's made even more difficult by the fact that you can't debug it easily. Writing a thunking layer is beyond the scope of this discussion, but Microsoft has provided some code for performing "universal" thunks to DLLs. The code is included with many of their SDKs and development environments, and on the Microsoft Software Developer Network CDs. The best approach to take is to try to avoid using third-party 16-bit DLLs whenever possible. Many developers are rapidly switching to Win32 libraries, which will link directly with your program without having to thunk.

Installation Issues for Win32s

Win32s is a combination of DLLs and 32-bit VXD modules that are installed in the WINDOWS and WINDOWS\SYSTEM directories through an installation program. You'll find Win32s and its installation program with every Win32 development system you can buy; it's redistributable without cost.

Win32s installs quickly, but requires you to restart Windows before you can run a Win32 program. Every day, there are more and more Win32 applications popping up that run using Win32s, so the chances of it already existing on your end-users' systems are increasing all the time. The polite thing to do is to check their systems for Win32s and update it if the version you have is newer. An easier thing to do is to check for Win32s, inform users if necessary that they must install Win32s before using your game, and provide the stock Win32s libraries and installation program along with your game.

Check your development environment for instructions for installing Win32s on your customers' computers and for creating an installation program that automatically installs Win32s and WinG.

Summary

In this chapter, I've introduced you to a few of the key points of developing 32-bit Windows programs. You learned about the fundamental differences between the Win16 API and the Win32 API—like wider data types and a flat memory model—and about some of the particular differences.

Developing 32-bit applications for Windows—whether you target Windows NT, Windows 3.1 with Win32s, or Windows 95—is straightforward and well worth the effort. Once you've gotten a taste of the simplified and speedy world of 32-bit programming, you'll never go back to 16 bits again!

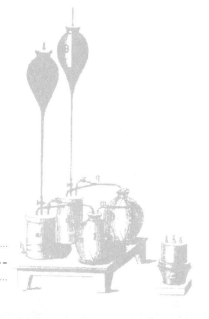

Part II

Advanced Gaming Concepts

Aequator
Ekliptik
I
H
E
C

15

Sprite Movies

[illegible] come si debbe fare le manovelle [illegible] le quali si muovono e [illegible]
e i gran pesi [illegible] [illegible] [illegible] [illegible] [illegible]
[illegible] nella [illegible] [illegible] alla manovella perchè quanto
la forza [illegible] più [illegible] l'omo più vale.

[illegible]

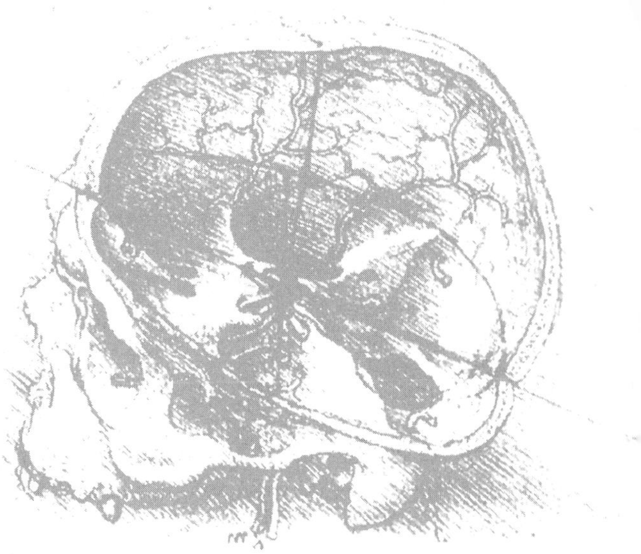

15

Sprite Movies

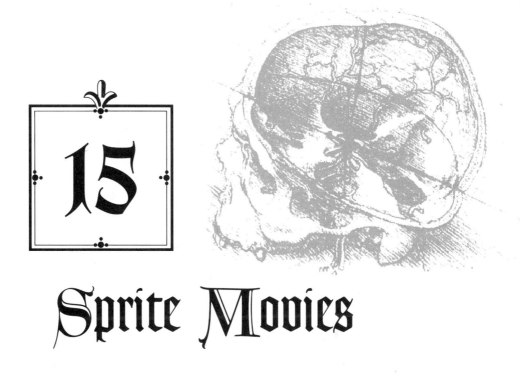

Now that we have a working Windows sprite engine, let's look at an enhancement that can make the engine considerably more useful for your game. As I'm sure you'll agree, the sprites could stand to be a little more interesting. *Animated sprites* (sprites that change appearance as they move) would be a significant improvement, and it turns out that they're easy to create.

Designing Animated Sprites

There are two basic ways to animate a sprite (that is, to change a sprite image at some interval as that image moves around on the screen):

- By computing new sprite images on the fly
- By playing back stored sprite images

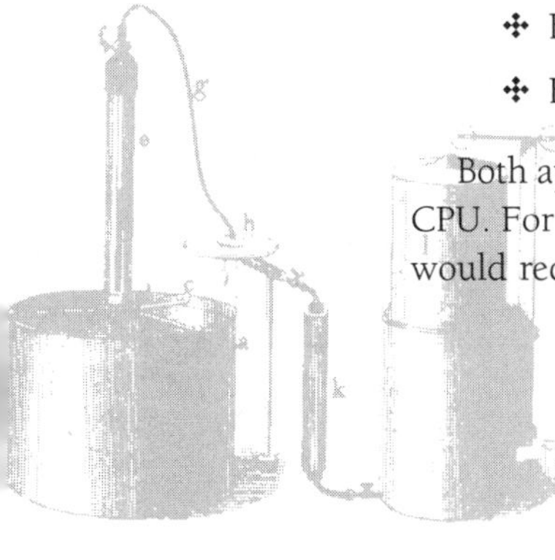

Both approaches have their place, but the first method obviously asks more of the CPU. For example, suppose you were trying to use sprites to help simulate 3D. This would require you to scale the sprites up or down to reflect their various distances from the viewer. Scaling bitmaps is a CPU-intensive operation and could have a significant impact on the overall speed of the game.

Playing back stored bitmaps is a technique that minimizes demands on CPU time by consuming more memory. It represents the classic speed-vs.-memory tradeoff. In situations where you have many sprites, they'll typically be small; to make them move quickly, you'll want to spend as little CPU time as possible changing their images. Keeping multiple images of each sprite in memory is a good approach in this case. It's also much simpler than creating efficient bitmap-scaling routines. For these reasons, I'll focus on implementing *stored* multiple-image sprites in this chapter.

To keep multiple images in memory for your sprites, you must devise a way to implement this scheme in software. There are several possible approaches, two of which I'll discuss here.

Linked Lists

One technique is to change a sprite from a single object in memory (represented by the SPRITE structure in the sprite engine code) to some sort of linked list of sprite objects, each with its own image. You could extend the current SPRITE structure to include a pointer to the next sprite image (frame) to be displayed. The program would continue to evaluate and display the list of sprite frames until it encountered a NULL pointer, signaling the end of the list of frames. At this point, the program would resume the normal walking of the sprite list (see Figure 15-1).

FIGURE 15-1

A linked list of sprites

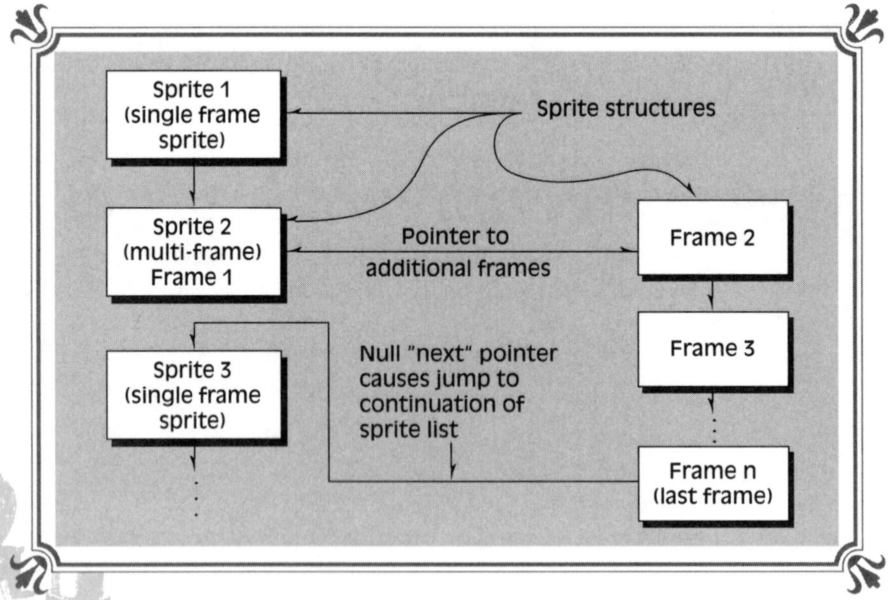

This approach has several advantages as well as disadvantages. One advantage is that it doesn't limit the sprite image—each image has a dedicated SPRITE structure that defines its size, speed, and so on. This method also allows you to switch images of the sprite easily—an advantage typical of a linked-list approach.

Among the disadvantages is the fact that this method isn't very memory-efficient. Not only does the image of each sprite have a separate SPRITE structure dedicated to it, but the DIB images for each frame occupy small chunks of noncontiguous memory, making memory fragmentation a potential problem. It also complicates the sprite-loading code. The list of frames must be built dynamically—you must devise some method for logically connecting all the frames of a given multi-image sprite.

Sprite Movies

Another approach would be to create sprites much like you would frames in a movie. Each such sprite image would be a section of one long bitmap (see Figure 15-2). Instead of using a separate SPRITE structure for each image, you would use the same structure for the whole "sprite movie," with the addition of a few variables that would keep track of the next frame of the movie to be played and so on.

This technique is more memory-efficient because it keeps all the images of the sprite together in a contiguous piece of memory and uses basically the same SPRITE structure for everything. The only disadvantages to this approach are that it makes it more difficult for you to change any one of the individual frames of the sprite movie (you'd have to copy new bits into the "film strip" between updates), and each sprite image must be the same size. This latter limitation isn't significant: You can always create a frame that's mostly transparent, making an effectively smaller sprite image.

FIGURE 15-2

A sprite movie

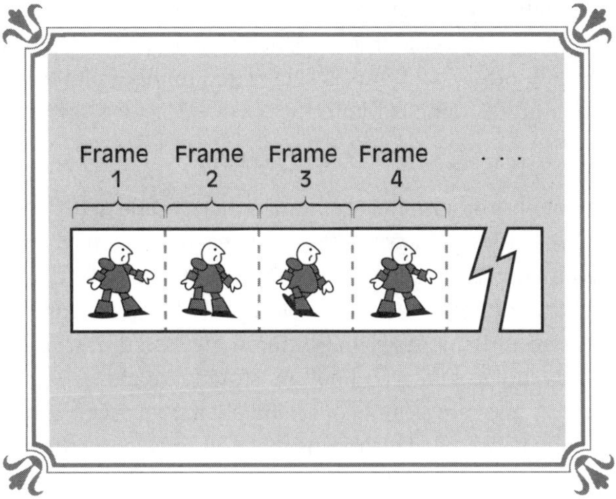

Of course, the strip must be wide enough to accommodate the widest sprite image, possibly wasting space, but this is a small sacrifice to make in return for speed and simplicity. In any event, you'll typically use multi-image sprites when you want an image for each orientation of a given player or game piece (for example, for a pair of computer-tossed dice, you might create a multi-image sprite containing a few dozen pictures of the die as it spins around), meaning that the sprite images would all be about the same size. The sprite-movie approach would waste no memory in these cases.

Incorporating Sprite Movies into the Sprite Engine

Let's suppose you've chosen to use the memory-efficient sprite movie. Next question: How do you choose which frame of a sprite movie to display? This will depend on your game. In the rolling-dice example, you might just play the movie from beginning to end (maybe looping it, if necessary), moving the position of the sprite as the movie plays. If your sprite movie represents the orientation of a particular game piece, you might play only one frame (or a subset of frames) that represents the current orientation of the piece. In any case, you'll need to have a very efficient way of displaying frames.

Displaying Frames Efficiently

If you think about the way images are stored in memory and how they get copied to the off-screen buffer, you might be able to guess how to store these sprite-image strips most efficiently. First, consider a long, horizontal movie strip. All the frames are the same height. An individual frame is some fixed number of pixels wide. The left-most column of any given frame is found by:

```
left_column = frame_width * frame_number;
```

Simple enough. You just create a bitmap that's `frame_width * number_of_frames` wide. Then, you draw your sprite movies in each frame, like you would in a conventional cel animation movie. But now think about the code that actually has to copy the data from one frame of the movie into the off-screen buffer before the data gets Blted to the screen. Remember that bitmaps are stored in *scan-line order* in memory; in other words, horizontal scan lines are stored one after another (see Figure 15-3).

Because scan lines are stored consecutively in memory, the memory for any given frame is widely dispersed. This means that you must copy the memory for the frame from the movie strip to the off-screen buffer one scan line at a time rather than in one big blast of bytes. A more efficient way of storing the movie would allow each frame

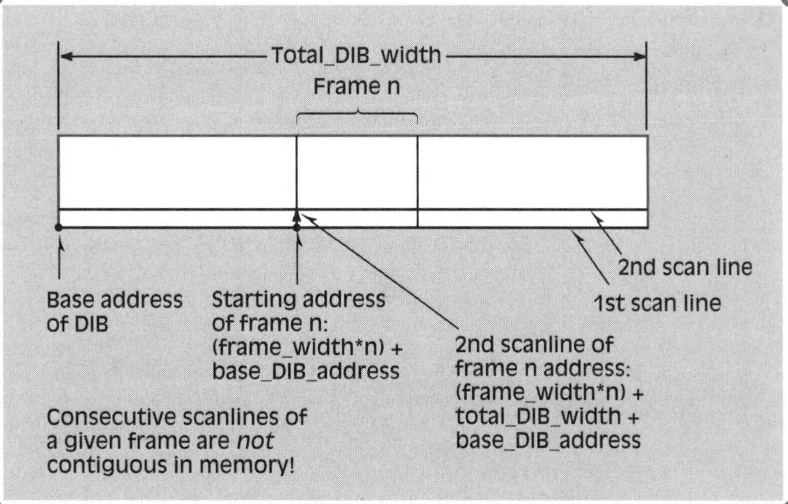

FIGURE 15-3

Bitmap memory storage

to occupy consecutive bytes of memory. But how do you store frames this way? In a *vertical* strip, of course. I'm sure you already thought of that.

Not only does storing the sprite movie as a vertical strip increase copying efficiency (this is a fairly minor improvement, really), it also makes it very simple to index to the frame you want to display. A given frame's starting memory address is simply:

```
start_address = movie_start_address +
                (frame_number * frame_height * storage_width);
```

For greater efficiency, you could reduce this to simply one multiplication and one addition, since `frame_height * storage_width` is a constant for a given sprite movie (see Figure 15-4). Remember from Chapter 13 that this calculation usually isn't anywhere near the critical path of CPU time, but it's an optimization that you might want to make if the calculation ever *did* get near the critical path.

It's easy to index into a vertical sprite movie strip to choose a given frame, so the code required to integrate sprite movies into the sprite engine is quite simple. More of the code has to do with choosing *when* to change the sprites than *how* to change them.

As I mentioned earlier, how you use sprite movies is really a game-design issue. You could use them to indicate the direction of a traveling game piece, in which case you'd repeatedly play the same frame until the piece changed direction (see Figure 15-5).

Or you could use a sprite movie for something like an explosion: It could start out with a large red and orange mass that would dissipate over the course of the strip (see Figure 15-6).

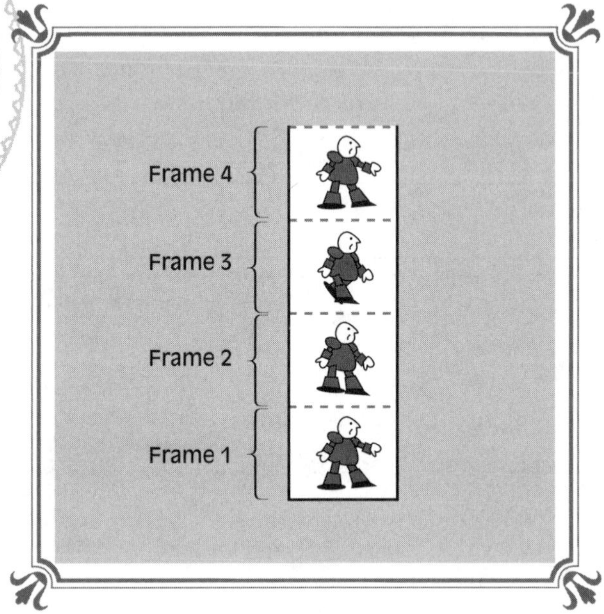

FIGURE 15-4

A vertical sprite movie

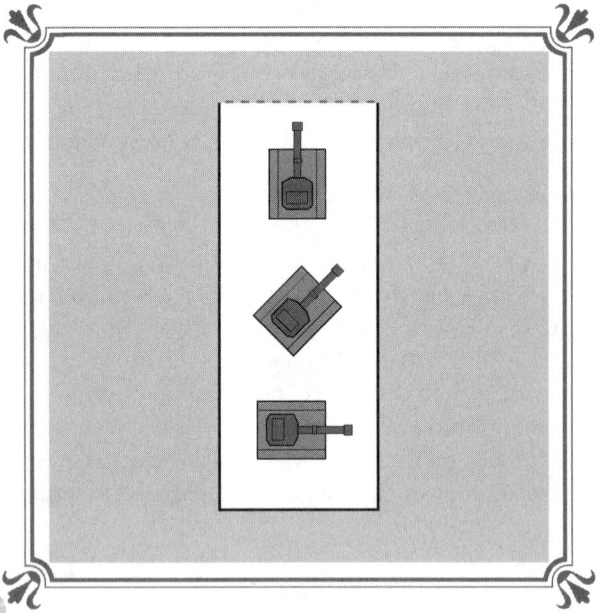

FIGURE 15-5

Sprite movies for orientation

FIGURE 15-6

Explosion sprite movie

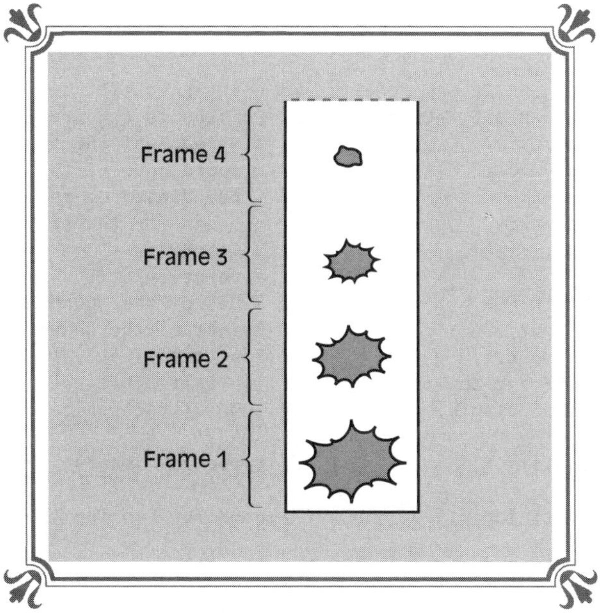

You could also use sprite movies to create animated missiles or random game-piece tosses. The applications are endless.

The code in this chapter will show you the basics of getting sprite movies up and running, along with a few ideas about how to use them. From there you should be able to tailor the code to your specific purpose.

Modifying the SPRITE Structure

The SPRITE structure holds all the local data associated with each sprite. Clearly, though, this structure must contain more information in order to accommodate sprite movies. What is it? A sprite movie isn't all that much different than a regular sprite—it's just a vertical strip logically divided into individual sprites. All the frames in a sprite movie are the same height and the overall height of a strip is stored as part of the DIB structure that makes up the sprite, so the only required variable is the number of frames in the strip.

That's not to say that a second variable wouldn't be handy. It would be useful to have an index to keep track of which frame should be played next. The value of the index could be based on some algorithm that decides which frame to show based on direction, position, or other parameter. The algorithm I show in this chapter will simply increment the index by 1 until it reaches the number of frames for the sprite movie, then reset it to the first frame. This will play the sprite movie in an endless loop, with one frame per iteration.

The modified SPRITE structure looks like this:

```
typedef struct _SPRITE {
    struct _SPRITE FAR *pNext;  // Pointer to the next item
    struct _SPRITE FAR *pPrev;  // Pointer to the previous item
    PDIB pDIB;                  // DIB image of the sprite
    int x;                      // x coordinate of the top-left corner
    int y;                      // y coordinate of the top-left corner
    int z;                      // z-order for the sprite
    int vx;                     // x velocity
    int vy;                     // y velocity
    int width;                  // Width of the bounding rectangle
    int height;                 // Height of the bounding rectangle
    BYTE bTopLeft;              // Top-left pixel value
    COLORREF rgbTopLeft;        // Top-left pixel color
    BOOL bSelectable;           // TRUE if the sprite can be selected by
mouse
    int multi;                  // Number of images if a multi-image
sprite
    int multi_index;            // Used for storing the current multi-
index
} SPRITE, FAR *PSPRITE;
```

The last two members, **multi** and **multi_index**, are the new variables for supporting sprite movies. Now, when should your code set and inspect these variables?

Loading Sprite Movies

It would be extremely handy if there were a way to store the number of frames in a multi-image sprite somewhere in the sprite file itself; perhaps in the DIB header, for example. Unfortunately, the BITMAPINFOHEADER that is part of every stored .BMP doesn't have any user data fields, so it would be hard to put the number of frames there. A sneaky person might stuff the number into one of the lesser-used variables, like **biXPelsPerMeter**. (Of course, this would hopelessly confuse any program that made use of the data in **biXPelsPerMeter**, but few imaging programs fall into this category.) To do this, you'd need to find a tool that allowed you to stuff an arbitrary value into the variable. The resourceful programmer could, of course, write a small tool that stamped the value into the file after the file had been created. A simple DOS tool would suffice:

```
/*
 * STAMPDIB
 *
 * Places a value in the biXPelsPerMeter field of a BITMAPINFOHEADER
 * structure within a .DIB file
 *
 * Usage: stampdib <file> <value>
 *        where <file> is the .BMP file to stamp and <value> is the
```

```
 *       number to stuff into the field.
 *
 */

#include <windows.h>
#include <stdio.h>
#include <stdlib.h>

int main (int argc, char *argv[])
{
    FILE *fp;
    int frames = 0;
    WORD wBytes;
    long fpos;
    BITMAPFILEHEADER BmpFileHdr;
    BITMAPINFOHEADER BmpInfoHdr;

    if (argc < 2) {
        fprintf(stderr, "Usage: stampdib <file> <value>");
        exit(1);
    }

    if ((fp = fopen(argv[1], "r+b")) == NULL) {
        fprintf(stderr, "Couldn't open file: %s", argv[1]);
        exit(2);
    }

    frames = atoi(argv[2]);

    printf("Stamping %s with %d...", argv[1], frames);

    wBytes = fread(&BmpFileHdr, sizeof(BmpFileHdr), 1, fp);
    if (wBytes != 1) {
        fprintf(stderr, "Failed to read file header");
        fclose(fp);
        exit(3);
    }

    //
    // Check to see if we have the magic "BM" at the start.
    //

    if (BmpFileHdr.bfType != 0x4D42) {
        fprintf(stderr, "Not a bitmap file");
        fclose(fp);
        exit(3);
    }

    //
    // Save the current position and read the BITMAPINFOHEADER.
    //
```

continued on next page

continued from previous page

```
    fpos = ftell(fp);

    wBytes = fread(&BmpInfoHdr, sizeof(BmpInfoHdr), 1, fp);
    if (wBytes != 1) {
        fprintf(stderr, "Failed to read BITMAPINFOHEADER");
        fclose(fp);
        exit(3);
    }

    //
    // Stuff the value in the header, fseek back, and write it out.
    //

    BmpInfoHdr.biXPelsPerMeter = frames;
    fseek(fp, fpos, SEEK_SET);
    if (fwrite(&BmpInfoHdr, sizeof(BmpInfoHdr), 1, fp) != 1) {
        fprintf(stderr, "Failed to write BITMAPINFOHEADER");
        fclose(fp);
        exit(3);
    }
    //
    // All done.
    //
    fclose(fp);
    printf("Done.\n");
    return 0;
}
```

There are many possible ways to store the number of frames in a sprite movie with the sprite bitmap. The STAMPDIB program listed here is just one option. The important thing is that the frame count be available when the sprite is loaded from within the **LoadSprite** function in SPRITE.C of the sprite engine.

Besides loading the sprite and setting the number of frames in the SPRITE structure, you'll need to fake out various parts of the sprite engine that deal with DIBs in order to accommodate sprite movies. Here's the modified **LoadSprite** function:

```
//
// Load a sprite.
// If no path is given, show a dialog box to allow the user to select the DIB.
//

PSPRITE LoadSprite(LPSTR pszPath, BOOL bRedraw)
{
    PSPRITE pSprite;
    RECT rc;
    LONG multi;

    dprintf2("LoadSprite()");

    //
```

```
// Allocate memory for the SPRITE information.
//

pSprite = (PSPRITE) ALLOCATE(sizeof(SPRITE));
if (!pSprite) {
    dprintf1("No memory for sprite");
    return NULL;
}

//
// Load the DIB image.
//

pSprite->pDIB = LoadDIB(pszPath);
if (!pSprite->pDIB) {
    goto $abort;
}

//
// Check to see if this file has been "stamped"
// as a multiframe sprite by stuffing a frame count
// in XPelsPerMeter.
//
multi = pSprite->pDIB->bmiHeader.biXPelsPerMeter;

pSprite->width = (int) DIB_WIDTH(pSprite->pDIB);
pSprite->height = (int) DIB_HEIGHT(pSprite->pDIB);

pSprite->x = 0;
pSprite->y = 0;
pSprite->z = 0;
pSprite->vx = 0;
pSprite->vy = 0;
pSprite->bSelectable = TRUE;
pSprite->pNext = NULL;
pSprite->pPrev = NULL;
dprintf4("Sprite is %u by %u", pSprite->width, pSprite->height);

//
// Map the color table so that it matches the one in the
// palette (which is the same as the background DIB).
//

ASSERT(G.pdibBkGnd);
MapDIBits(G.hpalCurrent, pSprite->pDIB, DIB_PBITS(pSprite->pDIB));

//
// Get the index and color of the top-left pixel
// (determines transparent color).
//

pSprite->bTopLeft = GetDIBPixelValue(pSprite->pDIB, 0, 0);
```

continued on next page

continued from previous page

```
    pSprite->rgbTopLeft = GetDIBPixelColor(pSprite->pDIB, 0, 0);
    dprintf4("Sprite top left: %2.2XH, %8.8lXH",
             pSprite->bTopLeft,
             pSprite->rgbTopLeft);

    // Multi-image sprite height adjustment
    if (multi) {
        pSprite->height /= multi;
        pSprite->multi = (int)multi;
        pSprite->multi_index = 1;
        // Fake out the height of the DIB. This is compensated for
        // in DIB.C's GetDIBPixelAddress.
        pSprite->pDIB->bmiHeader.biHeight /= multi;
    } else
        pSprite->multi = 0;
        pSprite->multi_index = 1;
    }

    //
    // Add it to the beginning of the sprite list.
    //

    if (G.pSpriteList) {
        G.pSpriteList->pPrev = pSprite;
        pSprite->pNext = G.pSpriteList;
    }
    G.pSpriteList = pSprite;

    //
    // Set the z-order somewhere in the middle.
    //

    SetSpriteZOrder(pSprite, 50, NO_UPDATE);

    //
    // Render the sprite and display it.
    //

    if (bRedraw != NO_UPDATE) {
        GetSpriteRect(pSprite, &rc);
        Render(&rc, UPDATE_SCREEN);
    }

    return pSprite;

$abort:
    if (pSprite) FREE(pSprite);


    return NULL;
}
```

Note the two simple changes. First, I set a local **LONG** variable, **multi**, to the **biXPelsPerMeter** field of the BITMAPINFOHEADER of the loaded sprite, where the frame count was stuffed by STAMPDIB. Later, the value is examined. If the value is not zero, the code specifies a series of adjustments to the values in the SPRITE and BITMAPINFOHEADER structures for the sprite. Let's examine that code in detail:

```
// Multi-image sprite height adjustment
if (multi) {
    pSprite->height /= multi;
    pSprite->multi = (int)multi;
    pSprite->multi_index = 1;
    // Fake out the height of the DIB. This is compensated for
    // in DIB.C's GetDIBPixelAddress.
    pSprite->pDIB->bmiHeader.biHeight /= multi;
} else {
    pSprite->multi = 0;
    pSprite->multi_index = 1;
}
```

First, we divide the **height** member of the sprite structure (previously set to the overall height of the DIB) by the value in **multi**. This makes **height** equal to the height of a *single frame* of the sprite movie. Next, we set the **multi** member of the SPRITE structure to the number of frames in the movie and set the current index (**multi_index**) to 1. (This index is 1-based rather than 0-based for reasons that I'll make clear later in this chapter.) Finally, we also set the height of the DIB as stored in the **biHeight** member of the BITMAPINFOHEADER to the height of a single frame. As the comment says, this is compensated for in **GetDIBPixelAddress** when the program looks up the address of a given pixel in the sprite movie.

Now that we've loaded a sprite movie, let's see how it's used in the main loop of the sprite engine.

Using Sprite Movies in the Main Loop

Remember that how you use sprites in a game depends to a large extent on the game's architecture. The sprite engine has a very simple main loop that increments the positions of the sprites by the value stored in member variables **vx** and **vy**, wrapping the sprite around the edge of the window if necessary. For this example, I'll keep things simple and just increment the sprite movie by one frame at each iteration, looping it back to the beginning when it's done.

Recall that the main loop for the sprite engine is in DRAW.C and is contained in the function **UpdatePositions**. Adding sprite-movie support to the function requires just four lines of code. Here's the entire function, with those four lines highlighted:

```
//
// Update sprite positions.
// (Main animation function)
//

void UpdatePositions()
{
    PSPRITE pSprite;
    BOOL bChanged = FALSE;
    RECT rcPos;

    pSprite = G.pSpriteList;
    while (pSprite) {

        if (pSprite->vx || pSprite->vy) {

            //
            // Add the old (current) position of the sprite
            // to the redraw-rectangle list.
            //
            GetSpriteRect(pSprite, &rcPos);
            Render(&rcPos, NO_UPDATE);

            pSprite->x += pSprite->vx;

            // Wrap sprites around one edge to the other.
            if ((pSprite->vx < 0) && (pSprite->x + pSprite->width < 0)) {
                pSprite->x = DIB_WIDTH(G.pdibBkGnd);
            } else if ((pSprite->vx > 0) &&
                      (pSprite->x > DIB_WIDTH(G.pdibBkGnd))) {
                pSprite->x = - (int)pSprite->width;
            }

            pSprite->y += pSprite->vy;
            if ((pSprite->vy < 0) && (pSprite->y + pSprite->height < 0))
{
                pSprite->y = DIB_HEIGHT(G.pdibBkGnd);
            } else if ((pSprite->vy > 0) &&
                      (pSprite->y > DIB_HEIGHT(G.pdibBkGnd))) {
                pSprite->y = - (int) pSprite->height;
            }

            // Increment the sprite index for multi-image sprites.
            if (pSprite->multi)
                pSprite->multi_index = (pSprite->multi_index+1 >
                                        pSprite->multi) ?
                                       1 :
                                       pSprite->multi_index+1;
            else
```

```
                pSprite->multi_index = 1;

            //
            // Add the new position of the sprite
            // to the redraw-rectangle list.
            //
            GetSpriteRect(pSprite, &rcPos);
            Render(&rcPos, NO_UPDATE);

            bChanged = TRUE;
        }

        pSprite = pSprite->pNext;
    }

    //
    // Render (with screen update)
    // if anyone changed position.
    //
    if (bChanged)
        Render(&rcPos, UPDATE_SCREEN); // Ask for the last one again.
}
```

The new code simply tests for a sprite movie (nonzero in `pSprite->multi`), then increments the `multi_index` or sets it to 1 if it's already on the last frame. Nothing could be simpler. But where, then, is the *real* work for handling sprite movies done? Only two other functions need to be modified to support sprite movies, one in DRAW.C and one in DIB.C.

You use the `RenderDIBBitsOffScreen` function to copy bits from a sprite (or the background image) to the off-screen buffer before the image gets Blted to the screen. By passing `RenderDIBBitsOffScreen` the `multi_index` value for a sprite, you can tell the function which frame of the sprite movie is to be copied to the buffer. `RenderDIBBitsOffScreen` appears in two places in DRAW.C: in the `RenderSprite-OffScreen` function and in the `Render` function. Looking at the latter, you see that `RenderDIBBitsOffScreen` is called to copy a portion of the background image to the off-screen buffer. I've added the new index parameter here:

```
    .
    .
    .

    //
    // Walk the draw-rectangle list.
    //

    pDrawRect = DrawList.pHead;

    while (pDrawRect) {
```

continued on next page

continued from previous page

```
        //
        // Render the background DIB to the off-screen DC.
        //

        RenderDIBBitsOffScreen(G.pdibBkGnd,
                               0, 0,
                               &(pDrawRect->rc),
                               // Image index = 1 for background.
                               1,
                               0,
                               FALSE);
        //
        // Draw the sprites.
        // Walk the list from the bottom (back) to the top (front).
        //

        pSprite = pLastSprite;
        while (pSprite) {
            RenderSpriteOffScreen(pSprite, &(pDrawRect->rc));
            pSprite = pSprite->pPrev;
    }
    .
    .
    .
```

Here the index passed is 1, since the background isn't a multi-image sprite. (Can you see ways to extend it?)

Looking at `RenderSpriteOffScreen`, you can also see where I've added the new index parameter:

```
//
// Render a sprite to the off-screen bitmap.
//

void RenderSpriteOffScreen(PSPRITE pSprite, LPRECT prcClip)
{
    RECT rc;

    if (!G.hdcWinG) return;

    dprintf4("RenderSprite()");

    //
    // See if the sprite rectangle is visible in the clip rectangle.
    //

    if (prcClip) {
        GetSpriteRect(pSprite, &rc);
        if (!IntersectRect(&rc, &rc, prcClip)) {
            return;
        }
    }
```

```
    RenderDIBBitsOffScreen(pSprite->pDIB,
                           pSprite->x,
                           pSprite->y,
                           prcClip,
                           // Set the y offset to the correct position
                           // for a multi-image sprite.
                           pSprite->multi_index,
                           pSprite->bTopLeft,
                           TRUE); // transparent
}
```

Here, the `multi_index` of the sprite being rendered is passed in to `RenderDIBBitsOffScreen` (remember that the loader code sets this value to 1 if the sprite isn't a multi-image sprite).

All that's left now is to modify `RenderDIBBitsOffScreen` (and one function that it calls, `GetDIBPixelAddress`) and the sprite-movie implementation will be complete. In fact, all we need to do to `RenderDIBBitsOffScreen` is to pass the new fifth parameter on through to `GetDIBPixelAddress`. Here's the function:

```
void RenderDIBBitsOffScreen(PDIB pDIB, int x, int y, LPRECT prcClip,
                            int index,
                            BYTE bTranClr, BOOL bTrans)
{
    RECT rcDraw, rcDIB;
    HPBYTE pStartS;
#ifndef FAST32
    HPBYTE pStartD;
#endif
    // Destination 48-bit pointer
    WORD DestSegment;
    DWORD DestOffset;
    long lScanS, lScanD;
    BOOL TopDown = (DIB_HEIGHT(G.pdibWinG) < 0) ? TRUE : FALSE;

    //
    // Intersect the clip rectangle with the off-screen DIB to make
    // sure we don't try to draw to any invalid coordinates.
    //

    rcDraw.top = rcDraw.left = 0;
    rcDraw.right = DIB_WIDTH(G.pdibWinG) - 1;
    // DIB_HEIGHT could be negative for a top-down DIB.
    rcDraw.bottom = abs(DIB_HEIGHT(G.pdibWinG)) - 1;

    if (prcClip) {
        if (!IntersectRect(&rcDraw, &rcDraw, prcClip))
            return;
    }

    //
    // Intersect the clip rectangle with the DIB rectangle.
```

continued on next page

continued from previous page

```
    //

    rcDIB.left = x;
    rcDIB.right = x + DIB_WIDTH(pDIB) - 1;
    rcDIB.top = y;
    rcDIB.bottom = y + DIB_HEIGHT(pDIB) - 1;

    if (!IntersectRect(&rcDraw, &rcDraw, &rcDIB))
        return;

    //
    // We have a sprite that is at least partially visible in
    // the clip rectangle.
    // Calculate the address of the first pixel of the bottom
    // scan line for the given index (if this is a sprite movie).
    //
    pStartS = GetDIBPixelAddress(pDIB, index,
                                 rcDraw.left - x,
                                 rcDraw.bottom - y);
```

Here, the index is passed to `GetDIBPixelAddress` as a new second parameter. All the real work (what little there is) is done in `GetDIBPixelAddress`, which is found in DIB.C:

```
HPSTR GetDIBPixelAddress(PDIB pDIB, int index, int x, int y)
{
    HPSTR p;
    long lWidth;

    //
    // Make sure it's in range; if it's not, return zero.
    //

    if ((x < 0)
    || (y < 0)
    || (x >= DIB_WIDTH(pDIB))
    || (y >= DIB_HEIGHT(pDIB))) {
        dprintf1("Attempt to get out of range pixel addr");
        return NULL;
    }

    //
    // Calculate the scan-line storage width.
    //

    lWidth = DIB_STORAGEWIDTH(pDIB);

    ASSERT(lWidth <= DIB_WIDTH(pDIB) + 3);
    ASSERT(lWidth >= DIB_WIDTH(pDIB));

    p = (HPSTR) DIB_PBITS(pDIB);
    p += (long)((DIB_HEIGHT(pDIB)*index)-y-1) * lWidth + (long)x;
```

```
    return p;
}
```

Here's where the straightforward nature of the task of implementing sprite movies is really apparent. The second parameter to `GetDIBPixelAddress` is the `multi_index` of the sprite movie, which was passed all the way down from the `Render` function. This index is the number of the frame to be rendered. Because sprite movies are stored in vertical strips, adding just *one multiplication* makes `GetDIBPixelAddress` return the proper address for the frame. Voila! Sprite movies!

Testing and Enhancing Sprite Movies

Now that you've implemented the basic characteristics of sprite movies, you can create a few .BMP files as vertical movie strips and test them out. There are plenty of programs available for creating 256-color .BMP files, but you'll need to make sure that the files you create have the proper vertical spacing to reflect the individual sprite size. Sometimes it's easiest to create the first sprite, copy and paste it into the next vertical frame (remember that the frames are played from bottom to top), and then modify it as necessary.

Once you've created the bitmap for a sprite movie, you can stamp it with STAMPDIB to tell the loader how many frames there are in the movie. Make sure you get this number right; if you stamp the file with more frames than the bitmap can accommodate, the code will index right off the end of the bitmap and crash with a GP fault! It wouldn't be difficult to check for this condition, of course, but this would cost some time in the slightly time-critical `GetDIBPixelAddress` function.

It should be clear how you can modify the code to use sprite movies to do different things. You could add a simple counter that increments the frames of the sprite movie less frequently, slowing down the frame rate. By changing the values in `vx` and `vy`, you would effectively change both the speed and direction of the sprite; you could use this information to select a frame of the sprite movie that represents the orientation of the sprite.

Summary

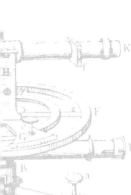

So far, the sprites in our sprite engine don't interact with one another—they float around on the screen passing over or under other sprites, depending on their z-order. While this may be useful for certain game characters, you'll often want sprites to react when they run into each other. Implementing this feature, usually called *collision detection,* is the subject of the next chapter.

16

Detecting and Reacting to Collisions

come tu vedi fare le manovelle ... le quali si movono e l'alza
e i grã pesi ... le ... sforzano ...
orzare nella ... della manovella ...
a forza ... più l'omo ...

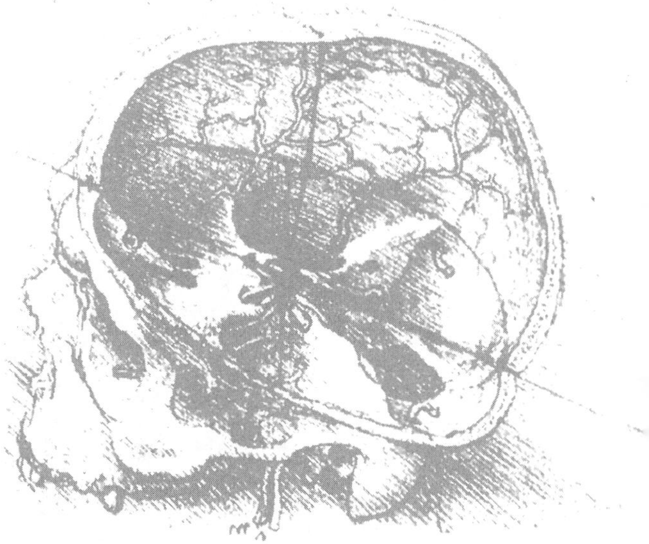

16

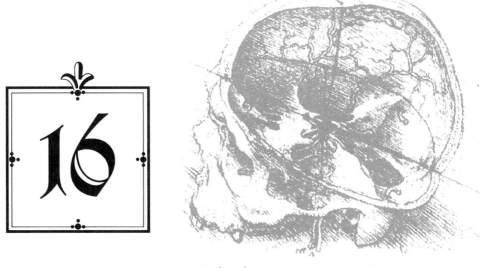

Detecting and Reacting to Collisions

Sprites that simply move around on a computer screen without interacting with one another are only so interesting to watch. Even if you add sprite movies to your game, you'll need to implement some kind of artificial intelligence if you want your program to avoid appearing repetitive and uninspired.

Probably the simplest, but most effective, behaviors to program are the reactions of objects to being hit by other objects—you might call it Newtonian-style artificial intelligence. In almost every game—and especially in two-dimensional sprite-based games—object collisions are a crucial part of play.

What Is a Collision?

It's important to think for a moment about what actually constitutes a collision in the context of a game. In a Newtonian world, when two objects attempt to occupy the same space at the same time, they collide. This is the kind of event you want to detect in your game. In a two-dimensional sprite-based world, collisions are relatively easy to define: Two (or more) sprites that overlap in any way are colliding. That means that for two sprites to collide, at least one opaque pixel of one sprite must overlap at least one opaque pixel of another sprite (see Figure 16-1).

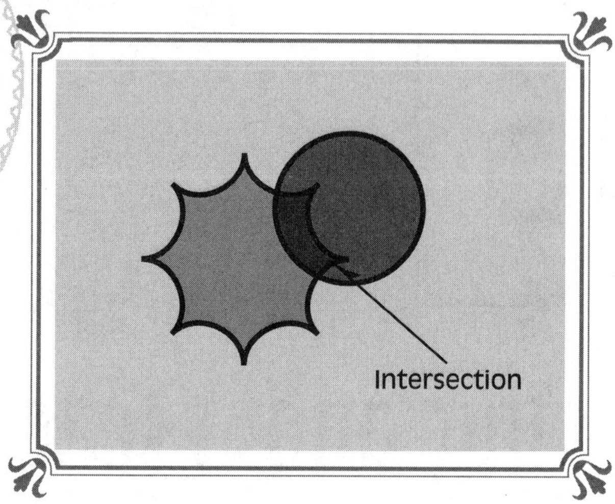

FIGURE 16-1
Intersecting sprites

The problem with this definition is that it requires a complete, pixel-by-pixel evaluation of each sprite to determine if a collision has occurred. If you methodically compare each pixel of a chosen sprite to each pixel of every other sprite, it will take you longer to detect collisions than it will to *draw* all the sprites—considerably longer, in fact. This is usually called an *n-squared algorithm*. Unfortunately, collision detection is an inherently *n*-squared kind of problem. The trick is to minimize the number of comparison operations that you must perform.

In fact, there *are* shortcuts that can significantly reduce the overhead required to detect an overlapping of two or more sprites. The most obvious shortcut involves comparing only the *bounding rectangles* of each sprite at the *n*-squared level. In the sprite engine, every sprite has a bounding rectangle that is used for generating the redraw-rectangle list for updating the display. You can use these rectangles to optimize the collision-detection process, as well—if the bounding rectangles of two sprites don't intersect, then the sprites don't intersect, either. Any rectangles that *do* intersect might represent sprites that have overlapping pixels (see Figure 16-2).

Of course, there are cases in which the bounding rectangles of two sprites intersect but the sprites have no intersecting opaque pixels (see Figure 16-3). In these cases, there's no shortcut for finding whether there is an actual intersection. You must test the pixels of one sprite against the pixels of the other. The most straightforward method here would be to test each pixel in one sprite against *every pixel* of the other sprite. This can be a very time-consuming process, though, especially if the sprites do not intersect or if the second sprite intersects only the "last" pixel of the first sprite. To find the intersection shown in Figure 16-4, for example, the algorithm would need to test every pixel in the first sprite against every pixel in the second sprite.

Fortunately, you can optimize even this test. If the bounding rectangles of two sprites intersect, then the only possible place their opaque pixels can overlap is in the

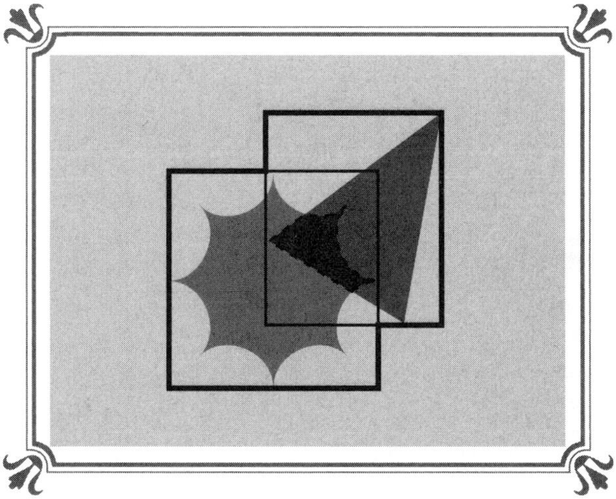

FIGURE 16-2

Intersecting bounding rectangles

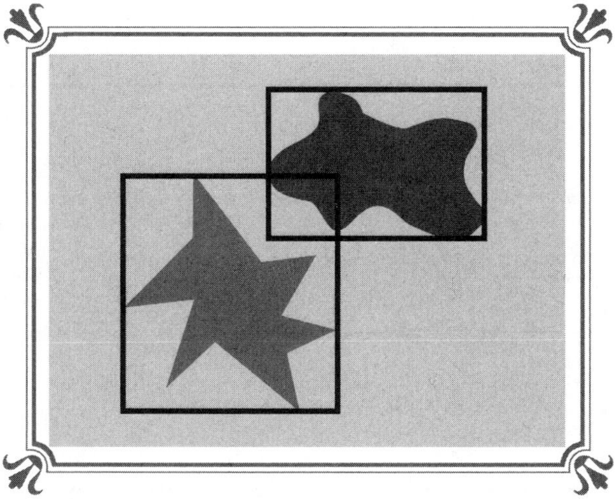

FIGURE 16-3

Intersecting bounding rectangles that do not contain intersecting sprites

rectangle that is the intersection of the two bounding rectangles (see Figure 16-5). As you might remember from Chapter 13, any algorithm that works on pixels is always going to be faster when it has fewer pixels to consider. Testing only the pixels within the intersecting box is going to be faster than testing all the pixels.

How Much Accuracy Is Necessary?

It is rarely necessary for a game to examine two entire sprites in pixel-to-pixel detail; usually, the bounding-rectangle-intersection test is sufficient to determine if there has been a collision. However, the characteristics of your sprites can make a difference

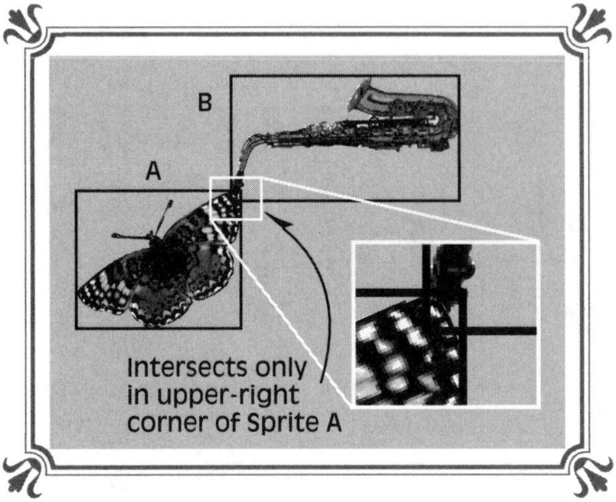

FIGURE 16-4

The most time-consuming collision of DIB sprites to detect

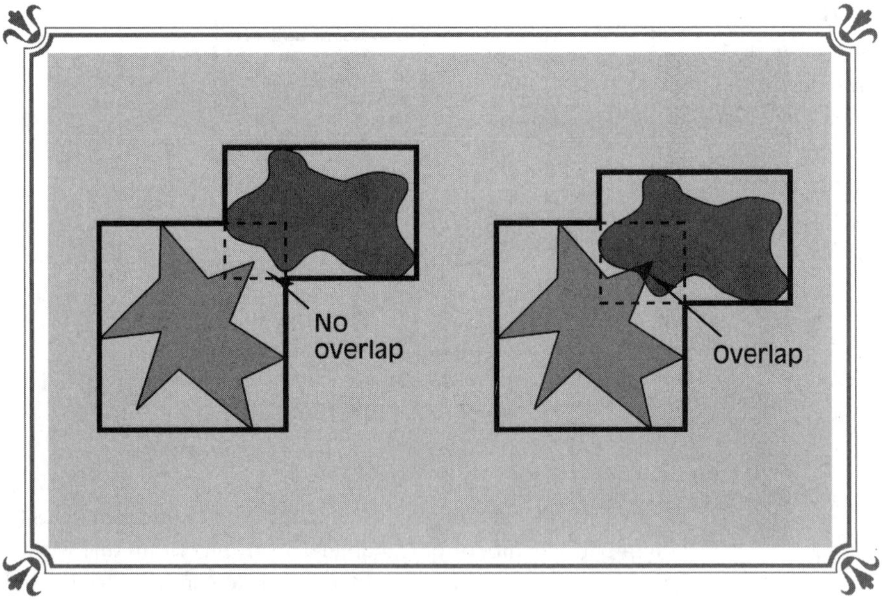

FIGURE 16-5

Testing the intersecting rectangle

here. For example, if the opaque parts of two sprites occupy only a small portion of their overall bounding rectangle, their collision might not look very realistic. (Of course, such sprites aren't using memory very efficiently, either!) Also, if one sprite is actually a sprite movie whose number of opaque pixels varies depending on the frame of the movie, a program that employs shortcuts may declare collisions when none appear to have taken place.

How accurate you make your collision detection really depends on how loose a definition of "collide" you're willing to accept. Most game algorithms favor speed over accuracy, because speed is generally much more important to play. However, you want to make sure your compromises don't impair the user's experience. Experimentation is sometimes the only sure way to tell how something will work in practice.

Collision-Detection Code

Enough theory—let's move on to the code. The first thing to do is to create a couple of new variables for the SPRITE structure to help with collision detection. Here's the new structure:

```
struct _SPRITE {
    struct _SPRITE FAR *pNext;  // Pointer to the next item
    struct _SPRITE FAR *pPrev;  // Pointer to the previous item
    PDIB pDIB;                  // DIB image of the sprite
    int x;                      // x coordinate of top-left corner
    int y;                      // y coordinate of top-left corner
    int z;                      // z order for sprite
    int vx;                     // x velocity
    int vy;                     // y velocity
    int width;                  // Width of the bounding rectangle
    int height;                 // Height of the bounding rectangle
    BYTE bTopLeft;              // Top-left pixel value
    COLORREF rgbTopLeft;        // Top-left pixel color
    BOOL bSelectable;           // TRUE if the sprite can be selected by
                                // mouse
    int multi;                  // Number of images if this is a multi-
                                // image sprite
    int multi_index;            // Used for storing current multi-index
    BOOL bCanCollide;           // True if this sprite can collide
    BOOL bHit;                  // This sprite has collided
} SPRITE, FAR *PSPRITE;
```

The last two members are new. The first of these, **bCanCollide**, is a Boolean you set to TRUE for every sprite for which you want to detect collisions. (Keep in mind that you might very well want to ignore collisions that occur between certain sprites.) The other new member variable is **bHit**, which the program sets when it discovers that the sprite has intersected another sprite.

Now that the sprite has a place to store some basic collision information, we need to initialize these variables when the sprite is loaded (in **LoadSprite** in SPRITE.C). Because the **bCanCollide** member can vary for each sprite, it would be a good idea to store this setting with the sprite file somehow, much as you stored the number of frames in a sprite movie. In fact, you can use the same technique, this time storing a 1 or a 0 in the **biYPelsPerMeter** member of the BITMAPINFOHEADER. For the sake of simplicity, I'll just initialize **bCanCollide** to TRUE here for sprites loaded with **LoadSprite** and assume that we care about collisions for all sprites:

```
.
.
.
pSprite->x = 0;
pSprite->y = 0;
pSprite->z = 0;
pSprite->vx = 0;
pSprite->vy = 0;
pSprite->bSelectable = TRUE;
pSprite->bCanCollide = TRUE;
pSprite->bHit = FALSE;
pSprite->pNext = NULL;
pSprite->pPrev = NULL;
dprintf4("Sprite is %u by %u", pSprite->width, pSprite->height);
.
.
.
```

Now, where do we put the actual test? The positions of the sprites are updated in the function **UpdatePositions**, so the test should obviously be somewhere near there. Since the test is based on the positions of the sprites, it makes sense that the program should update the positions of all the sprites before testing them for collisions. The test function is called **CheckForCollisions** and goes at the end of the main sprite list-walk loop in **UpdatePositions**.

```
.
.
.
    bChanged = TRUE;
    }

    pSprite = pSprite->pNext;
}
//
// Test for collisions at the new positions.
//
if (CheckForCollisions()) {
    //
    // Test hit sprites.
    //
    pSprite = G.pSpriteList;
    while (pSprite) {
        if (pSprite->bHit) {
            // Add update rectangle. Erase.
            GetSpriteRect(pSprite, &rcPos);
            Render(&rcPos, NO_UPDATE);
            // Do something to the sprite...
            .
            .
            .
        }
        pSprite = pSprite->pNext;
```

```
        }
    }
    .
    .
    .
```

The `CheckForCollisions` function does the real work, performing the necessary *n*-squared walk of the sprite list and setting the `bHit` variable to TRUE for sprites that collide. It returns TRUE if any sprites collided or FALSE if there were no collisions. You'll find `CheckForCollisions` in SPRITE.C.

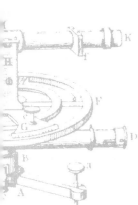

```
//
// Check for sprite-to-sprite collisions.
//
int CheckForCollisions()
{
    RECT r1, r2, rInt;
    int retval = FALSE;
    PSPRITE pTestSprite, pSprite;

    if (!G.pSpriteList)
        return FALSE;

    pTestSprite = G.pSpriteList->pNext;

    while (pTestSprite) {
        // First, can this sprite collide?
        if (!pTestSprite->bCanCollide) {
            pTestSprite = pTestSprite->pNext;
            continue;
        }

        GetSpriteRect(pTestSprite, &r1);
        pSprite = G.pSpriteList;

        while (pSprite) {
            // Don't test against self,
            // sprites that can't collide,
            // or  sprites that have already been hit.
            if (pSprite == pTestSprite || !pSprite->bCanCollide
                || pSprite->bHit) {

                pSprite = pSprite->pNext;
                continue;
            }

            GetSpriteRect(pSprite, &r2);
            if (IntersectRect(&rInt, &r1, &r2)) {
//#define TESTING
#ifdef TESTING
                HDC hdc = GetDC(G.hwndMain);
                FrameRect(hdc, &rInt, GetStockObject(BLACK_BRUSH));
```

continued on next page

continued from previous page

```
                    ReleaseDC(G.hwndMain, hdc);
                    MessageBox(NULL, "Collision!", "", MB_OK);
#endif

                    // Collision!
                    pTestSprite->bHit = TRUE;
                    retval = TRUE;
                    break;
                }
                pSprite = pSprite->pNext;
            }
            pTestSprite = pTestSprite->pNext;
    }
    return retval;
}
```

This function tests every sprite against every other sprite that can collide (note that a sprite is prevented from testing itself) to see if it intersects. **IntersectRect** does all the work here. There's also some conditional testing code that draws a black rectangle where the two bounding rectangles intersect and brings up a message box so that you can step through the test and watch the changing size and position of the intersection rectangle.

There are couple of things to note about this function. First, this version of it stops testing as soon as it finds there has been *one* collision with the current sprite (**pTestSprite**). This is another play-dependent decision. You could just as easily *increment* the **bHit** member variable for each hit detected and let the inner loop walk the whole list. Then **bHit** (which shouldn't be a Boolean in this case) would equal the number of other sprites that collide with the current sprite. For some games, this approach might be useful. It requires that the list *always* be walked through to completion, though. The example I've listed here walks the list only up to the first collision (if there is one).

Also note that this function doesn't compare sprites on a pixel-to-pixel level. If the collisions don't look real enough because there are large areas of transparent pixels inside a sprite's bounding box, you might want to add per-pixel testing. You should implement any such precise collision detection in the **IntersectRect** test. (This test, which is beyond the scope of this book, will probably need to be in assembly language.) If the sprites in your game move fast enough, you might not want to bother making your test this stringent. It will probably be difficult if not impossible for a player to tell the difference.

There's only one thing missing. Before we test all the sprites for collisions, we need to clear the **bHit** flag in each sprite at each round. The **ClearSpriteHitFlags** function in SPRITE.C does this.

```
//
// Clear the hit flags for all sprites.
//
```

```
void ClearSpriteHitFlags()
{
    PSPRITE pSprite = G.pSpriteList;
    while (pSprite) {
        pSprite->bHit = FALSE;
        pSprite = pSprite->pNext;
    }
}
```

This function is called just before the program walks the sprite list testing for collisions. Here's the entire **UpdatePositions** function (with the call to **ClearSpriteHitFlags** highlighted) for your reference:

```
void UpdatePositions()
{
    PSPRITE pSprite;
    BOOL bChanged = FALSE;
    RECT rcPos;

    pSprite = G.pSpriteList;
    while (pSprite) {

        if (pSprite->vx || pSprite->vy) {
            //
            // Add the old (current) position of the sprite
            // to the redraw-rectangle list.
            //
            GetSpriteRect(pSprite, &rcPos);
            Render(&rcPos, NO_UPDATE);

            pSprite->x += pSprite->vx;

            // Wrap sprites around one edge to the other.
            if ((pSprite->vx < 0) && (pSprite->x + pSprite->width < 0)) {
                pSprite->x = DIB_WIDTH(G.pdibBkGnd);
            } else if ((pSprite->vx > 0) &&
                       (pSprite->x > DIB_WIDTH(G.pdibBkGnd))) {
                pSprite->x = - (int)pSprite->width;
            }

            pSprite->y += pSprite->vy;
            if ((pSprite->vy < 0) && (pSprite->y + pSprite->height < 0))
{
                pSprite->y = DIB_HEIGHT(G.pdibBkGnd);
            } else if ((pSprite->vy > 0) &&
                       (pSprite->y > DIB_HEIGHT(G.pdibBkGnd))) {
                pSprite->y = - (int) pSprite->height;
            }

            // Increment the sprite index for multi-image sprites.
            if (pSprite->multi)
                pSprite->multi_index = pSprite->multi_index+1 > pSprite-
```

continued on next page

continued from previous page

```
>multi
                                    ? 1 : pSprite->multi_index+1;
            else
                pSprite->multi_index = 1;

            //
            // Add the new position of the sprite
            // to the redraw-rectangle list.
            //
            GetSpriteRect(pSprite, &rcPos);
            Render(&rcPos, NO_UPDATE);

            bChanged = TRUE;
        }

        pSprite = pSprite->pNext;
    }

    //
    // Clear sprite collisions from the last round.
    //
    ClearSpriteHitFlags();

    //
    // Test for collisions at the new positions.
    //
    if (CheckForCollisions()) {

        //
        // Change hit sprites into explosion sprite movies.
        //
        pSprite = G.pSpriteList;
        while (pSprite) {
            if (pSprite->bHit) {
                // Add update rectangle . Erase.
                GetSpriteRect(pSprite, &rcPos);
                Render(&rcPos, NO_UPDATE);

                // Do something here....
                .
                .
                .
                bChanged = TRUE;
            }
            pSprite = pSprite->pNext;
        }
    }

    //
    // Render (with screen update)
    // if anyone changed position.
    //
```

```
    if (bChanged)
        Render(&rcPos, UPDATE_SCREEN); // Ask for the last one again.
}
```

This `UpdatePositions` function updates the current position of all the sprites, clears their `bHit` flags, and then tests each sprite against every other sprite for collisions. You can see by running the program with a few sprites defined (and the test code in `CheckForCollisions` turned off) that this function doesn't appear to slow down the sprites at all. Compared to the operation of actually copying pixels, the process of testing a few rectangles takes very little time.

Now we can turn our attention to making the sprites do something interesting whenever we detect a collision.

Reacting to Collisions

Deciding what should happen when two sprites collide is a game-design issue. In many games, when two objects collide, one explodes. In other games, objects bounce when they encounter other objects. In still other games, an object just stops moving when it hits a stationary object. All these behaviors are easy to program once you have the capability of basic collision detection.

One of the simplest approaches is to delete one of the two sprites involved in a collision. This doesn't take much code at all, as you can see:

```
    .
    .
    .
    //
    // Test for collisions at the new positions.
    //
    if (CheckForCollisions()) {

        //
        // Change hit sprites into explosion sprite movies.
        //
        pSprite = G.pSpriteList;
        while (pSprite) {
            if (pSprite->bHit) {
                PSPRITE next = pSprite->pNext;
                // Add update rectangle -- erase.
                GetSpriteRect(pSprite, &rcPos);
                Render(&rcPos, NO_UPDATE);

                // Delete the sprite.
                DeleteSprite(pSprite);
                pSprite = next;
                continue;
                bChanged = TRUE;
```

continued on next page

continued from previous page

```
}
                pSprite = pSprite->pNext;
            }
    }
        .
        .
        .
```

This code simply deletes any sprite that has its `bHit` flag set.

Now, for a slightly more interesting effect, let's use the sprite-movies feature of the sprite engine to turn the sprite with a set `bHit` flag into a sprite movie of an explosion.

Substituting Sprites

Before you can substitute one sprite for another, you'll need to define a helper function called `ReplaceSprite` in SPRITE.C:

```
//
// Replace a sprite in the sprite list.
//

void ReplaceSprite(PSPRITE pSpriteOrg, PSPRITE pSpriteRepl)
{
    if (!pSpriteOrg || !pSpriteRepl)
        return;

    // Link the new sprite into the sprite list.
    pSpriteRepl->pPrev = pSpriteOrg->pPrev;
    pSpriteRepl->pNext = pSpriteOrg->pNext;
    // Keep the old sprite's position.
    pSpriteRepl->x = pSpriteOrg->x;
    pSpriteRepl->y = pSpriteOrg->y;

    DeleteDIB(pSpriteOrg->pDIB);

    // Substitute the new sprite.
    *pSpriteOrg = *pSpriteRepl;
}
```

As you can see, this is straightforward code. After a safety check, it copies the previous and next sprite links from the original sprite into the replacement sprite. It also copies the position of the original sprite into the replacement. (The replacement sprite shows up in the same place as the original.) It then deletes the DIB associated with the original sprite and assigns the replacement sprite to the original.

It's easy to replace one sprite with another. In fact, the most difficult part is simply *loading* the replacement sprite! The easiest way to do this is to create a "special" sprite whose pointer is held in the global structure:

```
//
// Global data
//

struct {
    char *szAppName;                    // Application name
    HINSTANCE hAppInstance;             // Application instance
    HWND hwndMain;                      // Main window handle
    PSPRITE pSpriteList;                // Pointer to the list of sprites
    PDIB pdibBkGnd;                     // Background DIB
    PDIB pdibWinG;                      // Off-screen WinG DIB
    HDC hdcWinG;                        // Main off-screen WinG DC
    HBITMAP hWinGBitmap;                // WinG bitmap to select into WinG DC
    LPVOID pOffScreenBits;              // Address of WinG bitmap bits
    UINT uiTimer;                       // Update timer
    HPALETTE hpalCurrent;               // Current application palette
    BOOL bShowUpdateRects;              // Show update rectangles.
    BOOL bCaptured;                     // Is the sprite captured?
    char szIniFile[_MAX_PATH];          // .INI file name
    BOOL bAutoUpdate;
    PSPRITE pSpriteExplode;             // Explosion sprite
} G;
```

The last member is a PSPRITE that will point to a loaded sprite movie. A slight modification (read "hack") made to the code in INIT.C (function `LoadScene`) that loads sprites from an .INI file makes it easy to identify the special explosion sprite movie:

```
    .
    .
    .
    //
    // Read each sprite entry and create the sprite.
    //

    p = szSprites;
    while (*p) {

        //
        // Load the sprite.
        //

        dprintf3("  Sprite: %s", p);
        GetPrivateProfileString(p,
                                "dib",
                                "",
                                szDIB,
                                sizeof(szDIB),
                                szFile);
        if (!lstrlen(szDIB)) {
```

continued on next page

continued from previous page

```
            dprintf1("No DIB= entry for sprite");

        } else {

            if (!lstrcmp(p, "explosion")) {
                // Load the explosion sprite into its special place.
                G.pSpriteExplode = LoadSprite(szDIB, FALSE, NO_UPDATE);
                G.pSpriteExplode->bCanCollide = FALSE;
                G.pSpriteExplode->vx = 0;
                G.pSpriteExplode->vy = 0;
                p += lstrlen(p) + 1;
                continue;
            } else
                pSprite = LoadSprite(szDIB, TRUE, NO_UPDATE);

            if (pSprite) {

                //
                // Get any other information.
                //
                .
                .
                .
```

In a real game, you would probably load the explosion sprite and other special sprite objects from the resource file. Using an .INI file just makes it easy to change sprite definitions without compiling the resource file and relinking.

Summary

You've seen how simple basic collision detection can be. The most challenging aspect is deciding what should happen when two objects collide. This reaction, which can be critical to the commercial success of your program, is a factor of game design more than anything else.

You've also learned that detecting collisions with great accuracy might not be as important as maintaining high-speed performance. How much information you need and what you do with it will be determined by the circumstances of your particular game. Oftentimes, it will be enough just to know that a collision has occurred. You can then specify any of a variety of actions—like the ever-popular explosion.

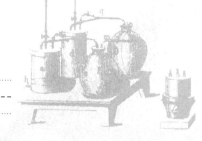

17

WinToon

[illegible] come tu debbi fare le manovelle [illegible] le quali si movano e lieva
e gran pesi [illegible] [illegible] sapere quanto [illegible]
forzare nella mano [illegible] per ma[illegible] a essa manovella perché quanto
la forza è più [illegible] più [illegible]

[illegible]

17

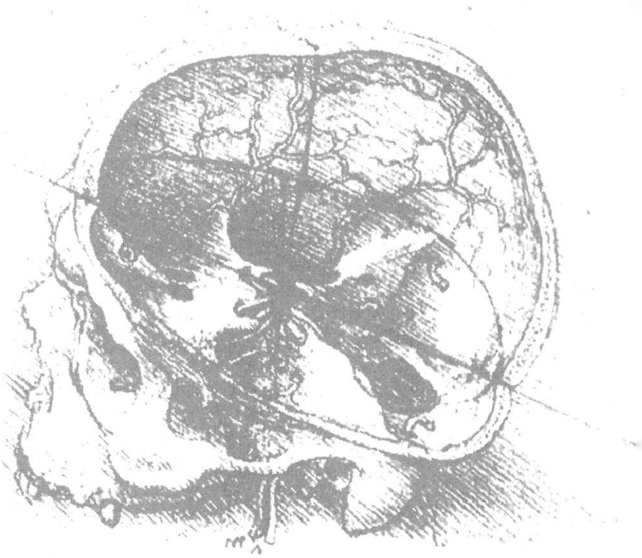

WinToon

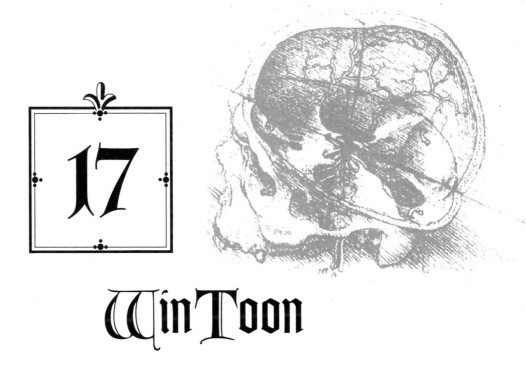

Traditionally, one of the primary issues for those programmers developing visually intensive titles for the Windows environment has been the lack of standard facilities for rendering animated graphics to the screen. This problem has been compounded by the slow video performance that results when you use the Windows GDI for bitmap manipulation. Over the last few years, the introduction of products like Video for Windows and accelerated video cards and drivers has helped to alleviate the speed problem, but the continued lack of standard facilities for quickly rendering complex graphics to the screen has forced most developers to write custom, project-specific tools to obtain the desired results.

Many of the developers who have been successful with Windows-based entertainment titles have had to begin by writing their own Windows-based sprite engines. Examples of such sprite engines include the Windows player for Broderbund's Living Books titles, as well as the engine used for 7th Level's TuneLand. Although they do the job, these engines are plagued by speed issues. They also experience compatibility problems with particular video cards. The engine for Lenny's MusicToons, for example, depended on knowing the exact layout of video memory, rendering this application incompatible with all but standard 8-bit color Windows video drivers.

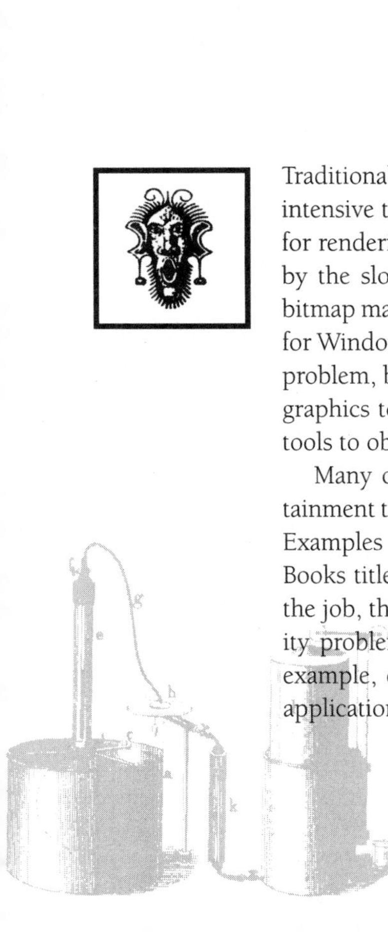

A solution of sorts came in late 1994 in the form of the WinToon animated sprite engine from the Microsoft Multimedia Developer Relations group. Based on technologies already present in Video for Windows and the newly released WinG accelerated graphics library, WinToon provides many of the facilities previously available only in a custom animated sprite engine. What WinToon offers is an easy method of overlaying animated sprites on a static background, synchronized with waveform audio. WinToon does not, however, provide the rest of the underlying logic that is necessary for creating a full title in the style of TuneLand or Living Books, nor all the facilities necessary for converting content into the format required for use in a WinToon-based title.

WinToon is available free of charge to developers. There are no run-time or licensing fees for shipping an application with WinToon. You can find a copy of the WinToon SDK on both the Multimedia Jumpstart and Developer Network Level 2 CDs, which are available from Microsoft Corporation. You can also download the SDK from the WINMM forum on CompuServe.

Bear in mind that WinToon 1.0 does have a few limitations. Currently, it is restricted to 8-bit color images and relies exclusively on the RLE compressor that comes with Video for Windows. At this time, you are also required to deal with all the performance and compatibility issues associated with WinG. (The release of new video drivers from most manufacturers of PC video boards, though, means that this last is really only a temporary problem.) If you can live with these minor inconveniences, WinToon can relieve you of the task of creating a custom sprite engine yourself.

How WinToon Works

WinToon is able to do what it does by rendering the video frames to the screen in a special order. WinToon starts this process by limiting the amount of data transferred from disk and the amount of screen area that needs to be updated. It then transparently draws the images on top of a specified background. You'll recall that when two bitmaps, the source or primary one of which contains pixels of a color defined as transparent, are merged into a single image, the transparent pixels are replaced by corresponding pixels from the destination or secondary bitmap. Figure 17-1 illustrates this concept. The images shown on the far left and in the center combine to produce the image on the far right. To achieve this result, I defined all white pixels in the image on the far left as transparent.

When you play a WinToon, you will usually specify a background image for WinToon to use when displaying video. This background image is the secondary, or destination, bitmap. The WinToon application will draw your WinToons transparently on this bitmap when it renders them to the screen. This approach has a few advantages. First, it requires only a single copy of the background to be stored in memory.

FIGURE 17-1

A simple example of transparency

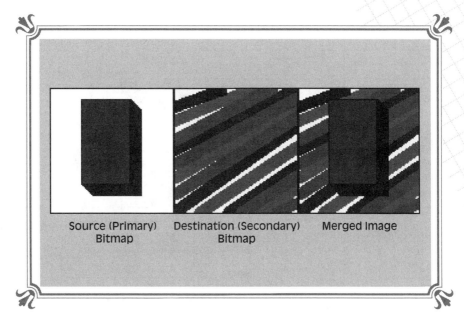

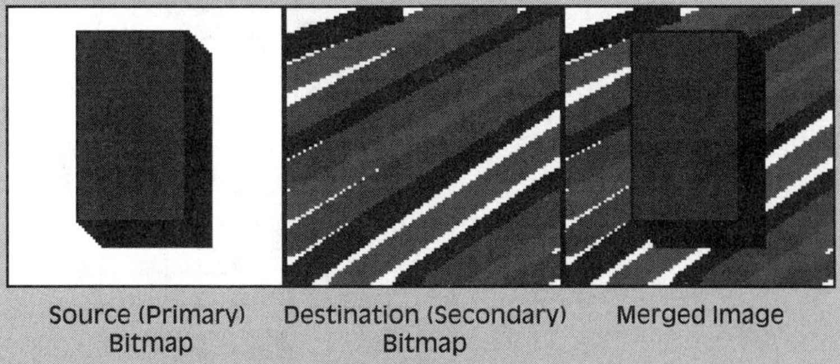

Second, it means that the WinToon pixels that before would have been made up of the background image are now a single color, allowing for greater compression and hence lower data-transfer rates. Finally, it allows you to use multiple backgrounds with the same WinToon, providing you with greater flexibility when authoring your title.

One of the ways that WinToon limits the amount of data being transferred from the disk is by using compressed images. Currently, WinToon supports only the RLE, or *run-length encoding,* compressor. This compressor looks at the scan lines of an image; instead of recording the color of each individual pixel, it records a pixel color and the number of pixels that contain that color. Figure 17-2 gives a graphical explanation of RLE compression. For images that consist of large areas of solid color (like cartoon characters), this compression method works rather well and can reduce the size of an image by as much as 10:1. But when dealing with anything more complex (in other words, images with wide and frequent variations in color), RLE quickly bogs down and can actually increase both the size and the load time of an image.

The RLE compressor is known as a "lossless" compressor—it does not throw away any data it receives, but instead returns an exact copy of the original data. Contrast this with compressors like Cinepack, Indeo, or JPEG, which return a reasonable facsimile, but not an exact copy, of the original images. While RLE can greatly reduce the size of an image, in and of itself it can't sufficiently cut the data-transfer rate of a sequence of images to an acceptable level.

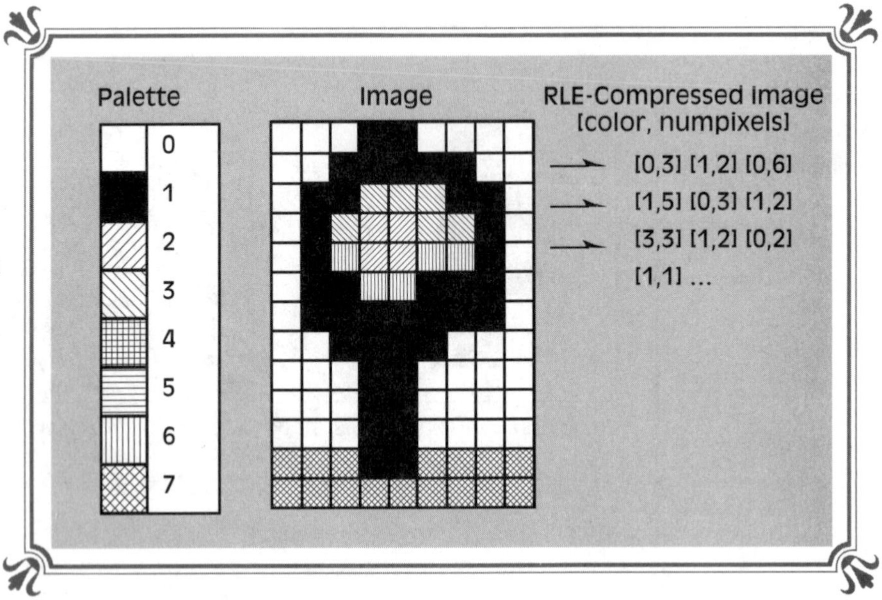

FIGURE 17-2

RLE converts a normal bitmap (consisting of a color entry for each pixel) into a series of number pairs

Video for Windows combines still-image compression with differential compression to further reduce the amount of data retrieved from disk. A differentially compressed sequence of images starts with a *key frame*—enough data to describe one complete image. The next frame consists of data describing only those pixels that changed from the previous frame. In movies, key frames are usually stored at certain intervals. All the frames in between the key frames are *differential frames*, which means that each is based on the frame preceding it. Figure 17-3 illustrates this concept. Differential compression by itself greatly reduces the amount of data that needs to be transferred from the disk, without degrading the quality of the image being displayed.

When WinToon renders frames to the screen, it uses WinG to handle the screen updates. This allows WinToon to substitute a composited bitmap for a full frame and render only the area that has changed. When building completed frames, WinToon uses its own custom BitBlt routines to build the final images. This permits it to use raw RLE data instead of requiring that the image be decompressed and analyzed pixel by pixel. This process reduces the amount of CPU time required to build a new, complete frame.

Finally, WinToon uses dirty-rectangle information read from the .AVI file to limit the actual screen area updated. (In WinToon, a dirty rectangle is a rectangular region of the screen that has changed from the last rendered frame and needs to be updated.) This information, which consists of only a few bytes per frame, is stored in a custom stream that WinToon defines at design time using the ScanAvi utility bundled with WinToon. ScanAvi analyzes the video frames in a normal .AVI file to determine what area changes from one frame to the next, and then uses the information to determine

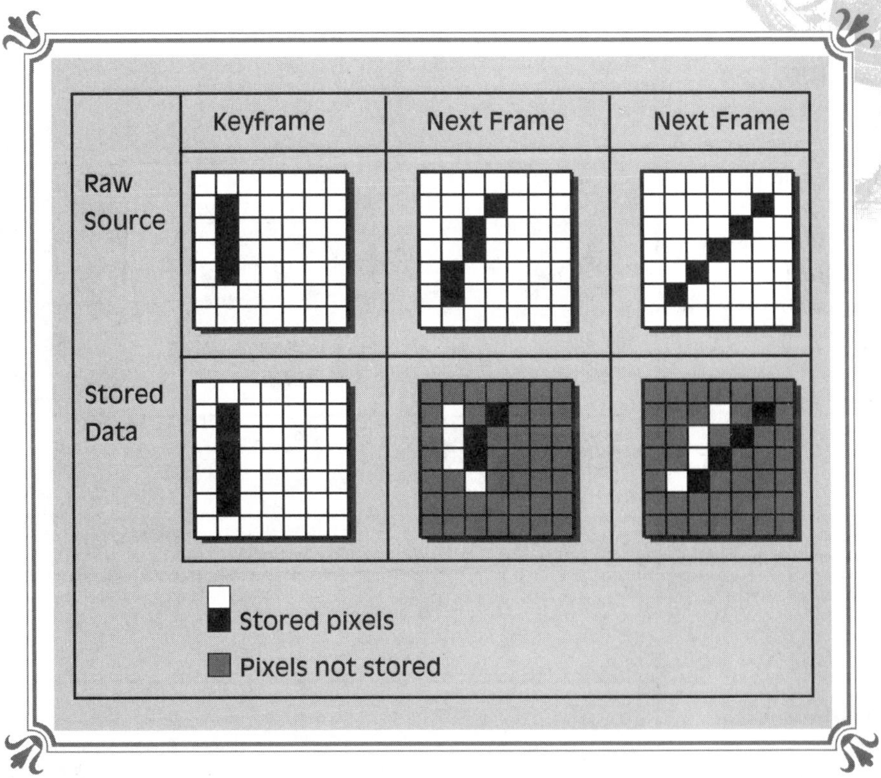

FIGURE 17-3

A sequence of differentially compressed images, showing the actual pixels stored for a key frame and two differential frames

the extents of the rectangle to be redrawn to the screen. This data is then stored in the custom stream. Figure 17-4 illustrates the process; notice the extra pixels added to erase those pixels of the first frame that are not used in the second frame.

Creating WinToon-Ready Content

Creating content that you can use with WinToon differs slightly from the normal process of creating content for use in an .AVI file. There is currently, of course, the 8-bit color limitation, but WinToon content also needs to be of the type that the RLE compressor can compress efficiently. Finally, it must be appropriate for the type of animation that WinToon provides. For example, material captured from video tape is not a good basis for a WinToon—there are great variations in color within each frame, and there are a large number of changes between frames. Drawn animation cels, which usually feature a relatively small and consistent set of colors, make for more appropriate content. Figure 17-5 provides some examples of good and bad source material for WinToons. The image on the right would compress and scan very easily,

FIGURE 17-4

Two consecutive WinToon .AVI-file frames and the rectangle required to update the screen

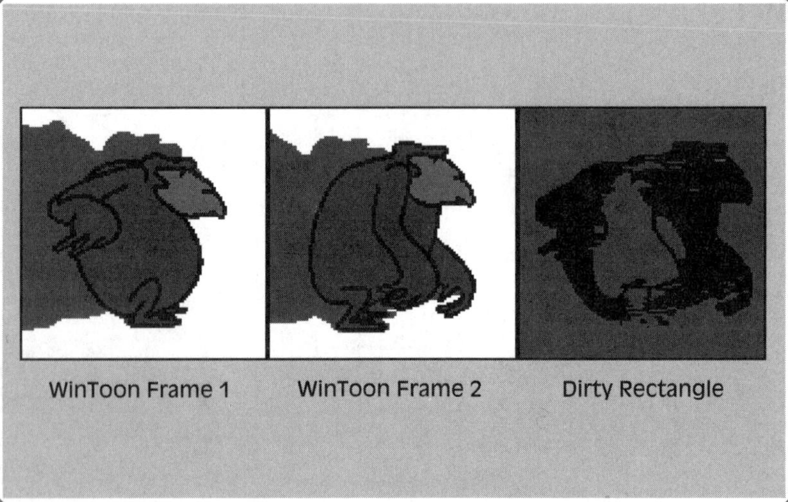

FIGURE 17-5

Evaluating source materials for WinToons

so it would be an ideal basis for a WinToon. The image on the left, however, would not be appropriate—it would be difficult to compress and would not scan for limited changes.

Creating Artwork for WinToons

Given the nature of the program, successful WinToons are usually cartoon-style animated characters or objects. One possible method for creating the source material would be to have professional animators create traditional cartoon cels, scan these cels on a solid background, bring each scanned frame into a bitmap editor, clean up the edges of the image, and reduce the colors in the image. A second possibility would be to create the artwork on the computer using animation-oriented software like Deluxe Paint, Autodesk Animator, or Disney Animation Studio, and then export the completed frames to bitmaps.

Before or after you've created the visual content, you will also need to create a soundtrack (if you want one) to play back with your animated sequence of frames.

Converting to an .AVI

Once your artwork and any accompanying soundtrack are finished, it is time to create the initial .AVI file from which your WinToon will be created. Several tools can do this, including Adobe Premiere for Windows and VidEdit. Here, I'll describe the process using VidEdit, since this tool comes with the Video for Windows SDK and is relatively easy to use.

Start off by determining the frame rate at which your cels will be running. This will help you synchronize your soundtrack. Generally speaking, this number should be a factor of 30 or 60 to ensure that Video for Windows does not have to deal with playing an odd number of frames per minute. (Video for Windows has been known to have problems with such frame rates.) Once you know your frame rate, place all your frames into sequentially numbered, individual .BMP files, starting at 0 (for example, FR0000.DIB, FR0001.DIB, and so on).

To create the .AVI file, follow these steps:

- Run VidEdit.
- Select Insert from the File menu (see Figure 17-6).
- From the File Type drop-down list, select DIB Sequence.
- Select the first file in your sequence of .BMP files (see Figure 17-6).
- Click on OK.

When you've finished creating the .AVI file, VidEdit should import all your frames into a new, video-only movie. Save a backup copy of your file, uncompressed, to be safe.

Next, you will need to change the frame rate of your movie. To do so, follow these steps:

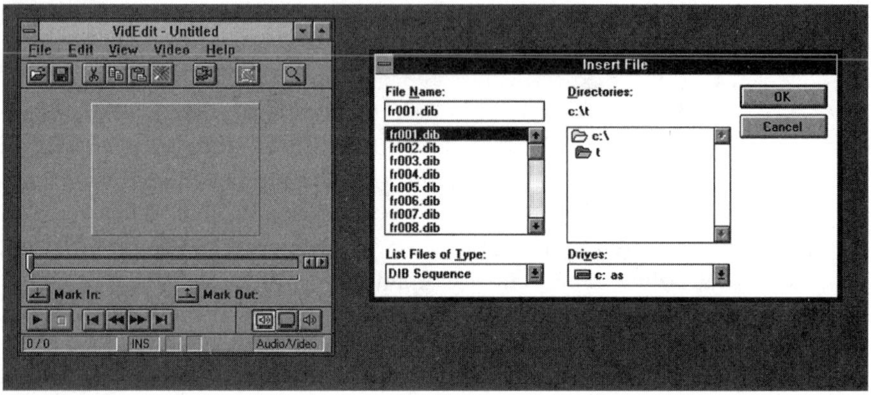

FIGURE 17-6

Inserting a numbered sequence of DIBs into a new .AVI file

- Select Synchronize from the Video menu.
- In the resulting dialog box (shown in Figure 17-7), enter the desired frame rate in the Video Speed field and enter 0 in the Play Duration field.
- Click on OK.

Your movie should now have the proper frame rate. Save it once again, uncompressed, to disk.

Now you can add your soundtrack (if you have one) to the movie. To do so, follow these steps:

- In the lower right corner of the VidEdit window are three buttons with icons for sound and video together, video alone, and sound alone. Click on the button showing the speaker icon (for sound alone).

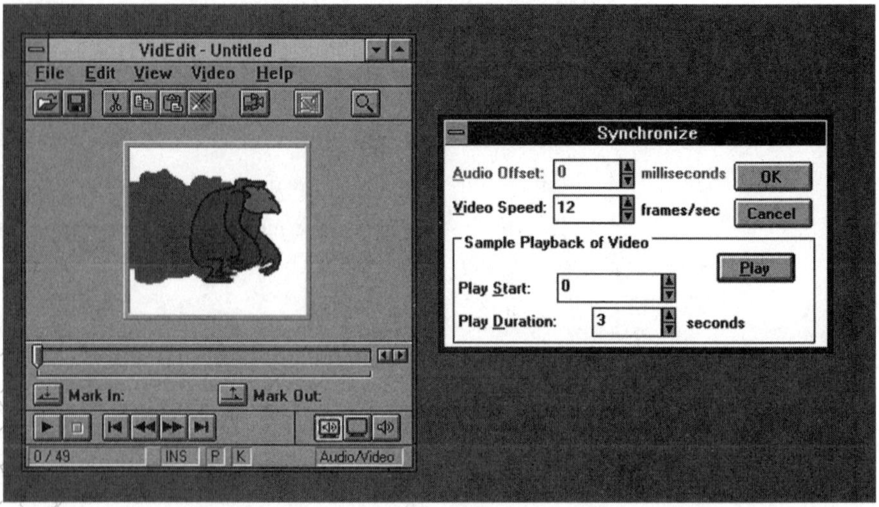

FIGURE 17-7

Changing the frame rate of an .AVI without discarding frames

- Set the frame selection to All by using the Set Selection command in the Edit menu.
- Select Insert from the File menu.
- Select Microsoft Waveform as the desired file type (see Figure 17-8).
- Select the .WAV file containing your soundtrack.
- Click on OK.
- You should now have a movie containing your soundtrack and your images. Play the movie to make sure that it synchronizes properly.
- If you need to adjust the frame rate or sound offset, use the Synchronize command in the Video menu.

When you've adjusted the file to your satisfaction, save an uncompressed copy.

The final step is to save a compressed copy of the file using the RLE compressor. Follow these steps:

- Select Save As from the File menu.
- Select the Compression Options button in the resulting dialog box.
- Click on Details. You'll fill in the resulting fields with the specifications for your final .AVI file.
- In the Video Compression Method field, select Microsoft RLE.
- Set the Quality slide to 100 percent.
- Fill in the Data Rate field. It should usually be set to 150 for single-speed CD-ROM drives or 300 for double-speed drives.
- Set the Interleaved Audio Every field to 1.
- For best performance when running from CD, instruct Video for Windows to pad the frames for CD-ROM playback.

FIGURE 17-8

Adding a soundtrack to an .AVI file

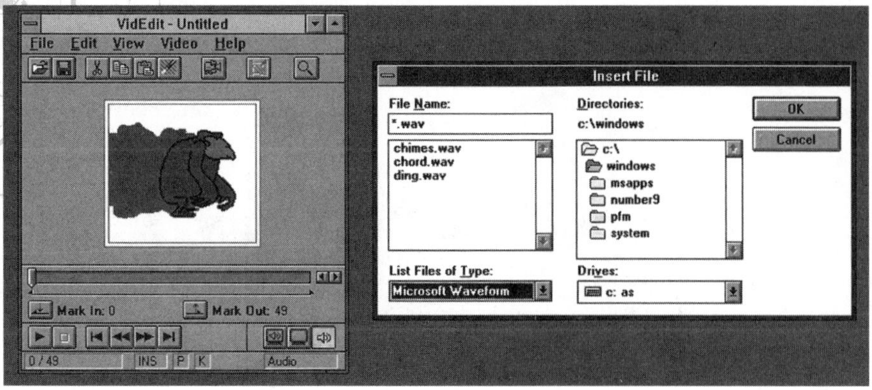

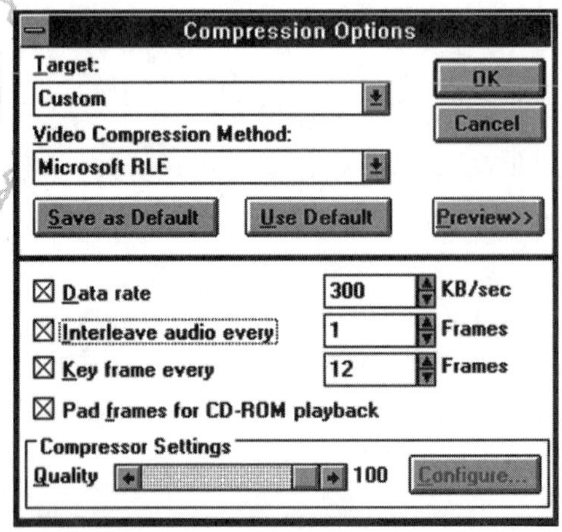

FIGURE 17-9

Changing the compression options for an .AVI file before saving it to disk

- Finally, you will need to set the number of frames between key frames. Generally, you should have no more than 1 key frame per second. So, for a movie with a frame rate of 12 frames per second, a key frame every 12 frames would be the practical minimum.

Your Compression Options dialog box should resemble the one I've completed in Figure 17-9. After following these steps, you will have an RLE-compressed movie that you can convert to a WinToon by using ScanAvi.

Using ScanAvi

ScanAvi is a utility that comes with the WinToon SDK. With it, you can create the third custom stream that will contain the dirty-rectangle information WinToon needs in order to render WinToons to the screen. Currently, ScanAvi will work only with movies you've compressed using the RLE compressor.

The easiest method for creating a WinToon is to start up ScanAvi and select Make Toon from the File menu. You will be prompted for the source and destination .AVI files, a log file name, and the scanning parameters. ScanAvi will then create a new .AVI file for you with the dirty-rectangle information WinToon requires. It is also possible to manually scan the .AVI file. See the WinToon documentation for more details on using ScanAvi.

Testing Your WinToons

The easiest way to test your completed WinToon, short of using it in your finished application, is to use the ToonApp application that is bundled with the WinToon SDK. This application allows you to create a .CTN file describing the hotspots and animation sequences in your WinToon .AVI file, and then run those hotspots and sequences on the proper background to see if they play correctly. The structure of a .CTN file is the same as that of a standard Windows .INI file. There are sections for scenes and hotspots, allowing you to specify background and foreground pictures, as well as the starting and ending frame indexes for animations.

ToonApp is almost a complete engine for a Living Books-style title, sans the state management required for branching and saving the current location in the application to disk. The C source code for ToonApp is included with the WinToon SDK for you to use as a reference when building your own applications.

Coding with WinToon

Adding WinToon to your application is, in most cases, as simple as handling a few WinToon-specific messages and loading and unloading WinToon movies. Once you've created a WinToon window and loaded a WinToon into it, you use standard MCI calls to control the playback of the movie. Here is a sample window procedure written in C of a simple WinToon application that plays a WinToon straight through from start to finish:

```
HTOON htoon;

LONG EXPORT WINAPI BasicToonWndProc(HWND hwnd, UINT message,
    WPARAM wparam, LPARAM lparam);
 {
    LONG ret;
    static UINT wm_ToonDraw = 0;
    WORD wMCIDeviceID;
    htoon = ToonFromWindow(hwnd);

    if (htoon && wm_ToonDraw == 0)
        wm_ToonDraw = ToonMessage(htoon);

    switch (message)
    {
    case WM_CREATE:
        // Create and attach a WinToon to this window.
      ret = ToonCreate(hwnd, lpCreate->cx, lpCrate->cy, 0);

        // Load an .AVI file into the WinToon window and start playing it.
        wMCIDeviceID = ToonOpenMovie(htoon, "TESTTOON.AVI", 255);
        mciSendCommand(hmovie, MCI_PLAY, MCI_MCIAVI_PLAY_WINDOW, NULL);

        return ret;

    case WM_DESTROY:

        // Destroy the WinToon window.
      if (htoon) ToonDestroy(htoon);
```

continued on next page

continued from previous page

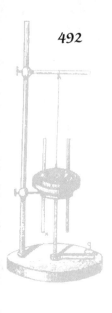

```
    //case ...
        // Your code here
    default:
        if (message == wm_ToonDraw)  //Message set with ToonSetMessage
            ret = HANDLE_WM_TOONDRAW(hwnd, message, wparam,
                   lparam, OnToonDraw);  //OnToonDraw is application-
defined.
        else
            /* ToonDefWindowProc defaults to DefWindowProc() */
            ret =  ToonDefWindowProc(hwnd, message,wparam,lparam);
        }

    return ret;
    }
```

This extremely basic window procedure creates a WinToon window, plays a WinToon at startup, and then destroys the WinToon when the window closes. It relies heavily on the default message processing of WinToon. **ToonDefWindowProc** defaults to the standard Windows message handlers, while handling all the WinToon-specific messages and any related Windows messages. The default window procedure for WinToon also takes care of handling messages like WM_ERASEBKGND, WM_PAINT, WM_PALETTECHANGED, and WM_QUERYNEWPALETTE. For more examples of window procedures, see the ToonApp source code in the WinToon SDK.

Installing WinToon on an end user's system is only slightly harder than executing a prebuilt install program. WinToon consists of a single DLL, WINTOON.DLL, which must be installed in the user's WINDOWS\SYSTEM directory (if it is not there already or is there in an older version). Remember to install the WinG run-time libraries *before* running WinToon. (See Chapter 11 for information on installing the WinG run-time libraries on an end user's system.) You must also link your application with WINTOON.LIB to gain access to the functions exported from WINTOON.DLL.

Using WinToon in Applications

Creating titles with WinToon is exceedingly simple; most of the work goes into creating code to manage navigation and the state of the application. You could in fact build a Living Books-style title almost entirely from the ToonApp sample code included with the WinToon SDK. All that you would need to add to this application would be static navigation buttons and a dialog box/menu interface for exiting the program and setting preferences such as sound volume.

You could generate a more exciting result by overriding several of the default WinToon message handlers to draw the elements of a WinToon movie in varying locations on the screen. This would allow for arcade- or adventure-style titles; you would simply use WinToon to handle all those animations you would traditionally handle with sprites. WinToon uses a custom BitBlt routine, so it would even be possible to perform some special effects at run time on the images being transferred.

What's Coming in the Future for WinToon?

The engineers at Microsoft are already developing WinToon version 2.0. Microsoft has even announced some of the possible additions. Here is a brief list of features you can expect to see in WinToon 2.0:

- Win32 (Win95/WinNT) support
- Greater-than-8-bit color support
- Support for all Video for Windows compressors

Summary

In this chapter, you learned not only what WinToon is, but how it works. You learned what types of content to use with this system, as well as the basics of how to include WinToon in your applications. For more detailed descriptions of the topics I've discussed here, see the WinToon SDK documentation. The WinToon SDK is included on this book's accompanying CD-ROM.

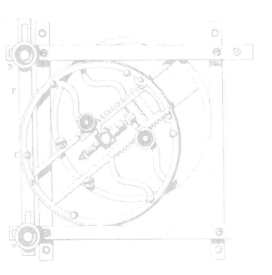

18

Game Smarts (AI)

[illegible]

[illegible]

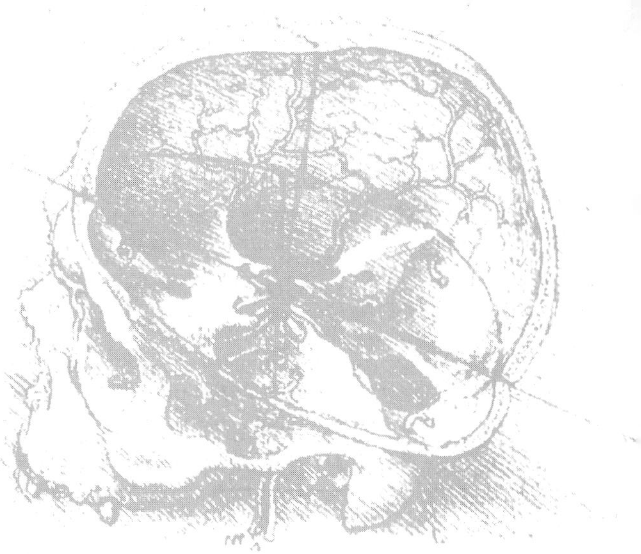

18

Game Smarts (AI)

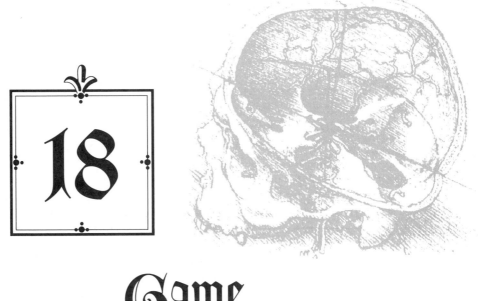

An electronic adversary worthy of the name is key to the success of any game. Surprising and seemingly intelligent actions on the part of your application are sure to hook and keep the interest of players. Whether it is deciding the next move on a chessboard or formulating tactics for a division of tanks, the game must afford the player a challenge. The programmer's job is not to bestow a game with true intelligence—that would be some trick—but to give the game enough tricks to keep the player entertained.

Game developers typically use only a moderate-sized subset of the artificial intelligence (AI) techniques available. They tend to stick to AI techniques that afford the best bang for the clock cycle—in other words, techniques that produce acceptably "intelligent" decisions *fast* rather than methods that have better results but are slower. In this chapter, I'll cover several of the basic AI techniques for injecting challenge and realism into a game.

Games Need Brains!

You've probably heard from time to time that a particular game is "too easy." If you examine the criticized game, you are likely to observe that it is, in fact, too *predictable* in its actions. The game's algorithm is simply not complex enough. Another way to arrive at this conclusion is to listen to the players who excel at these games: Most will say they have a plan they follow in order to win. In essence, they have discovered and are following the counteralgorithm. No wonder playing such games is boring: It's simply algorithm A against algorithm B. As you might expect, the advent of very sophisticated programs and users is making this type of game obsolete.

Many games do intentionally include some very "dumb" opponents, but there is a real difference between dumb and predictable. The latest first-person 3D action games tend to feature such a character. He's the one who disregards your enhanced platinum deflector shield and double-barreled ion rifle when he stands out in the open to get a clear shot at you with his pistol. These clods serve a clear and useful purpose. "Easy kills" like this provide the player an opportunity to practice before meeting more worthy opponents. Once having mastered these opponents, the player can virtually ignore them—they've done their bit to help the player better his or her skills in preparation for encountering significantly smarter and more powerful beasts.

Of course, at the other extreme you run the risk of implementing an algorithm that is unbeatable. For example, it would have been very easy to program the ghosts in Pac Man to have taken the shortest path to the player's destination, without realizing the consequences. (Refer to Figure 18-1 if you're too young to have had Pac Man's display indelibly printed on your memory.) The ghosts were frequently faster than the player, so death would have come swiftly and often. Fortunately, the designers recognized this pitfall and avoided it by finding methods for making the ghosts a bit more erratic in the early levels. This allowed 25 cents to furnish several minutes of play for even novice players.

FIGURE 18-1

Pac Man revisited

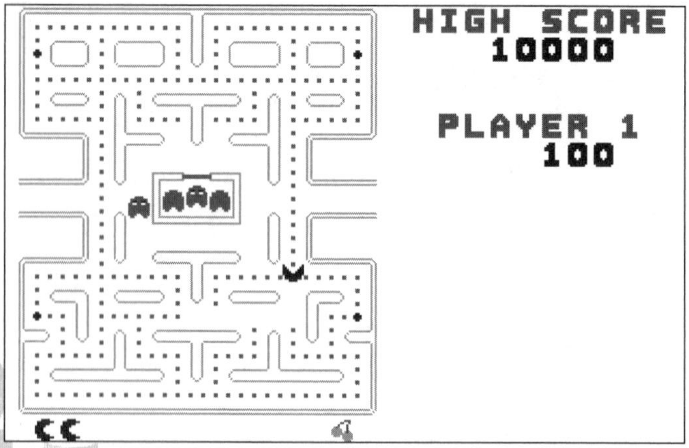

How Intelligent Should It Be?

Almost all games surfacing today feature some type of AI. Scaling your game's "intelligence" appropriately requires a great deal of care. To be successful, your game must provide just the right measure of challenge, and no more. Whether yours is a board, strategy, or action game, how you implement AI will have a distinct effect on its playability. Keep in mind that your game must be smart enough to challenge and amaze increasingly demanding players.

Board Games

Programmers usually endow board games with a sizable amount of artificial intelligence. They have been able to develop excellent algorithms that bring the level of computer play in some of these games close to that of human play. Very often, such games take advantage of an *intelligent search technique,* allowing the application to search through many options before choosing a suitable move. This technique is expensive to implement, but it often produces quite impressive results—in some cases, unbeatable ones.

Strategy Games

Obviously, the plethora of strategy games now on the market rely heavily on AI to produce stimulating combat situations. The algorithms are usually significantly more complex in this type of game than in most others; after all, the programmer must consider a great variety of tanks, planes, infantry, spaceships, and ogre platoons, each with its own strengths and weaknesses. To top it off, the implementation of the battlefield itself can make or break the game. Fortunately, given the "low action" requirements of most strategy games, programmers were able to find spare CPU time lying around to devote to advanced AI techniques. Thus, these games have been bestowed with algorithms for learning, evaluating, and searching, giving the illusion of significant intelligence on the part of the electronic opponent.

Action Games

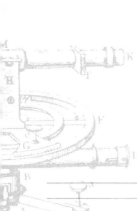

In the past, action games didn't rely on AI to the same extent other types of games did. Venerable Space Invaders' aliens, for example, simply zigzagged ever downward, regardless of what position the player took, dropping bombs with reckless abandon. But AI is adding another dimension of challenge to the new breed of 3D first-person games. These games are swarming with enemies who retreat when wounded and who ferret out and target a player's weaknesses. Some games even feature algorithms that analyze how the player acts and then formulate a personalized response. Welcome to the age where the program attempts to find *your* counteralgorithm.

Chasing, Evading, and Moving

Realistic motion improves the quality and believability of any simulation. By using AI techniques, you can make your game's creatures *appear* to act as if they were thinking entities. Creating this illusion of reality hinges on your program's ability to introduce random elements. How so? Well, consider this example. A player opens a door in a 3D simulation. All six of the creatures in the room always respond to such an action by sprinting directly at the player. The player suffers instant death, over and over and over. Sure, it's a great kill tactic—the computer probably loses only two or three of its creatures. But that's not really the point. The point is that the player always dies—and so, most likely, does his or her interest in the game.

By implementing a random element, you can ensure that the movements of your creatures imply that the creatures actually care about their own well-being. This makes the game playable. In other words, random motion can mitigate the effects of killer battle tactics while simultaneously creating a more realistic environment.

Realistic Movement

So what's needed for realistic movement? This, of course, depends on the nature of your game. Most creatures in DOOM, for example, head for the player but take a zigzagging path. This is simple and effective; it makes the creatures harder to hit, but allows them to advance.

Living creatures rarely move in a perfectly straight line. Consider a two-dimensional *xy* coordinate space. Straight lines are easy to come by—any point with an increasing *x* and static *y* component moves horizontally in a straight line. To introduce more erratic motion, we could just assign the *y* movement to a random value. This movement, though, would probably become *too* erratic and unrealistic. To remedy this problem, we can use the trigonometric functions SINE and COSINE to introduce curves:

```
x = SINE(f) * radius
y = COSINE(f) * radius  where f increases from 1 to 2p
```

If we plot these points, we'll get a circle with a size relative to *radius*. This doesn't do much to improve the situation, however; movement that follows a perfect circle is not much more realistic than movement that follows a perfectly straight line. We need a greater element of unpredictability.

Let's look at an example that might implement just the right degree of randomness. Say we have a game that features a firefly, and we need to find a convincing way for the bug to move. The illustration on the left in Figure 18-2 shows segments of several circles (in other words, arcs). By "pasting" these arcs together, we can create the path shown on the right in Figure 18-2. This erratic yet smooth path is similar to the kind a real firefly might follow.

By using different radii, we can create elliptical paths, producing movement that is even more realistic.

Simulating Creatures

Admittedly, movement that may be realistic for a firefly will not necessarily be realistic for an enemy in DOOM. The movement I've illustrated in Figure 18-2 is *quite* erratic and unpredictable. To tailor this to other creatures, we could "calm down" the algorithm by limiting the pool of available arcs. Or, because most creatures don't move in endless arcs, we could throw some straight lines into the mix. In any case, it's important that we preserve *some* degree of variety.

Let's build a sample program that will model a swarm of fireflies. (We can call it Bugs.) In this program, we'll simply move a designated number of fireflies (NUMBUGS variable) according to the arc method I outlined in Figure 18-2.

FIGURE 18-2

Combining arcs to create a smooth but unpredictable path

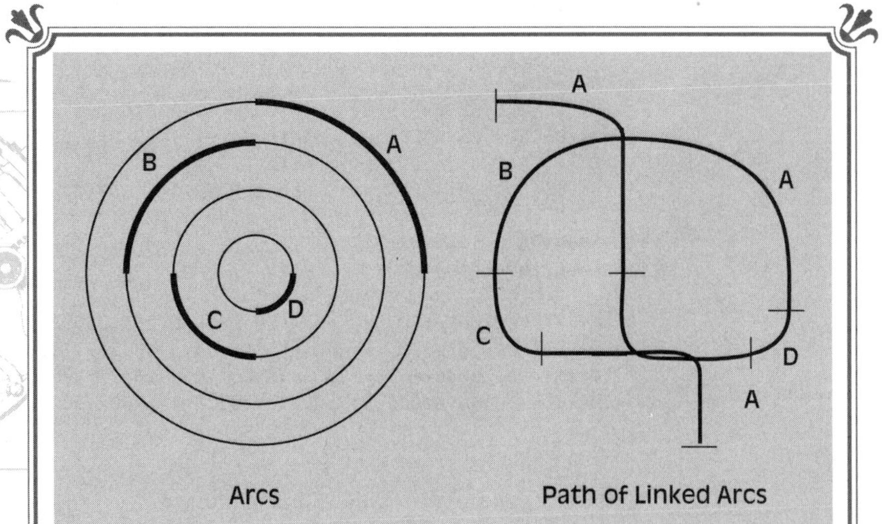

```
// Point array holds a plot point for each bug.
struct pt { int x,y; } point[NUMBUGS];

// Bug array holds a temporary arc and pivot for each bug.
struct abug { int xd,yd;              // Current angle in arc
              int xpivot,ypivot;      // Pivot point x and y
              int xlimit,ylimit;      // Max angle for this arc
              int xradius,yradius;    // Fluctuating radius value
              } bug[NUMBUGS];
.
.
.

// Bugs is implemented as a Windows screen saver. This is the main
// call routine.

void DoScreenSaver ()
{  int g;

    // Move all bugs except bug 0.
    for (g=1;g<NUMBUGS;++g)
      { // Erase the bug.
        SetPixel(hDC,point[g].x, point[g].y ,RGB(0,0,0));

        // Move the bug.
        movement(g);

        // Redraw the bug.
        SetPixel(hDC,point[g].x, point[g].y, RGB(0,255,0));
        }

    // Move bug 0 twice.
    SetPixel(hDC,point[0].x, point[0].y , RGB(0,0,0));
    SetPixel(hDC,point[0].x, point[0].y+1 ,RGB(0,0,0));
    SetPixel(hDC,point[0].x+1, point[0].y , RGB(0,0,0));
    SetPixel(hDC,point[0].x+1, point[0].y+1 , RGB(0,0,0));

    movement(0);
    movement(0);

    SetPixel(hDC,point[0].x, point[0].y,RGB(255,255,255));
    SetPixel(hDC,point[0].x, point[0].y+1 ,RGB(255,255,255));
    SetPixel(hDC,point[0].x+1, point[0].y ,RGB(255,255,255));
    SetPixel(hDC,point[0].x+1, point[0].y+1 ,RGB(255,255,255));
   }
```

The **DoScreenSaver** routine simply erases, moves, and redraws each bug. We accomplish the movement by piecing together arcs from ellipses in a random fashion. I've added more elements of erratic movement to account for the fact that fireflies often perform near-180-degree turns. This entailed imposing very little restriction on the program's choice of arcs, incrementing radii as an arc progressed, and effectively eliminating straight-line movement.

This code is for two dimensions, but I could have easily made it for 3D by adding a *z* coordinate. With this many fireflies in motion, however, this two-dimensional model does an admirable job of producing the illusion of 3D. Carefully designed two-dimensional movement algorithms often create this serendipitous effect.

```
// Movement routine - good stuff happens here
// Move whatever bug number is passed once according to its arc and so on.

 void movement (int g)
  { int x,y,xdist,ydist;

    // Check to see if x has exhausted its arc.
    // If so, pick a new arc and reset radius.
    if (++bug[g].xd >= bug[g].xlimit)
    { bug[g].xlimit = rand() % 350 + 10;
      bug[g].xARC   = 0;
      bug[g].xpivot = point[g].x;
      bug[g].xd     = bug[g].xlimit - (rand() % bug[g].xlimit);
     }

    // Check to see if y has exhausted its arc.
    if (++bug[g].yd >= bug[g].ylimit)
    { bug[g].ylimit = rand() % 350 + 10;
      bug[g].yARC   = 0;
      bug[g].ypivot = point[g].y;
      bug[g].yd     = bug[g].ylimit - (rand() % bug[g].ylimit);
     }

    // Calculate the new x and y offset.
    // sine/cosine * radius
    // (shift by 9 for fixed point math)
    x = (sine[bug[g].xd] * bug[g].xARC)>>9;
    y = (cosine[bug[g].yd] * bug[g].yARC)>>9;

    // Modify a bug's radius in real time, taking into
    // account the tightness factor.
    bug[g].xARC += (90-bug[g].xARC)/TIGHT;
    bug[g].yARC += (90-bug[g].yARC)/TIGHT;


// CHASE CODE HERE


    // Set the new x position.
    point[g].x = bug[g].xpivot + x;
```

continued on next page

continued from previous page

```
    // Allow for screen overlap.
    if (point[g].x < 0) point[g].x += screen.right;
    if (point[g].x > screen.right) point[g].x -= screen.right;

    // Set the new y position.
    point[g].y = bug[g].ypivot + y;

    // Allow for screen overlap.
    if (point[g].y < 0)  point[g].y += screen.bottom;
    if (point[g].y > screen.bottom)  point[g].y -= screen.bottom;
  }
```

The movement routine is really where the meat is. In our program, we've based firefly movement on an offset from a pivot point. Just as 3D graphics programmers often keep each object at its own local origin to facilitate operations such as rotation, we keep each bug at its own local origin to facilitate erratic arc combinations, producing a flurry around the pivot point. The program treats firefly 0 (array element 0) differently than the rest; it will be a target for other bugs to chase (you'll see this in a moment). The setting for the Number of Bugs option in the dialog box (screen saver setup) dictates how many fireflies are present. Running this program, you can see that the combination of elliptical arcs of differing radii gives each pixel an erratic but believable motion.

With very little modification, this code can make firefly 0 an object of affection. We simply change a firefly's direction so that it moves toward firefly 0 (by adding the code at the spot I've indicated in the previous listing). To do this, we could implement code such as:

```
if (point[g].x < point[0].x) point[g].x++;
  else point[g].x--;

if (point[g].y < point[0].y) point[g].y++;
 else point[g].y--;
```

Unfortunately, this simple method yields results that appear quite robotic: A firefly would take a perfectly diagonal path until either its *x* or *y* coordinate equaled that of firefly 0, and then it would proceed vertically or horizontally in a straight line to firefly 0. This is hardly what real fireflies do.

A slightly better method might be to use floating-point variables to keep track of the rise and the run from the given firefly to firefly 0:

```
Run  = point[0].x - point[g].x;
Rise = point[0].y - point[g].y;
```

Dividing both values by the larger of the two would cause the smaller to be less than 1 and the other to become 1. We could then add these offsets to the *x* and *y* coordinates. This method would work, but considering its detrimental effect on the ellusive randomness we've achieved, we might come to the conclusion that this code would be more appropriate for a heat-seeking missile than for a firefly.

An acceptable method for modeling erratic movement must include many random factors. When fireflies swarm around a light, there are always some individuals that remain a bit distant from the light, as if they were not particularly interested. To mirror this observation, we might use the following code:

```
// Get the distance to bug 0.
        xdist = abs(point[g].x - point[0].x) +1;
        ydist = abs(point[g].y - point[0].y) +1;

    // Be careful not to follow a beeline to bug 0
    // if the distance is greater than 5 and the bug "cares"
    // (in other words, the Swarm Factor hits).
    if ((abs(xdist-ydist) > 5) && (bug[g].xARC % SWARM))
     {
      // Prevent a diagonal path to bug 0.
      if (xdist>ydist/2)
      { if ((point[g].x > point[0].x) && (x > 0)) bug[g].xpivot--;
        if ((point[g].x < point[0].x) && (x < 0)) bug[g].xpivot++;
       }
      if (ydist>xdist/2)
      { if ((point[g].y > point[0].y) && (y > 0)) bug[g].ypivot--;
        if ((point[g].y < point[0].y) && (y < 0)) bug[g].ypivot++;
       }
      }
```

Initially, the program calculates the relative distance between the interested firefly and firefly 0. We have used the Swarm Factor setting (from the dialog box) to dictate how much a firefly should "care" about chasing firefly 0. Median values tend to produce a realistic swarm; the bulk of the population will be persistently intent on catching firefly 0, but there will always be a few stragglers who remain indifferent.

To prevent the fireflies from following a common path to the goal, we allow a firefly's *x* or *y* direction to "care" about the chase only as long as it is a relatively different distance from the *x* or *y* coordinate of firefly 0. This obviates the "beelining dilemma." We modify only the paths of those fireflies who are currently not heading for firefly 0. Because we have introduced randomness, some fireflies will "accidentally" head in the direction of firefly 0 anyway; we don't need to alter their courses. If the program determines that a given firefly *does* care, we move its pivot (not its current location) nearer the target.

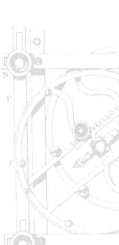

We can easily modify this procedure for use in 3D or to emulate any type of living creature's movements. It tends to create a sort of ambling effect. The chase implementation with application-specific modifications is also portable. Most creatures "care" much more about reaching their target than our fireflies do, so we'll need to make changes to facilitate the degree of their desire, but it will always remain true that algorithmic "beelines" do not adequately represent the actions of living creatures.

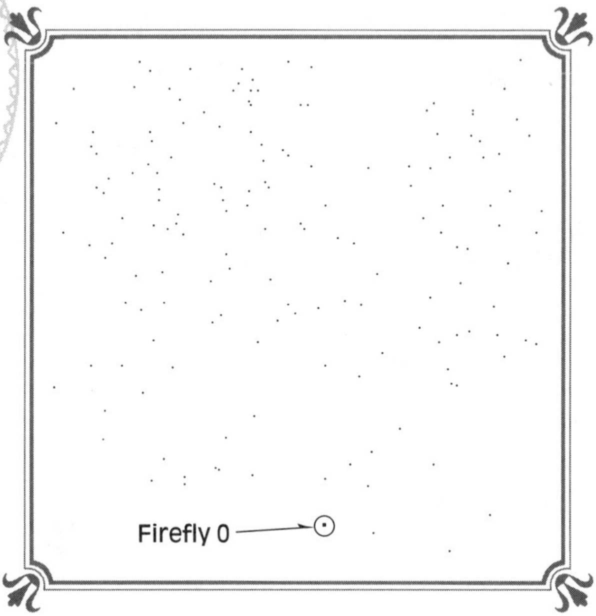

FIGURE 18-3

A legion of fireflies chasing firefly 0, "medium swarming"

Simulating Machines

You'll want to note that beelining *is* rather typical of the movements of many man-made machines. Most machines—including airplanes, autos, and yes, heat-seeking missiles—perform more predictable actions than do living creatures.

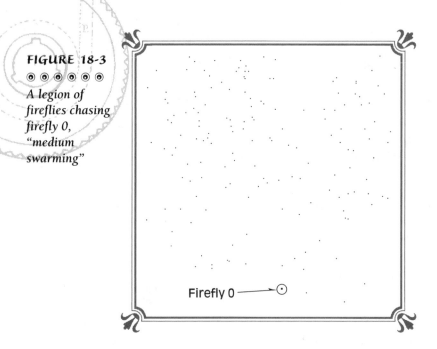

Two factors determine how machines move: speed and maneuverability. Although it may not be possible to outrun a heat-seeking missile, it may be possible to avoid it altogether. Machines that fly typically have poor maneuverability when compared to animals that fly.

Taking Size into Account

Modeling machine movement is analogous to modeling any large object movement. Fireflies are seemingly immune to the effects of inertia (of course this is not true, but to the human eye it appears that way). When modeling larger objects (machines, elephants, and so on), however, you must consider inertial factors in order to produce realistic actions. A common way to implement this is to assign directional vectors to each object. No explicit sines or cosines are used, yet all movement is subtly curved and flowing. We assign a maneuverability class as the maximum increment by which that directional vector can change at a given moment. The higher the maneuverability

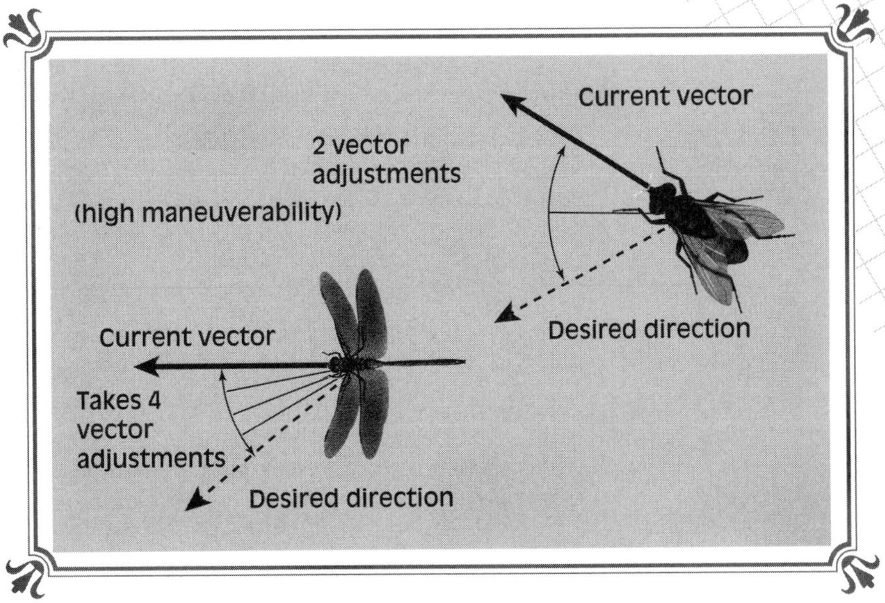

FIGURE 18-4
Inertial movement governed by vectors

increment, the faster that object can turn. Note that the faster the object is moving, the less impact the maneuverability increment will have at any moment, as Figure 18-4 illustrates.

The black firefly (predator) is chasing the red (prey). The movement algorithms take into account two distances: the distance from the firefly to the nearest wall and the distance from firefly to firefly. To implement the vector movements, we can simply replace the movement procedure in the Bugs program with this:

```
// Movement routine - good stuff happens here
// Modified movement procedure with directional vectors
void movement (int g)
  { int flag,t,d;
    long u,v;

    // Flag indicates whether bug is worried about the other bug
    // or hitting a wall--flag is initially set to other bug.
    flag = 1;

    // Multiply maneuverability to obtain a wall buffer zone.
    t=2000*turn[g];

    // Check to see if the bug is too close to any wall. If so, modify
    // the direction and modify the flag.
```

continued on next page

continued from previous page

```
if (point[g].x <50-t)
{ flag = 0;
  point[g].vecx += turn[g];
  point[g].vecy += ((point[g].vecy<0)?-turn[g]:turn[g]);
  }
  else if (point[g].y <50-t)
   { flag = 0;
     point[g].vecx += ((point[g].vecx<0)?-turn[g]:turn[g]);
     point[g].vecy += turn[g];
     }
  else if (point[g].x > 350+t)
   { flag = 0;
     point[g].vecx -= turn[g];
     point[g].vecy += ((point[g].vecy<0)?-turn[g]:turn[g]);
     }
  else if (point[g].y > 350+t)
   { flag = 0;
     point[g].vecx += ((point[g].vecx<0)?-turn[g]:turn[g]);
     point[g].vecy -= turn[g];
     }

// If the bug is worried about the other bug...
if (flag)
{ // A bit of erratic turning
  d = rand()%3 + 1;

  // Modify the bug to chase or evade (depending on the bug's number).
  if ((point[g].x > point[1-g].x))
                    point[g].vecx += (2*g-1)*turn[g]/d;
  if ((point[g].x < point[1-g].x))
                    point[g].vecx -= (2*g-1)*turn[g]/d;
  if ((point[g].y > point[1-g].y))
                    point[g].vecy += (2*g-1)*turn[g]/d;
  if ((point[g].y < point[1-g].y))
                    point[g].vecy -= (2*g-1)*turn[g]/d;
 }

// Enforce limit on maximum speed.
if (point[g].vecx > spd[g])  point[g].vecx = spd[g];
if (point[g].vecx < -spd[g]) point[g].vecx = -spd[g];
if (point[g].vecy > spd[g])  point[g].vecy = spd[g];
if (point[g].vecy < -spd[g]) point[g].vecy = -spd[g];

// Code to slow prey when it's not in danger
d = 1;
if (g)
 { u = point[0].x - point[1].x;
   u = u*u;
   v = point[0].y - point[1].y;
   v = v*v;
```

```
        u = sqrtl(u+v);
        d = u/100 + 1;
        }

    // Add movement.
    point[g].x += point[g].vecx/d;
    point[g].y += point[g].vecy/d;

    // Enforce window boundaries.
    if (point[g].x < 0) point[g].x++;
    if (point[g].x > 399) point[g].x--;

    if (point[g].y < 0)  point[g].y++;
    if (point[g].y > 399)  point[g].y--;

    }
```

This code continuously modifies the predator's vector to aim toward the prey, as long as the new vector will not result in an inevitable crash with the wall. The prey uses a similar technique to evade the predator. The prey also takes into account a "no danger" area: When the prey is an acceptable distance from the predator, it takes no measures to avoid the predator (in other words, its speed slows and it employs no special directional algorithm). Initially, the program gives the prey a higher maneuverability class than it does the predator. The difference in maneuverability, coupled with the fact that the prey doesn't "want" to be caught, means that the predator can never catch the prey, although their speeds are equal.

Taking Speed into Account

But what happens when the speeds are not equal? In a chase scenario, speed is the *single* most important variable. Assuming that all other factors are equal, we can be certain that in any encounter between two opponents, the one that has a distinct speed advantage over the other will usually win (in other words, the faster object will escape, catch, or destroy the slower object). It's only by modifying *more than one* other factor that we can significantly affect this advantage. Maneuverability, size, and intelligence all play important roles in a one-on-one scenario, but none is as crucial as speed.

Here are some guidelines to keep in mind as you work out the power relationships in your game:

- If the predator and prey are of comparable size and intelligence, but the predator is faster and more maneuverable, it will catch the prey.
- If the predator and prey are of comparable intelligence, but the prey is notably faster, the predator will not catch the prey.

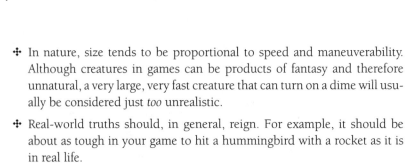

- In nature, size tends to be proportional to speed and maneuverability. Although creatures in games can be products of fantasy and therefore unnatural, a very large, very fast creature that can turn on a dime will usually be considered just *too* unrealistic.
- Real-world truths should, in general, reign. For example, it should be about as tough in your game to hit a hummingbird with a rocket as it is in real life.

Our evade program allows for experimentation with these factors. If you tinker around with it, you'll quickly find that although you can create quite ridiculous scenarios, a certain measure of balance is critical to realistic movement.

Searching

In order to analyze data and find optimal solutions—in other words, in order to consider all options and choose the best one—your program must be able to search. Searching in and of itself does not qualify as true artificial intelligence. AI comes into play when you are trying to improve a search technique, either by making it faster or by increasing its accuracy. When a program considers its next chess move, for example, it may search many possible moves. A human would immediately deem some of these moves ridiculous, but the algorithm built into the program is usually not sophisticated enough to eliminate even poor choices without at first exploring them. Actually, humans do something similar. Humans are typically just better trained to quickly tailor their searches to the more fruitful options, though.

Searches are limited to a *search space*. This is the domain in which the program or human is performing the search: For chess or tic-tac-toe, for example, the search space is the collection of all possible board configurations. To traverse the search space, we can hop from one board to the next, checking to see if each is the board we want. For our purposes, it's convenient to think of a single hop as being legal only if it takes us to a board that is just one move away from the current board.

Heuristics

As I just mentioned, searching all possible board configurations in the search space would be a naive approach. This kind of search assumes that no board (except the winning one) is better than any other. The program's goal in a tic-tac-toe search is to find any board where the program has three in a row and the player does not. Assuming that it doesn't find this configuration in the neighboring boards, an unsophisticated algorithm must search all neighbors of the neighbors and so on. As you might expect, such an algorithm could take a very long time.

A better solution would be to develop a board *heuristic*. A heuristic is a self-teaching, problem-solving algorithm. It forms an opinion, in terms of a value, of the viability of a given board configuration. In a tic-tac-toe game program, for example, the heuristic would assign a very low value to a board in which the opponent had three in a row (a loss situation for the computer). On the other hand, it would give a high value to a board that was set up for a computer victory.

Searching is necessary or desirable in many games, not just trivial applications such as tic-tac-toe. Consider the tank warfare simulation shown in Figure 18-5. The tank being fired on assesses its situation. Its back is to an enemy and its rear armor weak, so it decides to turn. Which way? Turning right would expose stronger armor to the enemy and turning left would allow the tank to take shelter behind a structure. A heuristic could efficiently evaluate the possible actions to determine the best option.

Sailing Through Search Space

Armed with our board heuristic, there's no game we can't win. We simply test all moves possible from our current position, make the best one, and repeat until we attain victory! Well, almost. Depending on the search space in question, we may need to check several more factors. Fortunately, you can adapt a heuristic to search only those areas that promise to produce the most likely chance for a computer win.

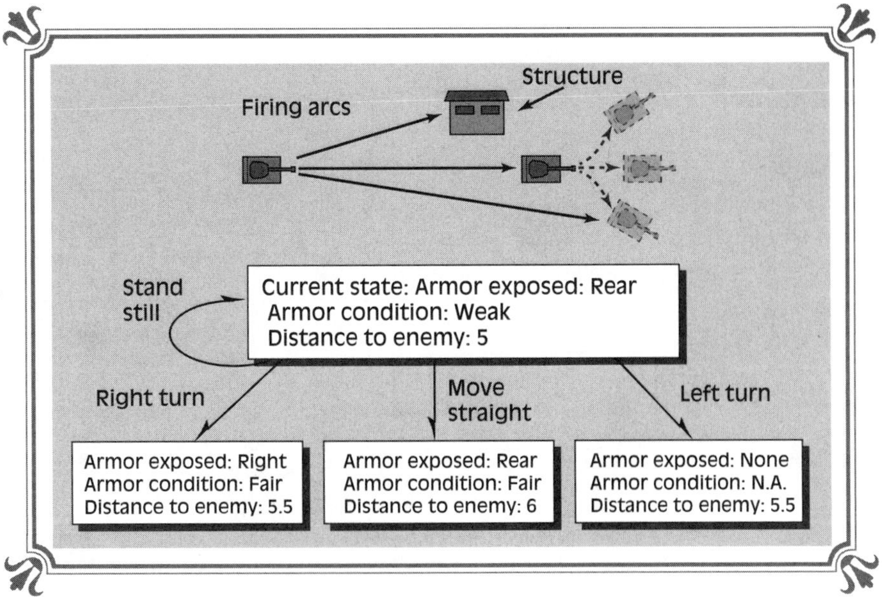

FIGURE 18-5

Searching through a tank's options

Figure 18-6 shows a classic AI problem, 15-puzzle. On the left, you can see one possible arrangement of the 15 tiles and 1 blank space in the square. The object is to slide the tiles around until they are in order, as shown on the right. Anyone who has played this game can testify to its difficulty. This stands to reason: There are approximately 2.09 x 10^{13} possible board configurations. Luckily for us, only half of those can occur on a correctly built board. (To put this number in perspective, assume for a moment that the world's fastest supercomputer could evaluate a million different 15-puzzle boards per second. In the worst-case scenario, it would take such a computer 4 months to search them all.) Clearly, we need to add some more AI features to the searching technique.

To solve the 15-puzzle, let's first decide on the heuristic. Obviously, the goal shown in Figure 18-6 is the best board. Any other board is bad. It could be argued, however, that some bad boards are worse than others. For example, a board where victory is only one move away is certainly not *all* that bad! A board that's two moves away is a bit worse, and so on. We can algorithmically define an appropriate heuristic in this way: For each tile that is in the correct position, add 1 point to the board's "goodness factor." (There are possibly better heuristics, but this one is simple and should prove adequate.) The goal state has a goodness factor of 16 (including the empty space), and every other board has a goodness factor that is less than 16. For example, our heuristic would say that the possible game state shown in Figure 18-6 has a goodness factor of 5.

We're not all the way there yet, though. Figure 18-7 shows a typical search tree; the state at the top, the *parent* state, is where our heuristic is currently searching. All

FIGURE 18-6

15-puzzle

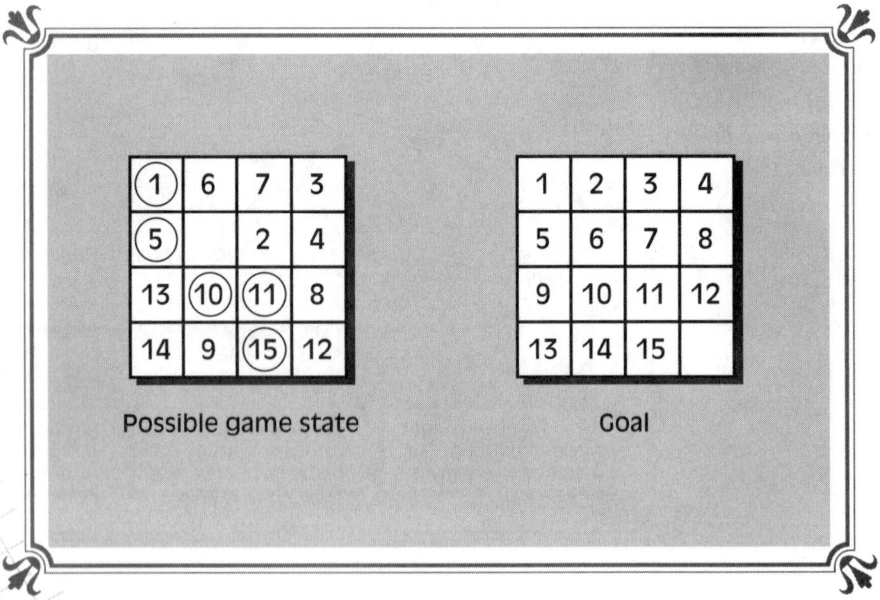

the possible moves the program can make are its *child* states. A serious problem arises when we implement our heuristic in this kind of structure. The heuristic will often find that the parent state is better than any of its possible child states (see Figure 18-7). Where to go from here? As humans, we know that sometimes things must get worse before they get better, but our heuristic doesn't have that information.

Very few searches can succeed if they consider local solutions only. In any case where the children of a state are worse than the parent, we want the heuristic to commence the search with the grandchildren. Of course, if the search is *still* not fruitful, we want the heuristic to move to the great-grandchildren, and so on. Better yet, we can modify the algorithm to perform a *depth-first* initial search—a search that looks through all specified levels at the same time, in hopes of reducing the effect local assessments have over the search. If the search still doesn't provide any viable solutions, we can continue the search at deeper levels. Whenever the search finds a descendant with a better (but not best) board configuration, that descendant becomes the new parent and the heuristic repeats the search.

This method is relatively straightforward, but it doesn't really take advantage of AI techniques. Only in its recognition of promising child states and its avoidance of locally optimal (and possibly misleading) solutions does our heuristic display any real elements of "intelligence." This technique is well suited to many problems, but it focuses only on tasks in which the computer is the only entity involved. Other games provide us with a greater challenge.

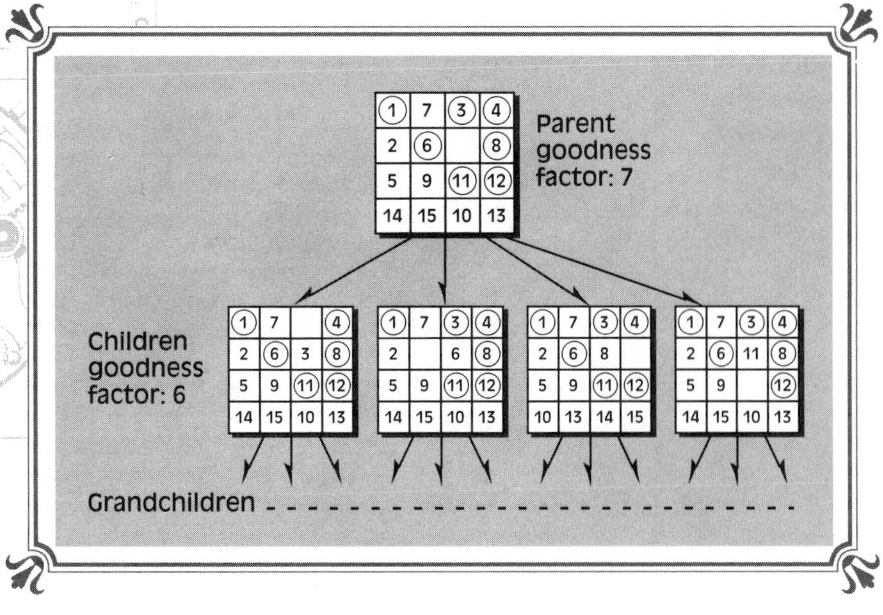

FIGURE 18-7

A 15-puzzle search tree

Multiplayer Considerations

Humans have a way of thwarting even wonderfully elegant search plans by making silly moves. Unfortunately, that's precisely what most game applications are supposed to handle—most programs need to search for moves that will win *despite* the actions of their human opponents. With this in mind, you can see that the search technique I just illustrated will be compromised if we try to implement it in a multiplayer situation: The computer is permitted only one move before the player is allowed to alter the program's assumptions in the process of making his or her move. It's easy to see how this might affect a board game such as chess or tic-tac-toe. If you look closely, though, you'll observe that it influences even action games, since the program must alternate between servicing the player's instructions and servicing its own (those of the monster, or whatever).

The human factor adds an unlimited quantity of the unknown to an algorithm's strategic decisions. Luckily, a most ironic method works exceedingly well in these situations: Simply make the naive assumption that the human will always make the best of his or her possible moves. In other words, the application prepares for the worst. If the human's play proves substandard, so much the better—this method will inherently take advantage of that.

Figure 18-8 shows a typical tic-tac-toe board and some of its descendants. The heuristic can *look* ahead as many moves as it wishes, but it can *make* only a move that is represented by one of the board's children. It assumes that the human will make

FIGURE 18-8

A search tree for tic-tac-toe

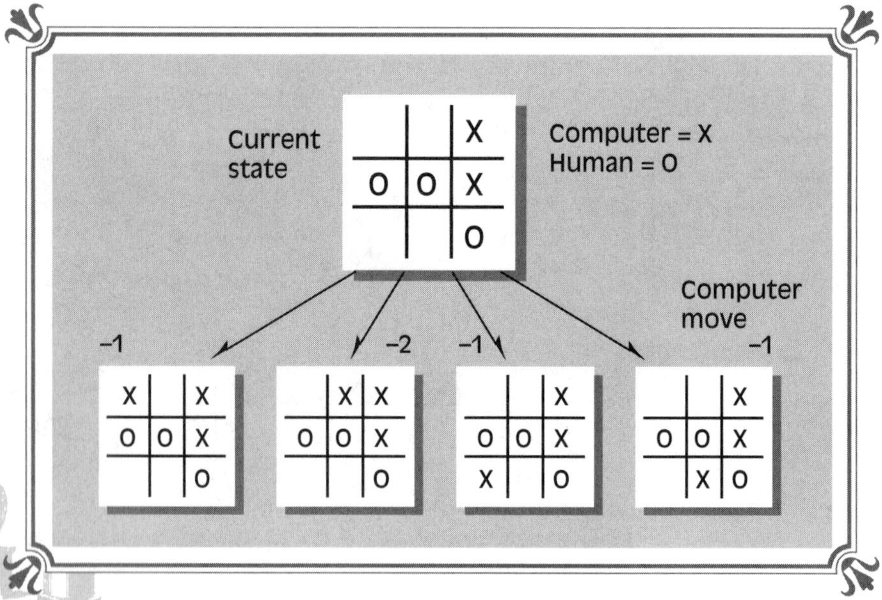

the best move in response. We can define such a heuristic in this way: Assuming the computer is X and the human is O, give a value of 99 to any board with a win-line (any row/column/diagonal of 3) that has 3 Xs, a value of 1 to any board with a win-line that has at least 1 X and no Os, a value of -1 to any board with a win-line that has at least 1 O and no Xs, and a value of -99 to any board with a win-line that has 3 Os. The evaluation function could simply consider the 3 rows, 3 columns, and 2 diagonals and apply this heuristic. This will yield the goodness factor of a board.

Min-Max

Finally, we can apply the *Min-Max* concept, which allows us to maximize the program's position and minimize that of the human. Figure 18-9 illustrates the different levels of computer and human moves. For each great-grandchild, the heuristic determines a goodness factor. As we move up the tree, each higher board takes on either the minimum or maximum goodness factor of its children, according to whether it is a computer or human move. The program alternates between its own moves and those of the human opponent until finally it reaches and chooses the first-level child with the maximum value as its next move.

You can see here the importance of searching ahead. If we had considered only the moves shown in Figure 18-8, the heuristic would have chosen board A, C, or D, since they have the best values. As you can see by looking at Figure 18-9, though, this strategy could have spelled disaster.

You can scale the "intelligence" of such a program by specifying, or allowing the player to specify, how deep to search. Tic-tac-toe has a relatively small search space, so allowing a tic-tac-toe program to search far in advance would produce a fast and effectively unbeatable algorithm.

We can produce a relatively generic piece of code to handle Min-Max searching:

```
struct changes { int changer,changec,value; } result;
struct aboard { char place[3][3];} board;
.
.
.
    // Computer's turn
    result = maxcheck(board,depth);

    // Make the move into the array.
    board.place[result.changer][result.changec] = 'X';
.
.
.
    // Maxcheck procedure for Min Levels of Min-Max
    struct changes maxcheck(struct aboard xboard,int depth)
    { int g,h;
```

continued on next page

FIGURE 18-9

The Min-Max concept applied to tic-tac-toe

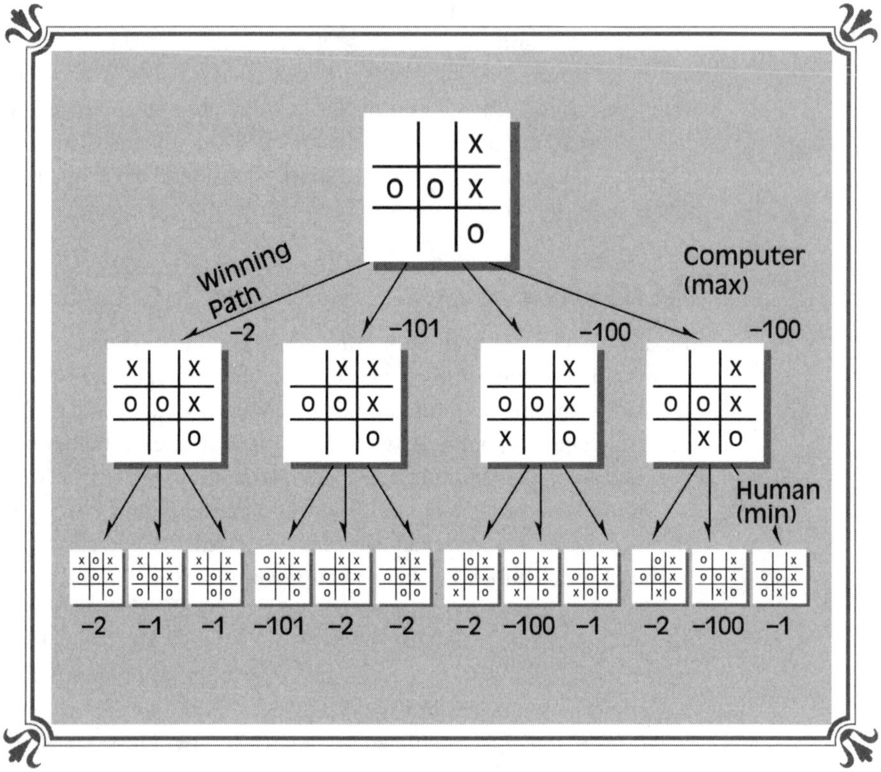

continued from previous page

```
struct changes ret,test;

// Defaults when called at maximum depth.
ret.changer = ret.changec = -1;
ret.value = -9999;
depth--;

// Has depth run out?
if (!depth)

  // This is deepest descendant. Return the board's value.
  { ret.value = evalboard(xboard);
    return ret;
    }

// Check each possible move.
for (g=0;g<3;++g)
  for (h=0;h<3;++h)
```

```
        // Limit the search to empty spots.
        if (xboard.place[g][h] == ' ')

          // Put in a "dummy" move and call mincheck.
          { xboard.place[g][h] = _X ;
            test = mincheck(xboard,depth);

            // Restore our "dummy" move.
            xboard.place[g][h] = ' ';

            // Was that move the best so far? If so, save the information.
            if (test.value > ret.value)
              { ret.value = test.value;
                ret.changer = g;
                ret.changec = h;
                 }
          }
    // Return the best move we found.
    return ret;
   }
```

When it is the program's turn to make a move in the game, it calls maxcheck with the current board and desired search depth as parameters. Maxcheck and mincheck will alternate back and forth, going deeper into the tree until the depth variable runs out.

Note mincheck's extreme similarity to maxcheck. In fact, to obtain a suitable mincheck procedure, you need only replace the three lines of bold in maxcheck with the following:

```
{ xboard.place[g][h] = _O ;    // _O  for human
test = maxcheck(xboard,depth); // Call maxcheck now.
.
.
.
if (test.value < ret.value)    // < , This is Min!
```

To apply this to many two-player games, you need only modify the code that dictates the program's possible moves. (For example, in tic-tac-toe, a player can move into any open space, but this is not true in chess.) Also, you must tailor the **evalboard** function to the particular situation.

Let's apply the Min-Max search technique to a more complex application. Recall Figure 18-5, which illustrated a tank warfare simulation. Figure 18-10 displays a possible heuristic and search tree for such a simulation. Here, the possibilities are formalized. As before, the program will opt to move its tank so that it will be hidden behind the barricade. The basis for this decision is clearer when you look at the Min-Max values.

FIGURE 18-10

Min-Max applied to a tank warfare simulation

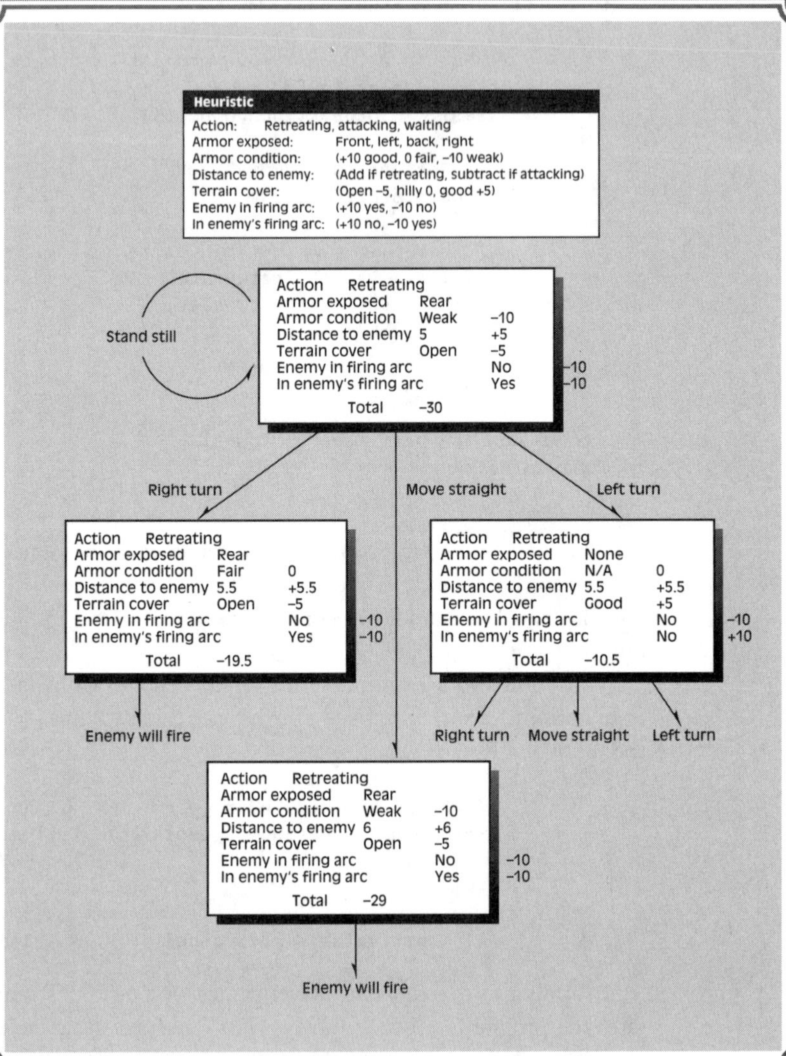

The most thought-provoking aspect of implementing a searching technique is the heuristic. We could include other elements in this heuristic; for example, we might want to evaluate "acceptable" damage (in other words, nonfatal hits that the electronic opponent might be willing to sustain because they improve the chances of winning). The program uses Min-Max at each level, either to dictate the computer's next move or to attempt to predict what the human opponent (whom the program assumes is smart) will do. A well-designed heuristic (in other words, one that you've taken care to closely tailor to the game in question) can provide surprisingly excellent results.

FIGURE 18-11

Alpha-Beta searching

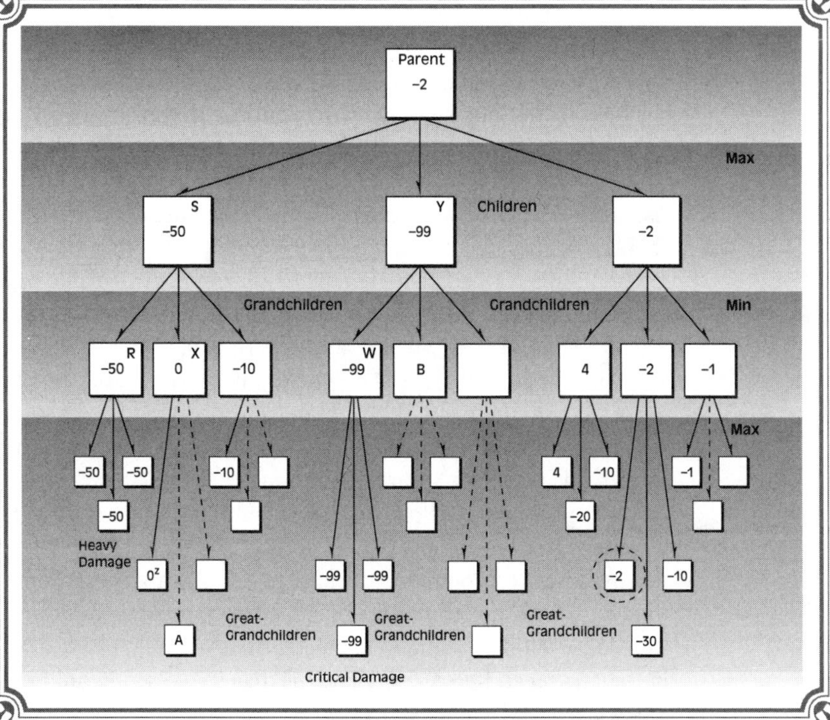

Alpha-Beta Searching

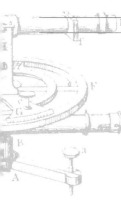

The AI technique *Alpha-Beta searching* can further improve the implementation of Min-Max. You can see the effects of Alpha-Beta "pruning" in Figure 18-10: The heuristic does not search past the conclusion "enemy will fire" for children 1 and 2 in the search tree. Under the basic Min-Max concept, our heuristic would continue this search to its obviously fruitless end. If we implement Alpha-Beta searching, though, the heuristic can watch for such dead-end situations and avoid spending time considering them. For small search spaces, such as the one necessary for tic-tac-toe, the size of the tree is not an issue; Min-Max should produce the same result and in about the same amount of time with or without Alpha-Beta pruning. When the search space is large (as it is for chess, Go, and so on), however, Alpha-Beta pruning becomes mandatory if the search is to be completed in a reasonable amount of time.

Alpha-Beta searching requires the use of two new variables. The alpha value monitors the Min moves (the computer moves) and the beta value monitors the Max moves (the human moves). Figure 18-11 shows an extended version of the search tree illustrated in Figure 18-10, with each node represented only by its heuristic value.

The many dotted lines represent connections to descendants the heuristic deemed to be of no value and therefore did not pursue, thanks to the cleverness of the Alpha-Beta search technique.

The first nonevaluated descendant is A (you can find it in the lower left portion of the figure). To understand why the heuristic doesn't bother to consider it, look at the value of its grandparent, S. The heuristic evaluates the first set of great-grandchildren (the "cousins" of A, at the far left) and finds them all to have the value -50 (heavy damage). The heuristic assigns this value to their parent, R, and grandparent, S. It then continues the search until it comes to the first of A's "siblings," the great-grandchild Z, valued at 0. The heuristic assigns this value to Z's parent, X. At this point, the heuristic decides not to evaluate any more of X's descendants. Why? This is a Max level, so if A had any value less than 0, Min-Max would ignore it. If A's value were greater than 0, Min-Max would still ignore it, but this time in the Min level, where the program would be looking at the lower value that has percolated up from A's cousins (the "heavy damage" family). In any event, A is destined for obscurity. The same holds true for A's unnamed sibling.

More pruning takes place at grandchild B. B's first sibling, W, has a value of -99, which the heuristic assigns to W's parent, Y. How does the heuristic know not to evaluate B (or its descendants)? Y's value of -99 is guaranteed to lose against S's -50 when the heuristic wraps things up by pushing a value from the Min level through to the top Max level. If B's value were greater than W's -99, it would be ignored by Max-Min in the Min level. If B's value were less than W's -99, it would be ignored by Max-Min when it reached the Max level, where we already know it must face S's value of -50.

The process of adding the Alpha-Beta searching technique to the Min-Max procedure is relatively straightforward. Keep track of an alpha variable for all Min push-throughs and a beta value for all Max values. The heuristic can rule out lower searches when the result of the first search is greater than the beta value or less than the alpha value. This technique often cuts the number of necessary board evaluations in half, which allows a search either to continue twice as deep or to run twice as fast as a straight Min-Max search.

Thoughts on Game Theory

Game theory has a long history, not only because games are a common form of entertainment, but because the strategies of play extend to many practical fields. The search techniques I've described are suitable for use in practical software designed to solve real problems.

Computer games have one simple goal: to entertain the player. To that end, the designer of any game must take into account the strengths and weaknesses of all players, electronic and human. Each has its own secret weapons.

The Computer Advantage

The act of developing an electronic player, whether it is a chess opponent or a fire-breathing demon, forces us to look seriously at what the computer can do. Two advantages of the computer are immediately apparent: It has a larger and more accurate memory than a human and it has a greater capacity for performing complex calculations rapidly.

A computer's memory, when the machine is operating correctly, is near perfect. A computer does not forget. Its recall is almost always faster than that of a human—it often retrieves data in under 100 nanoseconds and has the advantage of addressable memory. Human neurons fire an order of magnitude slower, and the process of recalling data usually excites many more neurons than necessary to retrieve the information. A good AI algorithm will take advantage of these differences. Heuristics will never overlook a viable move in their haste, strategy games will never misremember a weapon's range, and blackjack programs will never forget a face (um, player). Especially in games that have large environments, perfect memory becomes a distinct advantage.

Computers also excel at mathematical operations. In strategy games, electronic players can calculate the ranges, aspects, and damage potentials of all possible targets on the field in an instant.

Finally, there's one advantage that some people are distinctly uncomfortable considering: No matter the type of computer game, human players can't escape the fact that they are playing in the machine's own realm. Does the computer ever abuse the power this implies? Well, frankly, yes—but all in a good cause. Poker and similar games that are quite well suited to the organization of the human memory, for example, are difficult for computer algorithms to manage. Allowing the computer to occasionally cheat at such a game could give an overtaxed search technique a break, saving the human player from annoying waits. It doesn't hurt anything; after all, the program's primary goal is not to increase the electronic player's pot of imaginary money, but to challenge and entertain the human player. If peeking at the human's cards now and then provides a simple and effective means of increasing the entertainment factor, so be it. For games that have extremely large search spaces (such as chess, poker, and Go), controlled, unobtrusive cheating provides one method by which the computer can supply a challenge while retaining high speed.

The Human Advantage

An old maxim proves important even in the arena of computer games: Keep the customer happy. In order to keep the interest of a game player, the program must provide (at least every now and then) the player with a real sense of accomplishment, however small. So amid our discussion of all the techniques your program can employ to figuratively chop off human players at the knees and make them beg for mercy, we can't forget that it is the humans who are our customers. That means that our game applications had better allow humans a win once in a while.

Of course, not all the advantages belong to the computer. The human mind is, overall, a better computer than any existing electronic machine, and many types of games are much better designed for humans than they are for the machine. For example, there are approximately 10^{120} possible board configurations in chess, enough to dwarf the power of any electronic search technique. This number is greater than the estimated number of molecules in the visible universe, yet the human mind can prune the search tree in magnificent and relatively rapid ways to produce near-perfect moves. This is not a question of speed, but rather one of intelligence.

All other factors being equal, artificial intelligence has no chance against human intelligence. Any semblance of fairness is the result of the computer's home-turf advantage and the programmer's wily use of that high ground. In order to fulfill the only true purpose of a game—to entertain human players—you, as the programmer, will need to pull out all the stops just to make the encounter a sufficiently challenging and rewarding one.

Summary

The implemenation of AI into your game will have an important impact on its realism and playability. In this chapter, we covered some common AI techniques for computer games, and what makes them tick. Many computer games can get away with rather modest AI implementations and still provide a fair illusion of intelligence.

You should carefully implement AI into your game; given a chance, AI can be a memory hog. If your creation is a board game, it might not be a big concern. However, if you're designing an action game, you may need all the power you can get just to run the graphics. A fast, approximate AI algorithm may have to suffice. Whatever you end up doing, your game's AI should be smart, scalable, and challenging.

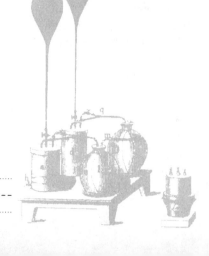

19

Backgrounds and Foregrounds

come debbe stare le manovelle ... le quali si movano e s'alza
... grave pesi ... le ... [illegible] ... saranno da bene
forzare nella ... per ... alla manovella perchè ...
la forza e più l'omo più vale.

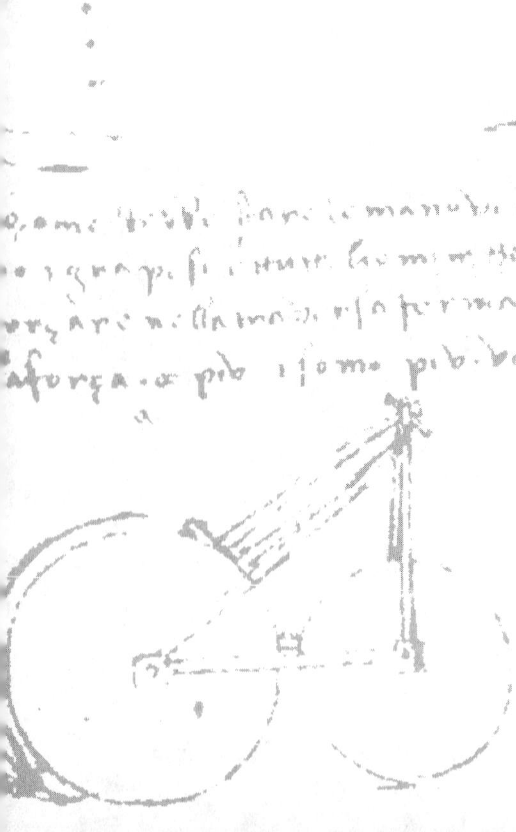

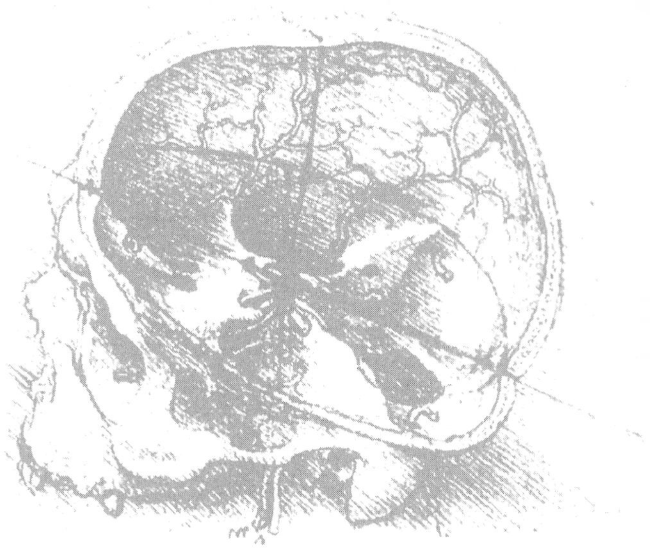

19

Backgrounds and Foregrounds

Beauty is but screen-deep. Fortunately for computer games, it doesn't need to go any deeper. The most important factor in a game is the challenge it provides, certainly, but prospective players will base their first impressions on the *looks* of a game. In this chapter, I'll give you an overview of the techniques you can use to create and enhance the visual aspect of your game's world and inhabitants.

Staying in the Background

Every game must have some kind of background. If the game does not involve scrolling (in other words, some type of background movement), then it's enough simply to place a well-chosen image or solid field in the background. Programs in this category include board games, such as Solitaire, and even some action games, such as the classic Asteroids.

If the game does require scrolling—Commander Keen, Duke Nukem, and DOOM are examples—you may need to invest considerable effort to accomplish a realistic effect. I'll cover 2D scrolling here and then move on to the latest craze, 3D scrolling.

2D Scrolling

Scrolling in 2D means moving in the *x* direction, *y* direction, or both. For simplicity's sake, let's first consider a game that scrolls in the *x* direction only. Many "side-flying" games are in this class.

WinG's ability to provide superfast Blts will give a 2D-scrolling game the punch it needs to scroll fast. Figure 19-1 shows the general concept behind partitioning the screen into *tiles*, *x*-by-*x*-pixel squares that each hold a chunk of the background.

It's often most economical to give your tiles dimensions that are multiples of 2; 32 by 32 pixels is a common tile size. It also makes life much easier if your playing area is some integer multiple of your tile size. For 32-by-32 tiles, a 640x480 playing area makes sense (15 tiles high by 20 tiles wide).

Notice in Figure 19-1 that the offscreen DC is wider than the onscreen DC. Typically, it is wider by a tile width on either side (making the offscreen DC of a 640x480 playing area with 32-by-32 tiles actually 704 pixels wide). These side buffers hold columns that the program may need to draw to the screen in the very near future.

Figure 19-2 shows the straightforward implementation of 2D scrolling. The procedure is as follows:

- Copy the background from one offscreen DC to another.
- Overlay the sprites.
- WinG Blt to the onscreen DC.
- Scroll the background DC by copying the image 1 byte to the left.

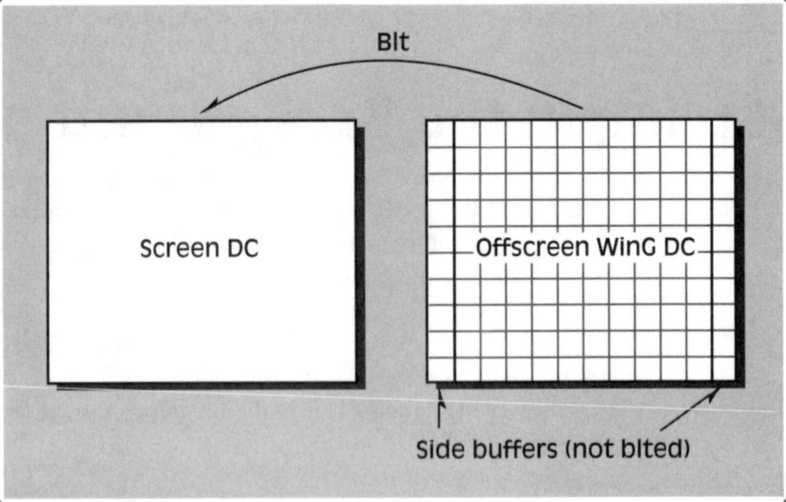

FIGURE 19-1

Blt with tiles and side buffers

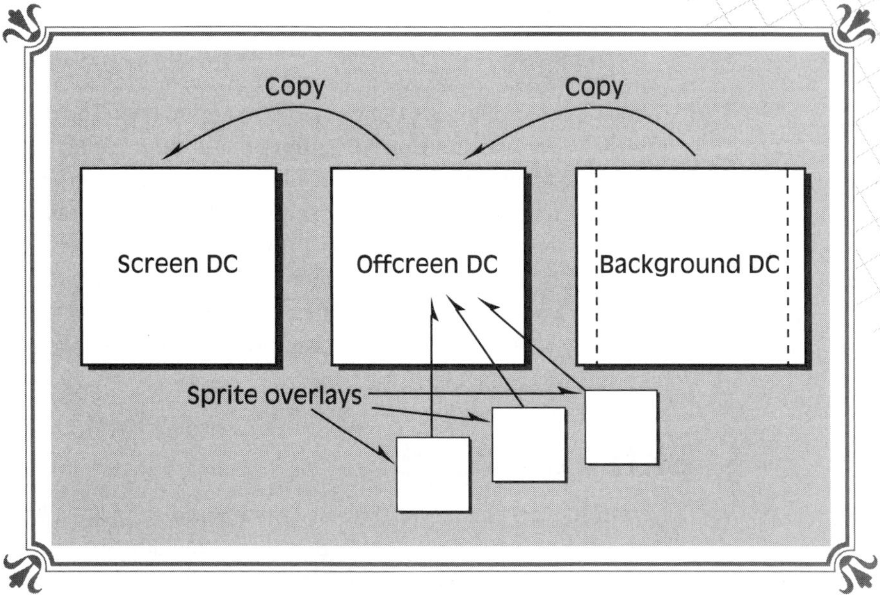

FIGURE 19-2

Drawing a scrolling screen

Your program can continue to work in this way (while of course processing any sprite movements) until the side buffer on the right is exhausted; in other words, until the column of spare tiles on the right has been moved onto the screen. At this point, your code must write a new column of tiles to this area. You can store the tiles to be written in a table, or even generate the tiles randomly if the background is general enough.

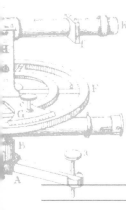

It's simple to convert this method for use with a vertically scrolling game. The side buffers move to the top and bottom of the DC, becoming row buffers. Even converting to scrolling in all directions is an easy process. Your code will have to accommodate diagonal movement, meaning that it must be able to handle filling row and column buffers simultaneously, but the overall idea is still the same.

There is still a fair amount of room for 2D scrolling games in the relatively untapped Windows market. WinG finally provides the tools you need to create such games.

Perception Regions

To make 2D scrolling more versatile, you can add *perception regions*. A perception region lets you scroll a portion of a screen at a different rate, making certain scenes appear more realistic.

To understand how perception regions work, consider what happens when you look out the side window of a car: The houses near the road go by in a blur, yet the mountains in the distance hardly move. To achieve this effect, you can create a fast-scrolling perception region to hold the houses and a slow-scrolling perception region to hold the mountains (see Figure 19-3).

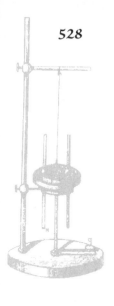

This technique has the added benefit of saving your program some time and trouble, since slow-scrolling areas requires less computation. The top region in our example might move once for every five times the bottom region moves. Otherwise, the processing is identical. This requires a bit more overhead in the code, but decidedly reduces the number of pixel writes, bringing down the overall cost.

You can also overlap the regions. To do this, you apply the *z*-order concept I described earlier in the book to background tiles.

However you choose to implement perception scrolling, it will only marginally complicate your code (good modularization will help). In exchange, it will enhance and speed your game's scrolling.

Enter da Vinci

Players form their first impressions of a game based on the quality of its graphics. This is the reason every team of game developers includes people who are specifically devoted to designing and beautifying this aspect of the program. Fortunately, there are many relatively simple techniques for producing quality graphics. Here, I'll concentrate on three ingredients critical to impressive-looking screens: texture, lighting, and color.

Texture

Texture adds a significant element of realism to surfaces. A carefully textured area can appear to be sand, stone, water, or most any other substance. Even simple textures

FIGURE 19-3

Perception scrolling

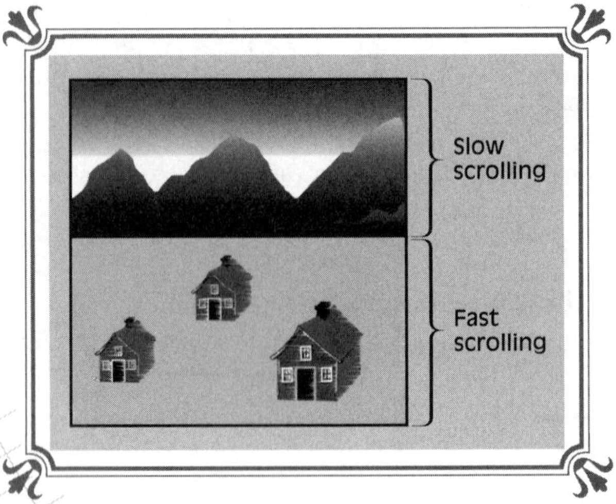

can greatly enhance the realism and beauty of a generated image. You can mathematically generate these simple textures. For example, you can create striped wallpaper by alternating *x* white columns and *x* black columns. You can place random dots for a stucco effect.

The cleanest and quickest way to simulate more complex textures is simply to scan in a picture of the texture you wish to add. Once you have a set "patch" of the texture, you can propagate it wherever you need it. You can even use this technique to apply scanned portraits to game surfaces. The cost of adding such features is extremely low, but these elements notably improve the overall effect.

Lighting

Careful use of lighting can also add a surprising degree of realism to even the simplest structures. The illustration on the right in Figure 19-4 displays a room with wallpaper and floor textures. These help give the room a 3D feel, but something is definitely missing. The illustration on the left in Figure 19-4 shows the exact same room after the image has been through a *radiosity simulator.* As you can see, the difference is striking. The 3D effect is obvious and the room looks quite "real."

Ray tracers and radiosity simulators do wonders for image quality, but at quite a slow pace. Real-time light-casting algorithms are typically too computationally expensive to consider necessary. If you believe your game would benefit from such precise modeling, though, run the lighting simulators ahead of time. You can save the results and simply display them during game time. Be warned, however: This technique

FIGURE 19-4

Realism produced by texture and lighting

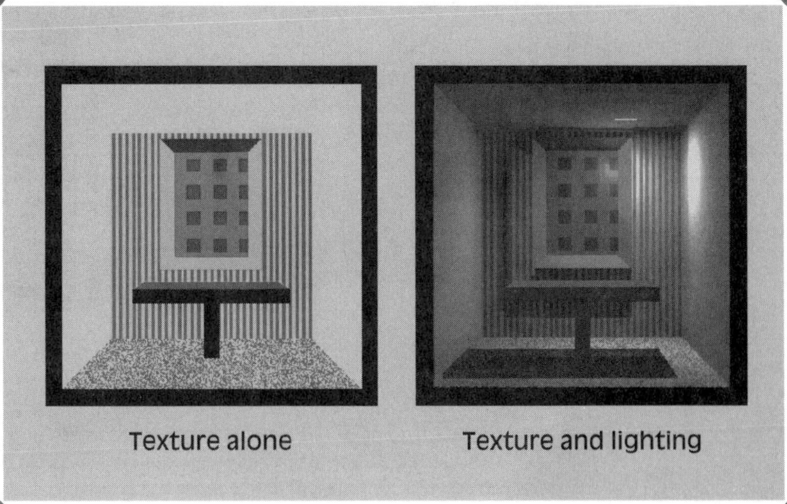

saves you some execution-time computations, but could significantly add to the game's disk requirements. Besides, there are ways to achieve similar effects without using full-fledged lighting simulators.

By carefully designing your graphics, you can often produce a respectable lighting effect at a low computational cost. Figure 19-5 shows two square grids. The first looks flat and "drawn," while the second has a 3D appearance that makes it "feel" more real. At the right, you can see an enlargement of one of the blocks of the "3D" grid. Two sides are outlined in black pixels and the opposing sides are outlined in white. This simple pattern of color gives the illusion of light coming from a specific direction. If you've developed any Windows applications, you've already used this technique for creating that environment's distinctive buttons and scrollbars. You can apply this method to many other graphic elements, as well.

Color

Last but certainly not least, you'll want to consider the use of color when you are developing your artwork. The video mode of the player's computer will dictate the maximum number of colors available to you, the designer. Video cards with large amounts of RAM produce good resolutions with up to 16.7 million colors, but many users will have video cards that produce only 256 (or even a measly 16) colors. Some program designers simply instruct their applications to refuse to run if only 16 colors are available; depending on your game, you may find that this is a necessary (if

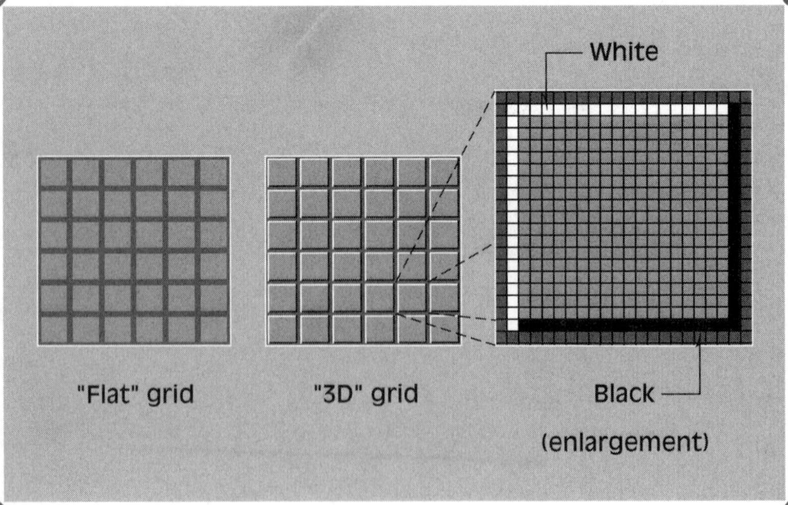

FIGURE 19-5

Creating a simple but effective illusion of light

unfortunate) strategy. Systems with 256 colors are slightly more manageable, but can still cause the programmer headaches.

Why do you need so many colors? Complex art, textures, and shading all demand it. To create a realistic shading effect, you may well need ten different blues (and ten reds, greens, yellows, and so on). Scan in just one color image and your program's color requirements may shoot through the roof—the scan program will probably need a huge range of colors just to adequately represent the image.

Given the demands of your program and the limitations under which it may be asked to run, it's imperative that you partition your color usage carefully. Otherwise, you may find that you don't have a broad enough color range for the elements of your game. By using contrasting colors in much the same way you use textures, you can create a wonderful illusion of complexity within the confines of limited-resolution environments. Above all, don't forget simple rules. If your background is blue, for example, make sure your sprites are some color that is quite different—in other words, don't let your colors swamp each other.

The 3D Wave

3D is definitely the future of computer games. Students of geometry have been able to do the necessary calculations for centuries, but desktop computers have only now reached a point where they can implement the math in real time. As computers speed up, it is likely the trend from 2D to 3D games will kick into high gear.

The Z Factor

Fortunately, becoming a part of this wave is not all that difficult: To get from 2D to 3D, you add a *z* (depth) coordinate to a 2D game's *x* (width) and *y* (height) coordinates. That's not to say that the jump from 2D to 3D is entirely without obstacles. Your program will need to perform an enormous number of calculations, usually as part of tedious matrix operations. A detailed discussion of this aspect of implementing 3D is beyond the scope of this book (there are many titles that focus on 3D graphics alone), but I'll cover what you need to get going. For advanced manipulations, consult any solid book on computational geometry or computer graphics.

The trademark example of 3D graphics is a spinning cube. Even WinG provides an example of this cornerstone demo. Figure 19-6 shows a 3D definition of a cube (for the sake of clarity, the cube is centered around the origin). The first step in modeling something such as this in 3D is to determine the cube's points in 3D space. (Right now, we're concerned only about the points that define the cube; we'll plunk in the lines between the points in a moment.)

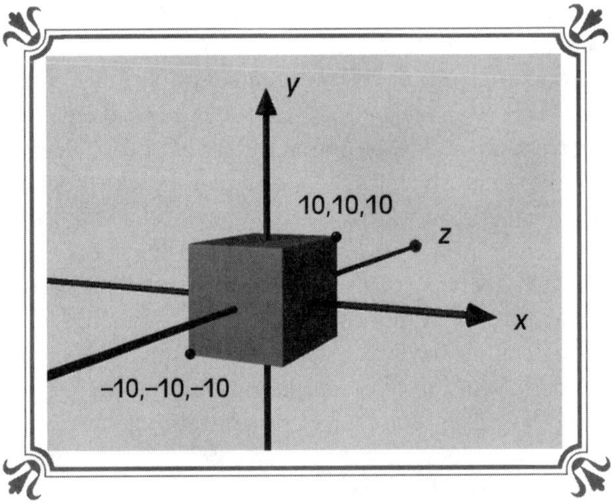

FIGURE 19-6

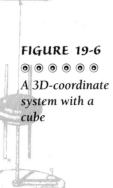

A 3D-coordinate system with a cube

The equation for projecting the points of a 3D object onto a 2D plane (in other words, for mapping a 3D object to the screen) is a simple one:

```
point2d.x = point3d.x/point3d.z;
point2d.y = point3d.y/point3d.z;
```

In other words, you divide the 3D object's *x* and *y* coordinates by its *z* coordinate to get the 2D equivalents.

We're not finished yet, though. Next, we need to multiply the whole mess by a distance value. This will dictate how far from the viewer the image is portrayed. We also need to do something about the negative 2D *x* and *y* values our calculations have yielded. (There are no negative screen coordinates in 2D.) The simple solution is to add half the screen's width to the *x* values and half the screen's height to the *y* values. Thus, our final screen formula becomes:

```
point2d.x = DIST*point3d.x/point3d.z + SCREENX/2;
point2d.y = DIST*point3d.y/point3d.z + SCREENY/2;
```

Okay, but where in this vast 3D space is the screen, mathematically speaking? Unfortunately, by default, it is within the *xy* plane. This isn't good. If you look again at Figure 19-6, you'll see that this means the screen is *inside the cube!* Obviously, this won't do.

The simplest solution is to "cheat" by moving the cube. We can simply shuffle it down the *z*-axis a bit, as shown in Figure 19-7. Do this only for the display and after any rotations. The code to rotate a 3D object assumes the object is to rotate about the origin (point 0,0,0), so the points should be defined specifically around the origin, as they are in Figure 19-6. If you define the points as shown in Figure 19-7, the cube will rotate as a *whole* around the origin, like a planet around the sun.

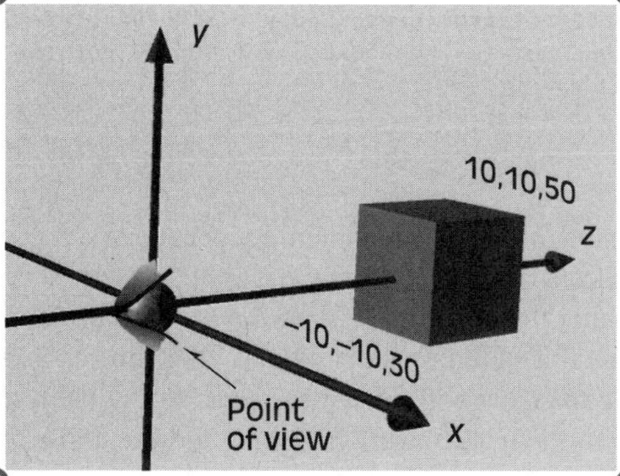

FIGURE 19-7

A cube translated down the z-axis

We rotate the cube using equations that essentially rotate the *points* of the cube around an imaginary sphere centered at the origin (sines and cosines abound). Here is a routine to do these operations:

```
struct pt3d { int x,y,z; } box[8],newbox[8];

void transform(int rotatex,int rotatey,int rotatez)
{ float tx,ty,tz;
  int g;

// Ensure the rotation angles are greater than 0 and less than 360.
rotatex = (rotatex + 360) % 360;
rotatey = (rotatey + 360) % 360;
rotatez = (rotatez + 360) % 360;

// Loop through all points (that's eight for a cube).
 for (g=0;g<NUMPT;++g)
  {
    // Rotation about the z-axis
    tx = COSDEG(rotatez)*box[g].x - SINDEG(rotatez)*box[g].y;
    ty = SINDEG(rotatez)*box[g].x + COSDEG(rotatez)*box[g].y;
    newbox[g].x = tx;
    newbox[g].y = ty;

    // Rotation about the y-axis
    tx =  COSDEG(rotatey)*newbox[g].x + SINDEG(rotatey)*box[g].z;
    tz = -SINDEG(rotatey)*newbox[g].x + COSDEG(rotatey)*box[g].z;
    newbox[g].x = tx;
    newbox[g].z = tz;
```

continued on next page

continued from previous page

```
    // Rotation about the x-axis
    ty = COSDEG(rotatex)*newbox[g].y - SINDEG(rotatex)*newbox[g].z;
    tz = SINDEG(rotatex)*newbox[g].y + COSDEG(rotatex)*newbox[g].z;
    newbox[g].y = ty;
    newbox[g].z = tz;
  }
}
```

You can see that 3D math gets a bit messy. This code actually implements the equations resulting from the matrix operations for 3D rotation. It is broken into three rotations, one each for the *x*-, *y*-, and *z*-axes. Successive calculations use the new values. Note that **box** will be the initial definition of the cube and will likely never change. Each call to **transform** will rotate the box and store the result in **newbox**. Besides the actual call to the line-drawing functions and the initial setup of the points, this code is all that's responsible for the amazing 3D cube.

Cheating

In most cases, the only way to squeeze out enough computing power to model your 3D virtual-reality simulator is to cheat—not in the sense of not playing fair, but in the sense of not quite giving what you promise. For example, if you bill your game as a 3D flight simulation yet you use 2D sprites for the enemy planes, then it's not really 3D, now is it? The player probably won't care, though; if it "looks" and "plays" 3D, then that should be good enough. There are many such "cheats" that allow a game to run faster without irritating players.

Programmers of the latest 3D first-person shoot-em-ups have figured out every trick in the book. Here are a few common methods:

- If the player is stationary, draw the wall textures accurately. As soon as the player begins to move, you can significantly decrease the quality of the textures; the player won't be able to detect the degradation during fast movement. If you've chosen the textures carefully, players won't perceive any gaps anyway (the human brain tends to "fill" such small holes). As soon as the player slows down the movement, start drawing pretty again.
- Drawing entire hallways gets expensive; make a habit of darkening hallways as they get deeper. After a certain distance, the hallway will grow too dark for the player to see. How about that—if it's too dark to see, then there's no need to waste computer time drawing anything.
- If the game takes place "outside," you can still take advantage of the hallway trick. Just use fog instead of darkness to obscure things that are beyond a certain distance.
- Avoid 3D calculations where possible by using 2D that "looks" 3D.

The nature and requirements of your game will dictate where you can implement cheats. It's very seldom that programmers implement full 3D models using every equation between the covers of an analytical geometry book. Use shortcuts whenever possible to speed your code. The hard-and-fast rule is this: "If it looks right, it is right. If it seems fast enough, it's not."

Terrain and Viewpoint

The most sophisticated backgrounds these days are realistic terrains modeled in three dimensions. To allow you to grasp the basic concepts of 3D modeling, I'll present techniques that constitute a "formal" implementation of 3D terrain. However, there is probably no game with 3D terrain that employs all these methods in such a rigid form. There are many places where you can optimize (and cheat) to speed things up significantly, and you should feel free to derive optimizations and cheats for your specific needs.

Modeling 3D Terrain

A common method for creating a 3D terrain that includes mountains, rivers, valleys, and so on relies on the use of *fractals*. Basically, the term *fractal* refers to entities with a notable amount of self-similarity. This self-similarity will often surface in a program as recursion. You can imagine that a fractal is, for all intents and purposes, simply the visual realization of a mathematical formula; if you want to model a mountain, then you must develop the equation for a mountain! Of course, these perfect modeling equations can't quite replicate the real world, but the results can still be admirable.

On the First Day

We'll start where every world-creating project starts: at the beginning. Like it or not, the world is made of triangles—well, at least this one will be. Figure 19-8 shows a transition of recursive subdivisions of a triangle. For each triangle, we calculate a midpoint along each of its edges. We then connect these midpoints, forming four smaller triangles within the original. (Typically, gamers are not used to having terrains bordered in a triangular shape, so we'll put two triangles together to form a more appropriate four-sided polygon. The subdivisions can occur without regard to this alteration.)

As you can see, this procedure could continue endlessly. To control it, you must decide on a feasible level of *granularity* for the terrain. The granularity determines the extent to which the triangles are subdivided. This is an important decision. A coarse granularity will afford the terrain only a few large triangles, making the terrain appear blocky, while a finer granularity will result in many more (smaller)

FIGURE 19-8

A triangle with recursive subdivisions

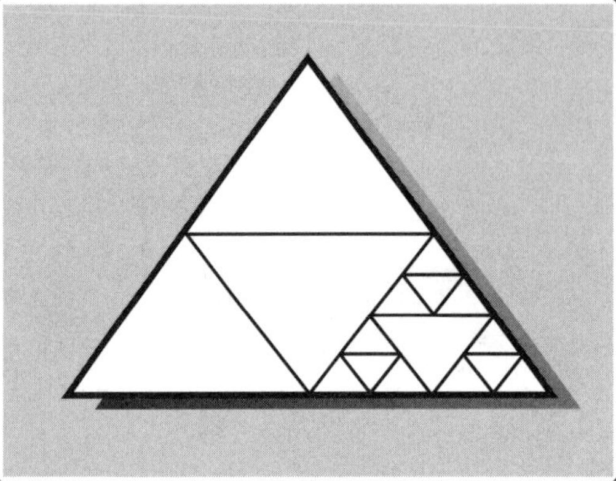

triangles, producing a much more realistic effect. However, more triangles mean more computation.

This is supposed to be a 3D terrain, so let's map these points (and triangles) into 3D space. In Figure 19-9, they are laid flat on a plane and projected back to 2D space. (Here again, I've pushed the entire field of triangles up the *z* coordinate so we can avoid messing with the viewpoint location.)

This is a flat plane. Every point has a unique *x* and *z* coordinate, but each point has the same *y* coordinate. Fine, no rocket science there. Now we need to loop

FIGURE 19-9

A flat image in 3D projection

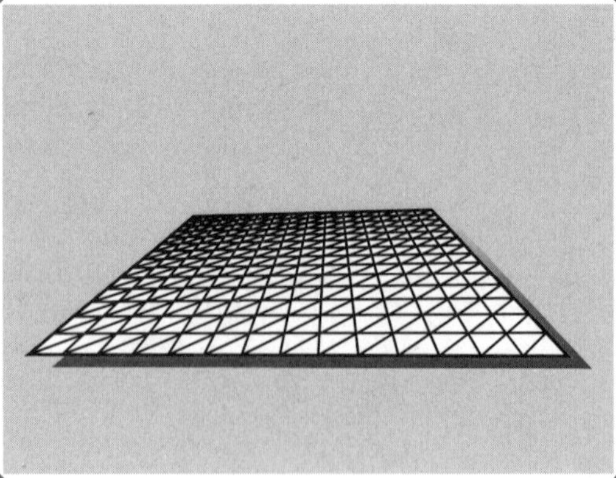

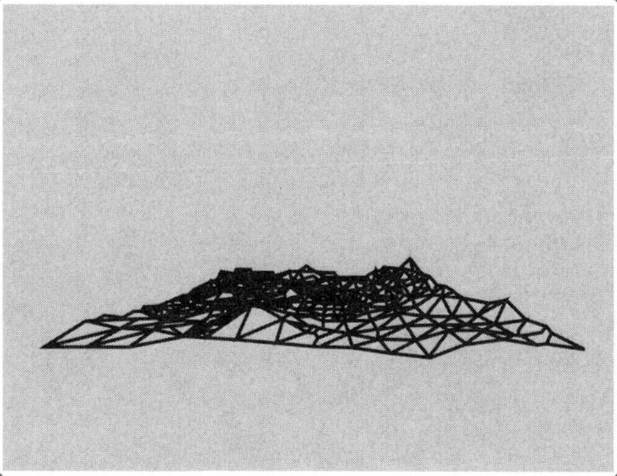

FIGURE 19-10
The terrain begins to emerge

through all the points and assign them a random (or controlled random) *y* coordinate. The effect is illustrated in Figure 19-10; in spite of the coarse granularity, the basic characteristics of the terrain are immediately evident.

Many programs that use this technique will take a few moments at the beginning of the game to generate the fractal landscape. Once the program creates the model and puts it in memory, the program need only refer to it as necessary—no further large-scale terrain generation is required.

Cheap Beauty

Figures 19-9 and 19-10 show a "wireframe" terrain. It serves to illustrate the idea, but a game's environment must look as real as possible, of course. Achieving this realism is no easy task. Considering its vast complexity, it would seem nature has been rather uncharitable to graphics programmers, who must attempt to model it. Fortunately, nature has afforded us a few small favors, too.

Consider what you know about snow and bodies of water, for example. You often see snow packs on mountain tops, while you usually find bodies of water in depressions at lower elevations. Figure 19-11 illustrates a simple method that allows you to put those observations to use when you are assigning colors to your terrain. The method relies solely on the value of a triangle's *y* coordinate (you can measure the *y* coordinate from any vertex). It fills any triangle above a certain *y* coordinate with white to represent snow, any triangle below a certain *y* coordinate with blue (water), and any triangle that falls in between the two *y* coordinates with green (trees). Obviously, this is pretty simplistic, but the point is that the frugality of this technique allows you room for further manipulations.

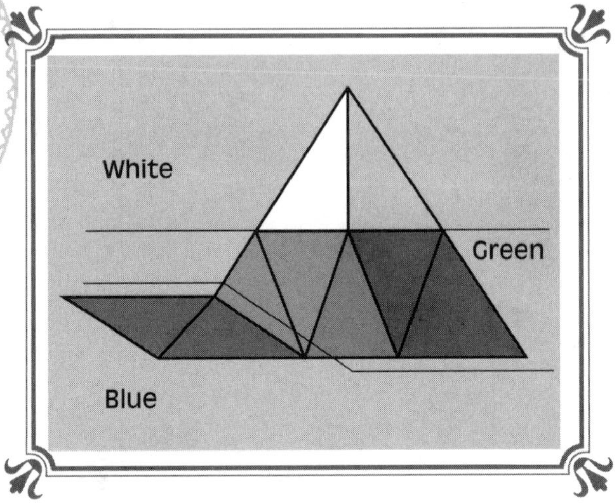

FIGURE 19-11
Partitioning snow, trees, and water

Trees Falling in the Woods

If a triangle resides on the side of a fractal mountain that is not exposed to the viewer, does it get drawn? Heavens to Betsy, no! At least it *shouldn't* get drawn, since it would later be overdrawn by the front side of the mountain. We can speed things up by not drawing items that don't matter. The cost of calculating whether something is on an opposing side of a hill or other object is (usually) insignificant compared to the cost of actually drawing a polygon.

Back to some geometry. Figure 19-12 shows a simple fractal mountain and the position of the viewpoint. Triangle N is visible to the viewer but triangle M is not. The figure also shows the *normal vectors* to triangles N and M, labeled n and m, respectively. The normal vector is a vector that is perpendicular to the plane in question. N and M are triangles, triangles have three points, and three points are all you need to define a plane—in other words, each triangle lies within a plane. (This is the reason the terrain is modeled out of triangles and not squares. Squares are dangerous: They have four points. Four points may not all lie in the same plane, and this would complicate the elegant equations you can use for planar surfaces.) Using the three points for triangle N, you can calculate the normal vector for each triangle with the formula

```
Normal.x = (B.y - A.y) * (A.z - C.z) - (B.z - A.z) * (A.y - C.y)
Normal.y = (B.z - A.z) * (A.x - C.x) - (B.x - A.x) * (A.z - C.z)
Normal.z = (B.x - A.x) * (A.y - C.y) - (B.y - A.y) * (A.x - C.x)
```

which you can manipulate to eliminate redundant calculations.

Once you've calculated the normal vector for a polygon, the next step is to calculate the vector from the viewpoint to some near midpoint of the triangle. This is a simple calculation:

```
View.x = midpt.x - respect.x
View.y = midpt.y - respect.y
View.z = midpt.z - respect.z
```

Figure 19-12 shows the result.

Now that you know these two vectors (the vector from viewpoint to midpoint and the normal vector), you need perform only one more calculation. Pumping these two vectors through a dot-product calculation, you will get a number between -1 and 1:

```
Dotp = (Normal.x * View.x)+(Normal.y * View.y)+(Normal.z * View.z)
```

If the number is negative, then it represents a triangle that faces the viewer (in other words, a triangle that should be drawn). If the number is positive, it represents a triangle on a plane not visible to the viewer (in other words, a triangle that should not be drawn). Taking the inverse cosine of this number will yield the angle between the two vectors.

The dot-product calculation can tell you a great deal about the relationship between two vectors. It may require a lot of work, but 3D terrains typically are not compute-bound, so this isn't usually a problem. Besides, by performing this calculation, you will save yourself the trouble of drawing an awful lot of hidden (and therefore useless) surfaces, resulting in a noticeable boost in speed.

You can implement the dot product this way:

```
// Calculate the angle of incidence.
// A,B,C are the points of the triangle.
// Respect: Is the point in question the viewpoint or light source.
```

continued on next page

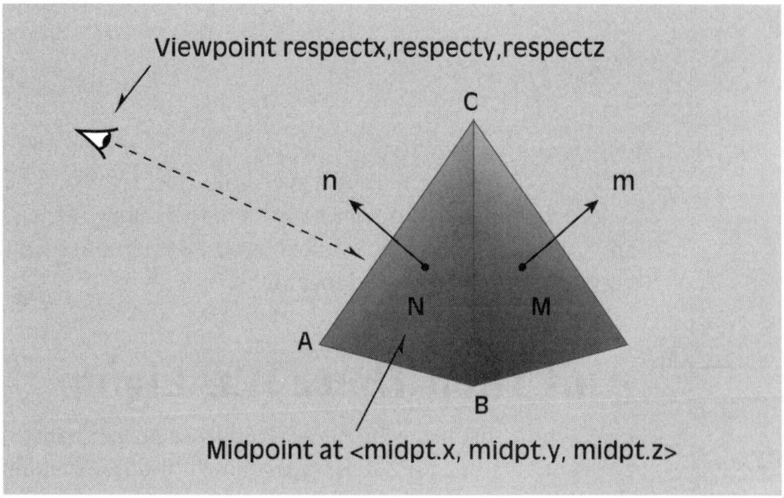

FIGURE 19-12

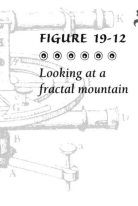

Looking at a fractal mountain

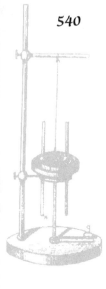

continued from previous page

```
float dotproduct(struct pt3d A, struct pt3d B, struct pt3d C,
                 int respectx, int respecty,int respectz)

{ // pt3d structure is int x,y,z;
  struct pt3d normal,midpt,view;
  float dotp;
  int j,k;

  // Calculate the normal vector for this plane (triangle).
  normal.x = (B.y - A.y) * (A.z - C.z) - (B.z - A.z) * (A.y - C.y);
  normal.y = (B.z - A.z) * (A.x - C.x) - (B.x - A.x) * (A.z - C.z);
  normal.z = (B.x - A.x) * (A.y - C.y) - (B.y - A.y) * (A.x - C.x);

  // Calculate a representative point in the triangle.
  midpt.x = (A.x + B.x + C.x)/3;
  midpt.y = (A.y + B.y + C.y)/3;
  midpt.z = (A.z + B.z + C.z)/3;

  // Calculate the vector from the viewpoint to the midpoint.
  view.x = midpt.x - respectx;
  view.y = midpt.y - respecty;
  view.z = midpt.z - respectz;

  // Get vector lengths.
  j = abs(normal.x*normal.x + normal.y*normal.y + normal.z*normal.z);
  k = abs(view.x*view.x + view.y*view.y + view.z*view.z);
  j = sqrt(j);
  k = sqrt(k);

  // Dot product
  dotp = (normal.x * view.x)+(normal.y * view.y)+(normal.z * view.z);
  dotp /= j;
  dotp /= k;

 return dotp;
}
```

A final note about the dot-product calculation: Be sure your application warrants it. It does cost something and it speeds up graphics only if it's possible to significantly reduce the number of triangles that need to be drawn. The choice all depends on the application. If your game features bumpy 3D terrain, then the dot-product calculation is almost always worth the trouble.

And Then There Was Light

Even simple shading techniques can enhance image quality significantly. The method I present here has a big advantage, though: It doesn't require any more math! Actually, it's not that calculating brightness doesn't require a bunch of nasty equations—

it's just that you have already done them. As I mentioned while discussing "hidden-surface removal," the dot product is the cosine of the angle of incidence (refer to Figure 19-12). This fraction can tell us how a triangle is oriented with regard to the light source. Figure 19-13 shows an example.

If a triangle's surface faces away from the light source, of course it will be dark. If a triangle's normal vector points directly at the light, then that triangle will be fully illuminated. If the normal vector is off by some angle (but still facing the light), then the triangle will be shaded to some degree. To determine this, we can reuse the dot-product code, giving it the vector for the light source to the triangle instead of supplying it the vector from the viewpoint to the triangle. Unless, of course, your viewpoint is at the same place as your light source. This is a bad idea in general, since the shading effect will be less dramatic.

Once you've calculated the dot product with respect to the light source, you can scale it into some shaded colors. A good choice might be to have 20 shades of gray, as shown in Figure 19-14. These "colors" can be defined in your palette (20 shades of each color may be too many if your game has a lot of colors). In our example, color 0 is black. As the color's number gets bigger, so does its brightness. Here, color 19 is pure white.

You can ignore any positive dot products, so that leaves values from 0 to -1. Multiply the negative dot products by -19 to produce values between 0 and 19 (you may need to do some slight rounding). Use the corresponding shades to fill the triangles.

There are more accurate lighting models, but they often slow down the game. This method has the distinct advantages of being simple and cheap.

FIGURE 19-13

Light source incidences and shading

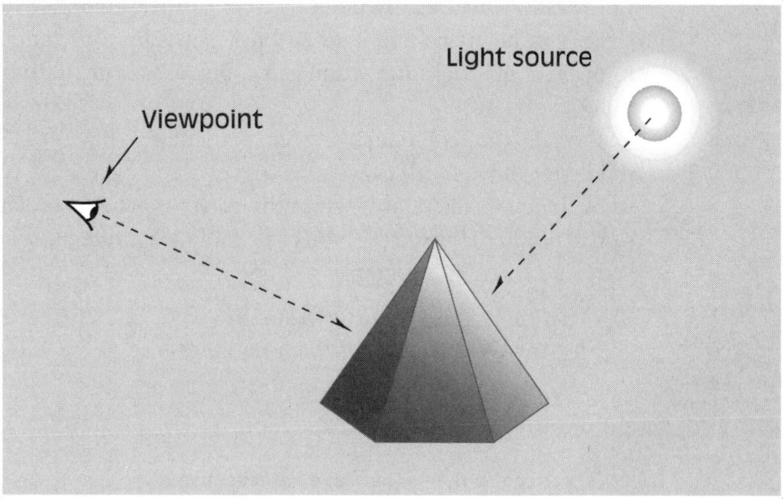

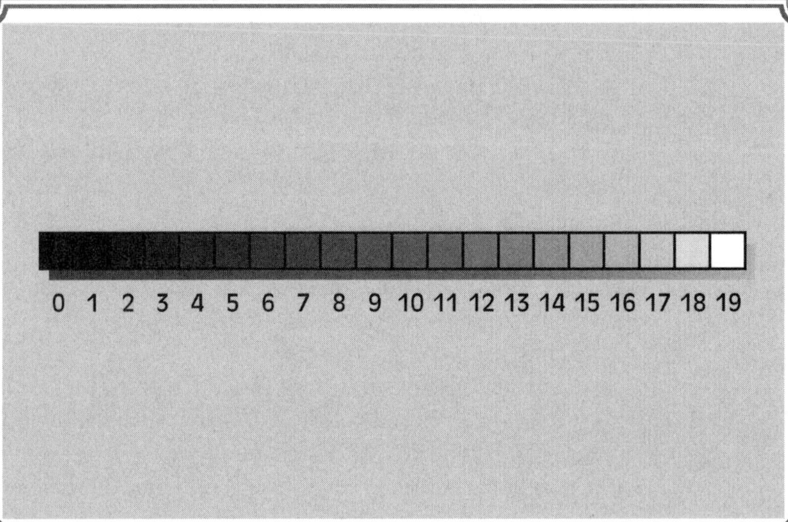

FIGURE 19-14

Shades of gray

Living Earth

PCs are now powerful enough (with a bit of cheating) to simultaneously model 3D terrain, control a legion of sprites, use artificial intelligence techniques, and simulate natural occurrences. Fly over the ocean in the Bullfrog Production's game Magic Carpet and you'll see my point. "Living earth" techniques such as water-wave modeling, ground morphing, and so on are usually too computationally expensive to implement in a real-time action game. But, as is evident from Magic Carpet, it can be done.

Overall, the techniques are not particularly difficult. They entail continuously modifying the *y* coordinates of the terrain in some preset manner. Note that this needs to be done regardless of whether the player is actually moving. To produce the illusion of fluidity, for example, you can simply substitute the following code for the flyby code in our terrain program:

```
// Code to produce "fluid" motion;
// in other words, colliding sine waves

void fluid()
{  int g,h,d;

// s controls one sine wave, d the other.
// Start s at an external counter value (X sine wave position).
   s = s1;
```

```
    s1 += GRIDSIZE;

// Loop through all points.
    for (g=0;g<GRIDSIZE;++g)
    { d = d1++;
      for (h=0;h<GRIDSIZE;++h)
      { // Start point3d at the standard place.
        point3d[g][h].y = (GRIDSIZE-h*3);

        // Add wave offsets. 6 defines wave amplitudes.
        point3d[g][h].y +=  6*sin(RAD((s%360)));
        point3d[g][h].y +=  6*sin(RAD((d%360)));

        // Changing these values will change the wave frequency.
        s+=1;
        d+=GRIDSIZE;
      }
    }
  }
```

This code (which you can optimize to your heart's content, by the way) sends two sine waves through each other. The effect is quite convincing.

Again, relying on tight code and cheats suited to your game will be your best option. For example, when the player is flying low over water (with no land in sight) does the viewpoint actually have to move? Wouldn't just dipping the viewpoint a bit and keeping the water waves undulating produce enough of an effect to "fool" the player?

Whatever effect you're after must be relatively straightforward, and it shouldn't require a large number of computations to determine *y* coordinates. The real trick is to accomplish these possibly expensive operations in a timely manner.

Motion Sickness

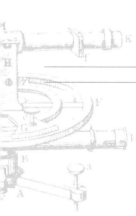

Superfast 3D games have been known to make players sick to their stomachs. This might appear to be a dubious distinction, but in fact it attests to the realism of such games. This kind of realism has its costs, though.

Your final product will represent a compromise between what you want to be in your background and what the processor will let you have. There are now games that have true 3D environments with fully rendered 3D enemies. They demand every ounce of power the player's computer can offer. Very fast CPUs are becoming the standard, but requiring a player to have a superfast machine will still limit your market somewhat. Consider this when you design your game. No matter what your decision, though, you should plan your implementation well and strive for a reasonable amount of realism.

And remember—if your game is so realistic it has people getting sick, gloat all you want, but tone it down a bit. Sick users don't play very long.

Right Up Front

Fortunately, foreground elements are often cheap compared to backgrounds. Standard foreground operations such as drawing sprites and using artificial intelligence techniques also usually aren't as nasty to implement as their background counterparts.

2D Sprites

The sprite engine we developed in Chapter 10 provides you with comprehensive code for moving and manipulating your sprites. But how do you actually create sprites? Here, I'll cover some guidelines for making your sprites attractive and easier to handle quickly.

First and foremost, you need to decide how big your sprites should be. Sprites themselves are usually not rectangular (see Doggie, which is included with WinG), but as I discussed in Chapter 10, they must reside in rectangular boxes. If you're a quick study, you might have guessed that the dimensions of a sprite rectangle should be multiples of 2. You're right. In this case, the important aspect is that multiples of 2 greater than 2 itself are divisible by 4. This allows your code to use doubleword copies at the assembly level. Doubleword copies are the fastest way to transfer data in x86 architectures. This stands to reason: Doubleword copies are 4 bytes, or 32 bits, so the code can make full use of the computer's architecture.

WinG's FAST32.ASM has the code for the **CopyDIBBits** routine. This routine simply copies one area of memory to another. Its authors couldn't be certain that the caller would always provide a rectangle with dimensions divisible by 4, so they had to make their code robust enough to handle a rectangle of any size. Unfortunately, this slows the routine down a little, as you can see in the first four assembly-language instructions in the following listing. The first two lines handle all the doublewords and the second two lines handle any extra bytes. There can be up to 3 extra bytes only, since 4 extra bytes would constitute another doubleword. If you can guarantee that your sprite copies will have widths divisible by 4, then you can remove the second two lines (and the associated code).

```
cdb_loop:

        ; ecx to hold the number of doublewords needed to copy
        mov ecx,ebx

        ; Copy the doublewords.
        rep movs dword ptr es:[edi], dword ptr ds:[esi]

        ; ecx to hold the number of "extra" bytes
```

```
; Maximum number of extra bytes possible is 3, since anything
; over 3 would be copied above as a doubleword.
; This line can be removed if the widths are divisible by 4.
mov ecx,eax

; Copy the bytes.
; This line can be removed if the widths are divisible by 4.
rep movs byte ptr es:[edi], byte ptr ds:[esi]

; Move the pointers to the next line.
add esi, dwScanS
add edi, dwScanD

; Have we done all the lines?
dec edx                   ; line counter
jnz short cdb_loop
```

As usual, it's a good idea here to save your optimization efforts for time-critical sections of code. (Incidentally, even if you leave the FAST32.ASM code untouched, a 32-byte-wide sprite will copy over faster than will a 31-byte-wide sprite.)

You may have noticed that although it makes a difference if the sprite width is a multiple of 2, the sprite height seems to be immaterial. Of course, you can copy shorter sprites in less time than you can tall ones. In this routine, though, there doesn't seem to be an advantage to a sprite height that is a multiple of 2. For this example, that is true. However, considering the huge number of calculations you'll probably need to make based on your sprite's height, it's wisest in the long run to make this dimension, too, a multiple of 2.

Colors and Images

Games require you to be a little exaggerated when it comes to color distinctions. A sprite that looks fantastic on the drawing program's display will end up disappearing if you put it in front of a game background of a similar color. Distinct colors are a must for clarity.

You can design sprites in several ways. It's most common to draw them by hand and this works well in many cases. You can even design acceptable sprites using the Paint program included with Windows, but you'll probably want to employ a slightly more comprehensive drawing package. It all depends on how sophisticated you need your sprites to be. Since WinG is biased toward games with 256 colors, there's a fair amount of flexibility for the artist.

Other methods include scanning 2D images (see Apogee's Rise of the Triad) or images of clay or similarly created "real" characters. Scanning helps you avoid a "cartoon" quality in your sprites but creates great challenges in the realms of sizing, color usage, and animated sequences.

3D Enemies

There are already games that provide a full 3D environment and 3D enemies. However, in many cases these sprites are quite blocky—in other words, they are made up of very few triangles. Blocky robots or angry polygons don't make thrilling enemies. In order to model more lifelike creatures, you need more triangles. Usually, a lot more.

No new math or techniques are involved in the creation of 3D enemies; you can just apply the 3D techniques I've already discussed in this chapter. Initially, the most difficult task is to define 3D coordinates that accurately describe the "being" you wish to model. There are some quite wonderful models of humanoid creatures in games today. Some of these models involve hundreds of triangles. If your game does not require significant screen scrolling and other expensive operations, then it's certainly feasible for you to implement such 3D entities. Again, you'll need to keep in mind the capacities of various processors and the limitations, if any, you are willing to accept.

Summary

As a finished product, your game will be the function of many variables. How you implement your background and foreground elements affects almost everything else. If you've decided to stick to a 2D game, you can devote a bit more time to the development of the game play. There is plenty of demand in the wide-open Windows game market for this type of game.

If you're dead-set on a 3D game, be ready to devote a lot of time to it. If you're a 3D novice, the introduction in this chapter should be enough to get you going. The code in this chapter is a good starting point.

In any case, be careful with your backgrounds and foregrounds. Graphics can slow down the fastest computers. WinG provides a great resource to speed up your game's graphics; if you use it intelligently, your game will fly!

20

Scoring and Saving

come trebbe fare le manovelle [illegible] le quali si movano e llaiza
[illegible] gran pesi [illegible] fa operano [illegible]
[illegible] nella man [illegible] nella manovella pegi [illegible]
la forza e più l'omo più vale.

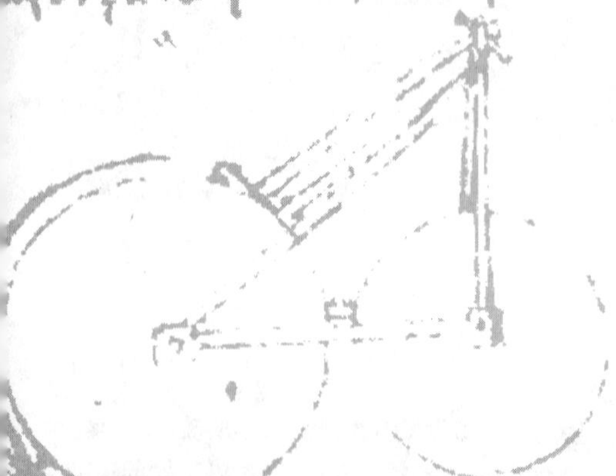

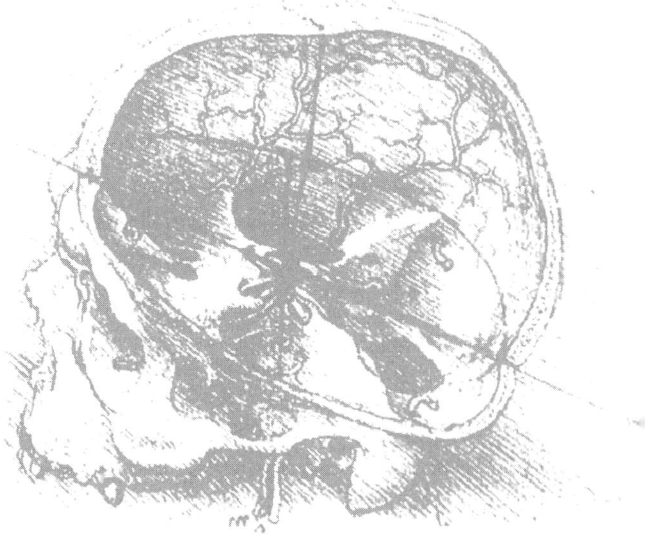

20

Scoring and Saving

At some point, every game designer must address the somewhat less romantic aspects of game creation. You'll need to make definitive decisions about how to deal with issues like scoring, saving, presenting, and protecting. In this chapter, I'll review the game industry's tried and true methods and suggest ways to set up your game.

Scoring

Nothing feeds a game's popularity like a feature that gauges a player's expertise. The most common methods for implementing such a measurement provide a numerical score. Typically, this score is displayed by an odometer that sits somewhere in a corner of the screen and madly calculates the results of the player's performance. The odometer and its close relatives have been the traditional mode for displaying video-game scores almost since the inception of these programs.

What Gratifies a Player?

The best method for determining what is a good gauge of a player's skills is to listen to the players themselves. What are people bragging about? Recently, gloating over a numerical score has been overshadowed by another kind of boasting: "I got to the eighth level!" Many successful games don't perform any scoring at all. Immediately after the release of DOOM, the Internet was swamped with posts proclaiming the names of the players who finished all ten levels first or who found certain secret doors. No scores were involved; these accomplishments themselves constituted effective gauges. Role-playing games also rarely rely on numerical scores. Instead, they provide the player with levels, novel magical items, and new monster challenges.

The beauty of these methods is that the rating system (and hence the bragging) is not directly tied to some implemented scoring mechanism. Instead, it is implicit in the game's design. The evolution of DOOM from Wolfenstein 3D provides a prime example of the power of this approach. Wolfenstein 3D had numerical scoring. The problem was, no one cared about the score; players all began referring to what *level* they were on as a measure of their skill. When Wolfenstein 3D's "successor," DOOM, was released, a scoring mechanism was nowhere to be found. This isn't to say numerical scoring doesn't have its place, but its effectiveness depends on the game's type. You can't always equate points with a sense of accomplishment.

Several key factors must be present before you can implement this style of accomplishment rating in place of numerical scoring. First, your application must be able to recognize that the player has completed a particular level, board, or section. The first-person 3D action games out today all do this quite well. When the player completes a level, the game stops and displays a message to that effect and then tallies statistics. This marker is associated with the "intended" gauges of skill. The designer expects (and hopes) the player will complete progressive levels and continue the quest.

If your game's design does not include explicit levels, then it is imperative that you implement a method of at least partitioning goals and acknowledging success. The developers of role-playing games often adopt this approach, usually because they have little choice. Such games take place in one big "world," not on leveled boards. They compensate the player's efforts by providing a visual reward when the player completes any so-called mini-quest. These mini-quests take the place of distinct levels.

Concealed items can provide another implicit gauge. A secret door or a buried treasure will furnish an element of surprise and adventure. Such items reward a specific approach to playing the game. Not every player will find this booty; those who search every last inch of your "world" are much more likely to locate these items than are those who fly through levels. By including concealed items, you can ensure that your program will gratify those who are methodical as well as those who race the clock, pleasing an expanded group of players.

Whichever method or methods you choose to gauge player expertise, be sure you include some mechanism for letting the player know how he or she is doing. A well-designed scoring system fuels word-of-mouth advertising for a game and gets players hooked.

What's It Worth?

If numerical scoring makes sense for your game and you decide to use it, make sure its implementation has a plausible organization. Obviously, if a critter that dies with 1 shot is worth 100 points, a mammoth that withstands 10 shots before it keels over had better be worth at least 1,000 points.

Determining a simple mathematical formula for your game's targets and then routinely applying it can help you ensure consistently representative point values. Figure 20-1 shows the point values for enemies in Battlezone, from Microsoft's Arcade series. The lowest level tank is worth 1,000 points; the super tank, 3,000. Assuming the

FIGURE 20-1

Battlezone scoring

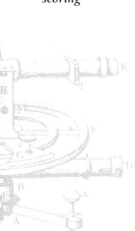

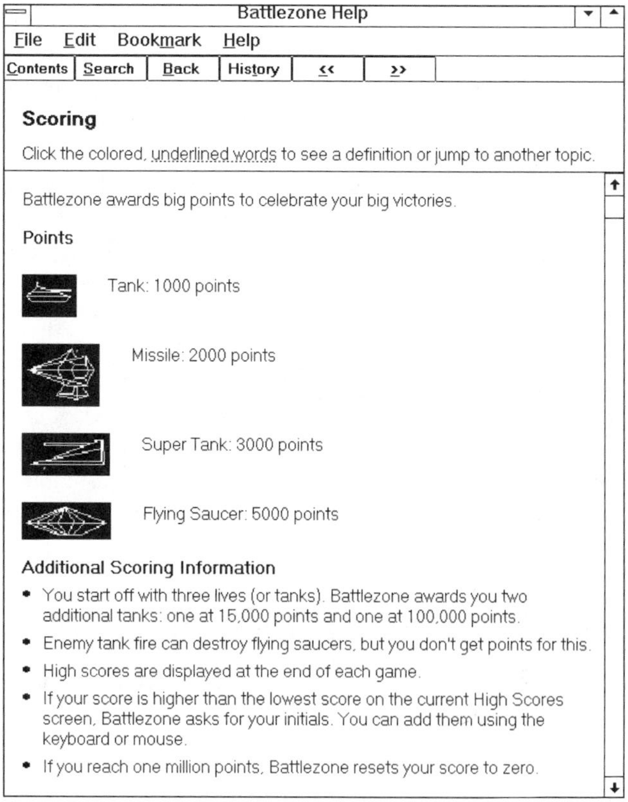

super tank has 3 times the speed and 3 times the firing rate of a normal tank, a mathematical formula for the point values in Battlezone might be:

Point Value = (Firing Rate * 500) + (Speed * 500)

Note that you can also apply this formula to the missile, assuming it has no firing rate but 4 times the speed of the basic tank.

Unfortunately, our formula doesn't seem to work for Battlezone's flying saucer, though: Although it's completely harmless, shooting down the flying saucer earns the player more points than does any other target. Of course, the flying saucer's function in the game is simply to provide bonus points, not a challenge. All the same, we'll need to modify our formula if we want to determine whether Battlezone's developers followed good game-programming practice. Assuming the flying saucer has twice the speed of a normal tank and that it is a "bonus" target, we can adjust the formula in this way:

Point Value = (Firing Rate * 500) + (Speed * 500) + (Bonus Item * 4,000)

Bonus Item will be either 1 or 0. The formula shouldn't change substantially even if Battlezone's developers were to add new components; the idea is to apply one fixed set of rules (in other words, the formula) to all point assignments. Future additions to the enemy arsenal that fit the formula would be consistent with the existing point-value structure. Once you've perfected such a point formula for your application, you will be able to keep a respectable level of consistency throughout the game by piping the attributes of any new targets through that formula.

Now let's look at the point values themselves. The lowest value is 1,000. Why 1,000? Why not 1 or 100? Well, the main reason is the fact that a score of, say, 18 doesn't sound too impressive. A score of 18,000 is likely to awe even a person unfamiliar with the game. Big numbers imply big accomplishments.

Creating Levels of Play

Levels of play that are challenging and thoughtfully constructed add to the fun and quality of a game. A level should represent a region of measurable advancement. Level specifics will depend, of course, on the game in question; however, some general points usually apply, regardless of the game type.

Make It Fair But Challenging

Once the game engine (the fashionable term) is complete, the artistic side of the game programmer must take over and design game levels that are nothing less than brilliantly creative and functional. Gamers have already seen it all; more importantly, they've seen the best. Levels must be fair and challenging, but it won't hurt if they are totally cool as well.

Action games and role-playing games typically follow a standard game-design template:

- First level: This should be short and sweet with only soft-shelled enemies. Keep in mind this is the level on which novices will learn. There's no need to get tricky and certainly no need to waste any surprises here, since new players will find everything novel and interesting (including what the game designer may consider seriously mundane).
- Middle levels: This is the main chance for your creative abilities to shine. A gradual increase in difficulty as the levels get higher is appropriate.
- Last level: Simply put, this should be unlike any other level and extremely difficult. No matter how expert, the player should still feel adequately challenged.

The developers of most every action and RPG game out there use this general template. It is difficult to stray from this logical approach and still design effective levels.

The Enemy

The most intuitive factors to consider when trying to strike a balance between difficulty and fairness are the quality and quantity of the enemies in your game. The player should encounter new and interesting enemies every so often as he or she advances. This, in and of itself, is a kind of reward for the player.

You should take extra care to increase the level of difficulty gradually enough to allow the skills of the player to grow. Ideally, every succeeding level will be more difficult than the last and slightly beyond the player's skill, providing a continual challenge. In order to assess the degree of difficulty and achieve a balance, you can again apply a formula. For each type of enemy or environmental hazard, assign a point value representative of its level of difficulty. With games that have numerical scoring, you can often just use the point values of the enemies (these values, if generated by a formula like the one I discussed in the previous section, should indicate how tough each enemy is). Then, develop a difficulty quota for each level: say, 10,000 for level 1, 20,000 for level 2, and so on.

Let's look at an example of this method. Microsoft's Battlezone puts you in command of a techno-tank that's in the middle of an alien battlefield where legions of enemies are attacking. (Refer to Figure 20-1 again if you need to refresh your memory of these enemies and their point values.) How did the makers decide when specific enemies would cross your path? Figure 20-2 shows some possible assignments for Battlezone's first level (Battlezone doesn't have specific levels but it does have "waves" that serve the same function). The quota for this level is 10,000 points, so the developers could include 10 standard tanks, 5 missiles, or 3 super tanks and 1 standard tank—or combinations thereof—and still remain under the quota.

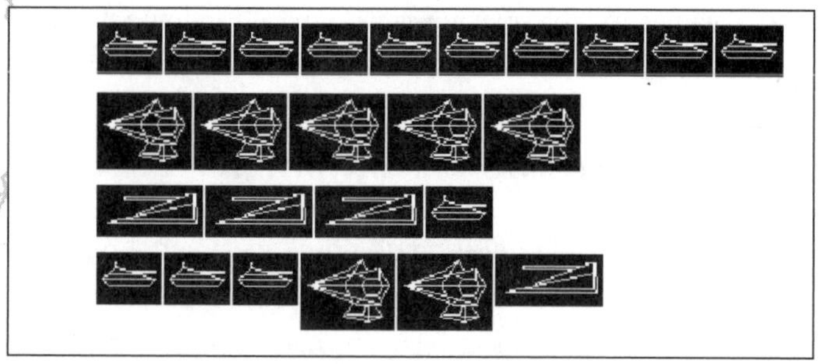

FIGURE 20-2

Some possible enemy configurations for "Level 1" of Battlezone

Granted, even if you use a difficulty formula, you must still take measures to implement the system intelligently. For example, novices would have quite a bit of trouble with an initial onslaught of three super tanks. The point system, though, can go a long way toward providing you with the information necessary in order to create consistent levels of difficulty.

Saving the Game's State

Regardless of the battle being fought, the planet being saved, or the ferocity of the drool-dribbling gorgon, one simple act can halt the action in any game: a call to dinner. Well, all right, there are an infinite number of reasons a user of your game might need to halt play and resume it at a later time. You need to take special care to prepare for this eventuality—there is little in the universe more frustrating for a player than losing his or her position in a game due to real-world events. Giving your program an unreliable saving mechanism is the straightest path to earning your game a poor reputation. If there is one piece of code you check and recheck to be sure it is devoid of bugs, make sure it's the code that deals with saving and reloading the game's state.

Size and Accuracy

Depending on the game, saving what the player is doing can be an arduous process. Your program might require significant amounts of information in order to be able to restore the "world" to its current state. This raises several serious concerns for the game programmer. First and foremost, you must ensure that the data saved is accurate. Your application should be able to restore the game to exactly the state it was in when the player left off; even minor changes can cause grave problems. Second, you should do everything in your power to make the saved game files as small as possible. For most games, this won't be a problem: Even without your intervention, the files will require only relatively small amounts of storage. Some situations, though, will demand a considerable amount of disk space. For these games, you will need to take extra steps.

Save the World

Saving the state of a game is analogous to freezing the "world" the player is in and writing it to disk. Many level-based games support a very simple game-saving methodology: They allow a player to save a game only at the beginning of a level. This way, the application need save only the level number and the player's current state. The program doesn't have to go to the considerable trouble of recording which monsters might be dead or which treasure might have been pilfered. When the application restores the game, it returns the player to his or her previous state (of health, wealth, and so on), but the game itself need only start fresh at a new level, using the saved level number to find its place. For many games, this is a cheap and acceptable solution.

A good number of games fall into a second category. These games have little to save, so the task is a relatively simple one. This category includes many action games and most board games (saving the 64 spots on a chessboard, for example, is no great problem).

And then there's the third category. This includes a large number of games that generate significantly greater state-saving concerns. Typically, games with elaborate worlds fall into this class. Strategy and role-playing games also belong to this group; it's notoriously difficult to create adequate saving mechanisms for these games. Unlike a level-based game, in which the application need not keep track of any levels the player has finished, adventure/role-playing games have towns, cities, and dungeons that a player can visit, change, and revisit at any time. And of course, if a player changes something about an environment, he or she expects it to stay changed, even through several restorations. Consider the simple act of dropping something. The player may drop the item in any town, in any building, in any room, and on any valid floor location in the entire game! The saved files for many adventure games can take up in excess of a megabyte each, simply because of the changes the player has made to the environment. The more the player plays, the more the environment changes and the larger the saved file becomes.

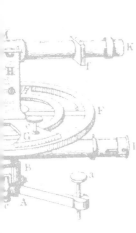

You can employ several strategies to help organize and limit the size of saved files for games that have "worlds" to keep track of:

- Employ a tree structure to organize the world. Tree structures have excellent algorithmic features and logically organize information.
- Keep everything in numbers that you can convert to base 2. If you have 257 different items in your game, for example, at all costs try to cut the number to 256 (in other words, 2^8) and store the item number in BYTE form, not INTEGER. Over the long haul, this could reduce the size of the

saved game considerably (not to mention make your program run faster and make it easier for you to code).

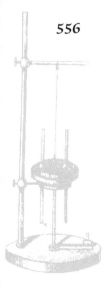

- Don't save what you don't need. If a particular aspect of the game has not changed, don't waste extra space by saving this redundant information. Load your initial game setup first and overlay the saved game.

The World on Disk

The organization of saved data can help simplify the task of loading the data and using it. Figure 20-3 shows a hex dump of a typical saved game file—if you were to dump the saved files of many of the popular games on the market, you would see something quite similar to this figure. (I discussed general Windows file I/O in Chapter 12; the focus here is on what the data looks like on disk.) This would be representative of how a file might look if written in C++ or Pascal. The data can be in one of two formats. On the right is the ASCII representation of data and the player's name. Important numbers are on the left (in hexadecimal). As long as the data is read in the same way it was written (and all necessary data was stored), the application should be able to restore exactly the world the player left.

Figure 20-4 illustrates a higher-level organization. Here, a world is organized in successively finer detail. This particular example models a role-playing game's world. If the player has not been to a specific city, then not only is that city not saved but neither are any of its elements. After all, there is no need to save information that

FIGURE 20-3

A hex dump of a saved game

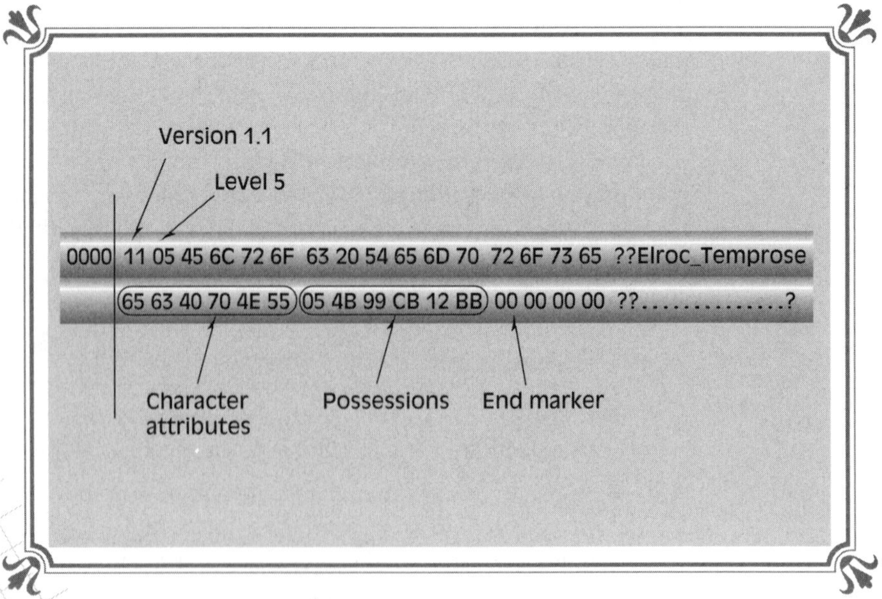

FIGURE 20-4

A possible organization for a saved game file

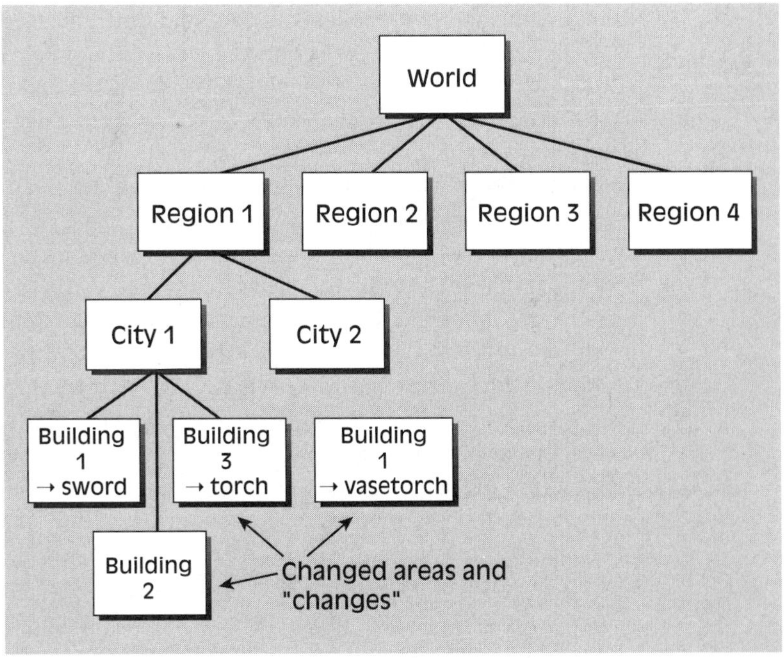

hasn't changed. Using this form of organization can conserve significant amounts of time and storage space when you are saving a game.

When called on to resume a saved game, the application should first reload the world to be restored as if it were a new game, and then overlay it with only the changes. Of course, saved games will increase in size as the player progresses. At some point, your application will need to store nearly the entire world.

Those Pesky Hackers

You've seen it before. The friend you always beat hands down in your favorite space combat simulator all of a sudden starts wiping up the cosmos with you. Last time you played him, he had a wimpy little space scooter and a 5-watt bump-laser—it was no problem to blow him away. But somewhere along the way he traded up to a biturbo battleship with heat-integration beams. How did he get them? Through hard work or clever bartering? You know better. He cheated—he changed the saved game.

No matter how hard you try, you cannot stop all hackers from getting into the saved game and deciphering its code. This stands to reason. Every hacker knows that even the game that incorporates an unbreakable encryption algorithm into its game-saving code has one Achilles' heel: The game itself must have the decryption algorithm. All the hacker has to do is sit back and watch the teacher you've provided.

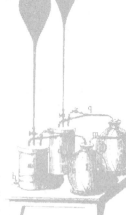

The saved game is the perfect target for modification. A hacker can examine and adjust it while the game isn't running. He or she has the luxury of being able to ignore subtle intricacies—simply changing a byte in a saved game can alter the balance of power.

The hacker problem can't be completely eradicated, but then again, who really cares? You may agree with those programmers who feel that it's not a big deal if hackers want to spend time and energy poking through bits to see how to get an extra couple of bullets. The only real damage done is to you, who is deprived of a certain measure of control over your application. For many developers, this isn't an issue of much concern.

Many of those developers who *are* perturbed by this perhaps minor dilemma, however, are now including "cheat" keys in their games. This permits players to cheat while still allowing the programmer control over the application. Initially, cheat keys might seem ridiculously counterintuitive. What player would forego using them? For some reason, though, they work. First, most people still play the game legally as a matter of pride. Second, hackers now rarely go to any lengths to crack a game in order to get a few extra powers the cheat keys already provide.

As a game designer, you might want to consider adding cheat keys to your application. Think carefully, though, before you take this step: If someone can use your cheat keys to attain a high score, the gaming community is apt to take a dim view of your game. It's in your best interest to instruct your game to disable any type of scoring (where possible) when it detects that a player is using the cheat keys. Otherwise, a high score in your game would be virtually meaningless, making players less inclined to "play to win" legally.

Compression and Encryption

If you're seriously intent on slowing down hackers, there *are* a few things you can do. An obvious tactic is to encrypt your saved game. As I mentioned, though, this is by no means a foolproof method—your game already includes the code for decrypting it. Of course, a decent encryption will prevent at least the less motivated and less skilled from figuring out your method.

Running a game to be saved through a compression algorithm, on the other hand, serves two purposes: Not only will this save disk space, but it will also provide its own method of encryption. Standard encryption methods are complex and tedious; implementing them simply to ensure the integrity of a saved game is overkill. However, considering the arguably more significant need to keep saved games small, you might find it worth the trouble to incorporate a compression algorithm into your application.

You may have some concerns regarding the speed of the compression and decompression processes. Overall, they shouldn't create a problem. When a player is saving a game, he or she is rarely expecting your program to perform at high speed; play is over, so the user isn't eagerly waiting for your application to get its act together. Besides, disk accesses are usually orders of magnitude slower than the process of decompressing data, so most of the time required to save or load a game is really devoted to waiting for the disk, not waiting for the CPU.

One word of warning: Be extremely careful when selecting a compression method. Several well-known algorithms are patented. You'll need written permission and will probably have to pay a substantial fee in order to use them. Fortunately, there are many algorithms that are available free of charge for public use. Standard Huffman or arithmetic coding are excellent choices. There are many superb references for these methods and compression in general; one of the best is *Data Compression: Methods and Theory*, by James A. Storer (Rockville, MD: Computer Science Press, 1988).

Copy Protection

Now that you've spent hundreds of hours developing, coding, and debugging the game of games, how do you deal with the ever-present threat of piracy? Well, as events in the industry have demonstrated, complete prevention of piracy is impossible (or at least impractical). You can, however, take many actions to slow the onslaught.

The Industry Standard

If you're still convinced that there must be some efficient way to stop pirates completely, consider the evidence. The large game developers in existence today still rely on relatively crude means to secure their products. Surely, this kind of money and talent would have developed a better method if one were possible. It may be that one of the remarkable minds out there will eventually hit on a scheme for granting invincible protection, but don't hold your breath: The odds look even bleaker when you consider that not only must a perfect protection mechanism stop pirates, it shouldn't noticeably increase the cost of the software or annoy legal users.

The Lesser of Two Evils

Many games today rely for their security on the manual-lookup test. The method is straightforward: Have the program require the user to look up a word or phrase in the manual and type it in. What does this prove? Well, at least that the user has a copy of the manual handy. How well does it work? Typically, software pirates have all the tools they need (computers, disk drives, and so forth) to easily copy the software, but they don't always have immediate access to a photocopying machine. This method,

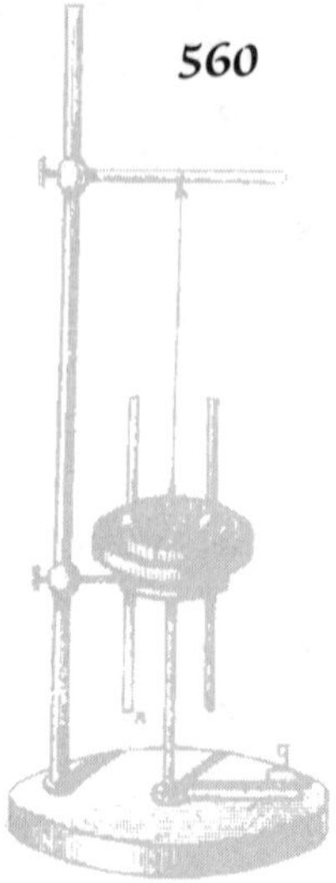

therefore, definitely has its merits and certainly annoys pirates. Unfortunately, it may also annoy legal users. When you consider the number of games that use this type of protection, however, it becomes clear that this scheme either doesn't irritate the legal users all that much or it must really thwart software piracy (to such an extent that developers are willing to risk alienating some legitimate players). In any event, this method is at least to some degree successful and for now is the standard.

Your System's Signature

A less common form of protection is *system signaturing*. Some games take a signature of the system on which they are installed and save this information. A signature might be a speed benchmark or a CMOS value check. From then on, whenever the game is started, it checks the machine's signature against the saved version. If the signatures differ, the program refuses to work and assumes it has been copied to another machine. In the case where a legal user has upgraded his or her system, the program usually tells the player to reinstall the application from the original disks. This method limits pirates to copying only the original installation disks. In other words, they cannot simply copy the software off one hard drive onto another machine; they must actually install it. This does not bother legal users until they upgrade their systems (which is typically not too often). The main drawback is that a signaturing method is difficult to implement reliably and can easily be fooled by new "DOS-compatible" operating systems. If a signaturing system starts going bad, users will have a hard time forgiving you.

Size Commands Respect

The recent crop of games on CD-ROM use their own intrinsic form of copy protection, which is afforded by their huge size. A CD can hold somewhere in the neighborhood of 600 MB of information; a game that incorporates video and sound can fill that up remarkably fast. Pirates may be sneaky and resourceful, but someone who doesn't want to spend the money to buy a legal copy of a game is not likely to have 600 MB of spare hard-disk space lying around.

Sharing, Giving, and Nagging

Shareware works on the "try before you buy" principle. Once a user has evaluated the software, the developer's hope is that the player will register the copy by sending the suggested compensation. Unfortunately, counting on the consciences of humans will rarely make you rich.

The most commercially viable shareware games implement some sort of incentive to register. For example, look at ID Software's DOOM, which was one of the most successful shareware distributions ever (although not the *most* successful—DOOM was distributed almost exclusively in compressed ZIP format and therefore boosted the demand for an even more broadly distributed shareware program, PKWARE's PKUN-

ZIP). Amazingly, ID Software simply gave away the first 10 levels of DOOM. The company ended the game, though, with an inoffensive message suggesting that these 10 levels should be registered and promising that those who registered would receive 20 more levels. Even so, it's estimated that only 1 percent—about 150,000—of the people who played DOOM actually registered it.

In an attempt to motivate users to register, some shareware authors resort to distributing their programs in the form of "nagware." This is shareware that displays a nagging window at some point during its execution, reminding you to register. Nagware usually encourages registration by frustrating its users. This can create some obvious PR problems. It is wise to be sure the user knows what benefits exist for registered users. Depending on your situation, these benefits might include technical support, updated releases, extra features, and more levels.

DOOM was an undeniable shareware success, but many shareware authors are not so fortunate. By and large, most shareware authors get few, if any, registrations. As you might expect, providing a quality product coupled with an incentive to register often produces the best results.

Thieves, Pirates, and Crackers

Game designers and programmers may be ingenious, but pirates are equally resourceful. Regardless of what means programmers resort to in order to protect their intellectual property, pirates find a way to steal it.

It's a simple matter for pirates to copy the many games (and possibly their manuals) that have little or no protection—it certainly doesn't take much brainpower. You shouldn't underestimate a pirate's ability to quickly find ways around any copy protections you implement, though. For almost every game that uses a manual-lookup test, for example, there exists a *crack* to circumvent this obstacle.

A crack is a program that is designed to modify another program (in other words, your game) in such a way as to destroy its copy protection. Smart crackers (people who write cracks) debug your program into assembly language and find where the copy protections are checked. Then they modify the code to disregard the protective mechanism. It would be illegal to change and distribute a copyrighted piece of code, but the act of writing a program whose sole function is to change another program is not a crime, at least for now. The debate on the Internet, where there are sites that are repositories just for cracks, is ever alive. Cracks are a little like radar detectors: They are not actually illegal in and of themselves, but they are sometimes used for illegal purposes.

Game companies have to a large degree accepted that some piracy will happen. It seems the effort involved in attempting to completely stamp out illegal copying is not worth it. It's been said that game companies use this excuse to keep prices higher. Whether that's true is immaterial; at least for now, piracy exists.

Summary

The methods that you choose to implement the administrative details of your game are largely a matter of personal preference. Overall, the type of game you create is not that important for these decisions. If you want your saved games well protected or your game ridiculously hard to pirate, then you must devote extra time to implement these elements. Again, a trade-off between implementation time and features rears its ugly head.

A good rule to follow is to not let any administrative elements get in the way of game play. You spent a great deal of time designing and programming your game. Don't let an overzealous copy protection scheme or unreliable saved game facility ruin a player's fun.

21

Entering the Third Dimension with OpenGL

o, ome ... fare le manovelle ... le quali si movano ... laiga
... gra ... le ... o ... saderano ... ne
... re nella ... a sia ... quella a sella manovella perchè ...
a forza ... pio ... omo pio ...

[illegible]

21

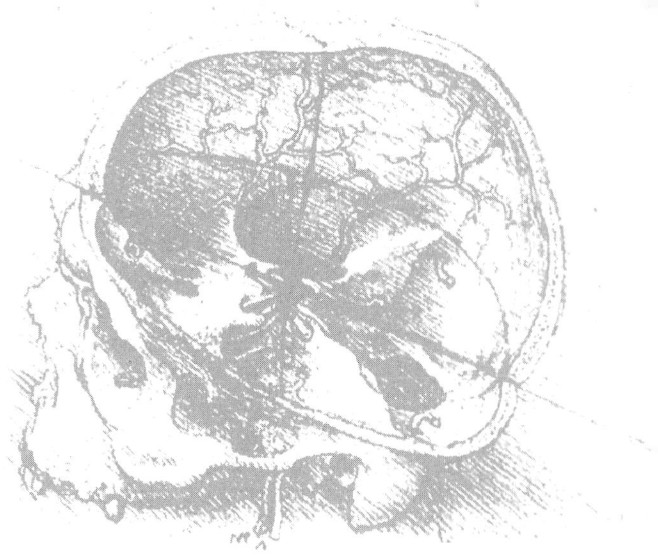

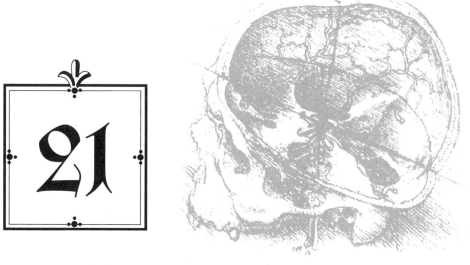

Entering the Third Dimension with OpenGL

In Washington, D.C., you can find street vendors who will take a Polaroid of you standing next to a life-size picture of the President. At first glance, it might be difficult to tell that the famous figure in the photo is just an image and not a real person. However, if the vendor were to shoot the picture from a slightly different angle, you would immediately perceive the lack of image depth that would indicate that the "President" was a fake—an imitation. The two-dimensional image is good for a laugh, but it's a disappointment compared to the real thing.

The majority of games and graphics programs available today are strictly 2D, meaning that their images are similar to photographs. Although such pictures may be beautiful, even breathtaking, they are obviously flat. The point of view is fixed. This sometimes makes it difficult for the player to evaluate the sizes of and relationships between the objects in the image. It also means that it's unlikely that he or she will ever be able to forget that this is just a game.

Adding the third dimension gives volume and depth to the objects depicted in the scene. It's a bit like turning a series of still photographs into a movie. In 3D graphics, objects can move and rotate. You can see the same setting from many different viewpoints. This can make your game much more interesting and challenging to play.

Why Is Depth Important?

When you paint a representational picture, you are creating one view of an object or objects. No matter what the environment in which the picture is shown or the position of the viewer, the observer is allowed to see those objects only from your viewpoint, with your highlights, shadows, and single viewing angle.

Constructing a 3D model means creating many views at once. The process is really more like sculpting than painting. Like a sculpture, a 3D model relies on spatial relationships, changing viewpoints, and depth. The viewer's perception of the artwork shifts as he or she moves and as the lighting conditions change, making it possible for the observer to take a much more active role in enjoying the work.

One of the fundamental advantages of 3D computer graphics is their ability to be viewed from any perspective. Two-dimensional images that are tilted and viewed from the side appear distorted. A 3D object merely looks different—perhaps completely different, as you can see in Figure 21-1. The four drawings seem to show different objects, but in reality, they are just different views of a cylinder cut obliquely.

As you can see, no single view provides enough information for the viewer to completely understand the shape of the object. Only certain specific views give *any* indication of the real shape of the item, in fact. Even a combination of several individual views might not clearly indicate the object's form. Allowing the viewer to walk around the object or rotate it while viewing it is the best way to convey the true structure of the object.

Seeing many different views of an object helps you to get a feel for that object rapidly. When we see an unfamiliar and intriguing item, we like to pick it up and explore it with our eyes and hands in order to understand it better. We inspect the

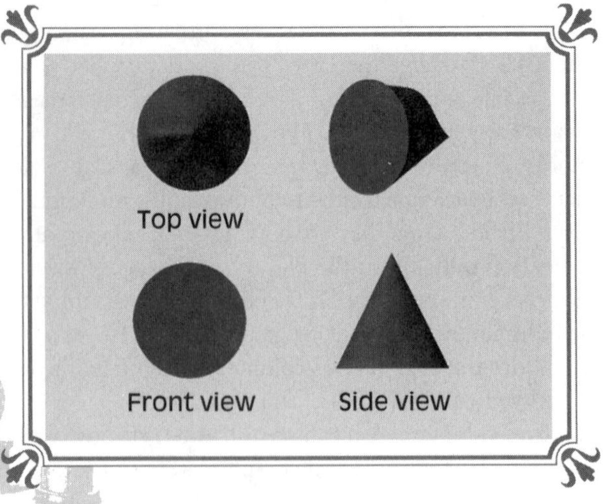

FIGURE 21-1
Four views of a single object

item visually and tangibly. How heavy is it? How much space does it take up? Does it open? Is it hollow, or could it be solid? Although we can't pick up a 3D computer model, we can explore it by changing either our point of view or the orientation of the model. An overhead view, for example, allows you to scope out the entire environment at once, while zooming in to view objects in detail permits you to become familiar with each item in the scene.

Creating the Illusion of Depth and Volume

No image shown on a TV or computer screen will ever be anything other than 2D—it is impossible to display three dimensions on something that exists in only two dimensions. However, you can make something on a computer monitor *appear* 3D.

There are several techniques artists and programmers use to give the illusion of three-dimensionality. One of the most familiar is perspective drawing, which involves the use of vanishing points and horizon lines. Its effectiveness is based on the fact that objects appear smaller and smaller as they recede into the distance (think of the familiar image of train tracks and telephone poles disappearing into a single point on the horizon). Figure 21-2 shows an example of this principle. In the left drawing, the person in the rear seems larger than the closer person, even though they are drawn exactly the same size. Our eyes deceive us; we expect objects in the distance to appear smaller than close objects do. The drawing on the right seems more natural, because the people are closer to the sizes we expect to see. To achieve

FIGURE 21-2

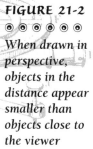

When drawn in perspective, objects in the distance appear smaller than objects close to the viewer

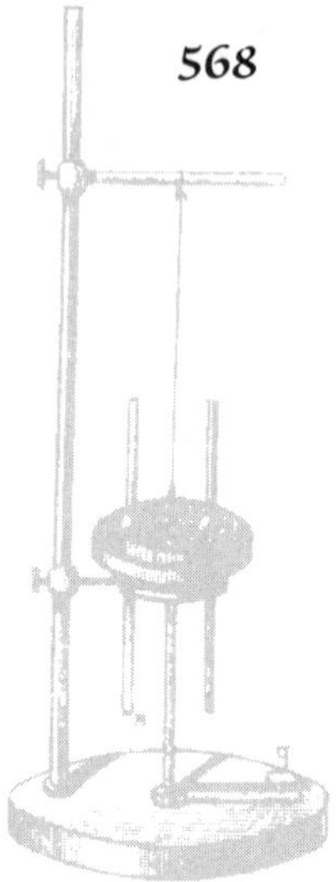

this effect in 3D computer graphics, you can use mathematical equations to precisely calculate the proper perspective.

Another trick for adding depth to an image is to make near objects *occlude* (cover) objects that are farther away. For example, we can tell which side of the tracks a far-off railway station is on (as well as the station's relative size) by watching to see whether the train moving in the distance passes in front of or behind the station.

One of the most powerful ways of making something appear 3D is to move the object in order to present many different viewpoints to the viewer. "Holding" an object in front of the viewpoint and rotating it is very effective. You can create this illusion of rotation by quickly showing a succession of images of the object, each with a slightly different point of view.

There are many other strategies for creating an illusion of three dimensions on the flat computer screen. In this chapter, I'll discuss a library of routines called OpenGL that provides you with mathematical techniques for producing a 3D environment and allows you to convert a true 3D scene to an appropriate 2D image.

An Introduction to OpenGL

OpenGL is a graphics library created by Silicon Graphics, Inc., the company responsible for building the computers and developing many of the programs used in the making of popular movies like *Jurassic Park*. SGI intended OpenGL to be a universal programming standard for 3D graphics, and it has been immensely successful. To date, Microsoft, IBM, DEC, and many other industry giants have adopted the OpenGL standard. (Currently, the OpenGL library comes with the Windows SDK for Windows NT only. However, it is anticipated to be available for both Windows 3.1 and Windows 95 by early Fall 1995. It is currently a commercial product, but is expected to come with any Win95 development package in the near future.)

There are other 3D programming libraries, but these have met with less-widespread acceptance. They include PEX (Phigs Extension to X) and HOOPS (from Ithaca Software). Although PEX is available for many platforms, not all versions implement all parts of the PEX graphics library. HOOPS, like OpenGL, is the same on all platforms it serves, but it has the disadvantage of being a proprietary standard. Recently, several new 3D APIs for personal computers have also appeared, including RenderWare from Canon, 3DR from Intel, and QuickDraw 3D for the Mac. The jury is still out on whether these new APIs will become popular for workstation-level platforms.

The Graphics Library

OpenGL gives a programmer access to hardware and software for creating 3D scenes for display on the monitor. It allows you to specify a viewpoint; render geometric forms with various colors, textures, and lighting effects; and animate those forms by rapidly modifying coordinates and redrawing the objects. You can use OpenGL for a variety of interactive programs, including engineering, simulation, modeling, and (of course) virtual-reality applications.

Because of the emphasis on interaction, OpenGL primarily contains routines for quickly drawing lighted and textured polygons. The most fundamental of the OpenGL library routines are those that allow the programmer to tell the computer where each vertex of a polygon is located (see Figure 21-3).

Most objects in the real world contain complex shapes and curves, of course, but it is faster to limit the representation of surfaces to flat facets or polygons, which OpenGL can handle more quickly and consistently than it can curved shapes. So what's a poor programmer to do? You can modify curved objects to create approximately corresponding polygonal objects, as I've shown in Figure 21-4. The object on the left is composed of complex curves. The object on the right is the simplified, polygonal version of the curved shape. This type of simplification is called *polygonization, faceting,* or *tessellation.*

Another set of frequently used library routines specify the surface properties of the polygons. OpenGL lets you select a color or colors for each of the polygons. You also use OpenGL calls to specify coefficients of reflection and the inclination of the polygons with respect to light sources. To achieve realistic lighting effects, you tell OpenGL the location and intensity of lights in the 3D environment and have its routines calculate the color of each polygon as OpenGL draws the polygon on the screen. (This

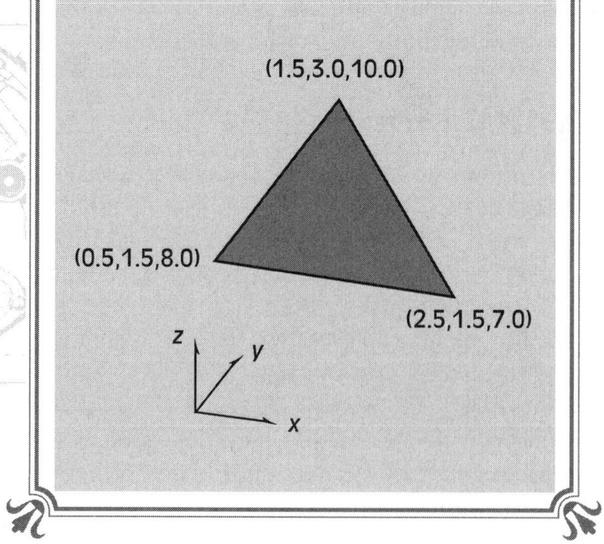

FIGURE 21-3

A triangular polygon defined by its three vertices

FIGURE 21-4

Tessellating curves to simplify them

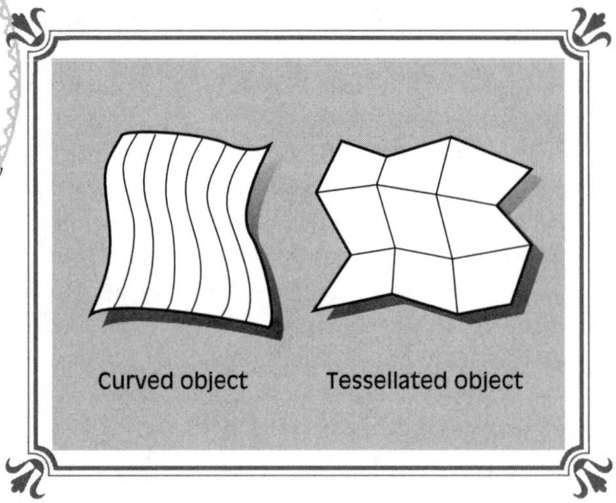

lighting model is encapsulated in the lighting routines in the library.) You can specify both highlight and diffuse light characteristics in the model of the object to produce an even more realistic rendering.

The programmer with a keen mind (or impaired judgment) might be interested in OpenGL's advanced palette of effects like texture mapping, blending, anti-aliasing, fog, and transparency. I'll discuss texture mapping in this chapter, but the remaining topics are beyond the scope of this book. If you experiment with these features on your own, it's important to remember that "interactivity" and "advanced effects" are mutually exclusive terms in the absence of hardware acceleration. It's also essential that you be intimately familiar with the basic concepts of OpenGL before you embark on an exploration of these topics.

The Utility Library

OpenGL provides a way to draw just about any scene. That doesn't mean, however, that it is convenient to use OpenGL for rendering in all cases. Like assembly language, OpenGL is powerful but sometimes difficult to use. Fortunately, the utility library of OpenGL includes routines for higher-level graphics operations that usually comprise several of the low-level OpenGL routines.

Say you want to render a sphere in OpenGL. The points that make up a sphere belong to the set that satisfies the equation $(x - a)^2 + (y - b)^2 + (z - c)^2 - d^2 = 0$, where d is the radius and the point (a,b,c) is the center of the sphere. But OpenGL has no way of taking that equation and turning it into a picture. First, you need to tessellate the sphere (create a polygonal approximation of the sphere) based on its mathematical representation. Doing so will produce a good result, but it's not a trivial task. This is where the OpenGL utility library comes to the rescue.

The utility library contains routines that can create spheres, cylinders, and disks, along with more complex objects like NURBS (non-uniform rational b-spline) curves and surfaces. These utility routines use OpenGL for drawing the surfaces on the screen, but they also include routines for creating and tessellating each object—jobs few programmers would want to do unaided.

In this chapter, I'll discuss the utility library only briefly; the routines in the library are easy to use once you have mastered the basics of OpenGL graphics programming.

OpenGL Basics

OpenGL begins where the window manager leaves off. After you open the window, you must create a GL rendering context into which OpenGL output can be sent. Unlike the DC, this rendering context can be created just once at the beginning of the program. It is deleted when the WM_DESTROY message is received. The rendering context uses information in the DC for setting up the viewport for the 3D rendering. If you resize the window, the rendering context must be notified so that OpenGL can reset rendering parameters pertaining to the scene.

Viewpoint

Once the rendering context is available for drawing, OpenGL needs a specification of the viewpoint. How far away should OpenGL draw objects? What is the aspect ratio of the window? The viewpoint specification indicates to OpenGL whether the scene will appear as though seen through a wide-angle lens, with significant distortion close to the edges of the window, or as though seen through a telephoto lens, with minimal difference in the apparent heights of near and far objects.

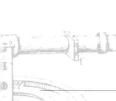

Geometry

After setting up the viewpoint, you can draw the geometric forms. Experienced OpenGL hackers liberally use *transformation matrices* (model-view, projection, and viewport matrices) to sprinkle forms around the environment. For instance, if you wanted to draw 100 pyramids on a 10x10 grid, you could define 100 pyramids and their associated polygons and move all the pyramids to their respective locations, or you could define a single pyramid and then keep telling OpenGL to draw the same pyramid over and over again, but in a different place each time. Later in the chapter, I'll discuss the pros and cons of transformations.

Polygons

As I mentioned earlier, every object you use OpenGL to draw must be composed of polygons. *Polygons* are planar (all the points lie on the same plane) and each can be

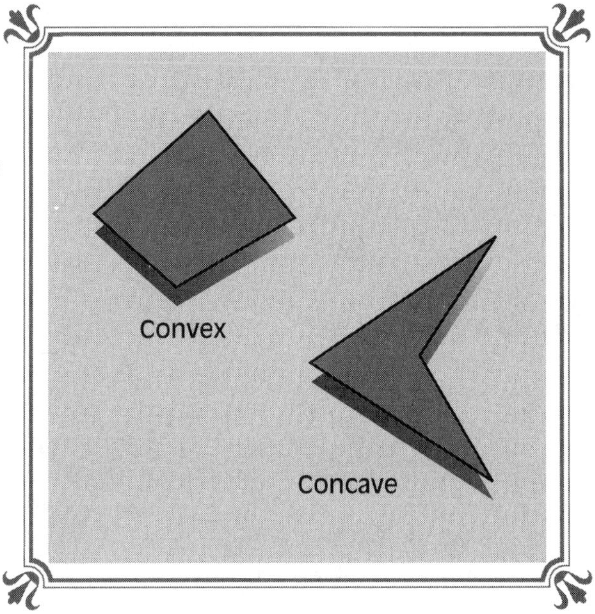

FIGURE 21-5

Convex and concave polygons

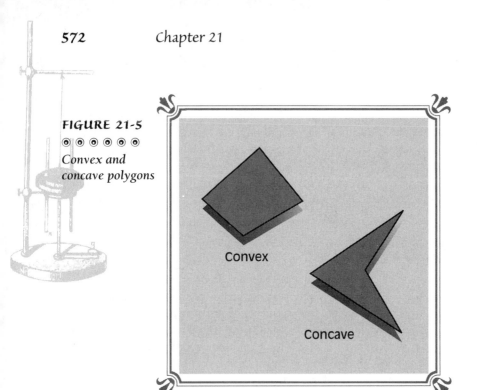

described by a series of points or vertices. Connecting the vertices in order will create the edges of the polygon. OpenGL likes only convex polygons. Concave polygons, like the one pictured on the right in Figure 21-5, give unpredictable results.

OpenGL can fill a polygon automatically. The fill color is determined by the color of the polygon and the current lighting conditions.

Normals

Human eyes are exceptional at distinguishing subtle differences between colors. Two side-by-side polygons drawn in slightly differing colors seem markedly distinct to us. Unfortunately, this ability means that the color differences that occur within *polyhedral objects* (objects made of polygons only) will be obvious, even when you don't want them to be. The sphere on the left in Figure 21-6 demonstrates this effect. (The code I used to create Figure 21-6 is included on the disk that comes with this book.) It has a faceted appearance—the face of each polygon is flat and rotated slightly from the orientation of the other faces. This is a poor way to represent a gently sloping surface.

One way to eliminate this faceted effect is to calculate the color of each polygon at the vertices of the polygon, instead of at the center of each face. Given the true *normal vector* (outward direction) of the surface at each vertex, OpenGL can calculate the color for that vertex and blend the color between vertices when it draws the polygon. Polygons that share edges also share vertices, so the edges on both polygons will be the same color and the eye will not discern the edge breaks.

Lighting

Our eyes are also proficient at integrating light. When we look at an object, our eyes combine information about:

- the color of the object
- the color of the light shining on the object
- the direction of the light shining on the surface
- the light's intensity
- the reflective and transmissive characteristics of the material

All this information is boiled down to a single color and intensity that is sent to the brain for more processing.

The analysis performed by our eyes for each individual color in a scene is well beyond the capabilities of even the fastest computers. In order to accomplish its goal, though, OpenGL must simulate that process effectively enough to create convincing 3D scenes.

The minimal OpenGL implementation allows you to use up to eight lights (of any color) in each rendered scene. You can place a light close to the objects, say by putting a lighted table lamp in the scene, or position the light at an infinite distance, creating an effect similar to sunlight. Unfortunately, calculating the effect of shadows cast by the lights is still prohibitively expensive and therefore unsupported by OpenGL. OpenGL doesn't mind if you want to draw shadows, but it won't lift a finger to help out.

FIGURE 21-6

Face normals yield a faceted surface, while vertex normals produce a smooth surface

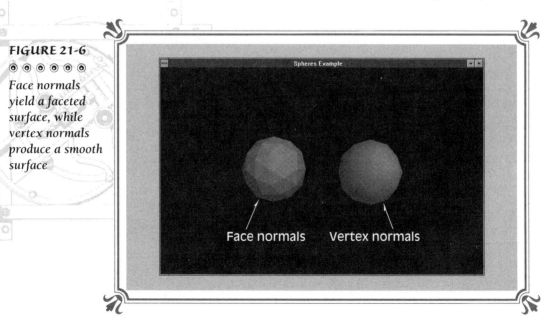

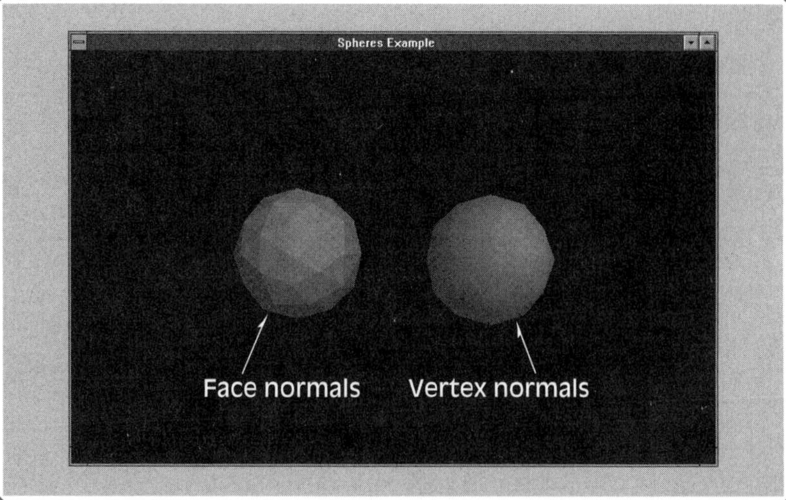

Materials

The final appearance of each set of polygons in a scene depends not just on the lighting and positioning, but also on the material properties of the polygons. When light hits a surface in the real world, a portion of that light is reflected, a portion is transmitted through the surface, and a portion is absorbed. A detailed simulation of real-world lighting effects would take a very long time, slowing down screen repaints and destroying any possibility of interactivity, but OpenGL does use simplified versions of real-world lighting effects in its calculations.

OpenGL simulates the effect of lights on surfaces by taking into account *diffuse reflection, specular reflection,* and transparency. Diffuse reflection is light that is reflected in many different directions due to the roughness of a surface—think of how light reflects off a crumpled piece of white paper. Specular reflection is light reflected directly from a light source to the eye of the viewer. The bright spots, or highlights, you see when you look at a highly polished surface like that of a billiard ball are due to specular reflection. Specular reflection is greatly reduced on rough, nonpolished surfaces.

Textures

Rendering 3D scenes takes time. To a certain extent, how much time the process takes is determined by the number of pixels and the number of polygons required for a scene. There is a trade-off between speed and scene detail. A complex scene will look better, but will take significantly longer to redraw than will a relatively simple scene.

Imagine drawing a tree using OpenGL's usual methods, for example. Each leaf would have to be a separate polygon. Given that, you can understand why the number of polygons used to render even a simple tree would bring the most souped-up graphics accelerator hardware to its knees.

An alternative approach to drawing complex objects involves a technique called *texture mapping.* Texture maps are images or bitmaps that are "painted" on polygons during rendering. Consider again our tree: If the tree is some distance from the viewer, instead of drawing individual leaves, you could draw a single tree-shaped polygon and paint the image of a tree on top of it. Texture mapping adds significantly to the realism of the scene, but is also an expensive operation. Watch the Windows NT Pipes screen saver perform with and without texture mapping to get a feel for the effect of texture mapping on speed.

Functions and Function Names

Many routines in OpenGL perform the same functions but differ in the type of data they accept as parameters. For instance, `glTranslatef()` and `glTranslatefv()` modify the model-view matrix in the same way. The *f* suffix on the name of the first routine indicates that the routine accepts floating-point values. The routine whose name ends in *fv* accepts a vector (or array) of floating-point values. Related OpenGL routines that accept different data types each have a suffix indicating the type that routine expects. Except in listings, I'll indicate these groups of routines in this chapter by using a generic group name, instead of using the specific data-type-dependent name. (For instance, I'll refer to both `glTranslatef()` and `glTranslatefv()` as `glTranslate*()`.)

OpenGL Is Not...

I've told you a lot about what OpenGL does and is, but not much about its limitations. The creators of OpenGL decided what the graphics library would be good at—quickly rendering geometric forms to give the illusion of three dimensions. In order to achieve the speeds necessary for interactive graphics, however, the developers of OpenGL purposely left out several expensive operations.

OpenGL Is Not a Ray Tracer

You've probably seen computer-generated images that look quite exquisite, perhaps even indistinguishable from a photograph. The scenes in the game MYST come to mind as an example of detailed and beautiful renderings. Although they are obviously not photographs of a real location, they have many subtle lighting effects that make them appear realistic.

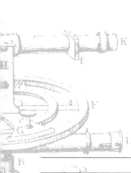

The curvature of glass or waves can create variations in the intensity of sunlight passing through glass or water. The dancing patterns of light shimmering on the bottom of a shallow pool require millions and millions of complex calculations to duplicate. A technique called *ray tracing* scans a scene over and over again looking for light reflecting between surfaces and refracting through transparent objects. The color of each pixel is considered and determined individually. The calculations for certain images take hours, or even days, to complete. OpenGL, for obvious reasons, makes no effort to provide the complex calculations required for ray tracing.

OpenGL Is Not a Window Manager

OpenGL's predecessor, GL, included commands for opening and managing windows, menus, and other GUI-related objects. The developers of OpenGL wanted to create a programming standard and API for 3D graphics, though, and so dropped some of GL's "extra" routines.

A 3D graphics program will require OpenGL calls to manage image generation and screen refreshing, as well as calls to open and move windows. Since they intended OpenGL to be a cross-platform standard, the OpenGL team was careful to avoid any routines that would be specific to a single window manager. The implication for the programmer is that porting a program from one platform to another will require at least a translation of window-management code, but no graphics code changes.

The Terminology of 3D Graphics

Some of the terminology of 3D graphics may be new to you. Articles and books written about 3D are often peppered with phrases like "z-buffer," "Gouraud shading," and other arcane terms. Fortunately, these usually refer to fairly simple concepts. In this section, I'll give you a working understanding of the language you'll encounter as you explore the world of 3D graphics.

Perspectives and Viewpoints

As I pointed out earlier in this chapter, all drawings on a computer screen are limited to two dimensions. In order to display a seemingly 3D image on the monitor, you must "paint" or "project" the image onto the screen as if the screen were a window into the 3D world (see Figure 21-7). There are several ways of projecting an image, but the two most popular are called *orthographic projection* and *perspective projection.*

Figure 21-8 compares orthographic and perspective projections. These views differ in how they represent parallel lines on the screen. In an orthographic view, an object's distance from the screen does not affect its drawn size. For instance, two equivalent blocks, one close to the viewer and one far away, will appear the same size

FIGURE 21-7

Painting a 3D image onto the 2D screen

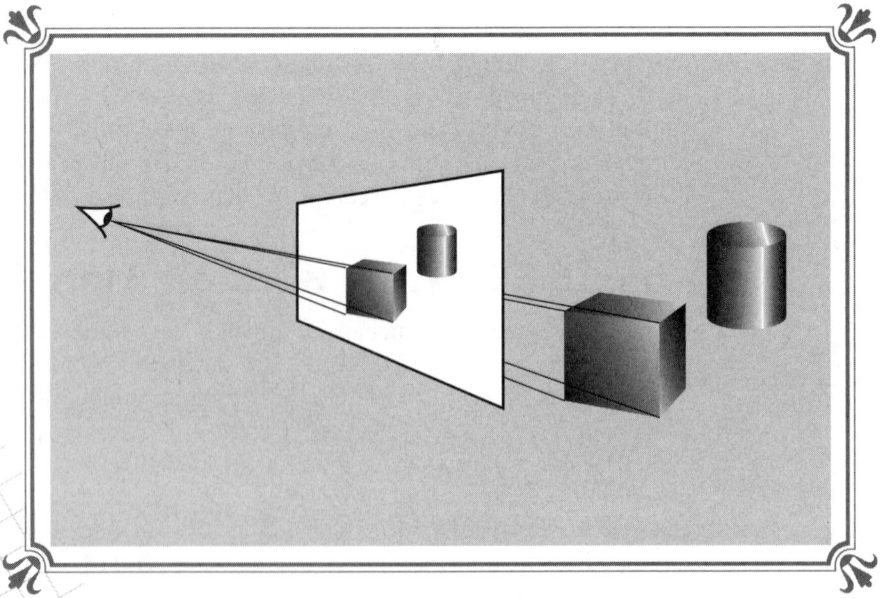

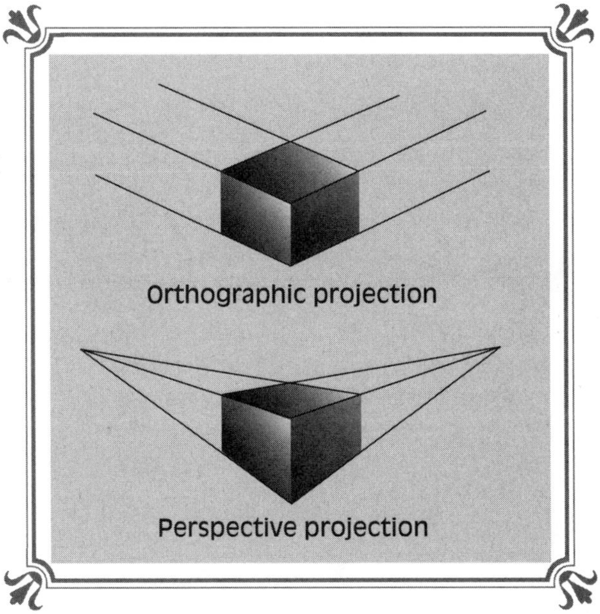

FIGURE 21-8

Comparing orthographic and perspective projections

FIGURE 21-9

As objects recede into the distance, they appear to grow smaller

on the screen. Here's another way to think of it: Imagine that the object in the scene is being pushed through the screen of the monitor. The edges of the object leave corresponding lines. Together, these lines constitute the silhouette of the object.

In perspective projections, objects that are farther away appear smaller, just like they do in real life. If you were to stand near a line of telephone poles, you would see this effect. Although all the poles are the same height, the far ones appear much shorter than do the ones close at hand, as you can see in Figure 21-9.

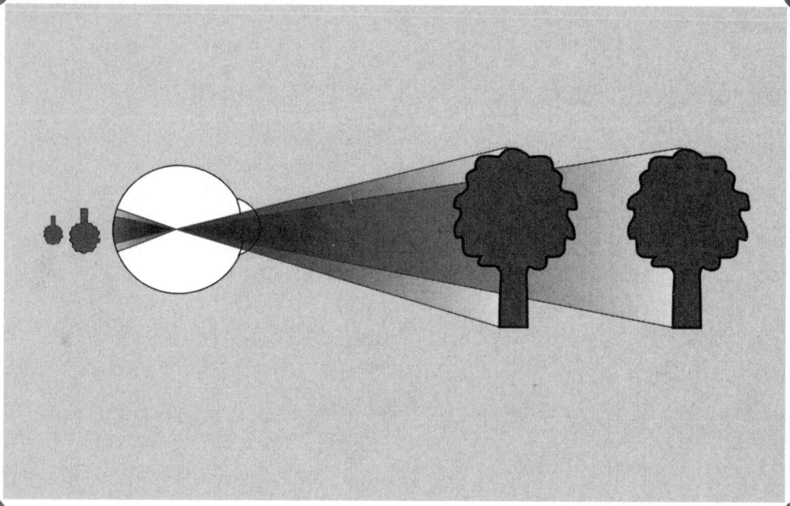

FIGURE 21-10

Objects at a greater distance from the eye appear smaller on the retina

Perspective projections mimic the eye's distance-perception mechanism. You can see in Figure 21-10 how this mechanism works. Even though the trees in the figure are the same size, the greater distance of the far tree causes its image on the retina to be smaller than the image of the closer tree.

Transformations

Transforming refers to moving, scaling, or rotating an object—changing its position, size, or shape. A transformation can be as simple as moving an object 5 inches in one direction, or as complex as making the object jump and spin about its center. Transformations create the magic of animation. I'll discuss transformations in detail in the section "Making Things Move."

Double-Buffering

To create the illusion of motion in an animated sequence, a program must quickly repaint the screen when either the viewpoint or an object in the scene moves. Unfortunately, it takes some time to draw each scene—the program can't create the image instantaneously. *Double-buffering* allows you to hide this limitation from the user.

To understand double-buffering, you need to know how the drawing process works. When it draws a scene, OpenGL follows steps a little like those you would take if you were drawing one frame of an animated sequence. The program uses memory as its scratch pad. This scratch pad is called a *buffer*. It clears the buffer, which is displayed on the screen, by filling the display memory with zeros. It then draws each element of the scene a bit at a time.

All this creates some obvious problems for the animator. When the screen fills with color, it detracts from the movement of objects in the animated sequence. Immediately after it colors the last pixels, OpenGL must erase the image to begin the process again, which means that the screen is blank much of the time.

With double-buffering, the program uses two drawing areas, or buffers. We look at one, the front buffer, while the program draws on the other, the back buffer. When the program has filled the back buffer with a new image, it simply switches the back and front buffers (or quickly copies the new scene to the front buffer, in the case of Windows NT). Then, while we are focusing on the updated image displayed in the front buffer, the program creates an even newer scene in the back buffer. This process is detailed in Figure 21-11.

The computer can paint into the back buffer, the front buffer, or both simultaneously. However, we can see only those changes being made to the image displayed in the front buffer.

Using an extra buffer for drawing improves the quality of the animation substantially. If the program completes the scenes in the back buffer quickly enough to allow it to update the front buffer at a rate of 15 to 24 frames a second or faster, the animation will appear smooth and will not flicker.

FIGURE 21-11

Using a back buffer to improve the flow of an animated sequence

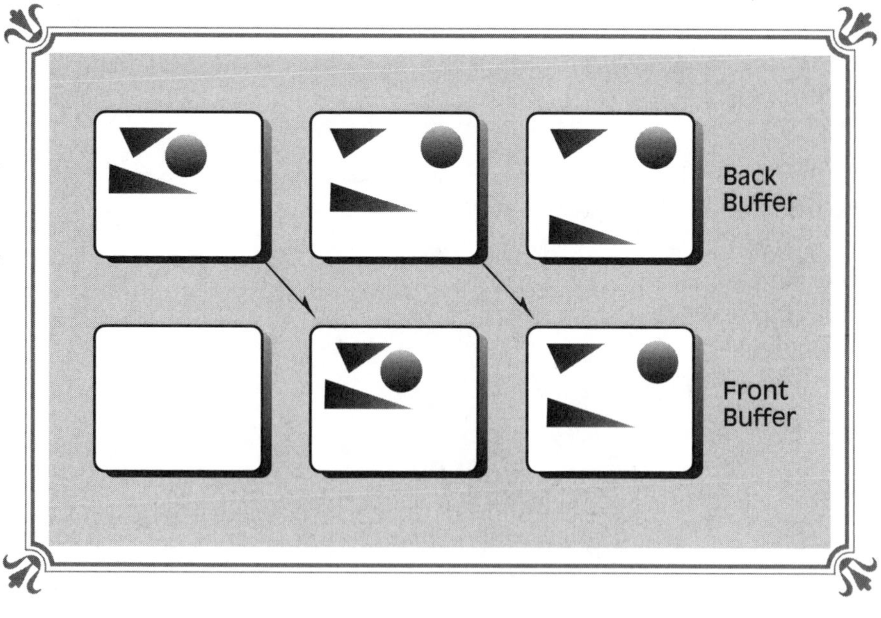

The Depth Buffer

Often, a painter will create the background of a work first and then add the foreground objects, painting over the portion of the background that will be hidden in the final composition. This is one method for placing close objects in front of far objects. In computer graphics, this back-to-front organization is called *painter's order.* Drawing in this way requires some additional work from the programmer.

The point of view in a 3D scene changes frequently. In order to use painter's order, you must continually maintain a list of objects ordered by distance from the viewer. Unfortunately, there are some scenes that are impossible to sort in this way. Consider the three triangles shown in Figure 21-12. Each triangle is both in front of and behind its neighbors, making it impossible to determine an order that would result in a final picture that's correct.

Even if all the objects in a scene can be put in order, you can't escape the fact that sorting is a very CPU-intensive operation. Usually, it must be done as a precalculated step, and not during the short time available to the program between rendering each frame.

A *depth buffer* addresses both of the problems of using painter's order. It's the most convenient way of keeping track of which objects cover other objects, because it allows the computer to record and store the depth of pixels as it draws a scene. It considers the distance of each pixel from the screen instead of sorting polygons and objects.

Illumination

In this context, the term *illumination* refers to the computations done by the computer to calculate the color and brightness of each pixel it draws on the screen. As I discussed earlier in this chapter, each polygon has surface characteristics and each light

FIGURE 21-12

These three triangles have no obvious distance order

illuminating the polygons has illumination characteristics. The program includes all these surface and light characteristics in the calculations for determining the color of the polygon. I'll cover the specific terms of the equations and the surface and lighting characteristics in some detail in the "Lighting and Materials" section.

Shading and Color

You can draw a polygon with a single color or with smooth gradations of color. Single-color polygons are called *flat-shaded polygons*. Flat shading is simple to execute, because the program need only replicate the same pixel values throughout the entire region of the screen occupied by the polygon. Unfortunately, objects that are flat-shaded appear faceted, like the surface of a cut gem. Faceted appearances are acceptable in some circumstances, but if you want a smooth surface, like that of a bowling ball, you will be disappointed with the results.

Gouraud shading creates a smooth color transition at the vertices of polygons. The program calculates the correct color for each vertex, and bases the final color of each pixel in the polygon on its distance from and the color of each vertex. Interpolating vertex colors takes some computing power and is usually aided by hardware acceleration.

Dithering is a technique where the computer combines individual colors to represent a color not available in the color palette. OpenGL dithers an image when it must display that image using a limited palette of colors. (OpenGL itself uses 8 bits of color resolution for the red, green, and blue parts of each pixel, making a total of 24 bits for all lighting and color calculations. It could easily display a full-color image with this much data, but many PC graphics adapters limit colors to a total of 256, because there are only 8 bits of data storage available for each pixel.) For example, if red (0xFF R, 0x0 G, 0x0 B) and white (0xFF R, 0xFF G, 0xFF B) are both available in the palette, OpenGL can create pink (0xFF R, 0x7F G, 0x7F B) by using alternating red and white pixels in equal amounts. To see an example of dithering, open the custom color selector in the Windows Color control panel while your PC is using an 8-bit (256-color) display mode.

Getting Our Feet Wet

Now that you have a basic understanding of some of the concepts of 3D graphics, let's dive in and get to work.

As you learned earlier in this chapter, there are certain routines required for setting up a 3D graphics window and drawing objects on the screen:

- First and foremost, you must initialize the graphics. This means creating a rendering context for OpenGL.

- You might need to create a special palette if you have 8 bits or fewer of color in your display adapter.
- Once you open and initialize the window, you must set up the viewpoint for the scene.
- Finally, you need to place and draw the objects in the scene.

Initializing the Graphics

To initialize the graphics, it's necessary to create a rendering context. This forms the link between OpenGL and the window. All OpenGL commands must pass through a rendering context, which contains all information pertinent to OpenGL.

In the main message loop of the **WndProc** function, after a DC is retrieved, the palette must be initialized. You don't need a palette for 24-bit graphics cards; the **managePalette** function, which I've listed here, does not allocate a palette for such cards. However, many machines use 8-bit graphics. For them, you must allocate a 256-color palette.

After creating the palette, you create a rendering context with the **wglCreateContext()** routine. The resulting rendering context will have the same pixel format as the DC. Notice that this routine starts with *wgl* instead of simply *gl*. All OpenGL commands start with the letters *gl*. Commands starting with *wgl* are those that are specific to the Windows environment.

```
// Window has just been created.
case WM_CREATE:

    // Get device context for drawing.
    devContextHdl = GetDC(winHdl);

    // managePalette returns NULL if 24-bit color is available.
    palHdl = managePalette(devContextHdl);

    // Create the rendering context.
    renderContextHdl = wglCreateContext(devContextHdl);
    wglMakeCurrent(devContextHdl, renderContextHdl);

    // Set up depth buffering, culling, perspective
    // projection, and lighting.
    InitOpenGLState();

    // It is essential to release the DC after
    // using it, because there are only five available for all
    // running applications.
    ReleaseDC(winHdl, devContextHdl);

    // Finished. Don't run DefWindowProc().
    return(0);
```

There is a significant difference between a rendering context and a device context. DCs are limited resources in Windows and you must release them (using commands like **ReleaseDC()** or **EndPaint()**) before returning control to Windows. A rendering context has no such restriction and can be retained in a static or global variable until the end of the program.

The command **wglMakeCurrent()** associates a rendering context with a DC and indicates that subsequent OpenGL calls should be displayed on that rendering context. You can release current rendering contexts with a call to

```
wglMakeCurrent(devContextHdl, NULL);
```

You can delete a rendering context by using the **wglDeleteContext** command:

```
// Delete the rendering context.
wglDeleteContext(renderContextHdl);
```

This command removes the rendering context from current status before deleting it.

I discussed the rather complex topic of palette management in Chapter 8, but I'll remind you here that if the graphics card you are using has fewer than 24 bits available, you must construct a palette that allows OpenGL to approximate 24-bit graphics. The **managePalette** routine listed here looks at the DC to determine the number and location of bit planes for each of the red, green, and blue colors:

```
static unsigned char colorConv[3][8] = {
    {0,255,0,0,0,0,0,0},
    {0,85,170,255,0,0,0,0},
    {0,36,73,109,146,182,219,255}
};


HPALETTE managePalette(HDC hdc)
{
    static PIXELFORMATDESCRIPTOR pfd = {
        sizeof(PIXELFORMATDESCRIPTOR),
        1,
        PFD_DRAW_TO_WINDOW | PFD_SUPPORT_OPENGL | PFD_DOUBLEBUFFER,
        PFD_TYPE_RGBA,
        24,
        0,0,0,0,0,0,
        0,0,
        0,0,0,0,0,
        32,
        0,
        0,
        PFD_MAIN_PLANE,
        0,
        0,0,0
    };

    LOGPALETTE *palPtr;
```

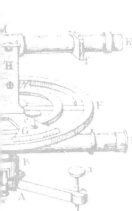

continued on next page

continued from previous page

```
HPALETTE palHdl;

int pixelFormat;
int numCols;
int i;
char rMask, gMask, bMask;
int rBits, gBits, bBits;

pixelFormat = ChoosePixelFormat(hdc, &pfd);
SetPixelFormat(hdc, pixelFormat, &pfd);

if (DescribePixelFormat(hdc, pixelFormat,
       sizeof(PIXELFORMATDESCRIPTOR), &pfd) == 0)
  return(NULL);

if ((pfd.dwFlags & PFD_NEED_PALETTE) == 0)
    return(NULL);

// Generate bit masks for each color.
rMask = (1 << pfd.cRedBits) - 1;
gMask = (1 << pfd.cGreenBits) - 1;
bMask = (1 << pfd.cBlueBits) - 1;

// Use nBits to index into colorConv matrix.
rBits = pfd.cRedBits - 1;
gBits = pfd.cGreenBits - 1;
bBits = pfd.cBlueBits - 1;

numCols = 1 << pfd.cColorBits;
palPtr = (PLOGPALETTE)
    LocalAlloc(LMEM_FIXED,
               sizeof(LOGPALETTE) +
               numCols*sizeof(PALETTEENTRY));

// Windows version number (0x300 for Win 3 or later)
palPtr->palVersion = 0x300;
palPtr->palNumEntries = numCols;
for (i=0; i < numCols; i++) {
    palPtr->palPalEntry[i].peFlags = 0;

    palPtr->palPalEntry[i].peRed =
      colorConv[rBits][(i>>pfd.cRedShift) & rMask];

    palPtr->palPalEntry[i].peGreen =
      colorConv[gBits][(i>>pfd.cGreenShift) & gMask];

    palPtr->palPalEntry[i].peBlue =
      colorConv[bBits][(i>>pfd.cBlueShift) & bMask];
}

palHdl = CreatePalette(palPtr);
LocalFree(palPtr);
```

```
    SelectPalette(hdc, palHdl, FALSE);

    RealizePalette(hdc);

    return(palHdl);
}
```

You must use this routine for 256-color modes. True-color modes (like 24-bit-color modes) do not use a palette.

First, **managePalette** requests the pixel format. If no palette is needed, the routine finishes and returns a NULL pointer. If a palette is necessary, the routine fills the palette with values that map the red, green, and blue bits in the palette index to reasonable values. Once the palette is filled with color values, the routine uses **CreatePalette()** to create a logical color palette. This color palette is put into the DC with **SelectPalette()**. Next, the routine **RealizePalette()** maps the logical palette entries into the system palette.

After the palette is initialized, **InitOpenGL()** sets up the OpenGL state. In this example, we turn on back-face polygon culling (I'll cover this subject later in the chapter) using the default values and we enable the depth buffer. We also turn on a single light **(LIGHT0)**, enable lighting calculations, and set up the properties for **LIGHT0**.

```
// Set up some lighting properties.
// LIGHT0 will be a directional light source.
GLfloat position[] = {-1.0f,2.0f,2.0f,0.0f};
// Define RGBA intensities for ambient, diffuse, and specular light.
GLfloat ambient[] = {0.2f,0.2f,0.2f};
GLfloat diffuse[] = {1.0f,1.0f,1.0f,1.0f};
GLfloat specular[] = {0.8f,0.8f,0.8f,1.0f};

// Set up the material parameters for the pyramid.
GLfloat ambient_mat[] = {0.5f,0.5f,0.5f,1.0f};
GLfloat diffuse_mat[] = {0.8f,0.6f,0.4f,1.0f};
GLfloat specular_mat[] = {0.2f,0.5f,0.2f,1.0f};
GLfloat shininess = 31.0f;

void InitOpenGLState(void)
{
    // Enable back-face culling using defaults.
    glEnable(GL_CULL_FACE);
    // glFrontFace(GL_CCW);
    // glCullFace(GL_BACK);
    // (These are default values, so the calls are
    //  commented out.)

    // Enable depth testing (z-buffer) using defaults.
    glEnable(GL_DEPTH_TEST);
    // glDepthFunc(GL_LESS)--Passes if the incoming z value
```

continued on next page

continued from previous page

```
    // is less than the current z value.
    // glDepthRange(0.0,1.0)--near clip plane == 0.0

    // Turn on lighting calculations.
    glEnable(GL_LIGHTING);

    // Turn on at least one light.
    glEnable(GL_LIGHT0);

// Install values in LIGHT0.
    glLightfv(GL_LIGHT0, GL_POSITION, position);
    glLightfv(GL_LIGHT0, GL_AMBIENT, ambient);
    glLightfv(GL_LIGHT0, GL_DIFFUSE, diffuse);
    glLightfv(GL_LIGHT0, GL_SPECULAR, specular);

    // Since we are using only one light and material for this
    // program, we will set up the light and material just once here.

    glMaterialfv(GL_FRONT, GL_AMBIENT, ambient_mat);
    glMaterialfv(GL_FRONT, GL_DIFFUSE, diffuse_mat);
    glMaterialfv(GL_FRONT, GL_SPECULAR, specular_mat);
    glMaterialf(GL_FRONT, GL_SHININESS, shininess);

    /*
       If we want to clear the screen with a color other than
       black, we could call this routine with values for R, G, B, and A
       different than 0.0.

       glClearColor(0.0f,0.0f,0.0f,0.0f);

       Default cleared color (0.0,0.0,0.0) is black.
       Default transparency (0.0) is opaque.

       If we want to clear the z-buffer or depth buffer
       with a value other than 1.0, we should call

       glClearDepth(1.0);

       Notice that depth, colors, and transparency values
       are limited to the interval [0.0,1.0].
      */

    return;
}
```

Setting Up the Viewpoint

There are three matrices that control the final view of the objects drawn on the screen: the model-view matrix, the projection matrix, and the viewport matrix. I'll describe each of the matrices in detail in the section "Making Things Move."

The code listed here is usually in the WM_SIZE message handler of a Windows program. It sets up the projection and viewport matrices so that the scene will fill the window with a perspective view.

```
#define FOV_Y   35.0  // Field of view in the y direction

void resetViewport(GLsizei width, GLsizei height)
{
    glMatrixMode(GL_PROJECTION);    // Prepare to write the projection matrix.
    glLoadIdentity();               // Put a 4x4 identity matrix to start.

    // Dire consequences await those who don't initialize the
    // matrix. The matrix from gluPerspective() is multiplied by the
    // current matrix.  If the current matrix is not the identity matrix,
    // who knows what lurks there?

    gluPerspective(FOV_Y, (GLdouble) width / (GLdouble) height, 0.1,
100.0);

    // 0.1 and 100.0 are the near and far clipping planes
    // respectively.  Objects more than 100.0 units away from
    // the camera are not drawn.

    // Set up the viewport.
    glViewport(0,0,width,height);

    return;
}
```

Before drawing anything, it is necessary to tell OpenGL the direction from which you will be looking at the objects. This information is stored in the model-view matrix and is initialized with the following code:

```
    glMatrixMode(GL_MODELVIEW);
    glLoadIdentity();
    gluLookAt(-3,3,6,0,0,0,0,1,0);
```

The first three values in the call to **gluLookAt()**, (-3,3,6), indicate the location of the camera in the scene. The second set of coordinates, (0,0,0), tell OpenGL that the camera should be pointing at the origin of the coordinate system. Finally, the last three values, (0,1,0), indicate that the *y*-axis should be pointing up when the scene is drawn on the monitor.

Drawing a Pyramid

The lighting setup is complete and the transformation matrices are initialized, so the only thing left to do for this simple example is to put the geometric forms into the scene. You define the color of the object before you draw it, using the **glMaterial*()**

routines, and then tell the computer where the vertices of the objects' polygons are so that OpenGL can draw the object on the screen.

```
// Points (vertices) that define a four-sided pyramid
static GLfloat vertex_list[][3] = {
    {1.0f,0.0f,0.0f},
    {0.0f,0.0f,-1.0f},
    {-1.0f,0.0f,0.0f},
    {0.0f,0.0f,1.0f},
    {0.0f,1.0f,0.0f}
};

// Normals for the five surfaces on the pyramid.
// The bottom square surface is made of two triangles.
// Normals must be of unit length.
static GLfloat normal_list[][3] = {
    {.57735f,.57735f,-.57735f},
    {-.57735f,.57735f,-.57735f},
    {-.57735f,.57735f,.57735f},
    {.57735f,.57735f,.57735f},
    {0.0f,-1.0f,0.0f}
};


void draw(void)
{
    glMatrixMode(GL_MODELVIEW);
    glLoadIdentity();
    gluLookAt(-3,3,6,0,0,0,0,1,0);


    // Clear the color and depth buffers.
    glClear(GL_COLOR_BUFFER_BIT | GL_DEPTH_BUFFER_BIT);

    // Draw the pyramid.
    glBegin(GL_TRIANGLES);

        // Draw the four sides.
        glNormal3fv(normal_list[0]);
        glVertex3fv(vertex_list[0]);
        glVertex3fv(vertex_list[1]);
        glVertex3fv(vertex_list[4]);

        glNormal3fv(normal_list[1]);
        glVertex3fv(vertex_list[1]);
        glVertex3fv(vertex_list[2]);
        glVertex3fv(vertex_list[4]);

        glNormal3fv(normal_list[2]);
        glVertex3fv(vertex_list[2]);
        glVertex3fv(vertex_list[3]);
```

```
        glVertex3fv(vertex_list[4]);

        glNormal3fv(normal_list[3]);
        glVertex3fv(vertex_list[3]);
        glVertex3fv(vertex_list[0]);
        glVertex3fv(vertex_list[4]);

        // Draw the bottom triangles.
        glNormal3fv(normal_list[4]);
        glVertex3fv(vertex_list[0]);
        glVertex3fv(vertex_list[3]);
        glVertex3fv(vertex_list[1]);

        glVertex3fv(vertex_list[2]);
        glVertex3fv(vertex_list[1]);
        glVertex3fv(vertex_list[3]);

    glEnd();

}
```

The **glVertex*()** routines tell OpenGL the vertices of each polygon. Since the code started with a call to **glBegin(GL_TRIANGLES)**, every group of three vertices designates a polygon. The normal vector for each polygon that is used by the lighting calculations is specified by a call to **glNormal*()**. Since the normal vector is the same for both bottom triangles, **glNormal*()** was only called once.

The last step is to tell OpenGL that you are done drawing the image and you would like to display it. When using double-buffering, the program must call **SwapBuffers()** before it shows anything on the screen. The code for the WM_PAINT message handler shows how **SwapBuffers()** is used. Take note that Windows NT doesn't really swap buffers—it quickly copies the back buffer to the front buffer. A second call to **SwapBuffers()** immediately after the first has an undefined effect. After a call to **SwapBuffers()**, you must assume that the back buffer is invalid.

```
    case WM_PAINT:

        // Get devContext and PAINTSTRUCT.
        devContextHdl = BeginPaint(winHdl, &ps);

        // Draw the scene into the back buffer.
        draw();

        // Show the newly drawn scene.
        SwapBuffers(devContextHdl);

        // Release the DC.
        EndPaint(winHdl, &ps);
        return(0);
```

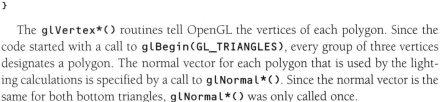

When you put all this code together, you end up with a lighted pyramid like the one shown in Figure 21-13. The complete source code for the tetrahedron program is included on the disk that comes with this book.

Making Things Move

The real appeal of 3D graphics is watching objects move—watching them bounce, spin, and hop around on the screen. The illusion of the third dimension is at its most convincing when objects circle each other or seem to fly out of the monitor. But how do you move objects in the world you have created?

As you already know, each object in a scene is made up of polygons, defined as a series of connected points. Each of these points has a location determined by three values: *x*, *y*, and *z*. You give motion to an object by transforming—in other words, by adjusting the positions of—its points. In 2D animation, you can make the polygon appear to slide across the screen by successively incrementing the positions of the *x* and *y* points. In 3D animation, where you can work with a *z* coordinate, motion toward and away from the screen is also possible. This, coupled with techniques that make objects appear smaller as they retreat and larger as they approach the screen, creates a very powerful effect.

When you use OpenGL, your game can keep track of where things should be drawn on the screen in relation to each other by using several transformation matrices. By setting values in each matrix, you tell OpenGL the location of the viewpoint, the position of each object in the scene, and how each object should move. Understanding how to use those matrices to get the effects you want is a complex topic. Once you comprehend a few basics, though, you should be on your way.

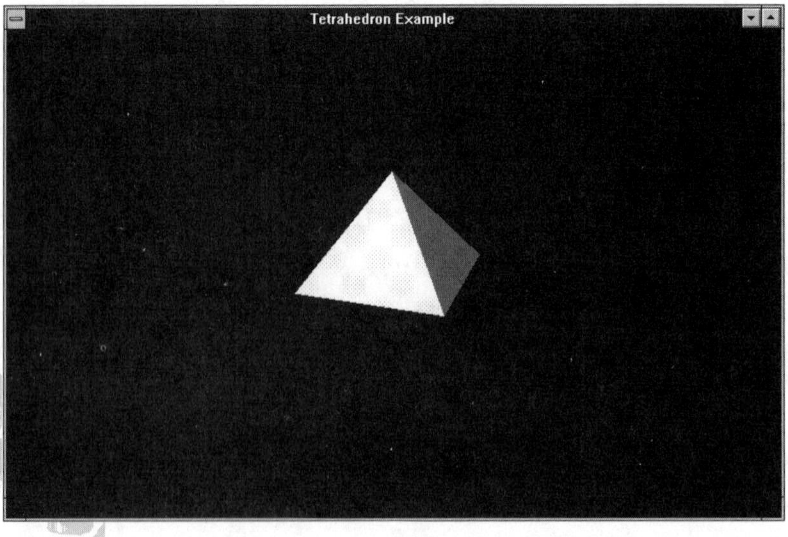

FIGURE 21-13

A tetrahedron illuminated with a single light, the output of our program

Your Directing Debut

Creating a 3D scene is a bit like making a movie. You, the programmer, are the director. The cast is made up of 3D objects—lists of colored, lighted polygons. You control the camera and the placement of each cast member. You might place a cube here, a sphere there. You might start with a close-up shot of the cube, and then zoom out to show the whole scene.

Placing objects in a scene, moving the camera or viewpoint, and zooming in and out are all transformations. OpenGL defines several types of transformations for building a 3D environment. In order to understand them, it is important to know a little about how OpenGL handles putting 3D elements on the screen.

When you set up a 3D scene using OpenGL, you do the following:

- Position the camera.
- Move all the models into place.
- Choose the lens type and adjust the zoom.
- Choose the size and aspect ratio of the final image.

These four steps are controlled by three transformation matrices in OpenGL. The transformation matrices contain the values necessary to move each polygon into the correct final position on the screen. Figure 21-14 shows the three matrices that transform models for the 2D screen coordinate system. Positioning the camera (viewing) and moving the models into place (modeling), transformations that are closely

FIGURE 21-14

Each object drawn on the screen is controlled by three transformation matrices

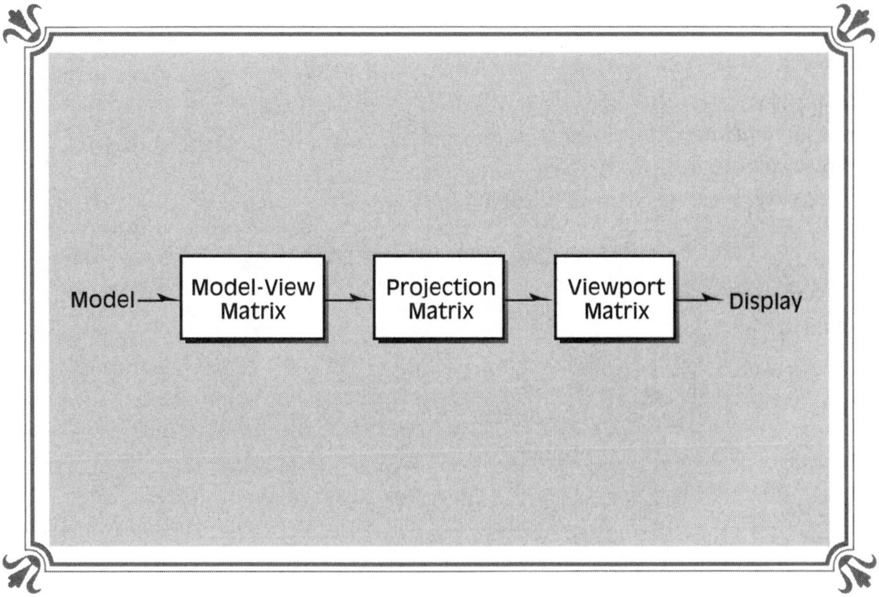

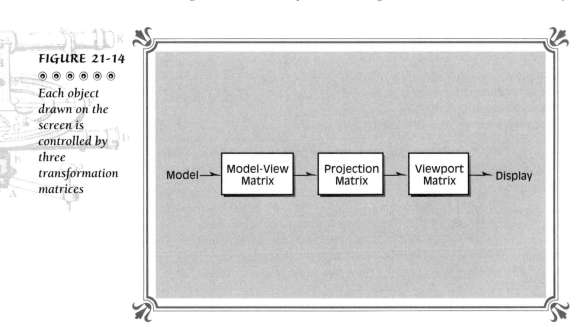

related, are both controlled by the *model-view matrix*. The second matrix, the *projection matrix,* is responsible for determining the type of camera lens and controlling the field of view and the amount of zoom. The third matrix, the *viewport matrix,* is responsible for the size of the final image and its placement in a window on the screen.

In this section, I'll concentrate on the model-view matrix. I'll cover the projection and the viewport matrices in "Projections and Viewports."

The Model-View Matrix

Initially, the camera starts out at the origin of the *world coordinate system,* looking down the negative portion of the *z*-axis. The world coordinate system is the right-handed coordinate system that is the default in OpenGL. If all three viewing matrices contain the identity matrix, the *x*-axis is the horizontal axis, the *y*-axis is the vertical axis, and the *z*-axis points toward the viewer. If the model-view matrix is equal to the identity matrix, only objects near the negative portion of the *z*-axis will appear on the screen when OpenGL draws them. Objects with positive *z* values will be behind the camera, so OpenGL will not draw them in the scene.

There are two ways to position objects so that they are visible on the screen. You can move and rotate the camera until it points at the object of interest, or you can move the object itself and place it in front of the camera. Moving the camera in one direction is just like moving every object in the scene in the other direction. Figure 21-15 illustrates this concept. Drawing A shows a 2-unit-wide cube centered at the

FIGURE 21-15

Moving the camera yields the same result as moving every object in the scene in the opposite direction

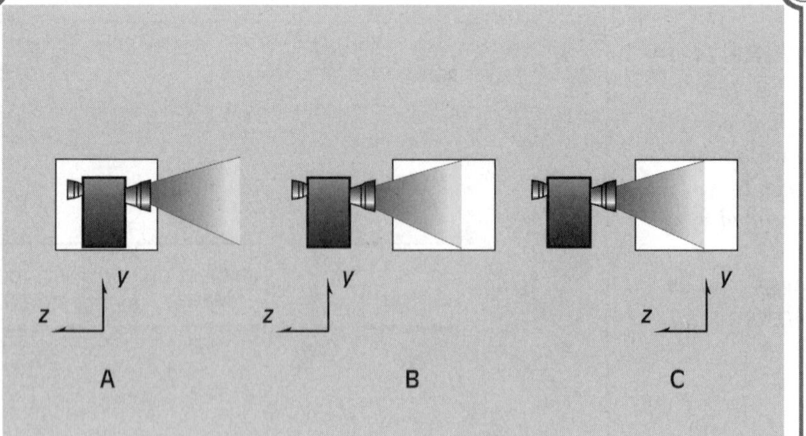

origin of the viewing coordinate system. The camera is in the middle of the cube. If you were to move the cube 4 units in the negative *z* direction, the camera would point at the center of one face of the cube, now 3 units away (as shown in drawing B in Figure 21-15). If you moved the camera 4 units in the positive *z* direction instead, the cube would look exactly the same on the screen as it would had you moved the cube 4 units in the opposite direction. See part (C) in Figure 21-15, and compare it to part (B). The viewer would not be able to tell whether you had moved the camera or the cube.

Look at the code for moving the camera:

```
double ptA[3] = {-1.0,-1.0,-1.0};
double ptB[3] = {1.0,1.0,1.0};

// Viewing transformation. Move the camera 4 units
// in the z direction. Viewing transformations are the
// inverse of modeling transformations.
glTranslatef(0.0,0.0,-4.0);
// Draw a cube from ptA to ptB (opposite corners).
DrawCube(ptA,ptB);
```

glTranslate*() takes 3 values that indicate the translation of objects in the scene. The 3 values correspond to the *x*-, *y*-, and *z*-axes. Moving the camera by 4 units means passing the vector (0,0,-4) to the **glTranslate*()** routine. It is absolutely essential to remember to invert the coordinates for viewing transformations.

Now look at the code for moving the cube:

```
// Modeling transformation. Move the cube 4 units in the negative z direction.
glTranslatef(0.0,0.0,-4.0);
DrawCube(ptA,ptB);
```

The code is exactly the same for both cases.

You must call any viewing transformations before calling any modeling transformations or drawing any objects. Transformations executed after objects are drawn have no effect on those objects.

You can translate, rotate, and scale models in a scene. There are provisions in OpenGL for requesting arbitrary transformations, but generally you will use only the **glTranslate*()**, **glRotate*()**, and **glScale*()** commands. I've just illustrated how **glTranslate*()** works. The subroutine **glRotate*()** takes 4 values that indicate the axis around which you would like to rotate an object and the number of degrees of rotation. The call **glRotatef(90.0,1.0,0.0,0.0)**, for example, causes OpenGL to rotate all objects drawn after this call by 90 degrees (a quarter turn) around the *x*-axis (1.0,0.0,0.0). The part of the object originally pointing in the *y* direction will point in the *z* direction. You can think of this as rotating the camera -90 degrees around the *x*-axis. Both transformations are done precisely the same way and have the same results.

You can scale—stretch, shrink, or reflect—objects along each of the 3 axes by using the **glScale*()** command. **glScale*()** takes 3 values that indicate the scale factor in the *x*, *y*, and *z* directions. Values greater than 1.0 stretch the object in the specified direction. Values between 0.0 and 1.0 shrink the object, and negative values create a reflected version of the object.

Here is the subroutine that draws the cube we called previously:

```
// Draw a cube aligned with the xyz axes defined by ptA and ptB.
void DrawCube(float ptA[3],float ptB[3])
{
    // Draw 6 quadrilaterals representing a cube.
    glBegin(GL_QUADS);
    glNormal3f(-1.0,0.0,0.0);
    glVertex3fv(ptA);
    glVertex3f(ptA[0],ptA[1],ptB[2]);
    glVertex3f(ptA[0],ptB[1],ptB[2]);
    glVertex3f(ptA[0],ptB[1],ptA[2]);

    glNormal3f(0.0,-1.0,0.0);
    glVertex3fv(ptA);
    glVertex3f(ptB[0],ptA[1],ptA[2]);
    glVertex3f(ptB[0],ptA[1],ptB[2]);
    glVertex3f(ptA[0],ptA[1],ptB[2]);

    glNormal3f(0.0,0.0,-1.0);
    glVertex3fv(ptA);
    glVertex3f(ptA[0],ptB[1],ptA[2]);
    glVertex3f(ptB[0],ptB[1],ptA[2]);
    glVertex3f(ptB[0],ptA[1],ptA[2]);

    glNormal3f(1.0,0.0,0.0);
    glVertex3fv(ptB);
    glVertex3f(ptB[0],ptA[1],ptB[2]);
    glVertex3f(ptB[0],ptA[1],ptA[2]);
    glVertex3f(ptB[0],ptB[1],ptA[2]);

    glNormal3f(0., 1., 0.);
    glVertex3fv(ptB);
    glVertex3f(ptB[0], ptB[1], ptA[2]);
    glVertex3f(ptA[0], ptB[1], ptA[2]);
    glVertex3f(ptA[0], ptB[1], ptB[2]);

    glNormal3f(0.0,0.0,1.0);
    glVertex3fv(ptB);
    glVertex3f(ptA[0],ptB[1],ptB[2]);
    glVertex3f(ptA[0],ptA[1],ptB[2]);
    glVertex3f(ptB[0],ptA[1],ptB[2]);

    glEnd();
    return;
}
```

To draw a cube centered on the origin, with sides 1 unit long, you would use the following code:

```
// Draw a single-unit cube centered at the origin.
float ptA[3] = {-0.5,-0.5,-0.5};
float ptB[3] = {0.5,0.5,0.5};

DrawCube(ptA,ptB);
```

You might draw 2-unit cubes separated by 1 unit along the *x*-axis by using 4 points:

```
// Draw 2-unit cubes separated by 1 unit along the x-axis.
float ptA[3] = {-0.5,-0.5,-0.5};
float ptB[3] = {0.5,0.5,0.5};

// Draw the first cube.
// Initialize the model-view matrix.
glMatrixMode(GL_MODELVIEW);
glLoadIdentity();
// Move the subsequent objects -1 unit along the x-axis.
glTranslatef(-1.0,0.0,0.0);
DrawCube(ptA,ptB);

// Draw the second cube.
// Reinitialize the model-view matrix.
glLoadIdentity();
// Move the subsequent objects 1 unit along the x-axis.
glTranslatef(1.0,0.0,0.0);
DrawCube(ptA,ptB);
```

Or, you could use a single cube (2 points) along with 2 transformation matrices, eliminating the need to store the extra cube data. The memory you save in this example is insignificant, but when a program uses many large 3D models, reusing data can be an advantageous strategy.

```
// Draw the first cube.
// Initialize the model-view matrix.
glMatrixMode(GL_MODELVIEW);
glLoadIdentity();

// Move the subsequent objects -1 unit along the x-axis.
glTranslatef(-1.0,0.0,0.0);
DrawCube(ptA,ptB);

// Draw the second cube.
// Move the subsequent objects 2 units along the x-axis.
glTranslatef(2.0,0.0,0.0);
DrawCube(ptA,ptB);
```

This moves the first cube 1 unit to the left and the second cube 2 units to the right—1 unit to compensate for the first translation and 1 unit for the actual move.

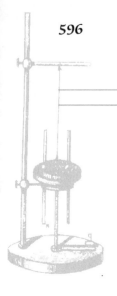

Multiple Transformations

For your game, you may need to draw a robot, a person, or some other *articulated figure*. An articulated figure is a complex model made of several smaller models, often called *hierarchical models*. When drawing hierarchical models, it's important to understand how transformations accumulate.

You know that when you multiply numbers, the order of the numbers is inconsequential; for example, 4∗5 is equal to 5∗4. This is not true in matrix operations, however—in general, A∗B is not equivalent to B∗A for matrices A and B. OpenGL converts all transformations to matrices and multiplies them by the current model-view matrix. For instance, the matrix created by a call to `glTranslatef(a,b,c)` is

$$\begin{bmatrix} 1 & 0 & 0 & a \\ 0 & 1 & 0 & b \\ 0 & 0 & 1 & c \\ 0 & 0 & 0 & 1 \end{bmatrix}$$

OpenGL multiplies this matrix by the current model-view matrix.

The order of transformations is important. Performing a rotation and then a translation would leave an object in a different position than if you were to implement the opposite sequence. For example, if you want to rotate a cube 45 degrees and then move it 3 units, you must call `glRotate*()` and then `glTranslate*()`. Calling `glTranslate*()` and then `glRotate*()` will produce a different result. Figure 21-16 shows the difference between the two calling orders.

Remember that OpenGL moves the local coordinate system of the object (indicated in Figure 21-16 by the smaller axes) when it moves the object. Rotating an object also rotates the coordinate system for subsequent translations and rotations.

Projections and Viewports

OpenGL has provided four projection transformation routines, `glFrustum()`, `glOrtho()`, `glOrtho2D()`, and `gluPerspective()`. They control the zoom factor and aspect ratio of the final view. All are helpful, but you will probably use `gluPerspective()` the most often. With it, you can cause a scene to look like it is being shown through a wide-angle lens or zoom the scene so that it seems almost like an orthographic or parallel projection.

A call to the `gluPerspective()` routine might look like this:

```
// Select the projection matrix.
glMatrixMode(GL_PROJECTION);
// Set up the projection transformation.
gluPerspective(fovy,aspect,zNear,zFar);
```

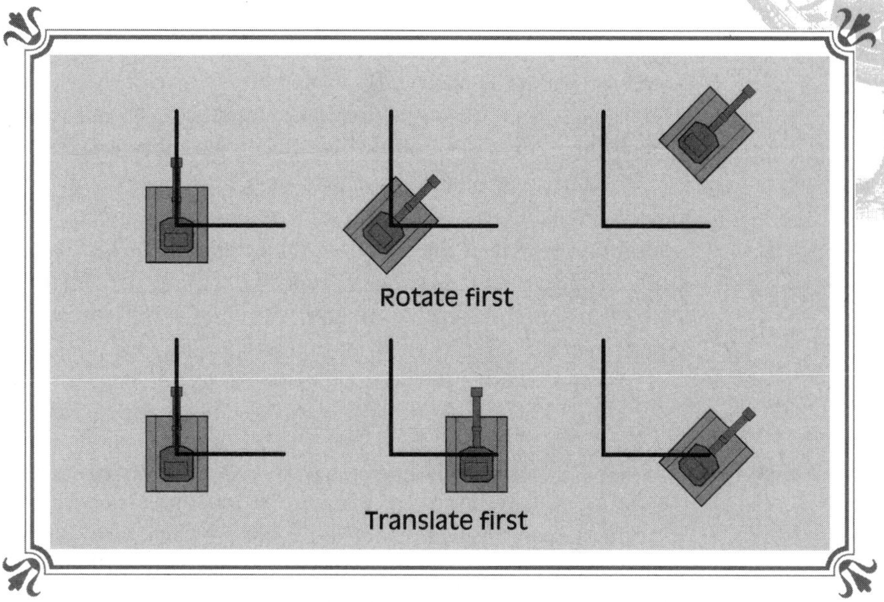

FIGURE 21-16

The same two transformations, applied in different orders

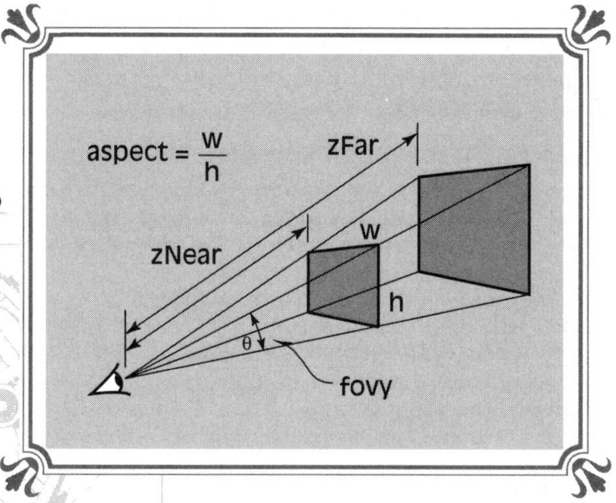

FIGURE 21-17

The arguments for the command `gluPerspective()`

Figure 21-17 shows the relationship of these arguments to the geometry of the viewer and graphics window. The first argument, **`fovy`**, which you specify in degrees, is the vertical field of view of the window. You should set it to the arc tangent of the height of the window divided by the distance from the viewer's eye to the screen (fovy = atan (W_{height} / eye_{dist})). It is usually between 18 and 30 degrees. Designers often slightly increase this value to emphasize the perspective effect.

The second argument, **`aspect`**, is the ratio of the horizontal field of view to the vertical field of view. A square window would have an aspect ratio of 1.0. This argument should equal the width of the window divided by the height (aspect = W_{width} / W_{height}).

zNear and **zFar** are the distances from the eye of the viewer to the near and far *clipping planes*. Objects outside of clipping planes do not appear in the scene, and objects intersected by clipping planes only partially appear on the screen.

The values in the viewport matrix are the last ones to influence the position of the objects on the screen. You use the **glViewport()** command to describe the position, width, and height of the portal on the screen into which OpenGL draws the final image. Typically, you call the **glViewport()** command with the full width and height of the available window, but sometimes you might want to restrict the drawing to just a portion of the window, in order to reserve an area for other user-interface elements or even other views.

```
// Setup the window for drawing the scene.
glViewport(0,0,width,height);
```

The coordinates for the **glViewport** command are specified in a window's client coordinate space instead of world display coordinates. In other words, the first two arguments, which refer to the origin of the viewport with respect to the client area of the window, are almost always (0,0).

The **gluPerspective()** and **glViewport()** routines are usually called when a WM_SIZE message is received from Windows—that is, when the program is started and again whenever the window is resized. The following code is an example of a WM_SIZE message handler for an OpenGL program:

```
case WM_SIZE:
    // Define the perspective transformation and viewport
    // on the screen. This is called once when the window is
    // first opened and again anytime the window is resized.

    // Get the width and height of the window.
    winWidth = (GLsizei) LOWORD (lParam);
    winHeight = (GLsizei) HIWORD (lParam);

    // Calculate the aspect ratio.
    winAspect = (double) winWidth / (double) winHeight;

    // Set up the projection transformation.
    // Select the projection matrix.
    glMatrixMode(GL_PROJECTION);
    // Initialize the projection matrix.
    glLoadIdentity();
    gluPerspective(28.0,winAspect,1.0,1000.0);

    // Specify the viewport.
    glViewport(0,0,winWidth,winHeight);

    return(0);
```

Setting Up a Scene

You, the director, decide how to set up a 3D scene. You can create the models of all your objects in the correct position and not use any transformations at all, but don't forget that any animation will require you to move some models. The model-view matrix makes it easy to move models and objects without changing the data defining those models. Using this matrix effectively will make your life as director much easier.

The projection matrix helps you specify how the scene looks on the screen. Do you want a perspective or an orthographic projection? Do you want the look of a wide-angle lens or a zoom lens? Once you have decided, you can select values for the `gluPerspective()` routine or one of its relatives.

Finally, the viewport transformation indicates where on the screen you want the image drawn. You can either fill the whole window or restrict the image to some smaller region of the window.

Of all the aspects of OpenGL, transformations and matrix operations are probably the most difficult to understand. The best way to really learn what these routines do and how they do it is to write many programs and experiment with different transformations. You should now have a good basic understanding of transformations, but before you become a transformation guru, you will have to do more than just get your feet wet—you'll have to dive in and start coding.

Lighting and Materials

Shine a flashlight on a wall in a dark room. Even if the color of the wall is uniform, the intensity of the light on the wall will change as you look from the center of the beam to the corner of the wall. The intensity and color of the light striking your eyes depends on many factors. The brightness and hue of the source are important, but these components are modulated by the color and reflective properties of the wall (or more precisely, of the finish on the wall).

You can create a picture of a wall by choosing colors carefully and applying them precisely; some expert painters select and apply colors so well that their final products are indistinguishable from photographs. We mere mortals, however, need help to make an image appear realistic. OpenGL is made for the artistically challenged. It incorporates a lighting simulation; instead of painting the lighting effects on a pixel-by-pixel basis, you can choose the lights and materials used in a scene and let OpenGL take care of creating the lighting effects.

To understand lighting effects, think of what happens to light as it leaves a source. Theoretically, the most light that can ever reach your eye is the amount leaving the source. But as light leaves a source, it spreads out. The farther your eye is from the source, the less light will enter your pupil. The intensity of the light is further reduced if you are looking not at the source, but instead at a reflection. Again, in theory, the largest amount of light that can be reflected off a surface is the total light striking that surface; in actuality, though, few surfaces are even close to being perfect reflectors. A white surface will reflect much of the light, but a dark gray or black surface will tend to absorb the light that strikes it. Thus, the actual amount of light striking your eyes depends on the intensity and color of the source, your distance from the source, the direction in which you're looking, and the properties of any reflecting surface.

In OpenGL, the appearance and color of a polygon depend not only on the color of the polygon but on the light illuminating that polygon, as well. OpenGL does not *simulate* the subtle real-world interaction of lights and materials, but it does quickly *model* the interactions in such a way as to give reasonable results most of the time.

Types of Light

OpenGL lighting calculations can specify four types of light: *ambient, diffuse, specular,* and *emissive.* You can use one of these types for environmental lighting, three for light sources, and one for defining surface properties or "materials."

When you examine an image, you can usually determine the locations of the light sources. Shadows and highlights give clues to the origin of a light. A sunny day is marked by distinct shadows. On a foggy day, the source of light is not apparent. There are no shadows and the light appears to be coming from everywhere at once.

Ambient light is light that seems to come from no particular direction. In OpenGL, the ambient light associated with a light source contributes to the brightness of every surface in a scene. You can also set ambient light in the environment, independent of any light sources. The environmental ambient light illuminates all surfaces, even in the absence of any specific lights. All surfaces in a given scene are equally well lighted by any ambient light, so ambient-light calculations do not take into account the position of the light source or the orientation of the surface. Each drawn surface has a value indicating how much the total ambient light can illuminate that surface.

Diffuse light is light that comes from a specific source but is scattered in all directions when reflected. If a surface is facing directly into a light source, it will be lighted by a diffuse light. A surface facing away from the source will not receive any diffuse light.

Specular light is light that travels directly from the source to your eyes. Specular reflection is directly reflected light. The brightness of specular reflection can be blinding. Think of a lake on a sunny day—most of the light that reaches your eyes from the surface of water comes from diffuse reflection, but when the water reflects the light of the sun directly into your eyes, that's specular reflection at work. Mirrors are the most common specular reflectors. A shiny sphere like a bowling ball or a pool ball will also show specular reflections as highlights (see Figure 21-18).

Emissive materials are those that are self-lighted. A surface that is emissive appears brighter than the nonemitting surfaces in a scene if all other material properties are

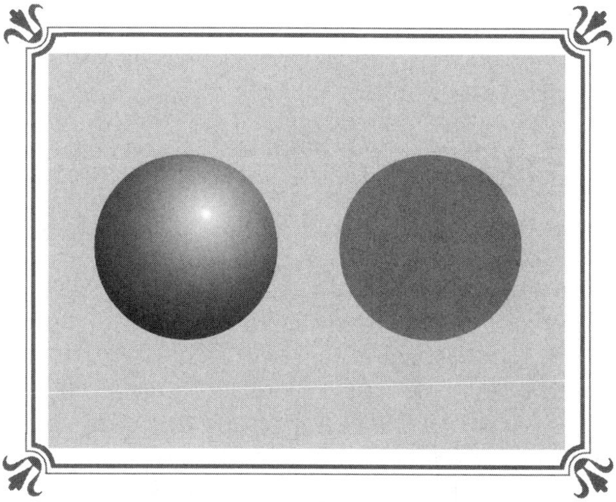

FIGURE 21-18

The specular reflection off the surface on the left identifies this object as shiny and spherical. It is difficult to tell if the object on the right is a circle or a sphere, dull or bright

the same for those surfaces. In OpenGL, even though an emissive surface looks brighter, it doesn't radiate light and contribute to the brightness of other surfaces. Emissive surfaces appear to glow and, unlike nonemissive surfaces, can be seen even when there are no active lights.

Lights in OpenGL have ambient, diffuse, and specular components. The numeric value of these components specify each light's contribution to the overall light in a scene. You can attenuate OpenGL lights by placing them farther away or concentrate their effects, making them like spotlights. Surfaces, too, have ambient, diffuse, and specular properties, as well as an emissive property. Materials have a "shininess" factor and can be partially or completely transparent. Spotlights and transparency are advanced topics that are beyond the scope of this book.

Light and Material Interactions

When you are first setting up lighting in OpenGL, the number of parameters can be overwhelming. To display one lighted surface, you have to provide up to three sets of parameters for the light and up to four for the surface material. The key to achieving the lighting you want is to have a fundamental understanding of what OpenGL does with all those parameters.

All properties work in a similar way. The final intensity of a surface's brightness depends on the amount of light available from the environment and the lights, and the properties of the surface. Let's look at ambient calculations as an example. Say that the maximum brightness of a surface is 1.0. The maximum ambient property of a light (Aln) or of the environment (Ae) is always 1.0. Therefore, the maximum total ambient light (At = Al0 + Al1 + … + Al7 + Ae) is 9.0. (Remember, you can use up to 8 lights per scene. However, you will rarely use all 8 lights at once and will even less frequently specify that all 8 lights and the environment have ambient values of 1.0.) This calculation uses the ambient value of the surface (As) to determine the final brightness of the surface, which is B = As * At. If either As is 0.0 or At is 0.0, the surface is not illuminated by ambient light. Since the maximum brightness is 1.0, values for B exceeding 1.0 are calculated as if they were just 1.0. In other words, a surface with an As of 0.2 and an At of 1.0 will appear as bright as a surface with an As of 0.4 and an At of 0.5.

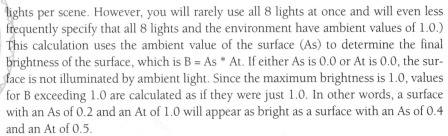

Color (RGB) is simply a separation of the three properties into red, green, and blue values. This means that our three parameters (ambient, diffuse, and specular) turn into nine parameters: R, G, and B values for the ambient property; R, G, and B values for the diffuse property; and R, G, and B values for the specular property. All calculations are done on a per-color basis and the final RGB color of the surface is the combination of all three sets of independent calculations.

Color plays an important role in determining how a surface looks in a specific light. A blue surface, for example, looks blue because it reflects very little red or green light. Shining a red light on a blue surface would be a waste of time, because all that red light would be absorbed by the blue surface—none would be reflected. In a scene that is lighted with red light, those objects that reflect red light will appear red, while all others will appear dark. Lighting a scene with a white light containing red, green, and blue wavelengths will cause objects to appear in their normal colors.

Defining Lights

Before you can calculate any lighting effects in OpenGL, you must use **glEnable()**:

```
glEnable(GL_LIGHTING);
```

You must also enable each of the lights individually. (Leaving every light disabled is a good way to keep your objects from showing up on the screen.) To turn lighting calculations back off again, use:

```
glDisable(GL_LIGHTING);
```

The subroutines

```
glEnable(GL_LIGHT0);
glDisable(GL_LIGHT0);
```

enable and disable **LIGHT0**, respectively.

You define the level of ambient environmental light by using the **glLightModel*()** routine. You can also use **glLightModel*()** to indicate to OpenGL the use of local or infinite lights and whether OpenGL should calculate lighting values for both sides of the polygons. The default value for the ambient light level is (0.2,0.2,0.2) for red, green, and blue. There is an additional value for alpha, which defaults to 1.0.

```
GLfloat lmodel_ambient[] = {0.2,0.2,0.2,1.0};
glLightModelfv(GL_LIGHT_MODEL_AMBIENT,lmodel_ambient);
```

sets the environmental ambient light values to the default. Changing the ambient light is as simple as changing the RGB values stored in **lmodel_ambient**.

For each individual light (**LIGHT0** through **LIGHT7**), you can set ambient, specular, and diffuse components by using **glLight*()**. The following code sets some values for **LIGHT0**:

```
GLfloat l0_ambient[] = {0.5,0.0,1.0,1.0};
GLfloat l0_diffuse[]={0.2,0.2,0.2,1.0};
GLfloat l0_specular[] = {0.2,0.2,0.2,1.0};
GLfloat l0_psition[] = {1.0,0.0,0.0,0.0};

glLightfv(GL_LIGHT0,GL_AMBIENT,l0_ambient);
glLightfv(GL_LIGHT0,GL_DIFFUSE,l0_diffuse);
glLightfv(GL_LIGHT0,GL_SPECULAR,l0_specular);
glLightfv(GL_LIGHT0,GL_POSITION,l0_position);
```

You can call the routines for setting lighting values anytime. There is a performance penalty for repeatedly changing the lighting parameters, but you are not prohibited from doing so. For the fastest performance, you should set up lights that you can use for your whole scene, and limit the number of changes necessary during the remainder of the program.

The position values you specify in the call to **glLightfv()** indicate the direction of an infinitely distant light or the position of local lights. The fourth value in the array, w, is 0.0 for infinite lights and nonzero for local lights. The position of a local light is (x/w,y/w,z/w).

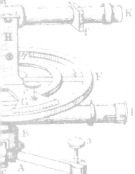

Specular-reflection calculations depend on the position of the light source, the position of the viewer, and the orientation of the surface. When lights are an infinite distance away, the lighting calculations are much simpler to perform. If speed is a factor, as it usually is, you should avoid using local light sources. Using **glLightModel*()** to turn on local lights will increase the realism of the lighting calculations, but will incur a performance penalty due to the more extensive calculations. To turn on local lighting, call

```
glLightModeli(GL_LIGHT_MODEL_LOCAL_VIEWER, GL_TRUE)
```

and then define some local lights to indicate that OpenGL should base the specular-reflection calculations and the intensity of the light striking the objects on local lights.

Defining Materials

You define surface properties (in other words, materials) by using the **glMaterial*()** routines. This code shows an example of a material property definition:

```
GLfloat ambient_mat[] = {0.8,0.8,0.8,1.0};
```

continued on next page

continued from previous page

```
GLfloat diffuse_mat[] = {0.5,0.4,0.3,1.0};
GLfloat specular_mat[] = {0.4,0.8,0.4,1.0};
GLfloat shininess = 63.0;

glMaterialfv(GL_FRONT,GL_AMBIENT,ambient_mat);
glMaterialfv(GL_FRONT,GL_DIFFUSE,diffuse_mat);
glMaterialfv(GL_FRONT,GL_SPECULAR,specular_mat);
glMaterialf(GL_FRONT,GL_SHININESS,shininess);
```

The shininess value specifies the brightness of the specular reflection. You can use it in conjunction with the specular color values for calculating the color of highlights in the scene. You can change the material properties anytime when drawing a scene; because of the performance penalty, however, it is better to draw all same-material polygons in a scene in succession.

Texture Maps

So far, I've talked mostly about painting polygons using either a solid color or colors that change smoothly along edges of a polygon. Often, though, it is necessary to draw very complex images—ones that would take thousands of polygons to render correctly if you were using flat or Gouraud shading. As I mentioned earlier in this chapter, you can use texture mapping for creating complicated shapes relatively easily. Texture mapping substantially enhances the realism of a scene while keeping the polygon count low.

Texture maps come in especially handy when you want to display maps, signs, or billboards in a 3D scene. Usually, it would be necessary to create a set of polygons or lines representing each letter and picture on such an item. Using a scanned or drawn digital picture of the item, however, you can display a single rectangle on the screen and have the text and pictures show up correctly.

Some home video-game machines, like the 3DO machines, and the majority of video arcade games have texture-mapping acceleration built in and use texture maps on most polygons. The disadvantage of texture mapping is that without hardware acceleration, this technique can reduce the speed of your application to the point where it is no longer interactive. However, you should keep in mind that high polygon counts are also an impediment to interactive gaming.

Creating Texture Maps

Texture maps are simply bitmaps. Normally, the entire image appears on the screen when you are working with a bitmap, as if there were a 1-to-1 correspondence between image pixels and screen pixels. Applying a texture map to an object works the same way, except you paint the image on the *object* instead of the screen.

You can create texture maps in memory or read them in from a file. Most often, you'll create your texture maps with 2D paint programs (like the Paintbrush application shipped with Windows) and store the texture maps on disk. The application that uses a bitmap reads it in from a file and applies it to the polygons as needed.

There are some restrictions on the images you can create as texture maps. The minimum 2D texture-map size is 64x64 pixels. The width and height of a texture map must both be multiples of 2. If you need to convert an improperly sized image to a valid texture map, use the OpenGL image-conversion routines (**gluScaleImage()** is one) that allow you to correctly adjust the size and aspect ratio of the image.

Before defining texture maps for use in a scene, you must enable texture mapping by using the **glEnable()** command:

```
glEnable(GL_TEXTURE_2D);
```

Once a bitmap is retrieved or stored in memory, you issue the command **glTexImage2D()** to prepare the graphics hardware for drawing the texture map on polygons. The format of the subroutine call for a 64x64 RGB image with 24-bit color is:

```
glTexImage2D(GL_TEXTURE_2 D   // Target - must be GL_TEXTURE_2D
             0               // Level - 0 indicates single level
             3               // Components - use RGB, but no alpha
             64              // Image width - in pixels
             64              // Image height - in pixels
             GL_RGB          // Image format - RGB values only
             GL_BYTE         // Format type - each color is 1 byte
             image);         // Pointer to texture image data
```

If you're interested in learning more about the **glTexImage2D()** command, consult the Windows NT online help for OpenGL.

Applying Textures to Objects

You apply textures to objects by indicating which image to use as the texture map and specifying texture coordinates for each point in the object. To create a brick wall, for example, you might draw a single image of a brick and use copies of that image to texture the entire wall. To indicate where to put each copy of the image, you would need to tell OpenGL how the texture map relates to each vertex in each polygon of the wall.

Texture maps are always assigned coordinates that start at (0,0) in the lower left corner of the image and increase to (1,1) in the upper right corner. To draw a single brick using the brick texture, you would draw a rectangular polygon whose 4 corners corresponded to the 4 corners of the texture map. The following code does just that:

```
glBegin(GL_QUADS);
glTexCoord2f(0.0,0.0);          glVertex3f(-1.0,-1.0,0.0);
```

continued on next page

continued from previous page

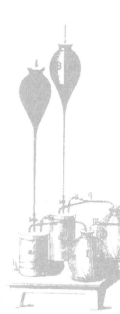

```
glTexCoord2f(0.0,1.0);          glVertex3f(-1.0,1.0,0.0);
glTexCoord2f(1.0,1.0);          glVertex3f(1.0,1.0,0.0);
glTexCoord2f(1.0,0.0);          glVertex3f(1.0,-1.0,0.0);
glEnd();
```

This code will produce a 2x2 rectangle on the *xy* plane, centered on the *z*-axis, that displays the entire texture map.

You specify the texture coordinates just prior to specifying each vertex coordinate. Individual texture-map pixels, or *texels,* usually do not correspond to single specific pixels on the screen. OpenGL gives you several controls for converting texels to pixels, a process called *filtering*. The simplest and quickest texel filter colors a pixel by using the texel that is closest to the center of the pixel. However, this often introduces artifacts. Like many programmers, you may want to use a more sophisticated filter.

A polygon can have only a single texture associated with it, but you can draw it using any texture map already defined or created. You can draw a single object made of multiple polygons using several textures.

Texturing Options

You can repeat textures over and over again on a polygon, as we did in the brick wall example. You can also *clamp* textures at the edges, using just the right-most and top-most texel values to fill the polygon instead of reproducing the texture image over and over. A brick wall drawn with clamped textures would show a single brick in the lower left corner with a solid color continuing toward the right and top of the wall.

Textures can completely replace every pixel in a polygon, or modulate the original color. The decision to replace or blend a polygon color with a texel color depends on the current texture mode. GL_DECAL mode replaces polygon color with texel values. GL_MODULATE and GL_BLEND modes combine the lighted color with texture colors. You will need to experiment with the different modes to find out which mode is most appropriate for your application.

You use the **`glTexParameter*()`** function to set texturing options, such as clamping or wrapping, and to set the texel filter type. You use **`glTexEnv*()`** to set the texture environment mode, which tells OpenGL how to integrate lighting effects with texture effects.

OpenGL can also generate texture coordinates automatically. Using OpenGL's texture-coordinate-generation feature, you can easily create contour maps for terrains and environment maps that look like shiny surfaces. You use **`glTexGen*()`** for setting this function.

The difference between simple shading models and texture-mapped scenes is often remarkable. However, using textures correctly is difficult, because of the many ways of applying them. If you plan to use texture maps in your application, you'll find it worthwhile to spend some time learning how each option affects the final appearance of objects.

Maintaining Interactivity

If you have run an OpenGL program under Windows NT, you know that you have time to clip your toenails while waiting for an animated sequence to finish. Without hardware acceleration, 3D graphics programs take a long time to generate an image. Some of the delay is due to the nature of the beast—3D graphics require complex, mathematics-intensive operations. However, part of the slowdown can be blamed on programmer mistakes and misunderstandings. Let's discuss a few of the topics that relate to slow graphics performance.

Filling Pixels

On a large monitor, there are a lot of pixels to manage. Few Windows users use less than 800x600 resolution, so there are at least 480,000 pixels to feed every time the screen is redrawn. If we also insist on 24-bit color mode, 800x600 translates to 1,440,000 bytes of information to address with every screen clear. Add a 32-bit depth buffer to that and an alpha channel (8 bits), and we're up to 2,840,000 bytes to fill. That's almost 3 MB of data every time we redraw the screen! If you could put data into average-speed memory chips at the fastest possible rate (~70 nanoseconds) 1 byte at a time, it would take you almost .20 seconds just to clear the screen between frames. It would take at least an additional .20 seconds to refill the screen with data, and the fill rate would limit your maximum frame rate for animation to about 2.5 frames per second—10 times slower than the rate used by film studios and required for smooth motion.

How do the big boys do it? Hardware acceleration is the key to speeding up the pixel-fill rate. A special memory-addressing mode that fills the memory with zero in parallel fixes the "clear screen" problem. The high-end graphics machines also split the task of coloring pixels between separate processors. The GLINT graphics boards do the pixel-filling job a little faster than it can be done in the main memory of the PC, because the memory is on the board itself.

For those of us who can only salivate and sigh at the thought of hardware acceleration, using a smaller window is also effective. Using one-fourth of the screen is a quick way to reduce the number of pixels that you need to fill. The Windows NT Pipes screen saver, for example, creates the illusion of working quickly by building the image incrementally as you watch. It rarely clears the screen and is drawing only a little bit on the screen at any one time.

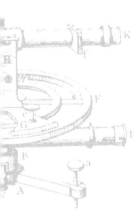

Traversing Polygons

Another slowdown in the drawing process occurs when the computer must grind through the polygons one by one to put them on the screen. Each triangular polygon has between nine and twelve 4-byte floating-point numbers that must be passed to the graphics hardware. Each floating-point number is involved in a series of calculations designed to figure out the final location of that polygon on the screen. Since your main processor is responsible for calculating those transformations, you may find that the redrawing speed is slower than you would like, even with a Pentium processor. In theory, the GLINT chip can handle up to 300,000 polygons per second, but the fastest CPUs can't begin to cope with that, because of the intensity of the floating-point calculations.

Transformations Without Matrices

Earlier in this chapter, you learned how to move objects by changing the modeling matrix instead of moving the individual vertices stored in the object. Every vertex in a scene must be passed through the model-view matrix before it is drawn on the screen. Fortunately, it makes no sense to move every vertex individually when creating animation effects. Transformations performed directly on the data are rare and almost always unnecessary. The proper use of the model-view matrix is the right way to avoid bottlenecks during animation.

Lighting Calculations

The lighting calculations OpenGL performs when lighting is enabled are quite expensive. The program must calculate each vertex's color using a formula that takes into account the properties of the surface and the color and intensity of each light in the scene. Once it finds the color at each vertex, OpenGL must smoothly vary these colors along the edges of the polygons. Again, this requires time. Turning off lighting effects and using flat shading sharply increases the refresh rate. Unfortunately, it also makes the final image not nearly as engaging. Determine what's appropriate for your application and scale your use of lighting calculations accordingly.

State Changes

Turning lighting on and off, changing material properties, and changing lighting parameters all require state changes in the OpenGL rendering path. These state changes are time-consuming. Sorting by object or material type before drawing can reduce the number of state changes per frame, thereby speeding up the redrawing just a bit.

Swapping Buffers

Swapping the back buffer and the front buffer (or in NT's case, blasting the pixels from the back buffer to the front buffer) takes time. Drawing into the front buffer is a way to eliminate that copy time. This technique is usually annoying, but you *can* use it effectively, as the Pipes screen saver shows.

Texture Mapping

Texture mapping is the king of processor hogs. Certainly, this technique adds a substantial amount of realism to a scene. When you perform it with special hardware, it can even be extremely fast. Unfortunately, texture-mapping hardware, although it has perhaps the most beneficial effect of all on image quality, is rare.

On the bright side, such hardware is beginning to gain popularity. The second-generation GLINT boards that use the 300TX chip will have some on board texture-storage memory to speed up the use of textures in scenes.

Culling

At any one time, the viewer is looking at only some of the objects in a scene. Usually, some objects will be either behind the viewpoint or hidden by other objects. Eliminating objects that the viewer can't see from the list of items to draw is one of the best ways to speed up an animation sequence or a game. Unfortunately, the viewpoint can change every frame for most 3D environments, so you must perform this "geometry culling" continuously. That can take up valuable CPU time, but the gains are generally much greater than the losses.

Another type of culling you can do directly in OpenGL is called *back-face culling*. OpenGL can tell by looking at the order of the vertices passed to it when drawing a polygon whether the polygon is facing toward or away from the viewer. Using the following code, you can tell OpenGL not to draw any polygons facing away from the viewer (obviously, discarding back-facing polygons will have no effect on the final image):

```
// Tell OpenGL that polygons with counterclockwise
// ordering on the screen are front-facing.
glFrontFace(GL_CCW);

// Cull (discard) the back-facing polygons.
glCullFace(GL_BACK);

// Enable culling.
glEnable(GL_CULL_FACE)
```

You can use `glDisable(GL_CULL_FACE)` to turn culling off when necessary.

Hardware Acceleration

The best way to speed up 3D programs is to throw money at them. (Surprise, surprise.) Hardware acceleration, though expensive, makes the single biggest difference in 3D applications. Sadly, accelerated 3D graphics boards using the GLINT chip cost as much as the computers they sit in. A significant contributor to that cost is the high-speed memory used for frame buffers and depth buffers. The prices may eventually come down, but don't hold your breath. Remember that the general population will not have access to hardware acceleration for some years and write your programs accordingly.

Display Lists

For an object you must draw over and over again, the drawing commands often remain the same. In fact, you might need to change only the values stored in the model-view matrix for such an object. If this is the case, you can "compile" the commands to display that object, including the vertex and material-property specifications, into a *display list*. A display list is a group of commands that OpenGL can preprocess for efficiency. You can create a display list by using the following set of routines:

```
unsigned int geomList;
// Just give me a single list number this time.
geomList = glGenLists(1);

// Begin compiling a new display list but don't draw it yet
// (GL_COMPILE_AND_EXECUTE would also draw it on the screen).
glNewList( geomList, GL_COMPILE);

// Draw all geometry here...

// Finished specifying OpenGL commands.
glEndList();

// Now execute the list.
glCallList(geomList);
```

To delete a display list, use this code:

```
// Delete a single list starting at geomList.
glDeleteLists(geomList, 1);
```

You can store almost all OpenGL commands in a display list.

Summary

Adding a third dimension to your images requires more than simply tacking another number on the end of a 2D vertex. In three dimensions, you must create and display models differently, consider lighting factors, and accommodate extra computing demands.

In this chapter, I've covered all the basics of OpenGL and 3D programming. But the best way to *really* learn the concepts of 3D graphics is to experiment with them.

Try creating some models. Start with something simple, like a pyramid. Play with the viewing parameters to see how each changes the appearance of your objects. Then try animating a simple robot or bouncing ball. 3D graphics is the wave of the future, so you might as well grab a board and dive in!

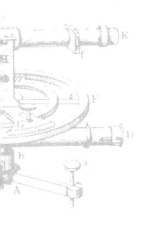

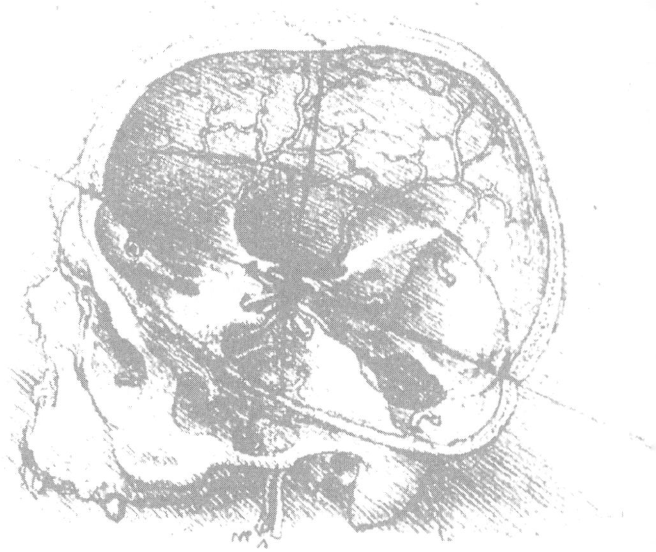

A

BugBots—Under the Lens

In this appendix, I'll explain how I structured and created the BugBots program and examine some interesting code snippets, concentrating mostly on those parts of the program that might not seem crystal-clear when you first read the source code. An executable version of BugBots, and the source code for the game, are included on the disk that accompanies this book. If you haven't run the game yet, it would probably be a good idea for you to do so before reading this appendix.

BugBots contains the main elements that you'll find in virtually any Windows game: animation and sounds. It also uses toolbars and multiple windows to provide a modern user interface. Figure A-1 shows the BugBots windows. The frame window and client window together make up the control bar. Modeless dialog boxes are used to create the animation stage (Stage dialog box), program editor (Edit dialog box), and the BugBot program list window (List dialog box).

These are the steps I followed when I created BugBots:

- I sketched the window designs on paper.
- I created code to create and open the windows.
- I added a scrollable background to the animation window.
- I added sprites to the animation window.
- I added sound.

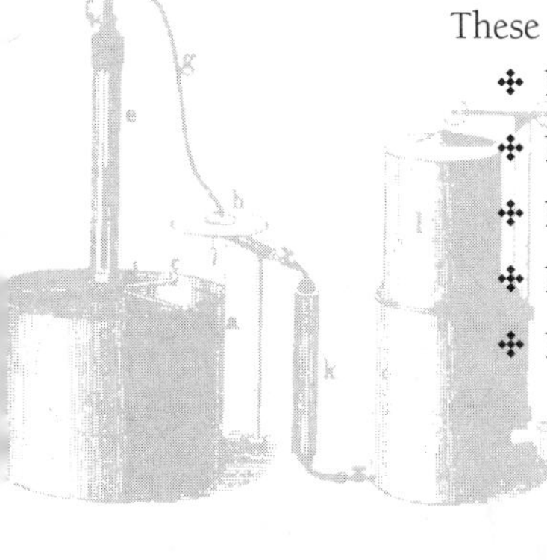

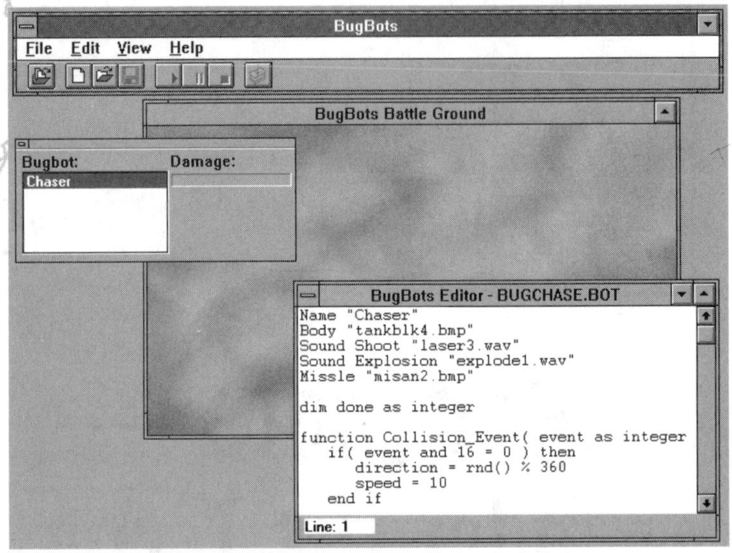

FIGURE A-1

BugBots' windows

Creating the BugBots Application Framework

BugBots is a moderately complex Windows application. The multiple windows, toolbars, and built-in program editor require that considerable attention be paid to the interaction and communication between the various windows components.

WINDOWSX.H and the Message Crackers

No, it's not a grunge group! Microsoft offers a set of tools that you can use to easily create a framework for a somewhat complex Windows application like BugBots. The file WINDOWSX.H contains a set of macros collectively referred to as message crackers. The message-cracker macros provide a convenient, portable, and type-safe mechanism for dealing with window messages, their parameters, and their return values.

The basic idea is that instead of having to pick apart message parameters with casts, HIWORD/LOWORD, and such, you simply declare and implement a function that has the properly typed parameters and return value. The message crackers pick apart the message parameters, call your function, and return the appropriate value from the window message.

The following message-dispatch code from EDITDLG.C shows how the message-cracker macros are used, and how simple and readable the resulting code is:

```
switch (msg)
{
    HANDLE_MSG(pedit, WM_COMMAND,  EditDlg_OnCommand);
    HANDLE_MSG(pedit, WM_SIZE,     EditDlg_OnSize);
    HANDLE_MSG(pedit, WM_CLOSE,    EditDlg_OnClose);
    HANDLE_MSG(pedit, WM_ACTIVATE, EditDlg_OnActivate);
    default:
         return EditDlg_DefProc(hwnd, msg, wParam, lParam);
}
```

As well as the message-cracker macros, WINDOWSX.H contains a number of other macros that make it much easier to deal with sending control messages in a type-safe and portable way. You can use the following code from the file EDITDLG.C to determine how many spaces to insert into a line when a user presses TAB:

```
int n = (start - Edit_LineIndex( hwndEdit,
Edit_LineFromChar(hwndEdit,start))) % SPACES_PER_TAB;
```

Although you do have to expend some effort to understand the code, consider the alternative, written without the benefit of the WINDOWSX.H macros:

```
int n = (start - (int)SendMessage( hwndEdit, EM_LINEINDEX, (WPARAM)
SendMessage(hwndEdit, EM_LINEFROMCHAR, (WPARAM)start, 0L), 0L))) %
SPACES_PER_TAB;
```

This is not the sort of code you want to read late at night after your third double-espresso!

Using MAKEAPP to Create the Application Framework

Some great programmer at Microsoft was thoughtful enough to provide a tool that creates an entire Windows program framework with a single comand line. The generated code uses the macros in WINDOWSX.H and creates a robust, extensible framework for your application. It's a source of never-ending wonder to me that the framework generator, MAKEAPP, is not used more often. I guess some Windows programmers just insist on doing the same old tedious tasks over and over again!

There are a number of ways to obtain MAKEAPP and related tools. I installed a copy from the Microsoft Developer's Network CD, but it is also available from the following on-line sources:

CompuServe

1. GO MSL.
2. Search for MAKEAPP.EXE.
3. Display the results and download.

Microsoft Download Service (MSDL)

4. Dial (206) 936-6735 to connect to MSDL.
5. Download MAKEAPP.EXE.

Internet (Anonymous FTP)

6. ftp ftp.microsoft.com.
7. Change to the \softlib\mslfiles directory.
8. Get MAKEAPP.EXE.

I created the BugBots framework by running MAKEAPP.BAT, copying the resulting DLG.C, and then using search-and-replace operations to produce the files STAGEDLG.C, EDITDLG.C, and LISTDLG.C.

MAKEAPP's template-based approach, plus the relatively small amount of manual editing required to create all the windows and dialog boxes used by BugBots, made it possible for me to move from working on the mechanics of the program to working on the appearance of it within an hour. If you want to spend your time working on cool sounds and graphics, and you don't care to write the same **CreateWindow** code over and over again, then you definitely want to get a copy of MAKEAPP before you start programming your own games. The time you spend finding and downloading it will be repaid before you've finished your first Windows game.

Program Initialization

All Windows programs begin execution when the startup library code calls **WinMain**. Like any typical Windows program, BugBots initializes data structures, creates windows, and then enters its message-dispatch loop. However, BugBots' initialization is somewhat complicated in that it initializes and creates three different windows: the frame window, client window, and animation window. After initializing the application's global data structure, **WinMain** calls **App_Initialize** to create and display the main windows.

```
int PASCAL WinMain(HINSTANCE hinst, HINSTANCE hinstPrev, LPSTR
lpszCmdLine, int cmdShow)
{
    //
    // Initialize the APP structure.
    //
    _fmemset(&g_app,0,sizeof(APP));
    g_app.hinst         = hinst;
    g_app.hinstPrev     = hinstPrev;
    g_app.lpszCmdLine   = lpszCmdLine;
```

```
    g_app.cmdShow       = cmdShow;
    g_app.hwndMain      = NULL;
    g_app.codeExit      = 1;        // Assume failure.
    g_app.fQuit         = FALSE;
    //
    // Initialize, run, and terminate the application.
    //
    if (App_Initialize(&g_app))
        App_Run(&g_app);

    App_Terminate(&g_app, (g_app.codeExit == 0 ? TERM_QUIT : TERM_ERROR));

    return g_app.codeExit;
}
```

Microsoft's MAKEAPP framework generator automatically provides code to initialize and service a Windows message hook for applications it generates. The message hook arranges for all windows messages, regardless of whether they are intended for a normal window or for a dialog box, to first pass through a single routine. After calling **App_InitializeHook** to install the message hook, **App_Initialize** calls **Frame_Initialize**, **Client_Initialize**, and **EditDlg_Initialize**. The frame, client, and program editor dialog boxes each require that a window class be registered prior to creation of the corresponding window. The existing **_Initialize** functions take care of creating the windows classes, although you can add other module-specific initializations to those functions.

Next, I started creating windows. The call to **Frame_CreateWindow** starts a chain of events that results in creation of the client and Stage dialog box windows. The four numeric parameters passed to **Frame_CreateWindow** determine the location and size of the window created. **App_Initialize** creates a frame window that is positioned at 10,0. The width of the frame window is hard-coded to be 620 pixels. The height is determined by current system settings, which may change from time to time. It is calculated to be the sum of the height of a caption bar (SM_CYCAPTION), the height of a menu (SM_CYMENU), and the height of the window's border (SM_CYFRAME), plus 30 pixels. The 30-pixel-high strip added to the vertical dimension of the frame provides a place for the client window, which is just high enough to display a toolbar.

Once the frame, client, and Stage dialog box windows were created, I made a call to **WaveMixInit** to initialize WAVEMIX.DLL. If you haven't installed WAVEMIX or if it is not functioning, **WaveMixInit** will return NULL and display an error message, but the program will run anyway. (The sound effects are nice, but optional.) If **WaveMixInit** returns a handle to the wave mixer, then **WaveMixActivate** is called to enable sound output. Later in this appendix I'll discuss WAVEMIX in detail.

```
BOOL App_Initialize(APP* papp)
{
    if (!App_InitializeHook(papp))
```

continued on next page

continued from previous page

```
        return FALSE;

    if (!Frame_Initialize(papp))
        return FALSE;

    if (!Client_Initialize(papp))
        return FALSE;

    if (!EditDlg_Initialize(papp))
        return FALSE;

    papp->hwndMain = Frame_CreateWindow(
            "BugBots",
            10, 0, 620, 30 +
                    GetSystemMetrics(SM_CYCAPTION) +
            GetSystemMetrics(SM_CYMENU) +
                    GetSystemMetrics(SM_CYFRAME),
            papp->hinst);

    if (papp->hwndMain == NULL)
        return FALSE;
    ShowWindow(papp->hwndMain, papp->cmdShow);

    if( (g_app.hWaveMix = WaveMixInit()) == (HANDLE)NULL )
        MessageBox(papp->hwndMain,
            "Could not initialize Wavemix","Error", MB_OK)
    else
            WaveMixActivate(g_app.hWaveMix, TRUE );
    return TRUE;
}
```

`App_Initialize` calls the following routine once, when the program first starts running. The height of the frame window is saved in the variable **`fixedHeight`** and is used to respond to the WM_GETMINMAXINFO that occurs while the frame window is being created.

```
HWND Frame_CreateWindow( LPCSTR lpszText, int x, int y, int cx, int
cy, HINSTANCE hinst)
{
    fixedHeight = cy;

    return CreateWindowEx(
            0L,
            "BugBots_Frame",
            lpszText, (WS_OVERLAPPEDWINDOW | WS_CLIPSIBLINGS |
WS_CLIPCHILDREN) & ~WS_MAXIMIZEBOX,
            x, y, cx, cy,
            NULL,
            NULL,
            hinst,
            NULL);
}
```

Between the time **CreateWindowEx** is called and the time control returns from that call, a WM_CREATE message will be sent to the new window. When that happens, a call is made to **Frame_OnCreate**. **Frame_OnCreate** calls **Client_CreateWindow**, which in turn results in a call to **Client_OnCreate** (surprise). After the frame and client windows have been created, **StageDlg_Do** is called. **StageDlg_Do** creates the window where the BugBot battle will take place.

```
BOOL Frame_OnCreate(FRAME* pfrm, CREATESTRUCT FAR* lpCreateStruct)
{
    pfrm->haccel = LoadAccelerators(lpCreateStruct->hInstance,
            MAKEINTRESOURCE(IDR_MAINACCEL));

    if (!pfrm->haccel)
        return FALSE;

    pfrm->hwndClient = Client_CreateWindow(pfrm->hwnd,
        0, 0, 0, 0,
        TRUE,
        0, NULL);

    if (!pfrm->hwndClient)
        return FALSE;

    pfrm->hwndStageDlg = StageDlg_Do(pfrm->hwnd);
    if( !pfrm->hwndStageDlg )
        return FALSE;
    return TRUE;
}
```

Toolbar Tips

I designed BugBots to emulate the appearance of Visual Basic. The main window looks like a toolbar with menus and the other windows can be sized and arranged on the screen independent of the main window. Figure A-2 shows the BugBots frame and client windows. The frame consists of the border, menu, and caption bar. The client window is the narrow vertical strip that contains the toolbar buttons.

Although Windows does not provide direct support for toolbar buttons, BugBots demonstrates an easy way to provide ones that look and act just like the toolbar buttons in other Windows programs. You can use techniques similar to those I used in

FIGURE A-2

The frame and client windows and the toolbar

BugBots to create all sorts of buttons: big buttons, little buttons, nonrectangular buttons, and even animated buttons.

```
typedef struct tagButtonDef
{
    int x;
    int y;
    int idNormal;
    int idPushed;
    int idGrayed;
    int idcmd;
} ButtonDef, FAR *LPButtonDef;
```

The client window code in CLIENT.C defines all the toolbar buttons for BugBots in a single array of **ButtonDef** elements.

```
static ButtonDef ToolButtonDefs[] =
{
    {  10, 2, IDB_PROJLISTNORMAL,  IDB_PROJLISTPUSHED,  IDB_PROJLISTGRAYED,
        CMD_PROGDLG },

    {  43, 2, IDB_NEWNORMAL,  IDB_NEWPUSHED,  IDB_NEWGRAYED,  CMD_FILENEW },
    {  66, 2, IDB_OPENNORMAL, IDB_OPENPUSHED, IDB_OPENGRAYED, CMD_FILEOPEN },
    {  89, 2, IDB_SAVENORMAL, IDB_SAVEPUSHED, IDB_SAVEGRAYED, CMD_FILESAVE },

    { 122, 2, IDB_PLAYNORMAL,  IDB_PLAYPUSHED,  IDB_PLAYGRAYED,  CMD_FILERUN },
    { 145, 2, IDB_PAUSENORMAL, IDB_PAUSEPUSHED, IDB_PAUSEGRAYED, CMD_FILEPAUSE },
    { 168, 2, IDB_STOPNORMAL,  IDB_STOPPUSHED,  IDB_STOPGRAYED,  CMD_FILESTOP },

    { 201, 2, IDB_COMPNORMAL,  IDB_COMPPUSHED,  IDB_COMPGRAYED,  CMD_FILECOMPILE }
};
```

The first two members of a **ButtonDef** element specify where on the toolbar a button will be located. The second, third, and fourth members are resource IDs for the bitmap images that will be used for the toolbar button. The last member defines the command associated with a toolbar button.

During the client window creation, **Client_CreateWindow** calls **TBInit**. **TBInit** calls **TBCreate**, as shown here, passing a pointer to the array of **ButtonDefs**:

```
    lpToolbar = TBCreate(papp->hinst, hwnd, sizeof(ToolButtonDefs) /
sizeof(ButtonDef), ToolButtonDefs);
```

If **TBCreate** completes without error, a pointer to a **Toolbar** data structure is returned. Happily, it isn't necessary to know anything about the **Toolbar** data structure to use toolbar buttons. The code in TOOLBAR.C contains a number of functions that manage the state of the toolbar buttons and test to see if a button has been clicked. All that's required in CLIENT.C is to intercept mouse messages and pass them on to the appropriate functions in TOOLBAR.C.

```
BOOL Client_OnLButtonDown(CLIENT *pcli, BOOL fDoubleClick, int x,
int y, UINT keyFlags)
```

```
{
    TBMouseDown(lpToolbar, x, y);
    SetWindowPos(g_app.hwndClient,
            HWND_TOP,
            0,0,0,0,
            SWP_NOMOVE | SWP_NOSIZE );
    return FALSE;
}

void Client_OnMouseMove(CLIENT *pcli, int x, int y, UINT keyFlags)
{
    TBMouseMove(lpToolbar, x, y);
}

BOOL Client_OnLButtonUp(CLIENT *pcli, int x, int y, UINT keyFlags)
{
    int idcmd = TBMouseUp(lpToolbar, x, y);

    if( idcmd != -1 )
        SendMessage(g_app.hwndMain, WM_COMMAND, idcmd, 0L );
    return FALSE;
}
```

When a user clicks an enabled toolbar button, the **TBMouseUp** function returns the command given in the corresponding **ButtonDef** element. If no enabled toolbar button is clicked, the function returns a -1. When the return value is something other than -1, **SendMessage** invokes the specified command.

Using the same command IDs for menu items as you use for the command buttons makes the programming really easy. **SendMessage** with **wparam** equal to WM_COMMAND and **idcmd** equal to some menu item's ID causes the application's main loop to dispatch the message as if it were actually generated by a menu.

Using the Sprite Engine

Once I'd finished with the mechanics of opening windows and servicing toolbar commands, it was time to get into the fun stuff! The sprite engine itself is somewhat limited in its support for animated sprites, but as you will soon see, it isn't too difficult to build new functionality on top of the existing engine. First we'll take a look at the fundamentals.

Sprite-Engine Initialization

All animation in BugBots takes place on the Stage dialog box window. During initialization, **StageDlg_OnInitDialog** calls **SpriteInit** and then loads the background image.

```
BOOL StageDlg_OnInitDialog(HWND hwndDlg, HWND hwndFocus, LPARAM lParam)
{
    SpriteInit(hwndDlg);
    LoadBackground("backgrnd.bmp", FALSE );
    g_app.hwndStage = hwndDlg;
    return TRUE;
}
```

`SpriteInit` simply takes note of the window handle passed to it and the size of that window. Those items will be used later, during animation. **LoadBackground** is where the sprite engine initialization really takes place.

```
void LoadBackground(LPSTR pszPath, BOOL bUpdateScreen)
{
    //
    // Delete the current sprite set.
    //
    DeleteSpriteList();
    //
    // Nuke any old DIB.
    //
    DeleteDIB(G.pdibBkGnd);
    //
    // Try to load the new DIB.
    //
    G.pdibBkGnd = LoadDIB(pszPath);
    if (!G.pdibBkGnd)
        return;
    //
    // Delete the old WinG DC and bitmap,
    // if they exist.
    //
    if (G.hdcWinG)
    {
        DeleteDC (G.hdcWinG);
        DeleteObject (G.hWinGBitmap);
        G.hdcWinG = NULL;
    }
    //
    // Create the WinG DC.
    //
    G.hdcWinG = WinGCreateDC ();
    //
    // Create a PDIB for the off-screen WinG bitmap.
    // Note that the bits are created elsewhere and
    // can't be accessed with the DIB_PBITS macro.
    // The header and color table are there as normal.
    // Free the old one (if it exists) first.
    //
    if (G.pdibWinG)
    {
        FREE (G.pdibWinG);
        G.pdibWinG = NULL;
```

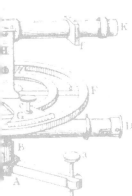

```
}
//
// Create a header and color table for the WinG bitmap, and
// copy contents into it from the background DIB.
//
G.pdibWinG = (PDIB) ALLOCATE (DIB_BISIZE(G.pdibBkGnd));
if (!G.pdibWinG)
{
    dprintf1("Couldn't allocate off-screen bitmap header");
    return;
}
_fmemcpy (G.pdibWinG, G.pdibBkGnd, (UINT)DIB_BISIZE(G.pdibBkGnd));
//
// Create a new palette based on the background DIB.
//
if (G.hpalCurrent)
    DeleteObject(G.hpalCurrent);
G.hpalCurrent = CreateIdentityPalette(G.pdibWinG);
//
// Map the bits of the background DIB to match
// the identity palette.
//
MapDIBits (G.hpalCurrent, G.pdibBkGnd, DIB_PBITS(G.pdibBkGnd));
//
// Find out what the best WinG DIB format is.
//
WinGRecommendDIBFormat ((LPBITMAPINFO)G.pdibWinG);
//
// Set height and width according to the recommended format
// (the multiply retains the top-down/bottom-up sense).
// Minimum size = 150x100
//
G.pdibWinG->bmiHeader.biHeight *= max (DIB_HEIGHT(G.pdibBkGnd), 100);
G.pdibWinG->bmiHeader.biWidth   = max (DIB_WIDTH(G.pdibBkGnd), 150);
//
// Create the bitmap; get the pointer to the bits.
G.hWinGBitmap = WinGCreateBitmap (G.hdcWinG,
                                  (LPBITMAPINFO)G.pdibWinG,
                                  &G.pOffScreenBits);

if (G.hWinGBitmap)
{
    // Select it in. I don't save the old bitmap.
    SelectObject (G.hdcWinG, G.hWinGBitmap);
} else {
    // Fail...
    DeleteDC (G.hdcWinG);
    G.hdcWinG = NULL;
    FREE (G.pdibWinG);
    G.pdibWinG = NULL;
}
//
```

continued on next page

continued from previous page

```
    // Draw the background to the off-screen DIB
    // and update the screen, if required.
    //
    Render(NULL, bUpdateScreen);
}
```

`LoadBackground` completely initializes WinG, loads a background image, and calls `Render`, which performs the initial screen update. You will be able to use this function as is in almost any Windows game you write.

Painting the Background

In response to various system events, or in response to the actions of BugBots itself, Windows will send WM_PAINT messages to `StageDlg`. `StageDlg`'s message-cracker macros dispatch the WM_PAINT message to `StageDlg_OnPaint`.

```
void StageDlg_OnPaint(HWND hwnd)
{
    PAINTSTRUCT ps;

    BeginPaint(hwnd,&ps);
    Render(NULL,TRUE);
    EndPaint(hwnd,&ps);
}
```

A call to `Render` is bracketed by a `BeginPaint`, `EndPaint` pair. When processing a WM_PAINT message, Windows programs must bracket their paint code with these two calls, or Windows will become confused about which windows need to be updated and which don't. The sprite engine's `Render` function takes care of displaying the background and any visible sprites.

Scrolling the Background

The BugBots background size is limited only by the size of the bitmap loaded for the background image. Depending on the background image's size and the hardware on which BugBots is running, the Stage dialog box's window may not be large enough to display the entire background at once. Instead of cluttering the animation window with scrollbars, BugBots allows the user to move the background around by using the arrow keys.

The message hook installed during program initilization turns out to be really handy here. Normally, Windows uses the arrow keys to move between controls on a dialog box. Since the animation window, `StageDlg`, is actually a modeless dialog box, Windows would not normally allow the programmer access to the arrow keys. However, the application framework created by MAKEAPP ensures this doesn't present a problem for us: It intercepts the arrow keys before the Windows dialog box handler sees them. `App_OnMsgFilter` calls `StageDlg_OnMsgFilter`, which then handles the arrow keys, as shown here:

```
BOOL StageDlg_OnMsgFilter(HWND hwndDlg, MSG FAR* lpmsg, int context)
{
    HWND hwndMsg = lpmsg->hwnd;

    //
    // If the message is destined for the dialog box or one of its
    // children, check for special key handling.
    //
    if (hwndMsg == hwndDlg || IsChild(hwndDlg, hwndMsg))
    {
        //
        // If F1 was pressed, post WM_COMMAND CMD_HELPABOUT
        // to the dialog box.
        //
        if( lpmsg->message == WM_KEYDOWN )
        {
        switch( lpmsg->wParam )
        {
                //
                // Left arrow
                //
                case VK_LEFT:
                    if( (G.bkgndXOffset += 8) > 0 )
                        G.bkgndXOffset = 0;
                    InvalidateRect(G.hwndMain, NULL, FALSE);
                    return TRUE;
                //
                // Up arrow
                //
                case VK_UP:
                    if( (G.bkgndYOffset += 8) > 0 )
                        G.bkgndYOffset = 0;
                    InvalidateRect(G.hwndMain, NULL, FALSE);
                    return TRUE;
                //
                // Right arrow
                //
                case VK_RIGHT:
                    if( (DIB_WIDTH(G.pdibBkGnd) + (G.bkgndXOffset -= 8))
< G.mainWndWidth )
                        G.bkgndXOffset = G.mainWndWidth -
DIB_WIDTH(G.pdibBkGnd);
                    InvalidateRect(G.hwndMain, NULL, FALSE);
                    return TRUE;
                case VK_DOWN:
                    if( (DIB_HEIGHT(G.pdibBkGnd) + (G.bkgndYOffset -= 8))
< G.mainWndHeight )
                        G.bkgndYOffset = G.mainWndHeight -
DIB_HEIGHT(G.pdibBkGnd);
                    InvalidateRect(G.hwndMain, NULL, FALSE);
                    return TRUE;
                case VK_F1:
```

continued on next page

continued from previous page

```
                    FORWARD_WM_COMMAND(hwndDlg, CMD_HELPABOUT, NULL, 0,
PostMessage);
                    return TRUE;
                }
            } else
                    return IsDialogMessage(hwndDlg, lpmsg);
        } else {
            return IsDialogMessage(hwndDlg, lpmsg);
        }
}
```

The important thing to remember when you're working with message filters in the application framework is to return the appropriate value from your message-filter function. In **StageDlg_OnMsgFilter**, TRUE is returned whenever a message is handled. Otherwise, the return value from **IsDialogMessage** is returned. The function **App_MsgFilter** in BUGBOTS.C relies on this behavior in order to determine when a window has handled a filtered message.

Sprites

Now that the program had a scrolling background, I was ready to add some sprites.

Sprite Initialization

When a user clicks the toolbar's Run button, the command message CMD_FILERUN is sent to the client window (see CLIENT.C), where it is dispatched to the **Client_OnCommand** function. Inside **Client_OnCommand**, a call is made to **Client_StartBots**.

```
static void Client_StartBots()
{
    int     i;
    int     multi;
    //
    //  For each possible BugBot
    //
    for( i = 0; i < MAX_BOTS; i++ )
    {
        LPBot lpBot = g_app.alpBots[i];
        //
        // Make sure the execution context is initialized.
        //
        contexts[i] = NULL;
        if( (lpBot != NULL) && (lpBot->bParsedOk == TRUE) )
        {
            //
            // We've got a valid BugBot program, so find the program's
            // entry point.
```

```
            //
            LPSym lpSym = SymFind(lpBot->lpGlobalSyms,"main");
            //
            // Make sure it's *really* a valid program.
            //
            if( lpSym != NULL )
                contexts[i] = InterpCreateContext( lpBot, lpSym);
            else
                continue;
            //
            // Place BugBot at random.
            //
            LineStart(  rand() % DIB_WIDTH(G.pdibBkGnd),
                        rand() % DIB_HEIGHT(G.pdibBkGnd),
                        0,
                        &lpBot->line );
            //
            // Load sprite, but free previous sprite if it exists.
            //
            if( lpBot->lpBodySprite )
                DeleteSprite(lpBot->lpBodySprite);
            //
            // Load the sprite's image.
            //
            lpBot->lpBodySprite = LoadSprite(lpBot->lpstrBodyname, 1, FALSE);
            //
            // Frames are square, so this calculation tells us how many
            // frames there are.
            //
            multi = lpBot->lpBodySprite->height / lpBot->lpBodySprite->width;
            //
            // Initialize the sprite.
            //
            lpBot->lpBodySprite->multi = multi;
            lpBot->lpBodySprite->multi_index = multi;
            lpBot->direction = 0;
            lpBot->speed = lpBot->curSpeed = 0;
            lpBot->lpBodySprite->height = lpBot->lpBodySprite->width;
            lpBot->lpBodySprite->pDIB->bmiHeader.biHeight /= multi;
            lpBot->lpBodySprite->type = SPRITE_IS_BUGBODY;
            lpBot->timeLastMove = timeGetTime();
            lpBot->frameScaler = 1;
            lpBot->damage = 0;
            lpBot->inCollisionEvent = FALSE;
            lpBot->inHitEvent = FALSE;
        }
    }
}
```

There are basically two things that need to be initialized for each sprite: the BugBot program and the BugBot's image. The BugBot program interpreter uses an "execution context" while running, which is really no different than an execution context in any

FIGURE A-3

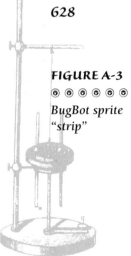

BugBot sprite "strip"

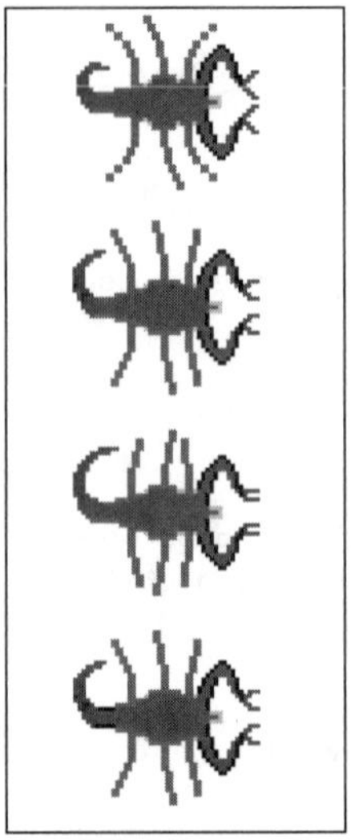

multitasking system. The state of the BugBot, including its program counter, stack pointer, and other run-time variables, is maintained in the execution context. The `SymFind` function that is called at the beginning of the `for()` loop in `Client_StartBots` locates the entry point for the BugBot program. Then `InterpCreateContext` is used to initialize the BugBot's execution context. Once the BugBot is initialized, it is placed, at random, on the field and its current location is initialized using a call to `LineStart`.

Next, the sprite's bitmap is loaded, using a call to `LoadSprite`. The support for multiple frames in the sprite engine is minimal, but it's usable under controlled conditions. `Client_StartBots` assumes that all frames are square and that multiple frames are arranged in a vertical strip (as shown in Figure A-3). These assumptions make it easy to figure out how many frames are contained in a sprite's bitmap: All that's required is to divide the bitmap height by its width to find the total number of frames. One thing to keep in mind here is that each BugBot can be oriented so that it "points" in some direction or other. I handled this by constraining each animation to four frames, which is the minimum number of frames required to provide realistic-looking leg movements.

Moving a Sprite

There are a number of things that need to be handled when the BugBot sprites are moving on the screen. The function `MoveBot` in RUN.C handles BugBot movement. The first task in `MoveBot` is to handle changes in velocity. Velocity changes are not instantaneous, so the following code takes care of changing speed gradually until the BugBot's final speed is attained:

```
    //
    // Time to change velocity?
    //
    if( lpBot->curSpeed != lpBot->speed && lpBot->timeLastVelChange + 1000 <=
timeGetTime() )
    {
        if( lpBot->speed > lpBot->curSpeed )
            lpBot->curSpeed++;
        else if( lpBot->curSpeed > 0 )
            lpBot->curSpeed--;

        if( lpBot->curSpeed != 0 )
            lpBot->msPerPixel = 100 / lpBot->curSpeed;
        else
            lpBot->msPerPixel = 0;
        lpBot->timeLastVelChange = timeGetTime();
    }
```

When **lpBot->curSpeed** is not equal to **lpBot->speed** (set by the BugBot speed = statement) and when it has been at least 1 second since the last change in velocity, the BugBot's speed is incremented by 1 and a new value is calculated for the BugBot's milliseconds-per-pixel parameter (**msPerPixel**).

After velocity changes are handled, the following code checks to see if it's time to move the BugBot and does so if required. The checks for **inCollision == FALSE** and **inHitEvent == FALSE** are required to prevent recursive firing of the corresponding events. The constant **FrameScale** and the BugBot variable **frameScaler** are used to reduce the rate at which frames change relative to a BugBot's velocity. If this were not done, the BugBot's legs would appear to move much too quickly relative to the distance it was traveling.

```
    if( (lpBot->msPerPixel > 0) &&
        (difftime > lpBot->msPerPixel) &&
        (lpBot->inCollisionEvent == FALSE) &&
        (lpBot->inHitEvent == FALSE) )
    {
        RECT rc;
        LINE curline = lpBot->line;
        int  newx, newy;
        int  frame;
        //
        // Time to change frames?
        //
        if( --lpBot->frameScaler == 0 )
        {
            if( --(lpBot->curFrame) < lpBot->firstFrame )
                lpBot->curFrame = lpBot->lastFrame;
            lpBot->lpBodySprite->multi_index = lpBot->curFrame;
            lpBot->frameScaler = FrameScale;
        }
        lpBot->timeLastMove = curtime - difftime % lpBot->msPerPixel;
        fMoved = TRUE;
```

The next section of code in **MoveBot** puts the BugBot's current position on the sprite engine's redraw list by calling **Render**. Passing a FALSE as the second parameter prevents any redrawing from occurring after all the BugBots have been moved. Then **LineNext** is called to change the BugBot's location, and collisions with walls are detected and handled.

```
//
// Put the sprite's current rectangle on the update list.
//
GetSpriteRect(lpBot->lpBodySprite, &rc);
Render(&rc,FALSE);
//
// Calculate the next position.
//
LineNext( &lpBot->line );
newx = lpBot->line.x;
newy = lpBot->line.y;
//
// Check for and handle wall-collisions.
//
if( newx < 0 )
{
    //
    // Hit the left wall.
    //
    newx = 0;
    collisions = 1;
} else if( newx + lpBot->lpBodySprite->width > DIB_WIDTH(G.pdibBkGnd) ) {
    //
    // Hit the right wall.
    //
    newx = DIB_WIDTH(G.pdibBkGnd) - lpBot->lpBodySprite->width;
    collisions = 2;
}
if( newy < 0 )
{
    //
    // Hit the top wall.
    //
    newy = 0;
    collisions |= 4;
} else if( newy + lpBot->lpBodySprite->height > DIB_HEIGHT(G.pdibBkGnd) ) {
    //
    // Hit the bottom wall.
    //
    newy = DIB_HEIGHT(G.pdibBkGnd) - lpBot->lpBodySprite->height;
    collisions |= 8;
}
```

Now that the BugBot has been moved and wall-collisions handled, **SetSpritePosition** is called to update the internal-position variables and **SpriteCollisionTest** is called to see if the BugBot has run into any missiles or other BugBots. If a

BugBot runs into a missile, **ExplodeMissile** is called to calculate the damage. If there is a collision with another BugBot, the previous position is restored and **NotifyCollision** is called. **NotifyCollision** will modify the BugBot's execution context so that the next instruction executed is the first instruction in the BugBot's **Collision_Event** routine.

```
//
// Move the sprite to a new position.
//
SetSpritePosition(
    lpBot->lpBodySprite,
    lpBot->line.x,
    lpBot->line.y,
    FALSE);
//
// Check for collisions with other sprites.
//
if( lpSpriteHit = SpriteCollisionTest(G.pSpriteList,lpBot->lpBodySprite) )
{
    if( lpSpriteHit->type == SPRITE_IS_MISSILE )
    {
        if( lpBot != (LPBot)lpSpriteHit->lpAppData )
            ExplodeMissile( lpSpriteHit, TRUE );
        if( lpBot->damage >= 100 )
            return FALSE;
    } else {
        newx = curline.x;
        newy = curline.y;
        collisions |= 0x10;
    }
}
//
// Automatic speed reduction for collisions
//
if( collisions )
{
    if( lpBot->curSpeed > 5 )
    {
        lpBot->curSpeed = 5;
        lpBot->msPerPixel = 100 / lpBot->curSpeed;
    }
    LineStart(newx, newy, lpBot->line.angle, &lpBot->line);

    NotifyCollision(lpCon, collisions);
}
```

The BugBot's new position is then finalized and a Boolean is returned to indicate whether the sprite has moved.

```
//
// Set sprite's position again; it may have changed.
//
```

continued on next page

continued from previous page

```
        SetSpritePosition(
            lpBot->lpBodySprite,
            lpBot->line.x,
            lpBot->line.y,
            FALSE);
    }
    return fMoved;
```

Sound

BugBots uses Microsoft's WAVEMIX.DLL to provide multiple simultaneous sound effects. WAVEMIX provides eight virtual sound channels, all of which are independently programmable. BugBots allows up to four contestant programs to execute at any one time. Using the **Sound** statement, a BugBot program can specify a sound to play when a BugBot shoots a missile and a different sound to play when the missile explodes.

Sound Initialization

Before you can use WAVEMIX, it must be initialized with a call to **WaveMixInit**. The following code from **App_Initialize** in BUGBOTS.C shows how to do this. **WaveMixInit** returns a handle that is required as a parameter to subsequent WAVEMIX calls, so it is saved in a global variable.

```
if( (g_app.hWaveMix = WaveMixInit()) == (HANDLE)NULL )
    MessageBox(papp->hwndMain,"Could not initialize Wavemix","Error", MB_OK);
else
    WaveMixActivate(g_app.hWaveMix, TRUE );
```

After the user clicks the Run toolbar button, the function **Client_StartBots** is called, as I described previously. The following code is used to initialize WAVEMIX channels for each BugBot that specifies a sound:

```
if( lpBot->lpstrShootName != NULL )
{
    lpBot->lpShootWave =
        WaveMixOpenWave(g_app.hWaveMix, lpBot->lpstrShootName, g_app.hinst,
WMIX_FILE );
    if( lpBot->lpShootWave != NULL )
        if( !WaveMixOpenChannel(g_app.hWaveMix, i, WMIX_OPENSINGLE ) )
            lpBot->uiShootChannel = i;
        else
            lpBot->uiShootChannel = 0xffff;
}

if( lpBot->lpstrExplosionName != NULL )
{
    lpBot->lpExplosionWave =
```

```
        WaveMixOpenWave(g_app.hWaveMix, lpBot->lpstrExplosionName, g_app.hinst,
WMIX_FILE );
    if( lpBot->lpExplosionWave != NULL )
        if( !WaveMixOpenChannel(g_app.hWaveMix, i * 2, WMIX_OPENSINGLE ) )
            lpBot->uiExplosionChannel = i * 2;
        else
            lpBot->uiExplosionChannel = 0xffff;
}
```

WaveMixOpenWave returns a handle to a WAVEMIX structure that is used by WAVEMIX while a sound is playing. **WaveMixOpenChannel** can be used to open a single channel, as it is in my code, or multiple channels, using WMIX_OPENALL. BugBots keeps track of whether a channel was opened successfully for a BugBot's sound by storing either the channel number or **0xffff** in BugBot's data structure. A value of **0xffff** means that either no sound was specified or that the channel could not be opened. As you can see, sound is handled as an optional element of BugBots. If the user has a soundcard, WAVEMIX, and the sound files, then the sound effects will work. Otherwise, the program will run without sound.

Making Noise

When a missile sound has been specified, the wave file for the BugBot program that's shooting is played, using the following code:

```
if( g_app.hWaveMix != 0 &&
    lpBot->uiShootChannel != 0xffff &&
    lpBot->lpShootWave != NULL )
{
    MIXPLAYPARAMS MixPlayParams;

    MixPlayParams.wSize = sizeof(MIXPLAYPARAMS);
    MixPlayParams.hMixSession = g_app.hWaveMix;
    MixPlayParams.hWndNotify=NULL;
    MixPlayParams.dwFlags=WMIX_CLEARQUEUE|WMIX_HIPRIORITY;
    MixPlayParams.wLoops=0;
    MixPlayParams.iChannel=lpBot->uiShootChannel;
    MixPlayParams.lpMixWave=lpBot->lpShootWave;
    WaveMixPlay(&MixPlayParams);
}
```

MixPlayParams is initialized in such a way that any previously started, but not yet complete, sound is terminated by WMIX_CLEARQUEUE. WMIX_HIPRIORITY tells **WaveMixPlay** to start the sound immediately. The other parameters in **MixPlayParams** let **WaveMixPlay** know which WAVEMIX session is making the call (multiple programs can open WAVEMIX at the same time), how many times to play the sound, and the channel and wave file to play. After the call to **WaveMixPlay**, the WAVEMIX will take care of playing the sound file–no further attention is required from the application.

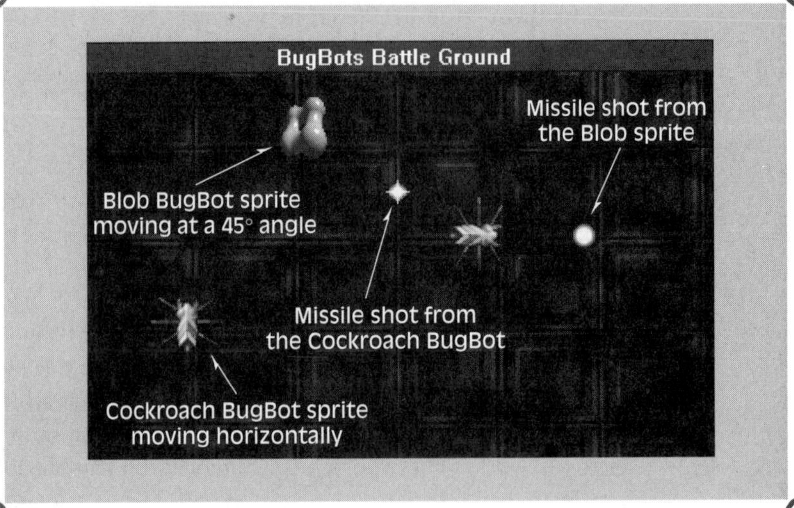

FIGURE A-4

A typical BugBot battle

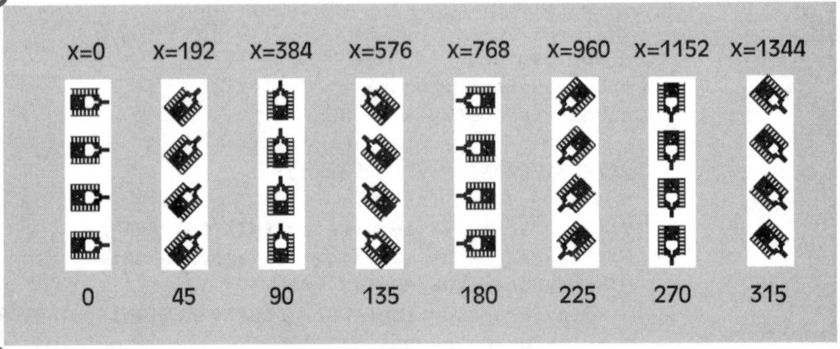

FIGURE A-5

The eight views of the BugBot sprite and the pixel starting point for each rotation

Summary

BugBots uses multiple windows and modeless dialog boxes to create a BugBot program editor and execution environment. Figure A-4 displays a typical BugBot battle in action, while Figure A-5 demonstrates the inner workings of the game by showing the range of motion of each BugBot sprite. Although the program isn't terribly fancy, it has all the elements that you are likely to need to use in a Windows game, and shows how to extend the sprite engine to support multiple sequences of multiframed animation.

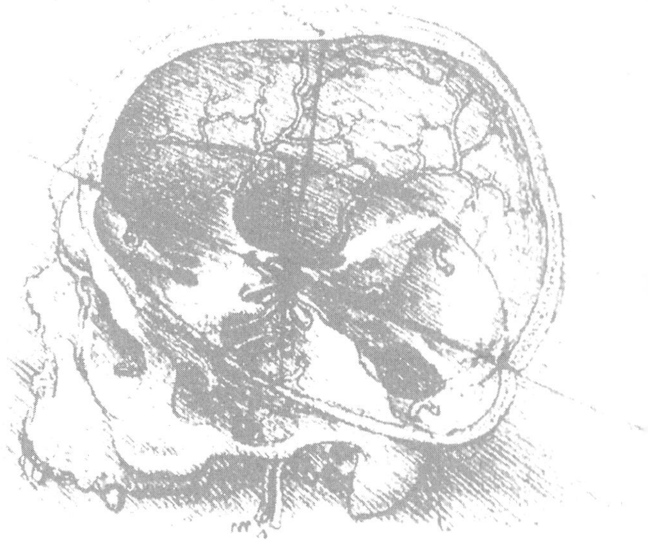

Index

D

G

M

n

X

Y

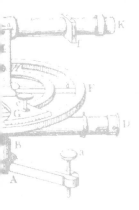

Z

ENVIRONMENTAL AWARENESS

Books have a substantial influence on the destruction of the forests of the Earth. For example, it takes 17 trees to produce one ton of paper. A first printing of 30,000 copies of a typical 480-page book consumes 108,000 pounds of paper, which will require 918 trees!

Waite Group Press™ is against the clear-cutting of forests and supports reforestation of the Pacific Northwest of the United States and Canada, where most of this paper comes from. As a publisher with several hundred thousand books sold each year, we feel an obligation to give back to the planet. We will therefore support organizations which seek to preserve the forests of planet Earth.